ARABIC THEOLOGY, ARABIC PHILOSOPHY

ORIENTALIA LOVANIENSIA
ANALECTA
152

ARABIC THEOLOGY, ARABIC PHILOSOPHY

From the Many to the One: Essays in Celebration of Richard M. Frank

edited by

JAMES E. MONTGOMERY

UITGEVERIJ PEETERS en DEPARTEMENT OOSTERSE STUDIES
LEUVEN – PARIS – DUDLEY, MA
2006

A CIP record for this book is available from the Library of Congress.

ISBN-10 90-429-1778-4
ISBN-13 9789042917781
D. 2006/0602/68

CONTENTS

Qur'ān

Paths to al-Ashʿarī

Al-Ashʿarī and the *Kalām*

Christian *Falsafa*

Avicenna and Beyond

Al-Ghazālī on Causality

EDITOR'S INTRODUCTION

The final sentence of the last scholarly work by Professor Richard M. Frank to have been published runs:

Ontology and logic are not separable the one from the other.[1]

This remarkable statement concludes an incisive and authoritative exposition of the term *ḥukm,* plural *aḥkām*, in the writings of the classical Ashʿarite masters, the architects of the formal theological system posterior to the eponym's death in 324/935 and prior to the *floruit* of al-Ghazālī. It forms one panel of a triptych of remarkable surveys of Ashʿarite ontology, stemming from the final stages of Professor Frank's professional career, the others being *The Ašʿarite Ontology: I. Primary Entities*, and *The Non-Existent and the Possible in Classical Ashʿarite Teaching*.[2] These works are characterized by scrupulosity in the recording of source references, subtlety and ingenuity in the exposition of ideas, and an astonishing sensitivity to the systematic implications and supple delimitations of Classical Arabic as a formal language for the speculative exploration of existence. Taken together they represent one of the most sustained endeavours to-date by any scholar to penetrate the formidable formalism of this system, predicated upon a reluctance to establish philosophical reasoning as an autonomous principle of theological speculation, a reluctance inherited from al-Ashʿarī's refusal to commit himself on a number of questions or to subject the godhead to an over-reductive analysis.

The prize of this formidable intellectual exercise is the sentence quoted above, in which 'logic' is to be understood as 'the formal and technical language of the classical Ashʿarīya', for whom being was univocal and ontology was truly nominalistic, deriving the impetus for their speculations from al-Ashʿarī's construction of 'a formal method based on the Arab grammarians' analysis of predicative sentences' which are

[1] *Al-Aḥkām in Classical Ašʿarite Teaching*, in: *De Zénon d'Élée à Poincaré. Recueil d'études en hommage à Roshdi Rashed* (*Les cahiers du MIDEO*, 1), ed. RÉGIS MORELON and AHMAD HASNAWI, Leuven: Peeters, 2004, p. 753-777 (p. 777): item no. 55 in the *Bibliography.*

[2] In: *Arabic Sciences and Philosophy* 9 (1999), p. 163-231: item no. 53 in the Bibliography; and in: *Mélanges de l'Institut Dominicain d'Études Orientales du Caire* 24 (2000), p. 1-37: item no. 54 in the *Bibliography.*

> Divided into three categories: (1) those that assert the existence of only the subject itself (*al-nafs*, *nafs al-mawṣūf*); (2) those that assert the existence of an 'attribute' (*ṣifah*, *maʿnā*) distinct from the 'self' of the subject as such; and (3) those that assert the existence of an action (*fiʿl*) done by the subject.[3]

We can trace this trajectory in Professor Frank's scholarship right back to his first encounter with the *Kalām* and his reluctance to acquiesce in its characterization as an apologetic exercise in hair-splitting quibbling and logic-chopping, combined with that remarkable *moment tournant* captured so brilliantly in 1981 when he demonstrated the full ontological implications for speculative theology of the system developed by the Arabic grammarians.[4]

Professor Frank's contribution to the Ashʿarīya alone would render the scholarly world deeply indebted to him. But of course, his legacy does not end there, for he has devoted the same considerable energies to the formative first centuries of the *Kalām* as a formal system, with particular emphasis on the emergence of the Muʿtazila and the school's first theological acme in the teachings of Abū ʿAlī and Abū Hāshim al-Jubbāʾī; has been among the first scholars fully and systematically to make use of the publication of sections of *al-Mughnī* of Cadi ʿAbd al-Jabbār; has made al-Ashʿarī the object of a number of studies spanning some thirty years; has established the influence of *Kalām* thinking on the theories of the *falāsifa*;[5] and has subjected to the most searching and penetrating scrutiny al-Ghazālī's cosmological and doctrinal affiliations, reading this influential thinker against the grain of his own reception history, in a manner that is not only controversial but refreshing and liberating — whatever the rights and wrongs of Professor Frank's al-Ghazālī, few will have brought such an impressive array of erudition to bear on his writings and paid him the greatest of all scholarly compliments, that of taking another thinker's thoughts *seriously*. And this is to say nothing of the works on the Syriac tradition and the Greek into Arabic translation movement. Indeed, an overview of his scholarly achievement will

[3] *Al-Ashʿarī*, in: *Encyclopedia of Religion*, ed. MIRCEA ELIADE, I, New York: Macmillan, 1987, p. 445-449 (p. 447): item no. 58 in the *Bibliography*. See also his *Ashʿarīyah*, in: *Encyclopedia of Religion*, ed. MIRCEA ELIADE, I, New York: Macmillan, 1987, p. 449-455: item no. 59 in the *Bibliography*.

[4] *Meanings are Spoken of in Many Ways: The Earlier Arab Grammarians*, in: *Le Muséon* 94 (1981), p. 259-319: item no. 32 in the *Bibliography*.

[5] See THÉRESE-ANNE DRUART, *Metaphysics*, in: *The Cambridge Companion to Arabic Philosophy*, ed. PETER ADAMSON and RICHARD C. TAYLOR, Cambridge: Cambridge University Press, 2005, p. 327-348 (p. 327).

be greatly facilitated by the initiative, under the editorship of Professor Dimitri Gutas of Yale, to publish, as part of the *Variorum Collected Studies Series*, three volumes of Professor Frank's major articles under the general heading *Texts and Studies on the Development and History of* Kalām.

In all of his studies on the Arabic-Islamic tradition, when once we have recognised the courage and enterprise demonstrated in embarking upon his study of the tradition of the *Kalām*; have celebrated the moral and intellectual integrity of his conviction that this tradition was anything but meaningless; have valued his repeated efforts to resist the appeals of approximation to Western theological traditions, especially when he has pointed to his own lack of success in such resistance — there is one feature which looms large and which I find irresistible: the prominent attention paid to the *ʿarabīya*, to Classical Arabic. It is hard to read a piece by Professor Frank without being deeply impressed by his command of the *ʿarabīya*, and without, in fact, having one's own knowledge thereof enhanced, challenged, revised or deepened. It is for this reason that I have chosen the principal title of this volume, *Arabic Theology, Arabic Philosophy*, with its slightly jarring repetition — for this is a theology (more customarily referred to as Islamic) which we should fail to appreciate, should we close our mind's eye for even one second to the *ʿarabīya* in which it is housed.

This volume of essays in celebration of Professor Frank's intellectual legacy had a strange birth, in that it originated with an invitation, over beer, at a meeting of the *American Oriental Society* in Toronto in March, 2001, which Tony Street and I attended. We extended an invitation to Professor Frank to visit the University of Cambridge and deliver a lecture. We were delighted when he accepted, and further deliberations led to the organization in the summer of 2002 of a conference under the general aegis of the School of ʿAbbasid Studies entitled, *Kalām and Philosophy: Problems and Perspectives*. The conference was a great success, but for one vital feature. Professor Frank in the end was unable to attend.

Some of the participants expressed a desire to publish their papers as part of a volume of Proceedings, which I decided to extend, by invitation, into a collection of papers in Professor Frank's honour. I should like to thank the contributors for their patience and support, but above all for the seriousness with which they approached the task of celebrating Professor Frank's achievements. The articles included in this volume are of the highest intellectual calibre and mark significant contributions to our understandings of an Arabic theology and philosophy. The authors have, in each and every instance, responded, variously and severally, to some facet of Professor Frank's work, be it his explorations of the Graeco-Syriac heritage, his theories concerning the Hellenization of the *Kalām* or (in a related instance) al-Ghazālī's reception of an Avicennan cosmology.

I should also like to take this opportunity to thank my contributors for enabling me (through assumption of the demands of editorship) to fulfil a personal debt of gratitude to Professor Frank for the extraordinary kindness he showed me on my first visit to the *American Oriental Society*, in Salt Lake City in Spring 1995.

JAMES E. MONTGOMERY
Trinity Hall, Cambridge.

YĀ KALĀM

RICHARD M. FRANK
The Catholic University of America

Min baʿdi mā quwwatin usarru bi-hī
aṣbaḥtu shaykhan uʿāliju l-kibarī

I was asked to talk about how I came to devote myself to the study of *Kalām* and how my work and my understanding of it progressed and matured over a number of years. What I shall have to say is quite informal, a short and slightly meandering account of my wandering about in a rather rich but largely uncultivated field. I should say at the outset that several of you folks have been very important to the progress of my work through your friendship and encouragement, in conversation and in your publications. When I came to prepare what little I have to say here, I looked back at what I have written and it seems to be rather scant by comparison with what a number of you have accomplished — for the most part a set of rather short pieces on a variety of particular though mostly related topics. And as is inevitable some of them contain blunders, inexact and sometimes erroneous interpretations, a few of which I corrected in subsequent papers where appropriate, but there are doubtless others of which I am unaware. Once something is published I tend to put it out of my mind and go on to other things, so that much of what I have written I haven't thought about for years and my memory of the content of all but the rather recent is not very good.

I had, even as an undergraduate, done a bit of philosophy, Plato and Aristotle and subsequently a course in which I read various parts of Plato's dialogues in Greek. Later, at the University of Rome, I read al-Fārābī's *Compendium of Plato's Laws* with Francesco Gabrieli and at the same time read *The Laws* in Greek. The earliest studies that I produced on Muslim philosophy were basically philological, one of them a piece in which I collected fragments of Isḥāq's translation of Aristotle's *De Anima* from Avicenna's glosses on the work — fragments that showed the characteristic precision of Isḥāq's work and that the complete translation that Badawī had attributed to him could not have been his.[1] I have always had a kind of fascination with words and language, and curiosities with the lexicon of early Muslim philosophical texts brought me to do some research on their possible origin and from this arose a study, published in 1958, concerning the origin of the technical term *annīya* (or *innīya* if you prefer).[2] The data display what I consider to be sound evidence of the influence of Syriac on some early Arabic philosophical works, including the *Theology of Aristotle*. Much later, in 1987, when *Le Muséon* asked for a short article for their 100th anniversary issue, I returned to the data that I had collected for the article on *annīya* and published the Syriac translations of a few passages of the *Enneads* found in the Syriac version of John of Scythopolis's glosses and comments on the Pseudo-Dionysius's *Commentary on the Divine Names*.[3] None of these fragments, alas, corresponds to anything in the *Theology of Aristotle*. Whether there was a Syriac work which underlay the Arabic of the *Theology* or maybe the style/syntax and technical vocabulary that were native to the original translators influenced the work I do not know — but I do think that it's a question which deserves some serious investigation.

About this time I read a few things — studies and texts — which had to do with *Kalām* and, my curiosity aroused, began to read more seriously some of the texts concerning the formative period of Muslim theology that were immediately available to me at the time. This was not totally new to me, for as a student I had read a good bit of al-Shahrastānī's *Kitāb al-Milal wa-l-Niḥal* with Levi della Vida. But now my attention was seriously focused on the early *Kalām* as such. What I read of the *Maqālāt* of al-Ashʿarī, the *Farq bayn al-Firaq* and the *Uṣūl al-Dīn* of al-Baghdādī, particularly concerning the dominant schools, sc., the Ashʿarites and the Muʿtazilites, seemed clearly to indicate that underlying and supporting the theses and arguments that were reported there must have been genuinely formal theoretical systems whose basic concepts, principles and structures were not clearly set forth in the manuals because of the elementary and disconnected way elements of the various theses and arguments were presented. So too the *Lumaʿ* of al-Ashʿarī and the *Tamhīd* of al-Bāqillānī are but elementary manuals that leave many important theoretical matters unexplained. My sense that this stuff ought to be seriously studied and understood was given some additional momentum by the insistence of several Orientalist colleagues that

[1] *Bibliography*, no. 14.
[2] *Bibliography*, no. 12.
[3] *Bibliography*, no. 41.

Kalām was little more than a superficial and relatively unsophisticated way of stating and of arguing and defending one or another point of basic religious doctrine: obviously one could not expect there to be a philosophically sophisticated theological system that was not manifestly based on or derived from one or another of the ancient or Hellenistic philosophical systems, and the absence of the Aristotelian logic was a clear indication that *Kalām* was no more than a kind of religious dialectic. Such was the common, though essentially uncritical, view, encouraged by some devotees of *Falsafa*.

So, I decided 'twere best to start at the beginning and the first piece I produced on early Muslim theology was an article on the Neoplatonism of Jahm b. Ṣafwān.[4] From there I went on to work on Abū l-Hudhayl and did a monograph on his metaphysics and a couple of years later a piece on his teaching concerning the divine attributes.[5] In the latter I showed the Neoplatonic influence of the *Quaestiones Christianae ad Graecos*, spuriously attributed to Justin Martyr, on his work. (This I had forgotten altogether until I found it cited in a recent article by Cristina D'Ancona.) About the same time I produced — with the encouragement of Goitein, I think — a somewhat detailed study on the nature of created causality as presented in al-Ashʿarī's *Lumaʿ*.[6] There are some things in this piece that may well need qualification or correction.

In the desire for the convenience of tidy unambivalences I had a naive tendency to look for neatly fixed precision in technical terms and expressions; but it takes more experience, more knowledge of, and a more cultivated sensitivity to, the style and usage of individual authors to get a proper knowledge and cultivated sense of their formal lexicon than I had at that time. This quest for exact and invariant terminology led to a rather poorly conceived article concerning the formal sense of *maʿnā* whose meaning, when employed as an ontological term, manifestly does not conform to its most common and normal uses.[7] When I think of this article I am reminded of a two line piece by Daniel Boulanger entitled 'retouche à la pensée' which reads: 'sous mes longues caresses / elle s'ouvre et délivre un bâtard'. Still perplexed by its formal *Kalām* usage I undertook at a much later date a study of the word in the works of the earlier lexicographers and grammarians which, albeit maybe of no major interest to students of philosophy or *Kalām* and maybe not to many oth-

[4] *Bibliography*, no. 20.
[5] *Bibliography*, nos. 2 and 24 respectively.
[6] *Bibliography*, no. 21.
[7] *Bibliography*, no. 22.

ers either, is, I think, of some genuine value for anyone interested in language as such and the ways in which 'meaning' was understood by Arab linguistic thinkers who were not (*wa-l-ḥamd li-Allāh*) directly influenced by foreign traditions.[8] It was only quite recently that the actual — or at least most plausible — origin of the use of *maʿnā* in the classical *Kalām* dawned on me, viz. its use in a loose sense of 'something' — a distinct entity that qualifies the substrate in which it resides; an abridgement for *maʿnan qāʾim fī l-dhāt/ fī l-maḥall* which is abridged to the single word. *Maʿnā* is thus associated with *maḥall*, whereas *ʿaraḍ* is associated with *jawhar*, the latter two being categorical terms.

After this I began to deal in what I should describe as a 'smallish way' with a few of the basic features of *Kalām* and with a couple of major theoretical topics too. One thing which was of considerable importance in how I learned to read the texts — in how I approached and sought to see and to understand the theoretical order and significance of what they said — should be mentioned here. It is that I had a number of close friends who were genuinely expert in a number of fields — several of them in physics and one in sociology of religion — but most importantly for my thinking about and trying to understand *Kalām*, a group of philosophical types, two of whom were specialists in Twentieth Century philosophy but also thought and wrote about classical and medieval thought. (I talk in the past here because one of them died a few years ago.) Most importantly they were primarily devoted to seeing and understanding philosophical issues and questions as such and then how as such they were seen and understood in the cultural and intellectual contexts of various historical periods. Our conversations were hardly ever formal — mostly talk over food and beer with topics shifting and sliding from university politics to philosophy, theology, and science. During this time, and later too, I read a goodly number of major philosophical works and various other things spoken of or recommended by my friends. All of this contributed to my understanding of *Kalām*. I became ever more aware that the Ashʿarite and Muʿtazilite metaphysical systems that developed from the teaching of Abū ʿAlī al-Jubbāʾī were unique, each in its own way, and that in reading and seeking to understand them one had to be careful not to let himself be guided by any outside system. From an early point in my work on *Kalām* I sought to avoid the use of language that evoked as such the concepts and constructs of other theoretical systems. The general problem of understanding the theoretical

[8] *Bibliography*, no. 32.

systems of classical *Kalām* and of rendering their formal terminology I discussed at some length in my presidential address to the American Oriental Society in 1996.[9]

The systems of different *Kalām* masters often differ significantly. With the Ashʿarites, for example, al-Ashʿarī's system is quite different from that of al-Bāqillānī, who in some works developed his own version of Abū Hāshim's concept of *aḥwāl*, and al-Juwaynī's system was again different, as were those of a number of lesser masters. As I came clearly to see somewhat recently, 'state' is, in most cases, not a proper translation for *ḥāl* in its technical use, and the sense of the concept differs significantly in the usage of al-Bāqillānī and al-Juwaynī and in that of ʿAbd al-Jabbār. One has, however, to be careful concerning language and terminology; al-Juwaynī's *Shāmil*, for example, is written in essentially normal *Kalām* style and language, whereas his *Irshād*, a short manual plainly written to impress somebody, is in a rather different style and occasionally with somewhat peculiar language, while his *Risālat al-Niẓāmīya*, written to honour the vizier, Niẓām al-Mulk, is written in another, conspicuously different style.

So, I was learning. The first thing that came out of all this was a short paper on the early development of *Kalām* delivered at the Third Congress of Arabists and Islamists held in Ravello in 1966.[10] It was at this meeting that I made the acquaintance of a number of colleagues with whom I was to form and maintain close contacts. Among the most important for my *Kalām* studies were Abūnā Anawati and Louis Gardet and the Sheikh Yūsuf[11] who doubtless remembers our being rebuked for sitting atop a column during a concert. The event that most stuck in my mind as one of the high points of the meeting was when a young man read a paper in which he sought to show that Greek poetry had a significant influence on Arabic poetry and Armand Abel, who was chairman of the session, thanked him for a paper that showed more creative imagination than the authors of whom he spoke. I attended also the following conferences in Coimbra, where I read a short piece on Abū Hāshim's theory of states,[12] and others in Brussels, and Sweden.[13] It was at the Coimbra meeting that Gerhard[14] and I got to know each other. In 1971 I

[9] *Bibliography*, no. 50.
[10] *Bibliography*, no. 23.
[11] Professor Josef van Ess of the University of Tübingen (Ed.).
[12] *Bibliography*, no. 25.
[13] *Bibliography*, no. 28.
[14] Professor Gerhard Endress of the University of Bochum (Ed.).

produced a paper on the questions of nature, creation, and causality in *Kalām* and *Falsafa* for a colloquium held in honour of Harry Wolfson. It is the only scholarly paper I ever produced which begins with a poem. The audience was unimpressed. The acts of the colloquium were never published so the study eventually appeared in a collection of essays assembled by Parviz Morewedge, who made several gratuitous emendations of his own without ever sending me any proofs.

All of these were short pieces that dealt with a few basic matters — relatively simple presentations of some of the things of which I was beginning to get a better understanding. Several other short pieces were written for one or another occasion at which my participation was requested and so appeared at odd intervals. One of them was on the nonexistent and the possible in Muʿtazilite teaching, also prepared for a volume that was never to appear and was published eventually in *MIDEO*.[15] Another on reason and revealed law in *Kalām* and *Falsafa* was prepared for the Festschrift in honour of Gardet and Anawati.[16]

Of considerable help to my reading of the *Kalām* texts was that for my own entertainment I read a lot of literary Arabic, poetry as well as prose, for one has to have a good knowledge and experience of the classical language as such if he is to work seriously in *Kalām*, or in *Falsafa* for that matter. (The so called *fuṣḥā* is not the classical language.) There came a point, however — I do not now remember precisely when or why — when I realised that for my understanding of *Kalām* a knowledge of classical syntax was not sufficient and that I had to read the early Arab grammarians, i.e., that in order to understand the language of the *mutakallimūn* properly one has to hear it as they heard it, not as the significance of its syntax and sentence structure is heard and unreflectively understood on the basis of another, unrelated language. So, I began at the beginning, with Sībawayh's *Book*. Understanding what he was saying and why proved to be more difficult than I had anticipated, but eventually much more rewarding as I came to see the remarkable insight and precision with which he conceived and formulated his rules and analyses. After a time you come to know what the author will say next regarding a particular question, but you don't really have it until later when you see and appreciate why, within the context of the system, that is what he must say. I might add here that one does well to use or at least to consult an Arabic lexicon,

[15] *Bibliography*, no. 54.
[16] *Bibliography*, no. 29.

e.g., the *Tāj al-Lugha*, and not to rely wholly on a dictionary that is into a European language.

Historically *ʿIlm al-Kalām* and *ʿIlm al-Naḥw* took shape together in the same intellectually creative environment as essentially native sciences. To come to know the two is to come to see the intellectual context of the one and of the other more clearly. And they thought and wrote in clear and correct Arabic. Notably, the logical reasoning of the *mutakallimūn* is in several respects dependent on the grammarians' analysis of predicational sentences and is, in fact, basically analytic. It is worth noting here that the question of language — of lexicon and syntax — is the main point of the famous dispute between Abū Saʿīd al-Sīrāfī and Mattā b. Yūnus. It is in no way a serious intellectual debate, albeit a number of scholars have naively taken it so, but rather a rhetorical boxing match, purposefully arranged in order to show that Mattā b. Yūnus is not very bright and that he and with him other devotees of *Falsafa*, including al-Kindī, are not capable of expressing themselves in clear and precise Arabic. *Naṭaqa, yanṭiqu* means to speak and speak clearly, and at the end of the dialogue the *manṭiqī* is reduced to silence. (Some have taken it that al-Sīrāfī does not like or appreciate Aristotle and the philosophical tradition, but they might get a somewhat different impression if they examined his *Commentary on Sībawayh's* Book.) The technical vocabulary of the *mutakallimūn* of the classical period, specialised and refined though it be, is not corrupted by the usage of translators; they never, for example, employ *sabab* as an equivalent of *ʿilla*. Later *Kalām*, however, came under the influence of elements of the *Falsafa* and its vocabulary, and this has caused problems to some scholars whose sense and understanding of *Kalām* were primarily founded on works such as al-Ījī's *Mawāqif* and al-Jurjānī's commentary; they failed to grasp the basic lexicon, structure, and sense of classical *Kalām*.

Eventually, having worked through a good deal of ʿAbd al-Jabbār's *Mughnī*, I produced several rather serious pieces on the teaching of the Muʿtazila, the first, on the autonomy of the human agent according to ʿAbd al-Jabbār, also prepared for a volume that never appeared and was ultimately published in *Le Muséon* in 1982.[17] *Beings and their Attributes* was a more ambitious work, some of the first section of which could do with some revision.[18] About the same time I prepared a couple of short pieces for two colloquia on moral theory, the one a general sort of essay

[17] *Bibliography*, no. 34.
[18] *Bibliography*, no. 4.

on moral obligation in classical *Kalām* and the other a rather short piece entitled 'Can God do what is Wrong?'[19]

By the time the latter two were completed, however, I had decided that the Ashʿarite tradition was obviously of far greater importance to the formation and history of Sunnī theology than was that of the Muʿtazila, however philosophically interesting the thought of the latter might be, and that it was to the works of the Ashʿarites that I should devote my efforts. The quest, again, was to understand their theology as such, not simply to display the primary theses along with the formalities of the systems. The theology of the systems extends beyond mere technical theological reasoning. One thinks, for example, of the use of Ashʿarite theological elements in al-Qushayrī's *Laṭāʾif al-Ishārāt* and the *ʿAqīda* pieced together out of various Ṣūfī statements and formulae that stands at the beginning of his *Risāla*. Save for a small portion of al-Juwaynī's *Shāmil* published in 1969, major texts of classical *Kalām* were not available, so off I went to spend a year with Abūnā Anawati in ʿAbbāsīya[20] while I worked in the Dār al-Kutub and some six weeks also with Dominicans in Istanbul where I read manuscripts mostly in the Süleymaniye and at Topkapi. As a result I acquired microfilms of a number of important Ashʿarite works.

Having now a goodly set of Ashʿarite texts I worked my way through them as time allowed, making indices and somewhat detailed notes as I had earlier done with the Muʿtazilite material. A number of my publications during this period dealt with a somewhat motley assortment of topics as were requested for particular occasions, meetings and colloquia. And I did a few texts, including some additions to al-Juwaynī's *Shāmil* found in a Tehran manuscript, microfilm of which was sent me by Mehdi Muhaqqiq.[21] I should maybe have edited the entire manuscript, but there was the problem of time, especially since there is the problem of identifying likely variants found in two compendia of the work. And I also published in *MIDEO* 18 an edition of al-Ashʿarī's *al-Ḥathth ʿalā l-Baʿth*, previously known as *Risālat Istiḥsān al-Khawḍ fī ʿIlm al-Kalām*, based on new sources, one of which, found in the *Ghunya* of al-Anṣārī, one of al-Juwaynī's students, gave the original title, sc., that which is found in the medieval bibliographies.[22] And I prefaced the text with a lengthy analysis of its formal structure as it seemed appropriate to

[19] *Bibliography*, no. 37 and no. 39 respectively.
[20] In Cairo (Ed.).
[21] Abū l-Maʿālī al-Juwaynī, *al-Kitab al-Shāmil fī Uṣūl al-Dīn*, Teheran 1981.
[22] *Bibliography*, no. 43.

call attention to the precision of al-Ashʿarī's argument as it seemed significant for our understanding of his status as the founder of the school.

At some point in the mid '80s I became interested in the work of al-Ghazālī, whose writings I had not looked at for years. I had bought a copy of his *al-Maqṣad al-Asnā* on the divine names and in reading it now for the first time was struck by his direct — in some places downright plagiaristic — use of Avicenna. Plagiarism is not at all uncommon in the writings of al-Ghazālī, but his use of Avicenna is of major significance to his theology. The first piece I wrote was in 1988 on his understanding of *Taqlīd* — here again for a colloquium whose acta were never published.[23] As I was rereading some of al-Ghazālī's other works, including parts of *Iḥyā' ʿUlūm al-Dīn*, it became clear to me that he was certainly not an Ashʿarite in any proper sense of the word. This resulted first in a paper for a colloquium held in Morigny in 1986[24] and subsequently was dealt with in some detail in my monograph, *Creation and the Cosmic System,* in which I set out the evidence for the dominance of Avicenna in major elements of al-Ghazālī's cosmology albeit he characteristically makes no serious attempt to deal with the philosophical difficulties involved.[25] His claim in the *Munqidh* to have achieved a complete understanding of logic and all the philosophical sciences is a bit fanciful to say the very least.

I attempted to set all this in context in *Al-Ghazālī and the Ashʿarite System* by noting that while a number of his works are manifestly addressed to different audiences there is a consistent identification of particular kinds or modes of religious discourse each one of which is distinguished as appropriate to individuals of a particular level of intellectual capacity and achievement.[26] The masters of *Kalām* are on a rather low level, while his own brand of neo-Platonising theology stands at the top. This fits with his analysis of *Taqlīd* — *Taqlīd* to various forms and genera of religious teaching according to the ability of the individual *muqallid*, while those of the highest level, like himself, are altogether free to pursue and to publish the 'insights' transmitted from the highest celestial sphere through the hierarchy of lower celestial spirits. This is quite different from the Ashʿarite understanding of the matter, which I had dealt with in an earlier study.[27]

[23] *Bibliography*, no. 48.
[24] *Bibliography*, no. 42.
[25] *Bibliography*, no. 5.
[26] *Bibliography*, no. 6. Some aspects of this are dealt with from another perspective in *Bibliography*, no. 52. There is a shorter version of this which was presented as a lecture at the University of Tunis: *Bibliography*, no. 51.
[27] Cf. *Bibliography*, no. 44.

After all this I turned back, so to speak, to the most basic metaphysical teaching of Ashʿarite *Kalām* of the classical period. This is not to suggest that I had or have any serious understanding of topics and questions I have not sought to investigate thoroughly, but I had come to a good understanding of a few very basic matters. Moreover, I had over a number of years accumulated a great quantity of data and thought that one of the most useful things I could do for those who were interested in *Kalām*, and particularly for those who wished to study the texts, was to set out a summary account of the fundamentals of their metaphysics along with a detailed examination of the technical terms and their formal use by several of the leading masters. This took some time to prepare and finally appeared under the title 'The Ašʿarite Ontology: I. Primary Entities'.[28] The 'I' was not necessarily intended to suggest that there was to be a 'II' but rather to indicate that only the rudiments were treated here. There was a short piece on the expression *lam yazal* which had appeared a bit earlier,[29] but that was simply another offshoot of my interest in the formal terminology of the texts but useful, I think, in that it illustrates the subtle differences between a number of early *mutakallimūn* in their conception and understanding of a primary theological question located and identified by a common, though sometimes in itself lexically ambivalent, expression. The article on primary entities was supplemented then by a study on the non-existent and the possible in classical Ashʿarite teaching, a topic that turned out to be a bit more complex — and certainly more interesting — than I had foreseen.[30] I do feel that these two studies make clear the high intellectual acuity of the major Ashʿarite masters. Al-Ghazālī, of course, considers them benighted, in part because they do not subscribe to the logic of the *falāsifa*, but their reasoning is consistently more rigorous than his. There has also appeared a short piece on the somewhat various senses of *al-aḥkām* and *al-aḥwāl* by different masters that I think will prove somewhat useful to those who would pursue the subject of classical *Kalām*.[31]

So — I spent most of my career in a field that most viewed as a theoretically rather unsophisticated kind of religious discourse that was unworthy of serious study. That attitude has changed, at least for those few interested in philosophy who know what it is.

[28] *Bibliography*, no. 53.
[29] *Bibliography*, no. 49.
[30] *Bibliography*, no. 54.
[31] *Bibliography*, no. 55.

BIBLIOGRAPHY[1]

Monographs:

1. *The Jeremias of Pethion Ibn Ayyûb al-Sahhâr*, Washington, D.C.: Catholic University of America Press, 1959 [partial publication of 1956 CUA dissertation: see also no. 15].
2. *The Metaphysics of Created Being according to Abû l-Hudhayl al-ʿAllâf. A Philosophical Study of the Earliest* Kalâm (*Uitgaven van het Nederlands Historisch-Archaeologisch Instituut te Istanbul*, 21), Istanbul: Nederlands Historisch-Archaeologisch Instituut in het Nabije Oosten, 1966 (also in: no. 8).
3. *The Wisdom of Jesus ben Sirach (Sinai ar. 155. IXth-Xth cent.)* (*Corpus Scriptorum Christianorum Orientalium*, 357-358: *Scriptores Arabici*, 30-31), Louvain: Secrétariat du Corpus Scriptorum Christianorum Orientalium, 1974.
4. *Beings and their Attributes. The Teaching of the Basrian School of the Muʿtazila in the Classical Period* (*Studies in Islamic Philosophy and Science*), Albany: State University of New York Press, 1978.
5. *Creation and the Cosmic System: al-Ghazâlî & Avicenna* (*Abhandlungen der Heidelberger Akademie der Wissenschaften. Philosophisch-historische Klasse*, Jhg. 1992, Abh. 1), Heidelberg: Carl Winter Universitätsverlag, 1992.
6. *Al-Ghazālī and the Ashʿarite School* (*Duke Monographs in Medieval and Renaissance Studies*, 15), Durham - London: Duke University Press, 1994.

Collections of articles:

7. *Philosophy, Theology and Mysticism in Medieval Islam: Texts and Studies on the Development and History of* Kalām, *Volume 1* (*Variorum Collected Studies Series*), Aldershot: Ashgate, 2005.

[1] This bibliography was compiled by Monica Blanchard and J.E. Montgomery, with the invaluable assistance of Dimitri Gutas, Thérèse-Anne Druart and Sidney Griffith.

8. *Early Islamic Theology: The Muʿtazilites and al-Ashʿarī. Texts and Studies on the Development and History of* Kalām, *Volume 2* (*Variorum Collected Studies Series*), Aldershot: Ashgate, 2006.
9. *Classical Islamic Theology: The Ashʿarites. Texts and Studies on the Development and History of* Kalām, *Volume 3* (*Variorum Collected Studies Series*), Aldershot: Ashgate, 2006.

ARTICLES:

10. *An Etymology of ʿΑΓΙΟΣ in a Work of Caesarius of Arles*, in: *Traditio: Studies in Ancient and Medieval History, Thought and Religion* 8 (1952), p. 387-389.
11. *A "Citation" from the Prophet Jeremias in Ibn Qutaiba and Tabari*, in: *Catholic Biblical Quarterly* 17 (1955), p. 379-402.
12. *The Origin of the Arabic Philosophical Term* Annîyah, in: *Les Cahiers de Byrsa* 6 (1956), p. 181-201 (also in: no. 7).
13. *Some Textual Notes on the Oriental Versions of Themistius' Paraphrase of Book Λ of the* Metaphysics, *Les Cahiers de Byrsa* 8 (1958-1959), p. 215-230 (also in: no. 7).
14. *Some Fragments of Isḥâq's Translation of the* De Anima, in: *Les Cahiers de Byrsa* 8 (1958-1959), p. 231-251 (also in: no. 7).
15. *The Jeremias of Pethion ibn Ayyûb al-Sahhâr*, in: *Catholic Biblical Quarterly* 21 (1959), p. 136-170 [partial publication of 1956 CUA dissertation: see also no. 1].
16. *The Description of the "Bear" in DN 7,5*, in: *Catholic Biblical Quarterly* 21 (1959), p. 505-507.
17. *The Literary Unity of* Sûrat al-Munâfiqîn *(63)*, in: *Catholic Biblical Quarterly* 23 (1961), p. 257-269.
18. *Social Evolution and the Human Species*, in: *American Catholic Sociological Review* 23 (1962), p. 310-323.
19. *A Note on 3 Kings 19,10.14*, in: *Catholic Biblical Quarterly* 25 (1963), p. 410-414.
20. *The Neoplatonism of Ǧahm ibn Ṣafwân*, in: *Le Muséon* 78 (1965), p. 395-424 (also in: no. 7).
21. *The Structure of Created Causality according to al-Ašʿarî. An Analysis of the* Kitâb al-Lumaʿ, §§82-164, in: *Studia Islamica* 25 (1966), p. 2-75 (also in: no. 8).
22. Al-Maʿnà: *Some Reflections on the Technical Meanings of the Term in the* Kalâm *and its Use in the Physics of Muʿammar*,

in: *Journal of the American Oriental Society* 87 (1967), p. 248-259.

23. *Remarks on the Early Development of the* Kalam, in: *Atti del terzo Congresso di Studi Arabici e Islamici, Ravello 1-6 settembre 1966*, Naples: Istituto Universitario Orientale, 1967, p. 315-329 (also in: no. 7).
24. *The Divine Attributes according to the Teaching of Abû l-Hudhayl al-ʿAllâf*, in: *Le Muséon* 82 (1969), p. 451-506 (also in: no. 8).
25. *Abu Hashim's Theory of 'States': its Structure and Function*, in: *Actas do quarto congresso de estudos árabes e islâmicos, Coimbra-Lisboa, 1 a 8 de setembro de 1968*, Leiden: Brill, 1971, p. 85-100 (also in: no. 8).
26. *Several Fundamental Assumptions of the Baṣra School of the Muʿtazila*, in: *Studia Islamica* 33 (1971), p. 5-18 (also in: no. 8).
27. *Notes and Remarks on the* Ṭabâʾiʿ *in the Teaching of al-Mâturîdî*, in: *Mélanges d'Islamologie. Volume dédié à la mémoire de Armand Abel par ses collègues, ses élèves et ses amis*, ed. PIERRE SALMON, Leiden: Brill, 1974, p. 137-149 (also in: no. 9).
28. *Al-Ašʿarî's Conception of the Nature and Role of Speculative Reasoning in Theology*, in: *Proceedings of the VIth Congress of Arabic and Islamic Studies Visby 13-16 August, Stockholm, 17-19 August 1972* (*Kungliga Vitterhets historie och antikvitetsakademien handlingar: Filologisk-filosofiska serien*, 15), ed. FRITHIOF RUNDGREN, Stockholm: Almqvist and Wiksell International, 1975, p. 136-154 (also in: no. 8).
29. *Reason and Revealed Law: A Sample of Parallels and Divergences in* Kalâm *and* Falsafa, in: *Récherches d'Islamologie. Recueil d'articles offert à Georges C. Anawati et Louis Gardet par leurs collègues et amis* (*Bibliothèque Philosophique de Louvain*, 26), ed. SIMONE VON RIET, Leuven: Peeters and Louvain-la-Neuve: Éditions de l'Institut Supérieur de Philosophie, 1977, p.123-138 (also in: no. 7).
30. Kalām *and Philosophy: a Perspective from one Problem*, in: *Islamic Philosophical Theology* (*Studies in Islamic Philosophy and Science*), ed. PARVIZ MOREWEDGE, Albany: State University of New York Press, 1979, p. 71-95.
31. Al-Maʿdūm wal-Mawjūd: *The Non-Existent, the Existent, and the Possible in the Teaching of Abū Hāshim and his Followers*, in: *Mélanges de l'Institut Dominicain d'Études Orientales du Caire* 14 (1980), p. 185-210 (also in: no. 8).

32. *Meanings are Spoken of in Many Ways: The Earlier Arab Grammarians*, in: *Le Muséon* 94 (1981), p. 259-319 (also in: no. 7).
33. *Attribute, Attribution, and Being: Three Islamic Views*, in: *Philosophies of Existence, Ancient and Medieval*, ed. PARVIZ MOREWEDGE, New York: Fordham University Press, 1982, p. 258-278 (also in: no. 9).
34. *The Autonomy of the Human Agent in the Teaching of ʿAbd al-Ǧabbār*, in: *Le Muséon* 95 (1982), p. 323-355 (also in: no. 9).
35. *Two Short Dogmatic Works of Abū l-Qāsim al-Qushayrī. First Part: Edition and Translation of* Lumaʿ fī l-Iʿtiqād, in: *Mélanges de l'Institut Dominicain d'Études Orientales du Caire* 15 (1982), p. 53-74 (also in: no. 7).
36. *Two Short Dogmatic Works of Abū l-Qāsim al-Qushayrī. Second Part: Edition and Translation of* al-Fuṣūl fī l-Uṣūl, in: *Mélanges de l'Institut Dominicain d'Études Orientales du Caire* 16 (1983), p. 59-94 (also in: no. 7).
37. *Moral Obligation in Classical Muslim Theology*, in: *Journal of Religious Ethics* 11 (1983), p. 204-223 (also in: no. 9).
38. *Bodies and Atoms: the Ashʿarite Analysis*, in: *Islamic Theology and Philosophy: Studies in Honor of G.F. Hourani*, ed. MICHAEL E. MARMURA, Albany: State University of New York Press, 1984, p. 39-53, 287-293 (also in: no. 9).
39. *Can God do what is Wrong?*, in: *Divine Omniscience and Omnipotence in Medieval Philosophy. Islamic, Jewish and Christian Perspectives* (*Texts and Studies in the History of Logic and Philosophy*, 25), ed. TAMAR RUDAVSKY, Dordrecht - Boston - Lancaster: D. Reidel, 1985, p. 69-79 (also in: no. 9).
40. Two Islamic Views of Human Agency, in: *La notion de liberté au moyen age: Islam, Byzance, Occident* (*Penn-Paris-Dumbarton Oaks Colloquia*, 4, session des 12-15 octobre 1982), ed. G. MAKDISI, D. SOURDEL, and J. SOURDEL-THOMINE, Paris: Société d'Édition «Les Belles Lettres», 1985, p. 37-49 (also in: no. 9).
41. *The Use of the Enneads by John of Scythopolis*, in: *Le Muséon* 100 (1987), p. 101-108 (also in: no. 7).
42. *Al-Ghazâlî's Use of Avicenna's Philosophy, in: Revue des Études Islamiques* 55-57 (1987-1989), p. 271-285 (also in: no. 7).
43. *Al-Ashʿarī's* «Kitāb al-Ḥathth ʿalā l-Baḥth», in: *Mélanges de l'Institut Dominicain d'Études Orientales du Caire* 18 (1988), p. 83-152 (also in: no. 8).

44. *Knowledge and* Taqlîd*: the Foundations of Religious Belief in Classical Ashʿarism*, in: *Journal of the American Oriental Society* 109.1 (1989), p. 37-62 (also in: no. 9).
45. *Al-Ustādh Abū Isḥāḳ: an ʿAḳīda together with Selected Fragments*, in: *Mélanges de l'Institut Dominicain d'Études Orientales du Caire* 19 (1989), p. 129-202 (also in: no. 9).
46. *Elements in the Development of the Teaching of al-Ashʿarī*, in: *Le Muséon* 104 (1991), p. 141-190 (also in: no. 8).
47. *The Science of* Kalām, in: *Arabic Sciences and Philosophy* 2 (1992), p. 7-37 (also in: no. 9).
48. *Al-Ghazalī on* Taqlīd*: Scholars, Theologians and Philosophers*, in: *Zeitschrift für Geschichte der arabisch-islamischen Wissenschaften* 7 (1991-1992), p. 207-252 (also in: no. 7).
49. "Lam Yazal" *as a Formal Term in Muslim Theological Discourse*, in: *Mélanges de l'Institut Dominicain d'Études Orientales du Caire* 22 (1995), p. 243-270 (also in: no. 7).
50. *Hearing and Saying what was Said*, in: *Journal of the American Oriental Society* 116.4 (1996), p. 611-618 (presidential address, delivered at the 206th meeting of the American Oriental Society, Philadelphia, Pennsylvania, March 19, 1996) (also in: no. 9).
51. *Contrastes entre trois systèmes: Muʿtazilisme, Ashʿarisme et Ghazālī*, in: *Les Cahiers de Tunisie / al-Kurrāsāt al-Tūnisīya* 49, no. 173 (1996), p. 85-104.
52. *Currents and Countercurrents*, in: *Islam: Essays on Scripture, Thought and Society. A Festschrift in Honour of Anthony H. Johns* (*Islamic Philosophy, Theology and Science*, 28), ed. PETER G. RIDDELL and TONY STREET, Leiden: Brill, 1997, p. 113-135 (also in: no. 7).
53. *The Ašʿarite Ontology: I. Primary Entities*, in: *Arabic Sciences and Philosophy* 9 (1999), p. 163-231 (also in: no. 9).
54. *The Non-Existent and the Possible in Classical Ashʿarite Teaching*, in: *Mélanges de l'Institut Dominicain d'Études Orientales du Caire* 24 (2000), p. 1-37 (also in: no. 9).
55. *Al-Aḥkām in Classical Ašʿarite Teaching*, in: *De Zénon d'Élée à Poincaré. Recueil d'études en hommage à Roshdi Rashed* (*Les cahiers du MIDEO*, 1), ed. RÉGIS MORELON and AHMAD HASNAWI, Leuven: Peeters, 2004, p. 753-777 (also in: no. 9).
56. *Yā Kalām*, in: no. 7 (above): see also p. 5-14 (of the present volume).

ENCYCLOPEDIA ENTRIES:

57. *Ḥāl*, in: *The Encyclopaedia of Islam, New Edition*, Supplement, Fascicules 5-6, Leiden: E.J. Brill, 1982, p. 343-348.
58. *Al-Ashʿarī*, in: *Encyclopedia of Religion*, ed. MIRCEA ELIADE, I, New York: Macmillan, 1987, p. 445-449.
59. *Ashʿarīyah*, in: *Encyclopedia of Religion*, ed. MIRCEA ELIADE, I, New York: Macmillan, 1987, p. 449-455.

REVIEW ARTICLES:

60. *The* Kalâm*, an Art of Contradiction-Making or Theological Science? Some Remarks on the Question*, in: *Journal of the American Oriental Society* 88 (1968), p. 295-309 (review of MICHEL ALLARD, *Le Problème des attributs divins dans la doctrine d'al-Ašʿarî et de ses premiers grands disciples* (*Récherches publiées sous la direction de l'Institut de Lettres orientales de Beyrouth*, 28), Beirut: Imprimerie Catholique, 1965).
61. *Ambiguities of Understanding*, in: *Journal of the American Oriental Society* 106.2 (1986), p. 313-321 (review of WILFRED CANTWELL SMITH, *On Understanding Islam: Selected Studies* (*Religion and Reason*, 19. *Method and Theory in the Study and Interpretation of Religion*), The Hague - Paris - New York: Mouton, 1981).

REVIEWS:

62. Review of: H.A.R. GIBB and HAROLD BOWEN, *Islamic Society and the West, Volume I, Islamic Society in the Eighteenth Century, Part 2*, New York: Oxford University Press, 1957, in: *Catholic Historical Review* 44 (1958), p. 98-99.
63. Review of: GEORGE M. LAMSA, *The Holy Bible from Ancient Eastern Manuscripts, containing the Old and New Testaments, translated from the Peshitta, the Authorized Bible of the Church of the East*, Philadelphia: A.J. Holman, 1957, in: *Catholic Biblical Quarterly* 20 (1958), p. 384-389.
64. Review of: JOHN H. MARKS — VIRGIL M. ROGERS, *A Beginner's Handbook to Biblical Hebrew*, Nashville: Abingdon Press, 1958, in: *Catholic Biblical Quarterly* 20 (1958), p. 389-390.

65. Review of: HENRI MICHAUD, *Jésus selon le Coran* (*Cahiers théologiques*, 46), Neuchâtel: Delachaux et Niestlé, 1960), in: *Catholic Biblical Quarterly* 25 (1963), p. 478-480.
66. Review of: J.-M. SOLÁ-SOLÉ, *L'Infinitif sémitique* (*Bibliothèque de l'École Pratique des Hautes Études, Section des Sciences historiques et philologiques*, 315) Paris: Champion, 1961, in: *Catholic Biblical Quarterly* 26 (1964), p.127-132.
67. Review of: LOUIS COSTAZ, S.J., *Dictionnaire syriaque-français, Syriac-English Dictionary, Qâmûs suryânî-'arabî.* Beyrouth: Imprimerie Catholique, 1963, in: *Catholic Biblical Quarterly* 26 (1964), p. 364-365.
68. Review of: BEN EDWIN PERRY, *Secundus the Silent Philosopher; The Greek Life of Secundus, Critically Edited and Restored so far as possible, together with Translations of the Greek and Oriental Versions, the Latin and Oriental Texts, and a Study of the Tradition* (*Philological Monographs*, 22), Ithaca: Cornell University Press, 1964, in: *Journal of the American Oriental Society* 86.3 (1966), p. 347-350.
69. Review of: FATHALLAH KHOLEIF, *A Study on Fakhr al-Dīn al-Rāzī and his Controversies in Transoxiana* (*Recherches publiées sous la Direction de l'Institut de Lettres orientales de Beyrouth, Série I: Pensée arabe et musulmane*, 31) Beyrouth: Dar el Machreq, 1966, in: *Bibliotheca Orientalis* 25 (1968), p. 229-233.
70. Review of: JOSEF VAN ESS, *Die Erkenntnislehre des 'Aḍudaddin al-Īcī, Uebersetzung und Kommentar des ersten Buches seiner Mawāqif* (*Akademie der Wissenschaften und der Literatur, Veröffentlichungen der orientalischen Kommission*, 22), Wiesbaden: Franz Steiner Verlag, 1966, in: *Journal of the American Oriental Society* 89.1 (1969), p. 278-279.
71. Review of: F.E. PETERS, *Aristotle and the Arabs, The Aristotelian Tradition in Islam* (*New York University Studies in Near Eastern Civilization*, 1), New York: New York University Press and London: University of London Press, 1968, in: *Journal of the American Oriental Society* 90.4 (1970), p. 556-559.
72. Review of: JOSEF VAN ESS, *Traditionistische Polemik gegen 'Amr b. 'Ubaid zu einem Text des 'Alī b. 'Umar ad-Daraquṭnī* (*Beiruter Texte und Studien*, 7), Beirut: in Kommission bei Franz Steiner Verlag, Wiesbaden, 1967, in: *Bibliotheca Orientalis* 28 (1971), p. 97-98.
73. Review of: MUHSIN MAHDI, *Alfarabi's Book of Letters (*Kitāb al-Ḥurūf*); Commentary on Aristotle's* Metaphysics. *Arabic text, edited*

with introduction and notes (*Recherches publiées sous la direction de l'Institut de Lettres orientales de Beyrouth, Série I: Pensée arabe et musulmane*, 46), Beyrouth: Dar El-Machreq, 1969, in: *Journal of the American Oriental Society* 92.2 (1972), p. 393-395.

74. Review of: FRANZ ROSENTHAL, *Knowledge Triumphant: the Concept of Knowledge in Medieval Islam*, Leiden: E. J. Brill, 1970, in: *Journal of the American Oriental Society* 93.1 (1973), p. 108-109.
75. Review of *Šurûḥ ʿalà Arisṭû mafqûda fî l-yûnânîya wa-rasâʾil uḫrà: Commentaires dur Aristote perdus en grec et autres épîtres* (*Recherches publiées sous la direction de l'Institut de Lettres orientales de Beyrouth; N.S., A: Langue et pensée islamiques*, 1), ed. ʿABDURRAḤMĀN BADAWI, Beyrouth: Dar El-Mashreq, 1971, in: *Journal of the American Oriental Society* 94.2 (1974), p. 245-247.
76. Review of: W. MONTGOMERY WATT, *The Formative Period of Islamic Thought*, Edinburgh: The University Press, 1973, in: *Bibliotheca Orientalis* 33 (1976), p. 69-74.
77. Review of: *Al-Mâturîdî, Abû Manẓûr Muḥammad ibn Muḥammad ibn Maḥmûd al-Samarqandî:* Kitâb al-Tawḥîd (*Recherches publiées sous la direction de l'Institut de Lettres orientales de Beyrouth*, Série I: *Pensé arabe et musulmane*, 50), ed. FATHALLAH KHOLEIF, Beirut: Dâr el-Machreq, 1970, in: *Orientalistische Literaturzeitung* 71.1 (1976), col. 54-56.
78. Review of: *Islamic Philosophy and the Classical Tradition: Essays presented by his Friends and Pupils to Richard Walzer on his Seventieth Birthday*, ed. S.M. STERN, ALBERT HOURANI, and VIVIAN BROWN, Columbia: University of South Carolina Press, 1972, in: *Journal of the American Oriental Society* 96.2 (1976), p. 287-290.
79. Review of: HANS DAIBER, *Das theologisch-philosophische System des Muʿammar ibn ʿAbbâd as-Sulamî* (*Beiruter Texte und Studien*, 19), Beirut - Wiesbaden: Franz Steiner Verlag, 1975, in: *Bibliotheca Orientalis* 38 (1981), col. 737-758.
80. Review of: HARRY AUSTRYN WOLFSON, *The Philosophy of the Kalam* (*Structure and Growth of Philosophic Systems from Plato to Spinoza*, 4), Cambridge - London: Harvard University Press, 1976, in: *Orientalistische Literaturzeitung* 76.6 (1981), col. 571-572.
81. Review of: A. ELAMRANI-JAMAL, *Logique aristotélienne et grammaire arabe. Étude et documents* (*Études muslumanes*, 26) Paris: Librairie Philosophique J. Vrin, 1983, in: *Journal of the American Oriental Society* 106.4 (1986), p. 826.

82. Review of: WILFERD MADELUNG, *Religious Schools and Sects in Medieval Islam*, London: Variorum Reprints, 1985, in: *Bibliotheca Orientalis* 43 (1986), col. 812.
83. Review of: MUHAMMAD B. ʿABD AL-KARIM (sic) AL-SHAHRASTĀNĪ, *Muslim Sects and Divisions: the Section on Muslim Sects in* "Kitab al-Milal w'l-Nihal", transl. A.K. KAZI and J.G. FLYNN, in: *Middle East Studies Association Bulletin* 20.1 (1986), p. 113-114.
84. Review of: DANIEL GIMARET and GUY MONNOT, *Shahrastani: Livre des religions et des sects. Traduction, avec introduction et notes* (*Collection UNESCO d'Oeuvres Représentatives, série arabe*), Louvain: Peeters and UNESCO, 1986, in: *Journal of the American Oriental Society* 110.1 (1990), p. 139-140.
85. Review of: *Sprachphilosophie in Antike und Mittelalter* (*Bochumer Studien zur Philosophie*, 3), ed. BURKHARD MOJSISCH, Amsterdam: Verlag B. R. Grüner, 1986, in: *Journal of the American Oriental Society* 110.2 (1990), p. 356-360.
86. Review of: TILMAN NAGEL, *Die Festung des Glaubens, Triumpf und Scheitern des islamischen Rationalismus im 11. Jahrhundert*, München: Verlag C.H. Beck, 1988, in: *Bibliotheca Orientalis* 47 (1990), col. 501-503.
87. Review of: HANS DAIBER, *Wāṣil Ibn ʿAṭāʾ als Prediger und Theologe: Ein neuer Text aus dem 8. Jahrhundert n. Chr.* (*Islamic Philosophy and Theology, Texts and Studies*, 2), Leiden: E. J. Brill, 1988, in: *Journal of the American Oriental Society* 111.4 (1991), p. 795-798.
88. Review of: JOSEF VAN ESS, *Theologie und Gesellschaft im 2. und 3. Jahrhundert Hidschra: Eine Geschichte des religiösen Denkens im frühen Islam*, I-II, Berlin - New York: Walter de Gruyter, 1991-1992, in: *Journal of the American Oriental Society* 114.4 (1994), p. 682-684.
89. Review of: ALNOOR DHANANI, *The Physical Theory of Kalām. Atoms, Space, and Void in Basrian Muʿtazilī Cosmology* (*Islamic Philosophy, Theology and Science, Texts and Studies*, 14), Leiden: Brill, 1994, in: *Journal of the American Oriental Society* 116.2 (1996), p. 318-321.
90. Review of DANIEL GIMARET, *Lecture muʿtazilite du Coran: Le Tafsīr d'Abū ʿAlī al-Djubbāʾī (m. 303/915) partiellement reconstitué à partir de ses citateurs* (*Bibliothèque de l'École des hautes études, Section des sciences réligieuses*, 101), Leuven: Peeters, 1994, in: *Journal of the American Oriental Society* 117.2 (1997), p. 382-384.

91. Review of: JOSEF VAN ESS, *Theologie und Gesellschaft im 2. und 3. Jahrhundert Hidschra: Eine Geschichte des religiösen Denkens im frühen Islam*, III-VI, Berlin - New York: Walter de Gruyter, 1992,1996, 1993, 1995, in: *Journal of the American Oriental Society* 119.2 (1999), p. 313-315.

Qur'ān

SEVEN QUR'ANIC EMENDATIONS

JAMES A. BELLAMY
University of Michigan

When Joseph's brothers return to their father and report to him falsely that Joseph is no more, they tearfully explain: *Innā dhahabnā nastabiqu wa-taraknā Yūsufa ʿinda matāʿi-nā fa-ʾakala-hu l-dhiʾb,* 'We went off *nastabiqu* and left Joseph with our things, and a wolf ate him' (12:17).

The problem of *nastabiqu* has been dealt with extensively by the late Franz Rosenthal in his article, Nastabiqu *in Surah 12:17*, in: *Studies in Judaism and Islam*, Jerusalem, 1981, p. 14-26. He discusses the possible meanings, the grammatical structure of the phrase; he reviews the translations, both medieval and modern, and he also discusses v. 12, *yartaʿ wa-yalʿab*, for which he notes several variant readings. He then makes a pertinent statement which can be applied to Qur'anic variants in general and can be usefully quoted here:

> The term 'readings' is appropriate, whether or not *q-r-ʾ* ought to be translated 'to read'. The differences derive from studying a written text. Nothing suggests that we are dealing here with direct oral tradition from the prophet. We have no means to ascertain which of the 'readings' goes back to him (p. 22f).

There is only one variant recorded for *nastabiqu*; Arthur Jeffery assigns the variant *nantaḍilu* 'compete, contend' to Ibn Masʿūd, which is odd, since it is not found in Ibn Khālawayh, who cites more than 200 variants from Ibn Masʿūd.[1] In discussing *nantaḍilu*, Rosenthal points out that

> we are faced with the problem of whether *nantaḍilu* can claim to be taken as a genuine variant, or whether it is merely an interpretation elevated to the status of a variant reading by attaching the name of Ibn Masʿūd to it (p. 19).

I think however that we can make a reasonable case for Rosenthal's second possibility. First of all, as noted above, it is not listed by Ibn Khālawayh, whose business it was to collect *shādhdh* readings. This means that either he did not know it, or, if he did, he did not regard it as a variant. Second, *nantaḍilu* does turn up in the commentaries. Al-Bayḍāwī

[1] ARTHUR JEFFERY, *Materials for the History of the Text of the Qur'an*, Leiden, 1937, p. 48. IBN KHĀLAWAYH, *Mukhtaṣar fī Shawādhdh al-Qurʾān*, Cairo-Leipzig, 1934.

defines *nastabiqu* as *natasābaqu* in running or shooting, and adds that sometimes Forms VI and VIII have the same meaning (*yashtariku*), as *intiḍāl and tanāḍul*.[2] Al-Ṭabarī says that some think that *nastabiqu* had the meaning of *nantaḍilu min al-sibāq* 'competing in a race'.[3] For al-Ṭabarī and al-Bayḍawī *nantaḍilu* was simply *tafsīr* and had no place in the text, whether *shādhdh* or canonical, for if they had known it as a reading, they would surely have mentioned it as such. It thus appears that *nantaḍilu* in *tafsīr* is older than it is in the textual tradition, and that it somehow slipped into the latter, and was then ascribed to Ibn Masʿūd. But even if we decide to grant *nantaḍilu* the status of a genuine variant, all is not lost, since we can now apply the principle of the *lectio difficilior*, which of course, favors *nastabiqu*; this does not mean, however, that it is totally correct and does not have to be emended.

The allusions in some of the commentaries to competition in running, shooting, and racing had their effect on the translations. For the translations down to Maracci and Sale, see Rosenthal, *Nastabiqu*, p. 14f. Here we shall cite only the recent ones: Bell: 'We went off trying who should be foremost';[4] Rosenthal comments, 'Bell attempts being non-committal and succeeds only in being ambiguous' (*Nastabiqu*, p. 16); Blachère: 'Nous étions parties pour lutter à la course';[5] Paret: 'Wir gingen weg um einen Wettlauf zu machen'.[6]

Towards the end of his article, Rosenthal touches on the difficulty the exegetes had in reconciling the playing and sporting of the brothers with their status as religious figures, especially of Joseph, for whom such a great future was in store (*Nastabiqu*, p. 24f.). He notes that these attempts failed and then concludes:

> It seems that we stand a much better chance of getting close to the truth if we follow the simple procedure of looking at 12:17 by itself in isolation and abide by the unpretentious proposal that *nastabiqu* there indicates hurried advance.

Rosenthal's explanation of the word, however, immediately invites serious questions, such as: 'hurried advance' to where? or for what purpose?, neither of which can be answered from the text as it stands.

[2] ʿAbd Allāh b. ʿUmar al-Bayḍāwī, *Anwār al-Tanzīl wa-Asrār al-Taʾwīl*, ed. Henri Fleischer, I, Osnabrück, 1968, p. 455.

[3] Muḥammad b. Jarīr al-Ṭabarī, *Jāmiʿ al-Bayān fī Tafsīr al-Qurʾān*, XII, Beirut, 1989 (Būlāq, 1323), p. 96 (ult.).

[4] R. Bell, *The Qurʾan: Translated with a Critical Re-Arrangement of the Surahs*, Edinburgh, 1937, p. 210.

[5] R. Blachère, *Le Coran: traduction nouvelle*, Paris, 1949, p. 465.

[6] R. Paret, *Der Koran: Übersetzung*, Stuttgart, 1962, p. 191.

In dealing with this and the other *qaṣaṣ* passages of the Qur'ān, one should not forget that they are all fiction; they never really happened. So one cannot speculate as to what Joseph and his brothers would have done under given circumstances; one can only speculate as to what Muḥammad could have thought pertinent to the story he was telling. It seems that Muḥammad did not have to cogitate long and hard to find the right words; rather they came to him quickly and spontaneously, and so should be immediately clear and appropriate. In this case, they should answer the questions raised above or show that they are not pertinent. Since none of the proposed meanings satisfies this requirement, we are justified in concluding that we are faced with a textual error. I would emend *nastabiqu* to *nastaqī*, that is *dhahabnā nastaqī*, 'we went off to draw water'. The *yā'* in *nastaqī* was mistaken for the final flourish of the *qāf*, and the extra minim was inserted to give some kind of meaning to the form. *Nastabiqu* may have been influenced by *istabaqā* in v. 25. Watering the animals is something that every desert-traveller has to do from time to time, and doubtless Muḥammad watered many camels during his career as a travelling merchant.

II

In Sūra 30:48 God says that he sends the winds to spread the clouds that bring rain (*wadaq*) to the people at which they rejoice. He continues in v. 49: *wa-'in kānū min qabli 'an yunazzala ʿalay-him min qabli-hi mulbisīna*, 'Although they before it was caused to descend on them before it were in despair'. The sentence seems to be somewhat garbled. Ibn Masʿūd omits *min qabli-hi*.[7] Al-Ṭabarī, as we would expect, accepts the text as it stands and says simply that *min qabli-hi* is added for emphasis.[8]

Barth says that *min qabli 'an* and *min qabli-hi* do not go well together and that the second phrase is just a variant of the first.[9] The translators take different approaches to the verse. Paret, p. 336 works both phrases into his translation: 'Während sie vorher, bevor er auf sie herabgesandt wurde, ganz verzweifelt waren'. Bell, likewise: 'Although … before it was sent down to them … before it they had been in despair'. Blachère refers to Barth and Ibn Masʿūd, and omits the second phrase as a doublet.[10]

[7] JEFFERY, *Materials*, p. 73.

[8] *Jāmiʿ al-Bayān*, XXI, p. 35.

[9] J. BARTH, *Studien zur Kritik und Exegese des Qurans*, in: *Der Islam* 6 (1916), p. 112-48. (p. 135f.).

[10] PARET, *Der Koran*, p. 336; BELL, *The Qur'an*, p. 398; BLACHÈRE, *Le Coran*, p. 428.

Here Ibn Masʿūd seems to be correcting (i.e. emending) the ʿUthmanic text. His elimination of *min qabli-hi* removes a disturbing anomaly. However, *min qabli-hi* is not necessarily a mistake. If *min qabli ʾan yuanazzala ʿalay-him* were dropped, *min qabli-hi* would make good sense and would not require any explication. In other words, each phrase is correct if used alone, but the two together cause trouble. So the questions come up: where is the mistake and what caused it?

Under such circumstance, I believe we are justified in looking for a different sort of mistake. I would emend *min qabli-hi* to *min wabli-hi*, 'of His (i.e. God's) rain'; the scribe failed to pick up his pen to make the break between the *wāw and the bāʾ*, thus converting the *wāw* into a *qāf*. Possibly he was writing hurriedly to keep up with the dictation. *Wabl* does not occur in the Qur'ān, but we do find *wābil*, which has the same meaning, three times, in Q. 2:264 and 265 *bis*. The text may possibly have read *wābil* with the *ʾalif* omitted. *Min* is the normal preposition used with *ablasa*, 'to despair' of. Translate: 'although they were in despair of His rain before it was made to descend on them'.

III

In Sūra 3:96 we find a mistake so obvious that it is surprising that it remained in the text. *Inna ʾawwala baytin wuḍiʿa li-l-nāsi la-lladhī bi-Bakkata mubārakan wa-hudan li-l-ʿālamīn*, 'The first house (of worship) that was established for the people is the one which is in Bakka, blessed and a guidance for the worlds'. Bakka, which is taken to be another name for Makka, seems really never to have been in use. Most commentators try to distinguish Bakka from Makka, and assume that the former is the sanctuary and that Makka is the name of the surrounding area.[11] Some however take just the opposite view. Al-Ṭabarī, IV, 4, calls on etymology to confirm the majority view. Bakka is the *faʿla*-form of the root *b-k-k*, of which the Form I verb means 'to crowd' and Form VI *tabākka* 'to crowd one another', so this must refer to the crowding that takes place only during the *ṭawāf* in the sanctuary during the *ḥajj* and not in the surrounding area.[12]

Noteworthy is the fact that there are no *shawāhid* for Bakka and that almost all the occurrences of Bakka occur in discussions of the Qur'anic passage. I have run across only one occurrence in a different context. Wahb

[11] YĀQŪT AL-RŪMĪ, *Muʿjam al-Buldān*, I, Beirut, n.d., p. 475.
[12] *Jāmiʿ al-Bayān*, IV, p. 4.

b. Munabbih (d. 110/728 or 114/732) says that God once declared: *Anā Allāhu dhū Bakka* ..., 'I am God, the lord of Bakka ... '.[13] Probably a lengthy search would turn up a few others, but not very many. I have not found any simple sentences such as 'I left Bakka' or 'I arrived in Bakka', and I am convinced that they do not exist, otherwise they would have been snapped up by the commentators. If Bakka had been in use during the lifetime of the Prophet, it is extremely unlikely that it could have been so completely forgotten in the short time between the end of the revelation and the beginning of *Tafsīr* that it turned into an insoluble lexicographical problem.

It is clear that the passage is wrong, and the necessary emendation is obvious. Read *bi-Makkata*. The *mīm* was badly written and mistaken for another *bā'*.

IV

In Sūra 2:259 we read a parable of a man who while travelling through a ruined village wonders how it can ever be revived. So God causes him to die (*'amāta-hu*); then He revives him and asks him how long he has slept. The man replies a day or part of a day: God tells him that he has been dead a hundred years, and continues: *fa-nẓur 'ilā ṭaʿāmi-ka wa-sharābi-ka lam yatasannah wa-nẓur 'ilā ḥimāri-ka wa-li-najʿala-ka 'āyatan li-l-nāsi wa-nẓur 'ilā l-ʿiẓāmi kayfa nunshizu-hā thumma naksū-hā laḥman*, 'Look at your food and drink, they have not altered, and look at your ass, so that we may make you a sign to the people, and look at the bones, how we shall raise them up and clothe them with flesh'.

The negative in *lam yatasannah* is disturbing since God presumably wants to convince the man that he has been dead a hundred years, but if his food and drink have not altered, this would confirm his belief that he had been dead only a short time. Moreover, if his ass has been reduced to bones, his food and drink must have long since vanished. Here I would emend *lam yatasannah* to *kayfa yatasannahu*. Aside from making better sense, the two *kayfa*-clauses are rhetorically more harmonious. The extension of final *mīm* in some old hands does not hang below the line of writing, but lies along the line, and so resembles the extension of *fā'*.[14] Emending initial *lām* to initial *kāf* is no problem.

[13] Abū l-Faraj ʿAbd al-Raḥmān b. al-Jawzī, *Kitāb al-Wafā bi-Aḥwāl al-Muṣṭafā*, Cairo, 1966, p. 34.

[14] See examples in B. Gruendler, *The Development of the Arabic Scripts*, Atlanta, 1993, p. 99.

It is perhaps worth noting that M. Pickthall in his translation of the Qur'ān omits the negative: 'Just look at thy food and drink which have rotted'. Pickthall would not have deliberately mistranslated the text — he was a pious Muslim — so his sense of what is appropriate must have obscured his view of the text as it stands.

V

A curious problem as regards the Prophet's conduct is presented by Sūra 12:3: 'We are telling you the best of stories in that we have revealed to you this Koran, although before it you were one of the negligent' (*wa-'in kunta min qabli-hi mina l-ghāfilīn*). The last phrase has been translated as follows: Bell: 'although before that thou wert one of the negligent'; Blachère: 'bien qu'avant cela tu aies certes été parmi les Insouciants'. Paret: 'du hattest vordem keine Ahnung davon'.[15] T. Nagel notes that Bell and Blachère translate literally, but that Paret misses the meaning of *ghafala* and suppresses the conjunction *wa-in*.[16] (In fact, Paret has translated the commentators rather than the Qur'anic text.) Following Ibn ʿAbd al-Kāfī (alive ca. 400/1000), Nagel assumes that the first three verses of Sūra 12 are a Medinese addition to the original Meccan Sūra. However, this does not touch the problem of the Prophet's heedlessness or negligence. One should ask why the Prophet in composing this passage should have admitted to having been negligent or heedless. What previous act or attitude could have troubled his conscience to the extent that he had to confess it in the Qur'ān? That this question has no merit will be proven by our emendation, which will show that the difficulty is a simple and easily solved textual problem.

Of the meaning of *ghafala* there is no doubt. In the *Tāj*, al-Zabīdī quotes two main authorities on *ghafala*: Sībawayhi: *taraka-hu ʿalā dhukr*, 'he omitted it despite remembering it'; and the *Kitāb al-ʿAyn*: *ghafalta-hu wa-'anta dhākir la-hu*, 'you omitted it heedlessly although you remembered it'.[17] Al-Rāghib al-Iṣfahānī defines *ghafala* as *sahw yaʿtarī l-insān min qillat al-taḥaffuẓ wa-l-tayaqquẓ*, 'neglect, which

[15] BELL, *The Qur'an*, p. 218; BLACHÈRE. *Le Coran*, p. 462; PARET, *Der Koran*, p. 190.

[16] T. NAGEL, *Medinensische Einschübe in mekkanischen Suren. Ein Arbeitsbericht*, in: *The Qur'ān as Text*, ed. S. WILD, Leiden, 1996, p. 59-68 (p. 61).

[17] MURTAḌĀ AL-ḤUSAYNĪ AL-ZABĪDĪ, *Tāj al-ʿArūs min Jawāhir al-Qāmūs*, XXX, Kuwait, 1965, p. 108.

affects a person through lack of care and alertness'.[18] He gives several examples of its use. No variants in the Qur'anic text are recorded.

The commentators, though they do not devote much attention to this problem, do go so far as to redefine the crucial word *ghafala*. Al-Bayḍawī says: *lam taḥṭur bi-bāli-ka wa-lam taqra' sam'a-ka*, 'it (i.e. the *qaṣaṣ*) never came to your mind, and it never impinged on your ear' (*Anwār al-Tanzīl*, I, p. 451). Al-Ṭabarī: *lā ta'lamu-hu wa-lā shay'an*, 'you don't know it, not a bit of it' (*Jāmi' al-Bayān*, XII, p. 90). This is a different sort of redefinition from those that sometimes lead to the correct meaning. Here the redefinition is wrong, and was clearly made to acquit the Prophet of the charge of negligence. Ignorance is no sin but negligence is.

I propose that we emend *al-ghāfilīna* in v.3 to *al-'āqilīna*, which requires no change in the *rasm* and only a minor change in the pointing, which, of course, was not indicated in the original. The translation of vv. 2-3 now runs as follows: 'We have revealed it as an Arabic Qur'ān, so that you (pl.) may understand (*ta'qilūna*). We shall relate to you (sg.) the best of stories, though you (sg.) beforehand were one of those who understood'.

The Prophet's people need the revelation to become knowledgeable, but the Prophet does not need the *qaṣaṣ*, since he is already wise far beyond the wisdom of his followers. The 'best of stories' in the end is really meant for the people, and the Prophet is about to transmit it to them. *Al-ghāfilīna* may have been influenced by *ghāfilūna* in v. 13.

VI

In Sūra 9:28 the Prophet rounds on the *mushrikūn*, saying that they are an abomination and that, after a year's time, they should not approach the sacred mosque. Then in v. 29 he turns his attention to the Jews and Christians, addressing the believers: 'Fight those who were given the book but do not believe in God and the last day, do not forbid what God and His messenger have forbidden, and do not practice the true faith, until they pay the *jizya 'an yadin*, being abased'. The somewhat vague expression *'an yadin* did not arouse much interest in the commentators. There are no variants. Al-Ṭabarī devotes less than three lines to *'an yadin*. He says that the idea could also be expressed by *'an yadi-hi* or *'an*

[18] AL-RĀGHIB AL-ISFAHĀNĪ, *Al-Mufradāt fī Gharīb al-Qur'ān*, Cairo, 1961, p. 362.

yadin li-yadin and likens it to expressions such as *kallamtu-hu faman li-fam* and *laqītu-hu kaffatan li-kaffa* (*Jāmiʿ al-Bayān*, X, p. 77). Al-Bayḍāwī is also very brief, but gives a few possible interpretations of *ʿan yadin* with differing meanings of both words: from a giving hand obediently (*munqādīna*); from their own hand without employing an agent; from their wealth; because of a hand that dominates them; in cash passed from hand to hand; after being favoured, since their salvation through the *jizya* was a great favour (*Anwār al-Tanzīl*, I, p. 383).

The translators are also cautious. Bell translates 'off hand', which seems to be an odd way of paying one's taxes. He adds a note saying that the exact meaning of the phrase is uncertain. Paret: 'aus der Hand', with a note: 'd.h. jeder für seine Person (?), oder: willig (? *ʿan yad*)'. Blachère: 'directement (?)'; note: 'L'expression, de sens incertain, est reçue le plus souvent avec cette valeur'.[19]

The uncertainty of the translators and the differing explanations of the commentators make it likely that we are facing a mistake. I would emend *ʿan yadin* to *ʿan burʾin*, 'after immunity', i.e. after they have been granted a guarantee of immunity and security. *Burʾ* is the equivalent of *barāʾa* (both are *maṣdars* of *bariʾa*), and although it does not appear elsewhere in the Qur'ān, *barāʾa* does occur twice, in Q. 54:43, and more to the point, as the first word of this Sūra. The sense is much better since the phrase *ḥattā yuʿṭū l-jizyata ʿan burʾin* extends the idea of *jizya* by including the reason behind it. One should keep in mind that there was no *hamza* in the Ḥijāzī dialect of Arabic that was spoken by the Prophet, and the sign for *hamza* was not invented until long after the first copying of Qur'anic texts. The mistakes *dāl* for *rāʾ* and *rāʾ* for *dāl* are common in later manuscripts. For several examples of *ʿan* in the meaning of *baʿd*, see al-Zabīdī, *Tāj*, XXXV, p. 422 f.

VII

Sūra 52 is largely devoted to descriptions of the blessings that will be heaped upon the believers in the hereafter, and the punishments inflicted on the *kuffār*. In v. 23 God promises the believers that in Paradise they *yatanāzaʿūna* (without *ʾalif*) *fī-hā kāʾsan lā laghwun fī-hā wa-lā taʾthīm*, which the translators render as follows: Bell: 'Therein they pass to each other a cup; There (in the garden) is neither vain

[19] BELL, *The Qur'an*, p. 177; PARET, *Der Koran*, p. 153; BLACHÈRE. *Le Coran*, p. 1083.

babble nor recrimination'. Blachère: 'ils se passeront dans ces jardins des coupes au fond desquelles ne seront ni jactance ni incitation au péché'. Paret: 'Sie greifen in ihm (Paradies) einer um den anderen nach einem Becher (mit Wein) bei dem man weder (betrunken wird und dummes Zeug) daherredet noch sich versündigt'.[20]

The translators were, of course, influenced by the commentators. The problem is with the verb *yatanāzaʿūna*. Al-Bayḍāwī explains that it means, 'they and their companions pass to one another a cup by pulling and tugging (*bi-tajādhub*)' (*Anwār al-Tanzīl*, II, p. 289). Al-Ṭabarī says the passage means, 'they give a cup of wine to each other, passing it alternatively one to another (*yatadāwalūna-hā*)' (*Jāmiʿ al-Bayān*, XXVII, p. 17).

Among the lexicographers, al-Rāghib al-Iṣfahānī is the most precise: '*Tanāzuʿ* and *munāzaʿa* are (the same as) *mujādala*; the two are used to express *mukhāṣama* (dispute, controversy) and *mujādala* (quarrel, dispute)' (*Gharīb al-Qur'ān*, p. 488). Al-Zabīdī equates *tajādhub* with *tanāzuʿ* (*Tāj*, II, p. 144), but in *Tāj*, XXII, p. 247 redefines the word by saying that figuratively (*min al-majāz*) it can be (the same as) *tanāwul* (receiving) and *taʿāṭī* (taking).

There are two reasons why we can consider *yatanāzaʿūna* a mistake. First, the verb appears six more times in the Qur'ān, and each time clearly contains the idea of controversy, disputing: Q. 3:152; 4:59; 8:43, 46; 18:21; and 20:62. Second, the idea is inappropriate here since controversy and disputes will lead wine drinkers to the very *laghw* and *ta'thīm*, which the end of the verse says do not occur in Paradise.

I would emend *yatanāzaʿūna* (spelled *ytnzʿwn*) to *yashrabūna*, 'they will drink'. The only real mistake occurred when *bā'* was misread as *ʿayn*, which may seem unusual, but many even more unusual mistakes can be found in later manuscripts, and here as elsewhere good sense must take precedence over palaeography. Cf. shortly before in v. 19: *kulū wa-shrabū hanī'an bi-mā kuntum taʿmalūna*, 'Eat and drink in good health as a reward for what you have done', and Q. 76:5: *'inna l-abrāra yashrabūna min kā'sin kāna mizāju-hu kāfūran*, 'The pious drink from a cup (of wine) mingled with camphor'.

[20] Bell, *The Qur'an*, p. 536; Blachère. *Le Coran*, p. 48; Paret, *Der Koran*, p. 439.

THE EMPTY ḤIJĀZ[1]

JAMES E. MONTGOMERY
University of Cambridge

The first published articles of Professor Richard M. Frank (hereafter: RMF) contain several which may surprise those familiar only with his mature work on the *Kalām*. Three broad categories can be discerned: philological excavations of textual cruces or linguistic obscurities in the Biblical and Christian traditions, from Caesarius of Arles to *Deuteronomy* and *Kings*, remarkable for their lexical tenacity so characteristic of RMF's work on the *Kalām*;[2] observations on the cultural and textual history of the early ʿAbbasid Arabic translations of the Bible, in particular the *Jeremias* of Pethion b. Ayyūb al-Sahhār, the subject of his 1956 Ph.D. at the Catholic University of America;[3] excavations in the Graeco-Arabica.[4] There are two articles which stand out, however. One is an article on the Qur'ān, of which more presently. The other, from 1962, is a treatment of the role of social evolution in the theological system of Teilhard de Chardin: *Social Evolution and the Human Species*.[5]

I read this latter article with some curiosity. I knew next to nothing of the work of Teilhard de Chardin. I was also intrigued to see what RMF

[1] This article has been rigorously peer-reviewed by two scholars whom I respect: Philip Kennedy and Garth Fowden. The infirmities of my Jahizian approach to argumentation which persist, persist despite their strictures and advice. I have often viewed the footnotes as an opportunity to explore issues apposite yet essentially tangential to the main points of my argument, especially in the section on the *wishāḥ*.

[2] Items 10, 16 and 19 in the *Bibliography* in this volume.

[3] Items 1, 11, and 15 in the *Bibliography*. See also item 3.

[4] Items 12, 13 and 14 in the *Bibliography*. These articles have excited much comment, especially item 14: see HELMUT GÄTJE, *Studien zur Überlieferung der aristotelischen Psychologie im Islam*, Heidelberg: Carl Winter, 1971, p. 28-44; *An Arabic Translation of Themistius Commentary on Aristoteles* De Anima (*Oriental Studies*, 2), ed. M.C. LYONS, Thetford: Cassirer, 1973, p. ix-xiii; DIMITRI GUTAS, *Avicenna and the Aristotelian Tradition. Introduction to Reading Avicenna's Philosophical Works* (*Islamic Philosophy and Theology*, 4), Leiden: Brill, 1988, p. 139 (on Ibn Sīnā's *marginalia* to the *De Anima*); *Aristoteles'* De Anima. *Eine verlorene spätantike Paraphrase in arabischer und persischer Überlieferung* (*Aristoteles Semitico-Latinus*, 9), ed. RÜDIGER ARNZEN, Leiden: Brill, 1998, p. 690-707. The materials discussed in *Bibliography* item12 have now been comprehensively surveyed in *A Greek and Arabic Lexicon*, ed. GERHARD ENDRESS and DIMITRI GUTAS, Fascicle 4, Leiden: Brill, 1997, p. 428-437.

[5] Item 18 in the Bibliography.

would make of the subject and I was not in the least disappointed. This piece contains, in so many ways, intimations of those features of the study of the *Kalām* tradition which I find most appealing about RMF's work. Firstly, we must study any thinker's system in its entirety and as an integrity:

> To treat a subject from the whole scheme of his subject — to cut out a piece from the middle of the bolt, as it were — is to distort both the place and the whole, for in removing it from the synthetic context which gives it its significance one takes away from it a great part of that profundity and, indeed, grandeur of scope which belongs to it. In isolation, without the overtones and resonances of the total context the piece becomes hardly different in any significant way from many similar patterns of contemporary thought (*Social Evolution*, p. 310).

Secondly, we must reflect upon the myriad ways in which humans respond, intellectually, emotionally and culturally, to 'the problem of reflective life':

> Each living culture or sociocultural unit (and I would not prejudice the real difficulty of empirically determining clear boundaries within the real order) whether in the past or the present, no matter how simple or complex, represents in a given collectivity of persons *a particular solution to the problem of reflective life*, a realized form of adaptation of the universal potential of reflective consciousness to a given 'environment' (*Social Evolution*, p. 312).

Thirdly, and to leap some thirty-four years to RMF's Presidential Address to the 206th Meeting of the American Oriental Society, 'language is being's house; man is lodged in its domicile':[6]

> Culture viewed as the formal structure of the adaptation of a social collectivity to a given 'environment', far from being 'mere convention' determines the modality of the existence of the members of the collectivity, in that it determines, within certain defined margins, the range and character of possible acts and that terms and framework within which these acts can be reflectively or non-reflectively lived and understood ... Culture furnishes the material and intellectual form through which human consciousness becomes intelligible to itself; the intelligible form in terms of which the infinite and indeterminate potential of human consciousness determines and defines its own existence (*Social Evolution*, p. 314-315).

[6] This is a translation of a dictum of Heidegger: see *Hearing and Saying what was Said*, in: *Journal of the American Oriental Society* 116.4 (1996), p. 611-618 (presidential address, delivered at the 206th meeting of the American Oriental Society, Philadelphia, Pennsylvania, March 19, 1996), item 50 in the *Bibliography*. For an early instance of interest in Heidegger, see *Social Evolution*, p. 314, note 13.

It is but a short step from 'culture' thus conceptualised in de Chardin's system to the following insight:

> Without language — without having meanings and thoughts present in articulate expression — we can't *have* sense and non-sense as such, can't make sense or commit nonsense. We can't even have the inexpressible as such, cannot have it in the sense of having it present to mind as something to recognize and reflect on, save as something presents itself in its recalcitrance to articulate presentation (*Hearing and Saying*, p. 613).

RMF has always been honest about the significance of his first encounters with *Kalām* and the perplexities which it presented to him. In responding to this bafflement, he seems to have drawn on several key features of his analysis of the role of social evolution and human-ness within the theology and Christology of Teilhard de Chardin.

And what of his article on the Qur'ān? Philological ease with the Qur'ān in his early articles on the Arabic Bible is ample testimony to a profound acquaintance with Islam's Holy Book on the part of RMF (items 1, 11 and 15 in the *Bibliography*)[7] and it is such profound acquaintance which precipitates one of the most fundamental insights RMF has brought to bear on the *Kalām*, that it must be considered as an intellectually sophisticated but credible response to the Qur'anic event, the fact of a divine revelation in Arabic:

> In the *kalâm* (and the term itself is resonant in the context), the origin of the questioning which is at the root of the science itself is perforce more self-consciously and more explicitly exegetical because of its explicit relationship to a revelation whose linguistic nature is not merely a fact among facts, something given and to be taken for granted, but an overarching fact, the awareness which must influence the view and conception of all facts.[8]

[7] In *Jeremias* (item 15, p. 139), RMF makes one of his many casual, matter-of-fact observations which will prove extremely fecund for future researchers: 'the common vocabulary of religion was pretty well set in so far as Arabic was concerned. It was based first and primarily on the Coran and then on the *ḥadîth* ... further the canons of correct usage (both in matters of vocabulary and syntax) were those of the nomads of the Arabian peninsula, those of the classical Bedouin poetry — the language of the desert. This implies two things if the translation is to remain within the compass of correct Arabic as measured by these norms: first that being a religious work it will have a definite 'Muslim' cast to it (for their religious vocabulary was that of 'the Book') and further that, if one were not to depart from this standard of usage, many typical expressions of the Syriac ... with its background of a settled, chiefly urbanized, agricultural society, would have to be recast'. Thanks largely to the brilliant investigations by Father Sidney Griffith of the implications of such an observation, the 'Qur'anic' quality of much early Christian theological writing in Arabic is a widely acknowledged 'fact'.

[8] *Beings and their Attributes. The Teaching of the Basrian School of the Mu'tazila in the Classical Period* (*Studies in Islamic Philosophy and Science*), Albany: State University of New York Press, 1978, p. 11 (item 4 in the *Bibliography*).

The article, *The Literary Unity of* Sûrat al-Munâfiqîn *(63)*, is almost unknown in Qur'anic studies: I can find no reference to it in, for example, the bibliographies compiled by Angelika Neuwirth or S. Parvez Manzoor.[9] Such neglect is entirely unwarranted, for this article is one of the first, to my knowledge, to challenge the critical shibboleth then prevalent in Qur'anic studies in the West that the *sūra*s of the Qur'ān were truly composite in a radical way, i.e. that they were essentially 'an inexplicable conjunction of disparate parts' (p. 258), represented so graphically in Richard Bell's translation, a work almost pathological in its dissection and dismemberment of the Holy Book. Of Bell's now completely discredited theories concerning the supposedly haphazard, gauche compilation of the Qur'ān, RMF notes that Bell:

> Carries his 'pieces-of-paper' hypothesis, which he works out in truly fantastic detail, to the point of eliminating all human activity and assuming the virtual impossibility that the composer of the piece in its present form either could or did exercise any conscious, rationally oriented judgment or intention in the work (*Literary Unity*, p. 266-267).

In the analysis of the short *sūra*, RMF's starting point is to note that 'a goodly body of the [Islamic, JEM] tradition' declares this *sūra* 'to have been composed on one occasion' (p. 258), and it is this which he tries to do justice to by exploring its implications. His sensitivity to the *sūra* as an integral unit of meaning is, of course, as we have seen in the case of Teilhard de Chardin, an instance of his approach to the integrity of any intellectual system however grandly conceived, and to this is added a refreshing insistence that 'each case must be examined on its own merits' (*Literary Unity*, p. 263), an insistence which was perhaps destined to gain some notoriety in RMF's radical reassessment of the debt owed by al-Ghazālī to the cosmology of Ibn Sīnā.[10]

Also refreshing are the rejection of 'statistical probability' as a literary hermeneutic ('a common, though often unstated, assumption of a certain "scientific" literary and textual criticism which all too often seems to confuse reality with the objectification of its own analytic

[9] ANGELIKA NEUWIRTH, *Koran*, in: *Grundriß der arabischen Philologie. Band II: Literaturwissenschaft*, ed. HELMUT GÄTJE, Wiesbaden: Reichert, 1987, p. 130-135; S. PARVEZ MANZOOR, *Method against Truth. Orientalism and Qur'ānic Studies*, in: *The Qur'ān. Style and Contents* (*The Formation of the Classical Islamic World*, 24), ed. ANDREW RIPPIN, Aldershot: Ashgate, 2001, p. 381-397.

[10] See further the comments of THÉRÈSE-ANNE DRUART, *Metaphysics*, in: *The Cambridge Companion to Arabic Philosophy*, ed. PETER ADAMSON and RICHARD C. TAYLOR, Cambridge: Cambridge University Press, 2005, p. 327-348 (p. 327).

process': *Literary Unity*, p. 262); the emphasis placed as much on the interpretive significance of the redactional process whereby the Qur'ān was given its final form as on 'the total consciouness of the prophet', together with the refusal to read the Qur'ān as the Old Testament ('the final redaction is, for the *Koran*, in great part if not virtually entirely, made either by the prophet, or within his immediate presence (though completed very shortly after his death) rather than by a school of disciples, suffering under a not altogether homogeneous prophetic tradition, often long after the death of the original author, as often in OT': *Literary Unity*, p. 266); the remark that composite structures are no less replete with meaning (here understood as 'authorial' intention) as are the parts of which they are composed (*Literary Unity*, p. 266); recognition of the rhetorical structure of Qur'anic utterance (in this case the 'homiletic') and of its unique capacity for stating the totality in the part ('the desire to talk always within the horizon of the total background': *Literary Unity*, p. 265); and avowal of the problems inherent in *situating* any particular *āya*, in view of the Qur'ān's 'consistent and conscious effort, as it were, to strip the events which may have provoked various revelations of their concrete detail and to describe rather the more generalized "situation"' (*Literary Unity*, p. 262), problems which are merely compounded by the tendency of 'much of the "historical exegesis of the *Koran* … the projection of the data of the book backwards into recollected situations' (*Literary Unity*, p. 263). RMF's solution to the question of literary unity is basically to interpret the Qur'ān through the Qur'ān, in this instance structurally rather than lexically.

In sum, this article deserves to be better known, for it contains a plethora of insights to the nature of Qur'anic discourse as well as numerous anticipations of many recent literary analyses of the Qur'ān, such as those of Michael Sells, Mustansir Mir, Neal Robinson or Angelika Neuwirth.

Sadly, RMF has never published, in extenso, any of his thoughts on the poetry of pre-Islamic Arabia: a smattering can be garnered from reading *Literary Unity*. This is not, then, through any lack of acquaintance: in many of the conversations which I have been privileged to have with him, he has been as likely to quote from the poetry of Labīd as from the tragedies of Sophocles or his beloved Rabbie Burns! It is also obvious from the emphasis throughout his life's work on the foundational importance of a proper and full appreciation of the *ʿarabīya* for anyone with ambitions to investigate the *Kalām*, that he includes poetry every bit as much as grammar within his definition of such knowledge.

When one allies the breadth of his linguistic erudition in Arabic to his intimate knowledge of Ancient Greek, Syriac and Hebrew, each consolidated by a proper philological training, the result is a scholar admirably equipped to deal with the linguistic demands of the Classical Arabic textual heritage, and sufficiently trained and prepared to see beyond the narrow confines of any of the more restricted, modern divisions of disciplinary specialisms.

Sadly, in the modern world, such a training is the exception rather than the norm and this has, I believe, led to an impoverishment of our intellectual vision. One area of the Classical Arabic heritage which has fared rather badly in the course of these developments is *jāhilī* poetry: a significant number of recent publications, aimed at the non-specialist, has given it such short shrift that I have felt impelled to protest. This contribution to a volume of essays in celebration of Professor Frank is both an apology of poetry and a plea for its continued relevance to any respectable study of not only Islamic origins but also the originary interests and notions of Muslim communities throughout the ages.

In the present work, I intend firstly to establish the semantic emptiness of the pre- and early Islamic Ḥijāz, a semiotic evacuation effected by the Qur'anic event, a religious, linguistic, cultural, social and spiritual eruption which led to the almost total obliteration of anything extra-Islamic (though not necessarily anything extra-Qur'anic) — with one major and, I submit, profoundly significant exception: the *qaṣīda* poetry of the *Jāhilīya*, accorded such a paradoxically privileged status in Allāh's definition of the Qur'ān as unlike any other discourse (or, in other words, inclusion through exclusion). The first stage of my argument will consider the pre-Islamic *qaṣīda*, amongst the most obdurate and recalcitrantly resistant of all Arabic art forms (with the single exception, perhaps, of the Qur'ān itself); indeed, it is hard to imagine any phenomenon less connected to the (Late Antique) world outside pre-Islamic Arabia than the *qaṣīda*. In the second stage of the argument, I investigate one instance in which the mature Islamic tradition responded to the empty Ḥijāz, by reflecting on the historical memory of the mythologizing of Imru' al-Qays by his poetic biographers. Despite the ʿAbbasid cultural relevance of the myth of Imru' al-Qays and the construction of his biography out of his verse, one facet of the process remains constant: al-Iṣfahānī and the tradition on which he draws read the life of Imru' al-Qays as fully and vibrantly part of the Late Antique world. In the third move of the argument, this act of reading drawn from the mature Islamic tradition will be compared with several readings of the Ḥijāz within and/or outwith the Late Antique oecumene taken from the modern, Western tradition. As conclusion to the argument, I aim to show how the *qaṣīda* can, in fact, be (or rather: ought to be) read so as to form part of the Late Antique phenomenon — so much so that those who pretend to study this phenomenon neglect this body of poetry to the scholarly detriment of their historical ambitions. *Qaṣīda* poetry is as fundamental to a fully contextualised understanding of Islamic origins as are vociferously promoted forms of Late Antique monotheism or intonations of Revelation as miracle.

If the notion of early 'Islam' suffers from conceptual vagueness,[11] the Ḥijāz, its topographical birthplace, is so indeterminate and so open to meanings as to be empty of meaning.[12] Our knowledge is entirely dependent upon either textual information provided by the later Islamic tradition or upon some snippets of a non-textual narrative which archaeology is beginning to provide. As a signifier, then, the Ḥijāz is empty.[13]

[11] Rejection of the interpretive liberties allowed by an essentialising and transcendental conception of 'Islam' is a mainstay of the works of Mohammed Arkoun. There is a very able study by CHASE ROBINSON of the enthusiasms for such a notion of Islam shared by Orientalists and Islamists: *Reconstructing Early Islam. Truth and Consequences*, in: *Method and Theory in the Study of Islamic Origins*, ed. HERBERT BERG, Leiden: Brill, 2003, p. 101-134. This article is also an important contribution to the methodology of the study of pre-modern Muslims, above all in the period of the Revelation. Robinson makes a convincing case for the abandonment of '"Islam" as a term of historical explanation' (p. 134). Unfortunately, the editor of the recently published *Cambridge Companion to the Age of Jusitinian*, Cambridge: Cambridge University Press, 2005, ed. MICHAEL MAAS, was unable (unwilling?) to heed his plea: Chapter 20, by FRED M. DONNER, is entitled *The Background to Islam*, p. 510-533. Fortunately, the contents of the chapter are not quite as dispiriting as the title might lead one to believe.

[12] My use of 'Ḥijāz' is fuzzy; it includes the mountain belt of the Ḥijāz, the Najd, the central plateau, and the Tihāma litoral and plains (the Ḥijāzī or Meccan Tihāma), though strictly speaking this latter is also 'empty': see the articles collected in *Arabian Archaeology and Epigraphy* 6 (1995); FRANCINE STONE, *Editorial*, in: *Arabian Archaeology and Epigraphy* 6 (1995), p. 212, notes that 'we must come to grips with a credible definition of Tihāma in the pre-Islamic period, both as a socio-economic and as a geographical region'. The Yemenite Tihāma is as 'empty' today as it was for Muslim authors during the classical period: see CHRISTIAN ROBIN, *La Tihāma yéménite avant l'Islam: notes d'histoire et de géographie historique*, in: *Arabian Archaeology and Epigraphy* 6 (1995), p. 222-235; A.F.L. BEESTON, *Sabaeans in Tihāma*, in: *Arabian Archaeology and Epigraphy* 6 (1995), p. 236-245; R.T.O. WILSON, *Some Notes on the Arabic Historiography of Tihāma in the pre-Islamic and Early Islamic Periods*, in: *Arabian Archaeology and Epigraphy* 6 (1995), p. 277- 285; MICHAEL ZWETTLER, *Maʿadd in Ancient Arabian Epigraphy*, in: *Wiener Zeitschrift für die Kunde des Morgenlandes* 90 (2000), p. 253, footnote 55; G. REX SMITH, *Tihāma*, in: *EI2*, X, p. 481-482 (p. 481).

[13] See further JOHN WANSBROUGH, Res Ipsa Loquitur: *History and Mimesis*, in: BERG, *Method and Theory*, p. 3-19 (especially p. 7-9). The issue of the non-Arabic sources is quite another matter, but hardly seem to me to fill an empty Ḥijāz.

I have purposefully excluded, for the moment, pre-Islamic poetry as a textual source of information and do not wish to embark upon a consideration of the ways in which the Qur'ān miraculously invites, whilst remaining obdurate to, interpretation and chronology. Although I welcome recent developments in the archaeological recovery of the pre-Islamic Ḥijāz as a means of reflecting upon and testing the text-based accounts (and, of course, vice-versa), and am not in a position to pass judgement upon its reliability (or assessments of its reliability) as material evidence in archaeological terms, there are difficulties in its use as evidence (principally those of narrative: Wansbrough's mimeticist position) — even admitting it as evidence does not avoid the epistemological problems of induction, whether it be those posed in *An Enquiry Concerning Human Understanding* by David Hume (we require an inductive argument to justify our use of inductive arguments when we reason from particulars to universals) or by Nelson Goodman (inductive arguments can be constructed to prove, for example, that emeralds are grue, i.e. both green and blue, or that children born after a certain date are immortal).[14]

Indeed, archeology does provide us with some hard, non text-based evidence (a coin, or a datable inscription or a building — 'factuality'), but our responses to that evidence are completely contingent upon the interpretative schemes we bring to bear ('meaning').[15] Thus, inscriptions from the Dome of the Rock have provided the evidentiary bases for completely divergent antithetical arguments for the date of the Dome's construction[16] and in several cases the textual tradition has been dragooned as explication of material evidence,[17] while Umayyad poetry is

[14] See ALEXANDER BIRD, *Philosophy of Science*, London: UCL Press, 1998, p. 18-19 and 165-186.

[15] Consider the following sequence of interpretive strategies deployed in the reconstruction of the history of the pre-Islamic coinage of the Ḥadramawt: 'numismatic studies allow us to establish the typological sequence of the ancient Hadramawt coinage ... The sequence and relative chronology of the series is based on typological studies. The absolute chronology of the series could be verified with the help of archaeological studies': ALEXANDER SEDOV, *Hadramawt Coinage, its Sequence and Chronology*, abstract of a paper presented at *The Seminar for Arabian Studies* held at the British Museum on the 22nd of July, 2005.

[16] For the best discussion of these *āyas*, see ESTELLE WHELAN, *Forgotten Witness: Evidence for the Early Codification of the Qur'ān*, in: *Journal of the American Oriental Society* 118 (1998), p. 1-14.

[17] See L.I. CONRAD, *Historical Evidence and the Archaeology of Early Islam*, in: *Quest for Understanding. Arabic and Islamic Studies in Memory of Malcolm H. Kerr*, ed. S. SEIKALY, R. BAALBAKI, P. DODD, Beirut: American University of Beirut, 1991, p. 263-282 (methodological reflections on problems arising from the use of 'medieval literary sources' by the excavators of Qaṣr al-Ḥayr al-Sharqī).

one of the many hermeneutic devices brilliantly brought to bear on Quṣayr ʿAmra by Garth Fowden.[18] And I am tempted to wonder at how great an influence the traditional 'textual' account has exerted on the intriguing survey of 'settlement patterns in Arabia in the period AD 565-570' conducted by G.R.D. KING, *Settlement in Western and Central Arabia and the Gulf in the Sixth-Eighth Centuries AD*.[19]

It is important to be clear on this point: the material and archaeological evidence for Arabia in the pre-Islamic period which has begun to emerge over the last three to four decades is truly exciting, but I find myself querying the use to which this evidence is occasionally put, or better the claims which are made for the evidence. The fascinating survey of precious metal mining in the Arabian peninsula offered by GENE HECK, *Gold Mining in Arabia and the Rise of the Islamic State*,[20] does not prove the veracity of the pre-modern Muslim sources which attest to an astonishing abundance of gold among the Meccans at the advent of Islam but rather indicates the plausibility of these materials (although as far as I can see, he musters only one gold mine which reveals traces of activity contemporary with the Prophet Muḥammad: Jabal Makhiyaṭ, circa 626 AD, p. 381), provides a welcome check on exclusive reliance on the silences of the non-Arabic textual sources, and should be a reminder of how little we really know and are likely to know.[21]

And it is the very elusiveness of the Ḥijāz as an empty signifier (afforced with the verificationism of Orientalism) which can, for example, enable Wael Hallaq to attack as 'Orientalist' the agreement expressed by some western scholars with the Islamic response to the

[18] GARTH FOWDEN, *Quṣayr ʿAmra. Art and the Umayyad Elite in Late Antique Syria*, Berkeley: University of California Press, 2004. A careful balance of material and textual (including epigraphical) evidence is conspicuous in the excellent survey of ROBERT G. HOYLAND, *Arabia and the Arabs from the Bronze Age to the Coming of Islam*, New York - London: Routledge, 2001.

[19] In: *The Byzantine and Early Islamic Near East, II: Land Use and Settlement Patterns*, ed. G.R.D. KING and A. CAMERON, Princeton: Darwin Press, 1994, p. 181-212.

[20] In: *Journal of the Economic and Social History of the Orient* 42 (1999), p. 364-395. See further his *'Arabia without Spices': An Alternate Hypothesis*, in: *Journal of the American Oriental Society* 123 (2003), p. 547-576, which aims to synthesize 'source documentation with extant physical evidence' (p. 550).

[21] Note the remark of CRONE, *Meccan Trade*, p. 89, that in the context of Persian silver mining in the Najd, 'Quraysh would seem to have been credited with commercial activities that were in fact performed by others'. See also the timely assessment of the *status quaestionis* by JEREMY JOHNS, *Archaeology and the History of Early Islam: The First Seventy Years*, in: *Journal of the Economic and Social History of the Orient* 46 (2003), p. 411-436; ROBERT SCHICK, *Archaeology and the Qur'ān*, in: *Encyclopaedia of the Qur'ān* (hereafter: *EQ*), I, p. 148-157.

Qur'anic vision of the heartlands of pre-Islamic Arabia as a wasteland devoid of any form of civilization (i.e. as the *jāhilīya*) while, in the process, promoting a most laudable and refreshing, but essentially (at least in traditional terms) un-Islamic, account of the peninsula.[22]

The very emptiness of the Ḥijāz as a signifier invites, indeed demands, a context: for, in the catchy formulation of Chase Robinson

> One may take the Ḥijāz out of the desert and put it into the mainstream of late antique ideas, or one may take the engineers of earliest Islam ... out of Arabia and put them in second/eighth- or third/ninth-century Iraq or Syria.[23]

There are a number of perspectives from which we can reflect upon the semantic indeterminacy of the Ḥijāz. I propose to think about the representative inhabitants of the area and the peninsula as a whole, the Bedouin, to review the biography of that most famous *jāhilī* poet, Imru' al-Qays of Kinda, to reflect upon Sasanid and Byzantine involvement in the area, and to investigate the wearing of the body-girdle among elite damsels depicted in pre-Islamic poetry.

The seductiveness of the Bedouin

There is a growing number of high schools in England which study 'Islamic Civilisations' as part of the History Curriculum. The Head of History at one school informed me that they had replaced study of the Roman Empire with Islamic Civilisations, in order to prepare the pupils for the study of the Palestinian-Israeli conflict later in their school career. One of the course books widely available is a Schools History Project publication, *Contrasts and Connections* (1991), part of the Year 7 curriculum, Discovering the Past.[24]

Pages 156-159 ('Arabia before Islam') focus on what is most immediately striking and significant about the geography of the Arabian peninsula: it is largely made up of a combination of sandy and stony deserts, and there are very few stretches of land where crops can be grown (detailed on a map, p. 158). Pages 156-157 stress the harshness of

[22] Wael B. Hallaq, *The Origins and Evolution of Islamic Law*, Cambridge; Cambridge University Press, 2005, p. 4 and p. 8-28 (respectively).

[23] Robinson, *Reconstructing Early Islam*, p. 132.

[24] Colin Shephard, Mike Corbishley, Alan Large and Richard Tames, *Contrasts and Connections*, London: John Murray, 1991.

the environment, its hostility to man and the survival problems of the inhabitants of the desert, the nomads — consider Question 5, for example: 'Why do you think Arabs felt they were living at the mercy of nature?' The general impression given on pp. 158-159 is that Arabia was 'backward and less united', as a result of the nomadism demanded by the physical conditions. Similar assumptions dominate the recent book of MOHAMMED A. BAMYEH, *The Social Origins of Islam. Mind, Economy, Discourse*,[25] as they do the profoundly influential and much respected work of MARSHALL G.S. HODGSON, *The Venture of Islam: Conscience and History in a World Civilization. Volume 1: the Classical Age of Islam.*[26]

For Hodgson, even Mecca embodies the Bedouin spirit of independence, almost untouched by the surrounding 'agrarianate high cultures': 'Bedouin Arabia, never incorporated ... into the great agrarian empires that had risen and fallen north of it for so long, was still a pocket of paganism'. In northern and central Arabia, 'such elements of high culture as were found there were merely bits of luster borrowed from the civilization of *Arabia Felix*, or from one of its rivals to the north'.[27]

An empty region is filled with empty people: 'in the pagan view the self was without a center, society without wholeness, and the universe barren of overall meaning'.[28] And what can be maintained of the people can be maintained of their belief systems: the Quraysh had forged an 'independent religious system, ... based on Bedouin ways, and ... neutral to all the confessional religious alliances'.[29] A developed version of this paradigm is BAMYEH's extraction of 'the ideology of the horizons' from what he terms the nomadic ode: 'such an ideology sees in the spectacle of the horizon not so much an inviting mirage as the most fundamental picture of the emptiness of grandiose human quests'; 'the emergence of sedentary societies did not necessarily entail the oblivion of the

[25] Minneapolis - London: University of Minnesota Press, 1999.

[26] Chicago: Chicago University Press, 1974.

[27] FRED M. DONNER, *The Early Islamic Conquests*, Princeton: Princeton University Press, 1981, p. 15.

[28] IRA M. LAPIDUS, *The Arab Conquests and the Formation of Islamic Society*, in: *Studies on the First Century of Islamic Society*, ed. G.H.A. JUYNBOLL, Carbondale - Edwardsville: Southern Illinois University Press, 1982, p. 49-72 and 212-214. Just how far this emptiness could determine how pre-Islamic Arabia was interpreted is well brought out by Jeremy John's excellent discussion of Creswell's and Caetani's theories concerning the 'house of the Prophet' in Medina: JEREMY JOHNS, *The 'House of the Prophet' and the Concept of the Mosque*, in: *Bayt al-Maqdis. Jerusalem and Early Islam*, ed. JEREMY JOHNS, Oxford: Oxford University Press, 1999, p. 59-112 (p. 72-79).

[29] HODGSON, *The Venture of Islam*, p. 157.

horizons of wandering'.[30] And empty people must have political systems which, if not quite empty, are at least impervious to change.[31]

The most extreme response to the emptiness of the Ḥijāz as signifier is that of Nevo and Koren for whom the Ḥijāz is literally empty: 'there are very few signs indicating that the Ḥijāz was much inhabited in the fifth to seventh centuries AD and certainly not by people using any form of Classical Arabic'; 'the Ḥijāz ... was a relatively empty area'. Their solution is to fill it with their interpretations of archaeological findings in the Negev, i.e. to read the Ḥijāz in terms of the Negev and Mecca in terms of Sde Boqer![32]

Nevo's epigraphic studies, which 'demand to be taken seriously',[33] display similarly deficient interpretative strategies as his archaeological work: in *Towards a Prehistory of Islam*,[34] in order to endow these epigraphical remains with meaning, he applies to them a version of the Wansbrough paradigm, by which he intends that the Muslim sources represent the culmination of the stages and processes whereby scriptural canonization was achieved and are thus the teleology of the tradition. In the end, what Nevo actually establishes is not the expression of a chronological sequence of beliefs from pre-Muḥammadan through Muḥammadan to Muslim but simply the hermeneutic viability of the paradigm he has adopted as his means of giving meaning to silent artifacts — this is most conspicuous when his classifications cannot accommodate as Qur'anic such phrases as *rabb al-ʿālamīna* and *al-nār*, by a process whereby for

[30] *The Social Origins*, p. 3-16 (quotations from p. 4 and 11).

[31] PATRICIA CRONE, *Slaves on Horses. The Evolution of the Islamic Polity*, Cambridge: Cambridge University Press, 2003, p. 24: 'and where the Central Asian tribes had a profuse and eclectic vocabulary of political titulature, the Arabs made good with *shaykh*, *sayyid*, and a few other terms'. ELLA LANDAU-TASSERON, *Alliances among the Arabs*, in: *al-Qanṭara* 26 (2005), p. 141-173, notes that 'the Arabic terms found in the sources, such as *qabīla*, *ʿashīra*, *ḥayy* etc. are inadequate because they have no fixed meanings' (p. 142, note 1). Yet as her study shows (and as studies of the fluidity and flexibility of Arabian genealogies demonstrate), this is an inappropriate form of 'nominalism': such laconic vocabulary is no indication that the society and social permutations it is intended to cover will be similarly sparse. Quite the contrary: it seems to me that the fluid and dynamic structure of tribal society ensures its elasticity (and hence its longevity) through the looseness of such concepts and the mutability of arrangements which the vocabulary can be made to cover.

[32] YEHUDA D. NEVO and JUDITH KOREN, *The Origins of the Muslim Descriptions of the Jāhilī Meccan Sanctuary*, in: *Journal of Near Eastern Studies* 49 (1990), p. 23-44 (quotations taken from p. 24 and 43). For devastating criticism of the interpretative shortcomings of their archaeological finds, see JOHNS, *Archaeology and the History of Early Islam*, p. 411-414.

[33] JOHNS, *Archaeology and the History of Early Islam*, p. 412.

[34] In: *Jerusalem Studies in Arabic and Islam* 17 (1994), p. 108-141.

something to qualify as Qur'anic it must be an exact *quotation* rather than an *allusion* or *echo*, i.e. the ways in which religious texts tend to infiltrate the popular consciousness and leave their imprint on languages. In other words, what does a phrase have to be to be counted as Qur'anic, in this scheme? Can we expect the same level of exactitude of a non-elite artifact as we do of an elite one? And how do we respond to such a disregard for (philological) exactitude in an elite artifact such as a poem? At a time when Muslims seem to have prioritized, in Qur'ān, Ḥadīth and poetry, *al-riwāya bi-l-maʿnā* (paraphrastic transmission) over *al-riwāya bi-l-lafẓ* (verbatim transmission), is exactitude the proper criterion by which to evaluate the material? And, to take two examples, how would we judge the Christian Arabic polemical text of the Second-Eighth Century, in defence of the Trinity, or the apologetic treatise of Nonnus of Nisibis (d. ca. 256/870), which bear the heavy imprint of Qur'anic language, partly by virtue of the Holy Book's domination of the *ʿarabīya* as a vehicle of expression, partly intentionally, in order to allow Christians greater facility in their debates with Muslims?[35]

[35] For examples of the varieties of Qur'anic quotation, allusion and echo in elite (prose and poetic) texts, see J.N. MATTOCK and J.E. MONTGOMERY, *The Metaphysical ʿUmar?*, in: *Journal of Arabic Literature* 20 (1989), p. 12-19; J.E. MONTGOMERY et al., *Revelry and Remorse: A Poem by Abū Nuwās*, in: *Journal of Arabic Literature* 25 (1994), p. 116-14; J.E. MONTGOMERY, *For the Love of a Christian Boy: A Song by Abū Nuwās*, in: *Journal of Arabic Literature* 27 (1996), p. 115-124; J.E. MONTGOMERY, *The Vagaries of the* Qaṣīdah. *The Tradition and Practice of Early Islamic Poetry*, Warminster: Aris and Phillips, 1991, Chapter Six; WADAD AL-KADI, *The Impact of the Qur'ān on the Epistolography of ʿAbd al-Ḥamīd*, in: *Approaches to the Qur'ān*, ed. G.R. HAWTING and ABDUL-KADER SHAREEF, London; Routledge, 1993; p. 285-313; on methods of transmission, see GREGOR SCHOELER, *Écrire et transmettre dans les débuts de l'islam*, Paris: Presses Universitaires de France, 2002; GREGOR SCHOELER, *The Oral and the Written in Early Islam*, trans. UWE VAGELPOHL, ed. J.E. MONTGOMERY, London - New York: RoutledgeCurzon, 2006; on their consequences for our reconstructions of the textual heritage: J.E. MONTGOMERY, *Editor's Introduction*, in: SCHOELER, *The Oral and the Written*; on the use of the Qur'ān in a very early Christian Arabic theological text, see: SAMIR KHALIL SAMIR, *The Earliest Arab Apology for Christianity*, in: *Christian Arabic Apologetics during the Abbasid Period (750-1258)*, ed. SAMIR KHALIL SAMIR and JØRGEN S. NIELSEN, Leiden: Brill, 1994, p. 57-114 ('the author is impregnated with the Qur'ānic culture', p. 109); see also, for example, SIDNEY H. GRIFFITH, *The Apologetic Treatise of Nonnus of Nisibis*, Article III in his: *The Beginnings of Christian Theology in Arabic. Muslim-Christian Encounters in the Early Islamic Period*, Aldershot: AshgateVariorum, 2002. Informed analysis of the apologetic, polemical and systematic adaptations and appropriations by ʿAbbasid Christian *mutakallimūn* of Islamic theology (*Kalām*), the *ʿarabīya*, and the Qur'ān, form the bedrock of Griffith's wonderful articles. The general background is covered in: SIDNEY H. GRIFFITH, *Arabic Christianity in the Monasteries of Ninth-Century Palestine*, Aldershot: Variorum, 1992. What I think we do have to take seriously in Nevo's epigraphical work is the evidence of Judaeo-Christianity and its expressions which he has brought to light. *How* we respond to this phenomenon is, once again, another matter entirely.

Yet there are some signs in the School's History Project textbook that Arabia was not a hermetically sealed geographical entity: the Map includes Damascus and an arrow pointing 'to Syria and the Byzantine Empire', suggests arrivals from India, and Source 5 is 'written by a Greek sailor in the first century', while we read on p. 158 that 'trade had brought many Jews and Christians to Arabia'.

The point which I wish to make is quite simple: this picture, which is fully consonant with the picture of pre-Islamic Arabia generally accepted among Muslims (it does, after all, highlight the miraculousness of the Qur'ān), is also the picture of pre-Islamic Arabia which one can easily find in much modern scholarship, although the sharpness of its outlines may vary from author to author (as such, it is an inheritance of the philologist founding fathers of the discipline of Islamic Studies who discovered in the *jāhilīya* a highly potent indicator of those features which for them typified the Arab mind). In volume 3 of the series *The Formation of the Classical Islamic World*, for example, entitled *The Arabs and Arabia on the Eve of Islam* and edited by FRANK PETERS,[36] we find in the 'Editor's Introduction', alongside recognition of the substantial movements of sedentarisation (and back again, for the process seems rarely to be stable) which took place in Arabia and acknowledgement that 'there is no lack of material evidence for the Arabs from outside the peninsula' (p. xii), an admission that this 'is evidence from the marches of Arabia' (p. xii), an emphasis on 'the nomadic life' and the consequent lack of unity among 'a nation of tribes', and, most importantly, the implication that the value of studying pre-Islamic Arabia consists largely in the information it can yield on the conditions in which Islam was revealed:

> the tribes of Arabia in both the pre-Islamic and Islamic eras have attracted the attention not only of historians but of anthropologists and political scientists, who see in them a stage en route or contributing to state formation, a topic of considerable interest in the development of Mecca and the Islamic *umma* (p. xiv).

The seductive appeal of the Bedouin is also evident in the almost schizophrenic presentation of material in Chapter 3 ('Arabia before Islam) of JONATHAN P. BERKEY's otherwise first-rate book, *The Formation of Islam. Religion and Society in the Near East, 600-1800*.[37] The following statements are telling:

[36] Aldershot: AshgateVariorum, 1993.

[37] Cambridge: Cambridge University Press, 2003, p. 39-49. There is a similarly 'schizophrenic' presentation of material in MAXIME RODINSON, *Mohammed*, Harmondsworth: Penguin, 1985, p. 11-37.

> A more effective social 'glue' was the blood-feud, which placed realistic constraints on the anarchy of nomadic life and limits on the endemic violence (p. 40);
> The moral order of their society depended less on reference to a framework of supernatural origin than it did to the exigencies of social life in the demanding world of their difficult environment (p. 41);
> It is in fact difficult to say much with confidence regarding pre-Islamic Arabian religion. The situation may not, however, be completely bleak. If we are to understand the rise of Islam, it may be that we can say *something* by looking beyond the particular condition of the Arabs to their place in the wider world of the Near East and of the cultural and religious patterns of late antiquity (p. 42-43).

A similar dichotomy is evident in Daniel Brown's recent book. Brown notes that 'the overall impression one gets from pre-Islamic poetry is that these are people in desperate need of Islam', an impression produced by the ways in which later Muslims recreated their pagan past 'as part of an national Arab conversion story'.[38] These are incantations of the supposed incompatibility of, say, Hellenism (or any other loosely or tightly coherent set of cultural assumptions and expressions) and what Fred Donner has called the 'solid Semitic bedrock', attacked so eloquently and persuasively by Glen Bowersock.[39]

Let us also note finally that pre-eminent in these accounts of the pre-Islamic Arabian peninsula is a shared sense of timelessness, of nomadism as representative of population patterns in the peninsula, of the perduration of this precarious nomadic existence as somehow beyond time and impervious to change, like a Platonic idea or a philosophical universal.[40]

According to Bamyeh, 'we are speaking of a terrain in which life repeats itself both endlessly and precariously',[41] while for J. Spencer Trimingham, the 'Arab humanism' of the nomads is so resistant to change that it allowed them 'to accept the type of Christianity which they met, since religion existed to be exploited by man, not to challenge and change man'.[42] And since the voice of this humanism was poetry, it

[38] DANIEL BROWN, *A New Introduction to Islam*, Oxford: Blackwell, 2004, p. 15.

[39] DONNER, *The Early Islamic Conquests*, p. 94; GLEN BOWERSOCK, *Hellenism in Late Antiquity*, Ann Arbor: University of Michigan Press, 1996, p. 71-82 (see especially p. 72).

[40] CRONE, *Slaves on Horses*: 'the history of Arabia ... is one of tribal immutability: there is not much to tell between the Arabia of the Bible and the Arabia of Musil's Rwala' (p. 23); 'the Arabs ... had enormous antiquity' (p. 24); 'the Arabs had lived in freedom from ethnic and social disturbance since very ancient times' (p. 24-25).

[41] *The Social Origins*, p. 3.

[42] *Christianity among the Arabs in pre-Islamic Times*, London - New York and Beirut: Longman and Librairie du Liban, 1979, p. 244.

too is for Trimingham (like many a student of pre-Islamic poetry before him), incapable of change, alteration and accommodation: 'religion ... was alien to the conventions of Arab poetry ... the profession of Christianity had not affected their mode of life or their poetry, *except on the surface*'.[43]

Yet the mooted representativeness of the nomad is in inverse proportion to the probable percentage of the population of the peninsula that may at any one time have been nomadic, even allowing for returns to nomadism after a period of sedentarisation: 'most Arabians ... are, and have been, settled people'.[44] And attentive readers will note that in several earlier sentences I slip from 'Bedouin' to 'nomadic', but might not demur, for the two are surely identical or at least indistinguishable. There is, however, a world of difference between the terms 'Bedouin' and 'nomad', and the use of the ethnonym Arab (or better: ʿArab) simply makes matters worse.[45] How, then, are we to refer to these representative (if empty) inhabitants of the empty Ḥijāz?

[43] Italics added: *Christianity*, p. 247. 'Arab humanism' is clearly a variant of Montgomery Watt's 'tribal humanism', endorsed as a Marxian hermeneutic so enthusiastically by RODINSON, *Mohammed*, p. 17. See the review of W. MONTGOMERY WATT, *Muhammad at Mecca*, Oxford: Clarendon Press, 1953 by G.H. BOUSQUET, *Une explication marxiste de l'islam par un ecclesiastique episcopalien*, in: *Hesperis* 41 (1954), p. 231-247; and WATT's riposte: *Economic and Social Aspects of the Origin of Islam*, in: *Islamic Quarterly* 1 (1954), p. 90-103. The immiseration of Rodinson's 'Beduin' who 'do not seem to have had much time for religion' and who 'were realists, without a great deal of imagination' (p. 16), 'half-starved and extremely anarchic' (p. 17) are very reminiscent of Marx's proletariat. By far the most imaginative and (in modern terms) theoretically ambitious study of Islamic origins and Mecca as a money-and trade-based society is BAMYEH, *The Social Origins*: see, for example, 'money, trade and abstract thought' (p. 20-33). He is, however, often uncritical and indiscriminate in his use of sources, optimistic in many of his interpretations, and does regularly over-egg his pudding.

[44] DONNER, *The Early Islamic Conquests*, p. 11. On Arabian nomadism: FRED M. DONNER, *The Role of Nomads in the Near East of Late Antiquity (400-800 CE)*, in: PETERS, *The Arabs and Arabia*, p. 21-33; HODGSON, *The Venture of Islam*, p. 147-151.

[45] Nomads: A.M. KHAZANOV, *Nomads and the Outside World*, trans. J. CROOKENDEN, Madison: University of Wisconsin Press, 1994; E.A. KNAUF, *Nomads*, in: *EQ*, III, p. 543-545; Bedouin: UTE PIETRUSCHKA, *Bedouin*, in: *EQ*, I, p. 215-218; Arabs: TARIF KHALIDI, *Arabs*, in: *Encyclopaedia of the Qur'ān*, I, p. 144-145; HOYLAND, *Arabia and the Arabs*, p. 85-112. To oversimplify, for the sake of clarity: in the two centuries or so before the life of Muḥammad, Arabian nomads are not to be presumed as necessarily identical with the Bedouin, though the latter, as people (rather than inhabitants) of the *bādiya*, could be represented as such, by non-Bedouins — thus a nomad is not necessarily a Bedouin and a Bedouin could, counter-intuitively, be settled for much of the year, and could also share some of the features of lifestyle which characterize the nomad (camel pastoralism, for example); while the ʿArab are those Bedouins who valorised the *ʿarabīya*, immortalised in *qaṣīda* poetry. It is the relationship between the ʿArab and the desert which I try to capture in my neologism, 'bedouinising'.

Recently, a most spirited and sustained defence of 'ʿArab' has been mounted by Jan Retsö, who speaks of a 'razzia-loving warrior caste' and imagines the ʿArab to form 'a socio-religious association of warriors, subject to a divinity or ruler as his slaves ... separate from ordinary settled farmers and city-dwellers, living in their own lots often outside the border between the desert and the sown' (p. 587).[46] The notion of a 'socio-religious association of warriors' (but one which celebrates the desert waste, wherever their residence may be) is appealing, but I cannot agree with his contention (p. 587) that the initiation rite described by Herodotus in the Fifth Century BC is that which the poet Labīd is said to have undergone:[47] after all, Herodotus mentions cutting off hair (with no indication of how much hair is removed), whereas Labīd has his head shaved but for a ringlet! In general, Retsö places too much faith in the possibility of the denotational continuity of the ethnonym *ʿarab* and does not really allow for its subsequent appropriation or adaptation as part of a deliberate act of identity manufacture.[48]

Mark Whittow has advocated replacing the term 'Arab' with the term 'Bedu', in accordance with contemporary anthropological and ethnographical practice ('those who see themselves and are seen by others as

[46] *The Arabs in Antiquity. Their History from the Assyrians to the Umayyads*, London - New York: Routledge, 2003, p. 583 and 587.

[47] He is influenced by the discussion of by S.P. STETKEVYCH, *The Mute Immortals Speak: Pre-Islamic Poetry and the Poetics of Ritual*, Indiana: Cornell University Press, 1993, p. 46-51. As Retsö himself notes (p. 606 and 619, note 81) hair-cutting is one of several initiations into the society of adults, originally belonging to the 'rites of puberty, wedding and entrance into adult society'. Thus, Labīd must become an adult before he can engage in the poetic battle. Head-shaving could mark both sacralisation and desacralisation: see G.R. HAWTING, *The Idea of Idolatry and the Emergence of Islam. From Polemic to History*, Cambridge: Cambridge University Press, 1999, p. 68-69 and 143, with further references. Yet JOSEPH HENNINGER, *Pre-Islamic Bedouin Religion*, in: PETERS, *The Arabs and Arabia*, p. 119 remarks that 'the offering of human hair was not a true sacrifice but a rite of passage, involving a transition from the profane to the sacred or in the reverse direction'. See also JOSEPH HENNINGER, *Zur Frage des Haaropfers bei den Semiten*, in his *Arabia Sacra. Aufsätze zur Religionsgeschichte Arabiens und seiner Randgebiete* (*Orbis Biblicus et Orientalis*, 40), Fribourg - Göttingen: Universitätsverlag and Vandenoeck & Ruprecht, 1981, p. 286-306.

[48] See the discussion of the observation that 'ancient observers generally associated the term "Arab" not with a language or culture but with an unsettled way of life' by FERGUS MILLAR, *The Roman Near East, 31 BC - AD 337*, Cambridge, MA: Harvard University Press, 1993, p. 221-222 and p. 511-515. For an example of ethnonymic slippage from the later tradition (Rūs and Ṣaqāliba), see JAMES E. MONTGOMERY, *Arabic Sources on the Vikings*, in: *The Viking World*, ed. STEFAN BRINK and NEIL PRICE, London - New York: Routledge (in press).

participating members of Arabic tribal culture'),[49] whereas M.C.A. Macdonald argues (in the context of North Arabia) for greater discrimination in the use of the label 'Bedouin'[50] and Michael Zwettler would establish 'its most restrictive' designation as 'the camel-raising and -riding Arab nomads of the late antique Near East'.[51] Walter Dostal, arguing for an Iranian (Parthian) influence for the saddle-bow and its associated weaponry and cultural complexes (including tent-types, customs and clothing), distinguishes between nomads, 'half-bedouins (breeders of small-cattle)' and 'full bedouins (camel-breeders)'.[52] The masters of *qaṣīda* poetry would represent the development of this last stage in the form of aristocratic 'rider-warriors' (the term is Dostal's: p. 14), adept at warfare with both horse and camel, implicated, to varying extents, in the imperial uses in North and Central Arabia of confederations of rider-warriors as mercenaries and characterized by developed military technology such as body armour and the lance.[53]

We can go further and identify these as the warrior elites of Maʿadd, if we accept the conclusions of the painstaking analysis of the ethnonym

[49] MARK WHITTOW, *Rome and the Jafnids: Writing the History of a 6th-c. Tribal Dynasty*, in: *The Roman and Byzantine Near East. Some Recent Archaeological Research* (*Journal of Roman Archaeology Supplement Series*, 31 [1999]), ed. JOHN H. HUMPHREY, Portsmouth, Rhode Island, 1999, p. 207-224 (p. 219 and footnote 33).

[50] *Was the Nabataean Kingdom a 'Bedouin State'?*, in: *Zeitschrift des Deutschen Palästina-Vereins* 107 (1991), p. 102-119 (see p. 102, note 2); I have been unable to consult his *Nomads and the Ḥawrān in the Late Hellenistic and Roman Periods: A Reassessment of the Epigraphic Evidence*, in: *Syria* 70 (1993), p. 303-413 (p. 327 and note 158). See also his *North Arabia in the First Millennium BCE*, in: *Civilizations of the Ancient Near East*, ed. J.M. SASSON, II, New York: Charles Scribner's Sons, p. 1355-1369. It is clear, however, that he would not agree with my desire to inflict such a vague tampering as 'Bedouinising' upon such 'an extremely loaded term' as 'Bedouin'.

[51] *Maʿadd*, p. 268, footnote 78.

[52] WALTER DOSTAL, *The Evolution of Bedouin Life*, in: *L'antica società beduina* (*Studi Semitici*, 2), ed. FRANCESCO GABRIELI, Rome: Istituto di Studi Semitici, 1959, p. 11-34 (p.12 and p. 29).

[53] DOSTAL, *The Development of Bedouin Life in Arabia seen from Archaeological Material*, in: *Studies for the History of Arabia, Part 1* (1979), p. 125-144 (p. 129): see also ZWETTLER, *Maʿadd*, p. 280-284, for a judicious assessment of Dostal's theories, Macdonald's critiques and Kuhnen's modifications (stressing the cavalry with the pack-camel as militarily and logistically ancillary); R.M. WEBSTER, *The Bedouin in Southern and South Eastern Arabia. The Evolution of Bedouin Life Reconsidered*, in: *Proceedings of the Seminar for Arabian Studies* 22 (1992), p. 121-134. On the elitism of the camel 'nomads', see HODGSON, *The Venture of Islam*, p. 150; FRED M. DONNER, *The Bakr b. Wāʾil Tribes and Politics in Northeastern Arabia on the Eve of Islam*, in: *Studia Islamica* 51 (1980), p. 5-38: 'the great majority of the groups within the B. Shaybān were nomadic or partly nomadic, and it was on this warrior aristocracy of powerful nomadic groups that the Shaybān's claims to leadership or noble status among the Bakr tribes rested' (p. 22).

Maʿadd advanced by Zwettler,[54] and I can see no cogent reasons for rejecting his meticulous and erudite sifting of the evidence, viz. that in the three centuries before Islam:

> the general population of predominantly camel-herding Arab bedouins and bedouin tribal groups — irrespective of lineage or place of origin — who ranged, encamped and resided throughout most of the central and northern peninsula ... and who had come to adopt the *šadād*-saddle and also, by the third century, to utilize it so effectively as a means of developing and exploiting within a desert environment the superior military advantages offered by horses and horse cavalry. Individuals or groups who identified with and comprised that population would have related themselves to it — and to each other — not as kinsmen, confederates or allies, but as colleagues, associates or cohorts in an amorphous, far-ranging, almost idealized aggregation of like-minded compeers and communities who shared many of the same social, cultural and ecological experiences, aspirations, opinions, and values.[55]

By the middle or the end of the seventh century, '*Maʿadd* entered the genealogical realm, where it became an eponym for the 'progressive' Northern Arabs'.[56]

In a book published in 1997, I proposed (in pursuance of some of these arguments) that we should in fact make a fundamental distinction between 'Bedouin' and 'nomad', and in the process I tentatively referred to *qaṣīda* poetry as 'bedouinising'. I am now much more convinced than I was then of the need to move beyond reading this poetry as a simple, and uncluttered, index of nomadic/bedouin life, as a miraculously transparent record of nomadic/bedouin existence, and to connect it with the process of the 'bedouinisation' of Arabia which marks the century and a half or so prior to the prophethood of Muḥammad, and which is connected with the centres of political power and cultural influence in the Arabian peninsula:

> The majority of pre-Islamic poetry, especially the most cherished and hence the supposedly most representative (was) ... composed ... in the seventh century by an intellectual[57] (bedouinising) elite connected with centres of

[54] *Maʿadd*, p. 223-309.

[55] *Maʿadd*, p. 285.

[56] *Maʿadd*, p. 285-286.

[57] By 'intellectual', which I admit may be something of an over-statement, giving the impression of arm-chair ideologues, I was trying to convey my deep admiration for the conceptual sweep of this movement's poetic ideology and its ability to manage comfortably abstract notions, such as the irrecoverability of time past and the emotional cancer of fatalism in terms of great immediacy. I cannot accept the materialist reading of *qaṣīda* poetry advocated by BAMYEH, *The Social Origins*, which I find to be too restrictive.

> political power and cultural influence in the Arabian Peninsula, traditionally conceived, for whom it was expedient to espouse matters nomadic. This poetry may have had its origins in nomadic poetry and may have engaged in the development of nomadic forms, but what we have today is Bedouin and not nomadic, if I can force such a distinction ... an Arabic poetry for Arabs, like an Arabic Qur'ān for Muslims in the religious domain, was an expression of poetic, cultural and political autonomy and pride.[58]

So convincing and satisfying is this picture of the *Badw* created in so much of the *qaṣīda* poetry of the *jāhilīya* that it has continued to cast its spell and enchant for some fourteen centuries.[59]

Looking back I can now see the influence exerted on my ideas by two articles in particular: WERNER CASKEL, *The Bedouinization of Arabia*, and G.E. VON GRUNEBAUM, *The Nature of Arab Unity Before Islam*, a work which contains the best (e.g. the application of the concept of *Kulturnation*) and the worst of his scholarship ('the general tenor of Bedouin life, atomistic, libertarian, devoid of larger purpose, and much in need of that heightening of its petty irrelevancies by which the poets lent it dignity'!).[60] These works consolidated my sense of the emergent political prominence of the Bedouin tribes gained from reading the excellent articles of M.J. KISTER.[61] However, I was unaware when I

[58] MONTGOMERY, *The Vagaries of the* Qaṣīdah, p. 258-259. See further JAN RETSÖ, *The Road to Yarmuk: The Arabs and the Fall of the Roman Power in the Middle East*, in: *Aspects of Late Antiquity and Early Byzantium*, ed. LEENART RYDÉN and JAN OLAF ROSENQVIST, Stockholm: Swedish Research Institute in Istanbul, 1993, p. 31-41: 'the most famous poets who were also, as a rule, great warriors, were either closely attached to these chiefs or direct descendants of them. The classical Arabic poetry and its language was created in this *milieu*' (p. 39-40). It is in terms of the appeal of the emptiness of the Ḥijāz as a signifier that we must consider the outlandish theory proposed by CHAIM RABIN, *On the Probability of South-Arabian Influence on the Arabic Vocabulary*, in: *Jerusalem Studies in Arabic and Islam* 4 (1984), p. 125-134, that the Arabs got their poetry from South Arabia, whose merchants, in their turn, 'could have transported to their own society certain features of Indian poetry' (p. 134).

[59] I would emphasize that this is a generalization and as such a simplification of the multifarious corpora of *jāhilī* poetry extant today, which also contains examples of popular, non-elite verse, as in the Hudhalī *dīwān*, for example, and codifications of the ideologies of Maʿadd, such as the *qaṣīda* poetry of Zuhayr b. Abī Sulmā. The consolidation of 'bedouinising' *qaṣīda*s led to the emergence of professional panegyrists, such as al-Nābigha al-Dhubyāni and al-Aʿshā Maymūn b. Qays.

[60] In: *American Anthropologist* 56 (1954), p. 36-46; and in: *Arabica* 10 (1963), p. 4-23, respectively. See the arguments against Caskel's theory of re-bedouinisation made by DOSTAL, *The Evolution of Bedouin Life*, p. 23-24.

[61] Articles such as *Al-Ḥīra. Some Notes on its Relations with Arabia*, in: *Arabica* 15 (1968), p. 143-169 (reprinted as Article III in: M.J. KISTER, *Studies in Jāhiliyya and Early Islam*, London: Variorum, 1980 and in: PETERS, *The Arabs and Arabia*); *Mecca and Tamīm (Aspects of their Relations)*, in: *Journal of the Economic and Social History of the Orient* 8 (1965), p. 113-163 (reprinted as Article I in: *Studies in Jāhiliyya*); *Mecca and*

wrote this book of the suggestion of Patricia Crone that Islam should be understood (in the words of Fred Donner) as 'a "nativist" (consciously Arab) identity movement'.[62]

My account of the consequences of 'foreign penetration characteristic of sixth- and early seventh-century Arabia' is not the engendering of Islam as a 'nativist movement ... as a primitive reaction to alien domination', for as CRONE herself acknowledges, 'the foreign presence is unlikely to have affected the majority of Arabs very deeply'.[63] A most potent reaction to this involvement and the emergence of the courts of Ghassān and Lakhm (like Kinda before them, confederations of elite warrior tribes acting as mercenaries in the employ of the imperial powers)[64] is the emergence of the Bedouin warrior as an expression of a complex of ethnogenetic ideals celebrated in 'Bedouinising' *qaṣīda* poetry.[65] Informed by a *Weltanschauung* of *muruwwa* (manly virtue), at the very heart of which lay a passionate and uncompromising adherence to *ʿirḍ* (honour),[66] set within 'a universal perspective where the paradigm

the Tribes of Arabia. Some Notes on their Relations, in: *Studies in Islamic History and Civilization in Honour of David Ayalon*, ed. M. SHARON, Jerusalem - Leiden: Brill, 1986, p. 33-57 (reprinted as Article II in his *Society and Religion from Jāhiliyya to Islam*, Aldershot: Variorum, 1990).

62 *The Background to Islam*, p. 515.

63 Islam as nativism: PATRICIA CRONE, *Meccan Trade and the Rise of Islam*, Princeton: Princeton University Press, 1987, p. 231-250. Quotations taken from p. 246, p. 247 and p. 249. Consider, however, the arguments of KISTER, in the articles mentioned above, who tends to view intertribal conflict as a direct consequence of Byzantine and Sasanid desire to divide and rule, while for RETSÖ, *The Road to Yarmuk*, 'the Islamic state in Medina can be interpreted in secular terms as an attempt to avoid circumvention of Arabia by excluding foreigners from controlling Yemen and abolishing the system of tribes being hired as mercenaries by outsiders'. In other words, from a non-religious perspective, Islamic Arabia is a declaration of independence, an unforeseen consequence of a long history of foreign interferences.

64 See the discussion in the next section and generally DONNER, *The Early Islamic Conquests*, p. 42-48. Ghassān and Lakhm were to Byzantium and Sasanid Iran what Kinda had been to Ḥimyar. The inability of the imperial powers to control their buffer zones and sometime mercenaries created the state of instability which led to the triumph of the Caliphate of Medina. WHITTOW, *Rome and the Jafnids*, argues that 'great power competition from the third century onwards had led to a phase of political development among the Bedu which transformed the previously unthreatening Bedu pastoralists into groupings capable of forcing the settled powers to take note' (p. 222-223).

65 See the similar but distinct assessment of HOYLAND, *Arabia and the Arabs*, p. 229-247 ('Arabhood and Arabisation'); further reflections on the emergence of the Bedouin as cultural norm in: JAMES E. MONTGOMERY, *The Deserted Encampment in Ancient Arabic Poetry: A Nexus of Topical Comparisons*, in: *Journal of Semitic Studies* 40 (1995), p. 283-316.

66 *Muruwwa*: see JAMES E. MONTGOMERY, *Dichotomy in* Jāhilī *Poetry*, in: *Journal of Arabic Literature* 17 (1986), p. 1-20.

for how one must live and die is founded on the principle of chance',[67] united yet differentiated by their scrupulous investment in the societal dynamics of genealogy, acquired and inherited (*ḥasab wa-nasab*), unanimous in their celebration of the possibilities of the *qaṣīda* and the *ʿarabīya*, these Bedouin warriors cherished their vehicles of war and chase, the she-camel and the horse, as well as their weaponry and armaments, and brought to perfection their mastery of the razzia and the hunt, informed by a notion of war as inseparable from religion.[68]

It was this complex which, among many other features, such as divine revelation in a linguistically dazzling Qur'ān, the messianic appeal of the apocalyptic (many of the Qur'anic echoes in early Arabic poetry are of eschatological *āyas*), the reformation of an ancestral Ibrahimic religion common to the speakers of the *ʿarabīya* centred on the Kaʿba in Mecca and the Islamicisation of the tribal *ghazwa* as the Muslim *jihād*, the divine mandate of which was corroborated by military successes), enabled Muḥammad to found a viable Islamic *umma*, an *umma* energized by tribalist patterns and practices, one which sought to recalibrate but not to dissolve or supersede them (contrary to what is sometimes maintained).[69] Moreover, the relationship of Prophet Muḥammad and the early Muslims to the poets and their poetry is complex and by no means as univocal as some responses to Qur'anic pronouncements on poetry might lead us to believe. That 'Bedouinising' *qaṣīda* poetry at its height, the emergence of the Arabian sanctuary of the Ibrahimic Kaʿba and an 'Arabic Qur'ān' are coterminous hardly seems a coincidence: these discourses crossfertilised each other remarkably, as their coexistence was explored, articulated and experimented with. In a simple sense, the Arabic of the *qaṣīda* poetry was a necessary condition for a divine revelation in Arabic.[70]

[67] NADIA JAMIL, *Playing for Time:* Maysir-*Gambling in Early Arabic Poetry*, in: *Islamic Reflections, Arabic Musings. Studies in Honour of Alan Jones*, ed. ROBERT G. HOYLAND and PHILIP F. KENNEDY, Oxford: Gibb Memorial Trust, 2004, p. 48-90 (p. 67).

[68] JAMIL, *Playing for Time*, p. 68.

[69] For an extreme statement of the exclusivist reading of the *umma*, against which I am reacting, see DONNER, *The Early Islamic Conquests*, p. 55-62 and passim (according to this view, embracement of Islam is akin to discipleship of Christ: the abandonment of all other social, cultural and ideological ties), and following him, FOWDEN, *Empire to Commonwealth*, p. 153. The intellectual and linguistic cosmos within which the contingencies and tensions of such a bold experiment were to be explored was that of the *ʿarabīya*: KHALIDI, *Arabs*.

[70] See generally MONTGOMERY, *Vagaries* (Chapter Six: *Poetry in the Early Islamic Period*), p. 209-257; MICHAEL ZWETTLER, *A Mantic Manifesto: the* Sūra *of 'The Poets' and the Qur'ānic Foundations of Prophetic Authority*, in: *Poetry and Prophecy: the*

The man who would be king

Consider how radically differently a picture of pre-Islamic Arabia is drawn in the following poetic *vita*, the biography of the most famous of all pre-Islamic poets the princeling Imru' al-Qays of the North Arabian branch of the South Arabian tribe of Kinda.[71] Such is his reputation that he is named in later Muslim tradition as the leader of the poets in Hell. What follows is principally a digest of the entry on Imru' al-Qays composed by the bureaucrat and scholar Abū l-Faraj al-Isfahānī (d. ca. 363/972) in his *Kitāb al-Aghānī al-Kabīr*, his Major Book of Songs.[72]

Beginnings of Literary Tradition, Ithaca - London: Cornell University Press, p. 75-119, 205-231; ALAN JONES, *Poetry and Poets*, in: *EQ*, IV, p. 110-114; and on the Kaʿba, see the two articles by URI RUBIN, *The Kaʿba: Aspects of its Ritual Functions and Position in Pre-Islamic and Early Islamic Times*; and: *Ḥanīfiyya and Kaʿba: An Inquiry into the Arabian Pre-Islamic Background of* Dīn Ibrāhīm, in: PETERS, *The Arabs and Arabia*, p. 313-347 and p. 267-294; together with DONNER's discussion of adherence to religious cults as social binding: *The Early Islamic Conquests*, p. 28. See, however, the counter arguments, largely concerning the problems of the semantic indeterminacy of the titles *allāh* and *rabb al-bayt* and the continued veneration at Mecca of Ḥubal and al-ʿUzzā, mustered by PAVEL PAVLOVITCH, Qad kunna (sic) lā naʿbudu 'llāha wa-lā naʿrifuhu. *On the Problem of the pre-Islamic Lord of the Kaʿba*, in: *Journal of Arabic and Islamic Studies* 2 (1998-1999), p. 49-74 (www.uib.no/jais).

[71] The Northern Kinda were Christian, despite al-Ḥārith's brief flirtation with Mazdakism: see TRIMINGHAM, *Christianity*, p. 276-278; the Kinda of the Ḥaḍramawt were Jews: M. LECKER, *Kinda on the Eve of Islam and during the Ridda*, in: *Journal of the Royal Asiatic Society* (1994), p. 333-356; *Judaism among Kinda and the* Ridda *of Kinda*, in: *Journal of the American Oriental Society*, 115 (1995), p. 635-650. In these extremely rich articles, Lecker documents the transition of Kindite supremacy from the Banū Ḥujr Ākil al-Murār, the branch to which Imru' al-Qays belonged (and who, according to IBN ḤABĪB, *Kitāb al-Muḥabbar*, ed. ILSE LICHTENSTÄDTER, Hyderabad: Dā'irat al-Maʿārif al-ʿUthmānīya, 1942, p. 267.5 owed their hegemony of the market at al-Rābiya in Ḥaḍramawt to their preferment by Quraysh [*bi-faḍl quraysh*]: see KISTER, *Mecca and Tamīm*, p. 156-157) to the Banū l-Ḥārith al-Wallāda, after the return to Ḥaḍramawt toward the end of the Sixth Century, and generally connected with the Persian conquest of South Arabia: see LECKER, *Ridda*, p. 336-337; GUNNAR OLINDER, *Āl al-Ǧaun of the Family of Ākil al-Murār*, in: *Le Monde Orientale* 25 (1931), p. 208-229 (on the Kinda of al-Yamāma and their demise: Arabic translation available in *Mulūk Kinda*, p. 181-208); M.J. KISTER, *The Campaign of Ḥulubān. A New Light on the Expedition of Abraha*, in: *Le Muséon* 78 (1965), p. 425-436 (reprinted as Article IV in *Studies in Jāhiliyya* (for Abū [l]-Jabr, of this dynastic branch of the tribe, who was the commander of Abraha's troops in 552, as mentioned in Inscription Ry 506). Kindite hegemony, in terms of its political structures, is variously described as 'a supra-tribal organization' (IRFAN KAWAR [SHAHID], *Procopius and Kinda*, in: *Byzantinische Zeitschrift* 53 [1960], p. 74-78 [p. 76]), as the 'nomad alliance-state of Kinda' (TRIMINGHAM, *Christianity*, p. 267) and as 'the first record of a properly Bedouin "monarchy"' (BAMYEH, *The Social Origins*, p. 46-52). That the ruling dynasties of Kinda experimented with a variety of political structures in the course of their long hegemony seems evident, and one should not underestimate the paradigmatic influence of the South Arabian kingdom of Ḥimyar: in so many ways, Kinda forms a bridge between Ḥimyar and Medina, whilst bearing many similarities with such

This biography is mythopoesis, driven in part by the desire to read biography into every verse of poetry transmitted under the name of Imru' al-Qays.[73] While I am primarily interested in the picture which al-Iṣfahānī draws, a picture in which the Ḥijāz and pre-Islamic Arabia are completely and comprehensively integrated into the Late Antique world, my concern is also with mythopoetic memory as opposed to the chimera of 'historical' accuracy.[74]

But first, ponder the following case of mistaken identity. Ibn al-ʿAdīm (d. 660/1262) recounts the following anecdote of the ʿAbbasid Caliph al-Ma'mūn (r. 198-218/813-833) in what purport to be his own words:

> I passed through Ankara ... and I saw the image [i.e. the statue] of Imru' al-Qays ... The Greeks in Ankara had made an image of [him] as they do with those they venerate.[75]

tribal confederations as the Tanūkh (on the formation of which in al-Baḥrayn, see AL-ṬABARĪ, *Ta'rīkh al-Rusul wa-l-Mulūk*, ed. M.J. DE GOEJE et al., I, Leiden: Brill, 1879-1901, p. 746.5-7; *The History of al-Ṭabarī, Volume IV. The Ancient Kingdoms*, trans. MOSHE PERLMANN, Albany: SUNY, 1987, p. 129; IRFAN SHAHID, 'Tanūkh', *EI2*, X, p. 190-192; TRIMINGHAM, *Christianity*, p. 267, footnote 63, mistakenly substitutes Taghlib for Tanūkh). I have not been able to consult CHRISTIAN ROBIN, *Le Royaume ḥujride, dit 'Royaume de Kinda', entre Ḥimyar et Byzance*, in: *Comptes rendus des scéances de l'Académie des Inscriptions et Belles-Lettres* 1996, p. 665-714. The complexities involved in studying tribal politics through such a fluid tradition as genealogy at this present remove are well brought out by DONNER, *The Bakr b. Wā'il Tribes*. For an exemplary study of such issues, see ZWETTLER, *Maʿadd*.

[72] ABŪ L-FARAJ AL-IṢFAHĀNĪ, *Kitāb al-Aghānī al-Kabīr*, IX, Cairo: Maṭbaʿat Dār al-Kutub al-Miṣrīya, 1936, p. 77-107.

[73] See JULIA BRAY, *ʿAbbasid Myth and the Human Act: Ibn ʿAbd Rabbih and Others*, in: *On Fiction and* Adab *in Medieval Arabic Literature*, ed. PHILIP F. KENNEDY, Wiesbaden: Harrassowitz, 2005, p. 1-54.

[74] ALBRECHT NOTH and LAWRENCE I. CONRAD, *The Early Arabic Historical Tradition. A Source-Critical Study*, Princeton: Darwin Press, 1994, p. xi: 'Arabic-Islamic historical tradition contains much which, however richly it may inform us about the perceptions and views of later times, reveals nothing *per se* about the historical object of the discussion'. Compare the approach of MICHAEL ZWETTLER, *The Poet and the Prophet: Towards Understanding the Evolution of a Narrative*, in: *Jerusalem Studies in Arabic and Islam* 5 (1984), p. 313-388: 'some crucial issues of early Islamic history and culture can be glimpsed between the lines of the evolving narrative representation of the confrontation between Prophet and poet' (p. 319). The extent to which the biography is exegetical of remarkable verses in the poet's *dīwān* can easily be appreciated from a perusal of the scrupulous connection of *khabar* with originary *bayt* carried out by GUNNAR OLINDER, *The Kings of Kinda*, in: *Lunds Universitets Årsskrift* 23/6 (1927), p. 94-118; Arabic translation, with valuable notes: *Mulūk Kinda min Banī Ākil al-Murār*, trans. ʿABD AL-JABBĀR AL-MUṬṬALIBĪ, Baghdād: Maṭbaʿat al-Ḥukūma, 1973, p. 152-180. For Olinder, however, the *bayt* provides corroborative documentary evidence for the *khabar*.

[75] Quoted from MICHAEL COOPERSON, *The Grave of al-Ma'mūn in Tarsus: A Preliminary Report*, in: *ʿAbbasid Studies*, ed. J.E. MONTGOMERY, Peeters: Leuven, 2004, p. 55. See further IRFAN SHAHID, *The Last Days of Imru' al-Qays: Anatolia*, in: *Tradition and Modernity in Arabic Literature*, ed. I.J. BOULLATA and T. DEYOUNG, Fayetteville:

It is improbable that the statue which al-Ma'mūn admired was a likeness of a pre-Islamic prince-poet erected in Ankara, and it has been suggested that what he may have been referring to was a pagan monument (possibly the Augusteum, temple of Roma and Augustus).[76] What then are we to make of the Caliph's imaginings? We could begin by noting that, in a bold act of cultural supremacy, the Caliph who is credited the most in our sources, both ancient and modern, with sponsoring the comprehensive translation into Arabic of the Greek and Late Antique intellectual heritage, is in little doubt as to the fact that the Arabs (as symbolized by their most famous poet and most tragic hero) have eclipsed the Rūm (an ethnonym which also includes what we would understand as Roman antiquity) to the point that they have dedicated a monumental statuary to Imru' al-Qays, one instance of the multiple facets of early ʿAbbasid identity of which this interpretative act of appropriation is the product. But is this little more than wishful thinking on the part of a Caliph who considered himself to be God's mouthpiece on earth? Or might there be some other reason for the Caliph to think that Imru' al-Qays was a figure of such importance to the Greeks? In other words, who was Imru' al-Qays and why was he in Ankara?

The second question is readily answered: his presence in Ankara is a biographical exegesis of the occurrence of the toponym *anqira* (rare in *jāhilī* poetry), in a piece of *rajaz* verse which was read as the last verses declared by Imru' al-Qays on his deathbed.[77] Such exegesis is the very inspiration of the narrative elaborations of this life.

University of Arkansas Press, 1997, p. 207-222, a modern application of the exegetical principles underpinning al-Iṣfahānī's biography, in which he is hoist with his own petard, having in an earlier publication criticized another scholar's reconstruction of Imru' al-Qays's biography as an 'unhappy attempt in accepting from the Arabic tradition accounts whose quality ranges from the purely fictitious and imaginary to the highly dubious and hypothetical', and the incorporation of them as 'established facts into a historical account deriving from a primary source': IRFAN KAWAR (SHAHID), *Byzantium and Kinda*, in: *Byzantinische Zeitschrift* 53 (1960), p. 57-73.

[76] CLIVE FOSS, *Late Antique and Byzantine Ankara*, in: *Dumbarton Oaks Papers* 31 (1977), p. 77 (reference taken from SHAHID, *The Last Days*, p. 221).

[77] References are to the three basic editions of his poems: *The Divans of the Six Ancient Arabic Poets*, ed. W. AHLWARDT, London: Trübner, 1870 (the reference is to poem number, then verse); *Six Early Arab Poets. New Edition and Concordance*, ed. ALBERT ARAZI and SALMAN MASALHA, Jerusalem: Max Schlossinger Memorial Series, 1999 (the reference is to the marginal numbers and the subsequent numbering of the lines: as this is a reissue of Ahlwardt's edition, the marginal numeration refers to his original pagination); *Dīwān*, ed. MUḤAMMAD ABŪ L-FAḌL IBRĀHĪM, Cairo: Dār al-Maʿārif, 1958 (reference is to poem number, then verse number, then page). For the *bayt*: (Ahlwardt) poem 28.4 (Arazi-Masalha, 133.17; Ibrāhīm, poem 94.4, p. 349). It is by no means certain that Ankara is meant by *anqira* and the *rajaz* verses are extremely

Imru' al-Qays's name means, 'the man of al-Qays',[78] and he is accorded two other titles, *al-malik al-ḍillīl*, the errant princeling, and *dhū l-qurūḥ*, the man of the weeping sores (*Agh.*, p. 78.2-3). Dates of birth and death are not, of course, to be expected,[79] though he is said to have been born among the tribe of Asad, and to have lived in either the fort of al-Mushaqqar located in al-Yamāma[80] or a fort located in the area designated in classical Arabic as al-Baḥryan, i.e. East Arabia, and the north-western litoral of the Persian Gulf in particular (p. 78.6-7).

Al-Iṣfahānī's begins his composite account (p. 78.15-79.3)[81] of the poet's life with the career of his great-grandfather, ʿAmr al-Maqṣūr, whose mother is alleged to have been one of the royal family of South Arabia, known as the Tubbaʿ (p. 79.5), and it is with the help of the kings of Ḥimyar that the founder of the dynasty, ʿAmr's father, Ḥujr Ākil al-Murār is said to have taken control of the tribes of northern and

non-committal and vague, containing nothing, beyond a future tense, to hint at a deathbed utterance. These are the kind of verses which posed the ultimate exegetical and imaginative challenge for the biographers. Cf. also SHAHID, *The Last Days*, p. 211-213. On the technique of verbal correspondence between exegetical *khabar* and evidentiary *bayt* (in the form of a quotation, echo or allusion), see WERNER CASKEL, *Aijām al-ʿArab. Studien zur altarabischen Epik*, in: *Islamica* 4 (1931), p. 1-99 (p. 66-75, 'Das Verhältnis der Verse zur Prosa'); ZWETTLER, *Poet and Prophet*, identifies such accounts as '(usually) aetiological narratives' (p. 325, footnote 57).

[78] It has been suggested that this is a theophoric and would thus mean 'worshipper of the god al-Qays'. I am inclined to see it in the context of ancestor worship, as with a considerable number of other theophorics, such as the name of the Prophet Muḥammad's grandfather ʿAbd al-Muṭṭalib, or the items on Medinan idolatry provided by al-Maqrīzī and discussed by MICHAEL LECKER, *Idol Worship in pre-Islamic Medina (Yathrib)*, in: PETERS, *The Arabs and Arabia*, p. 129-144. On ancestor worship: HENNINGER, *Pre-Islamic Bedouin Religion*, p. 109-128; on the problem of the theophorics: THEODOR NÖLDEKE, *Arabs (Ancient)*, in: *Encyclopaedia of Religion and Ethics*, I, p. 659-673 (p. 659-660); TILMAN SEIDENSTICKER, *Zur Frage eines Astralkultes im vorislamischen Arabien*, in: *Zeitschrift der Deutschen Morgenländischen Gesellschaft* 136 (1986), p. 493-511, especially, p. 503-506 and 508-509.

[79] SHAHID, *The Last Days*, p. 217 claims that 'the year A.D. 542 ... emerges as the one precise and certain date for the death of a pre-Islamic poet', and thus for the very history of the development of the *qaṣīda*. His evidence is pure exegesis tempered only by speculation and makes the foundations of a house of cards seem solid.

[80] On al-Mushaqqar, see IMRU' AL-QAYS, *Dīwān* (Ahlwardt) poem 20.7 (Arazi-Masalha, 128.15; Ibrāhīm, poem 4.5, p. 57; KISTER, *Mecca and Tamīm*, p. 130; 'a harbour-city frequented by merchants from Persia, an important base of Persian rule'.

[81] See S. BOUSTANY, 'Imru' al-Ḳays b. Ḥudjr', *EI2*, III, p. 1177, for the competing accounts of his biography (Kufan, Basran, and Baghdadi). ZWETTLER, *Poet and Prophet*, remarks that Ibn Qutayba provides two versions of the episode involving Kaʿb b. Zuhayr and Prophet Muḥammad (p. 322, footnote 33). For details relating to the members of this dynasty, see OLINDER, *The Kings of Kinda* (= *Mulūk Kinda*): Ḥujr: p. 39-46 (= p. 70-84); ʿAmr: p. 47-50 (= p. 85-91); al-Ḥārith: p. 51-69 (= p. 92-120); his sons: p. 70-93 (= p. 122-151); Imru' al-Qays: p. 94-118 (= p. 152-180).

central Arabia, known collectively as Maʿadd (p. 81.7-8).[82] Upon his death at the hands of the Ghassanid al-Ḥārith b. Abī Shamir (p. 81.11-12), ʿAmr is succeeded by al-Ḥārith, king during the rule of the Sasanid Qubādh b. Fayrūz (Kavād son of Perōz) (488-496, 498/9-531), in whose reign Mazdak preached his social and religious reforms.[83] Qubādh's support of the religious reform of Mazdak is shared by al-Ḥārith the Kindite but not by the Lakhmid governor of the military cantonment of al-Ḥīra, al-Mundhir b. Māʾ al-Samāʾ, who is ousted by Qubādh and replaced with al-Ḥārith (p. 79.4-14) in residence at al-Anbār (p. 80.5).[84] According to another version (that of Ibn Qutayba), al-Ḥārith owes his kingship to the last of the Tubbaʿ kings (p. 81.7-8).

[82] See ZWETTLER, *Maʿadd*: this article also provides *en passant* an excellent sketch of the history of Kinda in epigraphical and Greek sources: p. 241, 244-246 (Kinda in Ry 509), 248-250 (Kinda in Ry 506), 257-257 (Qays b. Salama). An inscription discovered and published by Ryckmans from the Fifth Century mentions Ḥujr son of ʿAmr King of Kiddat: see GONZAGUE RYCKMANS, *Inscriptions Sud-Arabes*, in: *Le Muséon* 69 (1956), p. 152; see also JACQUELINE PIRENNE, *L'Inscription «Ryckmans 535» et la chronologie sud-arabe*, in: *Le Muséon* 69 (1956), p. 165-181; IWONA GAJDA, *Ḥuğr b. ʿAmr roi de Kinda et l'établissement de la domination ḥimyarite en Arabie centrale*, in: *Proceedings of the Seminar for Arabian Studies* 26 (1996), p. 65-73 and Plate 1.

[83] M. GUIDI and M. MORONY, 'Mazdak', *EI2*, VI, p. 949-952; P. CRONE, *Kavād's Heresy and Mazdak's Revolt*, in: *Iran: Journal of the British Institute of Persian Studies* 29 (1991), p. 21-42; Z. RUBIN, *The Reforms of Khusro Anūshirwān*, in: *The Byzantine and Early Islamic Near East, III: States, Resources and Armies*, ed. AVERIL CAMERON, Princeton: Darwin Press, 1995, p. 227-298 (especially p. 228-231); JOSEF WIESHÖFER, *Ancient Persia from 550 BC to 650 AD*, trans. AZIZEH AZODI, London: I.B. Tauris, 1996, p. 208-210; GEOFFREY GREATREX, *Byzantium and the East in the Sixth Century*, in: MAAS, *Age of Justinian*, p. 482-486. The importance of the religious orientation of the (dynastic) elites of the Arabian confederations for tribal politics is well brought out by DONNER, *The Bakr b. Wāʾil Tribes*, p. 25-26. The situation is not too dissimilar, for example, from the adoption of Islam by the King of the semi-sedentary Volga Bulghār in the early Fourth/Tenth Century visited by Ibn Faḍlān: their Islam was at first confined to the ruling elite and was chosen as a politico-religious antidote to the Judaism of the Khazar aristocracy: see JAMES E. MONTGOMERY, *Ibn Faḍlān*, in: *Literature of Travel and Exploration: An Encyclopedia*, ed. J. SPEAKE, II, London: Fitzroy Dearborn, 2003, p. 578-580; *Travelling Autopsies: Ibn Faḍlān and the Bulghār*, in: *Middle Eastern Literatures* 7 (2004), p. 4-32. For all its appeal (in view of Mazdak's proposed pacifist abolition of personal property, and of marriage [as an index of personal property]), it is unwise to connect the Mazdakism of Imruʾ al-Qays's grandfather with the poet's notorious treatment of women as disposable sexual objects: see AL-TAHIR AHMAD MAKKI, *Imruʾ al-Qays*, in: *Arabic Literary Culture, 500-925* (*Dictionary of Literary Biography*, 311), ed. MICHAEL COOPERSON and SHAWKAT M. TOORAWA, Detroit etc.: Thomson Gale, 2005, p. 212-224 (p. 215). On al-Ḥārith, see TRIMINGHAM, *Christianity*, p. 269-273; KAWAR (SHAHID), *Byzantium and Kinda*.

[84] See KISTER, *al-Ḥīra*, p. 145 for this adoption of Mazdakism. Note that the reference to Ḥujr b. ʿAdī Ākil al-Murār's *zandaqa* in AL-YAʿQŪBĪ, *Al-Taʾrīkh*, ed. M.TH. HOUTSMA, Leiden: Brill, 1883, p. 299.1, is a textual emendation. The context is pre-Islamic chieftains and notables who were Christian!

Earlier in their kingly career, a branch of the Kinda had their base at Qaryat Dhāt Kahl ('the township with the shrine of the god Kahl'), famous today as Qaryat al-Faw the excavations of which were published by Ali al-Ansary,[85] 'an impressive town, comprising a market, palace, temple, tombs and houses,' with notables 'wealthy enough to commission fine frescoes and grand statues and to import high-quality objects of glass, metal and ivory'.[86] The Hellenism of these frescoes is discussed by Glen Bowersock, who speaks of how 'here in the center of the Arabian peninsula Hellenism inspired a hitherto unsuspected commemoration of local prosperity and culture'.[87]

Upon the accession of Khusraw as Anūshirwān (the Immortal Soul) to the Sasanid throne, bitterly hostile to Mazdak's religious reforms, according to our account, and the attendant return to favour of the Lakhmid al-Mundhir, al-Ḥārith is driven out of north-eastern Arabia by a contingent of Taghlib, Bakr and Iyād tribesmen under the leadership of al-Mundhir (p. 79.14-80.16). Imru' al-Qays's grand-father is said to have died in the territory of the Kalb (p. 81.1-6) in the year 528, but not before, according to another account, going 'over to the Byzantines, who assigned to him a phylarchate in Palestine' though subsequently having to abandon that territory too, after quarreling with 'Diomede, the *dux* of that province'.[88] Before his death, al-Ḥārith divided rule over the tribes of Maʿadd among his four sons, with Ḥujr, the father of Imru' al-Qays, accorded control over the Banū Asad and Ghaṭafān, and thus being lord of the territory traditionally known as al-Tihāma (p. 81.11-82.5).[89]

The most significant event in Imru' al-Qays's life is the death of his father Ḥujr at the hands of the Banū Asad. There are various accounts of this occurrence (p. 84.1-86.20), just as a number of reasons are adduced for the breakdown of relations between father and son before the former's death (p. 87.12-89.5), the favourite being the son's debauched and dissolute lifestyle. Imru' al-Qays is told of his father's murder while in the Yemen (p. 87.18), and the remainder of his life is devoted to fulfilling his vow of vengeance, in pursuit of an all-consuming vendetta.

[85] ALI AL-ANSARY, *Qaryat al-Fau. A Portrait of Pre-Islamic Civilisation in Saudi Arabia*, Riyadh - London: Croom Helm, 1982. See also his *Aḍwā' Jadīda ʿalā Dawlat Kinda khilāl Āthār Qaryat al-Fau wa-Nuqūshi-hā*, in: *Sources for the History of Arabia, Part 1*, 1 (1979), p. 3-11 (Arabic); BOWERSOCK, *Hellenism*, p. 74-75.

[86] HOYLAND, *Arabia and the Arabs*, p. 50.

[87] *Hellenism in Late Antiquity*, p. 75 and plates 12 and 13.

[88] IRFAN SHAHID, 'Kinda', *EI*2, V, p. 118.

[89] On Ḥujr, see TRIMINGHAM, *Christianity*, p. 275.

This vendetta takes him to the tribal confederations of Bakr and Taghlib, who provide him with short-lived assistance; then back to Lakhmid territory under the protection of his maternal cousin ʿAmr b. al-Mundhir (p. 92.2-8); then to Ḥimyar (p. 90.12-92.2) where another kinsman grants him assistance but dies and whence he is expelled by his kinsman's successor, Qarmal (p. 92.9-92.16). With the help of Marthad al-Khayr's troops and a disparate group of mercenaries, he is able to conquer the Banū Asad (p. 92.17-93.4), but now he is the hunted bounty of the forces of al-Mundhir the Lakhmid and a group of Sasanid heavy cavalry dispatched by Anūshirwān. Al-Ḥārith b. Shihāb of the Banū Yarbūʿ b. Ḥanẓala is unable to protect him and his clansmen against the threats of al-Mundhir (p. 93.6-14), and so Imru' al-Qays seeks refuge in the territory of Ṭayyi' (p. 93.14), among whom war breaks out, on his account (p. 96.10-11). He finally finds full protection at the fortress of al-Samaw'al in Taymā' (p. 96.17-99.4), where he is graciously received.[90]

It is at this point that a most remarkable incident in his life takes place — at Imru' al-Qays's request, al-Samaw'al writes to the Ghassanid phylarch al-Ḥārith b. Abī Shamir to secure him access to the court of Qayṣar, where Justinian (r. 527-565) welcomes him, gives him a royal lodging and then provides him with a large military force (the purpose of which is not specified, though reconquest of ancestral domains seems implied) (p. 99.4-10).[91] The hostility of the house of Asad, however, re-emerges

[90] See THOMAS BAUER, 'al-Samaw'al b. ʿĀdiyā', *EI2*, VIII, p. 1041-1042; RODINSON, *Mohammed*, p. 29; the poem by al-Aʿshā Maymūn in which the story concerning al-Samaw'al's sacrifice of his son to preserve his honour intact is mentioned has been translated by ALAN JONES, *Narrative Technique in the Qur'ān and Early Arabic Poetry*, in: *Journal of Arabic Literature* 25 (1994), p. 185-191. BAMYEH, *The Social Origins*, p. 276, implausibly interprets the incident in terms of the 'entrenched hold' of usury, rather than honour.

[91] This royal visit is unattested in any of the Byzantine sources and even SHAHID, *The Last Days*, p. 209 is constrained to concede 'that arguments may be advanced' for its occurrence and for its non-occurrence. It is an exegetically driven narrative response to the four occurrences of the regnal title *qayṣar* in the poet's *dīwān* (Ahlwardt, poems 13.4, 20.21 and 20.43, fragment 5.4; Arazi-Masalha, p. 123.3, 129.10, 130.13, 197.14; Ibrāhīm, poem 46.5, p. 213, poem 4.34, p. 65, and 4.47, p. 69, poem 54.8, p. 252), perhaps influenced by memories of the visit of an Amorkesos (Imru' al-Qays) to the court of Leo (r. 457-474) in the Fifth Century and of another Kindite, Imru' al-Qays's cousin Qays ibn Salama, discussed by IRFAN SHAHID (KAWAR), *On the Patriciate of Imru'-al-Qays*, in: *The World of Islam. Studies in Honour of Philip K. Hitti*, ed. J. KRITZECK and R. BAYLY WINDER, London: Macmillan, 1959, p. 74-82 (on the confusion, see p. 81-82); *Byzantium and Kinda*, respectively. See further his discussions in: *Byzantium and the Arabs in the Fifth Century*, Washington, DC: Dumbarton Oaks Research Library Collection, 1989, p. 59-91; *Byzantium and the Arabs in the Sixth Century*, I, Washington, DC: Dumbarton Oaks Research Library Collection, 1995, p. 158-160 and 187-188. D.G. LETSIOS, *The Case of Amorkesos and the Question of the Roman Foederati in Arabia in the Vth Century*, in: *L'Arabie préislamique et son environnement historique et culturel*

in the person of al-Ṭammāḥ, whose brother had been killed by our poet.[92] Whether through the conspirings of al-Ṭammāḥ, or a change of heart actuated by fear of the consequences of unleashing such a mighty force into the territory of the ʿArab under the leadership of such a singular individual, or because Imru' al-Qays was in secret amorous correspondence with Justinian's (non-existent) daughter and had composed shameful verses celebrating this amour (p. 99.10-14) (or had seen him in the bathroom), Qayṣar

> sent to him at that point a ceremonial robe, richly embroidered, stitched with gold, and soaked in poison, with the words, 'I have sent you a ceremonial robe which I myself have worn, in honour of you. When you receive it, don it as an auspicious blessing, and write to me to inform me of your progress from place to place'. He put it on when it arrived and he took great delight in it. But the poison quickly took effect and his skin started to fall off. This is why he was called the 'man of the weeping sores' (p. 99.14-100.2).

As a result of Justinian's 'shirt of Nessus', explicitly acknowledged by al-Iṣfahānī as an exegetical elaboration of the cognomen derived from the occurrence in his poetry of the substantive *qarḥ*,[93] Imru' al-Qays died in Byzantine territory sometime around 550 AD.

In Imru' al-Qays's poetry, the regal pretensions of this dynasty of Kinda (a tribe who, at the peak of their wealth and power, were able, a few centuries earlier, to mint their own coins) are combined with a celebration of the ideal of the noble, morally inflexible Bedouin, to provide a fusion of ideological, cultural and emotional values which contrasts sharply with the nomadic sterility and political chaos of the traditional picture of pre-Islamic Arabia. Before we leave this tragic and tormented figure, let us pause to reflect on the network of kinship represented by his clan of Kinda, which stretched from Ḥimyar in South Arabia to the court of the Sasanid emperor and his vassal Lakhmids in al-Ḥīra, from a Jewish poet-warrior in Taymā' to the Jafnid phylarchy in Syria and on to

(*Actes du Colloque de Strasbourg, 24-27 juin 1987)*, ed. T. FAHD, Leiden: Brill, 1989, p. 525-538 ('Amorkesos was not chosen by the Byzantines but imposed upon them by the circumstances', p. 538). For a possibly cognate instance of collective memory, see ZWETTLER, *Maʿadd*, p. 225, footnote 3, who suggests that al-Ṭabarī's reference to Nebuchadnezzar's invasion of the 'peninsular Arabs' is 'perhaps an imaginative retrojection of Shāpūr II's massive campaign against the Bedouins during the early fourth century'.

[92] This proper noun is taken from the phrase *la-qad ṭamaḥa l-ṭammāḥu* in Imru' al-Qays's *Dīwān*, where the definite substantive is clearly not intended as a proper noun: see (Ahlwardt) poem 30.13 (Arazi-Masalha, 135.7; Ibrāhīm, poem 13.13, p. 108).

[93] See *Dīwān* (Ahlwardt) poems 30.12, 32.3 and 4 (Arazi-Masalha, 135.6, 136.7, 136.8; Ibrāhīm, poem 13.12, p. 107, and poem 80.3 and 4, p. 339).

the court of Justinian. Moreover, his vendetta also involved most of the major tribes and tribal confederations in the peninsula, from the Christian Iyād to Bakr and Taghlib to the Banū Asad.[94]

The poet's *vita* also encapsulates some perdurable identity issues: the pre-Islamic notion of kingship which the Islamic notion of caliphate often accommodated, especially during the reign of the Umayyad dynasty (41-132/661-749-50); the heady admixture of Bedouin inflexibility and regal nobility; the demise of the dynasties of Kinda, Jafn and Naṣr and the waning of their sponsored religions in the peninsula; tribal identity and the negotiation of extended networks of influence; the enmity, mistrust and suspicion which later obtained between the Islamic imperium and the Byzantine and Sasanid empires.

However, Imru' al-Qays's various identities are so manifestly fashioned for him out of his poetry that we should also ponder the dynamics of the cultural tradition to which his biography belongs. In short, the biographies of pre-Islamic poets were constructed broadly in accordance with the scholarly principles refined in Qur'anic exegesis (*Tafsīr*), and specifically in accordance with that branch of exegesis and juridical thought known as 'the occasions of revelation' (*asbāb al-nuzūl*), the process whereby the dating of the verses of the Qur'ān were determined in correspondence with the biography of the Prophet Muḥammad. Every word of a poet's poetic oeuvre (his *dīwān*) was pored over with a view to finding clues that would facilitate the composition of biographies. The relationship between the validity of this method as exegesis and as biography is symbiotic, the success of the one justifying the applicability of the other and vice-versa.

Poetic vitae performed for the Islamic intellectual consciousness of the Eighth, Ninth and Tenth Centuries a function similar to the function of hagiographies and tales of the miraculous in the early medieval West:

[94] Among the many achievements with which the Arabian hegemony of the Kinda is credited is the creation of a 'high Arabic': see CASKEL, *Bedouinization*, p. 44 and generally SHAHID, *Kinda*, p. 118-119. According to Jan Retsö's theory of the creation of 'a professional class of warriors all over Arabia' by 'the hiring of professional soldiers by the Himyaritic kings from among the tribes', Kinda would be one of the many groups of professional soldiery which flooded the Arabian peninsula in the wake of the collapse of Ḥimyar in South Arabia: *The Road to Yarmuk* p. 39; for Kinda, see p. 38. See further HERMANN VON WISSMANN, *Ḥimyar, Ancient History*, in: *Le Muséon* 77 (1964), p. 487-489 (for Kinda under the reign of Shammār Yuharʿish III). WHITTOW, *Rome and the Jafnids*, p. 219-223 is an accomplished discussion of the impact which warrior-tribes could have on the complexion of the peninsula. Such martial prowess (among the Bedouin warrior elite) continued well into the early Islamic period: JOHN W. JANDORA, *Developments in Islamic Warfare: The Early Islamic Conquests*, in: *Studia Islamica* 64 (1986), p. 101-113.

they were 'ideal vehicles for the early medieval penchant for dramatizing abstract ideas and moral concepts'.[95] One of the abstract ideas which Imru' al-Qays's biography as it developed over time seems to have conveyed is captured in the case of mistaken identity, according to which al-Ma'mūn admired the statue erected by the Greeks in honour of the pre-Islamic poet in Ankara. A monumental statuary (so prominent a feature of Roman and Byzantine imperial architecture) dedicated to a failed pre-Islamic kinglet, admired by the Caliph who did the most to sponsor the acquisition of Greek science and philosophy in Arabic, himself an emblem of ʿAbbasid intellectual exuberance and confidence, is as much a declaration of a new world order as is the Dome of the Rock built by ʿAbd al-Malik (r. 65-86/685-705) in Jerusalem. Thus the statue is, like the mythic move which transferred the shirt of Nessos from Greece to Arabia, a cultural enunciation pronounced on the basis of an act of exegesis.[96]

I do not mean by this to account for Imru' al-Qays's biography simply in terms of the now standard modern exegetical strategy of legitimization: in other words, if there is a 'political impetus' behind this biography which 'is the key to its creation', it is of a general and not a specific nature, for this biography is only part of the wider ʿAbbasid phenomenon whereby such vitae were constructed, and clearly reflects the society's protean desire to fuse a multiple identity out of its pre-Islamic, Sasanid, Qur'anic, and Hellenistic heritages, by means of both the artifice and the artificiality of narrative, the literary (re)creation of 'the illusion of actuality' and the endowment of 'fragmented and disconnected events with meaning'.[97] A crucial feature of many Islamic biographies is that the anonymity of the fabricators entails the anonymity of their priorities of fabrication. Even in those cases when we can be confident that we are dealing with a composition of narrative units by one particular antiquarian (an Ibn al-Kalbī, for example), the practice, championed, for example, by al-Wāqidī, of employing combined reports tends to conceal more than it reveals.[98]

[95] CATHERINE CUBITT, *Memory and Narrative in the Cult of Early Anglo-Saxon Saints*, in: *The Uses of the Past in the Early Middle Ages*, ed. YITZHAK HEN and MATTHEW INNES, Cambridge: Cambridge University Press, 2000, p. 29-66 (p. 52).

[96] The same complex of notions is also evident in the famous *bayt* ascribed to Imru' al-Qays in which he refers to the *barīd*: see *Dīwān* (Ahlwardt) poem 20.48 (Arazi-Masalha, 130.18; Ibrāhīm, poem 4.38, p. 66); generally, ADAM SILVERSTEIN, *On Some Aspects of the ʿAbbasid* Barīd, in: *ʿAbbasid Studies* (*Orientalia Lovaniensia Analecta*, 135), ed. JAMES E. MONTGOMERY, Leuven: Peeters 2004, p. 23-32.

[97] Quotations taken from CUBITT, *Memory and Narrative*, p. 47.

[98] M. LECKER, *Wāqidī's Account on the Status of the Jews of Medina: A Study of a Combined Report*, in: *Journal of Near Eastern Studies* 54 (1995), p. 15-32. See further HAYDEN WHITE, *The Content of the Form. Narrative Discourse and Historical Representation*, Balti-

This 'positive identity' is diametrically opposed to a more pietist matrix of ideas appreciable in the sources according to which Imru' al-Qays is declared 'the standard[-bearer] of the poets to hellfire', a position based upon an interpretation of the ambiguous assessment of poets and poetry in the Qur'ān as one of outright hostility.[99]

Yet another complex of ideas, abstract and concrete, which fuelled this perfervid interest in pre-Islamic poetry and poets was their status as exemplary paragons of the *ʿarabīya*. We will search in vain for a nomadic identity in the case of Imru' al-Qays,[100] though he does, by virtue of his poetic pre-eminence, have an identity as a renowned craftsman of poems composed in the *ʿarabīya* and he is the paragon of the ʿArab warrior-poet elites who exploited its riches so captivatingly.[101] Like these warrior-poets, his identity, however multiple and mythic, is firmly anchored in the world of Late Antiquity.

more - London: Johns Hopkins University Press, 1987, p. ix, 1-4, 26-82; his approach in a nutshell (on Nazism and the Final Solution): *Historical Emplotment and the Problem of Truth*, in: *The Postmodern History Reader*, ed. KEITH JENKINS, London - New York: Routledge, 1996, p. 392-396; MATTHEW INNES and ROSAMOND MCKITTERICK, *The Writing of History*, in: *Carolingian Culture: Emulation and Innovation*, ed. ROSAMOND MCKITTERICK, Cambridge: Cambridge University Press, 1994, p. 193-220 (p. 201, 216); see also *The History and Narrative Reader*, ed. GEOFFREY ROBERTS, London - New York: Routledge, 2001.

99 Suzanne Stetkevytch's reading of the *akhbār* of Imru' al-Qays, whilst containing much which I find hard to accept, brings out admirably how the poet 'embodies the *jahl* (impetuosity) that was for Islam the essence of the pagan past, the seed of its moral and political undoing, and hence embraces all in the Jahiliyyah that was anti-Islamic': *The Mute Immortals Speak*, p. 241-285 (p. 284).

100 It should be remembered that although composer of the most famous pre-Islamic *qaṣīda* the picture which emerges from his poetic *vita* constructed for him is not that of an archetyp(ic)al nomad (despite the recent attempt of BAMYEH, *The Social Origins*, to establish him as such). This is nowhere as obvious as in his poetic dedication to the aristocratic (as opposed to the professional) hunt, itself not typical of the tradition: ZWETTLER, *Maʿadd*, p. 243-244, footnote 40, has connected the juxtaposition of aristocratic hunt and diluvian rainstorm in his *muʿallaqa* with the Ḥimyarite ritual hunt, success in which was 'believed to ensure a propitious rainfall'. A further uncustomary feature of this poet's *dīwān* is his preference for equine over camel description.

101 The hegemony of the *ʿarabīya* is a true, but not representative, account of the period under discussion. This is well captured in HERBJØRN JENSSEN's summary 'of the very little that can be known about Arabic before the dawn of Islam': 'we know that varieties very similar to classical Arabic were used for several hundred years before, extending over an area encompassing not only the Arabian peninsula but also parts of the Fertile Crescent. We also know that some of these varieties had sufficient prestige to be used for inscriptions and poetic composition. We do not, however, know who the users of these varieties were, what name they gave to their language, or for what other purposes, besides inscriptions and poetry, they may have used them. Nor do we know how great were the differences between the varieties in question since only one of them, classical Arabic, has been preserved for us in the form of a corpus of text and a systematic description': 'Arabic Language', in: *Encyclopaedia of the Qur'ān*, I, p. 130-131.

'On the tip of a rock, hemmed in ...'[102]

This poetic life writ large brings us to the third feature of the world of Late Antiquity most frequently touched upon in the standard scholarly works on the advent of Islam: the hostility which obtained between Byzantium and Persia, or better: the struggle to the death of two rival super-powers which is said to have weakened their resources to the point that they were incapable of resisting the onslaught of the Muslim raiders from the Ḥijāz,[103] and their various interferences in the three major regions of the peninsula. In other words, how one views the emptiness of the Ḥijāz will determine how one understands the Muslim conquests and, in a vicious circle, how one accounts for these conquests will support how one views the Arabs of the peninsula, for although, as Donner remarks, 'the causes for the conquest movement itself and the causes for its success' are not the same, these phenomena are synergetic.[104] For an empty Ḥijāz means, for Muslims, past and present, that the conquests are irrefragable proof of Allāh's support and the truth of the divine revelation (the kerygmatic paradigm), while for some scholars

> the Arab conquests were made possible by their opponents' weaknesses rather than by the power of the nascent Muslim armies[105]

[102] An abbreviated translation of *maʿkūfīna ʿalā ra's ḥajar bayna fāris wa-rūm* (on the tip of a rock, hemmed in between Fāris and Rūm), a dictum ascribed to Qatāda: KISTER, *al-Ḥīra*, p. 143. There is an unavoidable amount of duplication in this section of the discussion in section one ('The Seductiveness of the Bedouin') of this article.

[103] A 'classic' formulation (of this plausible but 'impressionistic assumption': BENJAMIN ISAAC, *The Army in the Late Roman East: the Persian Wars and the Defence of the Byzantine Provinces*, in: CAMERON, *States, Resources and Armies*, p. 125-155) is W.M. WATT, *Muhammad Prophet and Statesman*, London: Oxford University Press, 1961 (one of his many versions of this version of events); GEORGES H. BOUSQUET, *Observations sur la nature et les causes de la conquête arabe*, in: *Studia Islamica* 6 (1956), p. 37-52. For a sample of alternate readings, see ELLA LANDAU-TASSERON, *Features of the Pre-Conquest Muslim Army in the Time of Muḥammad*, in: CAMERON, *States, Resources and Armies*, p. 299-336; JAMES HOWARD-JOHNSTONE, *The Two Great Powers in Late Antiquity: A Comparison*, in: CAMERON, *States, Resources and Armies*, p. 157-226; ZEʿEV RUBIN, *The Sasanid Monarchy*, in: CAMERON, WARD-PERKINS and WHITBY, *Cambridge Ancient History*, p. 638-661, especially p. 659-661. BAMYEH, *The Social Origins*, p. 41-43 accounts for the emergence of Mecca as a mercantile success-story (rather than the conquests specifically) in terms of this imperial decrepitude.

[104] *The Early Islamic Conquests*, p. 8. I prefer to speak of Muslim rather than Islamic conquests in an attempt to avoid an over-deterministic prioritisation of 'Islam' at the expense of the agents in events, the Muslims.

[105] As LANDAU-TASSERON, *Features*, p. 299 remarks à propos the position of M. CANARD, *L'expansion arabe: le problème militaire*, in: *Settimane di Studi del Centro Italiano di Studi sull'alto medioevo* 12 (1965), p. 37-63, 309-335. See the careful discussion of FRED M. DONNER, *Centralized Authority and Military Autonomy in the Early*

for such empire building is simply unthinkable from within their notion of Arabia. Contrast this with the assertion by Michael Whitby that 'the Arabs took over territory by energetic conquest, not by default on the part of their opponents'.[106] A corollary is the extent and nature, or indeed the very incidence, of the involvement of Persia and Rome in the Peninsula.[107]

Thus, the ramifications of Crone's pivotal *Meccan Trade* is to place (the absence of) the peninsula firmly in the heart of the international arena rather than to 'presuppose the exteriority of Mecca and Arabia generally to the Byzantine-Iranian sphere',[108] in the words of Fowden, whose *Empire to Commonwealth* is a persuasive analysis of the situation and the position has been taken by many scholars,[109] though few have

Islamic Conquests, in: CAMERON, *States, Resources and Armies*, p. 337-360, building on the work done in his *The Early Islamic Conquests*, the 'Introduction' of which is a concise overview of the sort of issues involved in the denial 'that the "Arab conquest" was in any organic way related to the appearance of Islam' (p. 8).
The most prominent analyst of the *futūḥ* in terms of the kerygmatic paradigm is Larry Conrad: see LAWRENCE I. CONRAD, *The Arabs*, in: *The Cambridge Ancient History, Volume 14: Late Antiquity: Empire and Successors, A.D. 425-600*, ed. A. CAMERON, B. WARD-PERKINS and M. WHITBY, Cambridge: Cambridge University Press, 2000, p. 678-700: p. 679 and the references given in his footnote 7; for a survey of 'conquest' writings: AMIKAM ELAD, *The Beginnings of Historical Writing by the Arabs: The Earliest Syrian Writers on the Arab Conquests*, in: *Jerusalem Studies in Arabic and Islam* 28 (2003), p. 65-152. The kerygmatic paradigm is entirely consistent with Byzantine imperial ideology which viewed military victory as confirmation of the rightness of an emperor's rule: see MICHAEL MCCORMICK, *Eternal Victory: Triumphal Rulership in Late Antiquity, Byzantium and the Early Medieval West*, Cambridge: Cambridge University Press, 1986; see also MICHAEL MCCORMICK, *Emperor and Court*, in: *The Cambridge Ancient History, Volume 14*, p. 135-163 (p. 144, for the public acclaim of victories).

[106] MICHAEL WHITBY, *Recruitment in Roman Armies from Justinian to Heraclius (ca. 565-615)*, in: CAMERON, *States, Resources and Armies*, p. 61-124 (p. 122). Other articles in this volume are useful: ISAAC, *The Army in the Late Roman East*, p. 125-155; JOHN HALDON, *Seventh-Century Continuities: the* Ajnād *and the 'Thematic Myth'*, p. 379-423.

[107] Succinct is the account of HODGSON, *The Venture of Islam*, p. 151-153.

[108] See further CRONE, *Meccan Trade*, p. 46-50 for a digest of imperial interferences.

[109] SIDNEY SMITH, *Events in Arabia in the Sixth Century*, in: *Bulletin of the School of Oriental and African Studies* 16 (1954), p. 424-468; C.E. BOSWORTH, *Iran and the Arabs before Islam*, in: *The Cambridge History of Iran, III.1: The Seleucid, Parthian and Sasanian Periods*, ed. EHSAN YARSHATER, Cambridge: Cambridge University Press, 1983, p. 593-612 (p. 602-608); DONNER, *The Early Islamic Conquests* ('northern and central Arabia was for centuries the arena of two kinds of political struggle ... an ongoing competition among tribal confederations' and 'between the powerful tribal confederations ... and the great states surrounding' them: p. 48); CONRAD, *The Arabs*, p. 689-695; BERKEY, *The Formation of Islam*, p. 47. See further LAPIDUS, *The Arab Conquests*, broadly recapitulated in his *A History of Islamic Societies*, Cambridge: Cambridge University Press, p 37-53: the conquests as 'an integral part of the relationship between Arabia and Middle Eastern Societies', 'an evolutionary process' (p. 50) which 'rose directly

matched the boldness of Retsö: 'the trigger of the Arab conquest was thus Heraclius' triumph over the Sasanian Empire'.[110] As an example of the kind of activities that may have taken place, KISTER, *Al-Ḥīra* and *Mecca and Tamīm*, musters a fabulous array of source material in support of his proposition of close Persian involvement in the Ḥijāz. A dissident, though representative, voice is BAMYEH, *The Social Origins*, p. 5-6: 'with the exception of Yemen, the great powers of the time — the Romans, the Sassanids, the Abyssinians — displayed little interest in any part of the Arabian Peninsula'. This move is vital for him to stress the Arabian origins of Islam, as 'Mecca's location deep in the desert insulated the city from the fate of the other nascent trading centers that were annexed to such powers' (p. 6).

Now, al-Iṣfahānī's account of the Arabia of the tribe of Kinda tallies remarkably with Robert Hoyland's survey of Arabia during what he identifies as the 'Byzantine/Sasanian Period (c. 240-630 AD)'.[111]

This was the time when the coast of East Arabia emerged as a central locus of Sasanid sovereignty, with the establishment of centrally appointed provincial governors during the reign of Khusraw I (531-579 AD), and with control over the Arab tribes of the interior maintained through military incursions. There is also evidence of the spread of 'Nestorian' Christianity throughout the littoral and ultimately among the Arab tribes. Southern Iraq was the stronghold of the Ancient Church of the East and it was from al-Yamāma oasis that the counter-prophet Musaylima launched his evangelizing mission during the lifetime of the Prophet Muḥammad.[112] Moreover, Sasanid political influence presumably brought with it religious influence in the form of Mazda-worship (whether as Zoroastrianism, or Manichaeism or Mazdakism), the imperial religion of the Sasanid rulers.[113]

out of the conflict of different forms of religious, social and political organization in Arabia' (p. 66); WALTER E. KAEGI, *Byzantium and the Early Islamic Conquests*, Cambridge: Cambridge University Press, 1992; WALTER E. KAEGI, *Heraclius Emperor of Byzantium*, Cambridge: Cambridge University Press, 2003. For a survey of the issue of isolation or integration of the pre-Islamic Arabs, see WALTER DOSTAL, *Die Araber in vorislamischer Zeit*, in: *Der Islam* 74 (1997), p. 1-63.

110 *The Road to Yarmuk*, p. 41.

111 *Arabia and the Arabs*, to which the following discussion is heavily indebted. I have also found FOWDEN, *Empire to Commonwealth*, p. 100-137 especially informative.

112 DALE F. EICKELMAN, *Musaylima: An Approach to the Social Anthropology of Seventh Century Arabia*, in: *Journal of the Economic and Social History of the Orient* 10 (1967), p. 17-52.

113 See BERKEY, *The Formation of Islam*, p. 47; HOYLAND, *Arabia and the Arabs*, p. 27-32.

In South Arabia, both Byzantium and Seleucia-Ctesiphon endeavoured to exert influence over the kings of Ḥimyar, who in the Fifth Century, as al-Iṣfahāni's account of the *vita* of Imru' al-Qays makes clear, could boast of *de facto* rule over the Arab tribes to the point that they would style themselves 'kings ... of their Arabs of the highlands and of their coasts', by which is meant Central and Northern and East Arabia.[114] The early Fourth Century witnessed treaties between the Ḥimyar King Shammār Yuharʿish and the Sasanids, an exchange of ambassadors with the Ethiopian kingdom of Axum and the dispatch of Theophilus Indus as missionary on behalf of the emperor Constantius (r. 337-361). Relations between Axum and Ḥimyar deteriorated in the Sixth Century and led to the killing of the Martyrs of Najrān in 523 AD by the king of Ḥimyar, Yūsuf Dhū Nawās, a convert to Judaism who was himself killed by Ella Asbeha ruler of Axum. Ella Asbeha could not, however, maintain control over the province and following a rebellion, a Christian slave Abraha toppled the Axumian vassal Esimiphaeus. An inscription at the Maʾrib dam declares that he received embassies from five kingdoms — 'the Ethiopians, the Byzantines, the Persians, Mundhir of Lakhm, Harith ibn Jabala of Ghassan and his kinsman Abikarib ibn Jabala'.[115] It is Abraha who is reputed to have marched unsuccessfully on Mecca with an elephant in 552, described in *Sūra* 105 of the Qur'ān as a manifestation of divine favour in protection of His most beloved of sanctuaries.[116] In 559 AD, the Sasanids finally asserted unequivocal control over the Yemen in the form of the hero of popular oral legend, Sayf b. Dhī Yazan, and then in the form of an imperial governor Wahriz, terminating Ethiopian influence in the region once and for all. Religiously, South Arabia entertained not only its own, and very full, panoply of deities, but also contained communities of Jews and Christians, who were distinctly Monophysite (the credal allegiance of both Axum and Ghassān), despite the Chalcedonian aspirations of Byzantium eager to redeem them from the error of their ways: the Church of Ṣanʿāʾ, constructed by artisans and masons with mosaics and materials sent from Byzantium,

[114] HOYLAND, *Arabia and the Arabs*, p. 49.

[115] HOYLAND, *Arabia and the Arabs*, p. 55.

[116] LAWRENCE I. CONRAD, *Abraha and Muḥammad. Some Observations apropos of Chronology and Literary* Topoi *in the Early Arabic Historical Tradition*, in: *Bulletin of the School of Oriental and African Studies* 50 (1987), p. 225-240 (reprinted as Article IV in: *The Life of Muḥammad*, ed. URI RUBIN, Aldershot: AshgateVariorum, 1998, p. 41-56).

has been construed as an attempt to woo the South Arabian Christians from Monophysitism.[117] Mazda-worship was also to be found, in view of the extent of Sasanid involvement in the area (although once again its precise form is the matter of controversy).[118]

The corresponding period in the history of North and Central Arabia is exclusively dominated by the activities of the elite warrior confederations: the transhumant Ghassanids with their seasonal encampment at al-Jābiya (50 miles south-west of Damascus), Byzantine phylarchs, and the Lakhmids of al-Ḥīra, Sasanid kinglets and their perpetual warfare.[119] Despite (or perhaps because of) sharing a common ancestry, they not only waged war on one another but also competed ferociously as patrons of poets, their patronage of which did so much to provide the ʿArab warriors with an ideology of independence. Their Christian credal affiliations were also antagonistic, with the Naṣrids of al-Ḥīra following the Ancient Church of the East, and the Jafnids of the Roman *limes* opportunistic followers of Monophysitism.[120] Crucial in this overall development was the creation in the Sixth Century of 'super-chiefs' in the persons of al-Mundhir b. al-Nuʿmān (504-554) and al-Ḥārith b. Jabala (529-569).[121]

[117] HOYLAND, *Arabia and the Arabs*, p. 49-57; FOWDEN, *Empire to Commonwealth*, p. 109-116. On al-Qalīs, see AL-ṬABARĪ, *Ta'rīkh*, p. 934.4-936.8; *The History of al-Ṭabarī, Volume V. The Sāsānids, the Byzantines, the Lakhmids and Yemen*, trans. C.E. BOSWORTH, Albany: SUNY, 1999, p. 217-221); R.B. SERJEANT and R. LEWCOCK, 'The Church (al-Qalīs) of Ṣanʿā' and Ghumdān Castle', in: *Ṣanʿā': An Arabian Islamic City*, ed. R.B. SERJEANT and R. LEWCOCK, London: World of Islam Festival Trust, 1983, p. 44-48; BERKEY, *The Formation of Islam*, p. 45.

[118] See BERKEY, *The Formation of Islam*, p. 47.

[119] CONRAD, *The Arabs*, p. 692-693. The Ghassanids, like Kinda during its hegemonic period, were enclosed 'nomads', presumably with an integrated tribal structure: ZWETTLER, *Maʿadd*, p. 287, footnote 101; for the concept and associated tribal structures, see MICHAEL ROWTON, *Enclosed Nomadism*, in: *Journal of the Economic and Social History of the Orient* 17 (1974), p. 1-30 and ZWETTLER, *Maʿadd*, p. 255-256, footnote 59, with further bibliography. WHITTOW, *Rome and the Jafnids*, presses a distinction between dynasty and tribe and is strong on the permeabilities of nomadic and sedentary lifestyles.

[120] On the matter of credal allegiances, we should bear in mind the perceptive comments of FOWDEN, *Empire to Commonwealth*, p. 133: 'the greater the number of apparent contradictions one introduced into one's postion, the wider the choice of exits from the tight corners in which one was bound to find oneself'. IRFAN SHAHID has studied in meticulous detail the monophystism of al-Ḥārith b. Jabala: *Byzantium and the Arabs in the Sixth Century. Volume 1, Part 2: Ecclesiastical History*, p. 735-792. See however the important review by WHITTOW, *Rome and the Jafnids.* For an assessment of Byzantine policy involving the Ghassanids (as a threat to be contained), see MICHAEL WHITBY, *Greek Historical Writing after Procopius: Variety and Vitality*, in: *The Late Antique and Early Islamic Near East, I: Problems in the Literary Source Material*, ed. AVERIL CAMERON and LAWRENCE I. CONRAD, Princeton: Darwin Press, 1992, p. 25-80; HALDON, *Seventh-Century Continuities*, p. 403-405.

[121] See HOYLAND, *Arabia and the Arabs*, p. 78-83.

How we understand the Muslim conquests, be it as strategically and centrally coordinated and driven, and/or (as) energized by the universalizing expansionism of an (Islamic) monotheism afforced with the ideals of the aristocratic Bedouin warrior,[122] as nomadic migrations actuated by economic unsustainability, as random happenstance,[123] as imperial incapacity for countering the military novelty of the threat the tribal forces posed, as heralded by a globalising cultural discourse of Hellenism,[124] or

[122] A key implication of the argument presented in the first section of this paper is that the Muslim conquests of Syria and Iraq were in no small measure an expression of the conjunction of the 'Bedouinising' ethnogenetic matrix with the religious vision revealed in the Qur'ān. Cf. JOHN J. SAUNDERS, *The Nomad as Empire Builder: A Comparison of the Arab and Mongol Conquests*, in: *Diogenes* 52 (1965), p. 79-103; DONNER, *The Early Islamic Conquests*, passim for 'the idea that the conquests were the product of a definable movement having a powerful internal dynamic of its own, and traceable to a new religious ideology' (p. 8); RETSÖ, *The Road to Yarmuk*, p. 40.

[123] DONNER, *Centralized Authority*, designates the second scheme 'the ecological thesis' (p. 341-343) and the third 'the accidental thesis' ('the Arabs "found" themselves in possession of vast domains that, as an afterthought, they stitched together into an empire') (p. 344-345 and 359). The champions of the accidental thesis are: YEHUDA D. NEVO and JUDITH KOREN, *Methodological Approaches to Islamic Studies*, in: *Der Islam* 68 (1991), p. 87-101, amplified in their *Crossroads to Islam. The Origins of the Arab Religion and the Arab State*, New York: Prometheus Books, 2003. A subtle version of the 'accidental' thesis, and one which I find appealing for its emphasis on the contingencies and randomness of human action, is forwarded by BAMYEH, *The Social Origins*, p. 257-258 (responding to RODINSON, *Mohammed*, p. 37): 'it could be that an "Arab state", rather than being the "great need of the times", was in effect the unintended result of many developments based on pronouncements of less-profound needs. The emergence of a state out of this story can be understood in terms of structural imperatives coalescing out of unpredictable and unforeseen actions and counteractions rather than in terms of preexistent needs'.

[124] BOWERSOCK, *Hellenism*, argues that 'the legacy of Hellenism ... contributed to creating the foundations of Arab nationalism upon which Muḥammad was to build ... by bringing the Arabs together and equipping them with a sense of common identity' (p.73). The following claim is slightly more problematic: 'the emergence of Arabic court poetry was inspired by the Hellenic model ... in semitic terms pagan Arab poetry is in its complexity and rhythmic virtuosity the equal of the great Christian hymns in Syriac by Ephraem. Although both Syriac and Arabic are Semitic languages, outside traditions impelled them both to new eloquence. In the sense in which it may be said that Ephraem's hymns were Christian, the Arab odes were Hellenic' (p. 76-77). The process whereby the (indigenous) tribal pangeyric, such as many of those composed by ʿAmr b. Qamī'a and Zuhayr b. Abī Sulmā, became the court panegyric, such as those composed by al-Nābigha al-Dhubyānī, has yet properly to be studied: Hellenism (and for that matter Iranianism) contributed little to extant *qaṣīda* poetry, which remained resolutely 'Bedouinising', however much Iranianism and Hellenism may have set the ambience of courtliness in which these panegyrics were tested. For a study of a pre-Islamic court panegyric (the *Muʿallaqa* of al-Nābigha al-Dhubyānī) and two panegyrics of Prophet Muḥammad (Kaʿb b. Zuhayr and Ḥassān b. Thābit) see MONTGOMERY, *Vagaries*, p. 147-165 and p. 222-232 (respectively). Hellenism as a cultural determinant of Islam: BOWERSOCK, *Hellenism*, p. 76: 'Hellenism had played its irrevocable part in assisting the Arabs to discover a sense of their own national identity'; or p. 81: 'at least some of the roots of Islam were embedded in that local

as the unforeseen consequences of a multiplicity of decisions, discourses, responses and events, including the drive by the Medinan elite to control the ʿArab tribes, is intimately implicated in how we (re)construct imperial interferences in the peninsula and is inexorably determined by how we respond to the 'emptiness' of the Ḥijāz.

APHRODITE'S BODY CHAIN

A dispiriting development in many modern responses to the emptiness of the Ḥijāz (as signifier and as signified) has been the complete disregard of pre-Islamic poetry demonstrated by many of those who have recently chosen to recreate pre-Islamic Arabia. Thus Fred Donner can speak of an absence of 'contemporary documentation in the strict sense';[125] and I can find little mention of this poetry in representative articles by Lawrence Conrad or Chase Robinson;[126] Frank Peters begrudgingly notes that this poetry 'if it

Hellenism'. GARTH FOWDEN's emphasis on the profound links between universalism and monotheism (largely though not exclusively Hellenistic) is a productive way of reading certain aspects of Islamic origins: *Empire to Commonwealth. Consequences of Monotheism in Late Antiquity*, Princeton: Princeton University Press, 1993. See p. 137: 'both culturally and politically, Islam and its empire was already implicit in late antiquity'. In many ways, these represent amplifications of the ideas of C.H. BECKER, *Der Islam als Problem*, in: *Der Islam* 1 (1921), p. 1-21. See also AVERIL CAMERON, *The Eastern Provinces in the 7th Century AD. Hellenism and the Emergence of Islam*, in: *Hellēnismos. Quelques jalons pour une histoire de l'identité grecque. Actes du Colloque de Strasbourg, 25-27 octobre 1989*, ed. S. SAID, Leiden: Brill, 1991, p. 287-313 (for the difficulties involved in accounting for what 'Hellenism' may, in its multifarious senses, have been).

125 DONNER, *Background to Islam*, p. 511. It should be obvious by now that I can see no compelling reason to prefer such documentation (although I am not at all clear what it may be) to the 'large body of literary sources that describe what happened'. And poetry scarce merits a mention in his monograph, *Narratives of Islamic Origins. The Beginnings of Islamic Historical Writing*, Princeton: Darwin Press, 1998. HERBERT BERG, *The Development of Exegesis in Early Islam. The Authenticity of Muslim Literature from the Formative Period*, Richmond: Curzon, 2000, does not even (as far as I can see) mention poetry, even though it is a conspicuous exception to his observation that 'virtually everything we know of that period, whether historical, legal, exegetical, and so forth, comes to us in the form of *ḥadīth*s or texts with *isnād*s' (p. 224).

126 CONRAD, *The Arabs*; ROBINSON, *Reconstructing Early Islam*. It is one of the burdens of my argument that the poetry deserves more credit than Conrad's statement would allow: 'the relevant accounts, including a vast bulk of poetry, are frequently attributed to the pre-Islamic period or otherwise presented as describing events and conditions of that time, but apart from the Qur'ān the sources containing these accounts are at least two centuries later' (p. 679). In footnotes 40 (p. 684), 46 (p. 685) and 88 (p. 694), he does allow references to Zuhayr, Ḥassān b. Thābit and al-Aʿshā, and he has turned the poetry of al-Ḥassān to excellent use: *Epidemic Disease in Central Syria in the Late Sixth Century: Some New Insights from the Verse of Ḥassān ibn Thābit*, in: *Byzantine and Modern Greek Studies* 18 (1994), p. 12-58.

tells us little of their history is useful for reconstructing their society'.[127] This represents a remarkable decline in the fortunes of the poetry of the *Jāhilīya* from the days of Nöldeke, Goldziher and Lyall, for whom it was the very bedrock of their responses to the Qur'ān and the desert ʿArab (as it was for the ʿAbbasids and as it is for many modern Muslim scholars).[128]

And yet the *qaṣīda* and *qiṭʿa* poetry of the *Jāhilīya*, for all its vexed problems of authenticity and transmission, and for all the difficulties of interpretation it poses, can be read in such a way that it becomes remarkably informative of the material culture of the peninsula (techniques and materials for writing, for example, or luxury goods such as jewelry),[129] of the details of trade in the Persian Gulf,[130] or the practice and perils of pilgrimage,[131] or of those features of the Qur'ān which the *mukhaḍram* poets responded to emotionally, aesthetically and intellectually (primarily Qur'anic eschatology).[132]

Indeed, it strikes me as perverse that scholars can discuss the nature of *Jihād* and its relations to the tribal *ghazwa* without endeavouring to understand the conceptual universe of the *ghazwa* as represented so vigorously and stridently in the poetry of, for example, ʿĀmir ibn al-Ṭufayl of the ʿĀmir ibn Ṣaʿṣaʿa.[133] This is one area in which much modern scholarship is sorely deficient in comparison with the oft-berated philologists

[127] PETERS, *The Arabs and Arabia*, p. xiii. This marks a slight advance, I think, on his earlier statement: 'the classical ode of the Arabs is poor stuff for history' (F.E. PETERS, *Allah's Commonwealth. A History of Islam in the Near East, 600-1100 AD*, New York: Simon and Schuster, 1973, p. 45). Compare this, for example, with ALFRED BLOCH, *Die altarabische Dichtung als Zeugnis für das Gesitesleben der vorislamischen Araber*, in: *Anthropos* 37-40 (1942-1945), p. 186-204; or with the reconstructions of the poetic universe of self-identification by MALCOLM C. LYONS, *Identification and Identity in Classical Arabic Poetry*, Warminster: Gibb Memorial Trust, 1999; or with the boldly imaginative study of this warrior society's cosmology by NADIA JAMIL, *Playing for Time*.

[128] See, for one example among many, volume one of IGNAZ GOLDZIHER, *Muslim Studies*, ed. and trans. S.M. STERN and C. BARBER, I, London: Allen and Unwin, 1967-1971. C.J. LYALL could write an article entitled, *Ancient Arabian Poetry as a Source of Historical Information*, in: *Journal of the Royal Asiatic Society* (1914), p. 61-73.

[129] MONTGOMERY, *The Deserted Encampment*.

[130] See Chapter Five of MONTGOMERY, *Vagaries* ('An Arab at Sea'); a slightly different version: J.E. MONTGOMERY, *Salvation at Sea? Seafaring in Early Arabic Poetry*, in: *Representations of the Divine in Arabic Poetry*, ed. G. BORG and E. DE MOOR (= *Orientations* 5 [2001]), Amsterdam: Rodopi, 2001, p. 25-48. On trade in the Gulf, see TOURAJ DARYAEE, *The Persian Gulf Trade in Late Antiquity*, in: *Journal of World History* 14 (2003), p. 1-16.

[131] J.E. MONTGOMERY, *Arkhilokhos, al-Nābigha al-Dhubyānī and A Complaint against Blacksmiths - or, A Funny Thing Happened to Me*, in: *Edebiyât* 5 (1994), p. 15-49.

[132] MONTGOMERY, *Vagaries*, p. 209-257.

[133] His *dīwān* has even been translated into English!: *The* Dīwāns *of ʿAbīd ibn al-Abraṣ of Asad and ʿĀmir ibn aṭ-Ṭufail of ʿĀmir ibn Ṣaʿṣaʿah*, ed. C.J. LYALL, Cambridge: Gibb Memorial Trust, 1980 (1913).

of the late Nineteenth and the first half of the Twentieth Century.[134] In addition, this is in complete contradistinction to the tradition which this scholarship seeks to represent — a constant throughout the many generations of pre-modern Arabic poetry is that poetry is the *dīwān* of the Arabs and it behooves us to understand what those who lived, created and gave voice to these various traditions understood by poetry as 'register'.[135] Otherwise, we merely foist on this past one of the many modern concepts of history, distorting it beyond recognition in the process.

As an example, let me take the body chain, the *wishāḥ*.[136] In a *ḥāʾīya* Bishr b. Abī Khāzim al-Asadī describes his beloved Sulaymā as *haḍīma 'l-kashḥi jāʾilati 'l-wishāḥi*, 'slender-waisted, her body-girdle loose-(fitting)':

> The *wishāḥ* was an item of women's apparel wrapped around the waist and affixed, transversely, across the shoulders, which could be encrusted with jewels.[137]

It thus formed a cruciform shape around the wearer's breasts. There are numerous variations on this topos, in both pre-Islamic and later Arabic poetry, enough for us to be seduced by the assumption that the pre-Islamic instances of the image are as conventional as those which recur throughout the later tradition. The context of Bishr's verse is erotically charged, involving an exchange of saliva and a potent, though concise, description of a night of love-making.

During the Umayyad period such an assumption of conventionality would be without warrant. That it should also be unwarranted for the pre-Islamic *qaṣīda* is established by a detour to Hoxne in Suffolk, East Anglia and scrutiny of Aphrodite's body chain.[138]

[134] A welcome break with this trend is HOYLAND, *Arabia and the Arabs*, p. 211-219. A major achievement of PATRICIA CRONE and MARTIN HINDS, *God's Caliph. Religious Authority in the First Centuries of Islam*, Cambridge: Cambridge University Press, 1986, is the authors' inclusion of poetry within their evidence base. And I cannot commend highly enough Fowden's use of poetry to determine the intellectual universe of the patron of Quṣayr ʿAmra. And yet, the transmission of Umayyad poetry is no less *unreliable* (whatever that may mean) than that of the *Jāhilīya*.

[135] LYONS, *Identification and Identity*, designates this as 'register' poetry (see p. x-xi).

[136] My argument (which is positivistic in intent) in this section is very tenuous, probably tendentious and highly probabilistic. There are problems of geography and chronology which the extant remains do not properly allow me to bridge and I am reading these artifacts within a master narrative of pre-Islamic Arabia as an inflection of Late Antiquity. Indeed, in the case of Qusayr ʿAmra I even allow myself to read late Umayyad iconography in terms of the *Jāhilīya*.

[137] For the reference and discussion, see MONTGOMERY, *Vagaries*, p. 174.

[138] As will be apparent, this discussion, and the references, have been inspired by FOWDEN's wonderful study of the frescoes of Quṣayr ʿAmra in *Quṣayr ʿAmra*. My discussion is at its most conspicuously probabilistic here, because of my novitiate in Classical and

One of the most remarkable pieces of Roman-British jewellery is the Hoxne body chain, one of the two clasps of which is a gold solidus of the Emperor Gratian (r. 367-383 AD), which provides the terminus post quem for the item in its current form. It is:

> A kind of gold harness constructed of flat straps of loop-in-loop chain, two of which were worn passed over the shoulders, and two under the arms, joining at strap-unions on the chest and back of the wearer.[139]

In other words, it is a *wishāḥ*. But what do Bishr's (pre-Islamic) inamorata and the Fourth Century Roman Briton have in common? To begin with, despite the numerous instances of such body chains as represented in statuary, figure-work or poetry over the centuries, and several of them are astonishingly old, these body chains are actually quite rare:

> The type, although rare, is known to have existed centuries earlier in Hellenistic times and still to have been current in the Byzantine world as late as the sixth century. Representations of body chains in wear are well known in Roman art, from mosaics and decorated silver to terracotta figurines.[140]

Islamic iconography; because I have not personally visited Quṣayr ʿAmra; because of my regard for the work done on this complex by FOWDEN and others; and because 'what we now see on Quṣayr ʿAmra's walls is to some extent the product of modern interpretation' (FOWDEN, *Quṣayr ʿAmra*, p. 67, and Chapter One). I am emboldened however by two considerations: the sheer diversity of the interpretations conjured up by scholarship to account for (some aspect or other of) this most enigmatic structure; and because the complex is largely a 'floating' signifier, firmly anchored in a tradition which we understand very, very poorly; for 'although Quṣayr ʿAmra's paintings quite often seem to recall particular iconographical types from the art of the Roman East, we cannot always be certain that the debt is specific and conscious, partly because as yet we are imperfectly informed even about the vocabulary of late Roman art, let alone the sources and procedures of artists employed by the Umayyads' (FOWDEN, *Quṣayr ʿAmra*, p. 230).

[139] CATHERINE JOHNS, *The Jewellery of Roman Britain. Celtic and Classical Traditions*, London: UCL Press, 1996, p. 96. On the Hoxne treasure, see p. 217-218 and Colour Plate 6. For a Roman-British mosaic representation, see RANUCCIO BIANCHI BADINELLI, *Rome: The Late Empire. Roman Art AD 200-400*, trans. PETER GREEN, London: Thames and Hudson, 1970, p. 210, figure 198 (a mosaic of Dido and Aeneas from Low Ham, Taunton, Devon). A Byzantine body chain: KATHARINE R. BROWN, *The Gold Breast Chain from the Early Byzantine Period in the Römisch-Germanisches Zentralmuseum*, Mainz: Römisch-Germanisches Zentralmuseum, 1984 (which I have been unable to consult).

[140] JOHNS, *The Jewellery of Roman Britain*, p. 96. Figure 5.10 on p. 98 is an example, 'a terracotta figure from Egypt of Roman date showing a woman wearing a body chain'. Note that the woman is fully clothed, which is the exception in the representations of women clad in body chains with which I am familiar. Compare this with the following (Roman) images: the semi-nude woman with armlets, necklace and body chain in the Casa dei Vettii at Pompeii ('Il Supplizio di Dirce'): G.E. RIZZO, *La pittura ellenistico romana*, Milan: Fratelli Tres, 1929, p. 40, plate 66; Aphrodite (semi-nude, anklets,

So their prominence (indeed predominance) in any one tradition is highly significant in itself. Secondly, their rarity is also significant:

> The wearers generally appear to be goddesses — even Venus herself, as on the mosaic from Low Ham — or nymphs, rather than mortals. The type was apparently a long-lived and traditional one, but in all probability its use was very restricted, perhaps to women of exceptionally high rank, or to specific formal occasions.[141]

So, the wearers of body chains in the ancient and Late Antique worlds are presumably either divine (Aphrodite-Venus), supernatural (nymphs), women of the highest social rank or women (of variable social status?) perhaps enformed by the divine. It is unclear whether there is any connection between these presumptions and representations of the (body chain wearing) woman as naked or (partially) clothed (nakedness, especially of the breasts, being a conspicuous, though not exclusive, feature of depictions of Aphrodite), or whether nakedness or full clothing are idiosyncratic inflections which are to be contextualised for any given tradition, in any given occurrence.[142] Nudity is, of course, always culturally significant, though its precise significance is often lost on us.

bracelets, body chain, tiara, ear-rings) and Ares (Pompeii): RIZZO, *La pittura*, plate 104; Aphrodite (semi-nude, anklets, bracelets, armlets, necklace, tiara and body chain or pendant necklace) and Adonis (Pompeii): RIZZO, *La pittura*, plate 123; JOHN R. CLARKE, *Looking at Lovemaking: Constructions of Sexuality in Roman Art 100 BC - AD 250*, Berkeley - London: University of California Press, 2001, plate 12 (from the apodyterium of the Suburban Baths at Poempeii: a man performs cunnilingus on a woman clad only in a body chain); p. 168, figure 60 ('male-female couple on bed, bronze mirror cover found on Palatine, Rome [AD 69-79]: the woman, who faces the viewer, wears a necklace, body chain, armlets, bracelets and one visible anklet); p. 173, figure 64 ('male-female couple on bed, Casa dei Vettii, Pompeii'); see p. 315, note 60 for references to other depictions of body chains.

141 JOHNS, *The Jewellery of Roman Britain*, p. 96.

142 For a Classical Aphrodite with a body chain apparently made out of shells, see ANGELOS DELIVORRIAS, GRATIA BERGER-DOER and ANNELIESE KOSSATZ, *Aphrodite*, in: *Lexicon Iconographicum Mythologiae Classicae*, II.1, p. 86 = II.2, p. 78, figure 779; see also II.1, p. 109 = II.2, p. 110, figure 1083. The representation found at Khirbat Tannur near Petra during the era of Aretas IV (ca. 9 BC to 40 AD), does not sport a body chain, though 'son peplos est serré sous les seins par une ceinture', to achieve a slightly similar (though clothed) enhancement: FAWZI ZAYADINE, *Al-'Uzza-Aphrodite*, in: *Lexicon Iconographicum Mythologiae Classicae*, II.1, p. 167-169; II.2, p. 169-170 (figures 1-7) (II.1, p. 167). See also FAWZI ZAYADINE, *L'iconographie d'al-'Uzza-Aphrodite*, in: *Mythologie gréco-romaine, mythologie périphériques (Colloques internationaux du Centre de la Recherche Scientifique*, 593), ed. LILLY KAHIL and CHRISTIAN AUGÉ, Paris: CNRS, 1981, p. 113-118 and plates 1-11 (p. 115 and plate 3). Iconographical influence is detected by EVA BAER, *Female Images in Early Islam*, in: *Damaszener Mitteilungen* 11 (1999), p. 13-24 and plates 2-5 (p. 18) in the representation of the peplos in the statuary of Khirbat al-Mafjar.

Instances of body chain wearing beauties have also been found at Jerash in the Trans-Jordan (from the Late Imperial era),[143] at Ephesus (early Imperial era),[144] at ʿAmmān (date unknown),[145] in Coptic Egypt (Fourth Century AD),[146] at Herakleopolis (Ahnas) in Upper Egypt (among others) (early Fifth Century),[147] and at Ctesiphon (Sixth Century).[148]

Among the most remarkable are the 'Safaitic' rock-carving of a faceless woman clad in armlets and anklets and with two bands around her waist, surmounted by a hemisphere,[149] as in so many images of Aphrodite in which the crest of her shell birthplace is made to double as the canopy of the heavens, and with what appears to be a blazing star or planet over her right shoulder;[150] and a sequence of naked female figurines from Susa

[143] J.H. ILIFFE, *Imperial Art in Trans-Jordan. Figurines and Lamps from a Potter's Store at Jerash*, in: *The Quarterly of the Department of Antiquities in Palestine* 11 (1945), p. 1-26 (p. 10 and plate II, figures 25 and 26).

[144] BAER, *Female Images*, p. 14, figure 2.b; *Ephesos. Der neue Führer*, ed. PETER SCHERRER, Vienna: Österreichisches Archäeologisches Institut, 1995, p. 43, figure 5.

[145] MARIE-ODILE JENTEL, *Aphrodite (in Peripheria Orientali)*, in: *Lexicon Iconographicum Mythologiae Classicae*, II.1, II.1, p. 154-166; II.2, p. 156-169 (p. 159 = II.2, p. 164, figure 111); FOWDEN, *Quṣayr ʿAmra*, p. 231, figure 59. See also the figure from Syria: JENTEL, *Aphrodite*, II.1, p. 165 = II.2, p. 169, figure 244.

[146] JENTEL, *Aphrodite*, II.1, p. 158 = II.2, p. 163, figure 89.

[147] This is a limestone figurine, Cairo Coptic Museum no. 7033: see BAER, *Female Images*, p. 14, note 11. See also FLORENCE D. FRIEDMAN, *Beyond the Pharaohs. Egypt and the Copts in the 2nd to 7th Centuries AD*, Rhode Island: Museum of Art, 1989, p. 257, cat. No. 171 (fragment of a limestone frieze from a Fourth to Fifth Century tomb, the Nereid is 'elaborately coiffed ... clad in a cestus ... and holding a veil ... the deceased, upon her death, has become a nereid'); JOHN BECKWITH, *Coptic Sculpture, 300-1300*, London: Tiranti, 1963, figure 63 and p. 20 (a Nereid).

[148] RICHARD ETTINGHAUSEN, *From Byzantium to Sasanian Iran and the Islamic World. Three Modes of Artistic Influence*, Leiden: Brill, 1972, plate 6, figure 19: 'stucco reliefs with female dancers from the interior of large mansion in Ctesiphon, Iraq, Sixth Century' (p. 67). There is an unusual type of body chain worn by a woman on an Iranian silver vessel (dated to between the Eighth and Tenth Centuries) kept in the Hermitage at St. Petersburg, one which does not meet in the cleavage but runs down the woman's sides: see OLEG GRABAR, *The Formation of Islamic Art*, New Haven: Yale University Press, 1987, figure 99. See also the different necklaces-cum-truncated body chains worn by two dryads in a Coptic image from about the middle of the Fifth Century: BECKWITH, *Coptic Sculpture*, figure 66.

[149] Or a veil, or an extravagant hair style ....The 'canopy' is reminiscent of the veil flaunted by the Coptic Nereid from the limestone tomb and enchanting the dancing girl depicted on a Sasanian silver drinking cup: AURELIE DAEMS, *The Iconography of Pre-Islamic Woman in Iran*, in: *Iranica Antiqua* 36 (2001), p. 1-150 (p. 59 and figure 221), with references to further examples.

[150] MELCHIOR DE VOGÜÉ, *Syrie centrale: inscriptions sémitiques*, Paris: Baudry, 1868, p. 141, figure 402; SUSANNE KRONE, *Die altarabische Gottheit al-Lāt* (*Heidelberger Orientalische Studien*, 23), Frankfurt am Main: Peter Lang, 1992, p. 581, figure 3; FOWDEN, *Quṣayr ʿAmra*, p. 66, note 96. There are a number of such representations in both Safaitic and Thamudic and they have been subject to a bewildering variety of interpretations from

and dating from the Middle Elamite period (1450-1100 BC), which are understood to represent a quadripartite 'evolution towards steatopygy', i.e. excessive fat in the buttocks, though in this case the arms and thighs are also meant.[151]

In the first stage the woman is portrayed with slender hips, a pair of bracelets on each wrist, one anklet on each foot, and are adorned with a 'single *baudrier*';[152] in the second stage, her hips are fuller, the '*baudrier* is now crossed', i.e. it is a *wishāḥ*, 'a star shaped amulet rests on the chest while a rectangular jewel or clip holds the *baudrier* in place between the breasts' and 'stretch-marks are illustrated by means of two semi-circular carvings underneath the navel';[153] the third stage is typified by her broader shoulders and pronouncedly fuller hips than stages 1 and 2, while the body chain is still of the crossed type;[154] the figures of stage 4 have grotesquely steatopygous hips and arms, recalling 'an archaic tradition were (sic) women were violin or 8-shaped', and continue to

dancing girls to some sort of celestial being: see KRONE, *al-Lāt*, p. 299-303, for discussion with references; as far as I am aware, little attention has been paid to the body chain, the 'stretch marks' have not been properly identified and the coiffure of these figures would benefit from consideration of the description of the hair-do of the *ḥabashīya* (*zanjīya*) in the Muslim accounts of the annihilation of al-ʿUzzā, discussed below.

151 DAEMS, *Iconography*, p. 13. For a fantastic verbal realization of such steatopygous beauty see the *rāʾīya* by al-Marrār b. Munqidh, an Umayyad poet, preserved as number 16 in the *Mufaḍḍalīyāt*, especially verses 63-90, a verbal opulence totally in keeping with the frescoes of Quṣayr ʿAmra. That early Arabic poets often compared women with statuettes, see Imru' al-Qays Ahlwardt poem 52.9; al-Nābigha Ahlwart poem 7.16; al-Aʿshā Ahlwardt poem 18.5 and 32.9; SIEGMUND FRAENKEL, *Die aramäischen Fremdwörter im Arabischen*, Leiden: Brill, 1886, p. 271-272. I take the statues found at Qaryat al-Faw to be the kind of figure involved in the comparison: see AL-ANSARY, *Qaryat al-Fau*, p. 108, plate 1, and 120 ('statue of a lady ... made of brilliant white limestone'), though I would not rule out a representation of Aphrodite.

152 DAEMS, *Iconography*, p. 13 and 91, plate 47; see A. SPYCKET, *Les figurines de Suse. Mémoire de la Délégation Archéologique en Iran*, Paris, 1992, p. 157, figures 953-1019. For an earlier example of the single sash worn from left to right and wrapped around the neck (?), see DAEMS, *Iconography*, p. 11 and 90, figure 42, from the Shimashki period (2100-1900 BC).

153 DAEMS, *Iconography*, p. 13 and 91, plate 48; see SPYCKET, *Les figurines*, 1992, p. 165, figures 1020-1042. Cf. the figures of the goddess NĪN-ali, «la Dame de la Ville», from Dar-Untash reproduced in R. GHIRSHMAN, *Tchoga Zanbil (Dar-Untash), Volume II: Temenos, Temples, Palais, Tombes*, Paris: Geuthner, 1968, p. 18, figure 4 (G.T.-Z. 1143); plate 57 (G.T.-Z. 921, 937 and 939); plate 80 (G.T.-Z. 1031) and the discussion of the temple on p. 16-19. These stretch marks seem fairly consistent throughout the representations covered by DAEMS. Their presence in the Safaitic rock-carving suggests that it is to be connected with the Iranian rather than the Mediterranean tradition of body chain wearing damsels.

154 DAEMS, *Iconography*, p. 13 and 92, figure 49; SPYCKET, *Les figurines*, 1992, p. 168, figures 1043-1119.

wear the body chain.[155] At all four stages, the women are depicted as cupping their breasts with their hands. Daems reports the theory of Ghirshman that:

> These Middle Elamite Susa figurines were fetishes with the imagery of the fertility goddess Manzat and were kept by women during pregnancy to protect their unborn baby. Since most of these figurines were found broken in the streets during excavation, Ghirshman suggests that after childbirth, the figurines were no longer of any use and thus were thrown away.[156]

Daems also notes that the end of the Middle Elamite period marks a termination of the production in Susa of naked female figurines until their resumption there, as bone carvings, during the Parthian era.[157]

So, it seems that at some point this ancient Iranian body chain was transmogrified into the (body-)girdle of Aphrodite, a magical accoutrement which Homer describes as:

> the elaborate, pattern-pierced zone, and on it are figured all beguilements, and loveliness is figured upon it, and passion of sex is there, and the whispered endearment that steals the heart away even from the thoughtful.[158]

In bestowing her *caestus* on Hera, Aphrodite unbounds it from her breasts.

In the Early Arabic poetic tradition, the body chain becomes a powerful (if somewhat rare) symbol of eroticism. Pre-Islamic poets such as ʿAlqama b. ʿAbada, Bishr and al-Aʿshā, as well as Umayyad poets such al-Shamardal, al-Ṭirimmāḥ, al-Akhṭal and ʿUmar b. Abī Rabīʿa, describe their various love-interests as resplendent in their body chains.[159]

[155] DAEMS, *Iconography*, p. 13 and 92, figure 50; SPYCKET, *Les figurines*, 1992, p. 179, figures 1120-1133.

[156] DAEMS, *Iconography*, p. 13. See R. GHIRSHMAN, *La déesse nue élamite*, in: *Archäeologische Mitteilungen aus Iran* 1 (1968), p. 11-14 with Tafel 1 and 2 (p.12).

[157] DAEMS, *Iconography*, p. 14. I shall leave an account of the iconic development of an Iranian fertility fetish into the eroticisation of the Mediterranean Aphrodite body-girdle (approximately a millennium after it had apparently fallen into representational desuetude) to art-historians.

[158] HOMER, *Iliad*, ed. DAVID T. MONROE and THOMAS W. ALLEN, II, Oxford: Clarendon Press, 1978, Book 14. 214-218; the translation is that of RICHMOND LATTIMORE, *The Iliad of Homer*, Chicago: University of Chicago Press, 1951, p. 299-300. Note that the Greek here translated as 'zone' is *himas*, which can mean in the plural a 'harness' of a chariot: see the verse of Labīd discussed in MONTGOMERY, *Vagaries*, p. 174, note 235.

[159] For an inventory of occurrences, see MONTGOMERY, *Vagaries*, p. 174 and footnotes 235, 236 and 237. Plunging necklines, such as the promiscuous couture of the singing-girl (*qayna*) described by Ṭarafa in his *Muʿallaqa* (*raḥībun qiṭābu al-jaybi min-hā*), provoked the Qur'anic prohibition Q. 24.31 (*al-Nūr*). That they presumably belong to the same ambience of the body chain is indicated by figural representations of such singing and dancing girls on Sasanian silverware: DAEMS, *Iconography*, p. 59 and figures 223 and

Yet, it is difficult to tell in these instances whether the woman is naked, clothed or partially clothed. The eroticism of the contexts would imply some degree of nudity, but it is not clear to us, though it would presumably have been some fifteen centuries ago. Moreover, it rarely emerges at all clearly from many a *nasīb* of the pre-Islamic *qaṣīda* whether there is one *ḥabīb*, idealized and apotheosized, in a process whereby the multiple loves of the poets are transformed into an ideal type (a process which the subject women of Imru' al-Qays's *Muʿallaqa*, who are all different but who share their status as his conquests, seem to taunt and defy), of whether there are many, several and separate (and not simply in the sense of distinct individuals), not all of whom share the same standing in society — in other words, are some of these women slaves and concubines (such as Ṭarafa's singing-girl in his *Muʿallaqa*), are others free born (and hence elite) women (such as the inamorata of al-Shanfarā's *mufaḍḍalīya*), are yet others tribal dependents (i.e. not members of the aristocracy) or even prostitutes sacred to a deity?[160] These women are as elusive and evasive as the very language of love-making used in the *nasīb*.[161]

The fetishism of the Iranian figurines, combined with the ubiquitous late antique appeal of Aphrodite's iconography and its inflection in the early poetry of the Arabs, is fully realized in the most consummate visual celebration of the body chain extant in pre-modern Arabo-Islam, the hunting lodge and bath house complex built probably for al-Walīd b. Yazīd (r. 125-126/743-744) at Quṣayr ʿAmra in the Jordanian al-Balqā'. In several of these frescoes, women are depicted wearing the body chain, in various poses and various states of dress. The woman on the south soffit of the west arch of the hall is depicted semi-laterally, her upper body turning towards the viewer, one fist resting on her right buttock,

224. I leave it to others to decide whether the Qur'anic prohibition is to be considered as restricted (directed at a specific group of women characterized by the wearing of such garments, and thus as part of the Qur'anic attack on the socio-religious dimensions of alcohol consumption: the *qaṣīda* poets, like Horace and the Romans, drank after the *Persicos mores*) from which it can be extended to all women; or whether its current hermeneutic as unrestricted is its original sense. On 'restricted' and 'unrestricted' commands and prohibitions, see JOSEPH E. LOWRY, *The Reception of al-Shāfiʿī's Concept of* Amr *and* Nahy *in the Thought of his Student al-Muzanī*, in: *Law and Education in Medieval Islam. Studies in Memory of George Makdisi*, ed. JOSEPH E. LOWRY, DEVIN J. STEWART and SHAWKAT M. TOORAWA, Oxford: Gibb Memorial Trust, 2004, p. 128-149.

[160] Such women are discussed by JOSEPH CHELHOD, *Le sacrifice chez les arabes. Recherches sur l'évolution, la nature et la fonction des rites sacrificiels en Arabie occidentale*, Paris: Presses Universitaires de France, 1955, p. 155-159.

[161] See MONTGOMERY, *Vagaries*, p. 52-77.

the left arm raised slightly and bent back with index finger pointing down, adorned with anklets, bracelets, armlets, necklace, loin-cloth and body chain.[162] Very arresting are the women on the south soffit of the east arch of the hall. Their pose is full-frontal, and they gaze directly at the viewer, arms raised high above their head supporting a medallion, and bedecked with a body chain, a necklace, with three pendant leaves (?), bracelets and armlets, but wearing a shift or skirt covering the lower-half of their body.[163] Both sets of figures have been identified as dancing-girls. Of the first, Fowden notes that she is

> Like most of the Quṣayr ʿAmra women in that she has a rather slender torso and firm breasts, but heavy hips and fleshy thighs, calves and arms.[164]

In other words, she is a visual realisation of many a *ḥabīb* described in the *nasīb* of the pre-Islamic *qaṣīda*.

The third woman to wear a body chain is rendered on the northwest spandrel of the central aisle in the hall. She is reclining and pensive, her head resting on her left hand, her right arm outstretched, with open palm upturned. She is bedecked in a long skirt, but naked from the waist up save the now standard jewellery: one bracelet (?), armlets, necklace and *wishāḥ*:

> A hovering but wingless figure, more likely in this context to be an inept Eros than an apteral Victory hands her a crown.[165]

These life-size images remind Fowden of:

> The depictions of Victory (Nikē) holding up portrait medallions that were to be seen throughout the Roman Empire, including Syria and Jordan, and had deep roots in Greek artistic tradition.

Whilst noting that 'in attire they also recall an Aphrodite in a mosaic from a sixth-century mansion at Mādabā' he admits that:

> Their significance for the patron and artists ... is hard to guess. Probably they evoked nothing more specific than what they suggest to today's visitors, namely a courtly, opulent, and vaguely triumphal atmosphere, with a touch of irreverence in the topless and wingless Victories. If there was an allusion to some historical individual, the reclining woman who receives a crown, and whose undress ... virtually excludes her having been of free status, may have been some especially prized singing girl — such female

[162] FOWDEN, *Quṣayr ʿAmra*, p. 65, figure 17a.
[163] FOWDEN, *Quṣayr ʿAmra*, p. 65, figure 17b.
[164] FOWDEN, *Quṣayr ʿAmra*, p. 65.
[165] FOWDEN, *Quṣayr ʿAmra*, p. 74, figure 24.

> entertainers were by definition slaves. Though they resemble her, the women in the arch soffits are elegant space fillers, not portraits.[166]

Yet the resemblances between these women and the body-girdle clad Aphrodites which Fowden himself notes copiously throughout his work are so overpowering that it would be foolhardy to deny them an identity as instantiations of the goddess (or one of her nymphs).[167] Furthermore, the resemblances between these women and one type of the (several) manifestations of the beloved of the pre-Islamic *qaṣīda* are also so overpowering that it would be foolhardy to deny them a second identity as the *wishāḥ* wearing, highly charged and passionately eroticized *ḥabīb*. But are we dealing with the goddess herself (or one of her nymphs), or with concubines dressed as Aphrodite? Before we will be in a position to consider this question, we must consider the image which Fowden identifies as 'a late but powerful avatar, at the very heart of the Muslim caliphate ... of Aphrodite'[168] and ponder the worship of al-ʿUzzā in north and central pre-Islamic Arabia.

On the west wall of the hall there stands, in a position of great visual prominence, and without any verbal identification, a figure of a 'bathing beauty', her pose a combination of figures 17a and 17b, i.e. she is depicted full-frontally, her right fist rests on her right buttock and her left arm is arched at head height, with elongated index finger and pinkie pointing down.[169] Unlike them, she seems to wear a turban and a

166 FOWDEN, *Quṣayr ʿAmra*, p. 75.

167 See FOWDEN, *Quṣayr ʿAmra*, p. 59 (depictions of Aphrodite in bathing establishments, 'and often unclothed'); p. 60 (naked Aphrodite and nymph discovered at Scythopolis, by the River Jordan, cast there in 515 AD); p. 73 (echoes of Aphrodite in his figure 25, with a reference to JENTEL, *Aphrodite*, II.1, p. 155-156 = II.2, p. 157, figure 31); p. 146 (destruction of a statue in a bath house in Fusṭāṭ, in accordance with the edict of 103-4/721, promulgated by Yazīd II (r. 101-105/720-724). In a private communication, Fowden has urged caution: 'what could it possibly have meant to have been "dressed as Aphrodite"? There's a big gap between that and having just seen the image'. My response consists of viewing the late Umayyads as much through the lens of the *Jāhilīya* as of the Classical heritage. Fowden himself has proposed an intriguing answer to his question with regard to Dionysus and Aphrodite: *Greek Myth and Arabic Poetry at Qusayr ʿAmra*, in: *Islamic Crosspollinations*, ed. A. AKASOY, P. PORMANN, and J.E. MONTGOMERY (in preparation).

168 *Quṣayr ʿAmra*, p. 230.

169 FOWDEN, *Quṣayr ʿAmra*, p. 228, figure 57. On p. 233, Fowden suggests that her left hand is raised 'in order to pull back a curtain which hangs ... behind her' and lambastes this 'as pure ineptness on the part of the artist'. BAER, *Female Images*, p. 15, describes her as drawing a curtain. The ineptness is probably one of perspective, if we see her, for all her stasis, to be mimicking the manual gesture of the image depicted as figure 17a, as FOWDEN, *Quṣayr ʿAmra*, p. 233, note 20, remarks. Long fingers could be highly prized in a woman: ILSE LICHTENSTÄDTER, *Das* Nasīb *der altarabischen* Qaṣīde, in: *Islamica* 5 (1932), p. 18-96 (p. 90) refers to a verse of Imru' al-Qays. The terracotta Aphrodite from

pendant[170] rather than a body chain; like figure 17a she wears the slightest of loin-cloths, and like the other three figures she wears bracelets and armlets. If she, together with her three sisters, is not Aphrodite presiding over the luxuries of the bath,[171] her identity truly is a puzzle which Fowden has tried to solve by identifying her as the 'captive Sasanian princess', Shāh-i Āfrīd taken captive in Samarqand by Qutayba b. Muslim and rendered unto the caliph al-Walīd I (r. 86-96/705-715), subsequently becoming the mother of the caliph Yazīd b. al-Walīd (r. 126/744).[172] Whatever the truth

Sarageb (JENTEL, *Aphrodite*, II.1, p. 155-156 = II.2, p. 157, figure 31) is graced with improbably long fingers, two bracelets and one armlet. The position of her left arm is identical to that of the figure under discussion here.

[170] FOWDEN, *Quṣayr ʿAmra*, p. 232 and 235 places particular emphasis on the 'turban the bather appears to be wearing, with a round ornament on its front', so much so that he argues that it indicates 'that the artist had some particular occasion in mind'. It is possible that the ornamented turban is an Umayyad echo of the Iranian 'central protuberance' in the depiction of feminine coiffure, 'a type of hairdo where the hair is turned into a turban on the forehead, jutting forward at the centre': see DAEMS, *Iconography*, p. 11-12 and figures 41 and 45-46. In the Middle Elamite statuaries, 'the protuberance can be represented as a circle'. This coiffure lends support to the Iranian influence which FOWDEN detects in this figure, on which see next but one note. For Aphrodite with a pendant: the mosaic of (a bare-breasted) Aphrodite in the Hippolytus hall at Mādabā in Jordan (FOWDEN, *Quṣayr ʿAmra*, p. 77, figure 26), wears a splendid necklace couched between her breasts, an inflection of which tradition FOWDEN, *Quṣayr ʿAmra*, p. 230-231, not implausibly discerns in our similarly adorned bathing beauty: he refers to JENTEL, *Aphrodite*, II.1, p. 165 = II.2, p. 169, figure 244; the Umayyad brazier from al-Faddayn northwest of Quṣayr ʿAmra, surmounted with two figures of naked women, whom I presume to be Aphrodites, clad in pendant necklaces, armlets and bracelets, with right arms outstretched and holding a bird (a dove?) in their left (FOWDEN, *Quṣayr ʿAmra*, p. 78, figure 27); HENRY MAGUIRE, *The Good Life*, in: *Late Antiquity. A Guide to the Post-classical World*, ed. G.W. BOWERSOCK, P. BROWN and O. GRABAR, Cambridge, Mass.: Belknap Press, 1999, p. 238-257, figure 24, (a 'shell-shaped pendant'); BECKWITH, *Coptic Sculpture* figure 62, from circa 400 AD, is of an Aphrodite with a pendant necklace nestled in her cleavage; GRABAR, *Formation*, figure 82, a sculpture from the bath entrance at Khirbat al-Mafjar which has a prominent necklace, though not pendant between the breasts, armlet(s?) and a long skirt, in the manner of Quṣayr ʿAmra's figure 17b. Note the Iranian influence in this female's stretch marks visible above the waist of the skirt.

[171] I am not alone in reading this figure as *an* Aphrodite or as seeing her as an analogue of one of the other body-girdled figures in the complex, though I do not propose that any two of them depict the same woman; Aphrodite: see FOWDEN, *Quṣayr ʿAmra*, p. 232 (the painting is an allusion to 'iconographical types of Aphrodite, perhaps in particular to images that show the goddess at her bath with an attendant holding her clothes'); p. 240 (dismissal of Blazquez's suggestion that the panel represents the *maïoumas*, a ceremony in celebration of Dionysus and Aphrodite, part of the triumphal celebrations in Constantinople which may have taken place in the bath house of the Sophianai); p. 244 ('Shāh-i Āfrīd is depicted at a moment of exposure and humiliation, but also of triumph and as a new Aphrodite'); superficial similarities: p. 75 (between his figures 17b and 24); p. 235, note 21 (and the references given there: between his figures 24 and 57).

[172] FOWDEN, *Quṣayr ʿAmra*, p. 227-247. Incidentally, the Elamite figurines and the body chain at Ctesiphon corroborate Fowden's detection of Iranian influence in the bath house, but say little about his identification of the princess.

of these matters, and I think that Fowden's argument is here at its boldest and most speculative, be she a captive princess or a favourite dancing girl or most cherished concubine,[173] it is indubitable that she is depicted as Aphrodite and irrefragable that the goddess's (body-)girdle had bewitched the late Umayyad patron of this bath-house as it had ancient Greeks, Copts, Christians, Iranians and pre-Islamic Arabs.

Deep uncertainty governs what we know of the varieties of religious experience in the Arabian peninsula in the half millennium or so before the Qur'anic event.[174] Indeed, in the language of the Qur'ān itself, we are confronted with beings

> Who are naught but names which you have named, you and your fathers, on which Allāh has sent down no power — you simply follow conjecture and what <your> souls desire; even though guidance has come to them from their Lord![175]

Among the mysterious names mentioned in this same *sūra* of the Qur'ān (*āya*s 19 and 20), comes that of al-ʿUzzā:[176]

[173] See GRABAR, *Formation*, p. 154-155.

[174] W. ROBERTSON SMITH, *Lectures on the Religion of the Semites, First Series: the Fundamental Institutions*, London: Black, 1894; JULIUS WELLHAUSEN, *Reste arabischen Heidentums*, Berlin: Reimer, 1897; NÖLDEKE, *Arabs (Ancient)*; G. RYCKMANS, *Les religions arabes préislamiques* (*Bibilothèque du Muséon*, 26), Leuven: Publications Universitaires, 1951; HENNINGER, *Pre-Islamic Bedouin Religion* (originally published in 1959); WERNER CASKEL, *Die alten semitischen Gottheiten in Arabien*, in: *Le antiche divinità semitiche* (*Studi Semitici*, 1), ed. SABATINO MOSCATI, Rome: Istituto di Studi Orientali, 1958, p. 95-117; TOUFIC FAHD, *Le panthéon de l'Arabie centrale à la vieille de l'hégire*, Paris: P. Geuthner, 1968 (Chapter One: 'Conceptions religieuses de l'Arabie ancienne', p. 1-35); MARIA HÖFNER, *Zentral- und Nordarabien*, in: *Die Religionen Altsyriens, Altarabiens und der Mandäer* (*Die Religionen der Menschheit*, 10.2), ed. HARTMUT GESE, MARIA HÖFNER and KURT RUDOLPH, Stuttgart: Kohlhammer, 1970, p. 354-402; IḤSĀN ʿABBĀS, *Two Hitherto Unpublished Texts on Pre-Islamic Religion*, in: *La signification du bas moyen âge dans l'histoire et la culture du monde musulman* (*Actes du 8me Congrès de l'Union Européenne des Arabisants et Islamisants, Aix-en-Provence - Septembre 1976*), Aix-en-Provence: Edisud, 1976, p. 7-16; A.G. LUNDIN, *Die arabischen Göttinnen Ruḍā und al-ʿUzzā*, in: *Hudhud. Festschrift für Maria Höfner zum 80. Geburtstag*, ed. ROSWITHA STIEGNER, Graz: Karl-Franzens-Universität, 1981, p. 211-218; CHRISTIAN ROBIN, *Du paganisme au monothéisme*, in: ROBIN, *L'Arabie antique*, p. 139-155; PAVLOVITCH, *The pre-Islamic Lord*; HOYLAND, *Arabia and the Arabs*, p. 139-166; RETSÖ, *The Arabs*, p. 600-622 ('in spite of their great erudition, none of these writers has had any clear idea about what the Arabs were. They all describe the religion of the people(s) living in Arabia, not that of the Arabs', p. 616). The important articles of JOSEPH HENNINGER from over three decades are collected in *Arabia Sacra*.

[175] Q. 53.23 (*al-Najm*).

[176] WELLHAUSEN, *Reste*, p. 34-45; F.V. WINNETT, *The Daughters of Allah*, in: *The Muslim World* 30 (1940), p. 113-130; FAHD, *Le panthéon*, p. 163-182; JOSEPH HENNINGER, *Zum Problem der Venussterngottheit bei den Semiten*, in: *Anthropos* 71 (1976), p. 129-168; MICHAEL LECKER, *The Banū Sulaym. A Contribution to the Study of Early*

Have you seen al-Lāt and al-ʿUzzā; and Manāh, the third, the other?

In modern scholarship, this deity has enjoyed three (widely held) identities; the earliest attestable being that of a bilingual Aramaic-Greek inscription found on the island of Cos, and dated to the reign of Aretas IV (end of the First Century BC to first half of the First Century AD), in which al-ʿUzzā is equated with Aphrodite;[177] it has been associated with a manifestation of the planet Venus as the Morning Star;[178] and, through the venerable process of *Tafsīr al-Qur'ān bi-l-Qur'ān*, as one of *al-banāt li-Allāh*, the daughters possessed by Allāh.[179]

Yet despite a plethora of references to al-ʿUzzā in many of the languages of pre-Islamic Arabia, it is unclear whether there is any continuity of worship or even identity between the deity with this name of the Northern Arabs (the Ḥawrān, Sinai, and southern Mesopotamia [i.e. the Lakhmids of al-Ḥīra]), that of the Nabataeans (Petra), that of the central Arabs (Kinda at Qaryat al-Faw, Quraysh, and others, at al-Nakhla and Mecca), or that of the Southern Arabs. The Muslim sources in Arabic aver that there was an intimate, if not exclusive, devotion which

Islam, Jerusalem: The Hebrew University, 1989, p. 36-42; ZAYADINE, *L'iconographie d'al-ʿUzza-Aphrodite*; SUSANNE KRONE, *Die altarabische Gottheit al-Lāt* (*Heidelberger Orientalische Studien*, 23), Frankfurt am Main: Lang, 1992, especially p. 492-520 ('Die Gottheit al-ʿUzzā'); GERNOT ROTTER, *Der* veneris dies *im vorislamischen Mekka, eine neue Deutung des Namens "Europa" und eine Erklärung für* Kobar = *Venus*, in: *Der Islam* 70 (19993), p. 112-132; HAWTING, *Idea of Idolatry*, p. 130-149 (Chapter 6, 'The Daughters of God); JOHN F. HEALEY, *The Religion of the Nabataeans: A Conspectus* (*Religions in the Graeco-Roman World*, 136), Brill: Leiden, 2001, p. 114-119; M.C.A. MACDONALD and LAILA NEHMÉ, *al-ʿUzzā*, in: *EI2*, XI, p. 967-968.

177 HEALEY, *Religion of the Nabataeans*, p.117, strikes a note of caution. It is also important to bear in mind in this connection that Herodotus, *Histories*, 3.8, does not refer to Aphrodite by name but employs instead the epithet *ouraniē*, i.e. 'heavenly <female>'. HOYLAND, *Arabia and the Arabs*, p. 252 refers to the bilingual inscriptions which equate Dushara and al-ʿUzzā with Zeus and Aphrodite.

178 RETSÖ, *The Arabs*, p. 605-606: 'the star, *kawkabtā*, would thus be the male god, Dusares/Dionysus/Phosphoros/Eōsphoros/Lucifer'. The evidence of the text of John Damascene on the worship of the Morning Star and/as Aphrodite is unfortunately inconclusive, for the *kai* can be read both as epexegetical rather than copulative, or as copulative rather than epexegetical. See the sources given by J.B. SEGAL, *Arabs in Syriac Literature before the Rise of Islam*, in: *Jerusalem Studies in Arabic and Islam* 4 (1984), p. 89-123 (p. 112-114); and ROBERT G. HOYLAND, *Seeing Islam as Others Saw It. A Survey and Evaluation of Christian, Jewish and Zoroastrian Writings on Early Islam* (*Studies in Late Antiquity and Early Islam*, 13), Princeton: Darwin Press, 1997, p. 105-107 and p. 480-489.

179 MACDONALD and NEHMÉ, *al-ʿUzzā*, p. 968, note that 'the phrase *banāt Allāh* ... may originally have meant no more than "celestial beings"'. This article is a gem of common sense. See p. 967-968 for a survey of some of the other identities proposed for al-ʿUzzā; p. 968 for the four *āyāt* of the Qur'ān in which these 'daughters' are referred to.

obtained between the Quraysh of Mecca and this deity (it was also worshipped by, among others, Thaqīf, Khuzāʿa, Kināna), though their 'Meccocentricity' has recently been called into doubt.[180] These same sources are also confusing on the tribal guardianship of the deity's sanctuary, it being thought the preserve of both Ghaṭafān and the Banū Sulaym, two groupings not known elsewhere in the sources for their mutual amicableness.[181] In sum, beyond noting the proliferation across the centuries of the deity's name in a variety of languages and contexts, we can but conclude, with Macdonald and Nehmé that:

> It is possible, but at present unprovable, that al-ʿUzzā was considered by her worshippers to have some of the features of Aphrodite and/or to be in some way a manifestation of the planet Venus, but there is not enough evidence to establish exactly how she was conceived in any particular region or period.[182]

And yet before we lose Aphrodite's bewitching body-girdle altogether, let us ponder a detail of one of the several versions of the destruction of the sanctuary of al-ʿUzzā by the Muslim hero, Khālid b. al-Walīd, acting under the orders of Muḥammad, on the 25th of Ramaḍān in 8 AH (16 January, 630).[183] In the account given by al-Ṭabarī on the authority of al-Wāqidī, Khālid, having destroyed the complex (?: al-Ṭabarī's narrative is not clear), returns to the Prophet who sends him back to al-Nakhla, to do the job properly, because the first attempt was not accompanied by an apparition. As Khālid destroys the deity's 'house' (*bayt*) and smashes the idol, the priest (*sādin*) invokes the deity and 'against him there sallied forth a naked Ethiopian <woman>, wailing. He killed her and took

[180] HAWTING, *Idea of Idolatry*, p. 148. For the special relationship, see IBN AL-KALBĪ, *Das Götzenbuch Kitâb al-Aṣnâm*, ed. ROSA KLINKE-ROSENBERGER, Leipzig: Harrassowitz, 1941, p. 13.17, 16.14-17.8 (Arabic); HEALEY, *Religion of the Nabataeans*, p. 117 notes that there is 'some evidence in Byzantine Greek polemical texts that a relief figure of Aphrodite was located in the Kaʿba at Mecca', though their polemicism might temper, if not invalidate, their worth.

[181] LECKER, *Banū Sulaym*, p. 36; KRONE, *al-Lāt*, p. 501-503; ʿABBĀS, *Two Hitherto Unpublished Texts*, p. 10 posits a *ḥilf* between Sulaym and Ghaṭafān; HAWTING, *Idea of Idolatry*, p. 138-140. On the *ḥilf*, see LANDAU-TASSERON, *Alliances*.

[182] *Al-ʿUzzā*, p. 968.

[183] I have compared the versions of Ibn Isḥāq, al-Wāqidī, Ibn al-Kalbī and al-Ṭabarī: IBN ISḤĀQ, *al-Sīra al-Nabawīya*, ed. M. AL-SAQQĀ, I. AL-ABYĀRĪ and A. AL-SHALABĪ, Cairo: Muṣṭafā l-Bābī l-Ḥalabī, 1955, p. 436.8-437.7; AL-WĀQIDĪ, *Kitāb al-Maghāzī*, ed. J. MARSDEN-JONES, London: Oxford University Press, 1966, p. 873-874; IBN AL-KALBĪ, *Aṣnām*, p. 15.5-16.13; AL-ṬABARĪ, *Taʾrīkh*, I, p. 1648.1-9; *The History of al-Ṭabarī, Volume VIII. The Victory of Islam*, trans. MICHAEL FISHBEIN, Albany: SUNY, 1997, p. 187. There is a further account of the destruction of a deity's sanctuary at Buss recorded by AL-IṢFAHĀNĪ in his *Kitāb al-Aghānī*, XIX, Cairo: al-Hayʾa al-Miṣrīya al-ʿĀmma li-l-Kitāb, 1972, p.15.10-17.9; see KRONE, *al-Lāt*, p. 501.

such jewellery (*ḥilya*) as was on her'.[184] No other account which I have consulted mentions this jewellery, and the point in mentioning Khālid's requisitioning of them is not clear. Are they booty, or some special insignia of the deity, such as a *wishāḥ*, which would most definitely qualify as *ḥilya* and which was (in Arabian as well as other cultures) often encrusted with precious stones?[185] Or, put in narrative terms, is this a feature of the *khabar* which once was profoundly significant, but in which subsequently the tradition took next to no interest as it was deaf to its significance, its continued presence in the *khabar* a residue of an earlier account?

A recurrent feature among studies of the religious beliefs and practices of the pre-Islamic Arabs is the issue of astral cults, for which some scholars find ample evidence in Islamic as well as extra-Islamic materials, while others remain sceptical.[186] Central to every discussion of astral cults and star worship, is the equivalence of the deity al-ʿUzzā with the planet Venus, and specifically its manifestation as the morning star.[187] The question of whether al-ʿUzzā is to be equated with Aphrodite is quite a different matter from the identification of al-ʿUzzā with the planet Venus and the deity's consequent involvement in astral worship. And however we view the evidence as a whole, one thing is also clear, namely that to reject the existence of an astral cult in pre-Islamic Arabia

[184] The version of the story given in al-Wāqidī's *Kitāb al-Maghāzī* is constructed as an exercise in the psychology of Khālid b. al-Walīd. See the emendation of JOHNS, *'House of the Prophet'*, p. 94, note 150: *nāfishatin shaʿru-hā*, and note. FRIEDRICH STUMMER, *Bemerkungen zum Götzenbuch des Ibn al-Kalbî*, in: *Zeitschrift der Deutschen Morgendländischen Gesellschaft* 98 (1944), p. 377-394 (p. 379-380), has shown the Hellenistic-Christian origins of the exorcised demon as negroidal; see also FAHD, *Le panthéon*, p. 173-175.

[185] FOWDEN, *Quṣayr ʿAmra*, p. 261, and note 45, discerns in the story an awareness on the part of the 'Semitic population of Syria, and to a certain extent of Arabia as well ... of the iconography of the Greek gods'.

[186] See the excellent review of the Arabic materials in SEIDENSTICKER, *Zur Frage eines Astralkultes* ('über Strenkult im vorislamischen Zentralarabien nichts Sicheres bekannt ist', p. 509), who provides evidence of pre-Islamic reverence for the new moon (*hilāl*) which he connects with the pre-Islamic pilgrimage.

[187] JOSEPH HENNINGER, *Über Sternkunde und Sternkult in Nord- und Zentralarabien*, in: *Arabia Sacra*, p. 48-117 (p. 79-96), who restricts the equation to the Northern Arabs. See also his *Zum Problem der Venussterngottheit*; RETSÖ, *The Arabs*, p. 604 and 617, note 51, notes that the evidence of Theodor ban Kônî (Eighth Century AD) associates the ʿArbāyē with the worship of Nanī, whom he equates with Ishtar, and not with al-ʿUzzā: see p. 618, note 64 for further references. HAWTING, *The Idea of Idolatry*, p. 142 is guardedly cautious on the matter of the equation. KRONE, *al-Lāt*, p. 499 and 506-507 sees al-ʿUzzā worship as emanating from Nabataea and borne south into the central Arabian heartlands and South Arabia by the tribes of Ghaṭafān and Sulaym, whence it spread, becoming firmly established in Mecca.

is not the same thing as to deny the stars and other celestial bodies an important and deeply significant role in the cosmology of the *qaṣīda* poets and the warrior-elites who shared their *Weltanschauung*. The broad outlines of this cosmology and its Islamic adaptations have been brilliantly established by Nadia Jamil in two fantastic studies, to which I have briefly referred in Section One of this article:

> The universe is a gambling arena where Life is forever pitched against Death, and where men are obliged always to 'play' for the *rihān* of their life-interests. Some 'games' they win, and others they lose; but Death will always win the match.[188]

And further, should we refuse a divine association to the body chain clad damsels of the *nasīb*, this in itself does not mean that the wearing of the *wishāḥ* is without astral significance.[189]

That the wearing of the *wishāḥ* is not to be associated with the planet Venus but with the appearance of the stars of al-Thurayyā, the Pleiades, is suggested by a line of poetry in a long *lāmīya* by Imru' al-Qays:

> *Idhā mā 'l-thurayyā fī 'l-samā'i taʿarraḍat*
> *taʿarruḍa 'athnā'i 'l-wishāḥi 'l-mufaṣṣalī*
>
> When al-Thurayyā appears at an angle in the heavens,
> Just as the folds of the body chain divided <in sections, by gems> appear at an angle[190]

[188] Jamil, *Playing for Time*, p. 88. The paradigm for this 'covenantal duty to sacrifice for poorer dependents' (p. 62) is the *maysir* game of chance, and it resonates as a 'fusion between *maysir*-gambling and duty to a covenant centred on blood-relations' (p. 65): as such war is as much a game of chance as competing to feed the needy. See also her study, *Caliph and Quṭb. Poetry as a Source for Interpreting the Transformation of the Byzantine Cross on Steps on Umayyad Coinage*, in: *Bayt al-Maqdis. Jerusalem and Early Islam*, ed. Jeremy Johns, Oxford: Oxford University Press, 1999, p. 11-58.

[189] Thus Nabataean ear-rings which carry images of two eyes and a nose have been interpreted in terms of the iconographical image of the 'eye-idols' of al-ʿUzzā: J. Patrich, *'Al-ʿUzzā' Earrings*, in: *Israel Exploration Journal* 34 (1984), p. 39-46; Krone, *al-Lāt*, p. 509 and footnote 191; for a photograph, see Zayadine, *L'iconographie*, figure 1 (from Wadi Ramm).

[190] Ahlwardt 48.23 (= Arazi-Masalha 147.13; Ibrāhīm poem 1.24, p. 14). The translation aims to tease out the implications of the description. This image proved enormously popular among the Arabic poets of Umayyad Spain: see Paul Kunitzsch and Manfred Ullmann, *Die Plejaden in den Vergleichen der arabischen Dichtung* (*Beiträge zur lexicographie des Klassischen Arabisch*, 9), München: Bayerische Akademie der Wissenschaften, 1992, p. 35-36 and p. 36-38, numbers 1-4 and 6-12. For discussion of this verse and the efforts of the scholiasts to decipher its richness, see p. 149-152: my translation is consonant with what they term the scholiasts' 'Überinterpretation'; and for its astral extension to the 'belt' of Orion (Minṭaqat al-Jawzā') surrounding the 'breasts' of the Pleiades (al-Thurayyā), see p. 154-155. Other instances of Early Arabic poetry in which al-Thurayyā is associated with women's jewellery are nos. 28 (Yazīd b. al-

The Pleaides herald the onset of the rainy season. Thus Bishr b. Abī Khāzim:

Fa-lammā ra'aw-nā bi-'l-nisāri ka-'anna-nā
nashāṣu 'l-thurayyā hayyajat-hā janūbu-hā.

When they saw us in al-Nisār like
the mighty rain clouds of al-Thurayyā whipped up by their south wind.[191]

The destructive 'rain-clouds' of this poet's raiding tribe are a savage, ironical image characteristic of how the poets understand the dynamics of this cosmology: rain as life and death; lofty nobility as protected by unassailable might (i.e. as dependent upon slaughter), and by unbridled generosity as potentially destructive of the bestower. And the rainy season is a propitious time for sexual dalliance, which can also be morbidly destructive.[192]

The cosmology of which this complex is so integral and expressive a component and in the poetic universe of which meteorological phenomena are conceptualized in terms of the camel and its slaughter in *maysir* is sophisticated.[193] Thus when al-Thurayyā function as a temporal signifier, the poetic contexts in which they do so are important, for they too express notions of plenitude, military might, nobility and eroticism, notions which are present in the majority of the twenty-six Pleiades similes from Early Arabic and Umayyad poetry collected by KUNITZSCH and ULLMANN, *Die Plejaden*:

Eroticism: nos. 154 (Muʿaqqir al-Bāriqī), 270 (al-Farazdaq: Pleiades as gazelles as women as prey) and 345 (al-Kumayt b. Zayd): see also the *bayt* of Dhū l-Rumma on page 32;

Ṭathrīya); 42 (al-Ashhab b. Rumayla); 95 (al-Ḥuṭay'a); 350 (Suḥaym); 351 (Qays b. al-Khaṭīm). Cf. also the panegyric by Usayd b. ʿAnqā' (no. 341) and the discussion on p. 22 of the Pleiades as the 'head' of a woman in relation to other stars referred to as *al-kaff al-jadhmā'* and *al-kaff al-khaḍīb* and as *al-dhirāʿ*.

[191] BISHR B. ABĪ KHĀZIM, *Dīwān*, ed. ʿIZZA ḤASAN, Damascus: Wizārat al-Thaqāfa, 1960, poem 3, verse 11; KUNITZSCH and ULLMANN, *Die Plejaden*, p. 23-24 and p. 32. See JAMIL, *Playing for Time*, p. 73-74, for whom 'these two verses ... create a malignant "rain-cloud-mill"'. Al-Thurayyā can also herald a period of winter hardship: KUNITZSCH and ULLMANN, *Die Plejaden*, p. 31. See AL-AZRAQĪ, *Kitāb Akhbār Makka*, ed. F. WÜSTENFELD, I, Leipzig: Brockhaus, 1859, p. 79.21-22 (*wa-qāla la-hum ʿAmr inna rabba-kum yataṣayyaf bi-l-Lāt li-bard al-Ṭā'if wa-yushattiw bi-l-ʿUzzā li-ḥarr al-Tihāma*).

[192] See my review of KUNITZSCH and ULLMANN, *Die Plejaden*, in: *Journal of the American Oriental Society* 114 (1994), p. 687.

[193] See KUNITZSCH and ULLMANN, *Die Plejaden*, nos. 273 (Muhalhil b. Rabīʿa) and 408 (in which the booty is to be understood as camels: Khufāf b. Nudba). In general, they take what we might call a 'univocal' approach to this complex of imagery, especially on p. 147-154: thus 'das Tertium comparationis können die Lichtpunkte, das Leuchten oder der Glanz sein' (p. 148). In so doing, they do not allow room for the wider semantic and conceptual universe of which the similes are part.

Plenitude: nos. 214 (?Ḥassān b. Thābit), 242 (Abū Qays b. al-Aslat), 295 (Dhū l-Rumma);
Lofty nobility and unassailable might: nos. 200 (ʿAbd Allāh b. al-Zabīr), 302 (ʿAbd al-Raḥmān b. al-Ḥassān), 303 (Dhū l-Rumma), 304 (Kharqāʾ al-ʿĀmirīya), 305 (Anonymous), 412 (al-Ṭirimmāḥ). To these I would add the descriptions of troops of riders in nos. 316 (Khidāsh b. Zuhayr) and 327 (al-Shamardal) — cf. also the association of al-Thurayyā with the 'cistern of death' (*ḥawḍ al-mawt*) in a verse by Abū Ṣakhr and the tribal hierarchy of al-Ḥārith b. Ḥilliza, quoted on p. 33 and 34.[194]

Of the remainder, the sieve of no. 156 (Bishr b. ʿAmr b. Marthad) is obscure; the Pleiades are associated with the assaults of Time (*ghawāshin*) by Jarīr (no. 353), evoking Qurʾān 88:17 (*al-Ghāshiya*), in which the *ibil* were glossed by some *mufassirūn* as *saḥāb*, clouds, to the scorn of al-Naẓẓām;[195] and in a famous simile (no. 283) Dhū l-Rumma compares the Pleiades with a 'son of water' (*ʾibn māʾ*) soaring high in the sky above, understood as a water fowl of some sort, which makes me think of *al-gharānīq al-ʿulā*, the highest *gharānīq* (cranes, swans or herons?), of the Satanic Verses in the account of the revelation of Qurʾān 53 (*al-Najm*), in the first verse of which the incipient oath *wa-l-najm* is understood by some exegetes to mean al-Thurayyā,[196] and in verses 19-20 of which the three divinities of Allāt, al-ʿUzzā and Manāh are invoked.[197] A verse of Labīd's confirms the religiosity of the cosmology:

[194] See Jamil, *Playing for Time*, p. 75-77 and 86-87; *Caliph and Quṭb*, p. 22 (on the *ḥawḍ*).

[195] Al-Jāḥiẓ, *Kitāb al-Ḥayawān*, ed. ʿAbd al-Salām Hārūn, I, Cairo: Muṣṭafā ʾl-Bābī al-Ḥalabī, 1938, p. 343.13-14; Jamil, *Playing for Time*, p. 71, note 94.

[196] Kunitzsch and Ullmann, *Die Plejaden*, p. 27-29. Ilse Lichtenstädter, *A Note on the* Gharānīq *and Related Qurʾānic Problems*, in: *Israel Oriental Studies* 5 (1975), p. 54-61, discusses the association of the Daughters of Allāh, the *gharānīq* and the occasional gloss as 'delicate youth', 'noble people' and tentatively proposes 'a solution on the lines of the saga of water nymphs' (be it in the form of birds or nymphs) who assume human form upon quitting their watery habitat (p. 60-61). Her reference to the paradisiacal geese (*iwazz al-janna*) which, in Abū l-ʿAlāʾ al-Maʿarrī's *Risālat al-Ghufrān*, Ibn al-Qarīḥ observes metamorphosing into firm-breasted maidens (*jawārī kawāʿib*) and whose poetic and musical prowess the Shaykh puts to the test, suggests the longevity of this series of associations: divine being, water-fowl and beautiful woman (note also the sly reference to *ṣanam min aḥjār*: p. 205.3): Al-Maʿarrī, *Risālat al-Ghufrān*, ed. ʿĀʾisha ʿAbd al-Raḥmān Bint al-Shāṭiʾ, Cairo: Dār al-Maʿārif, 1950, p. 204.7-207.2; Gregor Schoeler, *Die Vision, die auf einer Hypothese gründet: Zur Deutung von Abū ʾl-ʿAlāʾ al-Maʿarrī's* Risālat al-Ġufrān, in: *Problems in Arabic Literature* ed. M. Maroth, Piliscsaba: The Avicenna Institute of Middle East Studies, 2004, p. 27-41.

[197] See Uri Rubin, *The Eye of the Beholder*, Princeton: Darwin Press, 1995, p. 156-166 (p. 159). Hawting, *Idea of Idolatry*, p. 147 notes the ritual formula which 'began, according to the report in the *Aṣnām*, with a slight variant upon K. 53:19-20 and then finished with the "high-flying cranes". The tag … may have an existence independent of the "satanic verses" story, and perhaps of Ibn al-Kalbī's report too'.

Wa-l-nujūmu 'l-latī tatāba'u bi-l-lay
li wa-fī-hā dhāta l-yamīni 'zwirārū
Dā'ibun mawru-hā wa-yaṣrifu-hā l-ghaw
ru ka-mā yaṣrifu l-hijāna l-duwwarū

Which Jamil renders as:

> And the stars that succeed one another by night, inclining westward [as they sink], follow a steady beaten track, directed by the law of their setting, as the idol of circumambulation dictates the movement of [worshipping] white-skinned women.[198]

The earthly 'mill' (*raḥā*), 'the corporate body of the covenant and its machine of war' (p. 68), which is also the celestial 'mill', 'has a centre equated with a sacred stone of ritual circumambulation' (p. 70). Thus it rotates around the *quṭb* — the chieftain of the tribe, the pole of the heavens and the betyl.

So, then, is the body chain wearing siren of the *qaṣīda* poets associated with al-ʿUzzā and is al-ʿUzzā, consequentially, associated with al-Thurayyā? One place in which to look for an answer is al-Ḥīra of the Lakhmid dynasty of Nasr. I have mentioned previously in Section One my theory that al-Ḥīra is one of the principal settlements in the environs of which the ideologies of Bedouinising *qaṣīda* poetry were forged.[199] The rulers of this cantonment seem to have oscillated between (Nestorian?) Christianity and al-ʿUzzā worship, as Arabic and non-Arabic sources attest, with al-Mundhir III (r. 503-554), al-Mundhir IV (r. ca. 574-580) and al-Nuʿmān III (r. 580-602) especially conspicuous for their devotion to al-ʿUzzā.[200] In one *khabar*, al-Nuʿmān refers a case of litiga-

[198] JAMIL, *Playing for Time*, p. 70; see also *Caliph and Quṭb*, p. 19 (a verse by ʿĀmir b. al-Ṭufayl) and p. 30.

[199] Clearly, the Hudhalī poets do not fit too comfortably in his scheme, and the deity seems to have exerted some appeal for several of their poets. The nature of Sasanian influence in Mecca and Kister's account of Mecca's contacts with al-Ḥīra do not invalidate the proposition, while the Hudhalī poets reveal that the *wishāḥ* should be kept in the Ḥijāz proper and not merely a northern buffer-zone.

[200] MACDONALD and NEHMÉ, *al-'Uzzā*, p. 968, provide the basic references; NÖLDEKE, *The Arabs (Ancient)*, p. 660 refers to the testimonies of Isaac of Antioch (worship of *al-Kawkabtā*) and Procopius, while KRONE, *al-Lāt*, p. 512-513 notes the testimony of Evagrius that al-Nuʿmān III of al-Ḥīra had in his possession a gold image of Venus, on which see HENRI CHARLES, *Le christianisme des Arabes nomades sur le Limes et dans le désert syro-mésopotamien aux alentours de l'hégire*, Paris: Ernst Leroux, 1936, p. 60; RETSÖ, *The Arabs*, p. 602 and 617, notes 31 and 32; HOYLAND, *Arabia and the Arabs*, p. 252-253, note 7. TRIMINGHAM, *Christianity*, p. 157, 193-194, 198 and 254-255, discusses these sources. The text of a famous letter which al-Mundhir b. Mā' al-Samā' sent to Kisrā, describing the captive girl taken from the Jafnid al-Ḥārith b. Jabala (r. ca. 529-569) who accompanied it, specifically mentions her *wishāḥ*: see AL-ṬABARĪ, *Ta'rīkh*, I, p. 1025.16-1026.17 (*gharthā l-wishāḥ*, p. 1026.5); *History of al-Ṭabarī, Volume V*, trans. C.E.

tion to al-ʿUzzā for settlement while in another, al-Mundhir III is said to declare his devotion to Allāt and al-ʿUzzā, a combination of divinities which is not unattested in the verses of the *qaṣīda* poets who, together with the warrior elite to which they belonged and for whom they declaimed their verse, revelled in the paradoxes and oxymorons of fertility, sensuality, war and destruction which a merging of these identities allowed them to express.[201]

Another place to look is the dome of the caldarium of Quṣayr ʿAmra, the ceiling of which is decorated with a fantastic fresco of the Zodiac after a model in a Greek astronomical manuscript; for all its Hellenistic reinterpretation, the *jāhilī* complex of the planetary association of inamorata, Aphrodite and astral lore was not lost on those who masterminded the iconography of the lodge, if they are read as perpetuators of the *Jāhilīya*.[202]

And yet another place to look is in the Qur'ān, which, whilst not furnishing an answer, may offer us a brilliant but grimly ironic clue. Verses 4 and 5 of *Sūrat al-Masad* (Qur'ān 111) run:

BOSWORTH, p. 353-354; FOWDEN, *Quṣayr ʿAmra*, p. 238. That the features of this remarkable verbal tour-de-force are entirely consonant with the Early Arabic *nasīb* is bought out by LICHTENSTÄDTER, *Nasīb*, p. 89-91. KRONE, *al-Lāt*, p. 504-505 briefly surveys the tribal affiliations of individuals with theophorics which included al-ʿUzzā. Her results show 16 occurrences for Quraysh but 14 for Bakr b. Wā'il (10) and Taghlib (4) who occupied North-Eastern Arabia and Mesopotamia.

201 ABŪ TAMMAM, *Hamasae Carmina*, ed. G. FREYTAG, II, Bonn: Lechner 1847-1851, p. 116.15-16 (al-Nuʿmān); *Aghānī*, II, p. 104.6-9 (al-Mundhir b. Mā' al-Samā' swears an oath by al-Lāt and al-ʿUzzā). WINNETT, *The Daughters of Allah*, p. 128 discerns in al-Mundhir's sacrifice of 400 nuns to al-ʿUzzā 'the function of a war-goddess'. The richest discussion is KRONE, *al-Lāt*, passim, and p. 512 (for the equation of al-ʿUzzā with Atargatis), p. 512-513 (al-ʿUzzā as 'Kriegs- und Schutzgottheit' and her shared functions with al-Lāt) and p. 520 where she notes that central Arabia is the only region in which al-Lāt and al-ʿUzzā are fused, 'a creation of a later period', discerning therein monotheistic influence: see WELLHAUSEN, *Reste*, p. 31; HAWTING, *Idea of Idolatry*, p. 138 sees this as evidence of confusion rather than as a sign of creativity. For the *qaṣīda* masters of the *ʿarabīya* and the Nasrids of al-Ḥīra, the biparous aspect of life and death epitomized by al-Lāt and al-ʿUzzā, captured perfectly the complex nature of their cosmology and *Weltanschauung*. See also LUNDIN, *Die arabischen Göttinnen*, p. 216, who makes a similar observation of the goddess ʿAthtarta/Ishtar. KRONE's discussion (*al-Lāt*, p. 515) of the *ḥadīth* of the Prophet Muḥammad who offers to protect Zayd al-Khayl al-Ṭā'ī from al-ʿUzzā and the 'black horse' (which she understands as having played a role in the cult of al-ʿUzzā) affords an opportunity to reconsider the symbolic dimensions of the horse in the poetry of Imru' al-Qays and ʿAlqama b. ʿAbada. According to JAMIL, *Playing for Time*, p. 83-88; *Caliph and Quṭb*, p. 24, horses, storms/water and destructive raids are associated in a fecund matrix of imagery.

202 FOWDEN, *Quṣayr ʿAmra*, p. 42-44, figure 10. In a private communication, Fowden has expressed his reservations concerning such a connection.

wa-'mra'atu-hū ḥammālatu/a 'l-ḥaṭab: fī jīdi-hā ḥablun min masad
And his woman, the porter of kindling wood: on her neck a rope of fibres.[203]

The Abū Lahab of this *sūra* was, evidently at a very early stage, identified with Muḥammad's paternal uncle ʿAbd al-ʿUzzā b. ʿAbd al-Muṭṭalib. The theophoric naturally led some *mufassirūn* and *akhbārīyūn* to connect this *sūra* with *sūra* 53, in which al-ʿUzzā is mentioned. Thus Ibn al-Kalbī's version of Abd al-ʿUzzā's declaration to the *sādin* of al-ʿUzzā's sanctuary at al-Nakhla of his devotion to the deity comes after the account of the Satanic Verses; or Abū Lahab's son is said to have died after he had repudiated the revelation of *Sūrat al-Najm*. Clearly, then, al-ʿUzzā loomed large in the minds of a number of the readers of this *sūra* in the formative first two centuries after the *Hijra*.[204] Just how prominently she loomed becomes obvious in some of the glosses of the phrase *ḥabl min masad*. Qatāda (d. 117/735), and al-Ḥasan al-Baṣrī (d. 110/728), are said to have interpreted this as referring to a *qilāda min wadʿ* (or, *kharz*), 'a necklace made of cowries' (or, shells), while for Saʿid b. al-Musayyab (d. 94/713), *masad* stands for *jawhar*, precious stones.[205] Now, what these examples of exegesis tell us is not necessarily that such ornamentation is the butt of the Qur'ān's parody (this is an especially obscure and polyvalent sample of the Revelation) but that it was how these Umayyads visualized the accessories of a woman in the service of al-ʿUzzā when they responded to the influence of the theophoric in their exegesis of these verses.

Aphrodite's body-girdle is the goddess of love's most potently enthralling accessory and she may have bewitched me into hearing echoes of her celebration, if not indeed worship, among (some) *qaṣīda* poets of pre-Islamic Arabia. That the Ḥijāz seems not as empty now as it did before may also be part of her spell.

What remains, however, is that Arabic *qaṣīda* poetry is a necessary though by no means sufficient condition for the miracle of an Arabic Qur'ān.

[203] See generally URI RUBIN, *Abū Lahab and Sūra CXI*, in: *Bulletin of the School of Oriental and African Studies* 42 (1979), p. 13-28. Footnote 73 on p. 25 explains the reasons for the divergent vocalizations of the epithet *ḥammāla*; with *jīd* compare, for example, the verse from Ṭarafa's *Muʿallaqa* quoted in note 159 above, p. 83-84.
[204] RUBIN, *Abū Lahab*, p. 14 and 24 respectively.
[205] RUBIN, *Abū Lahab*, p. 27-28, for discussion and references.

Paths to al-Ashʿarī

LE VOCABULAIRE PHILOSOPHIQUE DE L'ÊTRE EN SYRIAQUE, D'APRÈS DES TEXTES DE SERGIUS DE REŠ'AINĀ ET JACQUES D'ÉDESSE

Henri Hugonnard-Roche
Institut des Traditions Textuelles, CNRS

Dans une très fine étude portant sur l'origine du terme arabe *annīya*, parue dans les *Cahiers de Byrsa*, Richard Frank a consacré plusieurs pages à l'étude du vocabulaire syriaque de l'être, en particulier aux traductions syriaques des expressions grecques τὸ ὄν et τὸ εἶναι, comme sources possibles du mot arabe étudié.[1] Les quelques remarques qui suivent, consacrées à l'étude de textes syriaques touchant au vocabulaire de l'être et à des notions voisines, se veulent ainsi un hommage aux recherches remarquables d'acuité faites par Richard Frank, et elles se situent en quelque manière dans leur prolongement, même si elles ne visent pas à l'explication du mot arabe susdit.[2]

Notre propos se limitera ici au domaine syriaque, et nos remarques porteront sur les textes de deux auteurs des VIe et VIIe siècles respectivement: Sergius de Reš'ainā (mort en 536) et Jacques d'Édesse (mort en 708). Tous deux ont fait œuvre philosophique, le premier en composant notamment un commentaire sur les *Catégories* d'Aristote, le second en traduisant ces mêmes *Catégories* (ou en révisant une traduction antérieure du VIe siècle). Jacques d'Édesse, de plus, composa un manuel (*Encheiridion*)[3] touchant la signification et l'usage de plusieurs mots

[1] R. Frank, *The Origin of the Arabic Philosophical Term* Anniyya, dans: *Cahiers de Byrsa* 6 (1956), p. 81-201.

[2] Sur les différents emplois philosophiques du mot *annīya* chez les auteurs de langue arabe, voir la brève note de A. Hasnawi, *Anniyya ou Inniyya (essence, existence)*, dans: l'*Encyclopédie Philosophique Universelle, Les notions philosophiques*, II, Paris: Presses Universitaires de France, 1990, p. 101-102. Sur les mots ou les expressions grecques, dont *annīya* et les expressions formées à l'aide de ce terme sont les traductions, voir le relevé très détaillé et précis donné dans *A Greek and Arabic Lexicon (GALex), Materials for a Dictionary of the Mediæval Translations from Greek into Arabic*, éd. G. Endress and D. Gutas, I.4, Leiden: Brill, 1997, p. 428-436.

[3] Le terme *Encheiridion* figure en translittération syriaque au premier mot du titre dans le manuscrit unique qui conserve le traité (Londres, B.L., *Add.* 12154, fol. 158v-164v): voir l'édition procurée par G. Furlani, *L'ΕΓΧΕΙΡΙΔΙΟΝ di Giacomo d'Edessa nel testo siriaco*, dans: *Rendiconti della R. Accademia Nazionale dei Lincei, classe di sc. morali, storiche e filologiche*, s. VI, 4 (1928), p. 222-249.

syriaques se rapportant aux notions de «nature» (*kyānā*), d'*ousia*,[4] de «substance individuelle» (*qnūmā*), de «par soi» (*yātā*), de «personne» (*parṣūpā*), et d'«espèce» (*ādšā*). Pour l'un comme pour l'autre de ces deux auteurs, les *Catégories* et le vocabulaire philosophique lié aux problèmes de l'être occupent donc une place importante dans leur activité savante.

Tous deux, d'autre part, sont comparables, d'une certaine manière, à d'autres auteurs de même époque (ou à peu près), soucieux eux aussi de questions touchant au vocabulaire de l'être, parmi lesquels on pourrait citer Boèce: l'un, Sergius, par son ambition de commenter l'œuvre d'Aristote, en particulier son œuvre logique, l'autre, Jacques, par la rédaction de son «manuel» dans lequel un travail tout à la fois philologique et philosophique est fait sur le vocabulaire lié aux questions théologiques, qui rappelle un travail analogue fait par Boèce dans ses traités théologiques, où le vocabulaire de l'être est analysé.[5] D'autres rapprochements, à l'évidence, pourraient être suggérés entre le traité de Jacques d'Édesse et ceux de philosophes ou théologiens de langue grecque: on peut penser, en particulier, à un auteur de peu d'années postérieur à Jacques, à savoir Jean Damascène (c. 655 - c. 745), qui dans plusieurs de ses ouvrages s'attache à l'examen précis de questions relatives au vocabulaire de l'être, et des notions voisines.[6]

S'agissant des traités de Sergius et de Jacques, nous ne prendrons en considération ici que des fragments de leurs œuvres, sans nous attacher à les replacer systématiquement dans le champ culturel, philosophique ou théologique, qui est le leur (notamment pour Jacques d'Édesse), ce qui déborderait très largement le propos des présentes remarques. Nous examinerons seulement quelques éléments de vocabulaire, en essayant de porter attention aux aspects philosophiques qui y sont attachés. Nous commencerons, en suivant l'ordre chronologique, par Sergius de Reš'ainā.

[4] Nous rendrons en translittération latine les mots syriaques qui sont eux-mêmes des translittérations du grec dans les ouvrages cités, sans les écrire en lettres grecques. Nous réserverons l'usage de l'alphabet grec aux mots grecs que nous introduisons nous-même dans notre exposé.

[5] Voir, en particulier, le traité *Contra Eutychen et Nestorium*, dont on trouvera le texte latin avec traduction française dans BOÈCE, *Traités théologiques*, éd. A. TISSERAND, Paris: GF Flammarion, 2000 (p. 62-121).

[6] Voir, entre autres ouvrages, la *Dialectica* (ou *Capita Philosophica*) où sont exposées les définitions néoplatoniciennes ou patristiques du vocabulaire philosophique en usage notamment dans les controverses christologiques, ou encore le *Contra Jacobitas*: on trouvera une bibliographie complète sur la vie et les œuvres de l'auteur, dans la notice de V.S. CONTICELLO, *Jean Damascène*, dans: *Dictionnaire des Philosophes Antiques*, éd. R. GOULET, III, Paris: CNRS, 2000, p. 989-1012 (désormais abrégé: *DPhA*).

C'est dans le second livre de son commentaire[7] que Sergius aborde véritablement le traité des *Catégories*, et cela sous l'angle de sa place dans l'initiation à la logique.[8] Celle-ci, en effet, comme le déclare Sergius, est «l'art de faire des démonstrations droites au moyen d'un syllogisme sur chacune des choses qui sont dans le monde»,[9] et puisque les syllogismes démonstratifs sont composés d'énoncés, eux-mêmes composés de dénominations simples, le premier apprentissage est celui de ces dénominations, sur lesquelles porte précisément le traité des *Catégories*.[10]

Le premier point examiné par Sergius à propos du traité est, conformément à la tradition, celui de son but. Afin de déterminer ce but, il part de la remarque qu'il y a trois sortes de choses simples, sur quoi peut porter l'ouvrage: les choses (*ṣebwātā*) simples qui sont dans le monde, ou les concepts (*re'yānē*) simples que nous avons d'elles, ou les expressions (*bnāt qāllē*) simples au moyen desquelles nous les signifions. Par cette manière d'aborder le texte, Sergius se situe clairement dans la tradition des commentateurs néoplatoniciens, et plus spécifiquement dans la suite de l'alexandrin Ammonius (comme d'autres éléments, sur lesquels nous passons ici, le montrent à l'évidence). Et les trois réponses possibles, en faveur de l'une ou l'autre des sortes de

[7] Sergius a composé deux «commentaires» sur les *Catégories*, l'un adressé à un certain Philothéos, l'autre, qui est un peu plus développé, adressé à un certain Théodore, qui collabora aux travaux scientifiques de Sergius (ses traductions de plusieurs traités médicaux de Galien): c'est ce second commentaire que nous considérons dans la présente étude. Sur l'œuvre de Sergius, nous renvoyons à notre ouvrage: *La logique d'Aristote du grec au syriaque. Études sur la transmission des textes de l'*Organon *et leur interprétation philosophique*, Paris: Vrin, 2004 (en particulier, p. 123-132).

[8] Une traduction italienne partielle du commentaire de Sergius a été donnée par G. Furlani, *Sul trattato di Sergio di Rêsh'aynâ circa le categorie*, dans: *Rivista trimestrale di studi filosofici e religiosi* 3 (1922), p. 135-172. Traduction française et étude du prologue (manquant dans le manuscrit de Londres, B.L., *Add.* 14658, utilisé par Furlani) et du livre premier du traité de Sergius, dans Hugonnard-Roche, *La logique d'Aristote du grec au syriaque*, p. 165-231. Le livre premier porte sur des questions placées traditionnellement en préliminaire à l'étude d'Aristote (division de la philosophie, division des ouvrages d'Aristote, statut de la logique comme partie ou instrument de la philosophie).

[9] Le texte étant inédit, nous donnerons les références aux manuscrits de Londres, B.L. *Add.* 14658 (*L*), de Paris, BnF, syriaque 354 (*P*) et du manuscrit 606 du fonds Mingana à Birmingham (*M*): pour la phrase citée, voir donc *P* 15r, *M* 62v (en cette partie du texte, le manuscrit *L*, que nous utiliserons aussi dans la suite, présente une lacune due à la perte de feuillets).

[10] Il s'agit d'une présentation traditionnelle de la division de la logique, dont chaque partie est mise en correspondance avec l'un des traités de l'*Organon*, en sorte qu'une justification théorique est ainsi fournie à l'ordre de lecture des traités dans le cursus scolaire: voir nos remarques et les sources citées (Ammonius et al-Fārābī) dans notre ouvrage *La logique d'Aristote du grec au syriaque*, p. 255-256.

choses simples mentionnées plus haut, sont tirées de passages du texte aristotélicien, comme chez Ammonius.

Ceux d'abord qui disent que le traité porte sur les choses simples elles-mêmes s'autorisent d'un passage des *Catégories*, qui s'énonce, dans le texte de Sergius, comme ceci:

> Parmi les choses (*ṣebwātā*), certaines existent de manière universelle (*gawānā'īt itayhēn*), certaines <existent> de manière particulière (*iḥidāyā'īt*), et certaines encore possèdent la subsistance par elles-mêmes (*qyāmā d-yāthēn qānyān*), et certaines subsistent par celles-là (= les précédentes) (*b-hālēn d-metqaymān*).[11]

Il n'y a pas, dans le traité des *Catégories*, de texte identique à celui-là, c'est-à-dire dont la version syriaque de Sergius serait la traduction exacte. Quant aux deux traductions connues des *Catégories* en syriaque, elles ne contiennent pas non plus un texte identique à celui de Sergius.[12] Le passage du traité des *Catégories*, auquel se réfèrent les commentateurs grecs lorsqu'ils traitent de la même question que l'auteur syriaque, est celui de *Catégories* 2, 1a20 *sq.*:

> Τῶν ὄντων τὰ μὲν καθ' ὑποκειμένου τινὸς λέγεται, ἐν ὑποκειμένῳ δὲ οὐδενί ἐστιν ... .

Il s'agit du texte fameux, dans lequel Aristote introduit la quadripartition des étants (ὄντα), obtenue en croisant les deux caractéristiques suivantes, à savoir: celle d'être dit ou non d'un sujet et celle d'être ou non dans un sujet.[13] Les deux traductions syriaques sont fidèles au grec et ne comportent pas la «variante» de Sergius. Le texte de celui-ci présente, en somme, une division des choses (le mot *ṣebwātā* étant pris dans son sens le plus large, non limité aux existants matériels) en quatre sortes d'entités, par le moyen d'une double opposition: d'une part, l'opposition de l'universel au particulier correspond à la division aristotélicienne entre «ce qui est dit d'un sujet» et «ce qui n'est pas dit d'un sujet», tandis que l'opposition de «ce qui subsiste par soi» à «ce qui subsiste par autre chose» correspond

[11] Cf. le texte des manuscrits *L* 5ra, *P* 19v-20r, *M* 66r.

[12] Les deux traductions syriaques conservées sont une traduction anonyme datant du VIe siècle et la traduction de Jacques d'Édesse: nous nous permettons de renvoyer encore à notre ouvrage *La logique d'Aristote du grec au syriaque*, chap. I: «Sur les versions syriaques des *Catégories* d'Aristote», p. 25-37 (qui reprend un article paru dans le *Journal Asiatique* 275 (1987), p. 205-222), et chap. II: «Jacques d'Édesse et sa réception d'Aristote», p. 39-55.

[13] Sur cette quadripartition et le vocabulaire employé par Aristote, lire de judicieuses remarques dans ARISTOTE, *Catégories*, éd. F. ILDEFONSE et J. LALLOT, Paris: Éditions du Seuil, 2002, p. 297-303.

à la distinction aristotélicienne entre «ce qui n'est pas dans un sujet» et «ce qui est dans un sujet».[14] Par le croisement des oppositions mentionnées par Sergius, on obtient la même quadripartition des étants, ou choses, que celle obtenue par les critères aristotéliciens.[15]

Les différents mots syriaques utilisés par Sergius dans le passage cité, ceux de la racine *īt* et ceux de la racine *qwm*, se rapportent donc, semble-t-il, à deux modes distincts de signifier l'être: les premiers signifient simplement l'existence en tant qu'elle est considérée sous le mode de l'universel ou du particulier, tandis que les seconds se rapportent à la «subsistance», par quoi les οὐσίαι se distinguent des accidents.

Dans le commentaire d'Ammonius sur les *Catégories*, on trouve une présentation de la quadripartition des étants par Aristote, qui est proche de celle de Sergius. Ammonius résume, en effet, le texte d'Aristote par la double division suivante:

> Ἔστι δὲ ἡ διαίρεσις αὕτη· τῶν ὄντων τὰ μέν ἐστι καθόλου, τὰ δὲ μερικά, καὶ πάλιν τῶν ὄντων τὰ μέν ἐστιν οὐσίαι, τὰ δὲ συμβεβηκότα («La division est celle-ci: parmi les étants, les uns sont universels, les autres particuliers, et encore parmi les étants les uns sont *ousiai*, les autres accidents»)[16].

Mais Sergius, à la différence d'Ammonius, introduit le terme signifiant ce par quoi se caractérisent les οὐσίαι, à savoir la «subsistance par soi».

Philopon, pour sa part, reprend la division dans les mêmes termes qu'Ammonius, puis il utilise les critères que fournit cette division, pour en déduire la division suivante:

> τῶν γὰρ ὄντων τὰ μέν εἰσι [sic] καθόλου οὐσίαι, τὰ δὲ καθόλου συμβεβηκότα, καὶ τὰ μὲν μερικαὶ οὐσίαι, τὰ δὲ μερικὰ συμβεβηκότα … («Parmi les étants, les uns sont des essences universelles, les autres des accidents universels, et les uns sont des essences particulières, les autres des accidents particuliers»).[17]

[14] Sur ce point, voir plus loin l'explication, que nous rapportons sommairement, de PHILOPON, *In Cat.*, p. 27.7-9 BUSSE.

[15] L'équivalence des présentations d'Aristote et de Sergius est rendue parfaitement claire, si l'on porte attention à la remarque faite par A. DE LIBERA, *Prédication*, dans le: *Vocabulaire européen des philosophies: dictionnaire des intraduisibles*, éd. B. CASSIN, Paris: Éditions du Seuil, 2004, p. 1010. A. DE LIBERA écrit: «Contrairement à ce que suggère l'intuition, 'être dit d'un sujet' ne signifie pas 'fonctionner comme prédicat dans une proposition', mais 's'appliquer à une pluralité', c'est-à-dire 'être universel', et donc, par là même, 'être susceptible de fonctionner comme prédicat dans une proposition' (de fait, un particulier ne se prédique pas). Interpréter 'se dire d'un sujet' dans le sens d''être prédicat', c'est prendre l'effet pour la cause: c'est parce qu'il s'applique à une pluralité que ce qui est dit d'un sujet est susceptible de figurer ensuite comme prédicat dans une proposition».

[16] AMMONIUS, *In Cat.*, p. 25.5-6 BUSSE.

[17] PHILOPON, *In Cat.*, p. 28.21-23.

Philopon, un peu plus loin, fait le lien entre le langage aristotélicien de la division des étants (être dit d'un sujet / être dans un sujet) et celui des commentateurs (essence, accident), en donnant les équivalences permettant de passer de l'un à l'autre. À propos de l'appellation ἐν ὑποκειμένῳ par laquelle Aristote désigne l'accident, il remarque: αὐτὸ γὰρ καθ' αὑτὸ ὑποστῆναι οὐ δύναται, δέεται δὲ ἄλλου πρὸς ὕπαρξιν, τοῦτ' ἔστιν οὐσίας («en effet, il ne peut subsister par soi, il a besoin d'autre chose pour exister, à savoir une essence»); l'essence, au contraire, dit-il, Aristote la désigne par οὐκ ἐν ὑποκειμένῳ, car elle n'a pas besoin d'autre chose pour exister: οὐ γὰρ δέεται ἑτέρου πρὸς ὕπαρξιν.[18]

La comparaison de ces explications de Philopon avec le passage de Sergius que nous avons traduit plus haut montre clairement, pensons-nous, que les termes syriaques *qyāmā d-yāthēn* expriment la même idée que l'expression grecque καθ' αὑτὸ ὑποστῆναι.

La suite du texte de Philopon explicite, d'autre part, le déplacement effectué par Sergius dans l'expression de la division des étants. Philopon écrit, en effet:

> τῶν δὲ δύο διαιρέσεων τούτων ἡ μέν ἐστιν ἀπὸ τοῦ τρόπου τῆς ὑπάρξεως, ἡ δὲ ἀπὸ τοῦ τρόπου τῆς κατηγορίας, καὶ ἀπὸ τοῦ τρόπου τῆς ὑπάρξεως ἡ λέγουσα τῶν ὄντων τὰ μὲν εἶναι ἐν ὑποκειμένῳ, τὰ δὲ οὐκ ἐν ὑποκειμένῳ, ἀπὸ τοῦ τρόπου δὲ τῆς κατηγορίας ἡ λέγουσα τῶν ὄντων τὰ μὲν καθ' ὑποκειμένου, τὰ δὲ οὐ καθ' ὑποκειμένου λέγεται[19] («de ces deux divisions, l'une est selon le mode de l'existence, l'autre selon le mode de la prédication: selon le mode de l'existence, celle qui dit que, parmi les étants les uns sont dans un sujet, les autres ne sont pas dans un sujet; selon le mode de la prédication, celle qui dit que, parmi les étants, les uns sont dits d'un sujet, les autres ne sont pas dits d'un sujet»).

La division selon le mode de l'existence (ὕπαρξις) est celle qui se rapporte à la distinction entre ce qui subsiste par soi et ce qui a besoin d'un sujet (au sens existentiel) pour exister (πρὸς ὕπαρξιν), la division selon le mode de la prédication (κατηγορία) est celle qui se rapporte à la distinction entre l'universel et le particulier (où le particulier est le sujet de la prédication au sens logique). Dans le texte de Sergius traduit plus haut, la première division est la division philoponienne selon la prédication, tandis que la seconde division est la division philoponienne selon l'existence.[20]

[18] PHILOPON, *In Cat.*, p. 29.7-9.

[19] PHILOPON, *In Cat.*, p. 31.9-14.

[20] Le mot ὕπαρξις, tel qu'il est employé ici par les commentateurs néoplatoniciens, signifie l'inhérence d'un prédicat à un sujet, dont il est question dans le texte des *Catégories*.

Venons-en maintenant aux deux autres opinions sur le but du traité des *Catégories*, telles qu'elles sont reprises par Sergius. L'une, qui déclare que le traité s'occupe des expressions simples, se rattache à la phrase d'Aristote: τῶν λεγομένων τὰ μὲν κατὰ συμπλοκὴν λέγεται, τὰ δὲ ἄνευ συμπλοκῆς,[21] qui se trouve littéralement traduite. Ni l'opinion ni son expression verbale ne soulèvent de difficulté pour Sergius et nous ne nous y arrêterons pas.

En revanche, la troisième opinion qui voit dans le but du livre le traitement des concepts simples, demande des explications préliminaires, selon Sergius. C'est alors que l'auteur introduit, dans le cours de son commentaire, un exposé sur les genres et les espèces, à propos de quoi, dit-il, les philosophes ne furent pas d'accord entre eux. Sous cet intitulé de problème «sur les genres et les espèces», c'est en fait d'une version du problème que l'on a pris l'habitude de nommer problème des universaux, d'après sa dénomination en latin médiéval, qu'il s'agit.[22] Sur ce problème, l'opinion des platoniciens est la première que Sergius présente, dans les termes suivants:

> «Ils (les platoniciens) disent, en effet, que toute chose (*ṣbūtā*) qui est naturellement (*kyānā'īt*) dans le monde a une certaine forme (*ādšā*) <qui est celle> de sa substance individuelle (*qnūmā*), et elle possède (*qānyā*) aussi une forme (*ādšā*) auprès de son créateur (*bāruyāh*), qui est pour elle la subsistance (par soi) (*qyāmā d-yātā*), par laquelle elle a été imprimée et est venue ici à la génération (*hwāyā*)».[23]

Dans cette formulation, Sergius use de plusieurs termes techniques pour rendre compte de l'opinion platonicienne. La chose, dont il s'agit, est l'*item* quelconque caractérisé par sa présence dans le monde comme «étant naturel»: le mot *kyānā'īt* («naturellement») est une traduction du grec φυσικῶς. Cet être physique est pourvu d'une forme (*ādšā*, transposition syriacisée du grec εἶδος), qui est celle de son être singulier réellement existant dans le monde matériel. Deux plans, comme on sait, sont

[21] *Cat.*, 1a16-17.

[22] La source ultime de ce problème portant «sur les genres et les espèces» est le fameux questionnement par lequel Porphyre ouvre son *Isagogè*, pour l'abandonner aussitôt: «Tout d'abord concernant les genres et les espèces, la question de savoir (1) s'ils existent [ὑφέστηκεν] ou bien s'ils ne consistent que dans de purs concepts [ψιλαῖς ἐπινοίαις], (2) ou, à supposer qu'ils existent, s'ils sont des corps ou des incorporels, et, (3) en ce dernier cas, s'ils sont séparés ou bien s'ils existent dans les sensibles et en rapport avec eux —, voilà des questions dont j'éviterai de parler... », cité d'après PORPHYRE, *Isagoge*, trad. A. DE LIBERA et A.-Ph. SEGONDS, introd. et notes par A. DE LIBERA, Paris: Vrin, 1998, p. 1.

[23] Cf. les manuscrits *L* 5rb l. 27-36, *P* 20v, *M* 66v.

distingués par les platoniciens, celui du monde des objets physiques, et celui des formes de ces objets auprès du créateur, ou démiurge.[24] La chose dans le monde matériel est pourvue d'une forme, celle de son être singulier dans le monde, que le texte nomme *qnūmā*. Cette forme est l'empreinte reçue de la forme auprès du créateur, qui est désignée comme «subsistance par soi» (*qyāmā d-yātā*); c'est par empreinte de celle-ci que la forme a été engendrée dans le monde des objets physiques, ce que Sergius note par l'emploi de *hwāyā* (génération).[25]

Un troisième état de la forme est celui qui lui advient dans la pensée (*tar'itā*, qui équivaut ici au terme grec ἐπίνοια, employé dans le même contexte par les commentateurs grecs de l'*Isagogè*[26]), où sa subsistance (*quyyāmā*) est produite à partir de la réception, dans la mémoire, des formes appréhendées dans le monde sensible. La forme existe (*neštkaš*) donc de trois manières: dans la pensée du démiurge, dans les choses, et dans la pensée de celui qui les connaît.[27]

Les exemples — tirés des commentaires grecs — donnés ensuite par Sergius, pour illustrer la théorie néoplatonicienne des trois états de l'universel qu'il vient de rappeler, sont l'occasion pour lui d'introduire d'autres termes syriaques à usage technique. Ainsi, dans l'exemple de

[24] Dans la suite du texte, Sergius emploie régulièrement le mot *'budā*, dans lequel on peut légitimement voir un équivalent du grec δημιουργός. Sur la distinction platonicienne des deux types de réalités, voir notamment *Phédon*, 78d-79a.

[25] C'est une version simplifiée de la théorie platonicienne des formes (ou idées) que présente ici Sergius. La relation entre les formes et le démiurge est plus ou moins complexe, en effet, selon les auteurs, dans les diverses phases du médio-platonisme et du néoplatonisme: voir H. DÖRRIE et M. BALTES, *Die philosophische Lehre des Platonismus. Platonische Physik (im antiken Verständnis)* (*Der Platonismus in der Antike, Grundlagen-System-Entwicklung*, 5), II, Stuttgart-Bad Cannstadt: Frommann-Holzboog, 1998, p. 262-265 et les textes mentionnés dans ces pages. L'Idée platonicienne est caractérisée, de manière semblable à celle de Sergius, comme «subsistante par soi» (ὑφεστῶσα καθ' αὑτήν) dans des textes du PSEUDO-PLUTARQUE, *De plac. philos.* 1, 10 (882 D-E) Lachenaud (= AETIUS, 1, 10, 1-5 [Dox. Gr. 308a16-309a10]), du PSEUDO-GALIEN, *Plac. Phil.* 25 (Dox. Gr. 615, 12-16) et de STOBÉE, I, 134, 9-16 W.-H. (= AETIUS, 1, 10, 1-2 [Dox. Gr. 308b17-309b7]); voir DÖRRIE-BALTES, *Die philosophische Lehre*, p. 14-16 et 233-234.

[26] Voir, par exemple, AMMONIUS, *In Porph. Isag.*, p. 39, 14-15: τῶν ὄντων τὰ μὲν ὑφέστηκε, τὰ δὲ ἐν ψιλαῖς ἐπινοίαις ὑπάρχει ... L'opposition entre ὑπόστασις et ἐπίνοια a une longue histoire: voir, par exemple, les références (à propos du nombre ou de la grandeur géométrique) à ALEXANDRE D'APHRODISE, *In Metaph.*, p. 229.31-230.1 et 230.34-231.1, et à PLOTIN, *Sur les genres de l'être*, VI, 2, 13, 26-28, mentionnés par Ch. RUTTEN, *ΥΠΑΡΧΙΣ et ΥΠΟΣΤΑΣΙΣ chez Plotin*, dans: *Hyparxis e hypostasis nel neoplatonismo* (*Lessico Intellettuale Europeo*, 64), éd. F. ROMANO et D.P. TAORMINA, Firenze: Leo S. Olschki, 1994, p. 25-32 (à la p. 26).

[27] Sergius reprend donc ici la théorie néoplatonicienne dite, dans la tradition érudite, des trois états de l'universel: voir sur ce sujet, par exemple, A. DE LIBERA, *La querelle des universaux. De Platon à la fin du Moyen Âge*, Paris: Éditions du Seuil, 1996, p. 103-108.

l'artisan imprimant dans la matière les formes qu'il a dans la pensée et qui sont ensuite saisies par d'autres êtres humains, les formes des choses sont dites exister de trois manières, cette existence étant exprimée par le mot *meštakḥān* («existantes», où la racine verbale *škaḥ* correspond au grec ὑπάρχειν).[28] Sergius ajoute que les formes subsistent les mêmes dans les trois états — dans la pensée de l'artisan, dans les choses fabriquées, et dans la mémoire de celui qui les voit —, le mot signifiant cette subsistance étant alors *mqaymān* («subsistantes», où la racine *qwm* correspond alors au grec ὑφίσταναι). On notera au passage que la subsistance dont il s'agit ici n'est évidemment pas celle la subsistance au sens aristotélicien de ce qui n'a besoin de rien d'autre que soi pour exister.

Poursuivant son exposé de la conception qu'il dit platonicienne (et qui mêle des traits médio-platoniciens et néoplatoniciens) des états de l'universel, Sergius indique que «le fabricant de ce tout a formé les concepts de manière essentielle à propos des natures constitutives des choses» (*'budā d-hānā kul etra'ī ītyā'īt 'al maknuthēn d-ṣebwātā*). Entendons par là que le fabricant de ce tout qu'est le monde, c'est-à-dire le démiurge, a formé les concepts, selon l'essence des natures constitutives des choses. Le terme technique *ītyā'īt* (peu représenté dans la littérature syriaque)[29] est sans doute un équivalent du grec οὐσιωδῶς: il faut donc comprendre, probablement, la phrase de Sergius comme voulant dire que les concepts de l'essence des choses se trouvent dans la pensée du démiurge.[30]

Ces concepts (*re'yānē*), poursuit Sergius, aussitôt après qu'ils émanent de l'Étant en soi (*ayk man d-men ītyā nbahu*), sont les hypostases (*qnūmē*), à partir desquelles sont imprimées les choses du monde d'ici-bas. Dans le contexte platonicien syncrétique, où Sergius se place, le démiurge, dont il était question plus haut, est ainsi identifié à l'Étant en soi.[31] Le mot *ītyā*

[28] Voir, par exemple, le texte d'Ammonius, cité dans la note précédente. Nous reviendrons plus loin sur la traduction syriaque de ce terme grec à propos de Jacques d'Édesse.

[29] Voir les références dans le *Thesaurus Syriacus*, éd. R. PAYNE SMITH, I, Oxford: Clarendon Press, 1879, p. 174.

[30] L'idée que les formes intelligibles se trouvent dans la pensée du démiurge (ou de Dieu) est la conception usuelle des médio-platoniciens; voir, par exemple, ALCINOOS, *Didaskalikos*, 9, H 163: Ἔστι δὲ ἡ ἰδέα ὡς μὲν πρὸς θεὸν νόησις αὐτοῦ (= ALCINOOS, *L'enseignement des doctrines de Platon* [*Collection des Universités de France*], éd. J. WHITTAKER et trad. P. LOUIS, Paris: Les Belles Lettres, 1990, p. 20). Voir aussi les commentaires et références donnés dans DÖRRIE-BALTES, *Die philosophische Lehre*, p. 240-246. Sur le statut des formes auprès du démiurge, voir aussi, par exemple (pour une époque plus tardive), les remarques de PHILOPON, *In Physicorum* III, 4, p. 402.9 *sq.* VITELLI (πρὸς ταῦτά φασιν ὅτι πάντων μέν ἐστί τις ὁμοιότης κατ' οὐσίαν ἔν τε τοῖς εἴδεσι τοῖς ἐν τῷ δημιουργῷ ...).

[31] Le platonisme, comme on sait, identifiait Dieu à l'Étant en soi.

désigne cet Étant en soi, et le mot *qnūmē* désigne lesdites hypostases, dans un emploi qui est bien évidemment différent de celui qui est le sien pour désigner les étants individuels (par opposition aux essences universelles) de l'aristotélisme.[32]

Ces concepts qui sont auprès du démiurge, ajoute encore Sergius, les platoniciens disent qu'ils sont auprès de lui «hypostatiquement» (*qnūmā'īt*) ou en hypostase.

Enfin, ces concepts auprès du démiurge sont les genres et espèces premiers des choses, tandis que ceux qui sont engendrés (*hwāyān*) dans le monde physique, plus précisément dans la matière des choses naturelles (*hūlā da-kyānē*) à partir des précédents, sont dits «genres et espèces naturels des choses».

Ayant exposé les thèses platoniciennes sur le problème du statut des genres et des espèces, Sergius passe à l'exposé de l'opinion des péripatéticiens parmi lesquels, dit-il, se trouve Alexandre.[33] Sergius rapporte que les péripatéticiens refusent d'admettre les formes auprès du démiurge et ne reconnaissent que les deux autres types de formes (selon la typologie précédemment énoncée): ils nomment «naturelles» (*kyānāyā*, qui rend le grec φυσικά) les formes qui sont dans la matière (*hūlā*), et «intelligibles» (*re'yānāyē*, qui équivaut probablement au grec νοούμενα) et «dernières» (*'ḥrāyē*, traduction du grec ὑστερογενῆ) celles qui sont dans la pensée (*tar'itā*) et dans la mémoire. On observera que la présentation de l'opinion des péripatéticiens se fait tout naturellement dans le langage des commentateurs néoplatoniciens, puisque c'est d'eux que Sergius tire la matière de son exposé. Ainsi, lorsqu'il s'agit de préciser le statut des espèces dans la physique et dans la logique, Sergius utilise le même mot de «subsistance» pour indiquer que les espèces naturelles (qu'étudie le physicien) sont les natures et subsistances (*quyāmhēn*) des choses, et que les genres et espèces «intelligibles» (et «derniers») qu'étudie le logicien ont leur subsistance seulement dans la pensée et le discours.

Les remarques précédentes sont tirées d'un texte de Sergius dont l'intention est une explication du traité des *Catégories*, et non point un exposé à visée de prime abord lexicographique, à la différence du

[32] Sur l'histoire du mot ὑπόστασις et de ses diverses significations dans la tradition philosophique antique, on peut lire l'article détaillé de H. DÖRRIE, *Ὑπόστασις. Wort- und Bedeutungsgeschichte*, dans: *Nachrichten der Akademie der Wissenschaften in Göttingen, Philologisch-Historische Klasse*, 1955, p. 35-92.

[33] Cette mention du nom d'Alexandre d'Aphrodise suggère que Sergius a probablement utilisé, dans son exposé, une source précise, que nous n'avons pas identifiée.

second texte que nous allons brièvement examiner. Il s'agit du *Manuel* de Jacques d'Édesse déjà mentionné. L'ouvrage se présente, en son début, comme une étude de l'emploi du nom de «nature» (*kyānā*), étude qui est ensuite étendue aux termes utilisés pour la définition de la nature, c'est-à-dire *ousia*[34] et «substance individuelle», et enfin aux deux mots de «personne» et d'«espèce». Étant mises de côté les questions théologiques qui sous-tendent l'entreprise de clarification lexicographique de Jacques d'Édesse, auxquelles nous ne nous arrêterons pas, l'intérêt de ce texte tient en particulier à ce qu'il est dû à un savant fort bien informé des problèmes de la langue philosophique syriaque et de son évolution, et à un bon connaisseur en même temps de la langue grecque. Deux axes principaux de recherche conduisent l'étude de Jacques: d'une part, la recherche des significations des termes grecs correspondant aux mots syriaques (et dont ces mots syriaques sont éventuellement la simple translittération) et la comparaison du grec avec le syriaque; d'autre part, la comparaison des emplois que font des termes syriaques (voire des termes grecs syriacisés) les philosophes ou les logiciens profanes (littéralement «de l'extérieur»[35]) avec les emplois que font de ces termes les Docteurs de l'Église. L'étude se conclut, pour chaque terme, par la définition, ou les définitions, proposées par Jacques.

Le premier mot étudié par Jacques, celui qui, pourrait-on dire, suscite l'entreprise, est celui de «nature» (*kyānā*), ainsi présenté dès la première phrase: «Le nom de nature se dit, dans la langue grecque, de ce qui pousse ou croît».[36] Cette description, qui rapproche implicitement le mot grec φύσις du verbe φύειν en ce qu'il s'applique tout particulièrement aux plantes (φυτά),[37] reprend de fait la première des définitions données plus loin par Jacques, elle-même tirée de la *Métaphysique* d'Aristote:

[34] Le mot *ousia* figure toujours, dans le texte de Jacques, en transcription syriaque (*ūsia*) à partir du grec, sans être traduit, et nous le rendrons donc toujours par la transcription *ousia*.

[35] En syriaque: *hānūn da-lbar*. On rapprochera cette expression de son équivalent grec, οἱ ἔξω φιλόσοφοι, formule typique des écrivains ecclésiastiques. Voir, par exemple, un usage de l'expression grecque, dans un contexte semblable à celui du traité de Jacques, dans les *Capita philosophica* de Jean Damascène: cf. *Philosophische Kapitel* (*Bibliothek der Griechischen Literatur*, 15), éd. G. RICHTER, Stuttgart: A. Hiersemann, 1982, p. 209, n. 253, où le traducteur mentionne aussi l'usage, avec le même sens, de οἱ ἔξω σοφοί.

[36] Cf. FURLANI, *L'ΕΓΧΕΙΡΙΔΙΟΝ*, p. 224. Quelques années avant d'éditer le texte de Jacques d'Édesse, G. Furlani en avait donné une traduction italienne annotée: voir G. FURLANI, *Il manualetto di Giacomo d'Edessa (Brit. Mus. Manuscr. Add. 12 154). Traduzione dal siriaco e note*, dans: *Studi e materiali di storia delle religioni* 1 (1925), p. 262-282.

[37] Le rapprochement entre φύσις et φυτά «c'est-à-dire les choses qui croissent» est explicitement fait par Jacques d'Édesse, un peu plus loin dans le texte: voir FURLANI, *L'ΕΓΧΕΙΡΙΔΙΟΝ*, p. 226, lignes 16-21, et FURLANI, *Il manualetto*, p. 266.

> La nature (*kyānā*), ou *phusis*, est la génération (*hwāyā*), ou l'engendrement (*mawlādā*) des choses qui poussent ou croissent.[38]

Selon Jacques, le mot de «nature» se dit (chez les Grecs) des choses corporelles et animées, qui possèdent la faculté de croître et d'assurer la transmission de leur genre. En revanche, il ne se dit pas des êtres incorporels et immatériels, tels que Dieu ou les anges, ni des choses corporelles mais inanimées, telles que les pierres ou les quatre éléments premiers, ou du moins le mot de nature ne se dit de tous ces êtres et choses que par métaphore et usage (*ašīlā'īt wa-ḥšaḥtānā'īt*), du fait de l'usage qu'en ont fait les auteurs grecs profanes (*barāyē*). Quant aux Docteurs de l'Église, ajoute Jacques, ils l'ont utilisé non seulement pour les choses corporelles et animées, mais également pour l'Être increé (*ītyā lā baryā*), que les chrétiens appellent Dieu. Jacques emploie ici, notons-le, le même terme que Sergius avait utilisé pour désigner l'Être en soi des néoplatoniciens, c'est-à-dire le démiurge auprès duquel sont les formes des choses. Jacques, d'autre part, rapproche étymologiquement *kyānā* de *mkan*, qui signifie «adapté à, disposé pour» et il conteste, de ce fait, l'usage abusif qui est fait de *kyānā*, par ignorance de son étymologie, pour désigner Dieu. Puis, selon la pratique qu'il suivra dans son opuscule à propos de chacun des termes étudiés, Jacques énonce une série de définitions de *kyānā* ou *phusis*.

Les six premières, comme l'a bien vu G. Furlani, sont extraites de la *Métaphysique*, au livre Δ.[39] Sans les reprendre toutes ici, signalons celles qui nous renseignent sur l'emploi du vocabulaire de l'être.

La quatrième définition, qui s'énonce: «La nature (*kyānā*) est ce à partir de quoi d'abord existe (*itawhi*) ou advient (*hāwe*) l'ordre et la bonne proportion de quelque chose, lorsque sa puissance n'est pas changée ou modifiée»,[40] permet de spécifier ici l'emploi de *itawhi* dans le

[38] FURLANI, *L'ΕΓΧΕΙΡΙΔΙΟΝ*, p. 227; cf. ARISTOTE, *Métaphysique*, Δ, 4, 1014b16-17: φύσις λέγεται ἕνα μὲν τρόπον ἡ τῶν φυομένων γένεσις.

[39] Voir G. FURLANI, *Di alcuni passi della* Metafisica *di Aristotele presso Giacomo d'Edessa*, dans: *Rendiconti della R. Accademia Nazionale dei Lincei, classe di scienze morali, storiche e filologiche*, s. V, 30 (1921), p. 268-273; résumé dans Furlani *Il manualetto*, p. 276.

[40] Cette définition est tirée de *Métaphysique*, Δ, 4, 1014b26-27: ἔτι δὲ φύσις λέγεται ἐξ οὗ πρώτου ἢ ἔστιν ἢ γίγνεταί τι τῶν φύσει ὄντων, ἀρρυθμίστου ὄντος καὶ ἀμεταβλήτου ἐκ τῆς δυνάμεως τῆς ἑαυτοῦ (où Jacques, ou bien son modèle, a lu πρῶτον au lieu de πρώτου). On notera, sans s'y arrêter (car ce n'est pas ici le propos), que la traduction est infidèle au grec. Sur les définitions par Aristote de la *phusis*, qui sont reprises par Jacques d'Édesse, voir en particulier les commentaires donnés dans: ARISTOTE, *Métaphysiques, livre* Δ, éd. M.-P. DUMINIL et A. JAULIN, Toulouse: Presses Universitaires du Mirail, 1991, p. 153-161.

sens ordinaire de «existe», par comparaison avec *hāwe* pour «advient» ou «devient», où l'on retrouve la racine du mot *hwāyā*, utilisé dans la première définition pour désigner ce qui se dit en grec γένεσις.

La cinquième définition s'énonce comme suit: «la nature (*kyānā*) est l'*ousia* («l'essence») des choses qui existent par nature *(ūsia d-hānūn d-ba-kyānā itayhūn)*».[41] Pour la première fois, dans le texte de Jacques, apparaît le mot *ousia*, qu'il conservera toujours en translittération, sans jamais lui donner un équivalent syriaque.

La sixième définition fait également appel à l'*ousia*, de la manière suivante: «la nature est ce qui premièrement et principalement est *ousia* des choses qui ont en elles-mêmes le principe du mouvement, en tant qu'elles-mêmes».[42] Ces deux dernières définitions de ce qu'est la nature, pour les êtres du monde naturel, s'expriment donc dans les termes de l'*ousia*, et l'on peut trouver la source lointaine d'une telle approche dans la fameuse question posée par Socrate à Ménon sur ce qu'est une abeille περὶ οὐσίας (*Ménon*, 72a-b). L'assimilation de la nature à l'*ousia* aura une longue postérité, dans la philosophie comme chez les Pères de l'Église.[43]

[41] Cf. ARISTOTE, *Métaphysique*, Δ, 4, 1014b35-36: ἔτι δ' ἄλλον τρόπον λέγεται ἡ φύσις ἡ τῶν φύσει ὄντων οὐσία. Furlani traduit constamment *ousia*, dans le texte de Jacques, par *sostanza*, mais nous préférons ici «essence», pour conserver le lien étymologique, affirmé par Jacques dans son opuscule, avec le verbe εἶναι.

[42] Cf. ARISTOTE, *Métaphysique*, Δ, 4, 1015a13-15: ἡ πρώτη φύσις καὶ κυρίως λεγομένη ἐστὶν ἡ οὐσία ἡ τῶν ἐχόντων ἀρχὴν κινήσεως ἐν αὑτοῖς ᾗ αὐτά. Dans le texte syriaque de Jacques d'Édesse, nous interprétons les deux derniers mots *aw hānūn*, comme une transposition syriacisante des mots grecs correspondants, s'efforçant d'en rendre le sens, et non point comme une erreur sur ces mots, de la part de Jacques qui aurait confondu la conjonction ἤ («ou») avec la forme adverbiale ᾗ («en tant que»), comme le pense FURLANI, *Di alcuni passi della* Metafisica, p. 272 (et déjà p. 270 à propos de la troisième définition de «nature»).

[43] Sur les sens d'*ousia* dans les dialogues platoniciens, voir PLATON, *Ménon*, trad. M. CANTO-SPERBER, Paris: GF-Flammarion, 1993, p. 219-220 (qui traduit l'expression περὶ οὐσίας par «dans sa réalité», alors que nous préférons garder le terme «essence», puisque Jacques relie le mot grec étymologiquement à εἶναι). Sur la naissance du fameux «problème des universaux» dans ce texte du *Ménon*, voir A. DE LIBÉRA, *La querelle des universaux*, p. 51-56. L'équivalence entre φύσις et οὐσία est déjà posée, d'une certaine manière, par Aristote: cf. *Métaphysique*, Δ, 1015a13: καὶ ἡ φύσις οὐσία τίς ἐστιν (sur ce texte, voir le commentaire de A. JAULIN, dans ARISTOTE, *Métaphysiques, livre* Δ, p. 159-160); voir aussi d'autres passages signalés dans H. BONITZ, *Index Aristotelicus*, Berlin: Academia Regia Borussica, 1870, p. 545 b. Dans le commentaire d'ÉLIAS, *In Cat.*, p. 162.6 *sq.*, BUSSE (sur l'attribution à Élias, voir R. GOULET, «Élias», *DPhA*, III, p. 57-66), l'auteur indique que le mot οὐσία se dit de six manières, et selon l'une d'elles il désigne «la nature», par opposition aux accidents: τὴν μὴ ἐν ὑποκειμένῳ φύσιν τὴν ἀντιδιαιρουμένην τοῖς συμβεβηκόσιν.

Les définitions 7 à 10, dont la source n'est pas identifiée,[44] caractérisent la nature à l'aide de la notion de puissance qui est censée appartenir aux choses naturelles. De la première définition de ce groupe, qu'il est utile ici de citer: «la nature est la puissance constituante de quelque chose» (*ḥaylā mqaymānā dīleh d-medem*), il faut retenir, du point de vue de notre enquête, le terme *mqaymānā* qui pourrait traduire un mot grec tel que συστατική (ou συμπληρωτική). De la même façon que le mot grec συστατική dérive de συνίστημι, qui est apparenté à ὑφίστημι («subsister»), le mot syriaque *mqaymānā* est de la même racine que le mot *qyāmā*, que nous avons traduit par «subsistance». Remarquons, en effet, que c'est par l'expression διαφορὰ συστατική ἐστι τῆς τοῦ ζῴου οὐσίας que Porphyre désigne les différences constitutives de l'essence de l'animal («animé» et «doté de sensation»).[45]

La huitième définition réutilise le même mot signifiant «constituant» de la manière suivante: «La nature est la puissance qui se trouve fermement en quelque chose, qui a en elle constamment la faculté constituante d'elle-même» (*ma'bdānūtā mqaymānitā d-īteh*). Cette faculté constituante est manifestement ce par quoi la chose subsiste telle qu'en elle-même, ce que marque la communauté de racine entre «constituant» (*mqaymānitā*) et «subsistant» (*quyyāmā*).

Dans les deux définitions finales de «nature», que Jacques déclare avoir ajoutées aux précédentes et dont il est donc l'auteur, la nature est définie au moyen de l'*ousia*, comme ceci:

> «La nature est l'*ousia* qui est dans la subsistance (*quyyāmā*) de quelque chose».

Cette définition, précise Jacques, convient aussi aux choses inanimées, qui n'ont pas en elles la puissance d'engendrement.

> «La nature est la subsistance par soi de quelque chose (*quyyāmā d-yāteh d-medem*)».

[44] Furlani, *Il manualetto*, p. 276, déclarait n'être pas en état d'indiquer la source de ces définitions et nos propres recherches ne nous ont pas permis non plus d'identifier leur source. Rappelons que Jacques précise avoir trouvé les dix premières définitions chez les anciens, sans plus de précision: les six premières viennent de la *Métaphysique* d'Aristote, comme on l'a dit, mais les quatre autres restent à trouver.

[45] Voir Porphyre, *Isag.*, p. 10.5-6 Busse. Les diverses sortes de «différences» sont décrites par Porphyre, *Isag.*, p. 9.7 *sq.*, Busse. Une autre expression grecque, d'origine plotinienne, pour désigner les différences constitutives est διαφοραί συμπληρωτικαί: voir, sur ce point, Porphyre, *Isagoge*, introd. A. de Libera, p. xxxii-xxxiii. Les commentateurs désignent souvent ainsi les différences constitutives de l'essence: voir Porphyre, *In Cat.*, p. 95.22-23 Busse; Ammonius, *In Porph. Isag.*, p. 92.11-12 Busse.

Par ces deux formules, Jacques met au centre de la définition de la nature la notion de subsistance, et cela de deux manières: il s'agit de la subsistance dite «par soi» d'une chose (dans la dernière définition), ce qui est une autre manière de dire (en résumant, en quelque sorte, ce que dit la définition précédente) la subsistance d'une chose telle qu'elle résulte de l'*ousia* qui est en cette chose.[46]

Du fait qu'il a utilisé les mots d'*ousia* et de «subsistance» (*quyyāmā*),[47]dans les définitions de «nature», Jacques est conduit à s'interroger sur ces dénominations. Sans le suivre dans toutes ses réflexions, disons qu'il déclare équivalents les mots *ousia* (qui dérive de «exister», pour les Grecs, dit-il dans un curieux raccourci qui mélange grec et syriaque: *ūsia men hāy d-itawhi metemar*,[48] où *hāy d-itawhi* est l'équivalent de τὸ εἶναι) et *ītūtā*; chez les Grecs, *ousia* signifie «ce qui existe» (*haw mā d-itawhi*[49]), comme *ītūtā* en syriaque. Toutefois l'usage de *ītūtā* a cédé, en syriaque, dit-il, devant celui de *ousia*. Un équivalent est aussi, dit-il encore, la forme masculine *ītyā*, qui se dit de Dieu et des autres choses subsistantes par soi.[50]

L'*ousia*, étant le genre suprême, ne peut être définie par son genre et ses différences constitutives (*šuḥlāpē mqaymonē*, expression qui est une

[46] Notons que l'expression de «subsistance par soi» (*quyyāmā d-yātā*) était utilisée par Sergius pour caractériser les formes transcendantes, qui se trouvent auprès du démiurge, dans la conception platonicienne des «genres et des espèces», aussi bien que les réalités n'ayant besoin de rien d'autre pour exister: c'est de cette seconde acception que se rapproche ici l'usage que Jacques fait de la même expression.

[47] Notons que Farabi emploie le mot *qiwām* pour signifier la subsistance, notamment au sens où la subsistance des accidents dépend entièrement de l'existence d'une substance (ou sujet), sans laquelle lesdits accidents s'évanouissent: cf. *Al-Farabi's Commentary and Short Treatise on Aristotle's* De interpretatione, trans. F.W. ZIMMERMANN, London: Oxford University Press, 1981, p. 232 et n. 2. Il est vraisemblable que Farabi, par l'emploi du mot arabe *qiwām*, imite le syriaque *quyyāmā* plutôt que le grec ὑπόστασις, comme le dit ZIMMERMANN, *Al-Farabi's Commentary*, p. cxxx, n. 2. Signalons aussi que le mot hébreu *qiyyūm*, équivalent du syriaque *quyyāmā* et de l'arabe *qiwām*, se trouve aussi, avec le même sens de «subsistance», dans un ouvrage de Shem Tob ibn Falaquera: cf. M. ZONTA, *Un dizionario filosofico ebraico del XIII secolo. L'introduzione al «Sefer De'ot ha-Filosofim» di Shem Tob ibn Falaquera* (*Quaderni di Henoch*, 4), Turin: Silvio Zamorani, 1992, p. 39, 103-104 (nous remercions Madame Juliane Lay d'avoir signalé ce texte à notre attention).

[48] L'expression syriaque veut dire, semble-t-il, que *ousia* se dit à partir de τὸ εἶναι, dont la traduction syriaque est *hāy d-itawhi*.

[49] Cette expression syriaque est aussi une traduction usuelle du grec τὸ τί ἔστι, qui est une autre manière de dire l'essence, et il est possible que Jacques ait voulu faire référence à cette équivalence entre les deux formulations de l'essence, lorsqu'il a dit que *ousia* signifie *haw mā d-itawhi*.

[50] Nous n'examinerons pas ce que Jacques dit de l'appellation de Dieu, qui n'est pas notre objet ici.

traduction du grec des commentateurs: διαφοραὶ συστατικαί ou διαφοραὶ συμπληρωτικαί[51]). Jacques va alors donner de l'*ousia* quatre «définitions descriptives» (*ṯhūmē metrašmānē*).[52] La première est inspirée du texte des *Catégories*:

> «l'*ousia* est ce qui n'est pas dit d'un sujet, et n'est pas dans un sujet, mais est le sujet».[53]

La formule «mais est le sujet», ajoutée au texte aristotélicien, transforme une détermination essentiellement négative de l'*ousia* en détermination positive, mais en laissant ouverte la question de la nature de ce sujet: à cette question Boèce répondra en nommant le sujet comme *substantia*.[54]

La deuxième, qui est proche d'un texte du commentaire de Philopon sur les *Catégories*, est celle-ci:

> «l'*ousia* est ce qui, subsistant par soi (*mqaymat l-yātā*, expression qui est manifestement une traduction du grec αὐθυπόστατος), est aussi sujet pour les choses qui ne subsistent pas par soi (*d-lā mqaymān l-yāthēn*), et subsistent par elle (*d-bā netqaymān*)».[55]

La comparaison du texte de Philopon avec celui de Jacques permet de faire correspondre les mots syriaques de la famille de *quyyāmā* avec les mots grecs de la famille de ὑφίστημι, tandis qu'à εἶναι et ὕπαρξις devraient faire pendants les mots syriaques de la racine *īt*, au sens d'exister. Quant aux deux dernières «définitions» de l'*ousia* par Jacques, elles énoncent simplement que l'*ousia* n'est pas susceptible du

[51] Voir plus haut la note relative à la septième définition de «nature».

[52] Cette expression syriaque correspond à ce que les commentateurs grecs désignaient par le mot ὑπογραφή: cf. par exemple, PORPHYRE, *Isag.*, p. 3.20 BUSSE (ἡ τοῦ γένους ῥηθεῖσα ὑπογραφή).

[53] Cf. ARISTOTE, *Catégories*, 5, 2a11-13: οὐσία δέ ἐστιν ἡ κυριώτατά τε καὶ πρώτως καὶ μάλιστα λεγομένη, ἣ μήτε καθ' ὑποκειμένου τινὸς λέγεται μήτε ἐν ὑποκειμένῳ τινί ἐστιν. Contrairement à ce que dit FURLANI, *Il manualetto*, p. 279, le texte de la définition donnée par Jacques d'Édesse n'est nullement différent du texte de la traduction syriaque des *Catégories* qui lui est attribuée (éd. GEORR), c'est-à-dire du texte du manuscrit Sachau 226 (mentionné par Furlani, et le seul alors consulté par lui) et des autres manuscrits de la même version; cf. Kh. GEORR, *Les Catégories d'Aristote dans leurs versions syro-arabes*, Beyrouth: Institut Français de Damas, 1948, p. 256.

[54] Sur ce point, voir J.-F. COURTINE, *Note complémentaire pour l'histoire du vocabulaire de l'être (Les traductions latines d'ΟΥΣΙΑ et la compréhension romano-stoïcienne de l'être)*, dans: *Concepts et catégories dans la pensée antique*, éd. P. AUBENQUE, Paris: Vrin, 1980, p. 33-87 (aux p. 40-41).

[55] Cf. PHILOPON, *In Cat.*, p. 49.19-20: καὶ ἄλλως αὐτὴ [= οὐσία] μὲν αὐθυπόστατός ἐστι καὶ οὐ δεομένη τῶν ἄλλων εἰς ὕπαρξιν, αἱ δὲ ἄλλαι ἐν ταύτῃ τὸ εἶναι ἔχουσιν.

plus et du moins, et qu'elle est susceptible de recevoir les contraires.[56] Comme le remarque Jacques, toutes ces définitions se rapportent à l'*ousia* particulière, et non point à l'*ousia* universelle, car, dit-il, tous les logiciens donnent la priorité à la dénomination des choses particulières (*sū'rānē dīlānāyē*), c'est-à-dire des «substances individuelles» (*qnūmē*), et ils appellent «*ousiai*» les *ousiai* universelles par métaphore[57] et secondairement. Les Docteurs de l'Église, au contraire, appellent principalement «*ousiai*» les *ousiai* universelles.

Parmi les définitions que Jacques propose ensuite, en son nom propre, à la différence des quatre précédentes empruntées aux logiciens ou philosophes grecs, nous retiendrons de notre point de vue, qui est principalement celui de la lexicographie, rappelons-le, la huitième (dans le décompte total des définitions du mot),[58] qui s'énonce ainsi:

> «l'*ousia* est ce qui, étant dit d'une pluralité de choses, différentes numériquement et subsistantes par soi, donne le nom et aussi le 'ce que c'est' à toutes ces choses dont il est dit».

Cette définition doit manifestement être rapprochée du texte des *Catégories*, 2a19-21, où Aristote déclare que, «de ce qui se dit d'un sujet, nécessairement tant le nom que la définition se prédiquent du sujet».[59] Dans cette traduction française, le mot «définition» rend le mot grec λόγος. La définition de Jacques peut aussi être rapprochée d'une définition de l'espèce, donnée par Porphyre dans l'*Isagogè*, dans les termes suivants: «εἶδός ἐστι τὸ κατὰ πλειόνων καὶ διαφερόντων τῷ ἀριθμῷ ἐν τῷ τί ἐστι κατηγορούμενον».[60] L'*ousia* que définit Jacques étant évidemment une *ousia* seconde (en termes aristotéliciens), il est naturel que sa définition soit semblable à une définition de l'espèce. La comparaison des textes cités montre donc que l'expression syriaque *haw mā d-itawhi* («ce que c'est») est utilisée par Jacques dans

[56] Cf. Aristote, *Catégories*, 5, 3b33-4a9 et 3b24-32 respectivement.

[57] Sur l'emploi du mot «métaphore» dans un contexte proche, cf. Aristote, *Métaphysique*, Δ, 1015a7-12: φύσις δὲ ἥ τε πρώτη ὕλη ... καὶ τὸ εἶδος καὶ ἡ οὐσία ... . μεταφορᾷ δ' ἤδη καὶ ὅλως πᾶσα οὐσία φύσις λέγεται διὰ ταύτην, ὅτι καὶ ἡ φύσις οὐσία τίς ἐστιν.

[58] Voir Furlani, *L'ΕΓΧΕΙΡΙΔΙΟΝ*, p. 233 (pour le texte syriaque) et Furlani, *Il manualetto*, p. 271 (pour la traduction italienne que nous ne reprenons pas).

[59] Trad. Ildefonse et Lallot, p. 63 (φανερὸν δὲ ἐκ τῶν εἰρημένων ὅτι τῶν καθ' ὑποκειμένου λεγομένων ἀναγκαῖον καὶ τοὔνομα καὶ τὸν λόγον κατηγορεῖσθαι τοῦ ὑποκειμένου).

[60] Porphyre, *Isag.*, p. 4.11-12 Busse: «l'espèce est ce qui est prédicable de plusieurs différant par le nombre, relativement à la question: 'Qu'est-ce que c'est?'» (trad. A. de Libera et A.-Ph. Segonds, p. 5).

un sens technique pour rendre le grec τὸ τί ἔστι, qui est lui-même un équivalent de «définition» ou d'une partie de la définition (comme le genre).

La dernière des définitions de l'*ousia*, données par Jacques en son nom propre, s'énonce ainsi:

> «l'*ousia* est le par soi de toute chose et sa substance individuelle et sa nature» (*ūsia ītēh hī yāteh d-kulḥad wa-qnūmeh wa-qyāneh*).[61]

La relation entre *ousia* et nature a déjà été instituée plus haut par Jacques d'Édesse dans les termes de la définition de la nature comme *ousia* de ce qui subsiste, de la manière suivante: «La nature est l'*ousia* qui est dans la subsistance (*quyyāmā*) de quelque chose». La dernière définition de l'*ousia*, que l'on vient de citer ci-dessus, est la réciproque en quelque manière de cette définition de nature, et elle dit que l'*ousia* est ce par quoi toute chose (son «par soi») est ce qu'elle est: le «par soi» qui figure dans cette définition semble donc n'être rien d'autre que le τὸ τί ἦν εἶναι d'Aristote, comme invite à le penser cette formule de la *Métaphysique*: «pour chaque être, le *ti ên einai*, c'est ce qu'il est dit être par soi» (ἐστὶ τὸ τί ἦν εἶναι ἑκάστῳ ὃ λέγεται καθ' αὑτό).[62]

Viennent ensuite, dans le texte de Jacques, cinq définitions (sans présentation ni commentaire) de la «substance individuelle» (*qnūmā*), dont nous retiendrons les deux dernières qui mettent en relation les termes *qnūmā*, *quyyāmā* et *yātā*, de manière remarquable, comme suit:

> «la substance individuelle (*qnūmā*) est la subsistance particulière (*quyyāmā dīlānāyā*)» d'une part, et «la substance individuelle (*qnūmā*) est un par soi (*yātā*) indivisible» d'autre part.

Ce terme de «par soi» (*yātā*) est ensuite l'objet d'une seule définition, qui s'énonce ainsi:

> «le par soi (*yātā*) est ou bien l'*ousia* embrassant plusieurs substances individuelles (*qnūmē*) ou bien une seule certaine substance individuelle (*qnūmā*)».

Jacques apporte ensuite une précision terminologique importante:[63] ce qui est nommé *qnūmā* chez les Syriaques n'est pas nommé *qnūmā* chez les Grecs, mais *quyyāmā* (terme que nous avons traduit jusqu'à présent par

[61] Cf. FURLANI, *L'ΕΓΧΕΙΡΙΔΙΟΝ*, p. 233.20-21; nous ne reprenons pas la traduction de FURLANI, *Il manualetto*, p. 271.

[62] ARISTOTE, *Métaphysique*, Z, 4, 1029b13-14. Sur la notion de *to ti ên einai*, voir l'article portant ce titre, rédigé par J.-F. COURTINE et A. RIJKSBARON, dans: *Vocabulaire européen des philosophies*, éd. B. CASSIN, Paris: Éditions du Seuil, 2004, p. 1271-1277.

[63] Nous résumons ici, en l'explicitant, l'exposé de Jacques: cf. FURLANI, *L'ΕΓΧΕΙΡΙΔΙΟΝ*, p. 234.9-235.12, et FURLANI, *Il manualetto*, p. 271-272.

«subsistance», et derrière lequel il faut voir, ici, le mot grec ὑπόστασις). Jacques dit donc que les Grecs utilisent ce qui veut dire «sub-sistance»[64] pour dire «substance individuelle». Les Grecs, précise-t-il, dérivent *quyyāmā* de *mqayyam* («sub-sistant»), au contraire de ce que font les Syriaques. En effet, dit Jacques, on ne sait pas d'où dérive le mot syriaque *qnūmā*. Quant au mot grec, il ne signifie pas purement et simplement «sub-sistance» (*quyyāmā*), mais «subsistance sous quelque chose» (*quyyāmā da-tḥēt medem*).[65] Jacques, tout en écrivant un équivalent syriaque du mot grec, pense évidemment à la forme composée ὑπό-στά-σις. De cela, Jacques infère que le mot doit désigner ce qui est toujours l'espèce inférieure, c'est-à-dire une chose particulière, et qu'il ne désigne pas un universel. Il précise encore ses remarques en ajoutant que le mot *quyyāmā* — entendons ὑπόστασις — signifie (pour les Grecs) «un certain individu qui subsiste par soi» (*lā metpasqānā medem da-mqayyam l-yātā*), c'est-à-dire «une certaine *ousia* particulière» (*ūsia medem dīlā-nāytā*) et «une certaine nature particulière» (*kyānā medem dīlānāyā*).

À propos du mot *yātā*, auquel il s'intéresse ensuite,[66] Jacques entend corriger une erreur trouvée dans certains écrits (non précisés), provenant du grec, selon laquelle *ousia* est dit de «est» (*itawhi*, par quoi il faut entendre le grec ἔστιν) et *yātā* de «se trouve» (*škiḥ*, par quoi il faut entendre le grec ὑπάρχων). Selon Jacques, il est inexact que ce mot *yātā* se dise de *škiḥ*, pas plus chez les Grecs que chez les Syriaques, mais chez les uns et les autres *yātā* est dit, tout comme *ousia*, de «est». L'auteur laisse entendre aussi que les traducteurs du grec en syriaque sont à l'origine de l'emploi de deux mots en syriaque. Devant rendre dans cette langue les deux mots grecs utilisés pour signifier l'être, ils ont employé *itawhi* pour l'un et *škiḥ* pour l'autre, qui sont respectivement en grec l'un εἶναι (transcrit par Jacques sous la forme *'yn'*) et l'autre ὑπάρχειν (transcrit sous la forme *hūp'rkyn*), le premier venant du nom *ousia*, le second du nom *huparxis* (translittéré par Jacques sous la forme *hūp'rksīs*). Les traducteurs laissèrent alors le nom *ousia* tel qu'il est en grec (c'est-à-dire en le transcrivant seulement) et ils l'utilisèrent en syriaque (comme le font les Grecs), mais le

[64] Nous marquerons l'emploi particulier du mot syriaque *quyyāmā* par Jacques, comme traduction du mot ὑπόστασις, dans le présent contexte étymologique, en l'écrivant sous une forme qui signale sa composition étymologique en grec, à savoir «sub-sistance».

[65] Nous avons conservé la traduction de *quyyāmā* par «subsistance», par souci de cohérence, mais il faut ici prendre *quyyāmā* comme le simple substitut syriaque de ὑπόστασις.

[66] Nous résumons à nouveau, en l'explicitant, l'exposé de Jacques: cf. FURLANI, *L'ΕΓΧΕΙΡΙΔΙΟΝ*, p. 235.13-237.19, et FURLANI, *Il manualetto*, p. 272-273.

nom d'*huparxis*, tout en sachant qu'il est dit de ce qui est, ils le traduisirent par *yātā*. Quant aux docteurs de l'Église, dit Jacques, ils utilisent *yātā* parfois avec le sens de «*ousia* universelle» *(ūsia gawānāytā)*, parfois pour désigner des choses particulières (*sū'rānē dilānāyē*), c'est-à-dire un individu, autrement dit une «substance individuelle» (*qnūmā*). Voulant mettre les choses au clair, au terme de son examen du mot *yātā*, Jacques reprend sa propre définition, qu'il avait donnée d'entrée de jeu, à savoir: «le par soi (*yātā*) est ou bien l'*ousia* universelle qui comprend plusieurs substances singulières (*qnūmē*) ou bien une certaine substance individuelle». Il complète ensuite cette définition par une autre, dans laquelle il a simplement remplacé *ousia* par «nature», à savoir: «le par soi (*yātā*) est une certaine nature particulière (*kyānā medem dilānāyā*) ou bien une nature universelle (*kyānā gawānāyā*) comprenant plusieurs natures». Cette transformation est légitime, du fait que Jacques a mis en évidence plus haut l'équivalence, pour lui (et largement acceptée), entre «nature» et *ousia*.

Les deux derniers mots examinés par Jacques sont *parṣūpā* (transposition du grec πρόσωπον) et *ādšā* (transposition du grec εἶδος), à propos desquels Jacques procède comme dans les cas précédents, en examinant l'étymologie et les usages. Pour en venir directement au résultat, disons qu'il indique que le mot *parṣūpā* («personne») se dit d'une «certaine chose particulière qui subsiste par soi» (*sū'rānā medem dilānāyā damqayyam l-yāteh*), c'est-à-dire d'une «substance individuelle» (*qnūmā*), ou bien d'une certaine représentation formée à partir de l'agrément de plusieurs personnes. Au premier sens, *parṣūpā* est donc strictement équivalent à *qnūmā* («substance individuelle»), tandis qu'au second sens plusieurs substances singulières sont comprises dans une «personne».

Quant à l'espèce, déclare Jacques, elle est dite chez les profanes (*hānūn da-lbar*) de ce qui comprend les «substances singulières» (*qnūmē*) et divise le genre, mais non pas des substances singulières elles-mêmes. La définition de l'espèce par les profanes, citée alors par Jacques, reprend exactement la définition de Porphyre, telle qu'on la trouve dans la traduction syriaque d'Athanase:

> «l'espèce est ce qui est prédiqué de plusieurs choses, qui diffèrent par le nombre, dans le 'qu'est-ce que c'est' (*b-hāy d-mānā medem itawhi*, expression qui est la traduction du grec ἐν τῷ τί ἐστι)».[67]

[67] On a vu plus haut que l'expression syriaque utilisée par Jacques d'Édesse dans un sens technique pour rendre le grec τὸ τί ἔστι était *haw mā d-itawhi*; cette expression est moins adéquate que celle utilisée par Athanase, qui rend plus exactement l'interrogatif grec τί, à l'aide de l'interrogatif syriaque *mānā*, inclus dans sa formule (au lieu du démonstratif *mā* dans celle de Jacques).

Quant aux Docteurs de l'Église, dit Jacques, ils donnent le nom d'espèce aussi à une certaine chose particulière, c'est-à-dire une «substance individuelle» (*qnūmā*).

*

* *

Dans cet opuscule remarquable qu'est l'*Encheiridion*, Jacques d'Édesse procède donc à un examen critique du vocabulaire syriaque de l'être. La visée de cette entreprise n'est pas explicitement dite dans le traité, mais elle est évidemment à relier aux disputes théologiques des siècles précédents et aux options diverses prises par les différentes communautés religieuses de langue syriaque. Le premier résultat de l'examen est de montrer la diversité des sens pris par les mots étudiés au cours de l'histoire et selon l'origine des utilisateurs. Un autre résultat est de suggérer que l'analyse linguistique peut conduire à dissiper certaines oppositions entre des thèses qui se fonderaient sur des acceptions différentes des mots employés par les tenants de ces thèses.

Les moyens de l'analyse sont de deux sortes. Les uns sont tirés de l'étymologie, en grec ou en syriaque, des mots étudiés. Ce qui permet de rapprocher certains termes entre eux ou d'en trouver le sens précis: ainsi Jacques déclare que l'on ignore l'étymologie de *qnūmā* («substance individuelle»), et il distingue ce mot de *quyyāmā* («subsistance») dont l'étymologie est bien connue. Un autre moyen d'analyse utilisé par Jacques est celui de l'usage des mots. Sur ce point, tout le traité marque une nette opposition entre l'usage général des Docteurs de l'Église et l'usage de ceux que Jacques qualifie de «profanes». Ces derniers sont, en réalité, comme Jacques le dit parfois et comme cela ressort de ses analyses, les «logiciens», ou plus généralement les philosophes grecs. Et le point à noter est qu'il donne lui-même la préférence à l'usage des logiciens, comme le montrent les définitions qu'il énonce en son nom propre pour les mots étudiés, — définitions qui reprennent largement celles desdits logiciens. Par là, Jacques témoigne implicitement de l'utilité, voire de la nécessité, de recourir à la logique grecque dans l'analyse des notions en usage dans la théologie.

Nous avons limité notre propos, ainsi que nous l'avions spécifié, à une étude lexicographique des mots employés par Sergius et par Jacques d'Édesse pour traduire des termes grecs techniques ou désigner des notions philosophiques d'origine grecque, platonicienne ou aristotélicienne. Il nous paraissait nécessaire, en effet, dans un premier temps, d'essayer de serrer au plus près l'usage que font les philosophes syriaques du vocabulaire qu'ils ont eux-mêmes institué ou repris de leurs devanciers, tels les Pères de l'Église notamment. Il faudrait évidemment poursuivre ensuite l'étude au-delà des aspects lexicographiques, auxquels nous nous sommes attaché. Nous nous bornerons seulement ici à évoquer quelques parallèles qu'il serait intéressant de mener avec d'autres œuvres, appartenant au même champ de recherche que celui de Jacques d'Édesse, auxquelles nous avons déjà fait allusion. Nous avons mentionné plus haut, en effet, l'œuvre de Jean Damascène, auteur de peu postérieur à Jacques d'Édesse, dont l'entreprise lexicographique menée dans les *Capita philosophica* présente bien des points communs avec celle de Jacques. On y trouve, en particulier, l'analyse comparative de notions telles que φύσις, οὐσία, μορφή, πρόσοπον, εἶδος. Et même si les positions théologiques de Jean, auteur 'chalcédonien', sont différentes de celles de Jacques, théologien monophysite et traducteur de Sévère d'Antioche, les rapprochements entre les deux auteurs, du point de vue de leur analyse du langage philosophique seraient suggestifs. L'attention portée par Jean aux questions de langage ne se rencontre d'ailleurs pas seulement dans les *Capita Philosophica*, mais dans tous ses ouvrages, et l'on peut tirer du *De fide contra Nestorianos*, pour ne prendre qu'un exemple, la remarque suivante, tout à fait comparable à celles que Jacques fait de son côté:

> «Ὥσπερ οὐσία καὶ φύσις ταυτόν ἐστι παρὰ τοῖς ἁγίοις πατράσιν, οὕτω καὶ ὑπόστασις καὶ πρόσωπον ταυτόν ἐστι».[68]

Naturellement, les Pères n'avaient pas attendu le VIe ou le VIIe siècle pour s'intéresser au vocabulaire des notions dont nous venons de parler, mais ce sont ici les démarches mêmes de Jacques et de Jean, que nous rapprochons, et leur commun souci de se reporter aux philosophes «de l'extérieur», particulièrement à la tradition des logiciens, que nous voulons ici souligner. Il se trouve d'ailleurs que, dans l'un des ouvrages de Jean Damascène, le *Liber de haeresibus*, nous sont conservés deux extraits d'un traité de Jean Philopon, le Διαιτητής, dans lesquels le philosophe néoplatonicien, qui fut aussi théologien monophysite, examine les notions de φύσις et de ὑπόστασις.[69] Dans le second de ces extraits,

[68] Cf. *De fide contra Nestorianos*, section 52, dans: *Die Schriften des Johannes von Damaskos, IV: Liber de haeresibus. Opera polemica* (*Patristische Texte und Studien*, 22), éd. B. KOTTER, Berlin - New York: W. de Gruyter, 1981, p. 252.

[69] Cf. *Die Schriften des Johannes von Damaskos, IV: Liber de haeresibus*, p. 50-55. Les extraits du traité de Philopon, conservés dans l'ouvrage de Jean Damascène, sont très probablement des additions ultérieures incluses dans les manuscrits du *De haeresibus*: voir U.M. LANG, *John Philoponus and the Controversies over Chalcedon in the Sixth Century, A Study and Translation of the Arbiter* (*Spicilegium Sacrum Lovaniense, Études et documents*, 47), Leuven: Peeters, 2001, p. 21.

Philopon estime nécessaire, avant de réfuter les thèses nestoriennes, de rappeler les définitions de «nature» et d'«hypostase», ce qu'il fait de la manière suivante:

> «[L'Église] considère donc que la nature est la définition commune de l'être des choses qui participent à la même essence: par exemple, celle de tout homme, c'est animal rationnel mortel possédant intelligence et science ... L'essence et la nature reviennent au même. Quant à l'hypostase, c'est-à-dire la personne, c'est l'existence autoconstitutive de la nature de chaque être.... Ce qu'il plaît aux Péripatéticiens d'appeler individus... les Pères de l'Église l'ont appelé hypostases ou parfois personnes».[70]

De fait, comme on le voit sur cet exemple, la démarche de Philopon, dans son traité, est également semblable à celles de Jacques d'Édesse et de Jean Damascène. Comme eux (et avant eux), Philopon a recours aux ressources de la logique, dont il a appris et commenté les éléments à l'école d'Ammonius, pour élucider le vocabulaire en usage dans les discussions théologiques, ainsi que l'écrit H. Chadwick:

> In the *Arbiter*, Philoponus offers his services as a trained logician who thinks it may tidy up the ecclesiastical garden if the confusing terminology of the Christological debate is analysed and sorted out. His posture is somewhat akin to that of the role assigned to the dialectician in Syrianus' commentary on the *Metaphysics*: 'The philosopher aims at the salvation of his hearers, the sophist at their bamboozlement. The logician is a tester of what you are saying, not someone laying done truth for you to accept'.[71]

On pourrait ainsi multiplier les rapprochements de textes parallèles, entre les auteurs cités, mais en prenant garde que des formules semblables recouvrent éventuellement des positions doctrinales fort différentes.[72] Pour nous en tenir au point de vue qui fut le nôtre, dans les

[70] Éd. Kotter, p. 51: φύσιν μὲν οὖν οἴεται τὸν κοινὸν τοῦ εἶναι λόγον τῶν τῆς αὐτῆς μετεχόντων οὐσίας, ὡς ἀνθρώπου παντὸς τὸ ζῷον λογικὸν θνητὸν νοῦ καὶ ἐπιστήμης δεκτικόν ... Οὐσίαν δὲ καὶ φύσιν εἰς ταυτὸν ἄγει. Ὑπόστασιν δὲ ἤγουν πρόσωπον τὴν ἰδιοσύστατον τῆς ἑκάστου φύσεως ὕπαρξιν ... ἅπερ ἄτομα προσαγορεύειν τοῖς ἐκ τοῦ Περιπάτου φίλον ... ταῦτα οἱ τῆς ἐκκλησίας διδάσκαλοι ὑποστάσεις, ἔσθ' ὅτε καὶ πρόσωπα προσηγόρευσαν. Les remarques de Philopon sont clairement comparables à celles de Jean Damascène, que nous venons de citer en grec (cf. note 68).

[71] Voir, H. CHADWICK, *Philoponus the Christian Theologian*, dans: *Philoponus and the Rejection of Aristotelian Science*, éd. R. SORABJI, London: Duckworth, 1987, p. 41-56 (à la p. 42) et cf. SYRIANUS, *In Metaph.*, p. 63.21 *sq.*, KROLL.

[72] S'agissant de Philopon, ses traités théologiques ne sont pas les seuls ouvrages à comparer avec le traité de Jacques, mais il faudrait aussi explorer plus systématiquement ses commentaires sur Aristote que nous ne l'avons fait. Mentionnons, par exemple, cette formule du commentaire *In Cat.*, p. 46.15-16: «ἡ γὰρ οὐσία αὐθυπόστατόν τί ἐστι», que l'on pourrait rapprocher de la dernière définition de l'*ousia* donnée par Jacques d'Édesse en son nom propre. Sur le vocabulaire philosophique de Philopon et son emploi

remarques précédentes — l'attention à une démarche lexicographique qui se veut rigoureuse, comme support des réflexions théologiques — il est impossible de ne pas mentionner encore, comme nous l'avons suggéré en commençant, la comparaison qui pourrait s'effectuer entre Jacques d'Édesse et Boèce.

Dans une page fameuse de son traité *Contra Eutychen et Nestorium*, aussitôt après avoir défini la personne comme «substance individuelle de nature rationnelle» (*naturae rationabilis individua substantia*), Boèce entreprend de comparer le vocabulaire latin des mots désignant les notions essentielles de la théologie avec le vocabulaire grec correspondant.[73] Il note, en particulier, que les Grecs appellent ὑπόστασις ou encore πρόσωπον ce que les Latins nomment *persona*, — faisant ainsi la même remarque que Philopon, Jacques d'Édesse ou Jean Damascène, comme on l'a vu plus haut.[74] Mais il observe aussi que les Grecs préfèrent appeler par le nom de ὑπόστασις la «subsistance individuelle» (*individuam subsistentiam*) de nature rationnelle ou, selon une autre formule, les «subsistances qui sont selon le mode du particulier» (*subsistentias particulariter substantes*).[75] On rejoint donc ici l'observation faite, de son côté, par Jacques d'Édesse — comme nous l'avons vu plus haut — que les Grecs utilisent le mot ὑπόστασις, auquel lui-même fait correspondre «subsistance» en syriaque (*quyyāmā*), pour dire «substance individuelle». Il y a, en effet, deux manières de considérer les mêmes réalités individuelles, ainsi que Boèce l'explique un peu plus loin: selon qu'elles n'ont pas besoin d'autres choses qu'elles-mêmes

dans ses ouvrages théologiques, lire Th. HERMANN, *Johannes Philoponus als Monophysit*, dans: *Zeitschrift für die Neutestamentliche Wissenschaft und die Kunde der älteren Kirche* 29 (1930), p. 209-264. Plus largement, sur la position de Philopon dans les débats théologiques, on se reportera désormais à l'ouvrage essentiel de U.M. LANG, *John Philoponus and the Controversies over Chalcedon*.

73 Voir BOÈCE, *Traités théologiques*, trad. A. TISSERAND, p. 74-83.

74 C'était, en effet, une remarque banale d'observer qu'il était courant, chez les écrivains ecclésiastiques, d'utiliser ὑπόστασις pour désigner ce que les philosophes nommaient du mot de «personne», comme le dit Boèce, ou de divers autres mots signifiant «substance individuelle», tels que *qnūmā* dans le syriaque de Jacques d'Édesse ou encore ἄτομος οὐσία dans le grec de LÉON DE BYZANCE, *De sectis* I, PG LXXXVI, 1093 A, cité d'après C. MICAELLI, *Natura e persona*, dans: *Atti del congresso internazionale di studi boeziani*, éd. L. OBERTELLO, Roma: Herder, 1981, p. 331. Sur l'emploi du mot ὑπόστασις chez les écrivains ecclésiastiques, lire, par exemple, JEAN PÉPIN, *ΥΠΑΡΞΙΣ et ΥΠΟΣΤΑΣΙΣ en Cappadoce*, dans: *Hyparxis e hypostasis nel neoplatonismo*, éd. ROMANO et TAORMINA, p. 59-78.

75 Nous reproduisons la traduction donnée par TISSERAND, dans BOÈCE, *Traités théologiques*, p. 79, mais on pourrait préciser en disant: «les subsistances qui sont substrat à titre particulier».

pour être, et elles sont alors dites subsistances particulières; ou selon qu'elles sont substrats pour des accidents, et elles sont alors dites substances (étant bien compris que sont désignées par ces appellations distinctes les mêmes *ousiai* premières).[76] Boèce précise encore, de la façon suivante, la correspondance entre grec et latin: *Nam quod Graeci* οὐσίωσιν *uel* οὐσιῶσθαι *dicunt, id nos subsistentiam uel subsistere appellamus. Quod uero illi* ὑπόστασιν *uel* ὑφίστασθαι, *id nos substantiam uel substare interpretamur*. Ce système de correspondance est homologue à celui que Jacques établit de son côté entre grec et syriaque, avec cette différence, toutefois, que Jacques ne mentionne pas le terme grec qui correspond à ce qu'il nomme *quyyāmā* («subsistance»). Il est peu probable pourtant qu'il n'ait pas connu le mot grec οὐσίωσις, qui était alors usuel dans le vocabulaire des Pères de l'Église.

Les remarques qui précèdent ne donnent sans doute qu'un aperçu fort incomplet du vocabulaire de l'être chez les auteurs syriaques, plus précisément chez les auteurs qui se réclament de la philosophie profane, c'est-à-dire grecque. Mais nous espérons cependant avoir contribué à éclairer l'emploi de certains mots syriaques, en nous attachant à des comparaisons aussi rigoureuses que possible entre les sources grecques et les textes syriaques que nous avons pris pour objet d'étude.

[76] Voir la traduction de TISSERAND, p. 79. Lire aussi, par exemple, ce qu'écrit Thomas d'Aquin sur ce point (*Summa theol.*, I, qu. 29, respondeo), où l'on retrouve l'équivalence terminologique entre «hypostase» et «substance individuelle»: «Selon en effet que [la substance] existe par soi et non dans un autre, elle est appelée subsistance: en effet nous disons que subsiste ce qui existe non dans un autre, mais en soi.... Mais selon ce qui est posé-sous des accidents, on l'appelle hypostase ou sub-stance... », cité dans la traduction de TISSERAND, dans BOÈCE, *Traités théologiques*, p. 203, n. 37. Lire aussi les pages consacrées à l'étude que Boèce fait des mots *essentia*, *subsistentia* et *substantia* dans le *Contra Eutychen et Nestorium*, par A. DE LIBERA, *L'Art des généralités. Théories de l'abstraction*, Paris: Aubier, 1999, p. 177-187.

THE ARABIC VERSION OF *ENN.* IV 7[2] AND ITS GREEK MODEL[1]

CRISTINA D'ANCONA
University of Pisa

One of the most incontrovertible, major achievements of the past century in the field of Greek philology is the edition of the *Enneads* by Paul Henry and Hans-Rudolf Schwyzer. Four books by Paul Henry prepared the way for their edition, all devoted to the transmission of the Plotinian writings: *Plotin et l'Occident*, on the knowledge of Plotinus's treatises in the Latin speaking world between the Fourth and Fifth Centuries;[2] *Recherches sur la Préparation Évangélique d'Eusèbe*, on their pre-Porphyrian circulation;[3] *Études Plotiniennes I*[4] and *Études Plotiniennes II*,[5] devoted respectively to the ancient *états* of the Plotinian writings[6] and to their medieval forms, i.e., to the analysis of the direct tradition.[7] This Herculean labour enabled Paul Henry and Hans-Rudolph Schwyzer to put at the disposal of the scholarly community the critical edition of one of the masterpieces of ancient philosophical literature.

[1] My warmest thanks are due to James Montgomery for his careful reading of this paper and for his invaluable help with the English. Marie-Odile Goulet-Cazé and Richard Goulet were so kind as to read a preliminary version: I would like to thank them very much for their remarks. I am solely responsible for its weaknesses.

[2] PAUL HENRY, *Plotin et l'Occident. Firmicus Maternus, Marius Victorinus, saint Augustin et Macrobe* (*Spicilegium Sacrum Lovaniense*, 15), Leuven, 1934.

[3] PAUL HENRY, *Recherches sur la Préparation Évangélique d'Eusèbe et l'édition perdue des œuvres de Plotin publiée par Eustochius* (*Bibliothèque de l'École des Hautes Études, Section des Sciences Religieuses*, 50), Paris, 1935.

[4] PAUL HENRY, *Études Plotiniennes. I. Les états du texte de Plotin* (*Museum Lessianum, Section Philosophique*, 20), Paris - Brussels, 1938.

[5] PAUL HENRY, *Études Plotiniennes. II. Les manuscrits des Ennéades* (*Museum Lessianum, Section Philosophique*, 21), Paris - Brussels, 1941.

[6] Henry's idea of a textual *état* runs as follows: 'Le terme, encore neuf en critique textuelle, a l'avantage d'être indépendent d'un vocabulaire parfois néfaste et presque périmé. Il ignore les "codices deteriores", les "fautes de copistes", les "bons" et les "mauvais" archétypes. ... C'est un terme flottant. Un seul exemplaire, archétype ou sous-archétype perdu, manuscrit-source ou apographe, peut avoir été successivement ou être simultanément porteur de plusieurs "états". Un seul et même "état" peut avoir été multiplié en plusieurs exemplaires médiévaux, ou être tout à la fois attesté par un papyrus du IVe siècle et reproduit par une édition du XXe': HENRY, *Les états du texte de Plotin*, p. xix-xx.

[7] As in most cases with ancient authors, the direct tradition of Plotinus's writings is provided by medieval manuscripts and their derivatives: see Section I.

Among the pieces of evidence of the indirect tradition of the Plotinian writings, Henry and Schwyzer took into account the Arabic version, the most substantial portion of which is known as *Theology of Aristotle*, during precisely those decades when it appears that the Arabic version of Plotinus generated a constellation of related texts.[8] Thanks to the cooperation of Geoffrey Lewis, Henry and Schwyzer were also able to include in the so-called *editio maior*[9] the English translation, facing the Greek, of all the Arabic texts stemming from Plotinus. In the process this collection of texts acquired the name *Plotiniana Arabica*, under which title it is presently known.[10]

Not only does the Arabic version of Plotinus share the features of every other item of the indirect tradition, it also emphasizes them: the indirect tradition reproduces Plotinus's thought and wording within the framework of an *ad hoc* quotation; the Arabic version, in turn, is a translation into another language and an adaptation to another, often radically different cultural and theological context. Under such circumstances, the

[8] P. KRAUS, *Plotin chez les Arabes. Remarques sur un nouveau fragment de la paraphrase arabe des Ennéades*, in: *Bulletin de l'Institut d'Egypte* 23 (1940-41), p. 263-295 (repr. in *Alchemie, Ketzerei, Apokryphen im frühen Islam. Gesammelte Aufsätze*, ed. RÉMI BRAGUE, Hildesheim - Zürich - New York 1994, p. 313-345). Kraus discovered in a Cairo manuscript, misattributed to al-Fārābī, an *Epistle on the Divine Science* which proved to trace back to Plotinus's treatises V 3[49], V 4[7] and V 9[5]. F. ROSENTHAL, in *Aš-Šayḫ al-Yūnānī and the Arabic Plotinus Source*, in: *Orientalia* 21 (1952), p. 461-492; 22 (1953), p. 370-400; 24 (1955), p. 42-65 (repr. in *Greek Philosophy in the Arab World. A Collection of Essays* (*Variorum Collected Studies Series*, 322), Aldershot, 1990) compared the *Epistle on the Divine Science* and the pseudo-*Theology of Aristotle* with the 'sayings' ascribed to the 'Greek Sage' in a series of doxographical reports related to the *Ṣiwān al-Ḥikma* tradition: the MS Oxford, Bodleian Library, Marsh 539, the *Muntakhab Ṣiwān al-Ḥikma* attributed to Abū Sulaymān al-Manṭiqī al-Sijistānī (editions: ABŪ SULAYMĀN AL-SIJISTĀNĪ, *Muntakhab Siwān al-Ḥikma et trois traités*, ed. ʿA. BADAWĪ, Tehran, 1974; D. M. DUNLOP, *The Muntakhab Ṣiwān al-Ḥikmah of Abū Sulaimān as-Sijistānī*, The Hague - Paris - New York, 1979) and the *Kitāb al-Milal wa-l-Niḥal* by AL-SHAHRASTĀNĪ (edition and translations: *Book of Religions and Philosophical Sects by Muhammad al-Shahrastani*, ed. WILLIAM CURETON, London, 1842-1846; Th. HAARBRUCKER, *Abu -'l Fath' Muh'ammad asch-Schahrastâni's Religionspartheien und Philosophen-Schulen*, Halle 1850-1851 (repr. Hildesheim, 1969); *Livre des religions et des sectes*, trans. D. GIMARET and G. MONNOT, I, Leuven, s.d. (1984); trans. J. JOLIVET and G. MONNOT, II, Leuven, s.d. (1993)).

[9] The so-called *editio maior* contains the full critical apparatus: PLOTINUS, *Opera*, ed. P. HENRY and H.-R. SCHWYZER, I (*Porphyrii Vita Plotini*; *Enneades* I-III), Paris, 1951; II (*Enneades* IV-V; *Plotiniana Arabica* ad fidem codicum anglice vertit GEOFFREY LEWIS), Paris - Brussels, 1959; III (*Enneas* VI), Paris - Leiden, 1973); the so-called *editio minor* was published with a reduced apparatus and, more importantly, with some revised readings in the text: PLOTINUS, *Opera*, ed. P. HENRY and H.-R. SCHWYZER, I (*Porphyrii Vita Plotini*; *Enneades* I-III), Oxford, 1964; II (*Enneades* IV-V), Oxford, 1977; III (*Enneas* VI), Oxford, 1982. The last volume of the *editio maior* appeared in print later than the first volume of the *editio minor*.

[10] PLOTINUS, *Opera*, II (1959).

task of determining the value of this *sui generis* kind of indirect tradition is by no means easy and verges on the desperate, if one takes into account the fact that the Arabic is not critically edited. In what follows I would like to try to contribute to this field of research by discussing an example from the Arabic version of *Ennead* IV 7[2], *On the Immortality of the Soul*. The reason for singling out this treatise lies, as we shall see in Sections I and II, in the fact that it contains a substantial portion of text which is lost in the direct tradition but preserved in the indirect one, both Greek (Eusebius) and Arabic (pseudo-*Theology of Aristotle*).

I shall first sum up the main data about the direct and indirect tradition of the *Enneads* (Section I). Then I shall outline the peculiarities of the Arabic indirect tradition against this background (Section II). Finally, in Section III, an example from the Arabic version of IV 7[2] will be discussed.

SECTION I

The extant Greek manuscripts of the *Enneads* are 57 in number: nine in Paris;[11] nine in the Vatican Library;[12] six in the library of El Escorial;[13] six in Vienna;[14] five in Venice;[15] four in Milan;[16] four in Munich;[17] four in Oxford;[18] two in Florence;[19] two in Madrid;[20] one in Berlin;[21] one in Cambridge;[22] one in Darmstadt;[23] one in Leiden;[24] one in Turin;[25] and

[11] References are given to the pages of HENRY, *Les manuscrits des Ennéades*, where the MSS are described. Paris MSS: p. 3-15; 45-62; 91-96; 97-101; 105-108; 135-148; 176-178; 179-183; 319.

[12] Vatican Library MSS: p. 44, 124-128; 156-162; 163-168; 196-198; 225-226; 250-251; 296-300; 318.

[13] El Escorial MSS: p. 114; 155; 184-185; 240-243; 246-247; 278-279.

[14] Wien MSS: p. 134; 227-239 (on this important MS see also H.-R. SCHWYZER, *Der Plotin-Codex Vindoboniensis Phil. Graec. 226*, in: *Rheinisches Museum für Philologie* 86 (1937), p. 270-285); 248-249; 264-271; 280-284; 285-286.

[15] Venice MSS: p. 63-72; 151-154; 214-224; 254-263; 290-293.

[16] Milan MSS: p. 37-43; 102-104; 287-289; 301-307.

[17] Munich MSS: p. 75-90; 109-110; 192-195; 205-213.

[18] Oxford MSS: p. 129-133; 203-204; 275-277; 308-317.

[19] Florence MSS: p. 16-36 (on this important MS see also H.-R. SCHWYZER, *Der Plotin-Codex Laurentianus 87, 3*, in: *Rheinisches Museum für Philologie* 86 (1937), p. 358-384) and 117-123.

[20] Madrid MSS: p. 111-113; 199-202.

[21] Berlin MS: p. 186-191.

[22] Cambridge MS: p. 272-274.

[23] Darmstadt MS: p. 73-75 (see also p. 75-90).

[24] Leiden MS: p. 244-255.

[25] Turin MS: p. 169-173.

one in Zeitz (Saxonia).[26] The oldest manuscript which has come down to us is Venice, Bibl. Marciana, *Gr.* 209, dating back to the Twelfth Century and containing only treatises IV 7, I 1 and IV 2.[27] Only two manuscripts date back to the Thirteenth Century: Paris, Bibl. Nationale, *Gr.* 1976[28] and Florence, Bibl. Medicea Laurenziana 87, 3.[29] Most manuscripts belong to the Fifteenth Century though some are younger. The archetype of the entire Plotinian tradition, namely, the 'premier ancêtre commun de tous les manuscrits du moyen-âge et de la Renaissance' traces back to a period between the Ninth Century at the earliest and the Twelfth at the latest.[30] From this ancestor — which may also have belonged in the famous *collection philosophique*[31] — four *états médiévaux du texte* arose, which represent as many 'forms' which the text acquired and whose testimonies are the groups or families in which the extant manuscripts fall.[32]

26 Zeitz MS: p. 174-175.

27 This MS, which in the Fourteenth Century came into the possession of Bessarion, also contains Aristotle's *De anima*, *De motu animalium*, *De sensu et sensibilibus*, *De memoria et reminiscentia*, *De somno et vigilia et divinatione per somnum*: see HENRY, *Les manuscrits des Ennéades*, p. 150-154.

28 See above, note 11.

29 On this important MS see SCHWYZER, *Der Plotin-Codex Laurentianus 87, 3*.

30 HENRY, *Les états du texte de Plotin*, p. 30: 'L'accord des divers groupes de manuscrits permet de reconstituer avec certitude l'état de l'archétype: c'est-à-dire, en remontant la tradition, du premier ancêtre commun de tous les manuscrits du moyen-âge et de la Renaissance. L'archétype des *Ennéades* date au plus tôt du IXe siècle, au plus tard du XIIe. Tout comme il y a présomption que le texte des *Ennéades*, publié par Porphyre, est celui de Plotin, il y a présomption que le texte de l'archétype est celui des *Ennéades*, l' "original" vrai de la tradition manuscrite'. Henry, also suspected the existence of a 'double tradition directe', on the grounds of the variant readings in Treatise 21 (according to the chronological series), which bears other peculiar features relating to its place in Porphyry's edition (p. 36-40). The details are complicated and lie beyond the scope of this paper, but it is worth mentioning that Henry's idea of a 'double tradition directe' was connected with the hypothesis of the 'récension d'Eustochius': see p. 16.

31 On the *collection philosophique* see L.G. WESTERINK, *Damascius. Traité des premiers principes*, I, Paris, 1986, p. lxxiii-lxxx; L.G. WESTERINK, *Das Rätsel des untergründigen Neuplatonismus*, in: *ΦΙΛΟΦΡΟΝΗΜΑ. Festschrift für Martin Sicherl zum 75. Geburtstag: von Textkritik bis Humanismusforschung*, ed. D. HARLFINGER, Padeborn, 1990, p. 105-123; H.-D. SAFFREY, *Nouvelles observations sur le manuscrit Parisinus graecus 1807*, in: *Studies in Plato and the Platonic tradition. Essays presented to John Whittaker*, ed. M. JOYAL, Aldershot - Brookfield, 1997, p. 293-306 (repr. in *Le Néoplatonisme après Plotin*, II, Paris, 2000, p. 255-266); M. RASHED, *Nicolas d'Otrante, Guillaume de Moerbeke et la "Collection philosophique"*, in: *Studi Medievali* 43 (2002), p. 693-717. According to H. ARTS, *De scholiën op vijf Griekse filosofen, Plato, Plotinus, Olimpiodorus, Ammonius en Proclus*, thèse de licence, Louvain, 1962, quoted by WESTERINK, *Damascius*, I, p. lxxv, n. 2, the archetype of the *Enneads* belonged in the *collection philosophique*.

32 For the definition of 'état' in this context see HENRY, *Les états du texte de Plotin*, p. xx; for the relationship of the extant families of MSS and the 'états', see p. 31: 'L'archétype des *Ennéades* a donné naissance à quatre états médiévaux du texte, dont les

The comparison with the indirect tradition dealt with in the *États du texte de Plotin* made clear, in Heinrich Dörrie's words, that

> Die Handschriften sind also ungewöhnlich gute Zeugen für den Plotin-Text des IV. Jahrhunderts ... Die Probe aus *Enn.* IV, 7 macht es wahrscheinlich, daß die Handschriften sehr nahe an das Ursprüngliche heranführen'.[33]

In fact, one of the major tasks of the *États du texte de Plotin* was to compare the medieval direct tradition with the ancient forms of the text, luckily available through an important indirect tradition. Its importance lies firstly in the fact that the quotations are both early and extensive; and secondly in the fact that the indirect tradition fills a gap in the direct tradition.

As we have just seen, the archetype of the direct tradition stems at the earliest from the Ninth Century; but the first quotations from Plotinus's writings stem from a contemporary source, Porphyry, and a quasi-contemporary one, Eusebius of Caesarea.[34] In his Ἀφορμαὶ πρὸς τὰ νοητά, Porphyry quoted, literally and anonymously, many Plotinian passages.[35] Shortly after, i.e., in the first decades of the Fourth Century — some forty years after Plotinus's death (270 AD) and virtually contemporaneous with Porphyry's production of the *Enneads* out of Plotinus's treatises (ca. AD 300) — Eusebius of Caesarea quoted from Plotinus, naming his source.[36] In Book XI of his *Praeparatio evangelica*

relations sont difficiles, probablement impossibles à préciser .... Il se peut qu'à l'origine de ces groupes, il y ait d'autant d'exemplaires matériellement distincts, chacun l'œuvre d'un copiste, chacun l'ancêtre d'une famille. Il se peut aussi que tous ces états ou quelques-uns d'entre eux ne représentent que les transformations successives d'un seul et même exemplaire, corrigé par des réviseurs successifs, puis recopié directement à diverses époques par les scribes de nos manuscrits'.

[33] H. Dörrie, review of P. Henry, *Les états du texte de Plotin* and *Recherches sur la Préparation Évangélique d'Eusèbe*, in: *Göttingische Gelehrte Anzeigen* 12 (1938), p. 526-539 (p. 535).

[34] In addition to the Fourth Century Greek sources just mentioned (Porphyry, Eusebius), there are the Fourth Century Latin sources (mostly Marius Victorinus and Augustine) and the Fifth Century Greek sources (Cyrillus of Alexandria and Theodoret of Cyrrhus), which will not be taken into account here.

[35] Henry, *Les états du texte de Plotin*, p. 43-67, compared the Porphyrian quotations with their sources. See also H.-R. Schwyzer, *Plotinisches und Unplotinisches in den Ἀφορμαί des Porphyrios*, in: *Plotino e il neoplatonismo in oriente e in occidente* (*Atti del convegno internazionale Roma, 5-9 ottobre 1970*), Rome, 1974, p. 221-252 and C. D'Ancona, *Les Sentences de Porphyre entre les Ennéades de Plotin et les Éléments de Théologie de Proclus*, in: Porphyry, *Sentences*, Études d'introduction, texte grec et traduction française... ed. L. Brisson, I-II, Paris 2005, p. 139-274.

[36] The extensive quotation from IV 7 is introduced by the words ἐπάκουσον δὲ καὶ Πλωτίνου τὰ τοιάδε πρὸς τοὺς αὐτοὺς ἀποτεινομένου (*Praep. ev.*, XV, 21, 3 Mras: see Henry, *Les états du texte de Plotin*, p. 77). Henry, *Recherches sur la Préparation Évangélique d'Eusèbe*, p. 15, proposed 315 AD as the date for the composition of Eusebius's *Praep. Ev.*

he quoted several passages from V 1[10], and in Book XV he reproduced most of treatise IV 7[2]. In doing so, he unwittingly paved the way to make good the loss of a significant portion of this treatise which affected the archetype of the direct tradition. Fifty lines of what is today chapter 8^5,[37] missing in all the testimonies of the direct tradition, were recopied by Eusebius together with most of treatise IV 7.[38] The fact that at the end of this passage one can read five words which appear also in the MSS of the *Enneads* establishes that the passage did originally belong in Plotinus's text.[39]

Now, in the *Recherches* Henry had suggested that these fifty lines, albeit genuinely Plotinian, originally did not belong in the treatise but were added later, perhaps by Eustochius, perhaps on the demand of Plotinus himself;[40] but because P. Kraus noted that these lines are partly preserved in the Arabic version[41] — as we shall see in more detail below — in the *États du texte de Plotin* Henry acknowledged that their absence from the archetype of the *Enneads* was unintentional. However, he continued to stick to the main tenet of the *Recherches*, namely that Eusebius drew not from Porphyry's edition of the Plotinian treatises (our *Enneads*), but from a pre-Porphyrian edition of them, the so-called *recension d'Eustochius*.

Eustochius, as is well known, was the physician-philosopher who was in attendance on Plotinus at the time of his death and to whom the master addressed his last words, as recorded in the *Vita Plotini* by Porphyry.[42] However, in the *Vita Plotini* Porphyry also declares that some treatises of the master were sent abroad (in particular to Athens), a fact which implies that they were recopied and enjoyed the type of circulation which philolo-

[37] The subdivision of Plotinus's treatises into chapters is due to Ficinus, and in order to retain the traditional numbering Henry and Schwyzer numbered the text recovered from Eusebius as 8^1-8^5.

[38] Eusebius quoted extensively IV 7, from the beginning to Chapter 9, from a treatise which has 15 chapters according to Ficinus's subdivision: see the table, below p. 135.

[39] HENRY, *Les états du texte de Plotin*, p. 71. The words σῳζόμενον, καθόσον ἂν αὐτοῦ μεταλαμβάνῃ, ending the section preserved by Eusebius, appear also in the MSS of the *Enneads*: see the apparatus at p. 212 (*maior*, vol. II) and 157 (*minor*, vol. II).

[40] HENRY, *Recherches sur la Préparation Évangélique d'Eusèbe*, p. 128: 'Ces menus faits pourraient permettre de penser que lorsqu'il rédigea son traité, Plotin se garda délibérément d'attaquer la théorie de l'entéléchie, mais que plus tard, reprenant la question, il y fit insérér par Eustochius le fragment que cite Eusèbe, à moins que ce ne soit Eustochius lui-même qui l'y ait inséré de son propre chef'.

[41] P. KRAUS, *Un fragment prétendu de la recension d'Eustochius des œuvres de Plotin*, in: *Revue de l'Histoire des Religions* 113 (1936), p. 207-218 (repr. in: *Alchimie, Ketzerei, Apokryphen*, p. 301-312).

[42] *Vita Plotini*, 2.22-27.

gists call 'commerce d'amitié'.[43] That this circulation acquired the name *recension d'Eustochius* is mostly due to the existence of a scholion which corresponds with what is today identified as line 55 of IV 4[28], 29, a scholion which claims to mark the point where the treatise came to an end 'according to the edition of Eustochius', whereas in the edition of Porphyry it ended elsewhere.[44] On the other hand, in his comparison of that portion of IV 7 which is preserved by both the MSS of the *Enneads* and Eusebius, Henry had detected no less than 103 places where the text as testified by the MSS of the *Enneads* and as preserved by Eusebius differ from one another: he came to the conclusion that the differences could not reasonably be ranged under the heading of scribal mistakes.[45] This fact, taken together with the evidence of the scholion, led him to conclude that what he had in front of him in the MSS of the *Enneads* and in the *Praep. ev.* were two *états* of Plotinus's text: the edition Eusebius quoted from was the one of Eustochius, whereas the MSS stem from the edition by Porphyry, i.e., the *Enneads*.

The entire question of the *recension d'Eustochius* has been extensively dealt with by Luc Brisson and Marie-Odile Goulet-Cazé in the outstanding *Vita Plotini* of the Paris Team 76 of the CNRS. Both scholars agree that before the systematic edition provided by Porphyry, the Plotinian treatises received some form of circulation, though Luc Brisson credits Amelius, one of the disciples of Plotinus, with it, giving to Eustochius the role merely of an 'agent de transmission',[46] whereas

[43] So called by R. DEVREESSE, *Introduction à l'étude des manuscrits grecs*, Paris, 1954, p. 78; M.-O. GOULET-CAZÉ, *L'arrière-plan scolaire de la Vie de Plotin*, in: PORPHYRY, *La Vie de Plotin* (*Histoire des Doctrines de l'Antiquité Classique*, 6), by L. BRISSON et al., I, Paris, 1982, p. 231-327 (p. 284-287); see also T. DORANDI, *Le stylet et la tablette. Dans le secret des auteurs anciens*, Paris, 2000.

[44] The scholion runs as follows: ἕως τούτου ἐν τοῖς Εὐστοχίου τὸ δεύτερον Περὶ ψυχῆς καὶ ἤρχετο τὸ τρίτον. Ἐν δὲ τοῖς Πορφυρίου συνάπτεται τὰ ἑξῆς τῷ δευτέρῳ; see the discussion in L. BRISSON, *Une édition d'Eustochius?*, in: PORPHYRY, *La Vie de Plotin*, p. 65-69 and M.-O. GOULET-CAZÉ, *Remarques sur l'édition d'Eustochius*, in: PORPHYRY, *La Vie de Plotin*, p. 71-76.

[45] HENRY, *Recherches sur la Préparation Évangélique d'Eusèbe*, p. 73: 'L'examen minutieux des variantes de la péricope A du traité IV 7 et des extraits de V 1 permet d'affirmer avec grande vraisemblance que l'édition de Plotin dont Eusèbe se servit n'était pas celle dont dérivent les manuscrits de la tradition directe, à savoir l'édition des *Ennéades* préparée par Porphyre. En effet (1) les divergences que le texte d'Eusèbe présente par rapport à cette édition sont trop nombreuses pour qu'on puisse toutes les attribuer à la distraction des copistes'.

[46] BRISSON, *Une édition d'Eustochius?*, p. 69: 'Bref, avant l'édition porphyrienne des *Ennéades*, aurait circulé une édition chronologique des traités de Plotin, probablement réalisée sous la direction d'Amélius et à laquelle ferait allusion la scholie à *Enn.* IV 4, 29, 55 qui mentionnerait le nom d'Eustochius comme agent de transmission de cette édition pré-porphyrienne'.

according to Marie-Odile Goulet-Cazé if a pre-Porphyrian edition of Plotinus's writings had existed, it is Eustochius — as mentioned in the scholion — who must be credited with it.[47]

Whether it is to Amelius's notebooks that we ultimately owe the existence of an indirect tradition of Plotinus's writings, as maintained by Luc Brisson,[48] or to Eustochius, as mantained in the past by Paul Henry and in the French *Vita Plotini* by Marie-Odile Goulet-Cazé, for the present purposes it will suffice to bear in mind that the two versions of IV 7 that we can read in the MSS and *apud* Eusebius do ultimately trace back to one and the same source: the treatise written by Plotinus in its actual form — namely, *with* the part preserved through Eusebius — and recopied within his school in Rome. It was in the history of its transmission that the direct and indirect traditions of IV 7 diverged from one another. Let us recall the presence of the last words of the missing part in some MSS of the *Enneads*: this suggests that an accident befell the text of IV 7 which has come down to us through the archetype. Some folios were lost; hence, there is a gap of approximately eight pages in the Oxford edition of Plotinus, a gap which was filled by Henry and Schwyzer with Eusebius's quotation.

However, Eusebius is not alone in his task of transmitter. Until now, I have limited myself to mentioning the fifty lines of what is today chapter 8^5 missing in all the MSS, but transmitted by Eusebius, as the most striking difference between the direct and indirect tradition of IV 7. Now it is time, following in the footsteps of Henry and Schwyzer, to remind ourselves of the more complicated picture of the parallel transmission of this treatise in the direct and indirect traditions. To this end, I give in tabular form the conclusions reached by Henry in the *États du texte de Plotin*[49] and by Schwyzer in his study of MS Wien, Staatsbibliothek,

[47] M.-O. GOULET-CAZÉ, *Remarques sur l'édition d'Eustochius*, p. 75: 'N'importe quel disciple, du moins à partir d'une certaine époque, pouvait copier les traités plotiniens pour disposer d'un exemplaire personnel. Un disciple cependant se distingue à cet égard, c'est Amélius, parce que ses copies à lui, prises sur les autographes de Plotin eux-mêmes, sont les moins fautives, comme le reconnaît Porphyre lui-même .... Il est donc certain que circulaient dans l'École et en dehors de l'École des exemplaires assez identifiés au nom d'Amélius pour être comparés à d'autres, par exemple à ceux de Porphyre .... Mais si l'on veut soutenir la thèse de l'existence d'une édition préporphyrienne des traités plotiniens, je ne vois pas d'autre indice valable attestant cette édition que la mention de τὰ Εὐστοχίου dans la scholie et je n'en vois strictement aucun pour soutenir l'existence d'une édition d'Amélius'.

[48] On the role of Amelius in the transmission of Plotinus's writings according to Henry, see below p. 139-140.

[49] HENRY, *Les états du texte de Plotin*, p. 70-71.

Phil. Gr. 226,[50] retaining their sigla **A-D** for the four sections into which they subdivided the treatise.

IV 7(2)

Sections of the text	All the MSS of the *Enneads*	Some MSS of the *Enneads*	Eusebius
1.1, εἰ δέ – 8.28, δικαιοσύνη = **A**			
8.28, ἀνδρία – 8^4.28, ἁρμονία = **B**			
8^5.1, τὸ δὲ τῆς ἐντελεχείας – 8^5.52, μεταλαμβάνη = **C**			
9.1, ἡ δὲ ἑτέρα φύσις – 15.12 ἀπολωλυῖαι = **D**			

Leaving aside (for present purposes) section **A**, which is common to both,[51] and section **D** which was not recopied by Eusebius, it appears that the direct and indirect traditions are complementary: the lacuna in the MSS is filled thanks to Eusebius's extensive quotation. However, some MSS of the *Enneads* possess a part of the missing text, namely, section **B**, a fact which must be accounted for.

There are four MSS which contain section **B**, but one is *descriptus* and was not taken into account by Henry or Schwyzer;[52] hence, we have three MSS containing section **B** in the direct tradition of the *Enneads*. They all date back to the Fifteenth Century. Two of them belong to what

[50] SCHWYZER, *Der Plotin-Codex Vindoboniensis Phil. Graecus 226*.

[51] HENRY, *Les états du texte de Plotin*, p. 70: 'On se trouve donc ici en possession par excellence de deux "états" du texte, non pas directement de deux éditions antiques, car plusieurs fautes sont dues à des copistes, mais de deux archétypes qui dérivent l'un de l'édition de Porphyre, l'autre, d'une édition différente, probablement celle d'Eustochius'.

[52] The MSS are Paris, Bibl. Nationale, *gr.* 2082 (sigla: J; see HENRY, *Les manuscrits des Ennéades*, p. 135-148); Venice, Bibl. Marciana, *gr.* 240 (sigla: M; see HENRY, *Les manuscrits des Ennéades*, p. 214-224); Wien, Österr. Nationalbibl., *phil. gr.* 226 (sigla: V; see HENRY, *Les manuscrits des Ennéades*, p. 227-239). The MS Città del Vaticano, Bibl. Apostolica Vaticana, *Barb. gr.* 275 is *descriptus* on Venice, Bibl. Marciana, *gr.* 240 (see see HENRY, *Les manuscrits des Ennéades*, p. 225-226).

Henry called group *x*[53] and one to group *y*:[54] all three are important testimonies of the text and served, together with others, as the basis for the edition (*manuscrits-sources*).[55] Two of them make clear, one by means of a scholion and one through the arrangement of the writing on the folio, that section **B** counts as an addition.[56] Where does it come from? By comparing the text of section **B** in these MSS with the text of Eusebius, Henry in the *Recherches* proposed that the MSS of the *Enneads* which possess section **B** drew it from Eusebius, though not from the same MSS of the *Praeparatio ev.* which have come down to us.[57] This explanation was endorsed and even reinforced by Schwyzer, in his study of one of the MSS containing section **B**, namely, Wien, Österr. Staatsbibliothek, *phil. gr.* 226.[58]

Finally, another testimony of section **B**, contained together with section **A** in a miscellaneous MS of the Vatican Library, was singled out by Heinrich Dörrie in his review of Henry's *Recherches*[59] and was studied

[53] HENRY, *Les états du texte de Plotin*, pp. 31-32 and *Les manuscrits des Ennéades*, p. 115-116.

[54] HENRY, *Les états du texte de Plotin*, p. 32 and *Les manuscrits des Ennéades*, p. 149-150.

[55] The main features are summarised in the list of the *manuscrits-sources* provided by HENRY, *Les états du texte de Plotin*, p. 32-34: 'Le *Parisinus graecus 2082* (...), du XVe siècle, appartient à la même famille *x*, dont il forme une seconde branche. Il n'a pas de *marginalia*, mais, en revanche, contient, comme M et V, la péricope B du traité IV, 7. ... Le *Marcianus gr. 240* ... fut écrit, peu après C [i.e., the MS *Monacensis gr. 449*, written by the humanist Demetrius Triboles in 1465] par le même Démétrius Tribolès .... M est surtout important du fait qu'il contient la péricope B du traité IV, 7. ... Le *Vindobonensis phil. gr. 226* ..., du XVe siècle, est probablement antérieur à C et M et certainement indépendant d'eux, bien qu'il leur soit apparenté de très près. Entre autres extraits, il contient du folio 34 au folio 35 v, la majeure partie de la péricope B du traité IV, 7'.

[56] H.-R. SCHWYZER, *Das Plotin-Exzerpt im Codex Rossianus Graecus 986* in: *Rheinisches Museum für Philologie* 88 (1939), p. 367-379 (p. 368): 'Der Abschnitt **B** ist im M und V deutlich als Ergänzung gekennzeichnet, in M durch ein Scholion, das am Rande zu c. 8, Zeile 28 darauf aufmerksam macht, in V dadurch, daß der Abschnitt auf einem neuen Blatt beginnt und so an eine falsche Stelle geraten ist'.

[57] *Recherches*, p. 81-116. A summary of the conclusion reached in the *Recherches* is provided by Henry himself in *Les manuscrits des Ennéades*, p. 235-236: 'La péricope ne provient d'aucun manuscrit connu d'Eusèbe, ni même de leur archétype commun. Sans doute provient-elle d'un manuscrit de la *Préparation*, plutôt que directement d'une édition eustochienne de Plotin, mais elle est rentrée dans la tradition porphyrienne par l'intermédiaire d'un manuscrit de cette tradition ..., lequel est l'ancêtre commun de C, M et V et l'archétype subsidiaire où J a puisé le texte de la péricope **B**'.

[58] SCHWYZER, *Der Plotin-Codex Vindobonensis Phil. Graecus 226*, p. 270: 'Da die Hss. M und J den Abschnitt **C** nicht enthalten, ist es klar, daß die auf denselben Archetypus zurückgehen, wie alle übrigen Plotins-Hss., auf einen Archetypus, in dem durch Blattesausfall die erwähnte Lücke entstanden ist. Die teilweise Ergänzung der Lücke stammt anderswoher, und zwar entweder indirekt aus einer Eusebios-Hs. oder aus einer vollständigeren Plotins-Hs. Das erste ist bedeutend wahrscheinlicher als das zweite'.

[59] See above note 33. The MS is mentioned at p. 529 of Dörrie's review.

by Schwyzer.[60] The conclusions reached by Schwyzer and later endorsed by Henry[61] were that this excerpt too derives from a lost manuscript of Eusebius's *Praeparatio ev.*.[62] However, its scribe did not have recourse to a MS of the same family which was used by the scribes of the three relevant MSS of the *Enneads*, because the Vatican excerpt is independent of the other Plotinian MSS containing section **B**, and in turn the latter are independent of it.[63] More importantly, Schwyzer's scrutiny of this excerpt persuaded him that one of the main points on which the hypothesis of a pre-Porphyrian edition held by Henry in the *Recherches* rested required reconsideration.

Now, one of the main reasons to assume that Eusebius did quote from the pre-Porphyrian edition — the *recension d'Eustochius* — was the high number of variant readings (more than 100) in the text which they all had in common, namely, section **A**, of which both the Porphyrian edition and the allegedly pre-Porphyrian edition are extant. But since the text of the Vatican excerpt reduces this number to 10, Schwyzer came to see this as proof that the variant readings are peculiar to the MSS of Eusebius's *Praeparatio ev.* which were at Henry's disposal.[64] This fact hinted at an alternative explanation of the difference between the direct and indirect tradition,[65] according to which both texts stem from a unique ancestor: Plotinus's treatise IV 7 — the differences between the direct and indirect tradition are but the result of the manuscript transmission of the *Praeparatio ev.* On this assumption, one and the same version of Plotinus's IV 7 was edited by Porphyry in his systematic arrangement of the treatises (the *Enneads*) and was known to Eusebius,

[60] SCHWYZER, *Codex Rossianus Graecus 986*.

[61] HENRY, *Les manuscrits des Ennéades*, p. 324-339 (Appendice II: *Un fragment d'Eusèbe*).

[62] SCHWYZER, p. 373: «Daß T [i.e., the sigla given by Schwyzer, p. 369, to the MS Città del Vaticano, Biblioteca Apostolica Vaticana: *Rossianus graecus 986*] letzen Endes auf dieselbe nichtporphyrische Ausgabe wie die Eus.-Hss. (und die Plotin-Hss. JMV im Abschnitt **B**) zurückgeht, bedarf angesichts der zahlreichen Übereinstimmungen keines Beweises. Doch muß man darüber hinaus feststellen, daß T nicht direkt auf ein Exemplar dieser Ausgabe zurückgeht, sondern an einer (verlorenen) Eus.-Hs. stammt'.

[63] As shown by SCHWYZER, *Codex Rossianus Graecus 986*, p. 373-374.

[64] SCHWYZER, *Codex Rossianus Graecus 986*, p. 377: 'Der Wert von T liegt vielmehr im Abschnitt A .... Da T eine Rezension bietet, die die etwa 100 Abweichungen zwischen der porph. und der nicht-porph. Ausgabe um 10 vermindert, können wir sehen daß der Unterschied zwischen diesen Ausgaben geringer ist, als es bisher schien. ... Henrys Behauptung ... die nicht-porph. Ausgabe hebe sich deutlich von der porph. Ausgabe ab, erfährt durch T eine gewisse Einschrankung'.

[65] As recalled by SCHWYZER, *Codex Rossianus Graecus 986*, this alternative explanation was already surmised by Dörrie in his review of Henry's *États* and *Recherches* (p. 537).

who quoted it in full as long as the treatise met his interests, namely, until the end of what is today Chapter 8[5]. Later on, in the course of the medieval transmission of the *Enneads*, the archetype of the direct tradition lost some folios and IV 7 was transmitted only in a lacunose form, deprived of sections **B** and **C**, and some Fifteenth Century manuscripts filled the lacuna with Eusebius's text. It is true that some of these MSS bear a text which is remarkably different from that of the *Enneads*; but the Vatican MS is much more akin to the text of the *Enneads*, and this at least elicits the possibility that Eusebius too drew his text of IV 7 from the Enneadic version. In this case, the variant readings of all the Eusebian MSS apart from the Vatican MS would be peculiar to them and would provide no information about an alleged original difference between the text of IV 7 quoted by Eusebius and the Enneadic one.

This reconstruction, which can only be inferred from some suggestions by Schwyzer[66] and which was not accepted by Henry,[67] can be tested through a comparison with the other branch of the indirect tradition, namely, the one represented by the Arabic version of IV 7. As we shall see, the extraordinary importance of this branch of the indirect tradition lies in the fact that it not only contains section **B**, but also part of section **C**.

SECTION II

Paul Henry changed his mind on the nature, provenance and role of the *Plotiniana Arabica*. In the 1937 study of Plotinus's oral teaching, he advanced the idea that the Arabic version was but the record of the courses taught by Plotinus in Rome. The Arabic text is characterized by many blatant diverengences from the *Enneads* both in its arrangement and contents,[68] a fact which has been and still is accounted for as the

[66] See above note 64.

[67] HENRY, *Les manuscrits des Ennéades*, argued at p. 332-336 that the agreement of MS *Ross. gr.* 986 in so many places with the MSS of the direct tradition can only be the result of intelligent conjectures on the part of its scribe, and reached the conclusion, p. 339, that, 'Le fragment T ne réduit donc pas sensiblement l'écart entre les archétypes d'Eusèbe et de Plotin et, ni par son titre ni par ses leçons, ne constitue un élément essentiel dans la question des états antiques du texte de Plotin'.

[68] The difference between the Arabic version and the *Enneads* is so enormous that the editor of the Arabic, Fr. DIETERICI, albeit recognizing the Plotinian provenance of the doctrines of the pseudo-*Theology*, did not indicate any precise source in the *Enneads*: it was VALENTIN ROSE in his review of Dieterici's German translation (*Deutsche Literaturzeitung*, 1883) who first demonstrated the correspondence between the Arabic and Greek texts. Having studied the *Aristoteles pseudepigraphus* throughout his life, once Rose had in front of him Dieterici's German, it did not take him long to realize that the Greek model, albeit totally higgledy-piggledy, was Plotinus.

outcome of a later reworking of the original Greek text. Parting company with this explanation, Henry then argued that the Arabic was but the record of Plotinus's oral teaching, which travelled East thanks to Amelius's notebooks.[69] We are told in the *Vita Plotini* that Amelius recopied many writings of the master, that in 269 he left Rome for Apamea, taking the books with him, and that after his death they came into the possession of his adopted son Ostilianus Hesychius.[70] Henry interpreted this account as related to the written records of Plotinus's lectures and saw in Amelius's books the 'cours, dont la *Théologie* transmet le texte parlé'.[71] In his opinion, it was this *reportatio* of Plotinus's teaching, akin to (but by no means identical with) the text of the *Enneads*, which was bound to be falsely attributed to Aristotle many centuries later.[72] In the *États du texte de Plotin* (1938), Henry proposed the same explanation[73] but added several nuances[74] and even spoke of the pseudo-*Theology of Aristotle* as containing some 'extraits des *Sommaires et*

[69] Through a comparison of the pseudo-*Theology* in Dieterici's German translation with the Greek original, Henry claimed to have noticed in the Arabic paraphrase not only the traces of an oral style, but also doctrinal parallels with Alexander of Aphrodisias. Since we are told in the *Vita Plotini*, 14.13, that Alexander was read in Plotinus's class, he argued that the presence of such parallels could count as a trace of Amelius's notes not conveyed in the Porphyrian edition.

[70] Amelius left Rome two years before Plotinus's death; so, he did not have access to the last nine treatises Plotinus wrote during his last two years. The fact that not one of these last nine treatises is reproduced in the Arabic paraphrase counted as an additional proof in Henry's eyes; another was the fact that Emesa, the native town of Ibn Nāʿima al-Ḥimṣī, the translator into Arabic, is near to Apamea.

[71] *États*, p. xxvi, note 2. See also P. HENRY, *Vers la reconstitution de l'enseignement oral de Plotin*, in: *Bulletin de l'Académie Royale de Belgique, Classe des Lettres* 23 (1937), p. 310-342: see p. 326, where the pseudo-*Theology of Aristotle* is said to be a 'sténographie du cours' taught by Plotinus.

[72] HENRY, *Vers la reconstitution*, p. 316: 'Une œuvre grecque communément appelée la pseudo-*Théologie d'Aristote* ... a été considérée jusqu'ici par les orientalistes comme l'œuvre d'un disciple immédiat de Plotin, par tous les hellénistes comme une paraphrase tardive des *Ennéades*. En réalité, c'est un fragment — considérable — des σχόλια ἐκ τῶν συνουσιῶν, c'est-à-dire le texte intégral de certaines conférences de Plotin recueillies par Amélius'. HENRY was convinced that other late Ancient authors did convey the remnants of Plotinus's oral teaching: a full list is given in the *États du texte de Plotin*, p. xxvii. Among them, he devoted a study to the Fourth Century Platonist Dexippus: P. HENRY, *Trois apories orales de Plotin sur les Catégories d'Aristote*, in: *Zetesis. Album Amicorum door vrienden en collega's aangeboden aan Prof. Dr. E. De Strycker*, Antwerp - Utrecht, 1973, p. 234-265.

[73] Henry, *Les états du texte de Plotin*, p. xiv: 'Une œuvre arabe, le *Livre de la Théologie*, primitivement anonyme, devenue célèbre sous le titre de *Théologie d'Aristote*, n'est qu'un fragment des notes de cours d'Amélius, le principal disciple de Plotin, et nous restitue le texte original de vingt leçons du maître'. The *Theology* is also included under the heading *L'enseignement oral*, p. xxvii.

[74] HENRY, *Les états du texte de Plotin*, p. xxvi.

Arguments de Porphyre et … passages parallèles aux *Ennéades*'.[75] In the Introduction to the *Manuscrits des Ennéades* (1940), he repeated that the pseudo-*Theology of Aristotle* was the testimony to a stage of Plotinus's works which antedated the edition by Porphyry.[76] Although convinced that the Arabic *Theology* traced back to Amelius,[77] Henry also countenanced the idea that it contained the remnants of Porphyry's introductory writings — those κεφάλαια, ὑπομνήματα and ἐπιχειρήματα which he added, as we are told in the *Vita Plotini*, in order to help the reader of the *Enneads*. Perhaps Henry was thinking of some later reworker, who would have conflated Amelius's record of the courses taught by Plotinus together with Porphyry's auxiliary writings.[78] However, he proved to be ready to abandon this speculative reconstruction of the origins of the Arabic Plotinus. In 1941, a memorable study by Hans-Rudolf Schwyzer[79] provided the proof that the pseudo-*Theology of Aristotle* was created out of the *Enneads*, in precisely the same form as they were edited by Porphyry, and later on Henry declared his former reconstruction to be untenable and that the proofs given by Schwyzer were decisive.[80]

The importance of Schwyzer's demonstration lies not only in the fact that it ruled out speculations about the pseudo-*Theology* as the remnants of Plotinus's lectures allegedly preserved by Amelius, but also in that it paved the way to the understanding of the real nature of the pseudo-*Theology*. Independently of the various and at times conflicting

[75] HENRY, *Les états du texte de Plotin*, p. xxvi: on the alleged role of the ὑπομνήματα, ἐπιχειρήματα and κεφάλαια that Porphyry declares to have added to the *Enneads* in the creation of the pseudo-*Theology* see the *status quaestionis* by M. AOUAD, *La* Théologie d'Aristote *et autres textes du 'Plotinus Arabus'*, in: *Dictionnaire des Philosophes Antiques*, ed. R. GOULET, I, Paris, 1989, p. 541-590; M.-O. GOULET-CAZÉ, *L'arrière-plan scolaire*, and F. W. ZIMMERMANN, *The Origins of the So-Called* Theology of Aristotle, in: *Pseudo-Aristotle in the Middle Ages. The* Theology *and Other Texts*, ed. J. KRAYE, W. F. RYAN and C. B. SCHMITT, London, 1986, p. 110-240.

[76] HENRY, *Vers la reconstitution*, p. 322: 'Ce sont les *Ennéades* qui dépendent de la *Théologie*, ou plus exactement les écrits de Plotin publiés par Porphyre qui sont, en général, postérieurs aux cours recueillis par Amélius et partiellement conservés dans la *Théologie*'.

[77] In *Vers la reconstitution*, p. 332-333, HENRY surmised that Amelius himself might have been responsible for the subdivision of the text which appears in the Arabic, and which is totally different from the Greek original: 'Le groupement par sujets, l'Ame et l'Intelligence, aurait pu être déjà le fait d'Amélius. Il n'est même pas impossible qu'Amélius soit l'auteur du livre de Théologie qui a précédé la *Théologie d'Aristote*' (p. 332).

[78] HENRY, *Les manuscrits des Ennéades*, p. xlvii.

[79] H.-R. SCHWYZER, *Die pseudoaristotelische Theologie und die Plotin-Ausgabe des Porphyrios*, in: *Rheinisches Museum für Philologie* 90 (1941), p. 216-236.

[80] P. HENRY, *The Oral Teaching of Plotinus*, in: *Dionysius* 6 (1982), p. 3-12 (p. 5, n. 9).

reconstructions of the role played by Porphyry in the modifications which the Arabic text exhibits with respect to the Greek original, it is now commonly acknowledged that the Arabic text had as its antecedent his systematic arrangement of the treatises, and this is mostly due to Schwyzer's efforts.

In fact, the main purpose of Porphyry's edition lies precisely in that, as he himself declares, he wanted to produce a rational ordering of the treatises which Plotinus composed without any systematic intention, simply following the order of the topics dealt with in his morning lectures.[81] In his reordering, Porphyry claimed to have followed a double propaedeutic system. Firstly, in establishing the sets of treatises (each set representing an 'ennead', i.e., a group of nine treatises) he followed the pattern of the ascension from logic to cosmology and from the latter to metaphysics, the metaphysical domain being in turn structured according to the ascension from Soul to Intellect and the One.[82] Secondly, within each set he claimed to have arranged the treatises from the easier to the more complex.[83] In Porphyry's hands, Plotinus's philosophy became a system and this is the remote ancestor of the creation of the pseudo-*Theology of Aristotle*. What the Arab readers became acquainted with was a systematic corpus, leading from the sublunar to the suprasensible universe and ascending from Soul to Intellect to the First Cause, the One. Predictably, the parameters of the Arab reception of this systematic corpus would have been dictated by the attempt, for the doctrine of the First Principle, to display its harmony with the notion of *Tawḥīd* and, for the doctrine of the human soul and its immortality, its harmony with the eschatological concept of the Threat and the Reward.

Paul Kraus[84] and Franz Rosenthal[85] demonstrated that the Arabic version is a selection and adaptation of Plotinian materials whose author

[81] *Vita Plotini*, 24.1-16.

[82] See P. Hadot, *La métaphysique de Porphyre*, in: *Porphyre* (*Entretiens Hardt*, 12), Vandœuvres - Geneva, 1965, p. 127-163 (repr. in *Plotin, Porphyre. Etudes Néoplatoniciennes*, Paris, 1999, p. 317-353), and H.-D. Saffrey, *Pourquoi Porphyre a-t-il édité Plotin? Réponse provisoire*, in: Porphyry, *La Vie de Plotin*, II, p. 31-57, (repr. in *Le néoplatonisme après Plotin*, II, Paris, 2000, p. 3-48).

[83] This statement has no correspondence with reality: for instance, I 1[53], which opens the entire collection of the *Enneads*, is a desperately difficult treatise, presupposing an understanding of almost all the other writings by Plotinus — something which comes as no surprise, since it is the penultimate treatise which he composed. A similar remark might be made about the opening three treatises of *Ennead* VI, namely, the Treatise *On the Genera of Being*, VI 1-3 [42-44], one of the most technical and complicated of Plotinus's writings.

[84] *Plotin chez les Arabes*.

[85] *Aš-Šayḫ al-Yūnānī*.

consistently interpreted Plotinus's metaphysical tenets within the framework of a monotheistic theology. When Gerhard Endress edited the Arabic version of parts of Proclus's *Elements of Theology*, showing that the Proclus Arabus bears the same features as the Plotinus Arabus,[86] it became clear that both Neoplatonic texts were translated and rearranged within one and the same intellectual milieu, one which flourished in Baghdad towards the middle of the Ninth Century. Endress's linguistic and doctrinal analyses show that these adaptations were all produced within a circle whose leading personality was the first *faylasūf*, al-Kindī.[87] We should also note here that the Plotinian texts translated into Arabic come without exception from *Enneads* IV-VI, namely, from the three sets devoted by Porphyry to Soul, Intellect and the One. This counts as a confirmation that in the eyes of the Arab readers Plotinus's work did contain the exposition of a rational theology. Such is the scope of 'Aristotle's *Theology*', as explicitly stated in the *Prologue*, an introduction to the Arabic version which has no parallel in Greek and which places the *Theology* at the crowning glory of Aristotelian metaphysics.[88] F. W. Zimmermann rightly claims that Plotinus's *Enneads* IV-VI were meant to expound how the First Cause acts in creating and ruling the universe through Intellect and Soul, a topic lacking in Aristotle's *Metaphysics*[89] with which the *Theology* is explicitly associated in the *Prologue*.

[86] G. ENDRESS, *Proclus Arabus. Zwanzig Abschnitte aus der* Institutio Theologica *in arabischer Übersetzung* (*Beiruter Texte und Studien*, 10), Wiesbaden - Beirut, 1973.

[87] G. ENDRESS, *The Circle of al-Kindī. Early Arabic Translations from the Greek and the Rise of Islamic Philosophy*, in: *The Ancient Tradition in Christian and Islamic Hellenism. Studies on the Transmission of Greek Philosophy and Sciences dedicated to H. J. Drossaart Lulofs on his Ninetieth Birthday*, ed. G. ENDRESS and R. KRUK, Leiden, 1997, p. 43-76.

[88] ZIMMERMANN, *The Origins*, p. 122, maintains that the author of the *Prologue* is the translator himself, ʿAbd al-Masīḥ b. Nāʿima al-Ḥimṣī. In my *Al-Kindî on the Subject-Matter of the First Philosophy. Direct and Indirect Sources of al-Falsafa al-Ūlā, Chapter One*, in: *Was ist Philosophie im Mittelalter?*, ed. J. A. AERTSEN und A. SPEER, Berlin - New York, 1998, p. 841-855, I have argued in favour of al-Kindī's authorship; see also P. ADAMSON, *The Arabic Plotinus. A Philosophical Study of the Theology of Aristotle*, London, 2003, p. 35-40.

[89] In the *Kitāb al-Fihrist* (ed. G. FLÜGEL, Leipzig, 1871, p. 251.27; ed. R. TAJADDUD, Tehran, 1964, p. 312.14) IBN AL-NADĪM notes that Aristotle's *Metaphysics* was translated for al-Kindī, who in turn is said in the *incipit* of the *Prologue* to the pseudo-*Theology* to have 'corrected' this latter for Aḥmad, the son of the caliph al-Muʿtaṣim. On the interpretation of this 'correction' opinions vary: according to ZIMMERMANN, *The Origins*, it was only superficial and the real author of the changes that the Arabic exhibits with respect to Plotinus's text was the translator, Ibn Nāʿima al-Ḥimṣī: 'Ḥimṣī was responsible for all but a final crossing of 't's and dotting of 'i's carried out by Kindī' (p. 118). He is

However, the pseudo-*Theology of Aristotle* in itself, notwithstanding the intentions proclaimed in the *Prologue*, seems to have no definite plan; to be more precise, it seems to be totally chaotic. Conflicting explanations have been advanced for this, into which we are not compelled to enter here.[90] Still, it is germane to the present discussion to recall this point because, together with Schwyzer's demonstration, it elicits the following two conclusions: (i) IV 7 was translated into Arabic from a manuscript of the *Enneads* and (ii) it does not reproduce the order of the chapters as they are attested in any of these MSS. Let us first consider point (i).

From (i) one should naturally be led to infer that the Arabic version of IV 7 shares the lack of sections **B** and **C**. In fact, we have just seen that only those Greek MSS whose scribes had access to Eusebius's *Praeparatio ev.* partly fill the lacuna for section **B**, and that *no* Greek MS of the *Enneads* contains section **C**. But the Arabic, as Paul Kraus had already shown in 1939,[91] contains section **C**, at least in part: in Chapter III of the pseudo-*Theology*, lines 1-20, with the customary lexical and doctrinal adaptations, of what is today Chapter 8^5, namely, the one that we can read in Greek *only* thanks to Eusebius, are reproduced. The possibility that the translator of IV 7 into Arabic had access to a MS of the *Praeparatio ev.* and selected precisely those lines to fill the lacuna in the MS of Plotinus's IV 7 he had in front of him is pure speculation. Hence, the conclusion imposes itself that the Greek MS of the *Enneads* which the translator had at his disposal contained both sections **B** and **C**. This conclusion comes as no surprise if one thinks that the translation was made around 840 AD:[92] consequently, the Greek MS which the translator made use of antedated the archetype of the direct tradition which dates back to the Ninth Century at the earliest and to the Twelfth at the latest.

followed in this by ADAMSON, *The Arabic Plotinus*, p. 171-177; my guess is that al-Kindī made an attempt at producing a companion in rational theology out of the running translation of *Enneads* IV-VI made by Ibn Nāʿima al-Ḥimṣī. I have tried to argue this point in my *Pseudo-Theology of Aristotle, Chapter I: Structure and Composition*, in: *Oriens*, 36 (2001), p. 78-112.

[90] According to ZIMMERMANN, *The Origins*, the chaos in the Arabic text is the effect of the accidental dispersal of the leaves of the archetype and later reorganisation by an unknown reader, who was unable to understand the real nature of the text; I have tried to argue in favour of a different explanation in my *Ǧumlatu falsafatinā, l'ensemble de notre philosophie'. L'héritage de l'Antiquité tardive et son interprétation dans le Proème de la* Théologie d'Aristote, forthcoming in the proceedings of the conference *Science et philosophie arabes: méthodes, problèmes, cas*, Carthage, 28 novembre-2 décembre, 2000.

[91] See above, note 41.

[92] The *terminus ad quem* for the translation is given by the *incipit* of the *Prologue*, where we are told that the translation was 'corrected' by al-Kindī for Aḥmad, the son of the caliph al-Muʿtaṣim. The latter reigned between 833 and 842 AD.

Since it was the loss of some folios in this archetype which produced the lacuna in the direct tradition, the presence of sections **B** and **C** in the Arabic simply confirms what is in itself plausible, namely, that an earlier MS of the *Enneads* which was not affected by that loss reached Baghdad and provided the model for the translation into Arabic.

Although not surprising in itself, this fact entails significant consequences for the global picture of the transmission of Plotinus's text. What might have been understood as a minor detail under the assumption of Henry's former hypothesis of the non-Enneadic provenance of the pseudo-*Theology* becomes a much more significant point once we take into account the dependence of the Arabic Plotinus on the *Enneads*. If the translator into Arabic had at his disposal a MS of the *Enneads* now lost to us, which had not suffered the loss of folios in the central part of IV 7 which affects the Greek extant MSS, we can use the Arabic text to get a clearer picture of the transmission of IV 7. All in all, what the Arabic gives us is a testimony of the Enneadic text antedating the archetype. The testimonies of the treatise *On the Immortality of Soul* written by Plotinus around 254 AD and edited as the Seventh Treatise of *Ennead* IV by Porphyry around 300 AD can now be listed in tabular form as follows:

IV 7

Sections of the text	All the MSS of the *Enneads*	Some MSS of the *Enneads*	Eusebius	Arabic version of IV 7
1.1, εἰ δέ – 8.28, δικαιοσύνη = **A**				
8.28, ἀνδρία – 8^{4}.28, ἁρμονία = **B**				
8^{5}.1, τὸ δὲ τῆς ἐντελεχείας – 8^{5}.52, μεταλαμβάνῃ = **C**				
9.1, ἡ δὲ ἑτέρα φύσις – 15.12 ἀπολωλυῖαι = **D**				

Section **A** is common to all the direct and indirect testimonies of the text, even though the Arabic version lacks a considerable part of it (for this reason the relevant cell of the table has been shaded differently). Section **B** is missing in the direct tradition, quoted by Eusebius, translated into Arabic and preserved in some MSS of the direct tradition, which however do not depend for this section upon the Enneadic text, but upon Eusebius. Section **C** is missing in the direct tradition, quoted by Eusebius and translated into Arabic, with the exception of lines 28-38 of Chapter 8 and 20-52 of 8[5] (this absence is represented in the cell by the different shading). Section **D** is common both to the direct tradition of the *Enneads* and the Arabic version, but is lacking in Eusebius. The most obvious outcome of this state of affairs is that one can use the Arabic version as an additional testimony in reconstructing, by comparison with Eusebius's quotation, what the original Enneadic text might have been in sections **B** and **C**.

However, this does not mean that one can make use of the Arabic version to solve *cruces* in the Greek text, or at least not without qualifications. The Arabic is by no means a literal translation: it alternates literal quotations, more or less free paraphrases and independent passages. Consequently, what the Arabic text suggests or seems to suggest must always be carefully evaluated case by case against this background. In what follows, I shall confine myself to discussing an example taken from section **D**, which will serve to justify this cautious approach. However before proceeding to this discussion, it is necessary to address the question of the order of the Arabic text, namely point (ii) above.

Point (ii) merits attention because the differences between the Greek treatise and the Arabic version are important: firstly, the order of the Arabic text is different from the original; secondly, the Arabic version lacks two chapters of the Greek. The Plotinian treatise is scattered over three chapters of the pseudo-*Theology of Aristotle* and the passage 5.1-8.38 of the Greek is missing. One may infer from this that the Arabic version of IV 7 hardly fits with the idea that the Arabic stems from the *Enneads* as edited by Porphyry. The antecedent of the Arabic text of IV 7 might have been a defective MS, an intermediate source, or an adjusted text, whose testimony would consequently be of little or no value. The analysis of the structure of the Arabic version of IV 7 will suggest, I hope, a different explanation of the disorder of the Arabic with respect to the Greek. Let me first present schematically the layout of the text.

IV 7

Greek	Arabic
1.1-4.30	Pseudo-*Theology*, Chapter IX
8.38-8^5.20	Pseudo-*Theology*, Chapter III
13.1-15.12 (end of the treatise)	Pseudo-*Theology*, Chapter I

The beginning of the treatise is reproduced in Chapter IX of the pseudo-*Theology*, where it counts as the beginning of the chapter, under the heading *On the fact that the rational soul does not die*.[93] The central part, i.e., the one affected by the troubles in the direct tradition, is reproduced in Chapter III and I shall discuss the structure of this part of the Arabic version in greater detail immediately below. The end of the treatise is reproduced at the very beginning of Chapter I of the pseudo-*Theology*, under the heading *On Soul*.[94] Let us now focus on Chapter III of the pseudo-*Theology* and the way in which it reproduces the Greek text. In the Arabic version the text is topsy-turvy.

IV 7, 8-8^5

Greek	Arabic (pagination Badawī)
1 – 8.38-44 (end of the chapter)	48.8-17
2 – 8^1.1-9	48.17-49.9
3 – 8^1.9-35 (end of the chapter)	45.10-47.1
	47.1-6
4 – 8^2.1-15	47.6-48.8
5 – 8^2.15-22 (end of the chapter)	49.9-14
6 – 8^3.1-13	49.15-50.13
7 – 8^3.13-22	50.14-51.7
8 – 8^3.22-25	51.7-52.11
9 – 8^4.1-28 (end of the chapter)	52.12-54.6
10 – 8^5.1-20	54.7-55.10

93 In what follows I give the pages of both the *editio princeps* by Dieterici and the edition by ʿA. Badawī: F. Dieterici, *Die sogenannte Theologie des Aristoteles aus arabischen Handschriften zum ersten Mal herausgegeben*, Leipzig, 1882 (repr. Amsterdam, 1965); ʿA. Badawī, *Aflūṭīn ʿinda l-ʿArab. Plotinus apud Arabes. Theologia Aristotelis et fragmenta quae supersunt*, Cairo, 1966: the present passage, Dieterici, p. 125.4-130.11, Badawī, p. 121.1-129.7. The second part of Chapter IX of the ps.-*Theology* (Dieterici, p. 130.12-135.11; Badawī, p. 129.9-133.3) contains V 1(10), 11.1-12.20 (end of the treatise).

94 Dieterici, p. 4.12-8.3; Badawī, p. 18.11-21.7.

Chapter III of the pseudo-*Theology* totally coincides with the central part of IV 7. Unlike other chapters of the Arabic work, there are no excerpts from various Plotinian treatises[95] conflated here: the chapter limits itself to a reproduction of this part of IV 7 which, as we shall see, has a strong thematic unity. However, the author of the pseudo-*Theology* was keenly fond of a sort of cut and paste procedure and did not renounce it in this chapter. With the exception of 8^5, which is incomplete and coincides with the end of the Arabic chapter, there are no breaks or gaps in the sequence of the Greek text and the phrase 'end of the chapter' in the left column is meant to indicate this. However, the order of the Greek text is not reproduced in the Arabic. The beginning of Chapter III of the pseudo-*Theology* comes from 8^1.12-35. Then a passage from 8^2.1-15 follows. Next the Arabic goes back to 8.38-44, and then there is a passage from 8^1.1-11. It is only with the passage 8^2.15-22 that the Arabic begins to reproduce the correct sequence of the Greek text, and so it continues until the end of the chapter, which corresponds to line 20 of Chapter 8^5. Now if we start with the order of the Arabic text, and make it correspond with the sections of the Greek text numbered in the table above from **1** to **10**, we get the following picture:

IV 7, 8-8^5

Arabic	Greek
45.10-47.1	**3**
47.1-6	
47.6-48.8	**4**
48.8-17	**1**
48.17-49.9	**2**
49.9-14	**5**
49.15-50.13	**6**
50.14-51.7	**7**
51.7-52.11	**8**
52,12-54.6	**9**
54.7-55.10	**10**

Is this casual? One may be temped to answer in the affirmative. However, the reason why Chapter III of the pseudo-*Theology* begins with

[95] The most variegated is Chapter VIII of the pseudo-*Theology*, which conflates excerpts from VI 7, IV 4, V 1 and V 8; most of the chapters conflate excerpts from two Plotinian treatises.

text **3**, namely, with IV 7, 8^1.12-35 has much to do with the contents of these lines. In Armstrong's translation, the first nine lines of this Plotinian passage run as follows:

> By transferring, therefore, the powers of bodiless realities to bodies, they[96] leave nothing for the bodiless. But that bodies are able to do what they can do by bodiless powers is obvious for the following reasons. They will agree that quality is different from quantity, and that every body is of a certain quantity, and also that not every body is of a certain quality, as matter is not. But in admitting this they will also admit that quality in being different from quantity is different from body. For how without being of a certain quantity could it be a body, if every body is of a certain quantity? (IV 7, 8^1.9-17)

The corresponding Arabic text, namely, the beginning of Chapter III of the pseudo-*Theology*, runs as follows in Lewis's translation (Lewis's italics indicate the sentences which go back to the Greek text):

> Now that we have completed such introductory remarks as are necessary, concerning mind, the universal soul, the rational soul, the brute soul and the growing and natural soul, and have arranged the discussion on it in a natural order, following the way of nature, we shall now speak about the explanation of the quality (*māhīya*) of the soul. We begin by mentioning the doctrine of the Materialists (*al-jirmīyūn*), who think, in the error of their opinion, that the soul is harmony of the concord of the body and the union of its parts. We shall reveal the invalidity of their argument on this, and shall make plain the bad part of the doctrine held by their school. *For they transfer the faculties of the spiritual substances to the bodies, and leave the souls and the spiritual substances denuded of every faculty*. We say that *the acts of bodies take place only by powers that are incorporeal*, and these powers perform the wonderful acts, *and the proof of that is what we are going to tell*, God willing. Every body has quantity and quality, and *quantity is not the same as quality; nor is it possible for a body to be without quantity: this the Materialists (al-jirmīyūn) acknowledge*. If it is not possible for a body to exist without quantity, then quality is indubitably not a body; *how can quality be a body when it does not fall under quantity, if every body falls under quantity?* (Badawī, p. 45.1-15; Lewis's translation, p. 199-201).

The explicit ambit of the table of contents of the *Theology* as presented in the *Prologue*,[97] as well as the declaration of intent to use Plotinus's

[96] In this section of the treatise, running from 2.4 to 8^3.25, Plotinus is arguing against the Stoics, mentioned at the beginning of the section, 2.4-6, as those who say that soul is a kind of body: πρῶτον δὲ σκεπτέον, εἰς ὅ τι δεῖ τοῦτο τὸ σῶμα, ὃ λέγουσι ψυχήν, ἀναλύειν.

[97] In the Prologue (DIETERICI, p. 3.13-17, BADAWĪ, p. 7.7-11), the scope of the pseudo-*Theology* is described as follows (in Lewis's English translation, p. 487): 'Now our aim in this book is the discourse on the Divine Sovereignty, and the explanation of it, and how it

arguments in order to show the error of the 'corporealists' (*jirmīyūn*), indicate that section 8-8^5 of IV 7 was purposefully excerpted from the rest of IV 7. This part of the treatise was meant to provide the refutation of the materialist account of soul; Plotinus's argument that bodies can operate only thanks to bodiless powers was considered the strongest one to begin the discussion with. The change of the order of the Greek is the product of decision, not chance. I cannot discuss any more closely the details of the relocation of other text units, but it seems to me, on the basis of this passage, that it is fair to assume that if the text of this section of IV 7 does not reproduce the order of the Greek, this is not due to any peculiarity of the MS at the disposal of the translator, but to the editorial decision of the creator of Chapter III of the pseudo-*Theology*.

However, one must conclude that, albeit in good order, the MS of IV 7 at the disposal of the translator was incomplete. The extensive passage 5.1-8.38 is in fact missing in the Arabic in the form in which we presently have it. I have no strong argument against this, but would like to call attention to the fact that the beginning of the treatise does exist in Arabic as does the end (see the table at p. 146). Both gave rise, in the Arabic *Theology*, to chapters devoted to soul: the beginning of IV 7 is conflated with the end of V 1 in Chapter IX of the *Theology*, whereas the end of IV 7 is conflated with the beginning of IV 8 in Chapter I. As for the central part, the decision to extract passage 8.38-8^5.20 might have led to the discarding of passage 5.1-8.38. If so, the Arabic provides us with a version of IV 7 as it was written by Plotinus and edited by Porphyry. This version, albeit in disorder and lacunose, has the great advantage of supporting Eusebius in attesting to sections **B** and **C**.

However, this does not automatically allow us to use the Arabic as a test for decisions concerning *cruces* in the Greek text. Given the composite nature of the Arabic version, it would be inappropriate to establish any general rule. As a conclusion, I would like to give an example of a *crux* and the contribution that the Arabic version gives to its solution.

is the first cause, eternity and time being beneath it, and that it is the cause and originator of causes, in a certain way, and how the luminous force steals from it over mind and, through the medium of mind, over the universal celestial soul, and from mind, through the medium of soul, over nature, and from soul, through the medium of nature, over the things that come to be and pass away'.

SECTION III

In order to avoid the additional complication of including Eusebius's text in the comparison, the example will be taken from section **D**, namely, the end of the treatise which does not appear in Eusebius. For this section we have the direct tradition and the Arabic version, and in the Greek text we meet a passage which in the *editio maior* bears a *crux* which has been replaced by a conjecture in the *editio minor*. The *crux* occurs in chapter 14, lines 8-13, a passage where Plotinus is replying to a possible objection to immortality centered on the tripartition of the soul. Here is the text of the *editio maior*:

> Εἰ δὲ τὴν ἀνθρώπου ψυχὴν τριμερῆ οὖσαν τῷ συνθέτῳ † λυθήσεται, καὶ ἡμεῖς φήσομεν τὰς μὲν καθαρὰς ἀπαλλαττομένας τὸ προσπλασθὲν ἐν τῇ γενέσει ἀφήσειν, τὰς δὲ τούτῳ συνέσεσθαι ἐπὶ πλεῖστον· ἀφειμένον δὲ τὸ χεῖρον οὐδὲ αὐτὸ ἀπολεῖσθαι, ἕως ἂν ᾖ, ὅθεν ἔχει τὴν ἀρχήν.

And here is the text of the *minor*:

> Εἰ δὲ τὴν ἀνθρώπου ψυχὴν τριμερῆ οὖσαν τῷ συνθέτῳ λυθήσεσθαι <λέγεται>, καὶ ἡμεῖς φήσομεν τὰς μὲν καθαρὰς ἀπαλλαττομένας τὸ προσπλασθὲν ἐν τῇ γενέσει ἀφήσειν, τὰς δὲ τούτῳ συνέσεσθαι ἐπὶ πλεῖστον· ἀφειμένον δὲ τὸ χεῖρον οὐδὲ αὐτὸ ἀπολεῖσθαι, ἕως ἂν ᾖ, ὅθεν ἔχει τὴν ἀρχήν.

At variance with their customary practice, Henry and Schwyzer (henceforth, H-S) did not include this passage in the *Addenda et corrigenda*, the list of their changes of mind at the end of the *minor*. From the apparatus of the *maior* we learn that group *x*[98] as well as four MSS not belonging to it[99] read λυθήσεται, whereas group *w*[100] reads λυθήσεσθαι. Both texts are erroneous, the one with the verb in the future tense because the latter has no subject, τὴν ἀνθρώπου ψυχὴν being obviously inappropriate to serve as such a subject, and the one with the verb in the infinitive mode because, although consonant with τὴν ἀνθρώπου ψυχὴν, it is not governed by a verb. This must have been the feeling of Ficinus also, whose translation:

> Si autem oporteat animam hominis exsistentem trimembrem composito solvi

[98] See above, note 32.

[99] MSS Città del Vaticano, Bibl. Apostolica Vaticana, *urb. gr.* 62 (see HENRY, *Les manuscrits des Ennéades*, p. 156-162); Munich, Staatsbibl., *gr.* 449 (*Manuscrits*, p. 205-213); Venice, Bibl. Marciana, *gr.* 240 (see above, note 15); Wien, Österr. Nationalbibliothek, *phil. gr.* 226 (see above, note 14).

[100] See above, note 32.

implies that he read the infinitive λυθήσεσθαι (*solvi*) and provided a verb to govern it by understanding δεῖ after εἰ δὲ. The Greek text facing the Latin version in Creuzer's edition[101] reads εἰ δὲ τὴν ἀνθρώπου ψυχὴν τριμερῆ οὖσαν τῷ συνθέτῳ λυθήσεσθαι.[102] This is the text of the *editio princeps* by Perna (1580), who printed the infinitive of group *w*. In his critical note,[103] Creuzer claimed that it would have been possible to understand δεῖ, but H-S in the apparatus of the *maior* were quite sceptical about this. They also rejected the conjectures by Kirchhoff, who kept the infinitive and placed a lacuna after it, as well as by Vitringa and Müller, who tried to fill the lacuna with the conjecture λυθήσεσθαι <φήσουσι>, clearly thinking of Plotinus's reply καὶ ἡμεῖς φήσομεν. The reason why in the *maior* H-S where unhappy with these attempts at solving the *crux* and preferred to keep it was that, as they explain in the apparatus, the second part of the sentence bears no clear relationship with the first.[104] This fact led them to surmise that a major lacuna might have occurred, a lacuna which the *crux* points to and which cannot be filled — as in Vitringa's and Müller's attempts — on the grounds of the second part of the sentence. So they put a *crux* before λυθήσεται, the variant reading they adopted, in all likelihood because it is attested by a group, *x*, plus some other MSS independent of it. As for the other editors and/or translators, Bréhier accepted Vitringa's conjecture ('Dira-t-on que l'âme humaine, étant divisée en trois parties, se résoudra, puisqu'elle est composée?'), Harder kept the text as edited by Perna-Creuzer and understood the conjecture φήσουσι without putting it in the text[105] ('Wollen sie aber behaupten daß die menschliche Seele, da sie dreiteilig ist, infolge dieser Zusammensetzung sich auflösen wird … '), and Cilento accepted Vitringa's conjecture ('ma se diranno che l'anima umana, tripartita com'è, in seguito a tal composizione dovrà decomporsi … ').

[101] The Florentine edition of Ficinus's translation, published by Antonio Miscomini in 1492, is very rare; Ficinus's translation can be read alongside the Greek in the *editio princeps* of the *Enneads*, printed in Basel by Petrus Perna in 1559 and then again in 1580, as well as in the edition by F. CREUZER, Oxford, 1835 and Paris, 1855, all the while bearing in mind that CREUZER did not refrain from correcting Ficinus's translation here and there.

[102] PLOTINUS, *Enneades. Marsili Ficini interpretatione castigata*, ed. F. CREUZER and G. H. MOSER, Paris, 1855, p. 285.

[103] Vol. III, p. 257 of the 1835 edition, which I do not have available: I take this information from the apparatus *ad loc.* of the *editio maior* of the *Enneads*.

[104] In the apparatus *ad loc.* of the *editio maior*, p. 220, H-S commented on the *crux* as follows: 'sed fortasse plura interierunt, nam quae sequuntur in lin. 10-13 non plane refellunt protasin'.

[105] *Plotins Schriften*, trans. R. HARDER, I, Hamburg, 1956, p. 407: 'φήσουσι braucht nicht in den Text gesetzt zu werden, es läßt sich subintellegieren'.

Subsequently, a new conjecture was advanced by J. Igal: according to him, the original sentence was:

> εἰ δὲ τὴν ἀνθρώπου ψυχὴν τριμερῆ οὖσαν τῷ συνθέτῳ λυθήσεσθαι λεχθήσεται

but the scribe of the archetype wrote 'por un eror mecánico muy explicable' λυθήσεσθαι λυθήσεται, and both variant readings were reproduced separately in the subsequent tradition.[106] In the *minor* H-S did not accept Igal's conjecture, but they eventually agreed that the *crux* might have been solved by simply conjecturing a *verbum dicendi*. So, the revised text runs as follows:

> εἰ δὲ τὴν ἀνθρώπου ψυχὴν τριμερῆ οὖσαν τῷ συνθέτῳ λυθήσεσθαι <λέγεται>...

And here is Armstrong's translation of the entire passage, as edited in the H-S *minor*:

> But if it is said that the human soul, since it is tripartite, will be dissolved because of its composition, we too shall say that pure souls when they are set free abandon what was plastered on to them at their birth, but the others remain for a very long time; but when the worse part is abandoned, even it does not perish, as long as that from which it has its origin exists.[107]

From Ficinus's conjecture to the H-S *minor*, the meaning of the passage does not change substantially. As a matter of fact, whether one gives to the infinitive either the impersonal δεῖ as the governing verb, or a *verbum dicendi* as do Vitringa, Müller, Igal or H-S in the *minor*, the result is the same: the sentence is substantially sound and to the εἰ δὲ of its first part corresponds the καὶ ἡμεῖς φήσομεν of the second.

But it was precisely this correspondence which was questioned in the H-S apparatus of the *maior*. They suspected that a major lacuna had occurred, because they could not see any real relationship between the objection against immortality based on the tripartition of soul and Plotinus's reply, 'We too shall say that pure souls when they are set free ...'. As happens so often, Plotinus's reasoning is elliptical: the suspicion that something has been lost is nothing if not legitimate. Why on earth should the distinction between the destiny of the pure and impure souls solve the objection raised against immortality on the basis of the alleged

[106] J. IGAL, *Observaciones al texto de Plotino*, in: *Emerita. Revista de Lingüística y filología clásica* 41 (1973), p. 75-98 (p. 89).

[107] PLOTINUS, *Enneads* IV. 1-9, IV, Cambridge, Mass. - London, 1984, p. 391.

tripartition? Before trying to answer this question I would like to take into account the Arabic version. Here is it, in Lewis's translation:

> *Now the soul of man has three parts,* vegetative, animal and rational, *departing from the body at its decomposition and dissolution, but the pure clean soul which is not sullied or defiled by the defilements of the body, when it departs* from the world of sense, will return to these substances speedily and with no delay. *But the soul that has united with body and submitted herself to it* and become as if she were corporeal because of the *extent* of her immersion in the delights and pleasures of the body does not, when she parts from the body, *reach her own world until* by great toil *she has cast away* from *herself* every impurity and defilement that attached to her from the body. *Then does she return to her own world whence she came, but does not perish or cease to be,* as some think, *because she is attached to her origin,* even though she be far from it and remote.[108]

At first glance, the hope of finding in the Arabic the solution of the *crux* in the Greek is frustrated. Not only there is no trace of the entire question we have just discussed, namely, the alternative readings of the infinitive versus the future, but also the structure of the first sentence is altered: there is not even a trace of the hypothetical εἰ δὲ... or of the reply καὶ ἡμεῖς φήσομεν. In addition, as has been noted,[109] the Arabic version refers not to the Platonic tripartition of the soul,[110] as Plotinus unquestionably does, but to the Aristotelian one. The mention of the three parts 'vegetative, animal and rational' is clearly intentional and paves the way for the interpretation of the separability of the rational soul of *De Anima* III, 2, 413 b 24-27 as a claim for its immortality.[111] All

[108] Lewis's translation, p. 221; DIETERICI, p. 6.16-7.5, BADAWĪ, p. 20.12-21.2; see also PLOTINUS, *La discesa dell'anima nei corpi (Enn. IV 8[6]). Plotiniana Arabica (pseudo-Teologia di Aristotele, capitoli 1 e 7; "Detti del Sapiente Greco")*, ed. P. BETTIOLO et al., Padua, 2003, p. 227-228, Arabic text, and p. 273-275, commentary (our text is not a critical one, since we limited ourselves to checking the editions by Dieterici and Badawī against the three MSS which were accessible to us).

[109] See the discussion of this point in the commentary mentioned in the previous note.

[110] On the tripartition of the soul in the Platonic corpus and in ancient Platonism see the last volume of *Der Platonismus in der Antike* published by the late lamented MATTHIAS BALTES: H. DÖRRIE † - M. BALTES, *Der Platonismus in der Antike*, Band 6. *Die philosophische Lehre des Platonismus. Von der Seele als der Ursache aller sinnvollen Abläufe*, VI.1, Bausteine 151-168; VI.2: Bausteine 169-181; *Text, Übersetzung, Kommentar*, I, Stuttgart - Bad Cannstatt, 2002, p. 104-114 and 130-134 (texts and translations); p. 343-374 and 406-414 (commentary).

[111] *De An.* II, 2, 413 b 24-28: περὶ δὲ τοῦ νοῦ καὶ τῆς θεωρητικῆς δυνάμεως οὐδέν πω φανερόν, ἀλλ' ἔοικε ψυχῆς γένος ἕτερον εἶναι, καὶ τοῦτο μόνον ἐνδέχεται χωρίζεσθαι, καθάπερ τὸ ἀΐδιον τοῦ φθαρτοῦ. The Neoplatonic paraphrasis of Aristotle's *De Anima* translated into Arabic within the 'circle of al-Kindī' exhibits precisely this interpretation of Aristotle's definition of soul as the entelechy of the living

this, as important and informative as it may be about the nature, purpose and philosophical background of the Arabic Plotinus, seems to tell us nothing about its Greek antecedent. I would like to try to argue that this is not the case. Albeit not being a literal translation, the Arabic provides some important information about the cruciate passage.

The Greek text that the translator had in front of him must surely have contained the following elements of the first part of Plotinus's sentence:

> (i) τὴν ἀνθρώπου ψυχὴν = *nafs al-insān*; (ii) τριμερῆ οὖσαν = *dhāt ajzā' thalātha*; (iii) λυθήσεται or λυθήσεσθαι = *intiqād wa-taḥallul*

and the following elements of the second part:

> (iv) τὰς ... καθαρὰς = *al-nafs al-naqīya*; (v) ἀπαλλαττομένας = *idhan fāraqat*; (vii) τὸ προσπλασθὲν ἐν τῇ γενέσει = *'ālam al-ḥiss*; (viii) ἀφήσειν = *sa-tarja'u*; (ix) τούτῳ συνέσεσθαι = *qad ittaṣalat bi-l-badan*; (x) ἐπὶ πλεῖστον = *li-shadda*; (xi) οὐδὲ αὐτὸ ἀπολεῖσθαι = *min ghayr an tahlaka*; (xii) τὴν ἀρχήν = *bi-bad'i-hā.*

The interpretations and amplifications the Arabic version exhibits would deserve a detailed commentary, in particular the 'Aristotelian' shift in the rendering of the psychological tripartition. Still, what is germane to the present discussion is less the doctrinal background and purpose of the modifications of the Greek text than the structure of the sentence and its general meaning.

In the Arabic text, we are told that the human soul is tripartite *and* that the rational soul leaves the body when the latter dies. However, there is a difference among souls: the pure ones will return speedily, the impure ones will need great toil in order to get purified and reach the spiritual world. Once purified, even the imperfect soul will reach the spiritual world: the opinion of those who have maintained that it perishes is false, because, as remote as the impure soul might be from it, that world is its origin and it will in any eventuality return to it.

Such a rewriting contains many elements which misunderstand Plotinus's wording and thought, the most relevant of which lies in the 'Aristotelian' disguise. The focus of Plotinus's passage is the idea (at variance with so many Platonists who credited only the rational soul with immortality) that he also credits the inferior parts of the soul with immortality. But the Arabic passage contends, in purely Aristotelian

body: soul is substance because of its separability from body, and it is separable from body because it is immaterial. See R. Arnzen, *Aristoteles' De Anima. Eine verlorene spätantike Paraphrase in arabischer und persischer Überlieferung*, Leiden - New York - Cologne, 1998, p. 222-223.

vein, that it is the *rational* part which separates upon the death of the body. Another shift occurs in the understanding of the different destiny of souls: whereas Plotinus clearly alludes to the myth of the *Phaedrus*, with the different cycles to be accomplished before the soul is allowed to return to the realm of the intelligibles, depending upon whether or not one has practiced philosophy, in the Arabic version a clear allusion is made to its purification after death. All this is important and deserves more attention than these hasty remarks. But as far as the present question is concerned, it is even more important to notice that the Arabic posits the same relationship which we have in the Greek between tripartition and immortality. In a nutshell, soul is tripartite but this does not imply that it is perishable. Not only does the Arabic *not* suggest that the Greek as it has come down to us through the MSS is lacunose, but, in addition, it also hints that a *verbum dicendi* be supplied:

> ... Then does she return to her own world whence she came, but does not perish or cease to be, *as some think* (my emphasis).

Perhaps the Greek text Ibn Nāʿima al-Ḥimṣī had in front of him did not have the words λυθήσεσθαι <λέγεται> or <φήσουσι>;[112] but this is how he has understood the relationship between tripartition and the alleged mortality of soul. Some may infer from its tripartition that soul is perishable; they are at fault. Although tripartite, soul is immortal in its entirety. This is the basic structure of Plotinus's sentence, and the Arabic, notwithstanding the many changes it operates with respect to the Greek, still allows us to recognise it. No major lacuna in this Plotinian sentence, only another example of his customary condensation of thought and elliptical wording. There are cases in which the Arabic substantially helps in solving a textual problem in the Greek; cases in which it tells us nothing, because the translation is too free; and also cases like the present, in which it gives to the patient reader valuable information, which we can trace back to a model which antedated the archetype of the *Enneads*, about the original wording of a passage damaged in the entire tradition.

I would like to offer this modest exercise in reading Plotinus's text and its Arabic tradition to the scholar who taught us to follow patiently the traces of Plotinian texts and doctrines in Muslim theological literature.

[112] Richard Goulet, who was so kind as to discuss this point with me, suggests that 'as some think' may indicate a form like *οἴονται in the lost original.

GREEK INTO ARABIC: TRANSMISSION AND TRANSLATION

ROSHDI RASHED
Centre d'histoire des sciences et des philosophies arabes et médiévales, CNRS, Paris

Historians of Arabic science and philosophy, of whatever school, unanimously acknowledge the importance of the translation into Arabic of the Greek heritage. They know that to ignore this fact is to understand nothing of the emergence and development of these disciplines in Arabic, and subsequently, in Latin. This is not at all surprising: familiarity with the actual evolution of these areas of Islamic civilisation is what enables us to measure the impact of the Greek heritage — or, at the very least we need only rely on historical accounts and ancient biobibliographers such as Ibn Isḥāq al-Nadīm.[1]

We discover (even indirectly) from historical accounts of Greek science and philosophy just how extensively the Greek heritage was translated into Arabic. If the Arabic translations of Greek writings were to be neglected, a considerable quantity of the Greek heritage and a precious means of understanding it would be lost. Some of these writings are no longer extant in Greek or at best are only partially extant and now exist solely in the Arabic version. Study of the commentaries by Arab scholars and the progress they made in the disciplines covered by these writings constitutes an altogether better method of appreciation and of situating the contributions of their Greek predecessors in the history of a given discipline: Diocles, Apollonius, Ptolemy, Diophantus, Alexander of Aphrodisias, to name but a few.

Although the exceptional breadth of this phenomenon of scientific and philosophical transmission and its importance in the history of science and of philosophy are universally recognised, it has still not received anything like the attention it deserves. There are numerous texts still to be dealt with, and studies to be undertaken to investigate them thoroughly. Moreover, a change of perspective is required if this

[1] IBN ISḤĀQ AL-NADĪM, *Kitāb al-Fihrist*, ed. R. TAJADDUD, Teheran, 1971, in particular the Seventh Chapter: p. 299-360, and p. 417-425. English translation by B. DODGE, *The Fihrist of al-Nadīm*, New York, 1970. One of the earliest studies, now a classic, is MAX MEYERHOF, *Von Alexandrien nach Bagdad. Ein Beitrag zur Geschichte des philosophischen und medizinischen Unterrichts bei den Arabern*, in: *Sitzungsberichte der Preusischer Akademie der Wissenschaften* (*Phil.-hist. Klasse*) (1930), p. 389-429.

research is to follow more fruitful paths. Such a change is now beginning to take place, and it should be applied to methods as well as topics of research. Study of the transmission of the Greek heritage into Arabic from a purely philological angle — as is most often the case — is the surest route to losing sight of the essential points, which are: the motives behind the translation; the extension of its meaning; and the manifold forms it assumed. The examination of this phenomenon solely with a view to the restoration of those Greek writings which were totally or partially lost is to ignore its evolution completely. Once these studies, however legitimate and often locally important, have been generalised, they tend to become the trees which obscure the wood: that is, as soon as they are applied as the method of describing the evolution of the Greek into Arabic translation movement. Some recent research on this phenomenon has endeavoured to rectify this perspective.[2] We will attempt to present and examine this endeavour here.

Transmission and translation: locating the problem

1. Towards a New Approach

It is, then, a matter of no little urgency that the prevailing idea of transmission and translation be discarded forthwith and to that end two widely recognised elementary facts should be mentioned. Firstly, the new Muslim state encompassed the majority of the Hellenistic world: we are therefore talking about one people, but a people whose language and religion differed widely. They received as their heritage a body of knowledge, technical subjects and institutions — elements of a social and economic heritage connected with technical as much as institutional history. However, at the heart of this heritage, there is a body of what might be described as 'dormant' texts, as well as elementary instruction, notably in theology, astrology, alchemy or medicine. Secondly, this heritage is one among many which stemmed from different horizons

[2] R. Rashed, *Problems of the Transmission of Greek Scientific Thought into Arabic: Examples from Mathematics and Optics*, in: *History of Science* 27 (1989), p. 199-209; reproduced in: *Optique et mathématiques: Recherches sur l'histoire de la pensée scientifique en arabe* (*Variorum Collected Studies Series*), Aldershot: Ashgate, 1992, Article no. I. See also D. Gutas, *Greek Thought, Arabic Culture. The Graeco-Arabic Translation Movement in Baghdad and Early ʿAbbāsid Society* (2nd-4th/8th-10th centuries), London - New York, 1998; J.L. Kraemer, *Humanism in the Renaissance of Islam. The Cultural Revival during the Buyid Age*, Leiden, 1992².

(chiefly Persian, Sanskrit and Syriac). To ignore these facts is to neglect the important role played by practice, learning, technical subject matter and institutions in the circulation of knowledge; consequently the question of transmission would very soon be reduced to one of mere translation, whereby the Greek heritage would exist only in the form of books. In other words, one runs the risk of missing those things which are to be uncovered by sifting through the following branches of learning: elementary geometry, logistics, agronomy, hydrostatics, metrology — branches of learning destined later to become part of fully-fledged disciplines, or simply part of practical geometry. Obviously, this alone cannot explain the emergence and the development of science and philosophy in the new Islamic culture: nevertheless, it constitutes an important part of it.

It is not uncommon, however, for the act of translation to be presented as passive and scholarly, carried out in the same style, no matter what the subject. According to this presentation, there would be a translator (often a physician) with a knowledge of Greek who would translate Greek writings belonging to various disciplines not necessarily within his competence, haphazardly, depending on circumstances and the luck of the draw. Translation from Greek is thus a matter of pot-luck, subject to no constraints with regard to choice of book, or freedom to translate. Briefly then, if we adhere to this often tacit assumption, translators would have translated what they happened upon to the best of their abilities: and this would have been scholarly translation, since translated texts were used solely for teaching. Moreover, since at the time (according to this account) translation only required knowledge of Greek (if not Syriac), then the style of these translations would be uniform.

Such a description of transmission followed by translation is transformed into dogma, one that we encounter from time to time, particularly amongst modern biobibliographers.[3] If we are to believe its creeds, translation would be the first stage of a 'law' consisting of three stages succeeding one another logically and historically; first, translation for the acquisition of Greek science and philosophy; then in a second phase, assimilation of the knowledge thus acquired, before passing to the third stage; creative production. This naïve dogma arises from the same assumptions as the previous one: the consideration of translation as nothing other than a desire for acculturation.

[3] See for example F. SEZGIN, *Geschichte des arabischen Schrifttums*, V, Leiden, 1974, p. 25 ff.

Both the dogma and the premises on which it is predicated take several things for granted of which only two will be discussed here. The first is the concomitance of translation and innovation which has not been sufficiently emphasized. However, such concomitance obtains, to give just a few examples, in optics and catoptrics with al-Kindī, in the geometry of conics with al-Ḥasan b. Mūsā and his pupil Thābit b. Qurra (d. 901), and in numbers' theory with the latter. As we shall see, the phenomenon of concomitance unavoidably raises long-forgotten questions of the close relationship between translation and research, and the form which the translation takes, as well as its audience. The second thing which is taken for granted is related to the established but rarely discussed hypothesis of the strong bond of continuity between scientific and philosophical research in Antiquity and Late Antiquity, and the research which developed in Arabic. However this continuity had at best an infrequent effect and appears to have been both fragile and paradoxical.

2. Cultural Transmission, Intellectual Transmission

At an institutional level, there is the question of the arabicisation of the administration and of the organs of power, that is, the *Dīwāns*.[4] We have previously demonstrated that the arabicisation and the evolution of the *Dīwān* gave rise to the translation of logistics and encouraged research for its own ends. This in turn contributed to the conception of a non-Hellenistic discipline (i.e. algebra) with al-Khwārizmī. We have also shown how the culture of the *Dīwān*, so necessary for the training of a paper-based bureaucracy, created a social stratum whose linguistic and literary requirements as well as the demands of logistics, algebra and geometry, amongst other disciplines, stimulated both translation and innovative research.[5] It is therefore true that at this level, as in other sectors such as architecture and agronomy, a certain continuity is discernible. However, the situation is quite different when we turn to scientific research and philosophy. Whilst it is true to say that such research was very unusual

[4] R. RASHED, *Les recommencements de l'algèbre aux XIe et XIIe siècles*, in: *The Cultural Context of Medieval Learning*, ed. J.E. MURDOCH and E.D. SYLLA, Dordrecht, 1975, p. 33-60; reproduced in *Entre arithmétique et algèbre. Recherches sur l'histoire des mathématiques arabes* (*Sciences et philosophie arabes - Études et reprises*), Paris, 1984, p. 43-70, particularly p. 64 ff.

[5] ABŪ L-WAFĀ' AL-BUZJĀNĪ's book *The Arithmetical Requirements of the* Kuttāb (secretaries, administrators and bureaucrats), *the* ʿUmmāl (prefects, tax-collectors) *and others* belongs to this tradition: see the edition of A.S. SAIDAN, *ʿIlm al-Ḥisāb al-ʿArabī*, I, Amman, 1971.

and had vanished completely in both Alexandria and Byzantium,[6] in the Ninth Century, in Arabic, we witness a genuine scientific and philosophical renaissance, the foundations of which — linguistic, historical, philosophical and theological — had been solidly laid in the Eighth Century.

In short, Alexandria and Byzantium, as well as all the other cities of the known world (*oikumenē*), constituted a 'dormant library' for the new scientific community, a library rich in ancient manuscripts from Antiquity and Late Antiquity. All historical accounts are in agreement on this.[7] However, the absence of continuity at this level raises two intimately linked questions, only one of which concerns us at present. How are we actually to account for a renaissance which had been effected by leapfrogging centuries back to Apollonius and Aristotle, for example? What are the links between the transmission of the Greek heritage (and its translation in particular) and this renaissance? It is only really in the light of this scientific and philosophical renaissance that the issue of translation can be fully understood, for this is precisely the link which seems to provide the most efficacious means of understanding it.

The transmission of the Greek heritage into Arabic followed principally, but not exclusively, two paths which are complementary, for all their unequal importance and difference in nature. The first, as yet little explored, although familiar to historians of society and culture, is the one referred to earlier, that of professions, technical subjects, and institutions; in other words, the techniques, organisations and ideologies of the ancient citizens and inhabitants of the Greek-speaking Mediterranean that assured both their material and social existence. This first path is that of the transmission of the *Dīwān* translated into Arabic under Hishām b. ʿAbd al-Malik (724-743);[8] it is also the path taken by the processes of practical geometry and logistics, and by disciplines such as medicine, alchemy, astrology, agronomy, the military arts and

[6] J. F. HALDON, *Byzantium in the Seventh Century: The Transformation of a Culture*, Cambridge, 1990; H.D. SAFFREY, *Le chrétien Jean Philopon et la survivance de l'école d'Alexandrie au VIe siècle*, in: *Revue des Études Grecques* 67 (1954), p. 396-410; L.G. WESTERINK, *Anonymous Prolegomena to Platonic Philosophy*, Amsterdam, 1962.

[7] R. RASHED, *Les mathématiques infinitésimales du IXe au Xe siècle*. Vol. I: *Fondateurs et commentateurs*: *Banū Mūsā, Thābit ibn Qurra, Ibn Sinān, al-Khāzin, al-Qūhī, Ibn al-Samḥ, Ibn Hūd*, London, 1996, p. 142. See also TAMARA M. GREEN, *The City of the Moon*, Leiden, 1992. AL-MASʿŪDĪ's description in *Murūj al-Dhahab* (ed. C. BARBIER DE MEYNARD and M. PAVET DE COURTEILLE, revised by Ch. PELLAT, II, Beirut, 1966, p. 391-396, §§1389-1398) shows that any traces of Hellenism in Ḥarrān around the Third Century Hegira are essentially religious.

[8] AL-NADĪM, *Fihrist*, p. 303.

architecture. To this category belong treatises on elementary logic and theology which were necessary for religious teaching as it was conceived in Nestorian and Jacobite monasteries.[9] It is along this 'natural' path, ('natural' because it had been followed by Hellenised peoples for a thousand years), that we can see the translations of scientific texts in circulation.

The second path, much narrower, but better known, is that of the scholarly translation of philosophical and scientific writings from Antiquity and Late Antiquity. This path is distinguished from its predecessors in the history of translation, including Latin and Syriac, by its magnitude.[10] It would be unrealistic to believe that these two trajectories were self-contained and mutually exclusive. Various indicators point convincingly to the contrary, and future research will no doubt identify many intermediary stages that will allow us to discern all the more clearly this social phenomenon of heritage in transmission and translation. It is sufficient for the moment to identify one general and incontrovertible characteristic: the translation movement went hand in hand with the unification, arabicisation and islamicisation of the Muslim empire and its administration.

3. Scholarly Transmission: One Legend, Several Truths

The second path was, to all extents and purposes, officially 'opened up', if we are to believe the legend, by a dream of the mighty Caliph al-Ma'mūn. According to this legend, the Caliph dreamed he was engaged in conversation with Aristotle. The ancient biobibliographer al-Nadīm, having been told this episode, wrote:

> This dream was one of the most definite reasons for the output of books. Between al-Ma'mūn and the Byzantine Emperor there was correspondence, for al-Ma'mūn had sought aid opposing him. Then he wrote to the Byzantine emperor asking his permission to obtain a selection of old scientific

[9] One might consider the iconic figure of the Patriarch Timothy, who collaborated on the translation of the *Topics* of Aristotle from Syriac into Arabic which was commissioned by the Caliph al-Mahdī: see S.P. Brock, *Two Letters of the Patriarch Timothy from the Late Eighth Century on Translations from Greek*, in: *Arabic Sciences and Philosophy* 9 (1999), p. 233-246. See also J. van Ess, *Theologie und Gesellschaft im 2. und 3. Jahrhundert Hidschra. Eine Geschichte des religiösen Denkens im frühen Islam*, III, Berlin - New York, 1992, p. 22-28.

[10] H. Hugonnard-Roche, *Les traductions du grec en syriaque et du syriaque en arabe*, in: *Rencontres de cultures dans la philosophie medièvale*, ed. J. Hamesse and M. Fattori, Louvain-la-Neuve, 1990, p. 131-147.

> [manuscripts] stored and treasured in the Byzantine country. After first refusing, he complied with this. Accordingly, al-Ma'mūn sent forth a group of men, among whom were al-Ḥajjāj ibn Maṭar; Ibn al-Baṭrīq; Salmān, the director of the Bayt al-Ḥikmah; and others besides them. They brought the books selected from what they had found. Upon bringing them to him [al-Ma'mūn], he ordered them to translate [the manuscripts], so that they made the translation. It is said that Yūḥannā ibn Māsawayh was one of those who went to the Byzantine country.[11]

Al-Nadīm next recalls that the imperial model was imitated by many others. Similarly, the Banū Mūsā, protégés of al-Ma'mūn, sent the famous translator Ḥunayn b. Isḥāq (d. 877) to the 'Byzantine country' and he returned 'with rare books and unusual compositions, about philosophy, geometry, music, arithmetic and medicine'.[12] According to another version, it seems that one of the Banū Mūsā, the eldest (Muḥammad [d. 873]), had been part of an expedition to the Byzantine empire.[13] Several other historical sources describe missions sent to Byzantium, to Alexandria, and to the monasteries at the heart of the ancient Hellenistic world, in search of Greek manuscripts on science and philosophy, right through the Ninth Century and even later.

For all the legendary character of al-Ma'mūn's dream, it vividly captures how contemporary historians and biobibliographers appreciated that this translation movement was qualitatively different from any other which preceded it. It is this difference that we too must appreciate.

a. The Renaissance in Research

Ancient historians were aware that the translation movement came into being well before the reign of al-Ma'mūn (r. 813-833). To be more precise, before this period two stages of a preliminary phase can be discerned. A few fragments commented on by the biobibliographers tell us that translators had already been employed under the Umayyads. Witness the grandson of the founder of the dynasty, Khālid b. Yazīd (d. after 704) who asked one Stephanus to translate certain books on alchemy from Coptic and Greek. Al-Nadīm comments on this account in the following terms: it was 'the first translation in Islam from one language into another'.[14] This evidence has recently been challenged, but it at least has the merit of showing that ancient historians emphasized the

[11] AL-NADĪM, *Fihrist*, p. 303-304, in the translation of DODGE, *Fihrist*, p. 584.

[12] AL-NADĪM, *Fihrist*, p. 304, in the translation of DODGE, *Fihrist*, p. 584.

[13] IBN KHALLIKĀN, *Wafayāt al-A'yān*, ed. IḤSĀN 'ABBĀS, I, Beirut, 1978, p. 313.

[14] AL-NADĪM, *Fihrist*, p. 303. See also p. 419.

interest taken in translation by the scholars of this period and had assigned a special role to Khālid b. Yazīd.[15]

Another testimony, from the same al-Nadīm, serves to corroborate the first: this is the moment when, under the reign of the Caliph Hishām b. ʿAbd al-Malik, the *Dīwān* was translated from Greek into Arabic. It is also at this time when, under the reign of his father and on the advice of Khālid b. Yazīd, that currency was struck in Arabic and no longer in Greek; this is how Ibn al-Athīr and al-Nuwayrī report it.[16] A further testimony, in the same vein, confirms that at the end of the same century (the Seventh), Māsarjawayh translated a medical *compendium* by Ahrūn into Arabic.[17]

These scraps, for such they are, indicate that the transition to the arabicisation of the *Dīwāns* in particular, that is of the administration and its texts, coincided with certain translations undertaken as a result of individual initiatives, as a response to immediate practical needs. Other scraps, of indeterminate date, but which can very probably be situated between this period and the beginning of the next dynasty (the ʿAbbasid), point to the existence of translations, particularly in astronomy: for example Theon of Alexandria's translation of the *Introduction* to the *Almagest*, described by al-Nadīm as an 'ancient translation' (*naql qadīm).*

Arabicisation, which had already made considerable progress, continued to advance with the beginning of the ʿAbbasid dynasty. In addition, a political programme of monumental works was underway, as a result of the very displacement of the seat of the Empire and burgeoning urbanisation. Translation could not but increase and become more widespread. One name epitomizes this movement — that of the second ʿAbbasid Caliph al-Manṣūr (754-775).

Ancient historians agree in emphasizing the personal interest which al-Manṣūr took in astrology.[18] When he decided to found the new capital, Baghdad, he instructed astrologers to calculate the astral chart and to determine the most favourable moment to start work. Here we come across the names of Abū Sahl b. Nawbakht, Ibrāhīm al-Fazārī,

[15] M. ULLMANN, *Khālid ibn Yazīd und die Alchemie. Eine Legende*, in: *Der Islam* 55 (1978), p. 181-218.

[16] AL-NUWAYRĪ, *Nihāyat al-Arab fī Funūn al-Adab*, ed. M. AL-ḤINĪ, Cairo, 1984, p. 223-224; IBN AL-ATHĪR, *Al-Kāmil fī l-Tārīkh*, ed. C.J. TORNBERG, Beirut, 1965-1967 (= Leiden, 1851-1871).

[17] AL-NADĪM, *Fihrist*, p. 355.

[18] AL-MASʿŪDĪ, *Murūj al-Dhahab*, IV, Beirut, 1991, p. 333.

Māshā'allāh. The Caliph also summoned workers, artisans, experts on the law and geometers from various provinces, as many as were necessary for the realisation of this colossal project.[19] Let us dwell a while on this information. Abū Sahl b. Nawbakht is not only an astrologer; he is also a *mutakallim* — that is, a theologian-philosopher. In a text written in his hand, described by al-Nadīm, he presents a kind of legendary history of science, in which he sees its origins, both epistemological and historical, in Babylonian-Persian astrology.[20] Was this doctrine intended to justify the practice of astrology in which the Caliph himself believed? However, even this task required a true knowledge of astronomy and especially the composition of astronomical tables, or *zījs*. Al-Fazārī (second half of the Eighth Century) was not just a simple astronomer, but was also a mathematician. He composed and edited a *zīj*, but also wrote on astronomical instruments (astrolabes and sundials), something which required a solid knowledge of stereographical projections. It therefore seems possible that this group of astrologer-astronomers, accompanied by other geometers, could have carried out all the necessary surveys for the foundation of Baghdad, as well as calculating its astral chart.

New requirements came to light and form part of the backdrop, stimulating a particular programme of research: the composition of *zījs*, the exact representation of a sphere on a plane and so on. Although the disappearance of texts drastically deprives us of the sources that would have allowed us to evaluate this nascent research, there are definitely clues that alert us to a change in the climate. Al-Manṣūr could have received an Indian delegation containing an astronomer, in the presence of al-Fazārī to whom he could have given an Indian *zīj*. Al-Fazārī, along with Yaʿqūb b. Ṭāriq, could have been charged with adapting it into Arabic. A dubious story? Perhaps, but one which paints a picture of how one imagines the era to have been.[21] Another report (equally late — dating from 330/941), from a certain al-Akhbārī, as told by the historian al-Masʿūdī, also describes the interest that al-Manṣūr had in astrology, and that he was attended by Abū Sahl b. Nawbakht and al-Fazārī (as well as ʿAlī b. ʿĪsā, the astrolabe expert, and the youngest of the group by far).

[19] According to AL-NUWAYRĪ: 'He (al-Manṣūr) wrote to every country to ask that they send artisans and masons and he decreed that eminent, honest and just men, educated in jurisprudence and geometry, should be chosen' (*Nihāyat al-Arab*, XXII, p. 90).

[20] AL-NADĪM, *Fihrist*, p. 299-300.

[21] For a similar case, see AL-JĀḤIẒ, *Kitāb al-Bayān wa-l-Tabyīn*, ed. ʿA.M. HĀRŪN, I, Cairo, s.d., p. 88-93. French translation of the passage: M. AOUAD - M. RASHED, *L'exégèse de la* Rhétorique *d'Aristote: Recherches sur quelques commentateurs grecs, arabes et byzantins*, in: *Medioevo* 23 (1997), p. 43-189 (p. 89-91).

We read that al-Manṣūr 'is the first Caliph for whom books in foreign languages were translated into the Arabic language'.[22] Al-Akhbārī mentions some titles in translation, including the *Almagest*, the *Elements*, and Nicomachus of Gerasa's *Arithmetical Introduction*. He further writes that 'all the ancient texts in Greek, Byzantine, Pahlavi, Persian and Syriac' had been translated for him and 'that they [the books] had been distributed among people who had examined them and who were very keen to acquaint themselves with the knowledge which they contained'.[23]

Whatever the historical value of this late evidence, it does reflect the opinions of those who came after the reign of al-Manṣūr. Translations were commissioned at the behest of the sovereign, but in the background there was a certain amount of research requiring the translation of particular works, and accelerated arabicisation demanded the institution of a new library fit for an Empire which stretched from India to the Atlantic. And what are we to do with the books mentioned by al-Akhbārī? As far as the *Almagest* is concerned, nothing actually contradicts the accuracy of the information; in fact, it is corroborated by a passage from al-Nadīm, according to which al-Manṣūr's vizier, Khālid b. Barmak, instructed the preliminary translation, and which, on being found unsatisfactory, was later corrected at his behest.[24] Perhaps **this** is the translation in question. By contrast, the *Arithmetical Introduction* by Nicomachus was translated at first from Syriac, by Ḥabīb b. Bihrīz. However, he 'translated several books for al-Ma'mūn',[25] that is to say at least forty years later — which makes the evidence possible but improbable. We would also have to postulate a translation earlier than al-Ḥajjāj's first translation of Euclid's *Elements*, yet there is no other information available to confirm the existence of such a thing. The question therefore remains open.

The involvement of political power in soliciting translation from Greek and other languages; the establishment in Arabic of a library fit for the new world, a consequence, at least in part, of the continued arabicisation of the State and of culture for over a century and a half; the response to the needs of research: these were the imperatives to which translation had to respond at the end of the first phase and at the beginning of the second. Several ancient translations, until recently unknown,

[22] AL-MASʿŪDĪ, *Murūj al-Dhahab*, IV, Beirut, 1991, p. 333.
[23] AL-MASʿŪDĪ, *Murūj al-Dhahab*, IV, Beirut, 1991, p. 333.
[24] AL-NADĪM, *Fihrist*, p. 327.
[25] AL-NADĪM, *Fihrist*, p. 304.

must have belonged to this intermediary phase. We also know that al-Kindī possessed a translation of Archimedes's *Measurement of the Circle* which differed from the later translation based on a Greek manuscript.[26] Al-Kindī was also familiar with a translation of Euclid's *Optics* that was different to the one which has come down to us and which was most probably made before to this one. And finally, an ancient translation of the beginning of *Mechanical Paradoxes* by Anthemius of Tralles[27] has just been discovered.

The diversity of texts translated is striking: Euclid's *Optics*, Archimedes's *Measurement of the Circle*, works by Anthemius of Tralles. One could add other treatises. But as far as our actual knowledge goes, these are relatively short texts, but linked nonetheless to research, as we shall see. As for the translations, they are literal and rely on a terminology that would later be heavily revised during the second phase of translation (see below).

b. Institution and Profession: The Age of the Academies

This movement gathered momentum and accelerated into a second phase, during which translation became both *institution* and *profession*. Al-Ma'mūn's dream not only heralds its inception, but imbues it with meaning. Even at its apogee, at the beginning of the ʿAbbasid dynasty, the first phase of the translation movement cannot be confused with its successor, be it in terms of the number of translations, the diversity of texts translated, or the technical competence and increased specialisation of the translators. Translation became a scientific profession as well as an institution. There are various reasons for this transformation which began at the time of al-Ma'mūn and would burgeon with his successors. One reason which is often overlooked is the change in the encyclopaedia of knowledge: between the middle of the Eighth Century and the middle of the Ninth, there emerged various disciplines directly linked to the new society, its ideology and its organisation. For example, different fields of research were inspired by the need to have access to sacred texts and their interpretation. And so a whole spectrum of linguistic disciplines appeared, ranging from ethnolinguistics to lexicography based on actual phonological research and on combinatorial procedures. Thanks to al-

[26] R. RASHED, *Al-Kindī's Commentary on Archimedes'* The Measurement of the Circle, in: *Arabic Sciences and Philosophy* 3 (1993), p. 7-53.

[27] *Les catoptriciens grecs, I: Les miroirs ardents*, edited and translated with commentary by R. RASHED, Paris, 2000, p. 343-359.

Khalīl b. Aḥmad, they included grammar and philology.[28] Let us also keep in mind the development of the *Kalām*, a philosophical-theological science, with multiple schools and their various diversifications.[29] We should also note, for example, the different branches of history and the birth of the use of critical analysis as applied to evidence; the development of the hermeneutic sciences, especially that of the Qur'ān; the diverse logical and juridical sciences necessary for research into Islamic law, and so forth. Add to this algebra itself, as well as other disciplines born of practical needs and the administration of the Empire. The encyclopaedia of knowledge is therefore very different to that of Late Antiquity: al-Fārābī will later outline its contents in his *Classification of the Sciences*.[30]

If the new encyclopaedia reflects these disciplines and their diversity, as well as the culture of the time, it also points to a development which can be perceived from reading *Ṭabaqāt* works ('the classes of scholars') as well as ancient biobibliographies: a growth in specialisation. A scholar would belong principally to a profession, or sometimes two complementary professions, such as *mutakallim* (theologian-philosopher) and scholar of law. However, within the profession itself, a scholar would belong to one school or another: Kufa and Basra for example, for grammarians; Basra and Baghdad for theologian-philosophers.[31] These new disciplines, and the ever-increasing number of their specialists, constituted an audience with its own demands. The theologian-philosopher wanted to know more about philosophy, logic and even statics and physics, and wanted to understand them better.[32] The requirements of religion (determination of the direction of Mecca and the hours of prayer in such a vast empire) required new knowledge in astronomy. Progress

[28] R. RASHED, *Entre arithmétique et algèbre*, p. 253-257.

[29] R. M. FRANK, *The Science of* Kalām, in: *Arabic Sciences and Philosophy* 2.1 (1992), p. 7-37; J. VAN ESS, *Frühe Muʿtazilitische Häresiographie*, Wiesbaden, 1971. For an insight into the extent of the diversification of thought, see AL-SHAHRASTĀNĪ, *Livre des religions et des sectes*, translation with introduction and notes by D. GIMARET and G. MONNOT, Leuven, 1986.

[30] AL-FĀRĀBĪ, *Iḥṣā' al-ʿUlūm*, ed. ʿUTHMĀN AMĪN, Cairo, 1968³.

[31] From the outset these differences have been perceived as decisive. For the two fields mentioned, see ABŪ SAʿĪD AL-ANBĀRĪ, *Al-Inṣāf fī Masā'il al-Khilāf bayna l-Naḥwīyīn al-Baṣrīyīn wa-l-Kūfīyīn*, Beirut, 1987, and ABŪ RASHĪD AL-NĪSĀBŪRĪ, *Al-Masā'il fī l-Khilāf bayna l-Baṣrīyīn wa-l-Baghdādīyīn*, ed. M. ZIYĀDA and R. AL-SAYYID, Beirut, 1979.

[32] For example, Abū l-Hudhayl and his nephew al-Naẓẓām: see M.A. ABŪ RĪDA, *Ibrāhīm b. Sayyār al-Naẓẓām wa-Arā'u-hu l-Kalāmīya al-Falsafīya*, Cairo, 1946; A. DHANANI, *The Physical Theory of* Kalām. *Atoms, Space and Void in Basrian Muʿtazili Cosmology*, Leiden,1994.

in medical science was also needed to meet the demand for medicine in urban centres. Administrators of the *Dīwān* and private secretaries (a calling which grew into a true profession)[33] were the incumbents of positions which required command of a reasonably extensive general culture. In short, a wide audience for the disciplines and culture translated mainly from Greek and Persian was thus created. We also find a certain number of 'cultural' works among the books translated, dealing with topics such as the moral pronouncements of philosophers[34] or the interpretation of dreams.[35]

It is not long, in this second phase of the movement, before we see the institutionalisation of both translation and the Greek heritage. Facts and anecdotes abound, informing us that caliphs, viziers, princes, the wealthy, and even certain scholars, founded libraries and observatories and encouraged translation and research.[36] However, it has not been sufficiently emphasised that these new institutions housed not only individuals, as had previously been the case, but also groups, teams, often rivals and competitors.[37] Thus there were plenty of opportunities for the integration of the Greek heritage in the new scientific city. Take, for example, the House of Wisdom (*Bayt al-Ḥikma*) founded by al-Ma'mūn in Baghdad. It housed astronomers such as Yaḥyā b. Abī Manṣūr, translators such as al-Ḥajjāj b. Maṭar — who translated Euclid's *Elements* and Ptolemy's *Almagest* — and mathematicians such as al-Khwārizmī. Later we encounter, in another group linked to the same foundation, the three Banū Mūsā brothers, mathematicians and astronomers who financed and promoted translation; the translator of Apollonius, Hilāl b. Hilāl al-Ḥimṣī and the translator and mathematician, Thābit b. Qurra. We also know that groups of translators and scholars were formed around the Banū Mūsā, al-Kindī and Ḥunayn b. Isḥāq, to name but a few: other specialist groups worked in the same way in mosques, observatories and even hospitals.

[33] See for example IBN QUTAYBA, *Adad al-Kātib*, ed. A. FĀʿŪR, Beirut, 1988; AL-JAHSHIYĀRĪ, *Kitāb al-Wuzarā' wa-l-Kuttāb*, Beirut, s.d.

[34] For example, Ḥunayn b. Isḥāq's translation of *The Testament of Plato for the Education of the Young* in: L. CHEIKHO, *Traités philosophiques anciens*, Beirut, 1911.

[35] For example, Ḥunayn b. Isḥāq's translation of the *Book of Dreams* by Artemidorus of Ephesus: see the critical edition by TOUFIC FAHD, Damascus, 1964.

[36] M.G. BALTY-GUESDON, *Le* Bayt al-Ḥikma *de Bagdad*, in: *Arabica* 39 (1992), p. 131-150; Y. ECHE, *Les bibliothèques arabes publiques et semi-publiques en Mésopotamie, en Syrie et en Égypte au Moyen-Âge,* Damascus, 1967.

[37] Ancient bibliographers report conflicts between al-Kindī (and his collaborators) and the Banū Mūsā (and their group), for example.

The manner in which translation was carried out at this time reveals two related features of an especial importance. Conducted on a grand scale, it was not solely limited to writings with a practical aim; it quite often happens that translations from the first phase or even those from the beginning of the second phase were redone. Euclid's *Elements* was translated three times: the *Almagest* at least three times, and so on. The act of revising a translation was a response to changing criteria within the practice of translation. Translation became the work of individual members of schools and of competitive groups; the criteria for translation were no longer the same; the translator was no longer what he was during the first phase, but was doubly trained, both in languages and in philosophy and the sciences. But before we explain this evolution and ask who was translating, how he translated and why he did so, let us start by noting that translation did not follow any didactic order (from the easiest to the most difficult books), nor did it follow the chronological order of the Greek authors. There was certainly no predetermined plan that guided translation, though this is not to say that it was done haphazardly, in response to the discovery of books to be translated. Several contemporary accounts indicate on the contrary that works were chosen for translation before searching for the manuscripts required for the establishment of the text. Thus, Ḥunayn b. Isḥāq decided to translate Galen's *On Demonstration* before embarking on a search for manuscripts.[38] The

[38] The following is an autobiographical account by Ḥunayn b. Isḥāq of his search for a manuscript of Galen's *On Demonstration:* 'He [Galen] composed this work in fifteen books. His aim was to show the way forward in the matter of proofs. This was also Aristotle's aim in Book IV of the *Organon*. To date, none of our contemporaries has managed to obtain a complete set of this work, even though Jibrīl took great pains over his search, as did I in my zealous quest for this work in Mesopotamia, throughout Syria, Palestine and Egypt, even as far as Alexandria. I found nothing, except at Damascus where I discovered about half of the work, but it was incomplete and the books were not in any order. However Jibrīl discovered several books of this work, which were not the ones that I had found'. We can deduce from this account that searches took place not only in Byzantium, but throughout the whole of the ancient empire; that Alexandria, amongst other places, was visited in the search for Greek manuscripts; that the manuscript of such an important work as this was found in serendipitously in Damascus; that the translators themselves travelled independently of the great manuscript expeditions, such as the one dispatched by al-Ma'mūn; and finally that our knowledge of the translation movement from Greek into Syriac and Arabic is still not really adequate. These conclusions are confirmed by another account. Yaḥyā (Yūḥannā) b. al-Biṭriq, a member of the famous expedition sent by the Caliph al-Ma'mūn to Byzantium in search of Greek manuscripts, recounts how he was commanded by the Caliph to go in search of the manuscript of the *Sirr al-Asrār* (*Secret of Secrets*): 'the translator Yūḥannā b. al-Biṭriq said: I visited every temple where the philosophers had hidden their secrets; I visited every great ascetic, made wise by knowledge, thinking that he might have in his possession the object of my quest, until I came to the temple that Asclepius had had constructed. There I met a pious

same situation obtained when the Banū Mūsā wanted to have Apollonius's *Conics* translated.[39]

These features of the second phase of translation reveal a phenomenon that has gone unnoticed for too long: the close relationship between translation on a grand scale and active and innovative research. It is this relationship in particular which interests us here.

c. *An Ideal Translator: The Travels of Ḥunayn b. Isḥāq*

Before we examine this relationship, let us dwell a while on the training of this new generation of translators who were to transmit the essence of the Greek philosophical and scientific heritage right through the Ninth Century and especially during its second half. In contrast to the majority of their predecessors, these translators were neither enlightened amateurs familiar with an ancient language nor members of a profession (physicians or alchemists) capable of rendering into an approximate Arabic one of the books of their discipline. We are now confronted with true professionals, both in linguistic competence and scientific knowledge. The paragon, one might argue, was the famous Ḥunayn b. Isḥāq.[40] The account of his biography that has come down to us is of great interest: this colourful piece of literature, whether it be genuine or legendary, highlights the ideal characteristics of the new profession. (However, everything leads us to believe that this idealised journey bears more than a passing resemblance to historical reality.) A Christian Arab (Nestorian) born in 808 of a pharmacist father in Ḥīra, his travels began in Basra, where we see him perfecting his Arabic; he knew that the language of translation was not that of everyday use. His choice of Basra lies behind the legend that he met one of the greatest Arabic linguists: al-Khalīl b. Aḥmad.[41] In the story of his life, this

and devout ascetic, a man of surpassing knowledge and penetrating intelligence. Having made him aware of my goodwill towards him, I stayed as his guest and treated him with guile until I got him to entrust me with the books which were in his temple. Among them I found the book I had been looking for, the object of my quest which I coveted' (*Fontes Graecae Doctrinarum Politicarum Islamicarum*, ed. A. BADAWI, Cairo, 1954, p. 69).

[39] R. RASHED, *Les mathématiques infinitésimales du IXe au XIe siècle*. Vol. III: *Ibn al-Haytham, Théorie des coniques, constructions géométriques et géométrie pratique*, London, 2000, Chapter 1.

[40] See G. BERGSTRÄSSER, *Ḥunain b. Isḥāq über die Kunde syrischen und arabischen Galen-übersetzungen*, in: *Abhandlungen für die Kunde des Morgenländische Gesellschaft*, 1925. See also G.C. ANAWATI and A.Z. ISKANDAR, *Ḥunayn ibn Isḥāq*, in: *Dictionary of Scientific Biography*, XV, Supplement 1 (1978), p. 230-248.

[41] 'He [Ḥunayn b. Isḥāq] stayed there for some time and his master in Arabic was al-Khalīl b. Aḥmad' (IBN ABĪ UṢAYBIʿA, *'Uyūn al-Anbā' fī Ṭabaqāt al-Aṭibbā'*, ed. N. RIḌĀ, Beirut, 1965, p. 257 and 262).

legend is both initiatory and emblematic: his mentor in Arabic was none other than al-Khalīl b. Aḥmad himself. We next meet him in Baghdad, the scene of his scientific education proper, where he also studied medicine under the aegis of one of the greatest doctors of the time: Yūḥannā b. Māsawayh. It is here that our hero met his destiny. Banished by Ibn Māsawayh from his circle, Ḥunayn started his education afresh. This is the third stage. He went to one of the centres of Hellenism to perfect his knowledge of Greek — whether it was in the Byzantine empire or Alexandria, the biographers are unsure. He reappears a few years later, in Baghdad, reciting verses of Homer[42] by heart: symbolically, such mastery of Greek is most certainly a corollary to al Khalīl's earlier tutoring in Arabic.

Three distinct stages, therefore, and all necessary for the training of the new type of translator: henceforth a *translator-scholar*, one who knew Greek, Arabic, Syriac and the sciences. These important requirements find an echo in two facts. Firstly, science in translation was still a living science. In fact we will see later that translation was not carried out in order to rewrite the history of a scientific discipline, but rather actively to pursue a practical programme of research. Secondly, henceforth one of the tasks of the translator was to contribute to the development of scientific Arabic. This demanded linguistic research proper and in turn required an education and training similar to that received by Ḥunayn b. Isḥāq.

Ḥunayn then spent the rest of his life translating Greek medical works as well as several books of philosophy, some of which were required by the medical curriculum. During the course of this life of translation (the quality of which is universally acknowledged) he embarked on a programme of research into scientific Arabic. He is credited with translating one hundred and twenty-nine works, with two thirds being in Syriac and a third in Arabic. The disproportionate number of works in Syriac reflects the composition of the medical community at the time, and hence the nature of the demand. As most physicians were of Syriac origin and as they continued to hold positions as court physicians, so they were the ones who commissioned the majority of translations for practical or research purposes.[43] And in fact, where historical records provide the names of those who commissioned translations, we find Bakhtīshūʿ b. Jibrāʾīl, Salmawayh, Dāʾūd, and Yūḥannā b. Māsawayh, all of whom were Syriac physicians; and the Banū Mūsā, who were cultivated math-

[42] Ibn Abī Uṣaybiʿa, *ʿUyūn al-Anbāʾ*, p. 258.

[43] See H. Hugonnard-Roche, *L'intermédiaire syriaque dans la transmission de la philosophie grecque à l'arabe: le cas de l'*Organon *d'Aristote*, in: *Arabic Sciences and Philosophy* 1 (1991), p. 187-209.

ematicians. Ḥunayn b. Isḥāq also composed several medical works, as well as being a practising physician, in addition to a number of books on Arabic grammar and lexicography.[44] In order to comprehend the enormity of this output, let us note a second feature: the organization of translation and research into teams. There was a whole school organized around Ḥunayn, including his son Isḥāq, his nephew Ḥubaysh and ʿĪsā b. Yaḥyā, as well as the copyists al-Aḥwal and al-Azraq.[45]

This new type of translator, as we can see, is distinct not merely because of the exigencies of the linguistic and scientific training to which he responded, but also by his new tasks: research into both scientific Arabic as well as science. A gradual and latent transformation occurred as the century advanced, in embryo from the time of Ḥunayn b. Isḥāq: the change from *translator-scholar* to *scholar-translator*. This is the gulf which separates Ḥunayn from Thābit b. Qurra (d. 901).

d. Third Phase: From Translator-Scholar to Scholar-Translator

Thābit b. Qurra is one of the greatest mathematicians not only of Islam but of all time. He began life as a moneychanger. His mother tongue was Syriac, and he learned Greek and Arabic sufficiently well to translate works of astronomy, mathematics and philosophy. It was for his talents and linguistic knowledge that Muḥammad b. Mūsā, upon returning from a search for manuscripts in the Byzantine Empire, 'discovered' him in his native town of Ḥarrān (or in the nearby village of Kafr Tūtha) and brought him to Baghdad with him. Welcomed by Muḥammad b. Mūsā into his own home, he received instruction in mathematics under the aegis of the three brothers and especially the youngest, al-Ḥasan, a mathematician of genius. Once his education was complete, Thābit b. Qurra translated a considerable number of Greek treatises on mathematics, including Archimedes's *The Sphere and the Cylinder*, the last three books (now lost in Greek) of Apollonius's *Conics* and Nicomachus of Gerasa's *Arithmetical Introduction*. He also revised numerous translations — Euclid's *Elements* and Ptolemy's *Almagest*, among many others. Thābit b. Qurra also composed numerous works in astronomy and mathematics of such great importance that his sterling work as a translator almost pales into insignificance by comparison.

44 Ibn Abī Uṣaybiʿa mentions amongst his writings a book on grammar (*kitāb fī l-naḥw*) and a book on the classification of names of simple medicines (*kitāb fī asmāʾ al-adwiya al-mufrada ʿalā ḥurūf al-muʿjam*) (*ʿUyūn al-Anbāʾ*, p. 273).

45 Ibn Abī Uṣaybiʿa, *ʿUyūn al-Anbāʾ*, p. 260 and 270.

Between the translator-scholar such as Ḥunayn and the scholar-translator in the manner of Thābit, there is a whole 'intermediate' category, made up of eminent translators whose scientific training was as wide as it was deep: Ḥunayn's own son, Isḥāq b. Ḥunayn (d. 911) and Qusṭā b. Lūqā (d. beginning of the Tenth Century), among many others. Nonetheless, with this new phase of translation there was a noticeable change in educational requirements and in the criteria used in translating, and there was a major reinforcement of the links between scientific and philosophical research and translation. As we have remarked of Thābit, these are the very factors which fostered activities previously unheard of: the revision of ancient translations or those done by non-specialists.

TRANSLATION AND RESEARCH: A MULTIPLE DIALECTIC

If we ignore scientific and philosophical research, we will certainly fail to understand the Greek into Arabic translation movement. For this is what informed the choice of books translated, and drove its evolution. This statement is not a hypothesis of our own devising, nor is it an insight derived from the act of translation but from history. We will therefore select some examples from different disciplines, in order to illustrate and clarify as far as possible the dialectic of translation and research. The plethora of material and, of course, the limits of our own competence dictate our choice: we will limit ourselves principally to optics, geometry and arithmetic.

1. Concomitance and Transcendence: Optics and Catoptrics

Let us begin in a truly empirical fashion by listing the titles of major Greek works on optics and catoptrics translated into Arabic, along with their Arab translators.

1. Euclid's *Optics* was translated at least twice into Arabic; once before the middle of the Ninth Century. Al-Kindī composed a critical commentary on it at the beginning of his own research into optics.[46]

[46] R. RASHED, *Le commentaire par al-Kindī de l'*Optique *d'Euclide: un traité jusqu'ici inconnu*, in: *Arabic Sciences and Philosophy* 7.1 (1997), p. 9-57.

2. Ptolemy's *Optics*. The Greek original has been lost. The Arabic translation, most probably not produced before the end of the Ninth Century, is also lost. There remains only the Latin translation of the Arabic version, which was carried out by the Emir Eugene of Sicily.[47] From the documents available today, it seems that this work, and particularly the Fifth Book on refraction, came quite late in the development of optics, that is, during the Tenth Century (as part of the research conducted by al-ʿAlāʾ b. Sahl in particular).
3. The *Catoptrics* attributed to Euclid. It has been shown that fragments exist in Arabic, especially in a Ninth Century work written by Qusṭā b. Lūqā.[48]
4. Diocles's *Burning Mirrors:* only two propositions have been quoted by Eutochius.[49] The work is no longer extant in Greek, and we only have an Arabic translation,[50] which is relatively early if we are to judge by the vocabulary.
5. Anthemius of Tralles's *Burning Mirrors* (*Mechanical Paradoxes*). The extant Greek text is incomplete. This work was translated twice, perhaps three times, into Arabic; the first time before the middle of the Ninth Century, the second time rather later. At least one of the Arabic versions seems complete.[51]
6. *Burning Mirrors and the Abridged Conics*. This is an Arabic translation of a lost Greek book, by one Dtrūms, according to the Arabic transcription, who has yet to be identified.[52]
7. The *Bobbio Fragment* on burning mirrors. There is no trace of this text in Arabic.[53]

To this list can be added some titles of lesser importance, such as Hero of Alexandria's *Catoptrics*, fragments of which have survived in Arabic in an early translation.[54]

Such is the sum total of the texts on optics and catoptrics. Some conclusions are immediately obvious. The essential Greek works were

[47] A. Lejeune, *L'*Optique *de Claude Ptolémée dans la version latine d'après l'arabe de l'émir Eugène de Sicile*, Leuven, 1956.

[48] R. Rashed, *Œuvres philosophiques et scientifiques d'al Kindī*. Vol. I: *L'Optique et la catoptrique*, Leiden, 1996, Appendix 2, p. 541-645.

[49] R. Rashed, *Les catoptriciens grecs*, First Part.

[50] R. Rashed, *Les catoptriciens grecs*, p. 21.

[51] R. Rashed, *Les catoptriciens grecs*, Appendix, p. 343-359.

[52] R. Rashed, *Les catoptriciens grecs*, Chapter 2, p.155-213.

[53] R. Rashed, *Les catoptriciens grecs*, Chapter 4, p. 272 ff.

[54] Various writings in this tradition survive in Arabic: the Pseudo-Euclidean *On Mirrors*, for example.

known and translated into Arabic, some texts more than once. This is what we mean when we describe the translation phenomenon as large scale and multiple. Indeed, several treatises were translated into Arabic before the middle of the Ninth Century, and from the middle of that same century they were both studied and subjected to scientific scrutiny. For example, al-Kindī commented in minute detail on Euclid's *Optics* and the work of Anthemius of Tralles.[55] Moreover, it should not be assumed that the order of the translations conformed to the order outlined above; in fact the order which they followed was the order in which research was conducted. But before we discuss this point, let us begin by noting the differences between the two phases of translation, in order to distinguish the different criteria used. Anthemius of Tralles provides us with a good test-case.

It is certain that the first translation of Anthemius's *Mechanical Paradoxes* was carried out before the middle of the Ninth Century, right at the moment, it would seem, when research on burning mirrors was being conducted in Arabic. The works of al-Kindī and Qusṭā b. Lūqā in this area dispel any doubt on this point. Detailed examination of this translation reveals it to be literal, employing an archaic vocabulary long since abandoned even by al-Kindī himself. The second translation benefits from research which had in fact been undertaken, not only because it opts for a more exact and consistent lexicon, but also for an improved syntax, resulting in a more readable text.[56]

The difference between the two different types of translation did not go unnoticed at the time, even if its historical significance did. It is not by chance that in the Ninth Century and later the question of different styles of translation was raised. Al-Kindī debated the matter and his contemporary, the learned philosopher al-Jāḥiẓ, discussed it also.[57] We need only refer to al-Kindī's letter to a correspondent who had not understood Ptolemy's description of an instrument in the Fifth Book of the *Almagest:*

> You have asked me, O brother, may you be praised again and again!, to describe to you the instrument mentioned by Ptolemy at the beginning of Book Five of the *Almagest*, since you have doubts about the description he gives of this instrument and its use. Now, your doubts do not arise from a

[55] R. RASHED, *L'optique et la catoptrique d'al-Kindī.*

[56] See the Appendix for an illustration of this.

[57] AL-JĀḤIẒ, *Kitāb al-Ḥayawān*, ed. ʿABD AL-SALĀM HĀRŪN, I, Cairo, 1938-1945, p. 75 f. Cf. ABŪ ḤAYYĀN AL-TAWḤĪDĪ, *Kitāb al-Imtāʿ wa-l-Muʾānasa*, ed. A. AMĪN and A. AL-ZAYN, reproduction of the Būlāq edition, s.d., p. 112, 115-116,121. See also MUHSIN MAHDI, *Language and Logic in Classical Islam*, in: *Logic in Classical Islamic Culture*, ed. G.E. VON GRUNEBAUM, Wiesbaden, 1970, p. 51-53.

> fault in his exposition, but from the difficulty of the arrangement of his words, because he was such a learned and literate man that he was above and beyond observing the custom of the majority of people in the use they make of words; so much so that comprehending the arrangement of his words is difficult, even if the meaning is clear to those who undertake to translate his books from Greek into Arabic — the difficulty in the arrangement of the words is the reason why they are difficult for the translator to understand. Also, out of fear of conveying their own ideas instead of the meaning of his [Ptolemy's] words, and of allowing themselves to be seduced into making an error over conveying its true essence, they have been constrained to recreate the same order in Arabic, and to write in Arabic what each successive word means.
>
> In order to keep themselves free from error, the translators have been incessant in pondering, pursuing and disengaging the meanings they have obtained from this book. But not all of those who translated these books have been equally successful — only the most assured and those skilled enough in Greek not to lose two things at once: knowledge of the meanings of the book and the exactness of its words. In fact, those who try to interpret the sense of what they are translating, without understanding this sense, commit two faults simultaneously: they lose the meanings and they lose the words. And this is prejudicial to anyone who examines their translation in order fully to comprehend some of the insights of the author of the work.
>
> If, on the other hand, the translators capture for him the word as it is, even if it is difficult for him to comprehend, they allow him to comprehend the author's thoughts, even if they are only arrived at with much effort.[58]

This very important text describes for us, in the language of the day, the nature of translation from Greek into Arabic and discusses the two principal styles which we have identified. In addition to lexical difficulties, it is syntactical difficulties which predominate. Both features are the mark of a specialised language (in this case, astronomy). There are in fact two styles of translation: that of the translator who proceeds word by word, running the risk of losing the sense; that of the translator-scholars who attempt first to grasp the sense of the ideas; of this group, only those who are 'assured and skilled in Greek' succeed in not committing any errors. In the absence of this accomplishment (i.e. the style of Ḥunayn, Isḥāq and such), al-Kindī prefers the word by word approach.

The historical import of these reflections is clear, even if it is not pointed out by al-Kindī, himself in permanent contact with both types of translators. In fact, whereas the first phase of translation was often carried out in response to the needs of research in its infancy, the second

[58] AL-KINDĪ, *Risāla fī Dhāt al-Ḥalaq*, MS *Paris, Bibliothèque nationale*, no. 2544, fol. 56-60.

was generally linked to research which was already well advanced. Al-Kindī and his contemporary Ibn Lūqā are good examples for catoptrics. Being in possession of the first Arabic version of *Mechanical Paradoxes*, al-Kindī wrote a whole treatise on burning mirrors,[59] which was not only a critique of the numerous weakness of the Anthemius text, but included a host of new results. Ibn Lūqā was also engaged on research into catoptrics[60] and composed a treatise on burning mirrors. This is the period when most of the Greek treatises on mirrors were translated into Arabic, as a rigorous study of the vocabulary demonstrates. The progress in research made by al-Kindī and his successors led to a slightly paradoxical result: on the one hand it acted as an incentive to produce a better translation of *Mechanical Paradoxes*, which would then be used by al-Kindī's successors such as Ibn ʿĪsā (a minor author);[61] on the other hand, the role of the translated Greek texts was eventually relegated to being solely of historical value. Even if at the beginning of the Tenth Century scholars such as ʿUṭārid and Ibn ʿĪsā took an interest in them, by the end of the century, for Ibn Sahl, his contemporaries and successors they remained but a faint memory.

Burning mirrors represented only one chapter in Hellenistic optics. There was, for example, also optics proper: that is, the geometric study of perspective and optical illusions; catoptrics, which is the geometric study of the reflection of visual rays on mirrors; meteorological optics in which atmospheric phenomena such as the halo and the rainbow are studied. These are the divisions which al-Fārābī cites in his *Classification of the Sciences*. To the geometrical disciplines we must also add the theories of vision which characterized the activities of physicians and the treatises of philosophers. In all these areas, the Greek heritage was transmitted according to the model which has already been analysed for burning mirrors.

Historical research is not yet able to tell us which ideas on optics were transmitted by medical practice before the end of the Eighth Century. By contrast, towards the end of this period and during the first half of the Ninth Century, we encounter ophthalmological research undertaken by physicians such as Jibrāʾīl b. Bakhtīshūʿ (d. 828/829)[62] and after him Yūḥannā b. Māsawayh. This was of sufficient interest for Ḥunayn b. Isḥāq to compose for the medical community a compendium in which he

[59] R. RASHED, *L'optique et la catoptrique d'al-Kindī*.

[60] R. RASHED, *L'optique et la catoptrique d'al-Kindī*, Appendix II.

[61] R. RASHED, *L'optique et la catoptrique d'al-Kindī*, Appendix III, p. 647-701.

[62] AL-NADĪM, *Fihrist*, p. 354-355.

presented the contents of Galenic writings on the anatomy and physiology of the eye.[63] Ḥunayn also translated the pseudo-Galenic treatise, *On the Anatomy of the Eye*.[64] Did research into, and the practice of, ophthalmology stimulate the study of optics and catoptrics? This seems plausible, even if it is still too early to say. In any case, it is around this time that most of the principal Greek works on optics and catoptrics were translated — Euclid, Theon, Hero — (Ptolemy's *Optics*, in all probability, was not translated until the end of the century). The history of Arabic optics as inheritor of Greek optics (and Greek optics alone), was therefore essentially concerned with amending and critically revising its inheritance.

It is significant that in the middle of the Ninth Century, Euclid's *Optics* was not only available, but already the object of revision. We now know that, at this time, there was not one but two translations of the *Optics*. One of them exists in several manuscripts, and it often departs from the text of the two Greek versions known today, even in passages as fundamental as the preliminary definitions. This Arabic translation is the one which two mathematicians, Naṣīr al-Dīn al-Ṭūsī and Ibn Abī Jarrāda would comment on in the Thirteenth Century. The second translation is at least as old as the first, since al-Kindī used it in the middle of the Ninth Century. The identification of this version profoundly alters our conception of the textual history of Euclid's *Optics* as traced by Heiberg and which has been the subject of recent debate. In a nutshell, Heiberg distinguished between the *Optica Genuina* (*Vind. phil. gr.* 103) and the version he christened as 'by Theon', of which the oldest manuscript is the *Vat. gr.* 204. However, scholarship (W. Knorr, for instance) thought itself quite recently in a position to contradict this and to affirm that the text which Heiberg attributed to Theon (*Vat. gr.* 204) should be identified as Euclid's, with the *Optica Genuina* considered a later development of the version by Theon. However if we take account of the two Arabic versions, we are able to go one step further and demonstrate that there were not only two, but four, independent textual traditions of Euclid's *Optics*, and this leads us to conclude that none of these traditions preserved the correct version of Euclid's text.

[63] See his two books *Daghal al-ʿAyn* (*The Disorder of the Eye*) and *Fī Maʿrifat Miḥnat al-Kaḥḥālīn* (*On Knowledge of the Test of Oculists*). See M. MEYERHOF and C. PRÜFER, *Die Augenheilkunde des Juhana ben Masawaih*, in: *Der Islam* 6 (1915), p. 217-256 and especially M. MEYERHOF, *The Book of the Ten Treatises on the Eye ascribed to Ḥunain ibn Isḥāq (809-877 AD)*, Cairo: Imprimerie Nationale, 1928, p. 11-12.

[64] M. MEYERHOF, *The Ten Treatises*, p. 18 ff.; P. SBATH and M. MEYERHOF, *Livre des questions sur l'œil de Honain ibn Ishaq*, in: *Mémoires présentés à l'Institut d'Egypte* 36, Cairo, 1938.

Al-Kindī devoted to Euclid's *Optics* the first critical commentary we are aware of. The title of his book explains his intention in the clearest possible terms: *Rectification of the Errors and Difficulties due to Euclid in his Book* The Optics. But this book was preceded by another by al-Kindī: *On the Diversity of Perspectives.* Although lost in Arabic, this text has been translated into Latin as *Liber de Causis Diversitatum Aspectus (De Aspectibus).* The first quarter is devoted to the justification of the rectilinear propagation of rays of light using geometric propositions concerning shadows and the passage of light through slits. In this way, al-Kindī develops some comments in the prologue to the second version of Euclid's *Optics*, which Heiberg attributed to Theon. Whether or not this attribution is well founded matters little here. It is more important to bear in mind that in the middle of the Ninth Century at least the prologue, if not the whole piece, was known in Arabic. In the second part of *De Aspectibus*, al-Kindī reviews the principal doctrines of vision known since antiquity, before finally adopting the doctrine of emission, with a few amendments. This discussion shows that at the very least al-Kindī was acquainted with his predecessors' theories of vision. In the last part of *De Aspectibus*, he studies the phenomenon of reflection and establishes the equality of the angles formed by a direct ray and a reflected ray with the perpendicular to the mirror at the point of incidence. The demonstration is not only geometric but is also based on experiment. 'Proof based on experiment' belongs to a traditional language, traces of which can be found in the prologue of the *Optics* attributed to Theon and which was to be profoundly rearticulated at the beginning of the Eleventh Century by Ibn al-Haytham.

This brief survey of the contents of *De Aspectibus* is intended to demonstrate both the type of research being carried out in optics in the middle of the century as well as the distance separating it from Euclidean optics in the strict sense, which constituted the basis of its reception. In fact, it was only when *De Aspectibus* was finished that al-Kindī wrote his critical commentary of Euclid's *Optics*. The chronology of al-Kindī's writings on optics is clear: his critical commentary on *Optics* came after his own contribution in this area. This order explains, in part at least, the thinking that informs his critical commentary. Al-Kindī examines Euclid's definitions and propositions one after the other, in the light of his own results; he integrates criticisms he had already made of Euclid during the course of the preparation of his book, corrects what appears to him to be inexact, suggests other proofs which seem better to him, and attempts in his own way, and to the best of his abilities, to reveal the underlying ideas.

Al-Kindī's optical works and his works on burning mirrors are an outstanding example of the concomitance of research and translation of the Greek heritage. They also demonstrate the impossibility of reconstructing either the conceptual or the textual tradition of optics, without detailed and scrupulous scrutiny of the Arabic versions.

There are other examples besides al-Kindī in the Ninth Century. Qusṭā b. Lūqā, one of his collaborators and colleagues, was also interested in optics and catoptrics. He in his turn composed a treatise (though later, circa the 870s), entitled *On the Causes of the Diversity of Perspectives Produced by Mirrors*.[65] It deals with research into catoptrics, investigation of which reveals that Ibn Lūqā was familiar with Euclid's *Optics* as well as the *Catoptrics* attributed to him. In Chapter Ten, Ibn Lūqā seems to use the first proposition of the *Catoptrics* and again in Chapter Twenty-Two, traces of propositions 7, 16, and 19 from the same book can be identified. In the following chapter, we find proposition 2 from the *Catoptrics*, and in Chapter Twenty-Eight, proposition 5. While these references do not prove that Ibn Lūqā had in his hands an Arabic translation of the *Catoptrics*, they do strongly suggest that he had access to a source, at present unknown, which contained certain propositions in the book.

The second important treatise bequeathed to us from Greek optics is that of Ptolemy. We are sadly short of information when it comes to the dates and context of this lost translation. Al-Kindī's *De Aspectibus* has been thought to contain several passages 'which were manifestly inspired by expositions to be found in Eugene's version'[66] (i.e. the Latin translation from Arabic): this would make al-Kindī a *terminus ante quem* for the Arabic translation. But this does not seem correct to us. As we have shown, the prologue of the recension attributed to Theon[67] adequately accounts for what is to be found in the *De Aspectibus*. At present, the first evidence we have of the translation into Arabic of Ptolemy's *Optics* is quite late, towards the end of the Tenth Century, in the version of ʿAlāʾ b. Sahl.[68] As conjecture is our only recourse, we propose that this translation was done at the end of the Ninth or at the beginning of the Tenth Century. We further propose that the translation of this book was deemed desirable when research on refraction with

[65] R. RASHED, *L'optique et la catoptrique d'al-Kindī*, Appendix II.

[66] LEJEUNE, *L'*Optique *de Claude Ptolémée*, p. 29.

[67] R. RASHED, *Le commentaire par al-Kindī de l'*Optique *d'Euclide*.

[68] R. RASHED, *Géométrie et dioptrique au Xe siècle: Ibn Sahl, al-Qūhī et Ibn al-Haytham*, Paris, 1993. English translation: *Geometry and Dioptrics in Classical Islam: Ibn Sahl, al-Qūhī and Ibn al-Haytham*, London, 2005.

lenses developed in both optics and in catoptrics, as the works of Ibn Sahl testify. It is not by accident, then, that Ptolemy's Book Five held Ibn Sahl's attention. But for as long as we remain ignorant of the date of translation, any such statements, including our own, remain purely conjectural. Whatever the case, it remains true that progress in Arabic optics, with Ibn Sahl and Ibn al-Haytham (d. after 1040), meant that such translations came to be regarded as merely of historical interest and were but rarely salvaged from textual 'ship-wreck'.

In geometrical optics, we have seen how the various phases of the translation movement emerged. These phases, though easily recognisable, multiplied and overlapped each other. We can also notice a certain type of translation, a type which might be called *in medias res* insofar as it was directly linked to a programme of research and followed its development. Anthemius and Euclid were translated *in tandem* with the research conducted by al-Kindī, Qusṭā b. Lūqā and others. In turn, the progress of these studies brought about the re-translation of these self-same texts. In the case of the timing of the translation of Ptolemy's work, all the evidence suggests that it had to wait for the study of refraction to be underway.

2. Translation and Re-Reading: The Case of Diophantus

We will now turn to another type of translation, which cannot possibly be confused with the previous type insofar as in this instance translation was definitely not concomitant with research, but followed on from it after a certain period of time, and was carried out in order to enrich an active and fruitful programme of research already underway. This time, translation resembles the masterly recovery of an ancient text, which was to be reactivated and somehow re-interpreted in a way in which it was not initially intended to be read. Furthermore, with this type of translation, there was naturally neither revision nor any second translation: Diophantus's *Arithmetica* is a perfect illustration.

Diophantus of Alexandria, probably active in the Second Century, though there is no certainty over this point, composed an arithmetical compendium in thirteen books, probably modelled on Euclid's *Elements*. Diophantus's intention in his work is clear, and is stated explicitly in the preface of the first book: the construction of an arithmetical theory, ἀριθμητικὴ θεωρία. The basic elements of this theory are integer numbers considered as magnitudes of units, μονάδων πλῆθος, and fractional parts as fractions of magnitudes. These constituent elements of the theory are present not only 'in person', but also as types of numbers. The term εἶδος, translated into Arabic as *nawʿ* and later into Latin as *species*, cannot be rendered in the sense of 'power of the unknown'. In the *Arithmetica*, this idea deals equally and without distinction with indeterminate plurality and the power of a number of any plurality, i.e. one that is provisionally indeterminate. This last number is the 'unsaid' number (ἄλογος ἀριθμός). To get a better idea of this notion of 'species', it must be remembered that Diophantus refers to three 'species' of number: the line number, the plane number and the solid number. These species engender all other species which must ultimately be named after them. Thus the square-square, the square-square-square, the square-cube are all squares; the cubo-cubo cube is a cube. In other words, derivative species are only possible by composition, and the power of each must necessarily be a multiple of 2 or 3. In the *Arithmetica*, for example, when problems are set out, there is nothing to the power of 7, nor yet to the power of 5. In fact, the idea of a polynomial is quite absent. Thus, the composition of Diophantus's work becomes clear: it treats of combinations of these species, one with another, under specific constraints, and using elementary arithmetical operations. Resolution of a problem involves trying to pursue it in each case 'up to the point where there remains one species on both sides'.[69] Diophantus's *Arithmetica* is not a book of algebra, contrary to what one often reads, but an arithmetical treatise proper where one might look, for example, for two square numbers whose sum is a given square.

The second explanation which suggests itself concerns a work written during the reign of the Caliph al-Ma'mūn, between 813 and 833: al-Khwārizmī's *Algebra*. It is in this book that algebra was conceived for the first time as an autonomous discipline. Al-Khwārizmī, having defined basic terms and operations, studies algebraic equations of the first and second degree, together with associated binomials and trinomials, and the application of algebraic procedures to numbers and to geometric magnitudes, then finishes his book with indeterminate problems of the first degree. These problems are posed in algebraic terms and resolved using algebraic concepts. Al-Khwārizmī's successors, especially Abū Kāmil, carried out research into the chapter on indeterminate analysis as an integral part of algebra.[70]

[69] See our edition: *Diophante: Les Arithmétiques, Livres V, VI, VII*, Paris, 1984, p.103.

[70] R. RASHED, *Combinatorial Analysis, Numerical Analysis, Diophantine Analysis and Number Theory*, in: *Encyclopedia of the History of Arabic Science*, ed. R. RASHED, II, London - New York, 1996, p. 376-417 (= *Analyse combinatoire, analyse numérique, analyse diophantienne et théorie des nombres*, in: *Histoire des sciences arabes*, éd. R. RASHED, II, Paris, 1997, p. 55-91).

It is during the course of this research into indeterminate analysis as a chapter of algebra that Qusṭā b. Lūqā translated seven books of the *Arithmetica:* the first three correspond to the first three of the Greek version; the following four are lost in Greek; and Books 4, 5 and 6 in the Greek version do not seem to have been translated into Arabic.

These two preliminary explanations allow us to pose the problem of the translation of the *Arithmetica*. We are here concerned with a discipline, which was definitely not Hellenistic, but which had been established for half a century; a discipline one of the divisions of which dealt with indeterminate analysis. On the other hand we have a work (the *Arithmetica*) dealing with problems which, having been translated in terms of this new discipline, would become a part of it. However, this interpretation was not within the powers of any ordinary translator who happened to come along. Qusṭā b. Lūqā, the translator of the *Arithmetica*, had grasped the usefulness of Diophantus's book for research in this new discipline and in particular the section devoted to indeterminate analysis. It was he who provided the first algebraic — and anachronistic — reading of the *Arithmetica*. One can imagine without too much difficulty the impact of such a reading on the research programme and also on translation.

Before we begin our examination of these consequences, let us say a few words about the translator. Qusṭā b. Lūqā was a Greek Christian from Baalbek, who, according to al-Nadīm, was a good translator and knew Greek, Syriac and Arabic well.[71] Again according to the ancient biobibliographers, he was summoned to the capital, Baghdad, to participate in the Greek translation movement: he was there around the year 860. He therefore belonged to that slightly later generation of translators who, by virtue of cultural heritage and training, possessed an elaborate and polished terminology in many different areas of learning (among the different lexica at his disposal, algebra was foremost). He also belonged to the category of professional translator-scholars, who were drawn from different scientific disciplines, and therefore were well qualified to discern the meaning of the works which they were translating. The title of the works translated by Qusṭā which have come own to us reveal a wide range of skills, including 'minor astronomy' (Autolycus's *Heliacal Settings*; Theodosius's *Habitations*, *Of Day and Night*, and *Spherics;* Aristarchus's *On the Sizes and Distance of the Sun and Moon*). They also include Hero of Alexandria's *Baroulchos;* Archimedes's *The*

[71] AL-NADĪM, *Fihrist*, p. 304.

Sphere and the Cylinder; Alexander's commentary on *De Generatione et Corruptione*, as well as part of his commentary on the *Physics*. To these should be added Hypsicles's Books XIV and XV, both added to Euclid's *Elements*. Qusṭā seems therefore mainly to have translated books on mathematics and philosophy, subjects to which he had also contributed writings of his own.

This then was how Qusṭā b. Lūqā, with all the attendant skills of the translator-scholar, tackled the *Arithmetica*, sometime around the 870s. His translation is distinguished by its obvious algebraic look. It is as if Diophantus, in the eyes of the translator-scholar, were al-Khwārizmī's successor, and spoke his language. It is precisely al-Khwārizmī's lexicon which Qusṭā mines to express mathematical entities and operations in Arabic. We can discern Ibn Lūqā's interpretative bias in his choice of lexicon: his *Arithmetica* is a work of algebra. It is a bias that was to be long-lived: it is to be found in the work of Thomas Heath[72] and can still be found today.

Ibn Lūqā's choice is obvious from the very translation of the title of the work. Instead of *Arithmetical Problems*, προβλήματα ἀριθμητικά, which we find in the colophons of certain books as *al-Masāʾil al-ʿAdadīya*, the title is translated as *The Art of Algebra*, *Fī Ṣināʿat al-Jabr*. The original terms are also translated into terms used by algebraists, despite the inevitable semantic difference. The expression (ἄλογος ἀριθμός) was translated by Ibn Lūqā as 'thing' (*cosa*, *res*) that is 'the unknown' of the algebraists. This was a key concept in Diophantus's arithmetical theory, designating the provisionally indeterminate number which would necessarily be so at the end of the solution — a concept which caused modern translators such as Ver Eecke much embarrassment, who translates it as 'arithme'. The successive powers of this entity (δύναμις, κύβος, etc.) are also translated using algebraic terms: *māl* ('square'), *kaʿb* ('cube'), etc. Ibn Lūqā translates the term πλευρά; into Arabic as *jidhr* ('square root'), further marking the distinction between his own usage and that of Diophantus.

Operations are also 'algebraised'. So, when Diophantus formulates the first operation: προσθεῖναι τὰ λείποντα εἴδη ἐν ἀμφοτέροις τοῖς μέρεσιν ('add species subtracted to the two members'), Ibn Lūqā translated this by a single noun: *al-jabr*, the very word from which the discipline takes its name. In the same way, when Diophantus writes ἀφελεῖν

[72] See T. HEATH, *Diophantus of Alexandria: A Study in the History of Greek Algebra*, Cambridge, 1885.

τὰ ὅμοια ἀπὸ τῶν ὁμοίων, ('take like away from like'), Ibn Lūqā also translates this formula with a single word used by algebraists to describe this very operation: *al-muqābala*. After further investigation, we come to the conclusion that 'algebraisation' is a deliberate and systematic choice.

However this did not work for all of Diophantus's vocabulary and Ibn Lūqā was obliged to invent new terms and expressions, some of them to translate Diophantus's own terms for describing methods of resolution. He coined his own term when he translated ἡ διπλῆ ἰσότης, a concept dear to Diophantus, as *al-musāwāt al-muthannāh*, or 'double equality', which has all the semantic appearance of a Greek mathematical expression. In order to translate expressions of philosophical origin used by Diophantus, such as γένος, εἶδος, οἰκεῖον, φύσις, μέθοδος, Ibn Lūqā, himself a translator of philosophical opuscules, borrows the by then canonical lexicon of this discipline.

Thus, Diophantus's *Arithmetica* was translated using insights gained from al-Khwārizmī's *Algebra*. This translation is clearly distinct from the tradition of burning mirrors and optics; it is also distinct from the translation of Euclid's *Elements* and Ptolemy's *Almagest*. The question remains: what were the reasons for this translation and what inspired the translator to make this choice? The answer lies in the examination of the fate of the translation, and this will perhaps lead to a better understanding of the transmission of this part of the Greek heritage.

Initial research in Arabic into indeterminate analysis (today known as Diophantine analysis) had most probably been undertaken immediately after al-Khwārizmī. We have already noted that, in the last part of his book on algebra, al-Khwārizmī tackled some indeterminate problems. But there is nothing to indicate that he was interested in indeterminate equations *per se*, and in any case, indeterminate analysis did not actually appear in his work. The place it later occupied in Abū Kāmil's book, written around 880, its level of understanding,[73] and the references to other mathematicians who had worked in this area since al-Khwārizmī (whose writings are no longer extant), as well as the references to their own terminology, leave no doubt — Abū Kāmil was not the first, nor was he the only successor of al-Khwārizmī to have been actively engaged in the study of indeterminate equations. The conditions ripe for interest in Diophantus's *Arithmetica* can be said to have come into existence during half a century. On the other hand, read in the light of the

[73] RASHED, *Combinatorial Analysis* (= *Analyse combinatoire*).

new algebra, exactly as Ibn Lūqā would have read it, the *Arithmetica* falls right into place among works in progress on indeterminate analysis. The *Arithmetica* could even have given a boost to the development of this chapter in the history of mathematics, later described as: *fī l-istiqrā'*. The impact of the *Arithmetica* on Arab algebraists was thus more of the order of extension rather than innovation.

3. Translation as a Vector of Research: The Case of Apollonius's *Conics*

We have examined two traditions of translation: translation concomitant with, and in the same area as, current research and translation subsequent to a programme of research, which eventually integrated the work translated into what was (initially) a different tradition. There were three styles of translation: translation by 'amateur' translators, translation by professionals and translation by scholars — this latter style became increasingly dominant as the century progressed. But these traditions and styles were not exclusive: sometimes translation was not stimulated by one research programme alone, but by a whole range of activities, some of which did not properly speaking belong to the domain of the work translated. The work would in this case have been translated in furtherance of research into a cognate discipline as much as into other, fully or partly, established disciplines. An example of such a situation can be found in the translation of Apollonius's *Conics*.

The study of conic sections, of course, represents Hellenistic geometric research at an advanced level. Apollonius's *Conics* has been considered the most difficult mathematical work to have been inherited from antiquity. It comprises the sum total of knowledge of conic curves and surfaces produced by geometry since Euclid, Aristaeus the Elder, and so on, which was then enriched by Apollonius's own masterly contribution, especially in the last three books. This treatise would remain the most complete on this subject right up to at least the Eighteenth Century. Only seven of the original eight books remain: the eighth was lost quite early on, perhaps before Pappus[74] in the Third-Fourth Century. The remaining seven all survive in Arabic translation. The Greek text available is the one edited by Eutochius in the Sixth Century, comprising only the first four books.

[74] Rashed, *Les mathématiques infinitésimales*, III, Chapter 1.

Furthermore, at the beginning of the second half of the Ninth Century, mathematicians were dealing with problems requiring conic sections: problems posed in astronomy and optics (parabolic, ellipsoidal and conic mirrors); the determination of the area and volume of surfaces and curved solids, and such. One has only to read a list of the works of al-Kindī, al-Marwarrūdhī, al-Farghānī and the Banū Mūsā to be convinced. Al-Farghānī had recourse to conic sections in order to present the first demonstrative dissertation on the theory of stereographical projections necessary for the astrolabe. More important still is the trend of nascent research at the time, one which continued to develop throughout the century: from the Banū Mūsā on, there was a *simultaneous* interest in the geometry of conics and the measurement of curved surfaces and volumes. Thus the second of the three Banū Mūsā brothers, al-Ḥasan, came to write a treatise of enormous importance on the generation of elliptical sections and the measurement of their areas.[75] Al-Ḥasan devised a theory of the ellipse and elliptical sections by following a different method to that of Apollonius (the bifocal method). He considered the properties of the ellipse, as well as the different types of elliptical sections, as a plane section of a cylinder. According to the account of his own brothers, al-Ḥasan composed his treatise without any real knowledge of Apollonius's *Conics*. He only had at his disposal a faulty copy which he could neither have translated nor understood. Moreover, the method he followed is further proof, if proof were needed, of this account.

It is easy to understand the interest shown in the *Conics*; there was a general desire in all quarters to see the work translated, but then it became urgent to study this branch of geometry. The Banū Mūsā set about finding a translatable copy of Apollonius's work and after al-Ḥasan's death, his brother Aḥmad discovered in Damascus a copy of the Eutochius edition of the first 4 books. This is the decisive step which led to the translation of the seven books. Such an undertaking was not within the competence of any ordinary translator. It was originally the task of a team which had been set up, before it was taken in hand, this time by a scholar-translator: Thābit b. Qurra. He it was who translated the last three books: the most difficult, and according to Apollonius, the most original. He it was, most probably, who collaborated with the two surviving Banū Mūsā brothers, Aḥmad and Muḥammad, in the revision of the translation of the whole work.

[75] RASHED, *Les mathématiques infinitésimales*, I.

There is no doubt that this was the work of a team, particularly since it is known that other translators, such as Hilāl b. Hilāl and al-Ḥimṣī, participated in the translation.[76] Nevertheless, the undertaking remained very much a work of scholar-translators, with Thābit b. Qurra and the Banū Mūsā brothers acting at the very least as revisers. Supervised as it was by inventive scholars of the highest calibre, it should therefore not be confused either with ordinary translation or that of translator-scholars. Of course, as with the latter, this translation does indeed render into Arabic a Greek text perfectly understood and perfectly mastered. But this also confers a certain heuristic value on the work, in that translation by scholar-translators is a genuine means of discovery and of reorganizing knowledge. It takes on this new role because, of all the different types of translation, this is the one which is the most closely linked to research. To illustrate this new function, let us examine the work of Thābit b. Qurra, starting with his book *On the Sections of the Cylinder and its Lateral Surface*.[77]

In possession of the *Conics*, the collection of the seven translated books, in a sense he took another look at al-Ḥasan b. Mūsā's book. Apollonius's *Conics* served as a model for the elaboration of a new theory of the cylinder and its plane sections; his master's book provided him with the means for learning about geometric projections and transformations, which he in turn developed. In fact, Thābit b. Qurra was the first to take the step of considering the cylindrical surface as a conic surface and the cylinder as a cone with a summit projected to infinity in a given direction.

He begins the work by defining the cylindrical surface, then the cylinder, just as Apollonius in the *Conics* first defined the conic surface, then the cone. Thābit then follows the same sequence as Apollonius when making his definitions: axis, generator, base, right or oblique cylinder. If we examine the first propositions in Thābit's book, we can see that this pattern is continued.[78]

The *Conics* served as his model for the elaboration of his new theory of the cylinder, and it is to this end that he developed the study of geometric transformations. The incentive to translate the *Conics*, then, was embedded in the research led by al-Ḥasan b. Mūsā and his pupil Thābit b. Qurra. However, this research programme was not the

76 Rashed, *Les mathématiques infinitésimales*, III.

77 Rashed, *Les mathématiques infinitésimales*, I, p. 458-673.

78 Rashed, *Les mathématiques infinitésimales*, I.

only one being conducted at the time. Thābit and his contemporaries were also busy with geometric constructions using conics: notably the two means and the trisection of an angle. Astronomer-mathematicians, such as al-Farghānī, had recourse to conics in the study of projections, in order to draw up a rigorous theory for the figure of the astrolabe.

One might be led to think that the translation of the *Conics* is a special case, in view of the advanced level of geometry it contains. Obviously the level is significant, but this is not the main reason. Thābit b. Qurra also translated a book of neo-Pythagorean arithmetic: Nicomachus of Gerasa's *Arithmetical Introduction*,[79] and this was at a much lower level. Once again, all indications point to this translation being a part of this scholar-translator's research: in his famous theorem,[80] he elaborated what might be termed a descriptive statement made by Nicomachus into the first theory of amiable numbers. Thābit actually arrived at the devising of his new theory not only via Nicomachus, but also via the arithmetical books of the *Elements*. But given that a vast scientific culture was necessary in order for such research to be carried out, it only really grew and spread with the formation of the scientific city and its institutions. One of the means of this formation was, conversely, translation.

Once more, thanks to research carried out at the time, the translation of the Greek heritage advanced not only in material terms (i.e. one more text was added to the corpus), but also in terms of comprehension. Furthermore, the criteria of a good translation continued to evolve, which accounts precisely for the massive movement of retranslation and revision of translated works. In other words, retranslation and revision became two defining features of the Greek into Arabic translation movement. This is why Euclid's *Elements* was translated three times, with the last version being revised once more. The same is true for the *Almagest* and for some of Archimedes's writings, as well as some works on optics, for example. In fact, revision eventually became the norm, from the moment when al-Kindī revised some of the translations done by Qusṭā b. Lūqā and Thābit b. Qurra revised some of Isḥāq b. Ḥunayn's.

[79] NICOMACHUS OF GERASA, *Introduction arithmétique*, ed. W. KUTSCH, Beirut, 1958.

[80] F. WOECPKE, *Notice sur une théorie ajoutée par Thābit ben Qorrah à l'arithmétique spéculative des Grecs*, in: *Journal Asiatique* 4 (1852), p. 420-429.

4. Ancient Evidence of the Translation-Research Dialectic: The Case of the *Almagest*

Despite its highly technical character, the translation of the *Conics* does in fact more or less reflect the general situation. It is a concrete illustration of the reasons underlying the act of translation, of those which caused it to be taken up again and of those which ultimately brought about the revision of the translation. Give or take a few differences, which may be imputed to the nature and objects, as well as the requisite apodictic quality of the discipline, the same situation obtained in the other mathematical sciences, in alchemy and in medicine. For example, it was the same for astronomy too, as the situation obtained for the context of the translation of the magnum opus of ancient astronomy — the *Almagest*. Ibn al-Ṣalāḥ, the erudite scholar of the Twelfth Century, gives us a valuable account of this when he writes:

> There were five versions of the *Almagest*, in various languages and translations; a Syriac version which had been translated from the Greek, a second version translated from Greek to Arabic by al-Ḥasan b. Quraysh for al-Ma'mūn, a third version translated from Greek to Arabic by al-Ḥajjāj b. Yūsuf b. Maṭar and Halyā b. Sarjūn, also for al-Ma'mūn, a fourth version translated from Greek to Arabic by Isḥāq b. Ḥunayn for Abū al-Ṣaqr b. Bulbul — we have Isḥāq's original in his own hand — and a fifth version revised by Thābit b. Qurra from the translation of Isḥāq b. Ḥunayn.[81]

In the course of about a half century, we encounter at least three translations of the *Almagest*, plus a revision by one of the most prestigious mathematicians and astronomers of the age. During the Ninth Century, the whole corpus of Greek astronomy, with a few exceptions, was translated into Arabic. Equally significant is the fact that the two decades of the reign of al-Ma'mūn witnessed the production of two translations of the *Almagest*. This remarkable fact can only be understood within the context of an ongoing research project.

This project was described by an eminent astronomer of the day, Ḥabash al-Ḥāsib. Ḥabash begins by describing the state of research in astronomy before al-Ma'mūn. He notes that certain astronomers, without

[81] R. MORELON, *Eastern Arabic Astronomy between the Eighth and the Eleventh Centuries*, in: *Encyclopedia of the History of Arabic Science*, ed. R. RASHED, I, London - New York, 1996, p. 22 (= R. MORELON, *L'astronomie arabe orientale entre le VIIIe et le XIe siècle*, in: *Histoire des sciences arabes*, éd. R. RASHED, I, Paris, 1997, p. 37); IBN AL-ṢALĀḤ, *Zur Kritik der Koordinatenüberlieferung im Sternkatalog des Almagest*, ed. P. KUNITZSCH, Göttingen, 1975, p. 155.12-18 (Arabic text).

having 'produced a clear demonstration or a true deduction thereof', had posited a few principles and claimed to have attained great wisdom in knowledge of the sun, the moon and the stars.[82] Ḥabash is silent on the identity of these astronomers and their works. According to him, things remained like this until the time of al-Ma'mūn, at which point progress was made on the verification and comparison of different astronomical tables which had already been translated into Arabic: the Indian astronomic table (*zīj al-Sindhind*), the astronomical table of Brahmagupta (*zīj al-Arkand*), the Persian astronomical table (*zīj al-shāh*), the 'Greek canon', or Ptolemy's *easy tables*, as well as 'other *zīj*s'. This verification of the results from different astronomical tables gave rise to the following statement: 'each one of these *zīj*s is sometimes correct and sometimes strays from the path of truth'.[83]

Who conducted this early research? Ḥabash does not specify, but we do know that such activity had begun much earlier, with al-Fazārī, Yaʿqūb b. Ṭāriq and many others during the reign of al-Ma'mūn. Whatever the truth, it is after this process of verification and consequent to such a negative finding that al-Ma'mūn commanded Yaḥyā b. Abī Manṣūr al-Ḥāsib to

> revert to the base of the astronomical tables and gather together the astronomers and scholars of his time to collaborate on research into the fundamentals of this science, with the aim of rectifying it, given that Ptolemy had established the proof that it is not impossible to comprehend what the astronomers were trying to find out.[84]

The mathematician and astronomer Yaḥyā b. Abī Manṣūr al-Ḥāsib did what al-Ma'mūn ordered him to do. He and his colleagues took as their base text the *Almagest* and began, in Baghdad, to observe the movement of the sun and the moon at various times. After the death of Yaḥyā b. Abī Manṣūr, al-Ma'mūn ordered another astronomer, Khālid b. ʿAbd al-Malik al Marwarrūdhī, this time in Damascus, to conduct the first continuous observation in history (over one entire year) of the movement of the sun

[82] Ḥabash Al-Ḥāsib, *al-Zīj al-Dimashqī*, MS Berlin no. 5750, fol. 70r: *wa-qad waḍaʿa ṣinf min al-nās li-dhālika uṣūlan wa-'ddaʿū fī maʿrifat al-shams wa-l-qamar wa-l-kawākib ʿilman ʿaẓīman lam ya'tū ʿalay-hi bi-burhān wāḍiḥ wa-lā qiyās ṣaḥīḥ.*

[83] Ḥabash Al-Ḥāsib, *al-Zīj al-Dimashqī*, fol. 70r: *kull wāḥid min-hā yuwāfiqu l-ṣawāb aḥyānan wa-yabʿudu ʿan minhaj al-ḥaqq aḥyānan.*

[84] Ḥabash Al-Ḥāsib, *al-Zīj al-Dimashqī*, fol. 70r; *fa-lammā waqafa ʿalā dhālika amara Yaḥyā b. Abī Manṣūr al-Ḥāsib bi-l-rujūʿ ilā aṣl kutub al-nujūm wa-jamaʿa ʿulamā' ahl hādhihi l-ṣināʿa wa-ḥukamā' ahl zamāni-hi li-yataʿāwanū ʿalā l-baḥth ʿalā uṣūl hādhā l-ʿilm wa-l-qaṣd li-taṣḥīḥi-hi idh kāna Baṭlamiyūs al-Qālūdhī qad aqāma l-dalīl ʿalā anna dark mā yuḥāwilu ʿilmu-hu min ṣināʿat al-nujūm ghayr mumtaniʿ.*

and the moon.[85] It was during this period of active research in astronomy that Ptolemy's *Almagest* was translated twice. The same kind of analysis can be applied to the other disciplines linked to astronomy, such as research into sundials and the translation of Diodorus's *Analemma*, or spherical geometry and the translation of Menelaus's famous work.

Analysis such as this not only enables us to understand the modalities of the translation movement, but also allows us to predict its end — the point at which inherited science was overtaken by new research results and methods. This did not occur at the same time across all disciplines, however, though for a good number of them it happened at the turn of the century.

A PROGRAMMATIC CONCLUSION

Although fundamental works exist in this domain,[86] the question of the transmission of the Greek scientific and philosophical heritage into Arabic has still not been fully settled. These fundamental works can, with a few exceptions, be classified under the following headings: philology, philological archaeology, history. Philological research deals with the problems of lexicon and syntax created by translation into Arabic. Philological archaeology seeks to identify the real or 'virtual' Greek text lying behind the Arabic text, based on the postulate that lexical diffusion reflects conceptual diffusion. Historical research examines the impact of a translated text on the philosopher-scientists of classical Islam. Given that history and philology are necessary, any study of translation which invokes their authority should also consider the motivations and reasons for the translation as well as the choice of translator. This task requires us to look beyond al-Kindī, the 'first philosopher of the Arabs', to the theologian-philosophers *(al-mutakallimūn)* who preceded him or who were his contemporaries. As the example of Abū Sahl b. Nawbahkt, Abū l-Hudhayl and al-Naẓẓām (among many others) illustrates,[87] they were

[85] Ḥabash al-Ḥāsib, *al-Zīj al-Dimashqī*, fol. 70v.

[86] See M. Steinschneider, *Die arabishcen Übersetzungen aus dem Griechischen*, Graz, 1889; ʿA. Badawī, *Al-Turāth al-Yūnānī fī l-Ḥaḍāra al-Islāmīya*, Cairo, 1946; ʿA. Badawi, *La transmission de la philosophie grecque au monde arabe*, Paris, 1968; R. Walzer, *Arabische Übersetzungen aus dem Griechischen*, in: *Miscellanea Medievalia* 9 (1962), p.179-195.

[87] M.A. Abū Rīda, *Ibrāhīm b. Sayyār al-Naẓẓām*, Cairo, 1946; R.M. Frank, *The Science of* Kalām: J. van Ess, *Theologie und Gesellschaft*.

receptive, highly critical patrons interested in metaphysics, physics, biology and logic, in order to develop a deliberately rational discourse of their own. Al-Kindī himself had discovered in the writings of the Aristotelian Neoplatonic tradition a discipline which provided not only the basis of a rational discourse acceptable to all, but one which also lent itself to mathematical argument.[88] In all likelihood, this self-same milieu of theologian-philosophers will one day provide the key to understanding the reasons for the preliminary stages of the enormous philosophical translation movement as well their selection of works within the corpus of writings which is the Aristotelian Neoplatonic tradition.

APPENDIX

Anthemius wrote:

> τοῦ Η σημείου μεταξὺ τῆς τε χειμερινῆς ἀκτῖνος καὶ τῆς ἰσημερινῆς νοουμένου ὡσανεὶ κατὰ τὴν διχοτομίαν τῆς ὑπὸ ΕΒΓ γωνίας καὶ ἐκϐληθείσης τῆς ΗΖ ὡς ἐπὶ τὸ Θ σημεῖον [89]

We read in the first translation:

> *wa-li-yufʿal ʿalāmat Ḥāʾ wāsiṭatan bayna l-shuʿāʿ al-shatwī wa-shuʿāʿ al-istiwāʾ, ka-anna-hā qāṭiʿa wasaṭ zāwiyat Hāʾ-Bāʾ-Jīm wa-li-yukhraj khaṭṭ Ḥāʾ-Zāʾ ilā ʿalāmat Ṭāʾ.*
>
> … make the sign *H* in the middle between the ray of the winter solstice and the equinoctial ray, as if it cuts the middle of the angle *EBΓ*. Draw a straight line *HZ* up to point *Θ*[90]

The translator translates the Greek νοεῖσθαι as *faʿala* (to do) which is, to say the least, maladroit. In the unlikely scenario that he wanted to avoid a form of the verb *wahama* (to imagine, to conceive of) he could have opted for *jaʿala or kāna*. Note also his use of *ʿalāma* (sign), for the Greek σημεῖον, a rendering which was already quite rare by the Ninth Century, though it is encountered from time to time.

Let us examine the second translation of this same phrase:

> *wa-li-takun nuqṭat Ḥāʾ fī l-wasaṭ fī-mā bayna khaṭṭay Bāʾ-Hāʾ, Bāʾ-Jīm ʿalā niṣf zāwiyat Hāʾ-Bāʾ-Jīm. wa-nukhrij Ḥāʾ-Zāʾ ilā nuqṭat Ṭāʾ*

[88] R. RASHED, *Al-Kindī's Commentary on Archimedes'* The Measurement of the Circle.

[89] *Les catoptriciens grecs*, p. 350, 10-15.

[90] ANTHEMIUS, *Fī Ṣanʿat al-Marāyā l-Muḥriqa*, in: RASHED, *Les catoptriciens grecs*, p. 287.7-9.

> Let the point *H* be in the middle, between two straight lines *BE* (the line of the winter solstice) and the straight line *BΓ* (the equinoctial line), on the half angle *EBΓ*. Extend *HZ* to point *Θ*. [91]

Both the lexicon and the syntax of the second translation is more in keeping with Arabic usage and the language of geometrical optics.

Let us pursue this example a bit longer. The Greek text continues thus:

> ἐὰν τοίνυν κατὰ τὴν θέσιν τῆς ΗΖ εὐθείας νοήσωμεν ἐπίπεδον ἔσοπτρον, ἡ ΒΖΕ ἀκτὶς προσπίπτουσα πρὸς τὸ ΗΖΘ ἔσοπτρον λέγω ὅτι ἀνακλασθήσεται ἐπὶ τὸ Α σημεῖον [92]

The early translator rendered this into Arabic as:

> *fa-matā mā naḥnu tawahhamnā mir'āt dhāt saṭḥ mustawin fī mawḍiʿ khaṭṭ Ḥā'-Zā' al-mustaqīm mawqiʿan li-l-shuʿāʿ alladhī dalā'ilu-hu Bā'-Zā'-Hā' ʿalā mir'āt Zā'-Ḥā'-Ṭā', azʿumu anna-hu yuʿṭaf rājiʿan ilā mawḍiʿ Alif*

> So when we conceive of a mirror with a plane surface positioned on a straight line *HZ*, the place for a ray of light with signs *BZE* on a mirror *HZΘ*, I claim that it is reflected onto position *A*.[93]

Observe that the expression *fa-matā mā naḥnu tawahhamnā* is somewhat over-elaborate and does not appear to be entirely in keeping with Arabic syntax; it would be better to write *fa-matā tawahhamnā*. In the same way, it is more correct to use the preposition *ʿalā* instead of *fī*. The rest of the sentence is no better: after *al-mustaqīm* it should run *wa-kānat mir'āt Zā'-Ḥā'-Ṭā' mawqiʿan li-shuʿāʿ dalā'ilu-hu Bā'-Zā'-Hā'*, *fa-aqūl inna-hu yanʿakis ilā mawḍiʿ Alif.*

In this instance a literal translation has had a negative effect, and the use of the phrase *dalā'ilu-hu Bā'-Zā'-Hā'* is archaic, and was to be abandoned by later translators. In the same way *ʿaṭafa rājiʿan* for 'reflect' begins to disappear in the Ninth Century. Finally the use of *azʿumu* (I opine, I claim) instead of *aqūlu* (I say) for λέγω does not appear in translations from the middle of the Ninth Century.

In the second translation, the second phrase runs:

> *fa-in tawahhamnā saṭḥan mirā'īyan mawḍūʿan ʿalā mawḍiʿ khaṭṭ Ḥā'- Zā'-Ṭā', fa-inna-hu yakūn shuʿāʿ Bā'-Zā'-Hā, idhā waqaʿa ʿalā mir'āt Ḥā'- Zā'-Ṭā', yarjaʿ ilā nuqṭat Alif*

[91] Ibn ʿĪsā, *Kitāb al-Manāẓir wa-l-Marāyā l-Muḥriqa*, in: Rashed, *L'optique et la catoptrique d'al-Kindī*, p. 677.1-2.

[92] *Les catoptriciens grecs*, p. 350.14-17.

[93] *Les catoptriciens grecs*, p. 287.9-12.

> If we imagine the surface of a mirror positioned on a straight line $HZ\Theta$, then if the ray of light BZE falls on the mirror $HZ\Theta$, it returns to point A.[94]

This translation is less literal and whilst it does not adhere exactly to the letter of the Greek text (always supposing that we are dealing with exactly the same text, which is far from certain), it does convey the meaning in proper Arabic, using correct vocabulary and syntax.

[94] IBN ʿĪSĀ, *Kitāb al-Manāẓir wa-l-Marāyā l-Muḥriqa*, in: RASHED, *L'optique et la catoptrique d'al-Kindī*, p. 677.2-4.

Al-Ashʿarī and the Kalām

KALĀM ATOMISM AS AN ALTERNATIVE PHILOSOPHY TO HELLENIZING *FALSAFA*

A.I. Sabra*
Harvard University

The practitioner of *Kalām* will not grasp the dimensions of *Kalām*, and become a master and leader in his art, unless he brings what he knows well of the *Kalām* of religion to the level of what he knows well of the *Kalām* of *Falsafa*. Al-Jāḥiẓ, *Kitāb al-Ḥayawān*

Rationalism never shakes off its status of an experimental adventure. The combined influences of mathematics and religion, which have so greatly contributed to the rise of philosophy, have also had the unfortunate effect of yoking it with static dogmatism. Rationalism is an adventure in the clarification of thought, progressive and never final. But it is an adventure in which partial success has importance. Whitehead, *Process and Reality*

I. Introductory remarks

I.1. My concern is ultimately with the history of atomism and with the role of *Kalām* atomism in the history of Islamic intellectualism. My present task, however, is to focus on proposing an interpretation of the fundamental Ashʿarite view of the world through analysis of some Muʿtazilite positions which al-Ashʿarī himself carefully reported and eventually developed into what he believed to be a coherent view of the world as a world of contingent events — thus, I believe, in agreement with a basic intuition underlying the *Kalām* venture initiated by the Muʿtazila in the Eighth Century.

As far as the history of atomism is concerned, I will here simply point out the fact that, after the triumph of Aristotelianism over Democritean atomism in classical antiquity, the first strong and lasting resurgence of atomistic cosmology actually took place, not in Seventeenth Century

* A short version of this essay was presented in my absence by Jamil Ragep and Lorraine Daston on May 18, 2004 at the Max Planck Institute for the History of Science, Berlin, in a seminar directed by Professor Lorraine Daston on knowledge and belief. I am grateful to Professor Daston for comments and questions, some of which are addressed in the present version.

Europe, but in Eighth and Ninth Century Baṣra and Baghdad. That remarkable revival was the astonishing achievement conceived and diligently argued by the early Muʿtazilite 'thinkers', *nuẓẓār*, or *ahl al-naẓar*, or *mutakallimūn*, who, like the Seventeenth Century 'philosophers' and 'scientists' in Europe, were deeply concerned with theological questions. The details of exactly how this Eighth-Ninth Century episode came about is still largely shrouded in obscurity (as in some other early developments, e.g. the emergence of Arabic alchemy, or even of Arabic grammar). It has long been observed, however, that the Iraqi phenomenon frequently displayed traces or features of the early Graeco-Christian theological movements associated with Edessa in north-western Mesopotamia, which would point to Edessa as a remote origin of Islamic philosophical theology, just as pagan Ḥarrān, Edessa's close neighbour and determined rival, is known to have been one of the stages in the transmission of Greek astrology, astronomy and mathematics to Islamic culture. One undoubted medium in both lines of transmission was Syriac, but the facts of the transmission from Edessa have yet to be substantially explored, let alone made sufficiently clear.[1] But let me add at once that Arabic-Islamic atomism, though undoubtedly Greek in some of its features and forms of argument, was not what we would call 'Democritean'. The Arabic 'indivisible parts', or atoms, often look more like Leibniz's atoms than those of Democritus or Epicurus: as well as their spatial and 'mechanical' behaviour, they accommodate qualities like colours and flavours, even life and perception and knowledge.

I.2. With regard to the history of Islamic intellectualism, we face an entirely different story which unfolded in the broad daylight of a long stretch of well-documented history. In the Eighth Century, at Baṣra and Baghdad, the so-called Muʿtazila were already engaged in debates on

[1] J.B. SEGAL, *Edessa, 'The Blessed City'*, Oxford: Clarendon Press, 1970; J.B. SEGAL, *Edessa and Harran (Inaugural Lecture, 9 May 1962)*, London: School of Oriental and African Studies, University of London, 1963; H.J.W. DRIJVERS, *Bardaiṣan of Edessa*, Groningen: Rijksuniversiteit te Groningen, 1966, includes extensive bibliography; H.J.W. DRIJVERS, *The School of Edessa: Greek Learning and Local Culture*, in: *Centers of Learning: Learning and Location in Pre-Modern Europe and the Near East*, ed. H.J.W. DRIJVERS and ALASDAIR A. MACDONALD, Leiden, 1995, p. 49-59; G. VAJDA, *Le témoignage d'al-Māturīdī sur la doctrine des Manichéens, des Dayṣānites et des Marcionites*, in: *Arabica* 13 (1966), p. 1-38, 113-128; B. DODGE, *Mani and the Manichaeans*, in: *Medieval and Middle Eastern Studies in Honor of ʿAzīz Suryāl ʿAṭīya*, ed. SAMI M. HANNA, Leiden: Brill, 1972, p. 86-105; J. FÜCK, *The Role of Manicheanism under the Arabs*, in: *Arabische Kultur und Islam im Mittelalter* (*Ausgewälte Schriften*), ed. M. FLEISCHHAMMER, Weimar: H. Böhlaus Nachfolger, 1981, p. 258-266.

religion, politics and cosmology, as well as the defence of Islamic dogma against non-Muslim creeds. That began to happen during the Umayyad rule based in Damascus (40-132/661-750), and before the Graeco-Arabic translation movement in Baghdad was getting well under way during the reigns of the ʿAbbasid Caliphs al-Manṣūr (136-159/754-775) and al-Rashīd (170-193/786-809). The seventh Caliph, al-Maʾmūn, during whose reign (198-218/813-833) the translations from Syriac and Greek in science, medicine, mathematics and philosophy reached a culminating point, was also a patron of the rationalizing Muʿtazila. In fact al-Maʾmūn went so far as to support, even impose, the divisive Muʿtazilite thesis, rejected by traditionists and legists, that the Qurʾān, God's 'speech', was 'created'; and that policy of al-Maʾmūn's is known to have continued under al-Muʿtaṣim (218-22/833-842) and al-Wāthiq (227-232/842-847), before it was abandoned by al-Mutawakkil (232-247/847-861).[2] Thus

[2] See *Mawsūʿat Aḥmad Amīn*, a learned history of Islamic intellectual life in four parts consisting of nine volumes, and issued in many editions published in Cairo (Maktabat al-Nahḍa) and Beirut since 1929, that deserve more attention than they seem to have received in the West. See especially the first two parts, *Fajr al-Islām* (one volume, first issued in 1929), and *Ḍuḥā al-Islām* (three volumes). The other parts are titled *Ẓuhr al-Islām* (four volumes) and *Yawm al-Islām* (one volume). For the latest and most detailed study of the rise and early development of *Kalām*, see J. VAN ESS, *Theologie und Gesellschaft im. 2. und 3. Jahrhudert Hidschra: Eine Geschichte des religiösen Denkens in frühen Islam*, Berlin - New York: Walter de Gruyter, 1991-1995. See also D. GUTAS, *Greek Thought, Arabic Culture: The Graeco-Arabic Translation Movement in Baghdad and Early ʿAbbāsid Society (2nd-4th/8th-10th centuries)*, London - New York: Routledge, 1998 (includes extensive bibliography), esp. Chapters 3 and 4. Studies exclusively devoted to 'Islamic atomism' include: S. PINES, *Beiträge zur islamischen Atomenlehre*, Berlin: A. Hein, 1936, the book to which every subsequent writer on the subject is indebted; Arabic translation: *Madhhab al-Dharra ʿinda l-Muslimīn, wa-ʿAlāqatu-hu bi-Madhāhib al-Yūnān wa-l-Hunūd*, by MUḤAMMAD ʿABD AL-HĀDĪ ABŪ RĪDA (with the help of the author), Cairo: Maktabat al-Nahḍa al-Miṣrīya, 1946, has the advantage of presenting the quoted texts in the original Arabic; English translation: *Studies in Islamic Atomism*, trans. M. SCHWARZ and ed. TZVI LANGERMANN, Jerusalem: The Magnes Press, 1997; C. BAFFIONI, *Atomismo e antiatomismo nel pensiero islamico*, Rome: Herder, 1982; RICHARD M. FRANK, *Bodies and Atoms: The Ashʿarite Analysis*, in: *Islamic Theology and Philosophy: Studies in Honor of George F. Hourani*, ed. MICHAEL E. MARMURA, Albany: SUNY, 1984, p. 39-53; ALNOOR DHANANI, *The Physical Theory of* Kalām*: Atoms, Space, and Void in Baṣrian Muʿtazilī Cosmology*, Leiden, 1994. See also the book by RICHARD FRANK, *Beings and their Attributes. The Teachings of the Basrian School of the Muʿtazila in the Classical Period*, Albany: SUNY, 1978. Three substantial studies of individual 'atomists' are MUḤAMMAD ʿABD AL-HĀDĪ ABŪ RĪDA, *Ibrāhīm b. Sayyār al-Naẓẓām wa-Ārāʾu-hu l-Kalāmīya al-Falsafīya*, Cairo: Maṭbaʿat Lajnat al-Taʾlīf wa-l-Tarjama wa-l-Nashr, 1946 (on al-Naẓẓām's 'atomism' see below, comments on *Maq.*, 304.11-12); R. M. FRANK, *The Metaphysics of Created Being According to Abū l-Hudhayl al-ʿAllāf: A Philosophical Study of the Earliest* Kalām, Istanbul: Nederlands Historisch-Archaeologisch Instituut in het Nabije Oosten, 1966; and H. DAIBER, *Das theologisch-philosophische System des Muʿammar ibn ʿAbbād as-Sulamī (gest. 830 n. Chr)*, Beirut - Wiesbaden: Steiner, 1975.

two separate intellectual discourses came to be born and to have the chance of developing at roughly the same time, in the same region of the Islamic world, and with the active support of the ʿAbbasid rulers. The two discourses came to be distinguished in the Ninth and later centuries as the '*Kalām* of religion' (*kalām al-dīn*) and the '*Kalām* of philosophy' (*kalām al-falsafa*). But, as far as their cosmologies were concerned, the former definitely opted for a basic atomistic world-picture, while the latter followed the mainly Aristotelian paradigm vigorously transmitted and promoted by the translation movement. What the two discourses had in common was their adherence to argumentation as their method of discovery and persuasion — an essential characteristic which would seem to have been intentionally emphasized as such by inserting the term *kalām* in *both* of their appellations.[3]

From the Eighth and Ninth Centuries on, the history of philosophical thought in Islam was: (1) the history of puzzling out, utilising, and mastering a Greek philosophical legacy as expressed solely in Arabic idiom and syntax; (2) the history of what started as a theological philosophy born out of religious, political and moral debates, and frequently argued against sophisticated Christian sects or 'heresies', all expressed in the Arabic language of current educated speech and of the growing Islamic disciplines (especially law), and which assumed from the outset the attitude of opponent to Hellenizing *Falsafa*; and (3) the history of the inevitable and inevitably varied interactions of (1) and (2) at different times and in different places and circumstances throughout the Muslim world.

To illustrate: The first important devotee and energetic promoter of *Falsafa* and of the 'sciences' embraced by it (*al-ʿulūm al-falsafīya*),

[3] See the quote at the beginning of this paper, from AL-JĀḤIẒ, *Kitāb al-Ḥayawān*, ed. ʿABD AL-SALĀM MUḤAMMAD HĀRŪN, II, Cairo: al-Bābī al-Ḥalabī, 1965², p. 134.12-14. In the Thirteenth Century, the bio-bibliographer Ibn al-Qifṭī, in a notice on a Baṣrian Muʿtazilī named Muḥammad b. ʿAlī b. al-Ṭayyib, who died in Baghdad on Rabīʿ II, 436 AH (1044 AD) in the reign of the ʿAbbasid Caliph al-Qāʾim (422-467/1031-1075), and whom Ibn al-Qifṭī describes as 'a leader who was learned in the science of the *Kalām* of the ancients' (*kāna imāman ʿāliman bi-ʿilm kalām al-awāʾil*), 'sought to protect himself against his contemporaries by publishing his views in the form practised by the *mutakallimūn* of the Islamic religion' (*Taʾrīkh al-Ḥukamāʾ*, ed. J. LIPPERT, Leipzig, 1903, p. 293-294). It is worthy of note that Ibn al-Ṭayyib, who apparently tried to follow al-Jāḥiẓ's recommendation of a philosophically-enriched *Kalām*, felt obliged to conceal his appreciation of 'the *Kalām* of the ancients'. But of course al-Jāḥiẓ and Ibn al-Ṭayyib lived in two politically and intellectually different atmospheres. The generally typical situation is described by Alfred North Whitehead in the second quote at the beginning of this paper, from *Process and Reality*, corrected edition by DAVID RAY GRIFFIN and DONALD W. SHERBURNE, New York - London: Free Press, 1978, p. 9.

namely Yaʿqūb b. Isḥāq al-Kindī (died ca. 252/866), seemed to look above the *nuẓẓār*, promoters of the '*Kalām* of religion', to mature Greek doctrines and to rising humanistic ideals, and sometimes also experimenting with a kind of philosophical allegorization as a bridge between religion and *Falsafa*.[4] The 'Second Teacher' ('the first' being Aristotle), al-Fārābī (d. 339/950), was willing to assign to the *Kalām* of religion a position entirely subordinate and subservient to 'the true *Falsafa*'.[5] Avicenna (d. 428/1037) appears to have given *Kalām* more attention than his two prominent predecessors had done; but there is no evidence that he made any philosophical concessions to *Kalām* atomism, let alone a *Kalām* world-view.[6] The Cordoban Averroes (d. 595/1198) admitted that he only had a limited knowledge of *Kalām* largely derived from Ashʿarite writers, and declared himself unimpressed, even repelled by it. The Jewish Cordoban Maimonides (d. 602/1204) unambiguously endorsed the Muslim *falāsifa*'s view of *Kalām* as a brand of compromised rationalism.[7]

Hence the obvious importance of Ibn Khaldūn's statement in the Fourteenth Century that, by his time, works on *Kalām* and works on *Falsafa* appeared to be no longer distinguishable, whether in regard to terminology and forms of argument, or concerning concepts and doctrines considered by both the *mutakallimūn* and the *falāsifa*. In 1994 the present writer published an article provoked by that statement, and in which reference is made to consequences of the situation described by Ibn Khaldūn for the history of Arabic astronomy. But the subject is much

[4] See *Kitāb al-Kindī fī l-Falsafa al-Ūlā*, in: *Rasāʾil al-Kindī al-Falsafīya*, ed. MUḤAMMAD ʿABD AL-HĀDĪ ABŪ RĪDA, I, Cairo: Dār al-Fikr al-ʿArabī, 1950, p. 81-162; English translation: *Al-Kindī's Metaphysics*, trans. ALFRED L. IVRY, Albany: SUNY, 1974; new edition, French translation and notes: *Œuvres philosophiques d'al-Kindī, II: Métaphysique et Cosmologie*, trans. ROSHDI RASHED and JEAN JOLIVET, Leiden, 1998, p. 9-111; AL-KINDĪ, *Risāla ilā Aḥmad b. al-Muʿtaṣim fī l-Ibāna ʿan Sujūd al-Jirm al-Aqṣā wa-Ṭāʿati-hi li-Allāh ʿAzza wa-Jalla*, Arabic text, French translation and notes in: *Œuvres philosophiques*, p. 175-204; JOEL L. KRAEMER, *Philosophy in the Renaissance of Islam*, Leiden: Brill, 1986.

[5] See A.I. SABRA, *Science and Philosophy in Medieval Islamic Theology. The Evidence of the Fourteenth Century*, in: *Zeitschrift für Geschichte der Arabisch-Islamischen Wissenschaften* 9 (1994), p. 1-42 (p. 6, n. 8).

[6] MICHAEL E. MARMURA, *Avicenna and the* Kalām, in: *Zeitschrift für Geschichte der Arabisch-Islamischen Wissenschaften* 7 (1991/92), p. 172-206; PAUL LETTINCK, *Ibn Sīnā on Atomism: Translation of Ibn Sīnā's* Kitāb al-Shifāʾ, al-Ṭabīʿīyāt 1: al-Samāʿ al-Ṭabīʿī, *Third Treatise, Chapters 3-5*, in: *Al-Shajara* 4 (1999), p. 1-51.

[7] MŪSĀ B. MAYMŪN AL-QURṬUBĪ, *Dalālat al-Ḥāʾirīn*, ed. HÜSEYIN ATAY, Ankara: Ankara Üniversitesi, 1974, see esp. Section I.73, p. 199-232; MOSES MAIMONIDES, *The Guide of the Perplexed*, trans. S. PINES, with an Introductory Essay by LEO STRAUSS, Chicago: University of Chicago Press, 1963, p. 194-231.

too large and complex to be adequately explored in a few articles; and, as is well-known, the development noted by Ibn Khaldūn actually involved many influential authors in *Kalām* and *Falsafa* both before and after his time.[8]

I.3. The following discussions in this contribution are predicated on the assumption that Ashʿarism (at least as conceived by al-Ashʿarī himself and his immediate followers), rather than being a 'conservative' or so-called 'orthodox reaction' against the rationally oriented Muʿtazila, would be more correctly described as an intellectual ambition to render certain Muʿtazilī positions consistent with an ontology of events which itself incorporated an apparently coherent atomistic view which I have tried to identify below (under *Hypothesis: A World of Contingent Events*).

To elaborate briefly and generally on this statement: it should be known that:

> (*a*) al-Ashʿarī, and the Ashʿarites as a whole, retained the basic, all-important Muʿtazilī concept of knowledge (*ʿilm*) as the antithesis of *taqlīd*, a passive acceptance of authority in matters of thought and belief, and as a state of mind regularly *linked to* (though not, for the Ashʿarites, caused or engendered by) a prior activity to be performed by the individual knowing subject, an activity which both groups called 'thinking' or 'reasoning' (*fikr*, *naẓar*);[9]
> (*b*) both the Muʿtazila and the Ashʿarites accepted sense-perception as (1) a valid form of knowing (*ʿilm*), which (2) actually provided one of two foundations for two principal doctrines they claimed to prove in their capacity as practitioners of the new 'Science of *Kalām*', the other foundation being the 'necessary', *ḍarūrī*, or indispensable, propositions, some of which were identified with formal logic;
> (*c*) foremost among those principal doctrines were of course the existence of God from all eternity and the origination (*ḥudūth*) of the world at the beginning of time;

[8] SABRA, *Science and Philosophy*. See IBN KHALDŪN, *The Muqaddima of Ibn Khaldūn*, transl. F. ROSENTHAL, III, Princeton: Princeton University Press, 1967, p. 34ff.

[9] AL-QĀḌĪ ABŪ L-ḤASAN ʿABD AL-JABBĀR, *Kitāb al-Mughnī, XII: al-Naẓar wa-l-Maʿārif*, ed. IBRĀHĪM MADKŪR, Cairo: Wizārat al-Thaqāfa wa-l-Irshād al-Qawmī, 1960 (1962?); JOSEF VAN ESS, *Die Erkenntnislehre des ʿAḍudaddīn al-Īcī, Übersetzung und Kommentar der ersten Buches seiner* Mawāqif, Wiesbaden: Franz Steiner Verlag, 1966 (includes extensive bibliography); MARIE BERNAND, *La notion de* ʿilm *chez les premiers muʿtazilites*, in: *Studia Islamica* 36 (1972), p. 23-45; 37 (1973), p. 27-38; MARIE BERNAND, *Le problème de la connaissance d'après le* Mughnī *du Cadi ʿAbd al-Jabbār*, Alger: Société Nationale d'Edition et de Diffusion, 1982 (includes extensive bibliography); R. FRANK, *Knowledge and* Taqlīd: *The Foundation of Religious Belief in Classical Ashʿarism*, in: *Journal of the American Oriental Society* 109 (1989), p. 37-62.

(*d*) both the Muʿtazila and the Ashʿarites committed themselves to forms of atomism that put them sharply in opposition to all versions of the Aristotelianism embraced by the *falāsifa* of Islam, from al-Kindī and al-Fārābī to Ibn Sīnā and Ibn Rushd. The atomistic theses examined and defended by individual Muʿtazilite thinkers were not ready-made doctrines they had received in finished, well-defined and scholasticized forms; they consisted in fact of a variety of often clashing views which, inspired by age-old insights of Western and Eastern origins, they themselves struggled to articulate, often in discussions conducted in the common Arabic discourse of their own time and place;
(*e*) it is also clear that, in their initiatives, both Muʿtazilīs and Ashʿarīs were deeply involved in the religious, political, and cosmological issues generated by the claims and directives of the Islamic Revealed Book, and by the interpreters of Muslim law, and the actions of Muslim rulers;
(*f*) in literally all of these respects, the drives and motivations inseparably connected with the emergence of *Kalām* in the Eighth Century as an 'Islamic science' differed enormously from those that shaped the nearly contemporaneous rise of *Falsafa*, a set of grand doctrines of highly developed structures of thought all of which were made accessible to Arabic readers in translations of complete Greek texts and full Greek commentaries.

I.4. My present goal, however, is not to engage in a wide-ranging discussion aimed at establishing my underlying assumption itself, but rather to focus, tentatively but with a certain degree of precision, on examples of al-Ashʿarī's own understanding of certain Muʿtazilite doctrines, and on related examples of al-Ashʿarī's own criticisms, agreements or expansions of such doctrines, with the aim of elucidating some of the elements of what is intended to be a coherent view. My illustrative examples are accordingly derived from Hellmut Ritter's edition of al-Ashʿarī's *Maqālāt al-Islāmīyīn* and Daniel Gimaret's edition of the book 'dictated' by Abū Bakr Muḥammad b. al-Ḥasan b. Fūrak (d. 406/1015), entitled *Mujarrad Maqālāt al-Ashʿarī*. My present project would not have been possible to launch in the absence of these two magisterial editions which happen to complement one another in an unusual, perhaps unique manner in the extant *Kalām* literature. Al-Ashʿarī's *Maqālāt* is a clear, deliberately neutral and delicately expressed, though sometimes tantalizingly brief, account of Muʿtazilite doctrines and arguments as understood by one who had been brought up, so to speak, and practised in Muʿtazilite thought for many years before he dramatically announced (in 300/912-913) his desertion at the age of forty. As good luck would have it, Ibn Fūrak's book gives the definite impression of being a faithful, competent and intelligent account of al-Ashʿarī's own views or 'doctrines' (*maqālāt*) — a remarkable, unexpected match to the *Maqālāt al-Islāmīyīn* in clarity and precise reporting. To the selections chosen from these two books I have appended a relevant, albeit short and condensed, section from al-Ījī's influential *Kitāb al-Mawāqif* as a masterful text illustrating the situation described by Ibn Khaldūn.[10]

II. Hypothesis: a world of contingent events

Brief Statement of a Proposed Interpretation of the Ashʿarite View of the Created World, in Thirteen Propositions:

1. The world (*al-ʿālam*) is all that occurs (*kullu mā yaḥduth*).
2. Occurrences are events (*ḥawādith*) in space and time: all have space and time coordinates.
3. Occurrences consist of the coming into being of place-occupying entities called 'substances' (sing. *jawhar*), and of accidents (sing. *ʿaraḍ*) that may only reside (*taḥill fī*) or inhere (*taqūm fī*) in substances momentarily.
4. Substances are initially created (*tukhlaq*, *tubtadaʾ*, *tukhtaraʿ*) and subsequently re-created (*tuʿād*) at every moment of their span of existence.
5. Substances are of two types (*ḍarbān*): (1) 'simple' or 'individual' substances (sing. *jawhar basīṭ*, or *jawhar fard* or *munfarid*), called 'atoms' (sing. *juzʾ*, or *al-juzʾ alladhī lā yatajazzaʾ*: the part, or the indivisible part); and (2) composites of these, called 'bodies'.
6. Four accidents, known as *al-akwān*, the comings-to-be, completely describe the possible behaviour of substances *as place occupiers*: at every moment, a substance (atom or body) either (1) comes-to-be *in motion*, from one place to another, or (2) comes-to-be *at rest* in one and the same place; and, through motion and rest, a substance may (3) come-to-be *in contact with*, or (4) *in separation from*, another substance or substances.

[10] These three books, by al-Ashʿarī, Ibn Fūrak and al-Ījī, will respectively be referred to by the abbreviations: *Maq.*, *Muj.*, and *Maw.*: Abū l-Ḥasan al-Ashʿarī, *Maqālāt al-Islāmīyīn* [= *Maq.*], ed. Hellmut Ritter, Wiesbaden: Franz Steiner, 1963²; Ibn Fūrak, *Mujarrad Maqālāt al-Ashʿarī* [= *Muj.*], ed. Daniel Gimaret, Beirut: Dar El-Machreq, 1987; ʿAḍud al-Milla wa-l-Dīn ʿAbd al-Raḥmān b. Aḥmad al-Ījī, *Al-Mawāqif fī ʿIlm al-Kalām* [= *Maw.*], ed. Ibrāhīm al-Dusūqī ʿAṭīya and Aḥmad al-Hanbūlī, Cairo: Maṭbaʿat al-ʿUlūm, 1357/1938-1939.

7. Accidents acquire their *spatial positions* from their inevitable association with place-occupying substances.
8. Space and time, being neither substances nor accidents that *reside* or *inhere in* substances, are relations:
9. Space is an order of relations that happen to obtain between substance-occupied places (positions) at any moment.
10. Time is an arbitrary convention of correlating coincident or simultaneous events.
11. All occurrences are contingent, all of them being choices or free actions of a transcendent, unique, and omnipotent Agent:
12. In the created world of events, there are no Aristotelian substances, no natures or natural powers or forces, no forms or essences or necessities; there is only one, meta-physical, cause which acts without means or intermediate agents:
13. 'Creating', the act of a transcendent Being, 'is that which is created' (*al-khalq huwa l-makhlūq*).

III. Exploratory discussions of some principal topics:

Language Usage, Coming-to-be, Motion, Relativity of Space and Time, Nature, Creation

The following discussions are 'exploratory' in the sense that they are meant to be illustrative rather than exhaustive. They are, however, claimed to represent important and central positions of al-Ashʿarī and Ashʿarism.

Topic I: Language Usage as an Authority in Kalām *Argumentation*

Language usage has formed part of philosophical discourse from Plato and Aristotle to Wittgenstein. It is interesting to note that, while the *falāsifa*, as promoters and practitioners of ancient 'Greek philosophy', often had the task of constructing *ad hoc* expressions in Arabic to parallel Greek locutions which they read only in translation, the Muʿtazila seem to have established, from early on, a habit of invoking common usage of Arabic in support of distinct theoretical positions. Most of the Muʿtazila were Persians, but they wrote in Arabic, and they have been credited with important contributions to the theory and practice of Arabic rhetoric.[11]

[11] ʿAbd al-Ḥakīm Balbaʿ, *Adab al-Muʿtazila*, Cairo, 1959; Shawqī Ḍayf, *al-Balāgha: Taṭawwur wa-Taʾrīkh*, Cairo: Dār al-Maʿārif, 1976³.

The following are some examples of reference to language usage as a form of authoritative, philosophical argument:

1. At *Maq.*, 301.1-306.13, al-Ashʿarī refers to language (*lugha*) and to the language speakers (*ahl al-lugha*) as the basis of an argument by 'some' of the *mutakallimūn* (al-Ṣāliḥī is mentioned) who questioned the validity of attributing to an atom the 'name' *mumāssa* or *taʾlīf* (contact/touching, composition), which is one of the four modes of coming-to-be, unless the atom is actually in touch with another atom 'because the language users have not allowed the possibility of touching when there is nothing to touch'. For a reference to *ahl al-ʿarabīya* (speakers of the Arabic language), see *Muj.*, 245.18-23.
2. At *Maq.*, 304.8-10, al-Ashʿarī refers to 'some' *mutakallimūn* who take 'body' in the sense accepted by *ahl al-lugha*: namely, as that which is long, broad and deep, *without specifying a minimal number of atoms for the composition of body* (thus against, for example, Abū l-Hudhayl and Muʿammar).
3. The Muʿtazilite Muḥammad b. Shabīb, who affirmed the reality of both motion and rest as two distinct accidents, cites *ahl al-lugha* in support of understanding motion as departure (*zawāl*) from the abandoned place, a doctrine which he asserted to be due to the 'accommodation of language' (*ittisāʿ al-lugha*) and the 'established' ways of speaking (*Maq.*, 354.6-15). See also Topic III, on Motion.
4. The role of language figures prominently in a dispute between al-Jubbāʾī and his student/associate, al-Ashʿarī, as related by the latter (*Maq.*, 355.12-356.3); see also Topic III, on Motion.
5. Contrary to the usual trend, however, are Muʿammar's (d. 220/830) and al-Naẓẓām's dismissals of the authority of language (only in some cases?) as merely 'a manner of speaking' — the former in denying motion, the latter in denying rest (*Maq.*, 347.9-12; *Maq.*, 346.13-347.2; *Maq.*, 370.7-10).
6. For al-Ashʿarī himself, the common usage of language remained a principal argument at the basis of his analysis of motion and of his outright rejection of the philosophers' concept(s) of Nature (as well as the Muʿtazila's doctrine of 'engendering' [*tawlīd*]): see Topic V.
7. For an interesting example of the use, by al-Ashʿarī, of ordinary language in the heart of a discussion about the enduring (*baqāʾ*) of God and of bodies, see *Muj.*, 238.16-19; see also on *ahl al-lugha*: *Muj.*, 211.20-24; *Muj.*, 212.2.

The whole subject of language usage as a recognised argument in establishing *Kalām* doctrines deserves an extensive treatment for which there is no space here. It should be emphasized, however, that invoking the current Arabic language was not a fortuitous feature of *Kalām* argumentation but a tool which largely distinguished it from the discourse of the *falāsifa*.[12]

Topic II: The Doctrine of al-Akwān, Comings-to-be: Atoms as the Events of Coming-to-be in Place.

The doctrine of *akwān*, plural of *kawn*, which is the verbal noun from *kāna*, to be, or to come-to-be,[13] is a key doctrine in *Kalām* atomism which first appeared with the Muʿtazila, and which continued to play a critical role in Ashʿarite developments, a role which was even more fundamental and significant than has been recognized in modern studies. As expressed in our *Hypothesis* above, the four accidents called *akwān* together provide a complete description of the possible behaviour of 'substances' in space: at any moment *t*, an *existing* substance, whether atom or body, either (1) comes-to-be-*in-motion* by abandoning a prior place, thereby occupying another place, at *t*, or (2) comes-to-be-*at rest* in the place it occupied at the moment immediately preceding *t*; and, through motion *and* rest, a substance may (3) come-to-be *in contact with*, or (4) *in separation from*, other substances.[14] Contact is often referred to as *mumāssa*, touching, also *ijtimāʿ*, *taʾlīf*: composition or aggregation. Separation is also expressed as *mufāraqa* or *mubāyana*, i.e. a substance's coming-to-be separate or at a distance from other substances. *Mumāssa* or contact in fact covers the whole range of phenomena that involve

[12] See, e.g., al-Ījī's argument in his *Mawāqif* in support of 'the true doctrine' on body and against the Ṣāliḥīya and the Karrāmīya and Hishām, below, p. 262 and note 32.

[13] Al-Ashʿarī was aware of the distinction between *kāʾin* as a predicate, meaning '*X* exists', and as a copula, '*X* is "something or other"'; see comment on *Muj.* 43.12-14. In the latter case, to describe a thing as *kāʾin* is to ascribe to the thing the accident or occurrence of coming-to-be (*al-kawn*), or having-come-to-be, through which the thing has come-to-be *in-place*, 'if place is involved' (*idhā kāna makānun*). Behind this last condition is al-Ashʿarī's explicit and repeatedly stated belief that God can create a thing 'without the thing's being in a place' (*lā fī makān*). But al-Ashʿarī also admits that creating a thing without the thing's being in a place, though always within God's capacity, is beyond human understanding. (See *Muj.*, 43.12-14).

[14] In regard to (3) and (4): let (A_1, A_2) and (B_1, B_2) be two pairs of aggregated atoms at some distance from one another; at point of time *t*, let A_1 come-to-be in separation from A_2, and in-contact-with (B_1, B_2); at the same time *t*, atom A_2, having *come-to-be at rest* in its own former place, will also have come-to-be in separation from A_1.

touching or contiguity — like cohesion, pressure, impact, collision, etc., all understood as purely kinematical events. Some *mutakallimūn* thought of reducing all *akwān* to a single *kawn* by, for example, reducing contact and separation to either motion with a denial of rest, or to rest with a denial of *motion*. Some others reduced the *akwān* to contact. All four *akwān*, however, involve time as well as place, which makes explicit their common character as merely *events in space and time*. It is also clear that accidents/qualities, as *momentary* residents in substances, acquire their spatial positions, and hence their spatial coordinates, from their place-occupying subjects, namely the substances defined as place-occupiers. We are led to conclude that, as well as governing the behaviour of substances in space, the doctrine of *akwān* serves two principal purposes: it presents substances as events, or occurrences (*ḥawādith*) in time as well as place, and it anchors accidents/qualities as events in place as well as time. Obviously, *Kalām* substances should not therefore be confused with Aristotelian substances. And it is the *akwān* doctrine that lays the foundation of what we may regard as a basic decision to go in the direction of an ontology of events, rather than an ontology of 'things' that remain what they 'essentially?' *are* through change (see the discussion of 'creation' below, Topic VI). — *In other words, a substance (atom or body) is simply the* event *of an instantaneous coming-to-be* in place, *which makes it possible for another physical event to happen, namely the event of an accident's (or quality's) coming-to-inhere instantaneously in a* substance *(or* subject).[15]

[15] See the relatively late but clear statement in the *Tadhkira* (p. 88.10-89.3) of the Muʿtazilī Ibn Mattawayh in support of understanding substances as occurrences/events: '... let us ... state how a substance comes to exist (*kayfīyat wujūdi-hi*), which, according to us, happens by way of occurring (*bi-ṭarīqat al-ḥudūth*). — The foundation (*al-aṣl*/root) on which to base the proof that substances/atoms and bodies are new [= originated] is *the impossibility of freeing them from the occurrences* (*ḥawādith*) [*known as*] *al-akwān* (*the comings-to-be*) — for what is not separable from what is new, and does not precede it [in time], is also new. — And this is based on affirming the comings-to-be and their occurrence (as will be discussed in its proper place along with the *akwān*).

But let it be that we have to do here with something new/originated: then, that by means of which we know that no body can be separated from it is that we have shown that it can exist only in a place (*illā wa-huwa mutaḥayyiz*), and that what occupies a place must be *somewhere* (*fī jiha*), and that *that* can only happen through a coming-to-be (*wa-lā yakūnu ka-dhālik illā bi-kawn*). — That is made clear by our knowing that bodies must be either together or separate, and either in motion or at rest, and they cannot be conceived otherwise. But nothing imposes this judgement upon them except their coming-to-be-in-place. Therefore [this] judgement applies to them when they come to exist in place'. For Ibn Mattawayh's date and his *Tadhkira*, see our comment on *Maq.*, 316.1-7.

Al-Ashʿarī refers to the *initial creation* of substances by a number of terms, *ikhtirāʿ*, *ibtidāʾ*, *inshāʾ*, as well as *khalq*, to which act he ovbiously assigns a special status; and this leads to the question of how *kawn* and *creation* differ from one another. Al-Ashʿarī's answer, delivered in connection with his rejection of al-Naẓẓām's understanding of creation as a 'motion of endeavour', is simply the following: all motions (that is, all intelligible accounts of motion) presuppose a prior *being-in-place*; intitial creation does not. (See especially: *Maq*., 324.12-325.2; *Maq*., 346.13-347.8; *Muj*., 203.4-7; *Muj*. 291.3-6; *Muj*., 243.10-245.23.)

A question arises in connection with al-Ashʿarī's attribution of *baqāʾ* (enduring, persisting) to substances, i.e., atoms and bodies, as distinguished from accidents or qualities. If substances are at every moment coming to be in motion or at rest, then what can be meant by their 'enduring' beyond the assertion that coming-to-be (i.e., *kawn*) is an event that involves a *prior being-in-place*, while being created is an *initial* coming-into-existence that does not imply such a condition. It would seem, in light of this comparison, that a further function of *kawn* would be as an expression for the continued existence of what is simply defined as *'that which occupies place'*, whose *other characteristics* at any moment are the sum of accidents that come to inhere in the substance at that moment. That is to say, that 'enduring', for substances, is the persistence simply of their definition as place-occupying entities. There is no explicit argument to this effect in Ibn Fūrak's expositions of al-Ashʿarī's view, and the problem is made especially complicated by shifting the discussion back and forth between God and created bodies, as in the longest passage devoted to this discussion at *Muj*., 237.1-240.16. There, al-Ashʿarī is at one point reported to face a challenging question, 'so why don't you say, with respect to the enduring of body, that it endures by itself (*bāqī bi-nafsi-hi*) in the way that you say that God, *taʿālā*, endures by Himself?' (*Muj*., 239.11-12). — In fact, the correct and consistent answer to this question would appear to be to accept the proposed conclusion — in the sense that enduring, in God's case, is inferred from God's *definition* as a self-supporting being, and, in the case of body, from the *definition* of substance as that which occupies place, which definition of course holds through coming-to-be in motion and coming-to-be at rest. (See also *Muj*., 108.21-23.)

Topic III: Motion

In a general report by al-Ashʿarī on *Kalām* doctrines of motion (*Maq*., 353.16-356.3), he formulates the basic question posed by the Muʿtazila as the precise question of *where* the motion should be ascribed to the substance (atom or body) that is said to have moved from one place to another. The question is appropriate, being clearly suggested by the accepted, all-inclusive substance-accident ontology: if existents or world occurrences solely consist of substances and accidents/qualities/attributes, then, indeed: '*where* does the accident or quality motion come to inhere in the substance to which the motion is ascribed — in the first place or in the second?' Those who defined motion as departure (*zawāl*) from the first place, apparently the majority of the *mutakallimūn*, answered that, 'it is only in the second place that a substance can be said to have moved from the first, and therefore, it is only in the second place that the substance can be said to have acquired the accident/quality motion'. This obviously excluded the interpretation of motion as a 'state' accompanying the substance as it performs the transition from place to place (whatever the meaning that might be attached to this characterization, and ignoring problems raised by it — see *Maq*., 355.10-11). In particular, it would be misleading to try to elucidate the question asked and answered by the *mutakallimūn* in terms of the Aristotelian apparatus of potentiality, actuality, and perfection or completion. These terms certainly belong to an entirely different universe of discourse, and, looked at from the point of view of *Kalām* ontology, they should call to mind what Descartes says in his *Le Monde* (beginning of Chapter VII) where he quotes the Aristotelian definition of motion in Latin and French, adding that he does not understand it in either language. What the *Kalām* concept of motion as departure had in common with the Cartesian, anti-Aristotelian position was their insistence on elucidating motion exclusively in terms of place and time.

Muʿammar's equation, '*kawn* = rest' (*Maq*., 347.9-12; 355.1-2), and al-Naẓẓām's equation, '*kawn* = motion' (*Maq*., 324.12-325.2; 346.13-16), conveying a fundamental opposition expressed in a minimum number of words, sharply illustrate a feature of Muʿtazilite discussions as they have often reached us in short and frequently puzzling reports. Sometimes, however, one may be able to propose a plausible interpretation suggested by context which itself may lead to further inquiry and further elucidation. The equation attributed to Muʿammar is probably a case in point. Assuming the equation to apply primarily to atoms or indivisible parts, and assuming further that it implied an apparently prevalent conception of motion as departure (*zawāl*) from one place to another, we may write the statement, 'Atom *A* has moved from place p_1 to place p_2 at some time *t*' — in the form:

(*A* is in p_1 at time *t*) & (A is in p_2 at t_n), where t_n is the next moment immediately following *t* — so that, throughout "the motion," *A is at rest*, there being no moment between *t* and t_n.

Al-Naẓẓām went directly in the opposite direction, undoubtedly following a different line of thought, when he decided in favour of the dynamic concept of *iʿtimād*. I have translated *iʿtimād* by 'endeavour', a term proposed by Thomas Hobbes to render the Latin *conatus* (dictionary meanings: effort, exertion, endeavour; impulse, inclination, tendency). The Latin term was subsequently adopted by Leibniz and also translated by him into French (in his *Théodicée*) as *effort*.[16] The Arabic term, from the verb *iʿtamada* (*ʿalā*), to lean or press (against), was understood by Avicenna as equivalent to *mayl*, tendency or inclination, as in the 'natural' tendency of a heavy body to fall downwards, or the 'forced' or 'acquired' tendency of a thrown body to go upwards. Also in the Eleventh Century, Ibn al-Haytham (who was not a friend of *Kalām* or, at least, *Kalām* metaphysics) used *iʿtimād* in his mechanical analogies for explaining optical reflection and refraction.[17] In the *Kalām* tradition itself as reported by al-Ījī in the fourteenth century, *iʿtimād* came to be defined as 'that which entails (*yūjibu*) a body's counteraction (*mudāfaʿa, pushing back/resistance*) to what prevents/opposes (*yamnaʿu*) its motion in a certain direction'.[18]

[16] See G.W. LEIBNIZ, *The Labyrinth of the Continuum: Writings on the Continuum Problem, 1672-1686*, ed. and trans. RICHARD T.W. ARTHUR, New Haven and London: Yale University Press, 2001, p. 440-441 (Latin Glossary), also p. 494, 495.

[17] A.I. SABRA, *Theories of Light from Descartes to Newton*, Cambridge: Cambridge University Press, 1981², p. 72-76 and n. 14, and p. 93-97, n. 2; A.I. SABRA, ed., *The Optics of Ibn al-Haytham*, Arabic text of Books IV-V, Kuwait: National Council for Culture, Arts and Letters, 2002: see vol. II, p. 76-87 (explanation in dynamical terms of the reflection of light from smooth bodies). For the use of *mayl* in Avicenna see: S. PINES, *Études sur Awḥad al-Zamān Abu l-Barakāt al-Baghdādī*, in: *Studies in Abu l-Barakāt al-Baghdādī: Physics and Metaphysics* (*Collected Works of Shlomo Pines*, 1), Leiden: Brill, 1979, p. [1]-[95]; and on *iʿtimād* and *mayl*: p. [43]ff. See also FRITZ ZIMMERMAN, *Philoponus' Impetus Theory in the Arabic Tradition*, in: *Philoponus and the Rejection of Aristotelian Science*, ed. RICHARD SORABJI, Ithaca: Cornell University Press, 1987, p. 121-129; AHMAD HASNAOUI, *La dynamique d'Ibn Sīnā*, in: *Études sur Avicenne*, ed. JEAN JOLIVET and ROSHDI RASHED, Paris: Société d'Édition Les Belles Lettres, 1984, p. 103-123.

[18] AL-ĪJĪ, *Kitāb al-Mawāqif*, p. 125: *al-iʿtimād huwa mā yūjibu li-l-jism al-mudāfaʿa li-mā yamnaʿu-hu l-ḥaraka ilā jiha mā*. Al-Ījī adds that it had also been said (*qīla*) that endeavour is the '*mudāfaʿa itself*', and that [endeavour] had been defined by al-Ustādh Abū Isḥāq [al-Isfarāʾīnī], but asserted as something undeniable (*bi-l-ḍarūra*) by the Muʿtazila and many from our party, such as al-Qāḍī [al-Bāqillānī]'. Al-Ījī himself was of the opinion that denying endeavour is obstinate rejection of experience (*mukābara li-l-ḥiss*).

Al-Naẓẓām is reported to have said that, 'when a body endeavours [to maintain itself] in a place (*idhā 'ʿtamada l-jism fī l-makān*) we say that 'the body rested in the place', but not that rest is a quality (*maʿnā*) of the body other than its endeavour… ' (*Maq*., 346.13-15). This might seem to be just another way of stating the kinematic doctrine, shared by others, that rest is a coming-to-be (*kawn*) in one and the same place, that is, an occurrence that involves only two moments and one place. But, in explicating his position (and as an answer to the general question of '*where* does the motion occur when a substance moves from one place to another?'), al-Naẓẓām clearly asserts that it occurs in the first place *as an endeavour to move*, then, in the second, *as accomplished motion*. So that motion, for al-Naẓẓām, neither begins nor ends with 'rest' (*Maq*., 346.15-347.8; 354.1-5).

Al-Ashʿarī follows that (last) report on al-Naẓẓām with another on Ibn Shabīb (second half of the Ninth Century), who affirmed both motion and rest, the motion being 'endeavour' in the first place and 'departure' in the second, thus (like al-Naẓẓam) in accommodating the additional sanction of language usage (*Maq*., 354.6-15).

Now, al-Ījī tells us in concise and precise terms, that the '*mutakallimūn*' generally disagreed, not about the endeavour itself which, he adds, is attested by experience and experiment, but about *that hidden thing* that was supposed by some to 'entail' it (see al-Ījī's definition of endeavour quoted above). Al-Ījī mentions the important promoter of Ashʿarism in Nīshāpūr, Abū Isḥāq al-Isfarāʾīnī (d. 318/1027), as one who rejected endeavour in the sense defined above, but does not refer to al-Ashʿarī himself. There can be no question, however, about al-Ashʿarī's position, which is clearly reported in several places in Ibn Fūrak's *Mujarrad*. For example, at *Muj*., 211.20-24, al-Ashʿarī is said to have rejected al-Naẓẓām's account of initial creation as being a 'motion of endeavour', asserting instead that motion is, and must always be interpreted as a *kawn* requiring the thing in motion to have been first *in a place* from which it moved.

We are also told that al-Ashʿarī considered motion and rest as forming *one* class (*jins wāḥid*) of two members which are contraries, and therefore mutually exclusive (*Muj*., 211.25-212.2). And we are told that al-Ashʿarī maintained at the same time that the 'very *motion from* one place is the same as *rest in* another', and that in almost all of the above statements he cites the testimony of language (*Muj*., 212.3-9), actually asserting that endeavour (or what is called 'endeavour') is just a case of contact/*mumāssa* (which is a *kawn*), and explicitly rejects equating endeavour with gravity (*al-thiqal*) (*Muj*., 246.1-4; 275.7-17), thus against endeavour, nature and causality; see also Topic V, on Nature.

It should be clear that al-Ashʿarī's denial of al-Naẓẓām's dynamic concept of endeavour was a conscious and decisive step in the development of Ashʿarite philosophy of motion: it indicated a definitely intended banishment of all forces from the material world (see, in particular, *Muj*., 262.10-23); it was simply meant to block the way which the Muʿtazilite al-Jāḥiẓ in the Ninth Century had tried to open by strongly proposing to assimilate Muʿtazilite 'endeavour' to the *falāsifa*'s 'Nature'.[19]

Topic IV: Relativity of Space and Time

The concept of 'space', as distinguished from 'place', is conveyed more or less directly, and almost always without formal definitions, in terms used both by the Muʿtazila and the Ashʿarites: *makān*, *ḥayyiz*, *jiha*, *muḥādhāh*, *ḥulūl fī l-makān* (or, *shaghl* or *ishghāl li-l-makān*). This can partially be explained by the fact that Arabic lacks a special term for the English 'space' as distinguished from 'place'. *Faḍā*' (sometimes used by Fakhr al-Dīn al-Rāzī[20]) might have been used for space, as is done in modern Arabic; but *khalā*' and *farāgh* applied only to void or empty places. In the *Kalām* discussions, the burden of the distinction seems to have been usually thrown on *jiha* and *muḥādhāh*. Frequently, however, *makān* seems to have stood, ambiguously, for what we might understand as 'space'.

Throughout my translations, *makān* is rendered by 'place,' never by 'space'. For example, a substance *rests in* a place, and *moves from* place to place; similarly, a substance (atom or body) occupies place, or a place. I would have liked to render *ḥayyiz* by a term other than 'place' (if only to avoid frequently alerting the reader to my choice), but I could not find a more suitable word. I am not aware, however, of problems arising from this choice. *Ḥayyiz*, in the *Kalām* literature, may on some occasions have been meant to carry the meaning of *a finite volume of space*, but, as applied to individual substances or atoms, that meaning could not have been the accepted rule.[21]

[19] The assimilation of the *Kalām* concept of *iʿtimād* to the *falāsifa*'s Nature/*ṭabʿ* or *ṭabīʿa* is one of the themes of al-Jāḥiẓ's influential *Kitāb al-Ḥayawān*; al-Jāḥiẓ's views are frequently referred to by the Muʿtazilite ʿAbd al-Jabbār (d. 415/1025) in *al-Naẓar wa-l-Maʿārif*.

[20] See below p. 216, note 23.

[21] On the conflation of *makān* and *ḥayyiz* see the thesaurus by the great Eighteenth Century Indian scholar, MUḤAMMAD AʿLĀ B. SHAYKH ʿALĪ B. QĀḌĪ MUḤAMMAD B. MUḤAMMAD ṢĀBIR AL-FĀRŪQĪ AL-TAHĀNAWĪ, *Kashshāf Iṣṭilāḥāt al-Funūn*, I, Beirut: Dār Ṣādir, no date, p. 298-300, under *al-ḥayyiz*. On the author and his book see the article by R. SELLHEIM in: *EI*2, X, p. 98.

The crucial, explicit or clearly implied definition of substance, when applied to individual substance or atom, as *that which occupies place* (*yashghalu makānan*), must be understood as a postulate-defintion, just like Euclid's definition of point as 'that which has no part' (*sēmeion estin, ou meros ouden*), and nothing should be gratuitously added to what it actually asserts. In particular, we may not simply *assume* that an individual substance has size or shape; though composite substances, which also occupy places, of course have size and shape, but only by virtue of their being 'bodies' that extend in the three dimensions.[22]

Jiha is the term most frequently used in referring to the placement or localization of substances *in space* (in our translations from al-Ashʿarī's *Maqālāt* it occurs at *Maq.*, 316.1-7; *Maq.*, 316.8-9; *Maq.*, 316.10-12; see also: *Muj.*, 93.6-7; *Muj.*, 203.12-16, important). *Jiha* means *side* (as in left and right *side*), also *direction* and *region*. *Side* is obviously relational. *Direction* is, strictly, an angle. And region is a spot to be specified only by reference to other spots. The Arabic expression, *muntahā l-ishāra* (= *where you point to*), is helpful for elucidating substance-placement: it means the end, *muntahā*, or end-point, of the line along your stretched arm or finger, which point must be defined further as the intersection of that line with another, given line or surface. —As for *muḥādhāh*, it simply refers to the spatial relation of two points or atoms which face each other or stand in opposition to each other; in this sense the term can be translated as 'spatial opposition'. See especially *Maq.*, 316.1-7 and associated comments.

With these clarifications in mind there should be no difficulty in following passages that involve the terms listed above.

There is no discussion of time as such in Ibn Fūrak's *Mujarrad*. It is known however that time received much attention from the *mutakallimūn* in general.[23] Following is my translation of the passage in al-Ījī's *Mawāqif* on 'the Ashʿarite doctrine of time', which, as would be expected, clearly though briefly reveals its conventional nature:

> For the Ashʿarites, time is [any] emerging event taken to measure/determine another emerging event (*mutajaddidun yuqaddaru bi-hi mutajaddidun*); and the two may replace one another according to which one is [already] known to the questioner: thus, if someone asked, 'When did Zayd

[22] See 'Second Notice' in the 'Introduction: On the Divisions of Substance' to *Mawqif* IV (Texts in Translation IV.3, below).

[23] See, for example, FAKHR AL-DĪN AL-RĀZĪ (d. 606/1209), *Al-Maṭālib al-ʿĀliya min al-ʿIlm al-Ilāhī*, ed. AḤMAD ḤIJĀZĪ AL-SAQQĀ, Beirut: Dār al-Kitāb al-ʿArabī, 1987 (six parts in four volumes), of which Vol. IV, Part V is devoted to time and place.

arrive?', another might answer, 'At the rising of the sun', if the questioner had been aware of the sun's rising. If another asked, 'When did the sun rise?', the answer to one who was aware of Zayd's arriving might be, 'When Zayd arrived'. Thus [the time] will be different for different people. So that someone might say, 'I will be with you before you finish reading the book'; another might say, 'X stayed with me for as long as it took to spin a ball of yarn'; or a small boy might say, 'The eggs will be cooked when I have counted up to three hundred';... thus each will measure/determine [the time] by means of what is, for him, [already] measured (*kull bi-ḥasabi mā huwa muqaddarun ʿinda-hu yuqaddiru ghayra-hu*).[24]

Topic V: Nature

Amongst philosophical doctrines or positions, the single most frequently mentioned and denied by the early Muʿtazilites was one they referred to as the position of 'those who maintained the doctrine of natures' (*aṣḥāb al-ṭabāʾiʿ*), meaning the doctrine of the four elements of earth, water, air, and fire, and of the elementary qualities (hot, cold, dry, moist) associated with them. Also generally rejected by the Muʿtazila and the Ashʿarites was the concept of 'nature' as an innate power that appeared to them to be independent and incompatible with the idea of a single, transcendent and all-powerful Agent. But there was no unanimous agreement with regard to the concept of force or power as implied, for instance, by gravity as a *tendency* to motion in a certain direction. Nor was there agreement respecting the more general concept of *iʿtimād* (endeavour), promoted by al-Naẓẓām as a virtual motion (what he called 'motion of endeavour') which, together with the motion of translation or displacement (*nuqla*), permeated the material world from the moment of creation. As we have just seen in the discussion of motion, al-Naẓẓām in fact went so far as to maintain that creation itself was an instance of motion of endeavour.

The passage of al-Jāḥiẓ, from which the motto at the head of this essay is taken, goes on to exemplify what he considered to be mature *Kalām*: namely a discourse that reconciled established 'religious' Monism (*tawḥīd*) and a sophisticated, 'philosophical' doctrine of Nature (*ṭabʿ*). Such a synthesis would at least have been counted as one success for al-Naẓẓām, who generally failed to gain support from the *mutakallimūn* for his difficult notions of actually infinite division of body, the halts and leaps of substances in motion, and the interpenetration of matter. But that was not to be.

[24] AL-ĪJĪ, *Kitāb al-Mawāqif*, p. 112.

Al-Ashʿarī's denial of Nature is only one important part of his sweeping rejection of all forces, whether those maintained by the *falāsifa*/philosophers or by the Muʿtazila. They included, not only forces of endeavour and of gravity, but also the major doctrine of 'engendering' (*tawlīd, tawallud*), basically a form of causality which al-Ashʿarī believed to have definitely compromised the whole of the *Kalām* view of the created world. Al-Ashʿarī's own views are clearly and amply reported by Ibn Fūrak (examples follow this paragraph); and they are known to have been widely adopted by al-Ashʿarī's followers. They form one of the principal features of Ashʿarism. They have been recognized (correctly, I think) as a threat to specific forms of argument associated with *Falsafa*, and (in a sense) even a threat to the very concept of 'natural philosophy' as practised by the *falāsifa*. It would, however, be a misunderstanding of the consistent Ashʿarite position to interpret it as a departure from 'rational' or 'empirical' thinking. Such an interpretation would simply equate rationalism with pure 'Aristotelianism', or an Aristotelianism repaired by attaching some Neoplatonic themes! At any rate, the historical triumph of Ashʿarism over both Muʿtazilism and *Falsafa*, though neither complete nor inevitable, happened to mark the beginning of new directions and new debates for subsequent centuries of Islamic intellectual history.

In connection with the examples mentioned above, see: *Muj.*, 76.8-11; *Muj.*, 131.16-132.13; *Muj.*, 133.15-134-1; *Muj.*, 246.1-4; *Muj.*, 275.7-17; *Muj.*, 282.18-283.2. Other examples illustrating the use of language as an authority for denying the concept of nature are referred to in Topic I.

Topic VI: Creation

Kalām is a hybrid discourse which combines Euclidean postulational thinking (exemplified principally in the *Kalām* definition of substance), and themes derived from the Revealed Book. A prominent consequence of this synthesis can be seen in both Muʿtazilite and Ashʿarite cosmologies. To give a basic example: while someone philosophically restricting himself/herself to the Euclidean approach might hold that a world of 'created' events is new (*ḥādith*) simply because it is *always* new, the *mutakallimūn* all argued that the world is new in the sense that it initially came into being at a point in the past finitely removed from the present. As a result of this hybridization, however, there emerged a complex discourse that delved deeply into hermeneutic devices as well as appealing to abstract logical arguments, while both strategies frequently sought the support of empirical evidence. It is in this sense that *Kalām* may be called a 'religious philosophy'.

In the present section of this discussion I wish to point out a specific form of argument which we can call 'phenomenological', because it fundamentally involves descriptions and analyses of states and acts of consciousness for the sake of establishing distinctions to be used for elucidating certain *Kalām* positions. This kind of argument had been utilised widely by the Muʿtazila for establishing principal doctrines: such as the Muʿtazila's distinctive theory of knowledge; their explication of 'true' belief in terms of a self-conscious state of mind, called *sukūn al-nafs* (mental repose), which charatcerized the act of concluding a sound proof (which frequently takes the form of the Stoic *modus ponens*); their extensive analyses of divine actions by analogy with conscious human actions; and their elaborate doctrine of the 'createdness' of the Qurʾān as God's own 'speech'.[25] Much of these methods, excluding the last-mentioned

[25] All of these examples and others of a similar kind are extensively discussed in various volumes of ʿAbd al-Jabbār's *Mughnī*, especially those concerned with: *al-Irāda* (vol. VI. 2, Cairo: Wizārat al-Thaqāfa wa-l-Irshād al-Qawmī, 1962); *Khalq al-Qurʾān* (vol. VII, Cairo: Wizārat al-Thaqāfa wa-l-Irshād al-Qawmī, 1961); *al-Makhlūq* (vol. VIII, Cairo: Wizārat al-Thaqāfa wa-l-Irshād al-Qawmī, 196?), and most especially, *al-Naẓar wa-l-Maʿārif* (vol. XII, Cairo: Wizārat al-Thaqāfa wa-l-Irshād al-Qawmī, 1960 [1962?]). This last volume of over five-hundred pages is devoted to a long phenomenological discussion of 'knowing', 'thinking', 'believing', 'perceiving', 'doubting', etc., all analysed in terms of *taʿalluq*, in this case the term used as the Arabic equivalent of the English 'intentionality'. I will not resist the temptation to quote two small and remarkable passages that actually set forth the methodological approach of the whole volume (and much of the discussions in the other volumes just mentioned): 'You should know that a thinker (*al-nāẓir*) finds himself thinking, for he understands the difference between his being engaged in thinking and his other [conscious] states, in the way that he understands the differences between his states of believing and willing/desiring. And nothing is more evident than that which one finds oneself engaged in, because it ranks with perception (*fī ḥukm al-mudrak*) in having the same force of knowing/conviction (*al-ʿilm*)'; *iʿlam anna l-nāẓir yajidu nafsa-hu nāẓiran li-anna-hu yaʿqilu l-farq bayna an yakūna nāẓiran wa-bayna sāʾir mā yakhtaṣṣu bi-hi min al-aḥwāl ka-mā yaʿqilu l-farq bayna kawni-hi muʿtaqidan wa-murīdan. Wa-lā shayʾa aẓharu mimmā yajidu l-wāḥid min-nā nafsa-hu ʿalay-hi li-anna-hu fī ḥukm al-mudrak fī quwwat al-ʿilm bi-hi* (p. 5.3-6); And: 'You should know that thinking, like believing, must intend (*yataʿallaqu bi-*) something other than itself, and that it intends [its] objects according to their varieties. [Thinking] differs from believing in that believing intends [its object] as something of a [certain] description [say, that God exists]; whereas thinking intends, not a single description, but rather whether or not the thing is of a certain description, *or* of a contrary [description]' (*iʿlam anna l-naẓar ka-l-iʿtiqād fī anna-hu yataʿallaqu bi-l-ashyāʾ ʿalā sāʾir wujūhi-hā, wa-in kāna yukhālifu l-iʿtiqād fī anna-hu* [i.e. *al-iʿtiqād*] *yataʿallaqu bi-kawn al-shayʾ ʿalā ṣifa, wa-l-naẓar <u>lā</u> yataʿallaqu bi-ṣifa wāḥida, bal yataʿallaqu bi-<u>hal</u> huwa ʿalā ṣifa aw ʿalā ḍiddi-hā aw laysa huwa ʿalay-hā*) (p. 9.3-6).

provocative thesis, was taken over and developed by the Ashʿarīs. In the present study, however, my purpose is to illustrate the phenomenological argument in establishing the meaning of 'creating' as conceived by some of the Muʿtazila and adopted by al-Ashʿarī himself.

The question first posed by the Muʿtazila was whether *al-khalq* (the verbal noun from *khalaqa*, to create) is the same as (or identical with) *that which is created* (*al-makhlūq*), with some of the Muʿtazila answering in the affirmative. The English word 'creation' means both the 'act of creating' and 'the thing or totality of things created,' and so does the Arabic *khalq*. In what follows I usually translate *khalq* as creat*ing* to avoid an ambiguity that would render the question tautologous. The question thus concerns the relationship of an *action* of the Creator to an occurrence or coming-into-being of an event *in* the world. To answer the question the Muʿtazila were led to compare the act of creating with other acts of God, such as willing and commanding. Hence the analysis of relevant features of the structure of such acts in the arguments ascribed by al-Ashʿarī to a number of Muʿtazilīs:

Abū l-Hudhayl (d. 227/841-842)[26] held three theses: (1) that creating a thing is *distinct* from (*ghayr*) the thing; (2) that creating (from God) is God's willing/desiring the thing *plus* 'saying: "Be!", a command directed to the thing'; and (3) that God's act of creating is simultaneous with (*maʿa*) what is created but *not identical* with it (*Maq.*, 363.10-364.4). — ʿAbbād b. Sulaymān (d. ca. 250/864) would not accept thesis (1) because, he argued, 'what is created' is an 'expression' (*ʿibāra*) for the created thing *and* the act of creating at one and the same time (*Maq.*, 364.7-11). He agreed with Abū l-Hudhayl that creating involves the divine command 'Be!', but *not* that the command is *addressed to* the thing (which leaves unclear the nature of the command, and how it differs from willing/desiring, for example). Muʿammar (d. 215/830) (*Maq.*, 364.12-13) had on his part asserted the distinction between the act and what is produced simultaneously with it, and this had led *him* to assume an infinite series of creating acts all of which are nonetheless said to be simultaneous (and in fact identical) with one another (*Maq.*, 369.1-370.12, and especially *Maq.*, 272.1-373.12).

Two leading Muʿtazilites, al-Naẓẓām and al-Jubbāʾī, were among those who asserted the identity of the creating act and what is created. Their views are reported in lucid terms by al-Ashʿarī in the *Maqālāt*. For

[26] For Abū l-Hudhayl see the pioneering study by RICHARD FRANK, *Metaphysics of Created Being*.

al-Naẓẓām (*Maq.*, 365.1-7): 'willing,' (we may add, 'from both God and man') might be a 'commanding' (*amr*), or a 'judging' (*ḥukm*), both of which are obviously distinct from *that* which is commanded or judged; whereas 'creating', as the actual bringing into existence of what is created, cannot be divorced from *what* is being created; and the same holds for 'initiating' and 're-creating'. — In exactly the same vein, al-Jubbā'ī distinguishes God's act of willing from *what* God wills, and identifies 'acting' or 'doing' (*fi'l*) with *that which is acted or done* (*maf'ūl*) (*Maq.*, 365.8-11); in other words, there is no 'creating' without a corresponding 'created,' which in turn implies a 'creating'.

Al-Ashʿarī's position on creation as reported below by Ibn Fūrak seems identical with that of al-Naẓẓām and al-Jubbā'ī (*Muj.*, 58.15-16; *Muj.*, 91.17-18; *Muj.*, 224.6-10); which should not be surprising: their proposition is but a consequence of what became the Ashʿarite philosophico-theological view of the world as a world of events all of which are free actions of the Creator. Abū Ḥāmid al-Ghazālī (d. 405/1111) once expressed that same proposition in the course of a brief account of human knowledge as, ideally, a picturing in the mind of *all* existents, namely 'the heavens, the earth, the trees, the rivers' etc., — as follows:

> [T]he 'divine presence' (*al-ḥaḍra al-ilāhīya*) is an expression for the totality of existents, all of them being part of the divine presence; for nothing exists other than the Exalted God and His actions.[27]

It cannot be too stressed that for the Ashʿarite al-Ghazālī the above statement is not necessarily revealed only in a mystical experience, but as a result of argument shared by the founder of Ashʿarism and some prominent Muʿtazilīs.

IV. Texts in translation

All following translations are my own. They are as literal as I could make them without loss of comprehension. As is well known, however, translations always carry with them a certain amount of interpretation. To minimize possible misunderstanding, I have liberally supplied transliterations of Arabic terms and expressions within the body of the translated texts. Despite recent impressive developments, *Kalām* studies remain a field very much in need of an articulated methodology, or at

[27] Al-Ghazālī, *al-Mustaṣfā min 'Ilm al-Uṣūl*, I, Cairo: Būlāq Government Press, 1322 AH, p. 27.2.

least, substantial discussions of explicit methodologies suggested by the nature of the extant materials. The reader should not therefore be surprised by my occasional departure from current translations adopted by authorities in the field. Sometimes the translated passages are followed by notes in a smaller font in indented paragraphs.

The translations represent: (IV.1) selections of al-Ashʿarī's own understanding of Muʿtazilite doctrines as reported by him in his *Maqālāt al-Islāmīyīn*; (IV.2) selections of al-Ashʿarī's own beliefs and arguments as reported by Ibn Fūrak in *Mujarrad Maqālāt al-Ashʿarī*; and (IV.3) a chapter from al-Ījī's *Mawāqif*. It is fortunate that we have in these works at least two authoritative, and remarkably careful accounts of *Kalām* opinions, in reliable editions. The appended continuous section is from the fourteenth-century *Kitāb al-Mawāqif*, perhaps the richest, most compact, and influential 'textbook' of *Kalām*; the section further illustrates the consequential situation referred to by Ibn Khaldūn, and it illustrates an important stage in the interaction of Ashʿarite *Kalām* and *Falsafa*.

All selections are deemed relevant in different ways to basic questions of cosmology and therefore to my interpretation of Ashʿarite ontology as an articulation of a 'consistent' view of the world (*al-ʿālam*) that can be said to lie at the heart of *Kalām* atomism generally as a theory of contingent events. As intended by their author, the selections from al-Ījī's book simultaneously present some contrasts between basic doctrines favoured, respectively, by the *falāsifa* and the Ashʿarite *mutakallimūn*.

IV. 1: Excerpts from AL-ASHʿARĪ, *Maqālāt al-Islāmīyīn* [= *Maq*.].

The mutakallimūn *differed as to* what *body really is — in twelve doctrines* (*Maq*., 301.1-306.13 [*Selections*])

Body, indivisible part (atom), and substance are what accept accidents (*Maq*., 301.3-15):

— **Some** (***mutakallimūn***) said that body is what accepts (*yaḥtamilu*) accidents such as motions, rest, and the like, — so that no body exists that does not accept accidents, and nothing accepts accidents except body; — and they claimed that the indivisible part *is* a body that accepts accidents, and also that the meaning of 'substance' (*al-jawhar*) *is* that it accepts accidents; — that is the doctrine of **Abū l-Ḥusayn al-Ṣāliḥī**, who claimed that the [indivisible] part *is* a body that accepts all classes (*ajnās*) of accident, except that *taʾlīf* (composition, aggregation, contact) is not so called unless there comes-to-be an additional *ta'līf*/contact [in another atom], though one of the two [contacts] would validly apply to one [individual] part, — but we should not, following language [usage], call it *ta'līf*, since the language users (*ahl al-lugha*) have not allowed the possibility of touching when there is nothing to touch (*lam yujīzū mumāssata lā shay'*), saying that the name would apply only when another [body] is involved, ... and assimilating this situation to someone moving his jaws: if there is something in his mouth, then this is chewing, but if not, then that would not be called chewing.

The whole argument is an attempt to reconcile (or, run away from) the conflict between the asserted proposition that 'an atom accepts all classes of accidents', which means accepting a single quality (say, red) from any pair of contraries (red and any other colour) that make up every *jins*/class of accidents, and the fact that contact is an 'accident' that *must*, somehow, inhere at once in at least two atoms or bodies. The problem is endemic to every all-inclusive substance/accident ontology. For *jins*/class, see note to *Maq*., 308.16.

Body is a composite of indivisible parts (*Maq*., 302.1-4):

— **Some** said: body is body only because of [its] composition and aggregation (*li-l-ta'līf wa l-ijtimā'*); — and they claimed that when an indivisible part joins another indivisible part, then *each of them* is a body while being in the state of aggregation [with the other], because *each* is composed *with* the other; — but when they separate, then neither of them is a body; — that is the doctrine of **one of the Baghdādīs**, I think he is **'Īsā al-Ṣūfī**.

Compare with *Maw*., 'First Notice' in *Maw*., IV, 'Introduction: On the Division of Substance' (Texts in Translation IV.3, below).

The least body is composed of two indivisible parts (*Maq*., 302.5-9):

— **Some** said: 'body' means that it is composed (*mu'talif*) — the least body being composed of two parts; — they claimed that when two parts are composed, then neither of them is a body, but body is the two parts combined, it being impossible for composition (*al-tarkīb*) to be in a single thing (*al-wāḥid*), — thus a single thing accepts colour, taste, smell, and all accidents other than composition; I think this doctrine is due to **al-Iskāfī**).

Al-Ījī dismissed the whole debate among the Mu'tazila about the least number of parts/atoms that are necessary to compose a body as a 'verbal' controversy: see *Maw*. below, p. 262).

It is not possible to add a third betwixt two indivisible parts (*Maq.* 302.10-15):

— And **they** claimed that the doctrine of those who say (*qawl al-qā'il*), 'It is possible that a third [part] may be joined to the two [indivisible parts], is wrong and impossible, because each of the two occupies the other (*kull wāḥid min-humā mushghil li-ṣāḥibi-hi*), and if *each* occupies the other (*wa-idhā ashghala-hu*), then [one or] the other has no place, because if two parts have a single place, then a thing will have touched [occupied?] more than its [own] magnitude (*fa-qad māssa l-shay'u akthara min qadri-hi*), and if this were possible it would be possible for the world to be contained in one fist. And that is why he said: 'A thing does not touch (*lā yumāssu*) more than its [own] magnitude'; — that is the doctrine of **Abū Bishr Ṣāliḥ b. Abī Ṣāliḥ,** and of those who agreed with him.

Abū l-Hudhayl: the least that a body can be are six aggregated indivisible parts (*Maq.*, 302.16-303.6):

— **Abū l-Hudhayl** said: body is what has a right and a left, a back and a front, and a top and a bottom; — the least that a body can be are six parts: one a right and the other a left, one a back and the other a front, one a top and the other a bottom; — and [he said] that the individual, indivisible part [touches, *yumāssu*]* six parts similar to itself, and it moves and rests, and joins (*yujāmi'u*, comes together with) other [parts], and is subject to coming-to-be (*yajūzu 'alay-hi l-kawn*) and contact (*al-mumāssa*, touching), but cannot accept/carry colour, taste, smell, or any of the [other] accidents we have not mentioned, unless these six parts come together, and when they come together then they *are* the body and then they accept what we have described.

**yumāssu*, added by Ritter.

A single *composition/aggregation comes-to-be in the* two *aggregated parts* (*Maq.*, 303.7-8):

— **Some of the *mutakallimūn*** claimed that two indivisible parts [brought together] are together (*jamī'an*) subject to the composition/aggregation (*al-ta'līf*)*, — and that a single composition (*al-ta'līf al-wāḥid*) comes to be (*yakūnu*) in two places**; that is the doctrine of **al-Jubbā'ī**.

*'are together subject to the composition' (*yaḥillu-humā jamī'an al-ta'līf*): i.e. one and the same *ta'līf* inheres in *each* of the two indivisible parts, as explicitly asserted in the following sentence marked **.

Muʿammar: the least body is eight parts; corporeal properties are consequent upon an immanent 'nature' of parts in a certain combination (*Maq.*, 303.9-14):

— **Muʿammar** maintained that [body] is what is long, broad, and deep, — and that the least body is eight [indivisible] parts; — and when the[se] parts come together (*idhā 'jtamaʿat*), the accidents inevitably follow (*wajabat al-aʿrāḍ*), — and they [i.e. the parts] effect them (*tafʿaluhā*) by virtue of a necessitating nature (*bi-ījāb al-ṭabʿ*), — and each part effects in itself the accidents that inhere in it. — And he claimed that when a part joins (*inḍamma ilā*) a part, length occurs (*ḥadatha ṭūlun*), and that breadth comes-to-be (*yakūnu*) when the [two parts] are joined by two parts, and that depth occurs (*yaḥduthu*) when four parts come on top of (*yuṭbiqa ʿalā*) four parts, — and thus the eight parts [as a whole] come-to-be (*takūnu*) a body that is broad, long and deep.

An example of lucid reporting by al-Ashʿarī. To be noted is Muʿammar's concept of a necessitating nature (*ījāb al-ṭabʿ*) as the link between configurations of atoms and the 'accidents'/properties of length, length-and-breadth (= plane), and length-and-breadth-and-depth (= corporeity), all cases of *inḍimām* (coming together of atoms) or *mumāssa* (coming-to-be-in-contact), which is one of the four *akwān* or comings-to-be. Note the explicit synonymity, in this case, of *ḥudūth* and *kawn*.
Note the references by Ritter to *Sharḥ al-Ishārāt* (by al-Jurjānī) and to al-Baghdādī's *Uṣūl al-Dīn*: *Maq.*, p. 303.

Body is thirty-six parts that make up six arkān (*Maq.*, 304.1-7):

— **Hishām b. ʿAmr al-Fuwaṭī** maintained that *body* is thirty-six indivisible parts; — for he made it six *arkān* and made each *rukn* six parts; thus what **Abū l-Hudhayl** said to be a part, **Hishām** made a *rukn*; — and he claimed that touching/contact (*al-mumāssa*) cannot apply to parts, and that contacts belong to the *arkān* of which each *rukn* is six parts that are neither in contact [with] nor separate [from each other], — and that ['contact' and 'separation'] are only applicable to the *arkān*; — and, that that being the case, [body] can accept (*muḥtamil*) all the accidents such as colour, taste, smell, roughness, softness, coldness, and the like.

According to language usage, body is not a specified number of parts (*Maq.*, 304.8-10):

— **Some** said: body, [or] what the speakers of the language (*ahl al-lugha*) have called 'body', is what is long, broad, and deep; — and in [saying] this they did not specify a number of parts, even when (*wa-in kāna*) the parts of a body have a known number (*ʿadad maʿlūm*).

Hishām: body is *what exists* (*Maq*., 304.11-12):

— **Hishām b. al-Ḥakam** said that the meaning of 'body' (*jism*) is that it exists; and he said, 'By saying "body" I only mean that it exists, — and that it is a thing (*shayʾ*), — and that it supports itself (*qāʾim bi-nafsi-hi*, self-subsistent)'.

Al-Naẓẓām: the parts of a body have no assignable number (*Maq*. 304.13-15):

— **Al-Naẓẓām** maintained that body is what is long, broad and deep, and its parts have no designatable number (*ʿadad lā yūqafu ʿalay-hi*), and that there is no half that has no half, and no part that has no part; — the **Philosophers** defined body as that which is broad and deep [*sic*].

Actually infinite division, which is undoubtedly al-Naẓẓām's doctrine (see below), inevitably leads to the infinitely small, which, I believe, was also al-Naẓẓām's doctrine. Hence my translation of *ʿadad lā yūqafu ʿalay-hi* as a non-assignable/non-designatable number, that is not a determinate number at which one comes to a stop and says 'this is it'. Note that the Ninth Century Ṣābi'an mathematician Thābit b. Qurra (d. 288/901) readily accepted and defended the actual infinite in no uncertain terms. See A.I. SABRA, *Thābit b. Qurra on the Infinite and Other Puzzles: Edition and Translation of his Discussions with Ibn Usayyid*, in: *Zeitschrift für Geschichte der Arabisch-Islamischen Wissenschaften* 11 (1997), p. 1-33. As far as I know, all modern studies assume that al-Naẓẓām — alone among the Muʿtazila — rejected atomism, thus ignoring the possibility that he may have considered the atoms in a single body to be actually infinite in number, which, I think, is more than likely. His doctrine would then be that bodies are actually divided into an infinite number of parts, as distinguished from the philosophers' infinite divisibility 'in potentiality'. As al-Ījī said with his characteristic conciseness, 'For al-Naẓẓām, the parts are actual, and they are infinite' (*al-ajzāʾ bi-l-fiʿl wa-ghayr mutanāhiya*): *al-Mawāqif*, p. 186: see *Maw*. IV, *Marṣad* I, *Maqṣid* I, *Faṣl* 1, on 'simple body' (*Second Possibility*, below).

Body is the substance and the accidents all together (*Maq*., 304.16-305.4):

— **ʿAbbād b. Sulaymān** said that body is the substance and the accidents from which it is not separated, — and that such accidents from which [the substance] may be separated do not belong to the body and are distinct from it; — and he said that body is the place (*al-makān*), and argued that God, *taʿālā*, is not a body, saying that if He were He would be a place, and also argued that if He were a body He would have a half [and so on].

Body is a collection of accidents... (*Maq.* 305.5-306.11):

— **Ḍirār b. ʿAmr** said: that body is a collection of accidents that have been brought together and established and fixed (*fa-qāmat wa-thabatat*) so as to become a body that accepts [other] accidents ..., namely those that body cannot be free from *and* from their contraries, such as life and death, from both of which a body cannot be free, and such as colours and tastes, from every member of their *jins*/class the body cannot be free [at one and the same time], — and such as weight (*zina*), namely heaviness (*thiqal*) and lightness (*khiffa*), and also roughness and smoothness, heat and coldness ...

People differed about 'substance' and what it means — in four doctrines (Maq., 306.14-307.7*)*

— The **Christians** (*al-Naṣārā*) held that substance is what stands by itself (*al-qāʾim bi-nafsi-hi*), —and that whatever stands by itself is a substance, and every substance stands by itself (*Maq.*, 306.15-16).

— **Some Philosophers** said: substance is what stands by itself and accepts contraries (*al-qāʾim bi-l-dhāt al-qābil li-l-mutaḍāddāt*) (*Maq.*, 307.1).

'Contraries' = contrary qualities or accidents; see below, note to *Maq.*, 308.16.

— **Some** said: substance is that which, when it exists, carries accidents (*kāna ḥāmilan li-l-aʿrāḍ*), — the one who held this doctrine claimed that substances are substances by virtue of themselves (*bi-anfusi-hā*), — and they are known to be [characterizable as] substances [even] before they come into being, — the one who maintained this is **al-Jubbāʾī** (*Maq.*, 307.2-4).

— **Al-Ṣāliḥī** said: substance is what accepts (*iḥtamala*) accidents, — and for him a substance may exist without an accident being created by God in it, and without [actually] bearing accidents while being disposed to have them (*illā anna-hu muḥtamilun la-hā*) (*Maq.*, 307.5-7).

Al-Ṣāliḥī thus asserted the possibility of a 'bare' substance, namely a coming-to-be *in place*, which is free of other qualifying accidents. See above, Topic II.

[End of this section of *Maq*.]

*And [**People**] differed in regard to substances: are they all bodies, or is it possible for substances to exist that are not bodies? — in three doctrines* (*Maq*., 307.8-308.2).

Individual, indivisible substances do not have length, breadth or depth (*Maq*., 307.10-13):

— **Some** said: not every substance is a body, — and an individual (*al-wāḥid*), indivisible substance cannot be a body, — for body is that which is long, broad, and deep, unlike the individual substance. — That is the doctrine of **Abū l-Hudhayl** and **Muʿammar** and [the doctrine] espoused by **al-Jubbāʾī**.

Every substance is a body (*Maq*., 307.14):

— **Some** said: there is no substance that is not a body; — that is the doctrine of **al-Ṣāliḥī**.

Two types of substance (*Maq*., 307.15-308.2):

— **Some** said: substances are of two types (*ʿalā ḍarbayn*): composite (sing. *murakkab*) substances and simple/individual (sing. *basīṭ*), non-composite substances; — a non-composite substance is not a body, a composite substance is a body.

Here, 'some' includes Abū l-Hudhayl, Muʿammar, al-Jubbāʾī: see *Maq*., 307.10-13.

'Substances' are three ajnās (*Maq*., 308.16):

— **Some**, namely the **Marqūnīya**, said: that substances (*al-jawāhir*) are three distinct *ajnās*.

The Arabic *jins* (plural: *ajnās*) happens to be the term used by the translators of Aristotle, and hence by the *falāsifa*, for Aristotle's *genos*, the part common to 'essential' definitions of things that belong to different 'species': sing. *eidos*, *nawʿ*. That, of course, would not be the expected meaning of *jins* in *Kalām* literature, especially before the late mingling of

Kalām and *Falsafa* vocabularies referred to by Ibn Khaldūn (see Section I.2, 'Introductory Remarks', above); see the extensive discussion in RICHARD M. FRANK, *Beings and Their Attributes: The Teaching of the Basrian School of the Muʿtazila in the Classical Period*, Albany: SUNY, 1978, p. 72 ff, and associated notes). In the passages quoted below from al-Ashʿarī's *Maqālāt* and Ibn Fūrak's *Mujarrad*, the term *jins* and the plural *ajnās*, always translated as 'class' or 'classes', occur rather frequently in reports of doctrines held by the early Muʿtazila or by al-Ashʿarī: *Maq*., 301.3-15; *Maq*., 305.5-306.11; *Maq*., 307.1; *Maq*., 308.16; *Maq*., 309.1-2; *Maq*., 309.3; *Maq*., 309.4-8; *Maq*., 346.13-347.8; *Maq*., 372.1-373.12; *Muj*., 204.17-23; *Muj*. 211.25-212.2; *Muj*., 243.13-19. Here, at *Maq*., 308.16, and in the three following quotes, al-Ashʿarī presents *ajnās* as classes of 'substances', not accidents or qualities. This is misleading and, strictly speaking, wrong, as is plain from the examples cited at *Maq*., 309.1-2 (hot and cold, moist and dry) and at *Maq*., 309.4-8 (colours, shapes, etc.). — The *ajnās* are in fact classes of accidents or qualities which are also contraries and therefore mutually incompatible. Thus all colours constitute a single *jins* by virtue of the fact that the presence of one of them in a substance would imply the absence of all other colours. Similarly, with regard for instance to the philosophers' four 'natures' or elements and their constitutive properties, hot and cold are a single *jins*, and so are dry and moist, but not hot and moist, or cold and dry. And likewise for the properties listed at *Maq*., 309. 4-8, exemplifying al-Naẓẓām's doctrine. The list would obviously include motion and rest as contraries forming one *jins*.

It seems possible that the doctrine of *ajnās* was designed to sidestep discussions in terms of Aristotelian form and matter, or at least used for that purpose by the early *mutakallimūn*. The *Marqūnīya*/Marcionites were followers of Marcion, 2nd C. AD, the Christian bishop who first taught in Asia Minor before he moved to Rome in ca. 135. See IBN AL-NADĪM, *al-Fihrist*, ed. G. FLÜGEL, Leipzig, 1871-1872, repr. Beirut: Maktabat Khayyāṭ (n. d.), p. 328, 339 (on al-Marqūnīya).

'Substances' are of four ajnās (*Maq*., 309.1-2):

— **Some** said: substances (*al-jawāhir*) are of four contrary *ajnās*: hot and cold; moist and dry; — they are the **Proponents of Natures** (*aṣḥāb al-ṭabāʾiʿ*: those who hold the doctrine of the four natures).

'Substances' are of five ajnās (*Maq*., 309.3):

— **Some** said that substances (*al-jawāhir*) are of five contrary *ajnās*: four *ajnās* and a spirit/breath (*rūḥ*).

'Substances' are contrary ajnās *of indefinite numbers* (*Maq*., 309.4-8):

— **Some** said that substances (*al-jawāhir*) are contrary *ajnās*, some are whiteness, blackness, yellowness, redness, or greenness; and some are heat or coldness; some are sweetness or acidity; some are smells; some are tastes; some are coldness; and some are figures/shapes (*ṣuwar*); and some are spirits; — and they said: that all living [things] are one *jins*, and this is the doctrine of **al-Naẓẓām**.

What is possible for the individual substance (*Maq*., 312. 3-5):

— **Some** said that an individual, indivisible substance, by itself (*idhā 'nfarada*), accepts (*yajūzu ʿalay-hi*) what is acceptable by a body, such as motion, rest, taste, and smell; — they considered it impossible (*aḥālū*) that power/ability (*qudra*), knowledge, and life could reside/inhere in it while it is all by itself (*idhā 'nfarada*); — and they considered it possible that God might create a living (thing) without being endowed with *qudra*; — and considered it impossible for a substance to be free from accidents; — the one who maintains this doctrine is **Muḥammad b. ʿAbd al-Wahhāb al-Jubbāʾī**.

***People** differed as to whether it is possible* (hal yajūzu) *for body to be broken up, and to lose its aggregate character and become an indivisible part* (juz'an lā yatajazza'), *or not, and as to what may inhere* (yaḥillu) *in body — in fourteen doctrines* (*Maq*., 314.9-317.6 [Selections]).

Abū l-Hudhayl on body and atom (*Maq*., 314.12-315.6):

— **Abū l-Hudhayl** maintained that God, *subḥāna-hu*, may break a body apart (*yufarriqa-hu*) and abolish its aggregation until it becomes an indivisible part; — and that the indivisible part has no length or breadth or depth or aggregation or separation; — and that [an indivisible part] may come into aggregation with or separation from another [part]; — and that a mustard seed may be divided into two halves, then into four, then eight, until each of these parts becomes indivisible. — **Abū l-Hudhayl** allowed that the [indivisible] part (*al-juz'*) may be in motion or at rest, in isolation or in contact, by itself, with six other parts, or come into aggregation with or separation from other [parts]; — and that God may set it apart so that eyes can see it, by creating in us a seeing and perceiving of it; — but he [Abū l-Hudhayl] did not allow [an indivisible part] to have colour, taste, smell, life, power (*al-qudra*) and knowledge, saying that these are possible only for body ….

ʿAbbād b. Sulaymān: no atom can exist in isolation, etc. (*Maq*., 316.1-7):

— **Al-Naẓẓām** reported in his *Book on the Atom* (*fī kitābi-hi al-Juzʾ*) that **some[one]** claimed that the indivisible part [all by itself] is a thing (*shayʾ*) that has no length or breadth or depth and no *jihāt* [sides, directions]; — nor is it something that occupies places or may rest or move; nor can it be in isolation (*wa-lā yajūzu ʿalay-hi an yanfarida*); — and this is the doctrine held by **ʿAbbād b. Sulaymān**: — [who] said (*wa-yaqūlu*) that motion, rest, coming-to-be (*al-kawn*), occupying places, and having *jihāt* cannot be attributed to it [the indivisible part], nor can it be in isolation; — and [also] said that 'part' means that it has a half and that the half has a half [and so on] (*wa-yaqūlu inna l-juzʾ lā yajūzu ʿalay-hi l-ḥaraka wa-l-sukūn wa-l-kawn wa-l-ishghāl li-l-amākin wa-laysa bi-dhī jiha wa-lā yajūzu ʿalay-hi l-infirād, wa-yaqūlu maʿnā l-juzʾ anna la-hu niṣf wa-anna l-niṣf la-hu niṣf*).

The argument attributed to ʿAbbād is quite remarkable and, apparently, definitive. In what we might call a single-atom universe, the assumed atom 'in [absolute] isolation' is nowhere (*laysa bi-dhī jiha*), there being no other place-occupying substance to which it can be related in any way, such as right or left, or being in spatial opposition (*muḥādhāh*) to another substance, or being near or far, etc. From this it is inferred, not only that the atom *supposed* to exist has no *jihāt* (sides or directions), but also no *place* which it can be said to occupy, thus losing the very definition of substance. From this it follows that neither the *akwān*, nor even the very concept of '*being* in isolation', can be applied to it.

Compare *Muj*., 93.6-7, and especially, *Muj*., 203.12-16.

There is no harm in quoting here the following passage, on the relativity of *being somewhere* (*fī jiha*), from the book by the Fifth/Eleventh Century Muʿtazilī al-Ḥasan b. Mattawayh al-Najrānī, *Al-Tadhkira fī Aḥkām al-Jawāhir wa-l-Aʿrāḍ*, ed. SĀMĪ NAṢR LUṬF and FAYṢAL BADĪR ʿAWN, Cairo: Dār al-Thaqāfa li-l-Ṭibāʿa wa-l-Nashr, 1975, p. 62.3-9:

> 'A substance [S], when it comes to exist, must come to be *somewhere* (*fī jiha*), which means that it has come to exist in a situation (*ʿalā ḥaddin*) such that, if there were another substance [S'], then [S] would either be near or far from [S'], or to the right or left of it, or in one of the six directions (*ʿalā l-jihāt al-sitt*), without being where [S'] is located. This is a more effective expression than saying that '[S] exists in a place or in a spatial opposition (*fī makān aw fī muḥādhāh*) [with another subtance]', because place is what supports a heavy object and prevents the object's heaviness from engendering [i.e. bringing about] its fall. [The term] '*al-muḥādhāh*' is in the form '*mufāʿala*' from '*al-taḥādhī wa-l-taqābul*', namely being in [spatial] opposition. If only one substance existed, there would be no being-in-opposition. By being *somewhere* (*fī jiha*), a substance will possess a state (*ḥāla*) just as it possesses one by being in a place, but existence is distinct from both'.

The atom has a single jiha (*Maq*., 316.8-9):

— **Al-Naẓẓām** has reported **some** as saying that the [indivisible] part has a single *jiha*, and that [this] is so as in what appears of [visible] things, namely their surface that confronts you (*wa-ka-naḥw mā yaẓharu min al-ashyā', wa-hiya al-ṣafḥa allatī talqā-ka min-hā*).

This would seem to be an attempt, on the part of 'some', to rescue the concept of atom from aporias arising from the notion of indivisibility, by comparing *jiha* to the 'single' side or aspect of an object that reveals itself to the percipient without revealing 'other sides' of the object. This is one, perhaps rare and interesting, example of appealing to perception in a theoretical test of atoms.

The atom has six jihāt (*Maq*., 316.10-12):

— **Al-Naẓẓām** also reported that **some** had maintained that the part has six *jihāt* which are accidents that [inhere] in it, and that are distinct from it (*wa-hiya ghayru-hu*), — and that it is not divisible, and its accidents are distinct from it, and it is to [these *jihāt*] that the number [six] applies (*wa-ʿalay-h[ā] waqaʿa l-ʿadad*); while *it* [i.e. the part] is not divisible [along] its directions (*min jihāti-hi*) of above, below, right, left, front, and back.

The atom is qā'im *by means of things other than itself* (*Maq*., 316.13-317.2):

— * And he **[al-Naẓẓām]** reported [in his *Book on the Atom*] that **others** maintained that the part (*al-juz'*) stands (*qā'im*), not on its own [or, by itself, *bi-nafsi-hi*], nor by means of things (*wa-lā yaqūmu bi-shay' min al-ashyā'*) less [in number] than eight indivisible parts, — so that if someone raised a question concerning one part amongst them, then he would be asking about [that part's] being in isolation (*fa-innamā yas'alu ʿan infirādi-hi*) though it cannot be in isolation, while [the questioner] knows that the discussion is about the eight (parts), — ** since the eight [all together] do have length, breadth and depth: thus length *is* two parts, and length with length *is* a plane (*basīṭ*) that has length and breadth, and plane with plane *is* a [body] that has length, breadth and depth.

* See the following note ** which supports the translation of *lā yaqūmu* as *not self-subsistent*, or *has no independent existence*.
** '[body]', is suggested by Ritter as possibly a better reading than *jiha*, which appears as *j-n-h* in MS D.

Two is the least number of atoms to be imagined in combination (*Maq*., 317.3-6):

— And he **[al-Naẓẓām]** reported that **others** had maintained that parts are divisible until two [indivisible parts] are reached; — then, if you were to sever them, the severing would annihilate them; — and if you were to imagine one of them [by itself] you would not find it in your imagination, — and if you were to distinguish (*farraqta*) between them in the imagination, or otherwise, you would find only their annihilation. — That is the end of of what **al-Naẓẓām** has reported [in his *Book on the Atom*].

Muʿammar: man is an atom (*Maq*., 318.3-5):

— **Muʿammar** said that a human being (*al-insān*) is an indivisible atom (*juzʾ lā yatajazzaʾ*), — and allowed that knowledge, power (*al-qudra*), life, will/desire (*irāda*), and aversion may reside in it, but not [the qualities of] being in contact (*al-mumāssa*) or being apart (*al-mubāyana*), or motion, rest, colour or smell.

Al-Naẓẓām: parts are divisible ad infinitum (*Maq*., 318.6-8):

— **Al-Naẓẓām** said that there is no part (*juzʾ*) that has no part, and no portion (*baʿḍ*) that has no portion, and no half that has no half; — and that a part (*juzʾ*) is always subject to division (*jāʾiz tajziʾatu-hu abadan*) without end to the division (*wa-lā ghāya la-hu min bāb al-tajazzuʾ*).

Philosophers on actual and potential division (*Maq*., 318.9-10):

— **Some philosophers** said that a part is divisible (*yatajazzaʾ*), [and] that its division has a limit in actuality but has no limit in potentiality and possibility (*fī l-quwwa wa-l-imkān*).

Division doubted by sceptics (*Maq*., 318.11):

— **Sceptics** were in doubt (*shakka shākkūn*) [about division]: they said, 'We do not know (*lā nadrī*) whether a part (*juzʾ*) is divisible or not'.

The Greek Sceptics came to be known as *al-lāʾadriya*.

Al-Jubbāʾī: on hidden motion and tawlīd (*Maq*., 322.9-12):

— **Al-Jubbāʾī** maintained that a falling stone has halts/stops (*waqafāt*), — and maintained that there are hidden motions in a stretched bow and likewise in a built wall, — and that it is these motions that engender (*tuwallid*) the falling of the wall, — and that the motions in the bow and in the [stretched] chord are what engender the chord's rupture.

Al-Naẓẓām: all bodies are in motion: motion of displacement and motion of endeavour (*Maq.*, 324.12-325.2):

— **Al-Naẓẓām** said: all bodies are in motion (*mutaḥarrika*), and motion is of two [kinds]: a motion of endeavour (*ḥarakat iʿtimād*) and a motion of displacement (*ḥarakat nuqla*), — and so all [bodies] are really in motion though in regard to language [they sometimes can be said to be] at rest (*sākina*), — and motions *are* the coming-to-be (*al-kawn*) and nothing else [is]. — I [= **al-Ashʿarī**] have read in a book attributed to him where it said: I do not know what rest (*al-sukūn*) is unless it means that the thing has come-to-be (*kāna*) in a [given] place [at] two moments [one following the other], namely that [the thing] has moved in the [given] place [at] two moments [one following the other] (*taḥarraka fī-hi waqtayn*). — He claimed that bodies at the moment of their creation by God are moving with a motion of endeavour (*ḥarakat iʿtimād*).

Al-Naẓẓām: in the world, there exist only bodies and motions (*Maq.*, 346.13-347.8):

— **Ibrāhīm al-Naẓẓām** said: all human actions are motions and they are accidents (*aʿrāḍ*), — and 'rest' is said [to be an accident] only in a manner of speaking (*fī l-lugha*): when a body endeavours [to maintain itself] in the place [it occupies] for two [adjacent] moments (*waqtayn*), we say that [the body] has rested in the place, but *not* that rest is a quality (*maʿnā*) of the [body] other than the [body's] endeavour. — He claimed that the endeavours and the comings-to-be (*al-akwān*) *are* the motions, and that motions are of two types (*ʿalā ḍarbayn*): a motion of endeavour (*ḥarakat iʿtimād*) *in* a place, and a motion of displacement (*nuqla*) *from* a place; — and he claimed that all motions are one class (*jins wāḥid*), and that it is impossible for an entity (*dhāt*) to effect (*an yafʿala*) two different [i.e. contrary] actions.

In what has been reported of him, **al-Naẓẓām** claimed that length is what is long, and breadth is what is broad, — and he affirmed that colours, tastes, smells, sounds, pains, heat, coldness, moisture, and dryness are subtle bodies (*ajsām laṭīfa*), — and claimed that the place (*ḥayyiz*) of colour is [the same as] that of taste and smell, — and that subtle bodies may occupy (*qad taḥillu fī*) one and the same place, — and he affirmed no accident other than motion alone.

Muʿammar: Rest is the only kawn. *Accidents are distinct from bodies* (*Maq*., 347.9-12):

Muʿammar said: all *akwān* [comings-to-be] are rests, but some of them are said to be motions only in a manner of speaking (*fī l-lugha*), but in reality (*fī l-ḥaqīqa*) they are rests. — He affirmed that colours, tastes, smells, sounds, heat, coldness, moisture, and dryness are distinct from (*ghayr*) bodies.

ʿAbbād: Accidents are not bodies (*Maq*., 347.13–348.2):

— **ʿAbbād b. Sulaymān** affirmed that accidents are other than/distinct from (*ghayr*) bodies. If one asked him, 'Are you saying that motion is other than what is moving, and that black is other than what is black?', he would not accept that, and would say, 'My saying of a body that it is in motion is a statement about a body and a motion, and thus I cannot say (*lā yajūzu an aqūla*) that motion is *other* than what is moving (*ghayr al-mutaḥarrik*), since my saying 'is in motion' is a statement about a body *and* a motion; but I *do* say that motion is other than body.'

The mutakallimūn *differed about what motion and rest mean,*
(and about) where *these come to inhere in the body:*
in the first place or in the second? (*Maq*., 353.16-356.3).

Al-Naẓẓām on motion, kawn, *and* iʿtimād (*endeavour*) (*Maq*., 354.1-5):

— **Some** said that motion means what 'coming-to-be' (*al-kawn*) means, — and [that] all motions are endeavours (*iʿtimādāt*) some of which involve displacement (*intiqāl*, changing place) and some do not. — The one who holds this doctrine is **al-Naẓẓām**: he claimed that when a body moves from place to place, the motion occurs (*taḥduthu*) in the first [place], and [*this* motion] is the body's endeavours that entail (*tūjibu*) the coming-to-be (*al-kawn*) in the second [place], — and that the [body's] coming-to-be in the second [place] is the motion of the body in[to] the second [place].

Ibn Shabīb on motion and rest (*Maq*., 354.6-15):

— **Muḥammad b. Shabīb** affirmed [both] motion and rest, claiming that they are *the* comings-to-be (*al-akwān*), and [affirmed] that some comings-to-be (*akwān*) are motion and some are rest, — and that when someone moves to a second [place] it is his endeavour (*iʿtimād*) in the first place that entails [his] coming-to-be in the second [and his] departure (*nuqla* and *zawāl*) when the body has reached the second, — * in so far as the language speakers (*ahl al-lugha*) do not say of a body that it has abandoned [a first place] and passed (*muntaqil*) and moved from a first [place] until it has reached the second place. — Thus the quality (*maʿnā*) [i.e. motion] occurred in [the body] when it was in the first place, but 'departure' (*zawāl*) is [the term] applied to the body's coming-to-be in the second place — [this manner of speaking] being due to the accommodation of language (*ittisāʿ al-lugha*) and to our [practice of] speaking in the words people use and in the manner they adopt in their speech. — ** Thus the coming-to-be in the second place might be motion or rest, and, if motion, then it would entail a coming-to-be in the third place, *and, if rest, then it would be rest in the second place.*

* 'Has abandoned and passed and moved': *zāʾilan muntaqilan mutaḥarrikan.*
** The last, italicized, sentence is Ritter's emendation of the text, which is adopted here.

Muʿammar: kawn = *rest* (*Maq*., 355.1-2):

— **Muʿammar** said: the meaning of rest *is the* coming-to-be (*al-kawn*), — and there is no rest that is not *kawn* and no *kawn* that is not rest.

Abū l-Hudhayl: al-akwān *are distinct from motion and rest* (*Maq*., 355.3-7):

— **Abū l-Hudhayl** said that motions and rest are distinct from (*ghayr*) the *akwān* and the contacts (*al-mumāssāt*), — and that the motion of a body from a first place to a second occurs in [the body] when it is in the second place, when it has come-to-be [in it], — * and [*this* motion] is the body's having moved away (*intiqālu-hu*) from the first place and its having abandoned it (*khurūju-hu ʿan-hu*). — The resting of a body in a place is its persisting (*labthu-hu*) in it for two moments, — for, two places and two moments (*zamānayn*) are necessary for moving away from a place, and two moments [and one place] are necessary for resting [in it].

* See Ritter's note 5, p. 355.

ʿAbbād: motions and rests are mumāssāt (*Maq.*, 355.8-9):

— **ʿAbbād** said: motions and rest[s] are contacts (*mumāssāt*), — and he claimed that 'motion' and 'departure' (*zawāl*) mean the same thing.

Bishr b. al-Muʿtamir, his concept of motion (*Maq.*, 355.10-11):

— **Bishr b. al-Muʿtamir** said: motion occurs neither in the first place nor in the second; rather, the body moves by it (*bi-hā*) from the first to the second.

This is obscure.

Al-Ashʿarī disputing al-Jubbāʾī's doctrine of motion (*Maq.*, 355.12-356.3):

— **Al-Jubbāʾī** maintained that motion and rest are comings-to-be (*akwān*), — and that motion means departure (*al-zawāl*), — so that moving is nothing other than departing [or, having departed], — and that 'motion' does *not* have the meaning of *intiqāl*, — and that the non-existent motion (*al-ḥaraka al-maʿdūma*) is called 'departure' before its coming-to-be (*qabla kawn-ihā*) and is not called *intiqāl*.

I (**al-Ashʿarī**) said to him: But why don't you affirm (*tuthbitu*) every motion to be *intiqāl* in the way that you affirm every motion to be departure? He said, 'Because when someone moves (*ḥarraka* = shakes?) a rope hanging from a ceiling we say that the rope has shifted (*zāla*), swung (*iḍṭaraba*) and moved (*taḥarraka*), but would not say that it has changed place (*intaqala*)'. — So I said to him, 'Why not say that [the rope] has changed place in the air (*intaqala fī l-jaww*), as [in the way of] saying that it has moved, departed and swung?'. He did not come up with something that brings out the distinction.

[End of this Section in the *Maqālāt*.]

***People** differed as to 'creating a thing': is it 'the thing' or distinct from it?*
(*Maq.*, 363.9-365.12 [Selections]).

Creating, initiating, re-creating (*Maq.*, 363.10-364.4):

— **Abū l-Hudhayl** said that creating a thing, which is bringing the thing into being after its non-being (*takwīnu-hu baʿda an lam yakun*), is distinct from [the thing]; and that [creating] is [God's] willing [the thing] and saying to it 'Be!', [and that] creating is simultaneous with what is created when [the latter] happens (*wa-l-khalq maʿa l-makhlūq fī ḥāli-hi*); — and that it is not possible (*laysa bi-jāʾiz*) that God would create something which He does not will and to which He does not say 'Be!'; — and he affirmed that creating an accident is distinct from (the accident), and the same holds for creating a substance. — And he claimed that creating, which is a willing and a saying [of 'Be!'], does not [always] involve place (*lā fī makān*), — and claimed that composing (*al-taʾlīf*) is creating the thing *qua* composed, and that length is creating the thing *qua* long, and that colour is creating [the thing] *qua* coloured, — and that God's initiation of a thing (*ibtidāʾ Allāh al-shayʾ*) after its non-being *is* creating it, and it is distinct from [*the* thing], — and that re-creating (*iʿāda*) a thing is distinct from it and it is re-creating [the thing] after its annihilation. — And, that God's willing the thing is distinct from the thing, and His willing the faith is distinct from His commanding it; — and he affirmed that initiation is distinct from what is initiated, and re-creation is distinct from what is re-created, — and that initiation is God's creation of the thing for the first time, and that re-creation is creating it one more time.

One of many examples of lucid reporting by al-Ashʿarī.
My translation of *ghayr* oscillates between 'distinct' and 'other', but in most cases I have preferred 'distinct'.

ʿAbbād: is creating distinct from what is created? (*Maq*., 364.7-11):

— **ʿAbbād b. Sulaymān,** when asked, 'Do you say that creating is other than (*ghayr*) what is created?', replied, 'It would be wrong to say this, for "what is created" is an expression for a thing (*shayʾ*) *and* a creating'; — and he maintained that creating a thing is distinct from (*ghayr*) the thing, but not that creating is distinct from *what is created*; — and he maintained that creating a thing is a saying [of the command 'Be!'], as was **Abū l-Hudhayl's** doctrine, but not that God said *to* [*the thing*]: 'Be!', as **Abū l-Hudhayl** maintained.

Muʿammar on creating a thing (*Maq*., 364.12-13):

— **Zurqān** reported **Muʿammar's** claim that creating a thing is distinct from [the thing], — and that creating [presupposes another] creating, and so on to infinity (*wa-li-l-khalq khalq ilā mā lā nihāya la-hu*), — and that that [infinite series] comes to be (*wa-inna dhālika yakūnu*) at one and the same time.

See below, *Maq*., 372.1-373.12.

Hishām: 'creating' a thing is an attribute of it (*Maq.*, 364.14-15):

— **Hishām b. al-Ḥakam** is reported to have said that 'creating' a thing is an attribute of the thing (*ṣifa la-hu*) which is neither the thing nor distinct from it.

Bishr b. al-Muʿtamir: creating precedes what is created (*Maq.*, 364.16-17):

— **Bishr b. al-Muʿtamir** maintained that creating a thing is distinct from it, — and that creating precedes (*qabl*) what is created, — and it *is* God's willing the thing.

See the statements attributed to al-Naẓẓām and al-Jubbāʾī at *Maq.*, 365.1-7, and *Maq.*, 365.8-11.

Al-Naẓẓām: creating is what is created (*Maq.*, 365.1-7):

— **Al-Naẓẓām** maintained that creating (*al-khalq*), from God, *subḥāna-hu* — that is, the bringing into being (*takwīn*), *is* what is brought into being (*al-mukawwan*), namely *the thing* that is being brought into being (*al-shayʾ al-mukawwan*); — similarly, initiating (*al-ibtidāʾ*) *is* what is initiated, and re-creating (*al-iʿāda*) *is* what is re-created (*al-muʿād*); — but willing (*irāda*), from God, *subḥāna-hu*, could be the bringing into existence of the thing (*ījādan li-l-shayʾ*), or [it could be] a command (*amr*), which is distinct from what is willed, such as God's willing [for people] to have faith, namely God's commanding [the faith]. — Or, [willing] could be a judgement (*ḥukm*) or report (*ikhbār*) [from God], which *are* distinct from what is judged or reported, [such as] the willing of God, *subḥāna-hu*, to bring about the resurrection, which means that He has made a judgement and [has issued] a report concerning it. — Whereas initiating is what is initiated, and re-creating is what is re-created, namely creating the thing (*khalq al-shayʾ*) after annihilating it.

Al-Jubbāʾī: creating is what is created (*Maq.*, 365.8-11):

— **Al-Jubbāʾī** held that creating is what is created, — but that willing, from God, is distinct from what is willed, — and that man's action (*fiʿl*) is what is done by him (*mafʿūlu-hu*), but [man's] willing is distinct from what he wills; — and he maintained that God's willing the faith [from man] is distinct from commanding it, and from the faith, — and that [God's] willing to bring the thing into being (*irādatu-hu li-takwīn al-shayʾ*) is distinct from [the thing]. And I think that **someone** affirmed that creating is what is created but that re-creating (*al-iʿāda*) is distinct from what is re-created.

Abū l-Hudhayl: creating, saying 'Be!', and what is created (*Maq.*, 366.1-4).

— **Abū l-Hudhayl** maintained that creating, which is a composing (*ta'līf*) and a colour and a length and a being-such-and-such, are all created in reality (*makhlūq fī l-ḥaqīqa*) and effected (*wāqiʿ*) by a saying ['Be!'] and a willing, — but [maintained] that the creating which is a saying and a willing is not [itself] what is created *in reality* (*fī l-ḥaqīqa*), but rather what is said, in a figure of speech (*fī l-majāz*), to be 'created'.

Al-Maʿānī: *accidents or attributes*? (*Maq.*, 369.1-370.12):

***People** differed about* al-maʿānī (*qualities*) *that inhere in* (al-qā'ima fī) *bodies, such as motions and rest and the like — are they accidents* (aʿrāḍ) *or attributes* (ṣifāt)?

— **Some** said, 'We say they are attributes and do not say they are accidents, and we say they are qualities; — but we neither say they are the bodies nor say they are other than (*ghayr*) the bodies, because otherness (*al-taghāyur*) holds between bodies (*yaqaʿu bayna l-ajsām*)'. — That is the doctrine of **Hishām b. al-Ḥakam.**

— **Others** maintained, 'They [= qualities] are accidents, not attributes, because attributes are descriptions (*awṣāf*), namely what is said and spoken, such as saying, '*Zayd ʿālim qādir ḥayy*', whereas *al-ʿilm*, *al-qudra*, and *al-ḥayāh* are not descriptions, nor are motions and rest.

*And **they** differed as to why the qualities that inhere in bodies* (al-qā'ima bi-l-ajsām) *are called accidents*:

— **Some** said, 'They are called that because they happen to occur in (*taʿtariḍu fī*) bodies and inhere in them'. — These [latter people] denied that an accident could come to exist without being in a place (*lā fī makān*), or that an accident could occur without being in a body (*lā fī jism*), which is the doctrine of **al-Naẓẓām** and of many among ***ahl al-naẓar***.

— And **some** said, 'Accidents have not been called that because they occur in bodies (*taʿtariḍu fī l-ajsām*), since it is possible for accidents to exist without being in a body, and [generally] for events (*ḥawādith*) [to occur] without being in a place, such as time (*ka-l-waqt*), and willing, from God, *subḥāna-hu*, and such as persisting and ceasing to be (*al-baqā' wa-l-fanā'*), and creating a thing, which is a saying [of *kun* = be!] and a willing from God, *ta'ālā*'; this is the doctrine of **Abū l-Hudhayl.**

— **Some** said, 'Accidents have been called that only because they do not persist (*lā labtha la-hā*); and this appellation was taken from the saying of God, *'azza wa-jalla*: "This is a passing rain" (*hādhā 'āriḍun mumṭiru-nā*) (Q. 46:24), thus calling it *'āriḍ* because it does not linger; and (from) His saying: "You seek *'araḍ al-dunyā*" (Q. 8:67), thus referring to wealth as *'araḍ* because it is bound to disappear and depart'.

— **Some** said, 'An accident is called that because it does not inhere in itself and does not belong to the class of [things] that inhere in themselves'.

— And **some** said, 'The qualities that inhere in bodies are called accidents by a convention adopted by some of the ***mutakallimūn***, — and there would be nothing against rejecting this appellation on the authority of a Book or Tradition or Consensus of the Muslims or the language speakers' — this being the doctrine of many **thinkers** (*ahl al-naẓar*), including **Ja'far b. Ḥarb**.

'Abd Allāh b. Kullāb used to call the qualities that inhere in bodies 'accidents', and also 'things' (*ashyā'*), and 'attributes' (*ṣifāt*).

A benign infinite regress of qualities (*Maq*., 372.1-373.12):

And **people** *differed with regard to qualities* (al-ma'ānī):

— **Some** maintained that a body can only move, when it moves, on account of a quality (*li-ma'nā*), namely motion, without which [the body] would not be apt to move rather than not, nor would [the body] be apt to move at the time it does rather than at an earlier [time]. — They said, 'That being so, the motion too, in the absence of a quality on account of which there should be motion of [that same body], would not be apt to be motion of that body rather than of another'. — Thus [they concluded that] *that* quality's being one on account of which the motion should be a motion of *the* moved [body] is due to still another quality. — Now, qualities do not have a sum total, and they occur at one and the same time (*wa-laysa li-l-ma'ānī kull wa-jamī' wa-inna-hā taḥduthu fī waqt wāḥid*). — And the same can be said of blackness and whiteness and of black's belonging to one body rather than to another, and of white's belonging to one body rather than to another; and the same can be said in regard to the difference between black and white, and in regard to other *ajnās* and accidents according to their [doctrine], — [thus maintaining] the inevitability of affirming that, for [any] two accidents, whether mutually compatible or not, there exist qualities that have no sum total (*lā kull la-hā*). — [The same people also] claimed that the qualities that have no sum total are actions of the place which they occupy (*al-maʿānī allatī lā kull la-hā fiʿl li-l-makān alladhī ḥallat-hu*). — And similarly for what is said regarding a living or dead thing, when affirmed to be alive or dead: an infinity of qualities must be affirmed to inhere in it, since (*li-anna*) life cannot be the life [of the thing] rather than of another thing without [there being] a quality and without that quality's being due to another quality, and so on to no end. — That is the doctrine of **Muʿammar**.

— I have heard **one of the *mutakallimūn***, he is **Aḥmad al-Furātī**, claiming that motion is a motion of a body on account of a quality, and that the quality on account of which the motion is a motion of the [same] body occurred *not* on account of [another] quality.

— **Most thinkers** (*akthar ahl al-naẓar*) maintained that if we affirm a body to be in motion after its being at rest, then there must be a motion on account of which it moved, — and *that* motion belongs to the body, [but] not because of (*lā li-ajl*) the occurrence of a quality on account of which the motion belonged to [the body]; and they extended this doctrine to all other accidents.

Let R be an accident/quality, say, a certain colour red, that happens to inhere at a certain time t in a substance S: it is argued that, for a particular accident/quality R to have come to inhere in a particular substance S, at a particular time t, there must be a quality (*maʿnā*), call it R_1, on account of which R has come to inhere in S. By the same token, R_1 could not inhere in S without there being a quality R_2 on account of which R_1 has come to inhere in S at t. And so on to infinity. The infinite regress is, however, taken to be benign in the sense that the invoked qualities, though infinite in number, are identical with R in being the same colour red, and they all come to inhere in S at one and the same time. — This has sometimes been compared to Plato's 'third man argument'.
See Richard M. Frank, *Al-Maʿnā: Some Reflections on the Technical Term in the Kalām and its Use in the Physics of Muʿammar*, in: *Journal of the American Oriental Society* 87 (1967), p. 248-258; Daiber, *Muʿammar*, Indices, p. 570-571.

[End of this section]

IV.2: Excerpts from Ibn Fūrak, *Mujarrad Maqālāt al-Ashʿarī* [= *Muj.*]

In all quotations from Ibn Fūrak's *Mujarrad Maqālāt al-Ashʿarī*, the personal pronoun 'he' always refers to al-Ashʿarī himself.

Accidents do not endure/persist (*Muj.*, 12.22-13.3):

— [He maintained] that no accident can exist for more than one moment (*waqt wāḥid*), — * and that annihilation of an accident is not due to [the occurrence of] a contrary (*ḍidd*) [of the accident] or to an annihilating [agent] (*muʿdim*), — but, rather, its annihilation (*ʿadamu-hu*) must occur inevitably (*lā maḥāla*) in the second moment [of its existence] (*fī thānī waqti-hi*), it being impossible for [an accident] to exist through two adjacent moments (*fī ḥālayn muttaṣilayn*).

* For the meaning of 'contrary' see note on *jins*/class at *Maq.*, 308.16. See *Muj.*, 291.1-2.

Two meanings of kā'in (*Muj.* 43.12-14):

— [He maintained that] to describe (God) as *kā'in* has two meanings: one is to mean by 'His being' (*kawn*) the affirmation of His existence (*wujūd*); the other is to attribute to Him the coming-to-be (*al-kawn*) through which the *kā'in* has come-to-be-*in-place*, if place is involved, which, for Him, is not possible.

Note the recognition of the distinction between *kā'in* as a predicate, meaning '*X* exists,' and as a connector/copula. In the latter case, moreover, to describe a (created) thing as *kā'in* is to ascribe to the thing the accident or occurrence of coming-to-be (*al-kawn*), or having-come-to-be, *through which the thing has come-to-be*-in-place, 'if place is involved' (*idhā kāna makān*). Behind this last condition is al-Ashʿarī's explicit and repeatedly stated belief that God can create a thing 'without the thing's being in a place' (*lā fī makān*). But al-Ashʿarī also admits that creating a thing without the thing's being in a place, though always within God's capacity, is beyond human understanding.

Creating is what is created (*Muj.*, 58.15-16):

— ... Creating (*al-khalq*) is that which occurs (*al-ḥādith*, or what comes into existence), — which is impossible to have always been there (*azalī*).

Al-Ashʿarī's assertion here is equivalent to saying (with al-Naẓẓām and al-Jubbā'ī) that 'creating *is* what is created': *al-khalq huwa l-makhlūq*. See *Maq.*, 365. 1-7; *Maq.*, 365.8-11.

The Doctrine of Nature rejected (*Muj.*, 76.8-11):

— He denied the Doctrine of Nature (*al-qawl bi-l-ṭabʿ wa-l-ṭabīʿa*), and said that all occurrences (*al-ḥawādith*) are actions of God, by His choice and will and governance and estimation (*ikhtiyār*, *irāda*, *tadbīr*, *taqdīr*), — without any of these *entailing* (*mūjib*) another [intermediate] occurrence, or a nature that engenders it, — but, rather, all are His invention (*ikhtirāʿu-hu*) by His choice in the manner He chooses and knows.

Creating, doing, starting, inventing, etc (*Muj.*, 91.17-18):

— He equated, in a real sense (*fī l-ḥaqīqa*), between saying '*X* created', or 'did', or 'brought into existence', or 'started', or 'invented', [etc.] (= *khalaqa*, *faʿala*, *aḥdatha*, *anshaʾa*, *ikhtaraʿa* …).

Jihāt (*sing.*, jiha) *as spatial relations of substances* (*Muj.*, 93.6-7):

— … [He maintained] that the *jihāt* of a substance are the [indivisible] parts that surround it, and that *jiha*, according to him, can truly be attributed only to substance as that for which contiguity (*al-ittiṣāl*) and contact are possible …

Enduring (al-baqāʾ) *must inhere in that which endures/persists* (*Muj.*, 108.21-23):

— He maintained that enduring (*al-baqāʾ*) cannot be attributed to … any of the accidents, — and that what endures (*al-bāqī*) is that whose enduring inheres in it (*qāʾim bi-hi*), not in something else, — and that it is impossible for an accident to possess an endurance that inheres in something else.

'Nature' denied as a valid concept (*Muj.*, 131.16-132.13):

— He maintained that those who hold the doctrine of a Necessitating Nature or an Engendering Nature (*al-ṭabʿ al-mūjib wa-l-ṭabʿ al-muwallid*) are wrong — * for [he argued] that, if the Nature to which they refer was a created quality (*maʿnan ḥādith*), it would certainly belong to the *jins*/class [comprised of] substances and accidents … [131.21] But [in fact] [the **Natural Philosophers**] only invoke this empty expression [i.e., *ṭabīʿa* and *ṭabʿ*], without adding anything that yields a concept implying some [definite] characteristic or description (*maʿnan makhṣūṣ* *bi-ḥukm aw waṣf*). — If those who hold [this doctrine] are only capable of coming up with an utterance devoid of an intelligible notion, then what is understandable from [their] notion is [merely] that ordinary thing that habitually occurs in some way or other, — as [e.g.] when one says [of somebody] that 'he is good *by nature*,' or 'he is bad *by nature*,' when [that person manifests a particular behaviour] that is accustomed from him, but not because of a certain quality [in him] called Nature. — Accordingly when people are accustomed to the uniform occurrence of some accidents in some bodies, or in company with other accidents, they express this in terms of 'nature'; but that should not imply a particular quality, such as a power (*qudra*) that has an intelligible meaning or a particular characteristic or known varieties.

— He said, accordingly, that if someone asked him, 'If there was no necessitating Nature, and these occurrences happened through the creation and choice of their Creator, namely the Exalted God, would it then be possible for Him to choose creating them in some other manner?', he would say that several cases arise [for consideration]: some of [the occurrences] require by themselves a subject/substrate (*maḥall*) without which they could not occur, like the need of an accident to occur in a subject; and such a qualification (*ḥukm*) can neither be altered nor overturned. Some other occurrences may dispense with a subject though it may not now be possible [for us] to intelligize or perceive them without a subject, but it is possible for them to be created independently of and in isolation from any subject, as is [the case of] substance which in itself has no need for a subject.

> * Substances and accidents together make up one *jins* in the sense that an occurrence must belong to one or the other category but not to both (see note on *jins* at *Maq*., 308.16).
> Compare the last paragraph with *Muj*., 291.3-6.

Affinity of philosophical 'Naturalism' and Muʿtazilite 'Engendering' (*Muj*., 133.15-134.1):

— He maintained that the **Muʿtazilite** doctrine of Engendering (*tawallud*) and the **Natural Philosophers'** doctrine (*qawl al-ṭabāʾiʿīyīn*) are wrong in the same way, the two doctrines being assimilable one to the other; — and that both doctrines fail to guard against [viewing] the world as the work of an agent (*fāʿil*) deprived of knowledge and power and life, despite the manifest perfection and order and consummate design of the [existing] world. — For the way we have of knowing [those attributes of the world's Creator] is to argue *from* His [manifest] actions *to* Him; whereas [the **Muʿtazila**] would allow the occurrence of regular actions of perfect consistency and order without resort to a living, knowing, and powerful [Agent]. — As for the **Naturalists**, they allowed the occurrence of perfect actions (*afʿāl muḥkama*) to be initiated (*ibtidā'an*) without a knowing, powerful and living [Agent]. — * The **Muʿtazila**, on the other hand, allowed for [actions to occur] by way of engendering, so that, going farther than the **Naturalists**, they maintained the possibility of an action to occur in the absence of the [initiating] agent at the moment [of the action's occurrence], — ** meaning that [the occurrence] was due to the action of someone whose performance was a cause (*sabab*) that engendered [the occurrence] when [the performance] had ceased to exist. — Thus, by holding this doctrine, the **Muʿtazila** have committed a more grievous error [than the **Philosophers**'] that vitiated their [own] way of arguing for the existence of the world's Maker ....

A frequently cited example illustrating the argument in * and ** is that of someone's death being 'engendered' by a piercing arrow *after* the arrow's motion has been 'initiated' by the action of the archer who might even have been struck dead before the arrow has reached its target.

Bodies and atoms (*Muj.*, 202.13-15):

— ... He maintained that the bodies in the world are composed of indivisible parts (*ajzā' ghayr mutajazzi'a*), meaning that it is not possible (*lā yaṣiḥḥu*) for any part amongst them to have a half or third or quarter, nor can it be imagined (*lā yutawahhamu*) to be divided or fractionized (*yatabaʿʿaḍu*) into segments, fractions or parts.

Yatabaʿʿaḍu (from *baʿḍ*, some), to break up into fractions or portions. Clearly, al-Ashʿarī's statement is directed specifically against al-Naẓẓām's doctrine.

The indivisible part and the kawn *of coming-to-be*-in-place (*Muj.*, 203.4-7):

— He maintained that a single part/atom accepts all the accidents that may successively supervene upon it; — and that the [accident] by virtue of which [the part] comes-to-be-*in-place* — if place is involved, and which is a *kawn* (a coming-to-be), comes to exist and inhere in [the part] at every moment, whether [the part] is alone or in combination with other [parts]. — If the part comes to exist at the same time as (*maʿa*) another, then this situation (*al-maʿnā*) is [only] one of being-simultaneous-with the other; — if the other exists simultaneously, but not *in combination* (*mujtamiʿ*) *with* the part, then each of them is separated (*mubāyin*) from the other by virtue of that (*maʿnā*).

For the sense of *maʿnā* as used here, see *Maq*., 369.1-370.12; *Maq*., 372.1-373.12.

Length, aggregation, contact of atoms (*Muj*., 203.8-11):

— And he maintained that when a single part is brought together with another, then there will be in each a length which is an aggregation or contact or composition (*inḍimām wa-mumāssa wa-'jtimāʿ*). — In answer to [the question] — with respect to two atoms' being in composition or [being] long: 'Does one say of the two that they constitute a single composition or two?', he sometimes said that they are both long and aggregated by two lengths and two aggregations, and sometimes said that they are a single composition and a single [being] long.

An example of the problem due to interpreting relation as an inhering accident/property: *two* atoms make up length, therefore *each* has the property length.

Surrounding atoms/parts are the directions (jihāt) *of the surrounded atom* (*Muj*., 203.12-16):

— He maintained that a part, by itself and in isolation, has no *jiha*; if another part is created in touch with it (*muḍāmm la-hu*) then this [other part] will be a *jiha* of [the first], and the first will be a *jiha* of the other part, thus being on the right, left, behind, in front of, above, or below it. — He maintained that, 'the parts surrounding a part are the directions (*jihāt*) of that part'; — and considered a statement about the *jiha* of a part to be equivalent to a statement about the part's limit (*ḥadd*) and end (*nihāya*); he said that, 'The limit of a part is the part's *jiha* and *nihāya*', and that 'The part's *jiha* is distinct from it [i.e., from the part]'.

Colours are contraries, contacts are not (*Muj*., 204.10-13):

He allowed the existence of two contacts (*mumāssatayn*) [at once], but not two colours, in a single atom, the difference being that two colours are always contraries even when similar to one another, whereas two contacts are not contraries. — Clearly, it is not impossible for something to be in contact with one thing and separate from another, whereas it is always impossible for a thing to be made both black and white.

Atoms cannot be free from all compatible accidents [*Muj.*, 204.17-23]:

He maintained that a single part/atom (*al-juz' al-wāḥid*) may come into being apart from (*yaḥdutha munfaridan*) all other atoms, but cannot be exempt from all the accidents that may occur in it whether it is alone or in company with other atoms. — He maintained that the *kawn* in the atom while in isolation is that which would be *rest* if [the atom] came to be [in one and the same] place, or would be *motion* if it were previously in some place then in another without interruption; [the *kawn*] might also be a coming-to-be-in-contact or -in-separation, as with the case of coming-to-be-at-rest and -in-motion. [He also maintained] that aggregation and separation belong to one class (*jins*) and so are motion and rest. — He did not consider it impossible for two atoms to come-into-being separately or in aggregation.

See note on *jins* at *Maq.*, 308.16.

Corporeal dimensions as a kind of aggregation (*Muj.*, 205.18-19):

— He said that length is a kind of aggregation (*naw' min al-ta'līf*) and said the same about breadth and depth …

Quantities have lower but not upper limits (*Muj.*, 205.24-206.2):

— He maintained that augmentation and multiplication (*al-kibar wa-l-kathra*) have no limit of increasing, but that diminution and lessening have a limit at which they come to an end and cease to become smaller or lesser. — He compared that with counting (*ḥisāb*), in that [the former, namely augmentation and multiplication] have a beginning but no end, whereas [the latter: diminution and lessening] have an end of becoming fewer (*fī l-qilla*) but not of multiplying (*fī l-kathra*).

Thus al-Ashʿarī holds, clearly against al-Naẓẓām, that magnitudes and numbers have a lower but not an upper limit — see *Maq.*, 304.13-15 and associated note; *Maq.*, 318.6-8.

Gravity/weight (*Muj.*, 206.3-7):

— * Concerning his doctrine of the weight/gravity of an atom (*thiqal al-juz'*), he stated in the book *al-Nawādir*, in the course of discussion in the chapter on the atom, that the weight [of an atom] *is* the atom itself (*thiqalu-hu huwa huwa*) and is not due to something else, — and that a heavy [body] gains in weight through multiplication of the parts/atoms, [and] not through a quality, namely weight/gravity (*lā bi-maʿnan huwa thiqal*), — and that 'light' is a relative term (*min asmā' al-iḍāfa*), so that one says '*this* is heavy' and '*this* is light' relative to *that*. — But every atom *is*, of itself, heavy (*kull juz' fī nafsi-hi fa-thaqīl*). — He did not regard 'lightness' (*al-khiffa*) as a quality contrary to 'heaviness/gravity', but [rather considered] that they alternately apply to a substance according to this principle [of relativity] (*wa-yataʿāqabāni ʿalā l-jawhar ʿalā hādhā l-aṣl*)....

* 'Not due to something else' — here, I suppose, not due to a 'quality', on which see *Maq.*, 369.1-370.12; *Maq.*, 372.1-373.12.

Two atoms constitute a body; denial of interpenetration of substances (*Muj.*, 206.14-25):

— *... He said that the least that can be named 'body' are two [indivisible] substances in composition (*jawharān mu'talifān*). He considered it possible for the two to exist without being in composition [with one another], by coming-to-be in separation from one another. ... And he ... denied the doctrine of whoever held that the world is all full (*malā'*), saying that [the world] is interspersed with voids, in the sense that there are in the world empty places with no bodies in them; — ... he denied **al-Naẓẓām's** doctrine of interpenetration (*al-mudākhala*), and he asserted that two substances cannot exist in one and the same place (*maḥall*) ....

* Compare al-Ījī on 'the least number of atoms for composing a body', below p. 262 and note 32.
Note that *maḥall* could mean place.

Motion, moving, a thing in motion (*Muj.*, 208.13-14) (selections, their places in *Muj.* indicated by page and line):

— ... He held that a thing does not move (*lā yataḥarrak*) by the motion of its place, — and that whatever moves does so only by a motion that is in it.

This may be explicated as follows: standing on board a ship in motion as *my place*, I am kept stationary by my continual coming-to-be *at rest* in my place, while the ship moves by a continual coming-to-be *in-motion* from one place to another in water. (Simultaneously however I am in motion relative to an object on the river bank).

A body is not in motion at the moment of its creation (*Muj.*, 211.20-24):

— * (211.20-24) He maintained that [a body] cannot be in motion (*mutaḥarrik*) at the moment of its creation (*fī ḥāl ḥudūthi-hi*) — since saying that could not be supported by language [or] by reason (*min jihat al-lugha [wa-] lā min jihat al-ʿuqūl*). — For the language speakers (*ahl al-lugha*) say of a body that it is 'in motion' when, having been in some place, it passes (*intaqala*) from it to another; — whereas a body at the moment of its creation was not first in some place from which it moved to the other; — and, because of this, the body's coming-to-be (*al-kawn*) [in this case] is not called 'motion', but [something else, namely *kawn*] which has the sense of what is called 'motion'.

* The reading *[wa-] lā min jihat al-ʿuqūl* is supported by a parallel occurrence in the edition, p. 212.10.

— (211.25-212.2) He maintained that rest and motion are [one] class (*jins*) of coming-to-be to which the name[s] 'motion' and 'rest' are applied according to the way in which it [the event] occurs: if it is 'a coming-to-be *in* a place' then it is *rest in* [that place], and if it is 'a coming-to-be *away from* (*ʿan*) a place' then it is *motion from* (that place); thus the class (*jins*) is one but the meaning differs by way of language (*min ṭarīq al-lugha*).

See note on *jins* at *Maq.*, 308.16.

— (212.3-9) He maintained that the very *motion from* one place is the same as *rest in* another, and that the same thing can be at rest and in motion in two respects, ... as when someone leaves the road as he enters the mosque: his entering the mosque is the same as his leaving the road. And he maintained that 'rest' means nothing more than the thing's coming-to-be (*kawn al-kāʾin*) in the place it comes to occupy, without regard to a condition [tying the resting] to a single moment or two moments or three ...

— (212.14-20) And he held that 'occupying' [a place] (*al-ḥulūl*) and 'resting' [in a place] are the same ... And he cited the use of language in support of his doctrine of [place-]occupation ... And he said that the attribute of place-occupation truly applies only to substances, not to accidents ....

The Creator/al-Khāliq (*Muj.*, 224.6-10):

— ... 'The Creator' (*al-khāliq*) means that He acted through a pre-eternal power (*faʿala bi-qudra qadīma*) ....

Motion, rest, place-occupation (*Muj*., 234.3-5):

— He held that resting in a place is abandoning motion from it (*tark li-l-ḥaraka ʿan-hu*), and that one abandons moving in some direction (*ilā jiha*) by effecting motion in (*bi-an yafʿala ḥaraka fī*) another direction; — and that a [body's] moving *to* a place is resting *in* it, and that the body's resting in [the place] is its occupation of it.

Body does not endure through the endurance of its accidents (*Muj*., 237.10-11):

— Since we find that the accidents of body turn and change, then this is a proof (*dalīl*, sign) that the enduring of body is not [due to] the enduring of its accidents.

Substances and bodies may endure (*Muj*., 238.7-10):

He maintained that no accident can ever endure, — and that all substances and bodies may endure, — but they may be said to endure only at the second moment, not the first, of their coming into existence; — and that the consensus of the ***mutakallimūn*** in ancient and recent times has been that a body cannot be [said to endure] from the moment of its coming into existence (*fī ḥāl ḥudūthi-hi*).

Enduring is an accident which cannot endure (*Muj*., 238.16-19):

— He held that someone's saying, 'I am expecting Zayd to stay (*yabqā*)' means that he expects Zayd's *baqāʾ* to come to be one moment after another (*shayʾan fa-shayʾan*); — and he maintained that enduring (*baqāʾ*) is an accident which cannot endure (*ʿaraḍ wa-lā yaṣiḥḥu ʿalay-hi l-baqāʾ*), and that body always endures by the renewal of its endurance one moment after another (*ḥālan fa-ḥālan*).

Al-Ashʿarī's doctrines of akwān (*Muj*., 243.10-245.23) (selections):

— (243.10-12) Know that he maintained that coming-to-be (*al-kawn*) is a quality (*maʿnā*) on account of which a being (*al-kāʾin*) comes-to-be, *and* by means of which it comes-to-be-*in-place*, if place is involved (*al-kawn maʿnan la-hu yakūnu l-kāʾin kāʾinan wa-bi-hi yakūnu fī l-makān, idhā kāna makānun*); — and that [an *existing*] substance cannot be without *kawn*, just as it cannot be without colour; — and that *kawn* belongs to the individual substance (*al-jawhar al-munfarid*, or atom); — and that it is the quality on account of which a being (*al-kāʾin*) comes-to-be-*in-place*, if place is involved (*law kāna makānun*).

— (243.13-19) He maintained that motion and rest are of the class (*jins*) *kawn*, — and when *kawn* occurs in a particular way it is motion, and if in another way, it is rest. The way that gives *kawn* the name 'motion' is when it is a coming-to-be in a place after another without interruption (*bi-lā faṣl*). The qualification 'without interruption' is due to the fact that if [a thing] were in a prior place and then occurred (*ḥadatha*) in another place by way of re-creation (*al-iʿāda*), and is now in the [second place] by virtue of a [new] *kawn* in it, then *this* [subsequent] *kawn* will not be called 'motion', even though by means of it the thing has come-to-be in a place after its having come-to-be in the former place. Rather, *kawn is* motion when what had first come-to-be in a prior place is [now] in a second place without having been annihilated and [re]-created between the two [comings-to-be] ….

See note on *jins* at *Maq.*, 308.16.

— (243.20-244.3) He held that the second coming-to-be in the second place *is* the motion from the first; — * and he reported someone from our party as saying that the second *kawn*, along with the first, *is* motion, in the way that speech (*kalām*) or linguistic expression *is* [the concatenation] of a second letter with a [preceding] one. — But he [al-Ashʿarī] rejected this statement, saying that the second *kawn* in the second place is the motion itself, namely the motion *from* the first place and the rest *in* the second. — And he said that the motion itself *is* rest according to this account, and [thus] it is [both] a motion from the first place and rest in the second place.

* With regard to the argument in this sentence compare the meaningless sound *ʾa* with the word *ʾab* which means father.

— (244.4-5) He said that [a body] in motion presupposes two places, and that it cannot have moved [from] no-place or come to rest in no-place …

— (244.13-14) And he maintained that motion, change of place (*nuqla*), departure (*zawāl*), leaving a place, and taking-off and going-away from it — all of these are the same. …

— (244.20-21) And he held that the motion of body indicates that [the body's existence] had a beginning (*tadullu ʿalā ḥadathi-hi*), because [motion] entails that [a body's existence] will come to an end; and that which comes to an end by itself (*al-mutanāhī fī dhāti-hi*) must have been originated.

— (244.22-23) And he rejected as impossible the doctrine of whoever says that 'a motion [extending] from eternity' is motion, — and he held that motion cannot *be* motion unless it has occurred (*ḥadathat*), just as a substance cannot *be* a substance unless it has occurred (*ḥadatha*).

— (245.18-23) He did not consider *rest* to be anything more than the substance's occupying a place without [necessarily] lingering in it for two, or three [or more] moments. He maintained that qualifying this [occupation] with two or three [or more] moments is not an argument from the language users (*laysa bi-ḥujjat al-lughawīyīn*) or the way of the Arabic speakers (*ṭarīq ahl al-ʿarabīya*), but rather the reasoning of [theorizing] thinkers (*qiyās al-naẓẓārīn*). But [he maintained] that [the qualification] was invalid because [theoretical] thinking [in his view] has no way of naming a thing (*li-anna l-naẓar lā ṭarīq la-hu fī tasmiyat al-shayʾ*), and therefore there is no point in specifying amounts of duration [as a condition of rest] — just as when people say of someone that 'he rested/settled in a place or occupied it', or that 'he moved or departed from it', they mention — in the case of motion — only the change-of-place, and — in the case of rest — [only] the coming-to-be-in-place.

Iʿtimād (*endeavour*) *as a case of contact* (*Muj.*, 246.1-4):

— * He maintained that endeavour is a special case of contact (*mumāssa makhṣūṣa*) by being a contact [of one substance] with what lies under it in particular ways (*wujūh makhṣūṣa*). — He rejected the doctrine of those who held that endeavour is gravity (*al-thiqal*). We have [i.e., elsewhere in *Muj.*] reported his doctrine of gravity and his saying that gravity *is* the heavy [substance] *itself*, — and that it is not possible (*lā yaṣiḥḥu*) for an atom (*juzʾ*) to be heavier than an atom, or for a light [substance] to be lighter than a light [substance] except by comparison with (*bi-l-iḍāfa ilā*) something lighter or heavier than it.

This reduces *iʿtimād*, a force, or what is experienced as force, to one of the four *akwān*, which are purely kinematical events (in the present case, the event of coming-to-be-in-contact).
* Contiguity, cohesion, pressure, and collision would be examples of the *wujūh makhṣūṣa*/particular ways.

The akwān *and colours do not endure* (*Muj.*, 246.20):

— He considered it impossible for colours and *akwān* to endure.

Accidents do not endure for more than one moment (*Muj.*, 258.2-6):

— The characteristic [of accident] is that it is always (*lā maḥāla*) annihilated (*yuʿdamu*) in the second moment [of existence], — and that it is impossible [for accident] to exist through two contiguous moments (*ḥālayn wa-waqtayn muttaṣilayn*).

Denial of al-Naẓẓām's 'motion of endeavour' (*Muj.*, 262.10-23):

— He maintained that what **al-Naẓẓām** considered to be motion of endeavour (*ḥaraka hiya iʿtimād*) [in a body] at the moment of its creation by God — be He Exalted — *is* [in fact] rest. — Not maintaining that [the body] was [first] in a place from which it moved at the moment of its creation (*fī ḥāl ḥudūthi-hi*), he [al-Ashʿarī] would [rather] say that when [the body] was created (*khuliqa*) in a place, its coming-to-be in that place is to come-to-be at rest in it at the moment of creation *and thereafter as long as [the body] remained in it.* — He maintained that the very coming-to-be-in-place at the moment of creation belongs to the class (*jins*) consisting of *motion and rest*, even when it does not occur in the manner that calls for [one or the other of] these two terms: for the proper quality (*al-maʿnā alladhī yakhtaṣṣu l-jisma*), on account of which the body comes to occupy one place rather than another, is what is called *kawn*; and it is called 'motion' or else 'rest' according to the manner in which the substance has come-to-be in one place rather than in another. — And he maintained that the single substance (*al-jawhar al-munfarid*) has in itself that quality which, having occurred in one way, is rest, and having occurred in another, is motion. — He considered it impossible that a [substance] should be at rest or in motion without place being involved (*lā fī makān*). — He maintained that a [substance] in motion is in reality one in which the motion has come to inhere; — and that the part of a whole cannot be moved *by* the motion of the whole, but, rather, whatever part moves [must] do so by a motion that inheres in it, though one may loosely say that the whole moves by the motion of a portion of it. — * And he assimilated 'one who comes to move', to 'one who comes to know', in that [both] the moving and the knowing come to inhere in them.

'Knowing' and 'moving': is this a reference to the fact/observation that knowlege/knowing, unlike pain (for example), is *not* perceived/introspected as located/residing in some particular part of the knower's body? See *Maq.*, 369.1-370.12, and *Maq.*, 372.1-373.12, on *maʿnā*.

Iʿtimād, *nature, causality* (*Muj.*, 275.7-17):

— He considered impossible the doctrine of whoever says that the place of a thing resists/counteracts (*mudāfiʿ*) the thing's descent by [keeping] the thing at rest in itself: — he said that an inert thing (*jamād*) cannot (*lā yaṣiḥḥu*) counteract or impede (*yamnaʿu*), — and that an accident cannot engender an accident, — and that what prevents the thing's descent is [only] the occurrence (*ḥuṣūl*) of rest in it one moment after another (*ḥāl baʿda ḥāl*), — and that what is in it [i.e. in the falling thing] of [so-called?] endeavour does not *entail* (*lā yaqtaḍī*) the descent.

In regard to the meaning of 'endeavour' (*iʿtimād*), he maintained that it is no more than the settling/resting (*tamakkun*) of one substance in another as its place. — He said that ['endeavour'] is a name for *kawn* when it occurs in a particular way, namely as a particular [case] of being in contact (*mumāssa makhṣūṣa*). — He did not consider endeavour to be gravity — and we have [i.e., elsewhere in *Muj.*] made clear his doctrine of gravity; — and he rejected what the **Proponents of Nature** (*aṣḥāb al-ṭabāʾiʿ*) maintained regarding Nature, and the **Muʿtazilites'** doctrine of Engendering (*tawallud*) and of [intermediate] cause (*al-sabab*) as entailing the effect (*al-musabbab*) and of the Engendering of accidents by some accidents. — He maintained [instead] that [a substance] at rest, when it settles, does so by virtue of a [super-natural] power (*qudra*) which intiates the act of resting in it one moment after another (*awwalan fa-awwalan*), and not by means of an [intermediate or secondary] cause entailing [the rest] or on account of a quality (*maʿnā*) which engenders it.

One of the most revealing passages, reducing *iʿtimād*/endeavour as a natural dynamic force to *mumāssa*/contact, a *kawn* to be explicated only in terms of place and time.
For the term *maʿnā*, see *Maq.*, 369.1-370.12; and *Maq.*, 372.1-373.12.

Iʿtimād *in fire and in free fall* (*Muj.*, 276.1-4):

He rejected the doctrine of the **Philosophers** (*falāsifa*) and **Naturalists** (*ṭabāʾiʿīyūn*, Proponents of the Four Natures), and of the **Muʿtazila** who maintained that endeavour in a flame engenders the flame's motion upwards, and [that] endeavour in a stone engenders the motion downwards; — he said that all that is in them [i.e. in the flame and the stone] is created (*mukhtaraʿ*) by a powerful and wise [Being] who does what

He wishes to do without [intermediate] cause or manipulation (*muʿālaja*). — We have made clear [elsewhere] his [al-Ashʿarī's] way of denying the doctrine of Natures and his identifying it in meaning with the **Muʿtazila's** [doctrine of Engendering].

Denial of Nature and of Engendering (*Muj*., 282.18-283.2):

— You should know from what we have made clear to you regarding the [Muʿtazilite] doctrine of Engendering that he [al-Ashʿarī] denied that an accident can be engendered by another accident, — and that he maintained that all events (*al-ḥawādith*) are created (*mukhtaraʿa*) and initiated by God's choice, there being nothing in them that engenders another thing or event or occurrence that entails another, or an effect entailed by an [intermediate] cause. — He rejected the view of those who hold the doctrine of Nature: that it entails or causes or engenders. — He equally opposed the **Naturalists** and the **Muʿtazila** by denying their doctrine[s] of Engendering and of Nature, saying that each of these [two doctrines] derives from the other, and that whoever denies the action of Nature while accepting Engendering is committing a contradiction.

Accident (*Muj*., 291.1-2):

— … 'Accident' is the name for that which occurs (*yaʿriḍu*) in a body and does not endure (*lā yabqā*) in it …

Created things (*Muj*., 291.3-6):

— … Occurrences (*al-ḥawādith*), according to him [al-Ashʿarī], are of two [kinds]: — what occurs (*al-ḥādith*) is either that which requires a subject/substrate (*maḥall*) in order to occur, or that which occurs without needing a *maḥall*. The one that needs a subject belongs to the kind/*nawʿ* 'Accident'; the one that does not is called 'Substance' [atom], or it is a compound of substances [atoms] and is called 'body'.

This, for al-Ashʿarī, establishes the general meaning of *ḥādith*: *al-ḥādith* is (*a*) an individual substance or atom; (*b*) a body (or composite of atoms); or (*c*) an accident. An 'accident' is an occurrence in a subject (or substrate, *maḥall*); whereas a 'substance' is an occurrence, not in a subject, but *in a place* which it comes-to-occupy. An accident acquires space-coordinates only by being in a subject (called 'substance') which, by definition, has these coordinates. See end of *Muj*., 131.16-132.13.

[End of this section]

IV.3: Section from: AL-ĪJĪ, *Al-Mawāqif fī 'Ilm al-Kalām*, (p. 182-193):[28]

Mawqif IV: *On Substances*

Introduction: On the Divisions of Substance

As for the definition of substance (*jawhar*), you have known it from its divisions, and from the definition of accident (*ʿaraḍ*) which we will not repeat.

As for its divisions [they are as follows]:

The **Philosophers** (*ḥukamā'*) held that a substance, if it resides [in a subject or substrate] (*idhā kāna ḥāllan*), is form; if it is a subject (*maḥall*) of [the form], it is matter (*hayūlā*); if it is compounded of both, then it is a body; otherwise, when related to a body by way of managing or manipulating, then it is a soul or an intellect. — [All of] this pre-supposes the denial of the individual substance (*al-jawhar al-fard*, atom). But [for that account] to be complete, it would have to be shown, first, that [1] what resides (*al-ḥāll*) in something else *can be* a substance, and that [2], other than body, nothing is composed of two parts of which one resides in the other. But neither of these two [statements] has been established [by the **Philosophers**]. If we were to present [that doctrine] in a way that avoids this problem, we ought to say: a substance either has the three dimensions, and then it *is* a body, or it has not; and, for [any] part of [body], either it is actually in it (*kāna bi-hi bi-l-fiʿl*), then it is a form, otherwise it is a matter; if [that which resides] is not a part, then, if it manages the [body] it is soul or intellect.

The ***mutakallimūn***, however, held: that there is no substance except that which occupies place (*al-mutaḥayyiz*), as is already stated [in this book, *al-Mawāqif*]; and it is either divisible, and that is body, or it does not accept division (*lā yaqbalu l-qisma*) and that is the indivisible substance [or atom].

Two Notices

First Notice: Body is, for the majority [of the **mutakallimūn**], the composition of two [indivisible] parts (*majmūʿ al-juz'ayn*). For the **Qāḍī [al-**

[28] There are several editions of *Kitāb al-Mawāqif* which include the famous, extremely useful and widely used Commentary (*sharḥ*) by AL-SAYYID AL-SHARĪF ʿALĪ B. MUḤAMMAD AL-JURJĀNĪ (d. 816/1413). Two such editions are recently published: one, in three voumes, ed. ʿABD AL-RAḤMĀN ʿAMĪRA, Beirut: Dār al-Jīl, 1997; the other, in four volumes, ed. MUḤAMMAD ʿUMAR AL-DIMYĀṬĪ, Beirut: Dār al-Kutub al-ʿIlmīya, 1998. For more about the style and organization of al-Ījī's book see SABRA, *Science and Philosophy*, esp. p. 19 ff.

Bāqillānī], it is each of the two parts (*kull wāḥid min al-juz'ayn*), since it is in the [part] that the aggregation inheres (*li-anna-hu lladhī qāma bi-hi l-ta'līf*) — given that aggregation is an accident that, according to the principles admitted by our party [the Ashʿarites], cannot inhere in *two* parts [at once], because it is impossible for the one to inhere in the many. That is not a verbal dispute; rather, it is about whether there exists something (*amr*) distinct from the parts that should be identified with contiguity (*al-ittiṣāl*) or aggregation (*al-ta'līf*), as is affirmed by the **Muʿtazila**.

Second Notice: The individual substance has no shape (*shakl*) because [shape] is the figure (*hay'a*) of [either] a single enclosing boundary (*ḥadd*), and that is the sphere, or it is [the figure] made up of several boundaries, namely the polygon; and both are conceivable only in what has a part, for a boundary is a limit (*nihāya*), and limit is conceivable only with reference to *what has* a limit. The **Qāḍī [al-Bāqillānī]** said further that '[the individual substance] does not even resemble any shape, because similarity of shapes is identity in regard to shape, and, so, how can that which has no shape resemble another in shape?' — Others differed concerning the [supposed] similarity of the [individual substance] to the sphere on the pretext that the sides (*jawānib*) [of the former, like those of the latter], are not distinguishable; [and further refused the assumed similarity with the square] on the pretext that body can be composed from it without gaps; [and again refused similarity to] the triangle as the simplest of the polygonal figures.

Al-Āmidī held, and all agreed, that [the individual substance] has a certain measure (*la-hu ḥaẓẓ min al-misāḥa*) and therefore must have a limit (*fa-la-hu nihāya qaṭʿan*), — but that is subject to inquiry (*fī-hi naẓar*): for we do not grant that [the individual substance] has a limit (*lā nusallimu anna la-hu nihāya*); and even if that were granted, it would not follow from the individual substance's having a limit that the limit enveloped it (*tuḥīṭu bi-hi*), for then that which envelops and that which is enveloped would be assumed, and therefore [the individual substance] would be divided. — As for their saying, 'that [the individual substance] has a certain measure' (*la-hu ḥaẓẓ min al-misāḥa*), they might have meant by it that [the individual] substance has a quantity[?] of some sort (*ḥajm mā*); otherwise, [theirs] would be the doctrine that [the individual substance] is divisible in imagination (*wahm*), but not in actuality.[29]

[29] It is interesting that al-Ījī (following al-Bāqillānī) rejects doctrines stating that the indivisible part or atom has shape or even "something resembling shape". Al-Ījī further considers it a matter for discussion (*fī-hi naẓar*) whether or not to accept al-Āmidī's view that the atom has a 'certain measure' (*ḥaẓẓ min al-misāḥa*), 'for [the reason that] we do

Marṣad (i): *On Bodies*. Two Chapters:

Chapter 1. *On What Body Really Is* and *on Its Parts*:

[First] Five Propositions (*Maqāṣid*): **1-5**.

Proposition 1. *On the definition of body*:

The **Philosophers** use 'body', homonymously (*bi-l-ishtirāk*), in *two senses*:

One is 'natural body', given that body is investigated in natural science, and thus referring it to Nature (*al-ṭabīʿa*) as the principle of [all natural] effects (*al-āthār*). It has been defined as 'a substance in which it is possible to assume three dimensions (*abʿād*) that intersect at right angles'. We say 'possible' because it is not necessary (*lā yajibu*) that [certain/specific] dimensions should actually exist in it. As for *line*, it has no existence, especially in a sphere. As for *surface*, though inseparable from an existing body, which is necessarily finite, it is however not inseparable from the essence (*māhīya*) of body — it being possible to assume an infinite body without thereby depriving it of real corporeality, and without having to conceive body as a non-body.

[Following] is the meaning of 'right angle': if a line stands upright on another line, without inclining to either of the [latter's] two extremities, there will be produced on either side of [the standing line] two equal angles each of which is 'right'; if it inclines to one of the extremities, then one of the angles, called 'acute', will be smaller than the other, called 'obtuse'.

To picture the assumption of [three] dimensions in a body, we assume [first] a single dimension in the body at random — which is length; then another dimension at right angles with it in any direction (*jiha*) we wish — which is breadth; then a third intersecting the other two, which is determinate and conceivable only as one [i.e. in a single direction] — namely depth. This qualification (*qayd*) is not mentioned to distinguish

not grant that [the atom] has a boundary'. Al-Ījī then suggests the possibility of interpreting *misāḥa* as a *ḥajm* 'of some sort'. It is not clear, however, how *ḥajm mā*, in the sense of a finite 'volume', which must have size and shape, could help as a way out of the faced dilemma. It is therefore worth noting that later on in al-Ījī's book (Proposition 1, below, p. 261) the word 'quantity'/*kamm*, is used twice, either in place of *ḥajm* or as a synonym of it. 'Quantity', as distinguished from *ḥajm*/volume, can of course describe a non-extending entity, such as weight/gravity, that does not necessarily involve geometrical shape or size, while being designated by the point of intersection between the three dimensions.

(*tamyīz*) body, but to identify its essence (*li-taḥqīq māhīyati-hi*), for a substance accepting the three dimensions cannot be otherwise; and that which accepts dimensions in some other way can only be surface, to which [the term] 'substance' does not apply.

There are *doubts* (*shukūk*, aporias) that arise here, two of them *concerning the definition* itself:

The first aporia: 'the [proposed) definition is [actually] true of essence'; to which we would say [i.e. respond]: 'the essence accepts (*taqbalu*) [i.e., implies] corporeality and corporeality accepts the dimensions'.

The second aporia: '[the definition] is true of the imagined, mathematical body'; to which we would say: 'external existence is intended'.

Further, there are *two aporias regarding the definition as such*:

The first aporia: it has not been established that substance is a genus — as you have known from [our] discussion of the categories.[30] Now, it has often been said/objected, that 'substance is not a genus; otherwise, species under it would be distinguishable by substantial *differentiae*, since substance is not constituted of accidents, and [therefore, infinite] regress of *differentiae* would follow — as was shown with respect to existence'.[31]

It is [also] often said/objected, that 'substance is what exists, not-in-a-subject' (*al-mawjūd lā fī mawḍūʿ*); which includes two qualifications: [1] existence and its being accidental to existents (*ʿāriḍ li-l-mawjūdāt*), or else its belonging to the secondary intelligibles (*al-maʿqūlāt al-thāniya*); and [2] its not-being-in-a-subject, and that it is a nothing (*ʿadam*), not suitable for being a part of external existents.

It has been responded [to these objections] that the [proposed definition] is [meant to be] a description (*rasm*), not a definition (*ḥadd*).

The Second Aporia: The concept (*mafhūm*) of 'what accepts dimensions' is [either] something non-existent (*amr ʿadamī*), or else it is an accident inhering in some entity (*ʿaraḍ qāʾim bi-l-dhāt*), and therefore [it is the entity that] accepts [the accident]; but then the discussion would shift to the [entity's accepting it], and the [infinite] regress would follow. — It cannot be said, that 'what is impossible is the regress of *what pro-*

[30] *Kitāb al-Mawāqif*, p. 161 ff.

[31] *Kitāb al-Mawaqif*, Mawqif II: On General Matters (*al-umūr al-ʿāmma*), p. 41 ff.

duces the effects (*al-mu'aththirāt*), while *this* is a regress of the effects', because you have known that this kind of regress is invalid for (both) the **Philosophers** and the ***mutakallimūn***.

This may be answered [as follows]: 'acceptability (*al-qābilīya*) is a relation (*nisba*) distinct from that of which it is true [to say] that "it accepts, etc."', namely an entity which is a part of the body.

But now is the time for you to remember what we taught you regarding the manner in which genus and *differentia* are compounded, namely: that they are distinguishable only in the mind; that genus is something indeterminate, to be made definite by means of the *differentia*; and that to conceive the *differentia* is to represent the form (*ṣūra*) of what is indeterminate as a species. The *differentia*, on the other hand, is not something indeterminate that requires another *differentia* to make it definite, so that *differentia* would require another *differentia*; nor is it the concept itself, namely accident, but rather the special character of accepting [accident].

[*The second meaning of 'body'* is expressed by] calling it 'a mathematical body' because it is [also] investigated in the mathematical sciences (*al-ʿulūm al-taʿlīmīya ay al-riyāḍīya*), thus ascribing it to *al-taʿlīm* (teaching, *mathēsis*) because [people] began their teachings with it since it is easier and possessed of certain proofs that endow the soul with the capability to refuse conviction in their absence.

[The ***mutakallimūn***] thus defined 'body' as 'a quantity (*kamm*) accepting the three dimensions that intersect at right angles', the last qualifier being [included] here for [added] distinction. Were we to combine the [two definitions] in a single description (*rasm wāḥid*) we should say, 'body is what accepts, etc. [i.e. the three dimensions]', without mentioning 'substance' or 'quantity'.

So much for the **Philosophers'** [views]. As for the ***mutakallimūn***, you have known what we think of [their definition].

[Furthermore] the **Muʿtazila** said, 'Body is what is long, broad and deep', [regarding which] the **Philosophers** said, 'This defintion is invalid (*fāsid*), because a body is not a body by virtue of the dimensions that are actually in it', as we mentioned earlier. They said, further, 'If we take a piece of wax and make it one span in length and in breadth, then make it, for example, one cubit long and two digits broad, the former dimensions will have been taken away while the corporeality of the wax remains' — this they said on the basis of affirming [body to be] a quantity (*kammīya*); but, with regard to part[s], none has been introduced or removed; only some parts have been transferred from length to breadth.

We, however, would say: the intention [of the definition] is that length, breadth and depth *can be assumed* in the body, in the way that one says, 'body is what is divisible' (*al-munqasim*), meaning that it is what *accepts* division.

The Muʿtazila then disagreed as to the least [number of parts, or atoms] that body can be composed of:

> **Al-Naẓẓām** said: body can only be composed of infinitely [many] parts (*la yataʾallafu illā min ajzāʾ ghayr mutanāhiya*) — we shall come back to this;
> **Al-Jubbāʾī** said: [body is composed] of eight parts, by placing two [parts together] and then there is length (*fa-yaḥṣulu l-ṭūl*), and [placing] two parts on either side of it [i.e. of the length] (*ʿalā janbay-hi*), then there is breadth, then four above them, and then there is depth;
> **[Abū l-Hudhayl] Al-ʿAllāf** said: [body is composed] of six [parts], by placing three upon three.

The true [doctrine] is that it is possible (*yumkinu*) for [body to be composed] of four parts — by placing two [together], then placing a part beside one of the two, and placing another part above it. At any rate, what is composed of two or three parts is neither an individual substance nor a body, according to them, whether or not they allow the aggregation (*al-taʾlīf*) [of body] from *two* [parts]. The dispute is verbal, so let us move to what matters.[32]

As for doctrines like the one maintained by the **Ṣāliḥīya**, namely that [body] is what is self-subsistent (*al-qāʾim bi-nafsi-hi*), or by some of the **Karrāmīya**, that [body] is what exists, or **Hishām**'s doctrine that [body] is the thing (*huwa l-shayʾ*) — [these are] false (*bāṭil*), because they are enunciations (*aqwāl*) not assisted by language (*lā tusāʿidu ʿalay-hā l-lugha*): for one says (*yuqālu*), 'Zayd is more bulky (*ajsam*, from *jism*, body) than ʿAmr', that is (*ay*), larger in bulk (*ḍakhāma*) or extension of dimensions and in the aggregation of parts.

[32] It is clear that 'the true doctrine', here clearly stated, was meant to bring to an end a whole 'verbal' (i.e. useless) dispute which had exercised the minds of many of the Muʿtazila about the least number of atoms necessary for the composition of body. The 'true doctrine' implies a distinction between, on the one hand, 'aggregation' of atoms, which is possible with at least two atoms, and, on the other hand, 'body' *as that which extends in the three dimensions*, and which is possible to imagine as the configuration of four atoms. It is important to keep in mind al-Ījī's assertion that 'what is composed of two or three parts is neither an individual substance nor a body…'.

Proposition 2. *Body is* not *a totality of accidents brought together* (al-jism laysa majmūʿ aʿrāḍ mujtamiʿa), — *contrary to* ***al-Naẓẓām*** *and* ***al-Najjār*** *among the* ***Muʿtazila***, [and] on the basis of what you have known, namely that an accident cannot ever be self-supporting (*la yaqūmu bi-nafsi-hi*), but must ultimately stand (*yaqūmu*) in a substance.

In sum, [*their* thesis] is false. *They relied on Two Arguments*:

First Argument: substances *qua* substances are homogeneous (*mutajānisa*), but bodies differ [from one another] and, therefore, they are not just substances (*fa-laysat ʿibāra ʿan jawāhir*).

We say, rather, that substances differ in respect of what they are in themselves (*bi-dhawāti-hā*); and, because of this, we maintain that accidents do not persist/endure (*lā tabqā*) but substances do, as we shall explain.

You should further recognize that one who admits that substances are homogeneous (*mutajānisa*) cannot but make the accidents constituent of what body really is (*dākhila fī ḥaqīqat al-jism*), so that body would be a substance plus a collection of accidents.

Second Argument: if body exists, [then] accidents exist; and if it does not, they do not; and conversely.

Our response: Mutual implication does not signify unity/identity.

Proposition 3. *Simple body* (al-jism al-basīṭ) *accepts* (yaqbalu) *division:*

As to whether the parts [of which it is constituted] *actually* exist or not, and, in either case, whether they are finite or infinite, there are *Four Possibilities*:

First Possibility: The parts are actual and they are finite; that is the doctrine of the ***mutakallimūn***; it is the doctrine that body is [ultimately] composed of indivisible parts (*al-ajzāʾ allatī lā tatajazzaʾ*). For, if [all] parts were divisible (*mutajazziʾa*), then not all possible divisions would be actualized. The doctrine comes down to this: our doctrine that 'all possible divisions are actualized' entails that 'whatever [division] is *not* actualized is *not* possible'.

Second Possibility: The parts are actual (*bi-l-fiʿl*, in actuality) and infinite; that is **al-Naẓẓām**'s doctrine.[33]

Third Possibility: The parts are potential (*bi-l-quwwa*, in potentiality) and finite. That is the doctrine attributed to **Muḥammad al-Shahrastānī**, author of *Kitāb al-Milal wa-l-Niḥal*.

[33] See comments on *Maq*., 304.13-15.

Fourth Possibility: The parts are potential and infinite. That is the doctrine of the **Philosophers** (*ḥukamāʾ*).

Proposition 4. *On Two groups* (nawʿān) *of argument by the* **mutakallimūn**:

The First Group [of Arguments]: To show **(1)** that whatever is divisible (*kull munqasim*) has actual parts; then to show **(2)** that they are finite. There are [three] varieties [of argument] (*wujūh*) of **4(1)**: [namely **4(1)A**, **4(1)B**, and **4(1)C**, as follows]:

4(1)A: If what accepts division were *one*, then division of unity would follow (*lazima ʼnqisām al-wāḥid*). But the consequent is false; and [so is] the conditional. For it would follow that unity inheres in (*qiyām*) what accepts division; but division of the subject (*maḥall*) entails division of what inheres in it (*inqisām al-ḥāll fī-hi*), it being necessary that what inheres in one part is distinct from what inheres in another; and the *istithnāʾīya* [i.e. denying the antecedent] is evident, because 'unity' can only signify non-divisibility.

4(1)B: If what accepts division were *one*, then breaking it up would annihilate it; but the consequent is false. As for the implication (*al-mulāzama*), it is due to [the fact that] breaking would be to annihilate what a thing *is* and bringing out two [distinct] beings (*iʿdām li-huwīya wa-iḥdāth li-huwīyatayn*); for it is impossible that some definite thing should now be one sort of being then another. As for the falsity of the consequent, the reason is that it would entail that a mosquito's sting [is capable of] clefting the ocean, which is evidently denied by pure reason.

4(1)C: The partitioning sections (*maqāṭiʿ al-ajzāʾ*) are actually distinct, for a half-section is necessarily distinct from the third-, fourth-, fifth-section, and so on indefinitely, and this entails actual distinctness.

With regard to **4(2)**, *there are [three] varieties*: **4(2)A**, **4(2)B**, and **4(2)C**:

4(2)A: If distance (*al-masāfa*) were composed of infinite parts, then traversing it in a finite time would be impossible, and a fast[er] object would not catch up with a slow[er] one. The falsity of the consequent (*al-lāzim*) proves (*dalīl*) the falsity of the antecedent (*al-malzūm*).

4(2)B: It [i.e. what accepts division] is bounded by the two extremities; but it is impossible for what is [in]finite to be bounded by the two boundaries.

4(2)C: Aggregation must signify (*yufīd*) increase of volume (*ḥajm*), otherwise the volume of two [parts?] would equal the volume of one, and similarly for the volume of three, four, [etc.]; thus no volume would be obtained from the aggregation of parts, contrary to what is assumed. —If, however, aggregation signifies increase of volume, let it be aggregation of finite parts in all directions; therefore there would be volume (*ḥajm*) in all directions, which is body; therefore not every body is composed of infinite parts. — We then say: *this* body now has a finite volume and finite parts, while the body under consideration is that which has finite volume and infinite parts; but, no doubt, the volume will increse as the parts increase; and the ratio of volume to volume will be that of parts to parts; but the ratio of the volumes is one between two finite [magnitudes], whereas the ratio of the parts holds between a finite and an infinite [magnitude]; and so the ratio between two finite [magnitudes] will equal that between a finite and an infinite [magnitude] — which is a contradiction.

The Second Group [of Arguments], showing how body is composed of [parts] to begin with. Seven Arguments: 1-7:

Argument 1: The point exists; for, through it, lines touch (*idh bi-hā tamāssu l-khuṭūṭ*), and through it lines touch surfaces, and through it surfaces touch bodies; but for [something] existent to touch what does not exist is necessarily false. Moreover, [point] is the extremity of a line, line the extremity of a surface, and surface the extremity of a body; and the extremity of what exists exists. And, further, the point is not divisible. So we say that in the body there is a non-divisible existent that has position (*waḍʿ*); if it is a substance, then *that* is what we want to prove (*al-maṭlūb*); or else, it would have a non-divisible substrate (*maḥall lā yanqasim*), otherwise, that which occupies [the substrate] would be divisible, as has been shown repeatedly; and the regress could not continue but rather ends with substance, namely the indivisible part.

Argument 2: Motion exists, and divides into present, past, and future motions. We say then: that present [motion] exists, otherwise neither past nor future [motion] would exist: for the past [motion] is what was present, and the future [motion] is what will be present; and [the present motion] is not divisible, otherwise some part or parts of it (*baʿḍ ajzāʾi-hā*) could be *before* and some *after*, since [motion] is not of necessity a settled entity (*ghayr qārr al-dhāt*), and therefore not all of it would be present — and this is a contradiction (*khulf*). And the same would hold for all its parts, since no part [of it] would exist that is not present at some time or another; thus it is established (*fa-thabata*) that motion is composed of indivisible parts, and the same is true of distance because the one is coincident with the other. Or, we might say, [our conclusion follows] 'because if the distance is divisible then so is the motion over it, for the motion over half [the distance] is half the motion over [all of] it'.

Argument 3: Euclid demonstrated the existence of a least angle, namely that produced by the touching/tangency (*mumāssa*) of a straight line and circle which [angle] can neither be divided nor conceived except by affirming the [indivisible] part.

Argument 4: Let us assume a sphere that touches a plane surface, given that the sphere, the plane surface and their mutual touching are undeniably possible. Now, that through which the touching occurs is indivisible; otherwise it is either [divisible] in one direction (*fī jiha*) and then it is a line, or in more [than one] and then it is a surface, and [*this* must be plane] since it would coincide with a plane surface, and therefore the sphere would not be a sphere — which is a contradiction. We then assume the sphere to roll on the surface so as to touch it by every one of its own parts; then all the[se] parts are indivisible, which we wanted to prove.

Argument 5: We assume a line to stand perpendicularly to a line on which it passes: it will touch, through passing, all parts of the other line. But touching can only occur through a point, and therefore the traversed line is composed of points; and [as previously argued] the surface is composed of lines, and the body of surfaces; which is what we wanted to prove.

Argument 6: If bodies were not ultimately [reduced] to indivisible parts, then division of the heaven[ly sphere] and of the mustard seed would go on to infinity, and their possible respective parts would be equal (*sawā'*), which is untrue.

Argument 7: If the [indivisible] part did not exist a mustard seed would be divisible into an infinite [number] of slices that would cover the face of the earth and infinitely exceed it, which is necessarily false.

The preceding [argument(s)] might be questioned on dialectical [grounds], but should be convincing to a fair person.

Proposition 5. *The* **Philosophers'** *argument[s] that body is one and continuous and accepting division to infinity, rather than being composed of indivisible parts*:

Four Groups [of Arguments]: **5.1-5.4**:

5.1. *This relates to spatial opposition [of substances]* (al-muḥādhāh) *[and place-occupation]*: *Two Arguments* (wajhān): **A** and **B**:

5.1(A). Whatever occupies place (*mutaḥayyiz*) has a right and a left, necessarily distinct from one another.

5.1(B). If we compose a sheet (*ṣafḥa*) out of indivisible parts and hold it against the sun, the shining surface (*wajh*), i.e. the one towards the sun, is distinct from the dark one, towards us; this is also necessary/certain (*ḍarūrī*).

5.2. *This relates to touching* (al-mumāssa): *two arguments*: **A** and **B**:

5.2(A). If body were composed of indivisible parts then they would *not* be indivisible; and this is a contradiction. Explanation: The [part] at the middle of an ordered [row of parts] would prevent the two [adjacent] extremities from touching; for that through which [the middle part] touches one of the two extremities is distinct from that through which it touches the other; therefore [the middle part] is divided (*fa-yanqasimu*).

It cannot be said/objected: 'We do not grant this, because of the possibility of interpenetration (*al-tadākhul*)'; because *we* say: ' [your doctrine] is necessarily invalid; but [even] if it were granted for argument's sake, the place (*ḥayyiz*) of the two [place-occupying parts], and similarly of any larger number [of such parts], would be one; and thus there would be no ordering, no middle and no extremity; and the agglomeration [of parts] would not bring about a [certain] *volume* (*ḥajm*), contrary to what has been assumed. Moreover, interpenetration would come about after (*baʿda*) the touching/contact, it being certain that what[ever part] comes to meet [another] at [the moment of] touching is distinct from what comes to meet [the other] at [the moment of] complete interpenetration (*al-mudākhala al-tāmma*); and this would entail division'.

5.2(B). If a part were to pass over (*jāza ʿalā*) the meeting [point] of two [parts] (*ʿalā multaqā ithnayn*), then it would *not* be indivisible; but the antecedent (*al-malzūm*) is [taken to be] true; therefore the consequent (*al-lāzim*) is true; and the implication/entailment (*al-luzūm*) is evident because the [passing part] would not be touching both of the [adjacent parts] whole to whole; and that is just what division means.

As to the truth of the antecedent, there are [Three] Arguments (wujūh): **5.2(B)a**, **5.2(B)b**, **5.2(B)c**:

Argument 5.2(B)a: No doubt [the passing part] can move from one part to another; the motion will then be attributed to it either when (*ʿinda*) it is wholly at (*fī*) the first [of the two passed-over parts], or [at] the second, or at (*ʿalā*) the[ir] meeting [point]; the first two [suppositions] are false, because [they assume the motion to have taken place] either before it began or after it ended; the third [supposition] is the desired conclusion.

Argument 5.2(B)b: We assume a line of an even number of parts — say, six. We assume a part above one of the line's extremity, and another part below the other [extremity], and let the two parts move equably: then, the two parts, before they pass each other, will come to be opposite one another (*yataḥādhayān*), namely at the middle [of the line] since we assumed the equality of [their] motions, and *that* will be where the third and the fourth part meet.

Argument 5.2(B)c: We assume a line of an odd number of parts — [say, five], and assume those two parts placed above either one or the other of the [line's] extremities, then let them move equably: they will meet in the middle, namely the third part, and *that* will be where the two [parts] meet. But this [conclusion] may perhaps be blocked (*yumnaʿu*) by [saying] that the [two parts] would come to a stop [read: *yanqaṭiʿān*] before [reaching] the third, it being a condition of their moving that there be a certain empty [place] that accommodates the two parts.

5.3: *This relates to [considerations of] greater and less speeds* (al-surʿa wa-l-buṭʾ), and can be summed up [as follows]: *One of two things* follows, namely [1] denial of distinguishing motions by greater and less speeds, or [2] [asserting] the divisibility of parts; the first [1] is rejected, therefore the second [2] is asserted:

There are *two ways* of showing that one or the other of the *two things* [(1) and (2)] follows:

The *first way*: let the faster part (*al-sarīʿ*) cover one part, and that the slower part (*al-baṭīʾ*) has made no halts, on the basis of having shown that slowness is not due to interspersing halts. Therefore [the slower] has [indeed] been moving [throughout], and, therefore, it too has *either* covered one part, in which case the faster and the slower are equal [in speed], — which is [1]; *or* it has covered less than one part, and thus the part is divided, — which is [2].

The *second way*: which is to show that there are [two] concurrent motions (*mutalāzimatayn*), of which one is faster and the other slower, — thus freeing ourselves from appealing to [the argument that] 'slowness is not due to interspersing halts', but rather providing ourselves with what would afterwards support [that argument] — then: when the faster [motion] covers one part, and either [1] the second covers the same, then *this* would *imply* equality of the faster and the slower [motions]; or [2] [the second covers] less, and *this* would *imply* division of [the partially covered part]:

[This implication] takes **Six Forms**: **5.3(1-6)**:

5.3(1): *Considering the motion of the outermost periphery and of the polar [= innermost] circle of a millstone*: If the outer moves [continuously] while the inner makes halts, this would imply disintegration and division of the millstone into circles equal in number to its parts [along the radii] — even if the millstone were made of iron or something harder — as well as [the circles'] re-integration when the millstone stops and no effort would be great enough to loosen the parts. And while [breaking the millstone] would not be beyond God's power, its denial is asserted by reason (*al-ʿaql jāzim bi-ʿadami-hi*), as with all habitual occurrences (*ka-sāʾir al-ʿādiyāt*). It ought to be recognized that God, be He Exalted, has not created all these wonders in the millstone for the sake of confirming *your* doctrine!

5.3(2): *Considering a compass with three legs*, of which one is fixed while the other two turn around so as to draw two circles, an inner, smaller one, and an outer, larger one, both of which are completed and necessarily advancing together. In this situation, the breaking up [of parts] without scattering would be even more unlikely.

5.3(3): When someone stands on one heel and turns around it he will draw two circles, one by his heel, the other by his limbs. If you like, assume him to be stretching his arm: the tip of his finger will then draw a much larger circle. Now, we necessarily know that he does not interrupt his motion one part after another (*lā yanqaṭiʿu juzʾan juzʾan*). If you wish, assume this to be the case of two stars in the heavens, one close to the pole, the other on the ecliptic.

5.3(4): *The case of the sun and the shadow of a stick erected facing it*: the shadow will move, from morning to noon, over a determinate magnitude of the earth's surface, while the sun will have moved through a quarter of its orbit without interruption of the shadow's motion, — for the [solar] ray falls along a straight line, and halting the shadow would abolish the rectilinearity.

5.3(5): The case of a bucket attached to the extremity of a stretched rope (r_1) whose other extremity is fixed at the middle (*M*) of a well['s depth]; attached to the extremity of [another] rope (r_2) [fixed at the top (*T*) of the well] is a hook that reaches *M* [where it catches the first rope]. [By pulling up r_2] the hook and the bucket will rise to reach the top of the well simultaneously; and, therefore, the bucket will have covered the distance of the well's depth while the hook has covered half of it — certainly (*ḍarūratan*) without halting.

5.3(6): *The case of one part that moves [the distance of] one part on a mobile that moves [the distance of] one part*: Assume a line A[B]G, and assume a line DE upon A[B], and a part Z upon D; then, when D moves from A to B, E will have moved, by means of this motion, from B to G; but we have assumed that Z, which was opposite (*muqābil*) A, has moved to be now opposite G; then, Z will have moved [the distance of] two parts while D has moved [the distance of] one part; and, therefore, when Z moved [the distance of] one part, D will have moved [a distance] *less* than one part; — and in this is the desired conclusion.

The letters are muddled in the Cairo edition.

5.4: *Concerning matters relating to geometrical figures — Six Arguments* (wujūh) ***(1-6)***:

Argument 5.4(1): We assume a square made up of four lines each consisting of four parts, thus adding up to sixteen parts. Then each side of the square will be four parts; the diagonal also will be four parts; therefore the diagonal will be equal to the side, which is impossible as attested by experience (*al-ḥiss*) and geometrical demonstrations.

It cannot be objected, 'Why cannot the diameter be longer owing to void[s] (*khalā'*, vacuum) between [the parts]?'; for we would respond, 'If the void between every two parts accommodates a [whole] part, then the diagonal, now being seven parts, will be equal to two of the sides; and if [it accommodates] less, division will follow'.

Argument 5.4(2): [Consider] a right-angled triangle with each of the sides that contain the right angle being equal to ten parts; then we say, 'It has been proved that the square of the triangle's hypotenuse equals the sum of the squares of the sides; now, the square of each side is one hundred and the sum of the two squares is two hundreds, and so the hypotenuse is the root of two hundreds, that is, more than fourteen and less than fifteen; and this entails division of the part'.

Argument 5.4(3): [In] the same [right-angled] triangle: if we apply the top (*ra's*) of its hypotenuse upon [a point on?] one side, and stretch (*wa-madadnā*) its lower part (*rijla-hu*, its foot) from the other extremity [along the other side], then, undoubtedly, whenever something is [added along?] *this* side, something will be taken away off *that* side (*kulla-mā yanḥaṭṭu min hādhā l-ḍilʿ shay'un yakhruju min dhālika l-ḍilʿ shay'un*?); if the two are equal (*fa-in kāna mithla-hu*), it will follow that the hypotenuse is equal to what is applied to one side plus the remainder (*al-munṭabiq ʿalā ḍilʿ wa-l-fāḍil ʿalayhi*), which is equal to the other [side], thus the hypotenuse will be equal to the sum of the two sides — contrary to experience and geometry.

This [argument] belongs in some respect to category **5.3** [relating to considerations of greater and less speeds]. [34]

Argument 5.4(4): We have shown that the circle exists. Thus, assuming a circle whose circumference (*muḥīṭ*) consists of indivisible parts: if the exterior of the [circle] [i.e. of the circumference] is larger than its interior, then the part[s are] divided. Otherwise, it is *either* the case that there exists a void between any two [adjacent] parts — in which case, if the void's magnitude (*qadr*) accommodates a [whole] part, then the exterior of the [circle = circumference] will be double its interior, — which is belied by experience (*al-ḥiss*); and if the void's magnitude is less [than that], then division will follow. *Or*, it is the case that there is no void, then the interior of [the circumference] will equal its exterior, and [the interior] will equal the exterior of the other circumference enveloped by it, and the exterior of the enveloped circumference will also be equal to its [own] interior, and equal to a third, fourth, etc., circumference. Therefore the parts of the outermost circumference of a millstone would be equal to its polar [innermost] circumference — which is evidently false.

Argument 5.4(5): Euclid has proved (*barhana*) that the angle contained by two straight lines is divisible to infinity, [thus] denying the [indivisible] part.

Argument 5.4(6): He [Euclid) has proved (*barhana*) that every line can be bisected, thus assuming that any line made up of an odd number of parts will entail division of the middle part.

[*This is followed in al-Ījī's book by* **Propositions** (*Maqāṣid*) **6-8**, an *extended discussion of the* **Philosophers'** *doctrine of matter and form as the constituents of body*.]

[End of this section]

[34] I cannot claim to understand this argument, which I tried to follow in several editions, and about which al-Ījī seems to have had some reservation. For the clash of geometry and experience generally, the subject of **Proposition 5.4(1-6)**, see the illuminating remarks of ERWIN SCHRÖDINGER (with reference to Democritus), in his *Nature and the Greeks*, Cambridge: Cambridge University Press, 1954, Chapter 6, esp. p. 82 ff.

APPENDIX: NAMES AND DATES

ʿAbbād b. Sulaymān d. c. 250/864
ʿAbd al-Jabbār d. 415/1025
Abū Bishr Ṣāliḥ b. Abī Ṣāliḥ = Ṣāliḥ Qubba, d. second half of Third/Ninth Century
Abū Hāshim (al-Jubbāʾī) d. 321/933
Abū l-Hudhayl d. 227/841-2
Al-Āmidī d. 631/1233
ʿAmr b. ʿUbayd d. 143/762
Al-Ashʿarī 260-324/873-4-935
Averroes d. 595/1198
Avicenna d. 428/1037
Al-Baghdādī (ʿAbd al-Qāhir) d. 429/1037
Al-Bāqillānī d. 403/1013
Bardaiṣān, Bardesanes, of Edessa, d. 222 AD
Bishr b. al-Muʿtamir d. 210/825
Ḍirār b. ʿAmr d. 180/796
Al-Fārābī d. 339/950
Al-Fuwaṭī, Hishām b. ʿAmr d.?before 218/833
Al-Ghazālī d. 405/1111
Al-Ḥasan al-Baṣrī d. 110/728
Hishām b. al-Ḥakam d. 178/795
Ibn ʿArabī d. 638/1240
Ibn ʿAsākir d. 571/1176
Ibn Fūrak d. 406/1015
Ibn Ḥanbal d. 241/855
Ibn Khaldūn d. 808/1406
Ibn Kullāb, d. shortly after 240/855
Ibn Qayyim al-Jawzīya d. 751/1350
Ibn Rushd *see* Averroes
Ibn Shabīb, Muḥammad, d. second half of the Third/Ninth Century
Ibn Sīnā *see* Avicenna
Ibn Taymīya d. 728/1327
Al-Ījī, ʿAḍud al-Dīn d. 756/1355
Al-Isfarāʾīnī d. 318/1027
Al-Iskāfī d. 240/854
Jaʿfar b. Ḥarb d. 236/850-1
Al-Jāḥiẓ d. 255/868-9
Al-Jubbāʾī d. 303/915-6
Al-Jurjānī d. 816/1413
Al-Juwaynī d. 478/1085
Al-Kaʿbī d. 317/929 or 319/931
Al-Kindī d. ca. 252/866
Maimonides d. 602/1204
Mānī, founder of Manichaeism, d. 276 AD
Marcion, founder of the Marcionite sect (al-Marqūnīya), the first great Christian heresy, floruit 144 AD
Muʿammar d. 215/830
Al-Muḥāsibī d. 243/856
Al-Naẓẓām d. between 220/836 & 230/845
Al-Qalānisī d. second half of the Third/Ninth Century
Al-Rāzī, Fakhr al-Dīn d. 606/1209
Al-Ṣāliḥī, Abū l-Ḥusayn d. late in the Fourth/Tenth Century
Al-Shahrastānī d. 548/1153
Al-Ṣūfī, Īsā, 'one of the Baghdādīs' (*Maq.*, 302.4)
Al-Sumnānī d. 444/1052
Al-Taftāzānī d. 792/1390
Al-Ṭūsī (Naṣīr al-Dīn) d. 672/1274
Wāṣil b. ʿAṭāʾ d. 131/748
Zurqān, Abū Yaʿlā Muḥammad b. Shaddād d. either 278/891 or 279/892

ABŪ L-ḤUṢAYN AL-BAṢRĪ'S PROOF FOR THE EXISTENCE OF GOD

WILFERD MADELUNG
University of Oxford

In his book *Proofs for Eternity, Creation and the Existence of God in Medieval Islamic and Jewish Philosophy* (Oxford, 1987), H.A. DAVIDSON credits the philosopher Avicenna (370-428/980-1037) and the *Kalām* theologian Abū l-Maʿālī al-Juwaynī (419-478/1028-1085) with major refinement of the proof for the existence of God. He devotes a chapter to Avicenna's proof of the existence of a being necessarily existent by virtue of itself (p. 281-310), describes the failure of Averroes's critique of his proof (p. 331-335), and notes that

> A measure of the influence of Avicenna's proof is the fact that Necessarily Existent became an accepted synonym for God in Islamic and Jewish theology.[1]

Al-Juwaynī, according to Davidson, was the theologian who first 'fully and explicitly' recognized the need to prove the impossibility of an infinite regress of generated things. As the fourth principle in his proof of creation from accidents, he thus stipulated demonstration of '"the impossibility of generated things without a first [term]"' instead of the traditional proposition that what is unavoidably associated with generated accidents is itself generated (p. 144-146). Al-Juwaynī's version of the proof from accidents was adopted by al-Ghazālī, al-Shahrastānī, Maimonides and al-Ṭūsī (p. 145). Al-Juwaynī, moreover, employed a particularisation argument in his proof for the existence of God where he combined two motifs, the second of which 'must have been suggested to Juwaynī by Avicenna's analysis of the concepts *possibly existent* and *necessarily existent*' (p. 161).

Al-Juwaynī is also described as a great innovator in *Kalām* theology by M.M.A. Saflo in his thesis.[2] In agreement with Davidson, Saflo suggests that al-Juwaynī added the demonstration that temporal things must have a beginning and cannot regress infinitely as a fourth principle to the

[1] DAVIDSON, *Proofs for Eternity*, p. 387.
[2] M.M.A. SAFLO, *Al-Juwaynī's Thought and Methodology*, Berlin, 2000.

traditional proof from existence of accidents.[3] Al-Juwaynī was, moreover, the first theologian to use an argument of particularisation as a simultaneous proof for the existence of God and the creation of the world. This proof was vital for him to demonstrate that God was a freely choosing Creator endowed with a will.[4]

Davidson and Saflo were evidently not aware of the substantial reformulation of the *Kalām* proof for the existence of God by the Muʿtazilī Abū l-Ḥusayn Muhammad b. ʿAlī al-Baṣrī (d. 436/1044), whose name is not mentioned by them. Abū l-Ḥusayn al-Baṣrī's theological teaching was until recently largely unknown since his own works, except for his *al-Muʿtamad fī Uṣūl al-Fiqh* dealing with legal methodology, were lost or inaccessible, and quotations and references to him in later literature are sparse. His theological views can now be examined, however, in the extant parts of the *Kitāb al-Muʿtamad fī Uṣūl al-Dīn* by Maḥmūd Ibn al-Malāḥimī (d. 536/1141), the chief representative of Abū l-Ḥusayn's thought a century after his death.[5] Ibn al-Malāḥimī not only quotes Abū l-Ḥusayn frequently and at some length but expressly states at the beginning of his book that he intended to condense and supplement Abū l-Ḥusayn's major work, the *Kitāb Taṣaffuḥ al-Adilla*, in which he critically scrutinized the proofs and arguments used by the Muʿtazila and their opponents.

From Ibn al-Malāḥimī's detailed discussion it is evident that the proof for the existence of God as a freely choosing agent (*fāʿil mukhtār*) and the Creator of a temporal world was one of his major concerns that led him to novel theses and brought him into conflict with some of the established doctrine of his own Muʿtazilī school. This is confirmed by the recent discovery of a fragment of a treatise by the Jewish Karaite theologian Yūsuf al-Baṣīr (d. ca. 431/1040), a contemporary of Abū l-Ḥusayn al-Baṣrī, in which he polemically denounced the latter's proof for the existence of God from the point of view of the school doctrine of Abū Hāshim al-Jubbāʾī and Qāḍī ʿAbd al-Jabbār.[6] It may be noted that, in spite of Yūsuf al-Baṣīr's opposition, Abū l-Ḥusayn's doctrine was soon adopted by major Karaite theologians in Egypt.

[3] *Al-Juwaynī's Thought*, p. 167-168, 191-197, 205.

[4] SAFLO, *Al-Juwaynī's Thought*, p. 202-209. Al-Juwaynī was also treated as the first theologian to have developed the argument from particularisation by H.A. WOLFSON in his *The Philosophy of the Kalam*, Cambridge, Mass., 1976, p. 434-444.

[5] MAḤMŪD IBN MUḤAMMAD AL-MALĀḤIMĪ, *Kitāb al-Muʿtamad fī Uṣūl al-Dīn*, ed. M. MCDERMOTT and W. MADELUNG, London, 1991.

[6] An edition and study of the fragment is in preparation by S. Schmidtke and W. Madelung.

Ibn al-Malāḥimī describes two proofs for the existence of God offered by Abū l-Ḥusayn. The first one is a revised form of the traditional *Kalām* proof from accidents.[7] Like Avicenna's proof, however, it is based directly on the principle of causality in contrast to the analogy between the seen and the unseen world (*qiyās al-ghā'ib 'alā l-shāhid*) employed in the traditional proof. In substance Abū l-Ḥusayn's initial argument agrees with Avicenna's, although he uses, instead of Avicenna's terms 'necessarily existent' (*wājib al-wujūd*) and 'possibly existent' (*mumkin al-wujūd*), the traditional *Kalām* terms 'eternal' (*qadīm*) and 'generated' or 'temporal' (*muḥdath*, *ḥādith*).[8] Every generated thing (*muḥdath*), he states, requires a generator (*muḥdith*). Knowledge that something which occurs while it was possible for it not to occur must do so for some matter (*amr*), is necessary knowledge. This definition of *muḥdath* as contingent agrees with Avicenna's concept of *mumkin al-wujūd*, and Avicenna, like Abū l-Ḥusayn, held the causality implied in the argument to be known by self-evidence.[9] The generator (*muḥdith*), at least the ultimate generator, must necessarily exist and thus must be eternal.

The difference in the basic terminology used by Avicenna and Abū l-Ḥusayn despite the similarity of their initial argument is significant. With his Aristotelian conviction that the world must be eternal, Avicenna found the concept of *mumkin al-wujūd* most suitable since it lacked any connotation of temporality. The world could be possibly existent in itself, yet infinite in time and co-eternal with its ultimate cause, the Necessarily Existent in Itself. The term *muḥdath*, in contrast, expressed temporality, coming into existence after non-existence, and was inevitably opposed to eternity. Abū l-Ḥusayn used it, in consonance with the *Kalām* tradition, to express his conviction that the world was created by choice of its Creator and finite in time. Having established that bodies require a generator, he immediately proceeds to argue that this generator must be a freely choosing agent (*fā'il mukhtār*), not a necessitating cause (*mūjib*). An eternal necessitating cause, he maintains

[7] *Mu'tamad*, p. 167-169.

[8] It is at present uncertain whether Abū l-Husayn used Avicenna's terminology anywhere. Ibn al-Malāḥimī employs *wājib al-wujūd bi-dhāti-hi* and *mumkin al-wujūd bi-dhāti-hi* in his discussion of the claim that accidents are temporally produced (*Mu'tamad*, p. 87-88). The discussion, however, probably is a reformulation of Abū l-Ḥusayn's doctrine and is not based on a quotation. By the time of Ibn al-Malāḥimī, Avicenna's terminology was in common use in theology.

[9] DAVIDSON, *Proofs*, p. 299: 'the cause of generation is ... obvious, since no one, Avicenna is certain, can doubt that whenever an object comes into existence, it does so by virtue of something else'.

in agreement with the view of the philosophers,[10] cannot produce a temporal effect. The temporal body can be generated in time by an eternal being only by choice.

The presumption in this proof that bodies are temporally created and neither collectively nor in their material base eternal, as the materialists and Aristotelian philosophers held, had to be previously justified. The *Kalām* theologians commonly did so on the basis of their theory of accidents (*aʿrāḍ*) with three claims (*daʿāwī*). The first was the existence of such accidents which inhered in bodies and were the cause of their motion, rest, aggregation (*ijtimāʿ*), separation, colour, smell etc. The second was that bodies do not precede such existence, and the third that accidents are temporals (*ḥawādith*) which occur and vanish. When these claims had been verified, the conclusion was drawn that the bodies, since they do not precede these temporal accidents, must be temporal like them and subject to coming into existence and annihilation.

The *Kalām* theologians viewed these accidents as real entitative things (*maʿānī*) which are additional to atoms and bodies but normally require these as their substrate. Abū l-Ḥusayn denied the reality of such accidents, presumably influenced by the objections of the philosophers to this concept, and treated the qualities supposedly entailed by them as mere attributes (*ṣifāt*), changing characteristics (*aḥkām*) and states (*aḥwāl*) of the body. This did not significantly affect the method of his proof for the temporality of bodies based on the three claims of the theologians, and Abū l-Ḥusayn's teacher, Qāḍī ʿAbd al-Jabbār, in his *Kitāb al-Muḥīṭ bi-l-Taklīf* acknowledged that the 'proof by way of states' (*ṭarīqat al-aḥwāl*) equally led to knowledge of the temporal origination of the body but argued that the 'proof by entitative beings' (*ṭarīqat al-maʿānī*) was preferable.[11] He meant presumably that the traditional proof of the existence of God by analogy of the seen and unseen was complicated, though not rendered impossible, by any denial of the reality of accidents. Abū l-Ḥusayn, as noted, dispensed with the traditional proof. There were, however, followers of ʿAbd al-Jabbār like Yūsuf al-Baṣīr who radically denounced his denial of accidents and asserted that it destroyed the very basis of the proof for the existence of God.

[10] See AL-GHAZĀLĪ, *The Incoherence of the Philosophers*, ed. M. MARMURA, Provo, Utah, 1997, p. 13-14.

[11] Quoted by IBN AL-MALĀḤIMĪ, *Muʿtamad*, p. 157. See also p. 101, where this accommodating view of the *ṭarīqat al-aḥwāl* is attributed to scholars of the school of Abū Hāshim in general.

Abū l-Ḥusayn in turn refuted or criticized various arguments of the partisans of Abū Hāshim, including his own teacher ʿAbd al-Jabbār, in support of the *ṭarīqat al-maʿānī*.[12] He also criticized the school of Abū Hāshim for their treatment of the thesis that whatever does not precede temporal things must itself be temporally produced. It had evidently been realised in the school that the thesis holds true only if there is a first beginning of the temporals, but the response had in Abū l-Ḥusayn's view been inadequate. Abū Hāshim had claimed that any assertion of the existence of temporals without a first one contradicted itself in words and meaning, since the expression 'past temporals' contradicted the expression 'without a first', and if the opponents claimed that there was an eternal one among them, they contradicted their statement that they were temporals. Similarly ʿAbd al-Jabbār had affirmed that temporals without a first must contain one eternal and this would be inconsistent with their all being temporally generated. Abū l-Ḥusayn objected to both claims, pointing out that there was no contradiction in the mere assertion of a collective of temporals without beginning even though each temporal in it had a beginning. That the temporals in the world must in fact have had a first required a proof. His own proof was based on the argument that the existence of every temporal must be preceded by its infinite non-existence. Their totality then must also have been preceded by infinite non-existence and have had a beginning.[13]

Abū l-Ḥusayn's second proof for the existence of God quoted by Ibn al-Malāḥimī is a detailed argument from particularisation. Abū l-Ḥusayn initially notes that we observe all bodies to share in corporeality yet to differ in various respects, such as their division into the four elements earth, water, air and fire. There must be, he argues, some matter (*amr*) causing their difference, since otherwise none of them would be more likely (*awlā*) to belong to one element rather than another. In a lengthy disjunctive probe he arrives at the conclusion that the cause must be a powerful, freely choosing (*qādir mukhtār*) eternal agent who can be neither a body nor an atom (*jawhar*). The argument is formulated to counter any explanations and objections of the philosophers and reflects familiarity with Aristotelian cosmology and physics.[14]

Abū l-Ḥusayn al-Baṣrī must have been aware of the philosophical proof of the existence of God put forward by his contemporary Avicenna.

[12] *Muʿtamad*, p. 102-158. Some of the arguments of both sides will be analysed in the forthcoming study of al-Baṣrī's treatise.

[13] *Muʿtamad*, p. 89-93.

[14] *Muʿtamad*, p. 169-172.

He evidently appreciated its rational elegance and strength as well as its threat to the *Kalām* theological view of God as a Creator who produced and ruled the world by His deliberate choice. Yet his own intellectual formation cannot have been initially influenced by his encounter with Avicenna's thought. In his youth he studied Aristotelian physics, as S. M. Stern has shown, with the Christian logician Abū ʿAlī b. al-Samḥ (d. 418/1027), a pupil of Yaḥyā b. ʿAdī.[15] This was probably in the wider context of his study of philosophy and medicine. He was most likely the physician Abū l-Ḥusayn al-Baṣrī mentioned by Ibn Abī Uṣaybiʿa as an associate of the Nestorian physician, philosopher and Christian theologian Abū l-Faraj Ibn al-Ṭayyib (d. 435/1043).[16] Abū l-Ḥusayn presumably was not primarily attracted to philosophy and its theological thought. He had grown up as a Ḥanafī with a Muʿtazilī creed strongly endorsing belief in human free will and an almighty Creator God. Thus he approached his study of philosophy with a critical detachment and some time later attached himself to Qāḍī ʿAbd al-Jabbār, the eminent head of the Muʿtazilī school at the time, as a loyal yet equally critical disciple. He challenged and contradicted his teacher in his lessons (*dars*) on the basis of his previous philosophical training. ʿAbd al-Jabbār seems to have received his objections with an open mind and responded to them with equanimity. Some of his other students, however, were scandalized by Abū l-Ḥusayn's views and bold criticism of their revered teacher and, according to Yūsuf al-Baṣīr, even accused him of unbelief (*kufr*). Yet the aim of his criticism certainly was not to undermine any of the basic positions of Muʿtazilī theology. Rather he wished to defend them more effectively against the objections of the philosophers and other opponents.

Writing a generation after him, the Ashʿarī theologian al-Juwaynī must have been well acquainted with Abū l-Ḥusayn al-Baṣrī's Muʿtazilī thought. He does not seem to have mentioned him anywhere, presumably because he did not want to draw attention to the teaching of a representative of the rival school or to admit an indebtedness to him. Yet it

[15] S.M. Stern, *Ibn al-Samḥ*, in: *Journal of the Royal Asiatic Society* (1956), p. 31-41. The identity of the pupil of Ibn al-Samḥ with the Muʿtazilī theologian has repeatedly been questioned by D. Gimaret (*Abu'l-Ḥosayn al-Baṣrī*, in: *EIr*, I, p. 324 and Al-Shahrastānī, *Livre des religions et sectes*, trans. D. Gimaret and G. Monnot, I, Leuven: Peeters & Unesco, 1986, p. 289, n. 108). Gimaret is evidently right in rejecting the suggestion of some authors such as Ibn al-Qifṭī that Abū l-Ḥusayn was in reality a philosopher masquerading as a *Kalām* theologian. This obviously does not preclude the possibility of his having studied with Ibn al-Samḥ. His familiarity with philosophy went distinctly far beyond that of most theologians of his age.

[16] As suggested by Stern, *Ibn al-Samḥ*, p. 37-38.

is evident that much of the apparent originality of his theological thought had been broadly anticipated by Abū l-Ḥusayn. Al-Juwaynī adopted his views selectively and developed them independently in line with his own Ashʿarī creed. The crucial importance of demonstrating that temporals must have a first had been recognized by Abū l-Ḥusayn before al-Juwaynī. Like the latter, Abū l-Ḥusayn had insisted that mere reliance on the definition of 'temporal' and 'temporally produced' was not sufficient proof.[17] Al-Juwaynī followed Abū l-Ḥusayn's suggestion that the proposition of the impossibility of temporals without a beginning be included as a fourth claim in the proof of creation from accidents. He added, however, to the proof set forth by Abū l-Ḥusayn.

In his *Kitāb al-Irshād*, al-Juwaynī, having established the creation of the world, presents a proof for the existence of God that dispenses with the traditional analogy between the seen and the unseen and resembles closely that of Abū l-Ḥusayn.[18] Unlike Abū l-Ḥusayn, however, he upheld the reality of accidents, and the use of the traditional proof was not complicated for him by a closure of the *ṭarīqat al-maʿānī*. He affirms that the need of anything temporal, insofar as it may occur or not occur, for a 'particulariser' (*mukhaṣṣiṣ*) is self-evident and known by necessity, adding that this self-evidence rendered any probe (*sabr*) and investigation (*naẓar*) unnecessary. Like Abū l-Ḥusayn, he immediately goes on to argue that the particulariser must be a freely choosing agent, not a nature or a necessitating cause. Al-Juwaynī's use of the term *mukhaṣṣiṣ* here has led to the classification of this proof as one of particularisation.[19] In this sense, the proof of Abū l-Ḥusayn, who used the terms *amr* and *amr murajjiḥ* in place of *mukhaṣṣiṣ*, should equally be classified so. The description of God as a particulariser was obviously implied in the concept of a freely choosing agent. It may be preferable, however, to reserve the classification as proofs of particularisation to arguments based on the shape and order of the world such as Abū l-Ḥusayn's second proof and al-Juwaynī's proof in his *al-ʿAqīda al-Niẓāmīya*, which is based on the particular size of the world, the specific number of bodies in it and particular characteristics of bodies.[20]

[17] See SAFLO, *Al-Juwaynī's Thought*, p. 191.

[18] AL-JUWAYNĪ, *Kitāb al-Irshād*, ed. M.Y. MŪSĀ and ʿA.ʿA. ʿABD AL-ḤAMĪD, Cairo, 1369/1950, p. 28-29.

[19] WOLFSON, *Philosophy of the Kalam*, p. 434-436; DAVIDSON, *Proofs*, p. 161-162; SAFLO, *Al-Juwaynī's Thought*, p. 202.

[20] See WOLFSON, *Philosophy of the Kalam*, p. 435-438; SAFLO, *Al-Juwaynī's Thought*, p. 202-204.

Al-Shahrastānī summarizes a further particularisation proof of al-Juwaynī which, like Abū l-Ḥusayn's, starts out from the distinction of the four elements.[21] It proceeds, however, along a different line of argumentation than the latter, and it is unlikely that al-Shahrastānī here erroneously ascribed Abū l-Ḥusayn's proof to al-Juwaynī. The proof may well have been set forth in a work of al-Juwaynī that is no longer extant and reflect his endeavour to develop the idea of particularisation in various arguments. Al-Juwaynī probably was the first Ashʿarī theologian to provide a stringent proof of particularisation for the existence of God.[22] He certainly received the idea, however, from the Muʿtazilī Abū l-Ḥusayn al-Baṣrī.

[21] AL-SHAHRASTĀNĪ, *Nihāyat al-Aqdām*, ed. A. GUILLAUME, London, 1934, p. 12. Discussed by WOLFSON, *Philosophy of the Kalam*, p. 441-442; DAVIDSON, *Proofs*, p. 188.

[22] ʿAbd al-Jabbār severely criticized the use of certain arguments of particularisation (*takhṣīṣ*) by the Ashʿarīs in demonstrating the creation of the world, as has been discussed by R.M. FRANK, Kalām *and Philosophy: A Perspective from one Problem*, in: *Islamic Philosophical Theology*, ed. P. MOREWEDGE, Albany, 1979, p. 81-84. Various particularisation arguments for creation and a particularising agent were proposed, as noted by Davidson, by al-Māturīdī and by the Ashʿarīs al-Bāqillānī and ʿAbd al-Qāhir al-Baghdādī long before al-Juwaynī. Their arguments, however, lacked stringency. This was provided by al-Juwaynī with his affirmation of the self-evidence of the causality underlying the proof (DAVIDSON, *Proofs*, p. 159-161). The 'new motif' noticed here by Davidson was no doubt adopted by al-Juwaynī from Abū l-Ḥusayn al-Baṣrī's proof rather than suggested to him directly by Avicenna's analysis of the concepts *possibly existent* and *necessarily existent*.

UN CHAPITRE INÉDIT DE LA *TAḎKIRA* D'IBN MATTAWAYH SUR LES ILLUSIONS D'OPTIQUE ET AUTRES SINGULARITÉS DE LA VISION OCULAIRE

DANIEL GIMARET
Académie des Inscriptions et Belles-Lettres, Institut de France.

Un livre que Richard Frank connaît bien, et dont il a abondamment tiré parti notamment dans son *Beings and their Attributes* (Albany, 1978), est le traité (*taḏkira*, littéralement «memento») du théologien muʿtazilite Ibn Mattawayh[1] sur «les propriétés des substances et des accidents» (*aḥkām al-ǧawāhir wa-l-aʿrāḍ*). Ce traité, dont jusqu'à maintenant seule la première partie a été éditée,[2] est remarquable à un double titre. En premier lieu, considéré dans l'ensemble de la littérature des *mutakallimūn* (ou du moins de ce qui s'en est conservé), muʿtazilites ou non, il présente cette particularité rare, quasi unique, d'un ouvrage de nature proprement philosophique ou scientifico-philosophique. L'auteur y expose un système du monde, celui, du reste, en honneur chez la plupart des théologiens de son temps, et selon lequel l'univers est un composé de «substances» (c'est-à-dire d'atomes, dont sont faits tous les corps), toutes semblables entre elles, et d'«accidents» portés par elles, et d'où dérive l'infinie variété des êtres corporels (anges compris). Après, donc, une première section (*qawl*) traitant des dites «substances», Ibn Mattawayh passe en revue, méthodiquement, toute la série des accidents archétypiques depuis longtemps recensés par le *Kalām*, depuis la couleur et les autres accidents perçus par les sens jusqu'aux accidents spécifiques du vivant: désir, puissance, volonté, croyance, etc. De ce panorama cosmologique, Dieu n'est certes pas absent, bien au contraire. Mais s'Il intervient, c'est toujours, si je puis dire, de façon marginale, parce que tel ou tel développement l'exige. Il n'y a aucunement cette position centrale qu'Il aurait dans un traité classique de *Tawḥīd* ou d'*Uṣūl al-Dīn*, où tout part de Lui et retourne à Lui. Ici, c'est d'un *Kitāb Uṣūl al-Dunyā* qu'il conviendrait de parler!

[1] Dates inconnues, mais il était un des disciples directs du qāḍī ʿAbd al-Ǧabbār (m. 415/1025).

[2] Le Caire, 1975. La totalité de l'ouvrage est accessible dans deux manuscrits: Ṣanʿāʾ 562 (anciennement 210) et Milan, Ambrosiana C. 104, désignés ici respectivement par les lettres *ṣ* et *m*.

L'autre aspect remarquable du livre est qu'il représente pour nous l'ultime synthèse, et combien circonstanciée, des positions Ǧubba'ites en la matière, depuis les «deux šayḫ-s», Abū ʿAlī et Abū Hāšim, jusqu'à Ibn Mattawayh lui-même, en passant notamment par Abū ʿAbd Allāh al-Baṣrī, Abū Isḥāq b. ʿAyyāš, et leur disciple à tous deux, le qāḍī ʿAbd al-Ǧabbār. Cette richissime mine d'informations attend encore d'être sérieusement exploitée.

Au terme de son inventaire des accidents caractéristiques du vivant, Ibn Mattawayh a un dernier *qawl* consacré à la perception (*idrāk*) — bien qu'en vérité, en ce qui le concerne, il se refuse à considérer la perception comme un *maʿnā*, c'est-à-dire un accident (comme le sont, par exemple, la science ou la volonté), en quoi il prend le parti d'Abū Hāšim contre celui d'Abū ʿAlī. Pour lui comme pour Abū Hāšim, tout vivant est nécessairement percevant dès lors que sont remplies les conditions requises — existence du perceptible, bon état de l'organe sensoriel correspondant, absence d'empêchements — et il n'est donc nul besoin de supposer quelque «entité» (*maʿnā*) ou «cause» (*ʿilla*) à l'origine de cet «état» (*ḥāl*) que constitue pour tout vivant son «fait d'être percevant» (*kawnu-hu mudrikan*). C'est donc en réalité par simple commodité formelle que, symétriquement aux sections précédentes, Ibn Mattawayh parle ici d'un *qawl fī l-idrāk*, alors qu'il s'agit en fait d'un *qawl fī l-mudrik*.

Sur ce thème, après de longues — très longues... — considérations sur la perception en général, Ibn Mattawayh en vient aux diverses sortes de perception, selon qu'elles concernent tel ou tel des cinq sens fondamentaux: toucher, goût, odorat, ouie, vue. C'est, bien entendu, ce dernier mode de perception (*al-idrāk bi-l-baṣar*) qui fait l'objet des plus abondants développements.

L'optique d'Ibn Mattawayh — comme avant lui de toute l'école Ǧubba'ite — est fondée sur le principe du rayonnement oculaire (*šuʿāʿ al-ʿayn, šuʿāʿ al-baṣar*), une conception héritée des Grecs et qui, comme on sait, a longtemps prévalu.[3] Ses positions à cet égard sont fort proches de celles de son maître ʿAbd al-Ǧabbār telles que formulées dans le *Mughnī*.[4] Pour lui aussi, le processus de la vision consiste en ce qu'un rayonnement[5] — qu'il décrit comme «un corps subtil de la nature de la lumière» (*ǧism raqīq min qabīl al-ḍawʾ*) — se détache de

[3] Cf. l'article *Manāẓir* de A.I. SABRA dans l'*Encyclopédie de l'Islam*.
[4] ʿABD AL-ǦABBĀR, *al-Mughnī*, IV, Le Caire, 1965, p. 59-79.
[5] Ce terme me paraît ici plus indiqué que celui de «rayon».

l'oeil (*yanfaṣilu ʿan al-ʿayn*),[6] ou plus précisément de la pupille (*nuqṭat al-nāẓir*) et s'en va frapper l'objet à voir (*yaqaʿu ʿalā l-marʾī*) et entre en contact avec lui (*yattaṣilu bi-hi*). Ce rayonnement est plus ou moins puissant selon les individus, et chez un même individu, il est d'autant plus efficace qu'il est plus concentré (*muǧtamiʿ*). Cependant, la présence du rayonnement oculaire ne suffit pas à elle seule à ce que la vision se produise. Il lui faut l'aide (*mādda*) d'un autre rayonnement, venu de l'extérieur, celui, notamment, du soleil pendant la journée, d'une lampe pendant la nuit (mais d'autres corps aussi sont susceptibles d'émettre un rayonnement, par exemple l'eau, le verre, un miroir). C'est par la combinaison de ces deux rayonnements — lumière de l'oeil, lumière externe — que la vision se réalise.

Ce principe du double rayonnement permet à Ibn Mattawayh — on le verra dans l'extrait ci-dessous — de rendre compte de divers phénomènes relatifs à la vision: pourquoi nous voyons à travers le verre (noter ici l'emploi de *taraddada fī* au sens de «traverser»), comment un homme voit son visage dans le miroir,[7] comment se forme l'ombre portée, etc. Elle lui permet aussi d'expliquer — et c'est là pour lui autant de preuves de la réalité du *šuʿāʿ* — tout un ensemble d'illusions d'optique (*ḫaṭaʾ al-manāẓir*): inversion de la silhouette reflétée par l'eau, mouvement apparent de la rive par rapport au navigateur, de la lune par rapport aux nuages, miroirs déformants, réfraction,vision double, etc. Le recours au *šuʿāʿ* ne vaut pas cependant pour toutes les sortes d'anomalies visuelles, il en est (elles aussi mentionnées par ʿAbd al-Ǧabbār) qui exigent un autre mode d'explication: pourquoi, par exemple, la lune paraît-elle plus grosse qu'elle n'est à son lever et à son coucher? pourquoi un fruit plongé dans l'eau semble-t-il lui aussi augmenter de volume? pourquoi l'eau qui paraît blanche sous sa forme d'écume cesse-t-elle de l'être quand elle s'écoule? Ibn Mattawayh parle alors de mélange ou de voisinage (*muǧāwara*) d'atomes: au moment où la lune se lève ou se couche, les vapeurs (*buḫārāt*) qui s'élèvent du sol sont alors à son voisinage, et leurs atomes s'ajoutent aux siens, ce qui n'est plus le cas quand elle est à son zénith. Etc.

Il m'a paru intéressant, pour ce volume d'hommages à Richard Frank — et sans attendre une édition intégrale de la *Taḏkira* actuellement en cours mais qui risque de demander encore beaucoup de temps — d'en

[6] C'est-à-dire de chacun des deux yeux, d'où le dérèglement qui se produit en cas de strabisme.

[7] Un problème qui a depuis longtemps agité les théologiens, cf. AL-AŠʿARĪ, *Maqālāt al-Islāmīyīn*, éd. H. RITTER, Istanbul, 1929-1930, p. 434.

publier le chapitre qui suit, un chapitre qui, je pense, ne devrait pas manquer de piquer la curiosité du lecteur, et donner lieu aussi à d'utiles comparaisons avec les pages du *Mughnī* citées plus haut. Je livre ce texte sans autre commentaire — à mon grand regret. Richard connaît ma situation présente, qui ne me permet guère de faire mieux.

فصل

الذي بقي علينا من تمام الكلام في الشعاع وما يتّصل به أن نُبيّن الوجه في رؤية ما نراه، والوجه فيما لا نراه، والوجه فيما يقع من خطأ المناظر حتى يُخيَّل إلينا في الشيء أنه على صفة وليس عليها، إلى ما شاكل ذلك. ونحن نُبيّن القول في هذا الباب على ضرب من الاختصار.

أما رؤية أحدنا ما وراء الزجاج، فقد قال أبو هاشم فيه علتَين، إحداهما ما ذكره في نقض الإلهام وفي مسألة ابن البغدادي من أن الزجاج، من حيث اختصّ بضياء وصقالة، صار مُعيناً لنا على رؤية ما وراءه، وحل محل الآلات لنا في الرؤية ومُكمِلاً للحاسّة. ولهذا يفارق المرآة لأن داخلها ليس كظاهرها، فلا نرى بها [م٢٢٧ ب] ما وراءها. وكذلك الخزف وغيره. وأما الزجاج، فباطنه كظاهره، وذلك بيّن عند الكسر.

والعلة الثانية ما قاله في الجامع، وهي محكيّة عن أبي علي، من أنه، لما كان باطن الزجاج كظاهره في الصفاء، وكان فيه خلل على طريق الانعراج دون الاستقامة، فإذا وقع الشعاع عليه، تردّد فيه بأن يقع على الصفيحة الأولى، فيصادف خللاً [ص١٥٦ أ] على وجه الانعراج، ثم كذلك في جميع الصفائح حتى يبلغ ما وراءه، فنراه. وأما الخزف، فلخشونته يتشبّث الشعاع به. أما ثبوت ذلك في الزجاج، فظاهر لأنه، عندما يوضَع في مكان مُحمًى وفيه ماء، يرشح. وبمثل هذا يثبت الخلل في الخزف وغيره. وأما أن خلله على وجه الانعراج، فلأنه، لو كان على وجه[١] الاستقامة، لصار كالخروق التي في السجف الرقيق، وكُنّا نرى ما وراء الزجاج على حدّ ما نراه إذا كان من وراء[٢] سجف رقيق، وقد عرفنا التفرقة بينهما وأن رؤية ما وراء الزجاج أقوى من غيره.

١ م: سبيل.

٢ ص: ورائه.

ولا يجب على هذه الجملة أن نرى ما وراء الزجاج بعد زمان، لأن في الزجاج شعاعاً متردداً فيصير ذلك الشعاع متّصلاً بشعاع البصر، فنراه في أوّل وهلة كما نرى السماء في أوّل وهلة لمثل هذه العلة.

فإن قيل: «فهلا رأينا وراء النار، لأنها مختصّة بصقالة وضياء ؟»، قيل له: إن العلة المانعة من رؤية ما وراءها أمران، أحدهما أنها تتحرك وتضطرب على وجه الاتّصال، وتصير بمنزلة الماء إذا خُضخِض أنه لا نرى فيه الوجه. والثاني أن في النار أجزاءً مُظلِمةً، فلهذا يرتفع عنها الدخان ويسودّ ما يحترق بها. فإذا لم يخلص ضوؤها، فارقت حالها حال الزجاج. وهذا أولى من أن تُجعَل العلة في ذلك كثافة النار — على ما قاله أبو هاشم إن الشعاع، إذا كثف، صار كالنار وكقُرص الشمس فلا نرى ما وراءهما — لأنه لا يمكن القطع على أنّا، لو بلغنا موضع القُرص، لم نر ما وراءه، وأن كثافته أو كثافة النار تمنع من تردُّد الشعاع فيه.

وأما رؤية أحدنا وجهه في المرآة، فلأن شعاع العين يقع عليها وينعكس منها إلى الوجه. فتحل المرآة محل العين في أنه، إذا انفصل عنها شعاع ووقع على ما قابلها، صحت رؤية ذلك الشيء. ولهذا، لو أراد أن يرى القفا، لاحتاج إلى مرآتَين، إحداهما تُحاذي وجهه والأخرى تُحاذي قفاه، فيقع شعاع عينه على المرآة المُحاذية لوجهه، ثم ينعكس عنها إلى التي تُحاذي القفا، ثم ينعكس عن التي تُحاذي القفا شعاعٌ إلى القفا، فتصير رؤيته لها كرؤيته لوجهه عندما يقع شعاع عينه على المرآة ومنها ما[3] ينعكس إلى الوجه. ويجب أن تكون رؤية[4] الوجه في الوقت الثاني، لأنه ينفصل الشعاع عن عينه ويقع على المرآة ثم ينعكس عنها؛ وفي رؤية[5] القفا يتأخر وقتاً آخر. ولكن ضبط الأوقات لا يمكن، فيظنّ أن الكل وقع في وقت واحد.

وقد يقع في ذلك خلاف. فمن قال بإثبات الشعاع، مثل أصحاب الهندسة ومن يذهب مذهب الأوائل، وهو قول النظّام، قالوا بمثل ما

[3] كذا، ولعل الصواب: — ما.

[4] م: رؤيته.

[5] م: رؤيته.

قلناه. ومن لم يقل بذلك، مثل ما يُحكى عن أرسطو‹طا›لس[٦]، فإنه يقول بشكل في المرآة مثل شكل الوجه، فلهذا نراه. وهو قول أبي الهذيل، وإليه مال ابن الإخشيد وعلي بن عيسى[٧] من بين أصحابه.

وهذا قول بعيد، لأنهم إن حقّقوا ثبوت شكل المرئيّ في المرآة، فمعلوم أنّا نرى السماء والأجسام العظيمة في المرآة، ولا يجوز انطباع الكبير في الصغير.

وبعد فكان يجب، إذا حرّك أحدنا يمينه، أن يرى في المرآة كأنّ تلك الصورة يتحرك [م٢٢٨ أ] يسارها، وإذا حرّكنا اليد اليسرى، أن تتحرك منها اليمنى، لأن الشخصَين عند التقابُل تجب فيهما هذه القضية.

وبعد فإمّا أن يحصل مثل هذه الصورة بالعادة، فكان يصح الاختلاف؛ أو بأمر مُوجِب من طبع وغيره، وذلك باطل.

ومتى جعل هذه الصورة وراء المرآة، فيجب أن تكون مانعةً لنا من رؤيتها لكثافتها. فإن لم تكن وراءها، كانت بين الصفيحة الصقيلة وبين ما وراء المرآة، وذلك باطل.

واعلم أنّا، إذا نظرنا في المرآة، فلا بدّ من رؤيتنا للوجه على الحدّ الذي مضى. ولا بدّ من أن نراه بحيث هو، لأن الإدراك لا يتعلق بالشيء على ما ليس به. ولا بدّ من أن تكون رؤية الوجه بالمرآة أضعف من رؤيتنا لوجه غيرنا بالعين، لأنّا نراه بلا واسطة، ولأن جميع شعاع العين يتّصل به. وليس كذلك إذا رأيناه بالمرآة، لأن بعض الشعاع يتّصل بها.

وإنما موضع الكلام أن الذي يظهر في المرآة ما هو، على[٨] القطع على أن وجهنا ليس هو في المرآة نفسها؟ إذ ليس يمكن أن يقال «إنّا نظنّ أن فيها مثل الوجه»، لأنّا نقطع على خلافه. وعلى كل حال، فلا بدّ من أن يكون الذي يظهر يتخايل إلينا أنه بمثل صفة الوجه، وإن

[٦] ص، م: أرسطولس.

[٧] هو الرماني النحوي المفسّر.

[٨] م: مع.

قطعنا على خلافه، كما نقطع أن الأشجار غير مُنكَّسة وإن تخايلت إلينا كذلك، لأنّا نرى بالشعاع على ما تقدّم. والله أعلم بذلك.

واعلم أنّا، إذا نظرنا في المرآة وعرفنا الوجه، نرى المرآة أيضاً، لكن الأقرب، على ما قاله أبو هاشم، أنّا نرى المرآة في الحالة الثانية من حال رؤيتنا للوجه، إلا أن ضبط الأوقات لا يمكن. وكان من حقّه أن تنفصل في كل وقت من العين خيوطٌ من الشعاع وتتّصل بها خيوط، فيرى[٩] بالشعاع المنعكس من المرآة وجهه، وبما ينفصل من عينه المرآة في الوقت الثاني.

وقد قال أبو هاشم إن من الجائز أن تكون رؤيته للمرآة في الوقت الثاني لأجل أن الشعاع، إذا انفصل من العين واتّصل بالمرآة، تشبّث بها لخشونتها فيراها في ذلك الوقت بهذا الشعاع المتشبث بها، ولهذا تكون رؤية وجهه بالمرآة أضعف من رؤية غيره له بالعين، لأنه لا يرى وجهه بجميع شعاع عينه، [ص١٥٦ ب] لتعلّق البعض بالمرآة.

إلا أن هذا يوجب عليه أن لو بالغ الصَيْقَل في سدّ خللها وحُسن جلائها، حتى تصير بحيث لا خشونة فيها، أن[١٠] لا يراها لفقد تشبُّث الشعاع بها، وقد عرفنا خلافه.

فأما المرآة إذا بعدت، فلا تصح رؤية الوجه بها وإن انعكس عنها[١١] الشعاع، لأن البُعد يؤثّر في اجتماعه بل يتفرق ويتبدد، وعند القُرب لا يتبدد فيتّصل بالوجه. ولهذا، إذا كانت المرآة كثيرة الشعاع لتقعُّرها، صحت رؤية الوجه بها على بُعدها عنا.

فإن قيل: «فهل يجوز أن ينظر أحدنا في المرآة فيراها دون وجهه، بأن يمنع الله شعاعها من الانعكاس إلى الوجه؟»، قيل له: ذلك جائز في المقدور، ولكن الله تعالى قد أجرى العادة بخلافه، ونقضُ هذه العادة لا يصح إلا أن يُجعَل معجزةً لبعض الأنبياء.

فأما إذا نظر أحدنا في مرآة مقعَّرة فرأى وجهه عظيماً، فهو لأن بالتقعير يجتمع الشعاع، فيصير كبره وعظمه مُوجِباً لأن يتخايل إلى

[٩] أي الناظر في المرآة.

[١٠] كذا.

[١١] م: منها.

أحدنا أن وجهه عظيم. ولولا أنه يرى بالشعاع، لما صح ذلك. وأما المُقبَّبة من المرايا، فإن الوجه يُرى فيها صغيراً لأن الشعاع لا يجتمع فيها.

فصار كل ما كان من هذا الباب فاختلافه لأجل [م٢٢٨ ب] اختلاف حال الشعاع في موقعه. وعلى هذا، إذا نظر في السيف طولاً، رأى وجهه طويلاً، وإن نظر فيه عرضاً، رآه عريضاً.

وقد بيّنّا من قبل العلة في رؤية الكبير صغيراً من بعيد، وأن ذلك هو لاستدقاق طرف الشعاع المتّصل بالمرئيّ، أو ضيق زاويته والاعتبار بها[١٢] عند ضيقها واتّساعها، وعلى ما بيّنّا أن، عند تقريب حلقة الخاتم من العين، نراها أعظم مما هي[١٣] لسعة الزاوية، وإذا بعدت رُئيَت أصغر لضيق الزاوية.

وعلى العكس من ذلك، نرى القمر عند حال الطلوع وحال الغروب أعظم مما يكون عليه عند بلوغه كبد السماء، وكذلك الحال في الشمس. وإنما كان[١٤] كذلك لأن أجزاءً من البخارات ترتفع من الأرض فتُجاوره، وعند بلوغه كبد السماء يبعد فتُفارقه تلك الأجزاء.

ولمثل هذه الطريقة، نرى العنبة والإجاصّة في الماء أكبر مما هي[١٥] عليه، لجواز أن تُجاورهما أجزاء من الماء، فيتّصل الشعاع بالكل. والماء هو مما يتردد فيه الشعاع. ولمثل هذا نرى اللبن إذا ديف فيه الزعفران كأنه أصفر، لأن أجزاءه تُجاوره. ومعلوم في الجملة التباسُ الشيء بغيره عند التجاوُر أو الحلول، وتعذُّرُ الفصل بينهما والحال هذه.

وهذا هو الوجه في رؤية الصغير في الضباب عظيماً، أو المصباح من بعيد كبيراً. فإن أجزاء الضباب و[١٦] البخارات المرتفعة تتشبث به، فيُرى أكبر. وكذلك الجسم الذي يرفعه الآل في أوقات مخصوصة، تُجاوره أجزاء البخار فيُرى عظيماً. وكل هذا لضعف البصر عن التمييز بينه وبين ما جاوره.

[١٢] م: فالاعتبار بهذا.

[١٣] ص: هو.

[١٤] م: يكون.

[١٥] كذا.

[١٦] م: أو.

فأما إذا غمزنا على أحد العينَين[١٧] فرأينا القمر كأنه قمران، فذلك لأنّا بالغمز نقطع طرف أحد[١٨] الشعاعَين عن الآخر، فيصير ما من شأنه أن يتّصل كالخيط المتّصل منقطعاً. وإذا صار كذلك، اتّصل كل واحد من الشعاعَين بالمرئيّ على حدة، فيُخيَّل إليه أنه قمران. ولوكان يرى لا بالشعاع، لم يجب ذلك. ويُبيّن هذا أن الأحول الشديد الحَوَل يرى الشيء الواحد شيئَين، لأن الانقلاب قد صيّر كل واحد من الشعاعَين في جانب، واتّصل بالمرئيّ على حياله.

ولمثل هذه الطريقة، يرى الشخص الواحد في المرآة المُنشَقّة كأنه شخصان، لأن الشقّ يُزيل الشعاع عن نظامه فينقطع على حسب انقطاعه بالغمز.

فأما إذا نظرنا في الماء عند طلوع القمر فرأيناه كأنه قمران، فهو لأن شعاع عينه[١٩] يقع على الماء فيعكسه إلى القمر، ثم ينعكس عن القمر إلى ما قابله، فيُخيَّل أنه قمران.

وإنما نرى القمر كأنه يسيرُ عند سَيْر السحاب لأن الشعاع متّصل بالأمرَين، وهذه حال السحاب مع الكواكب. وأقطار القمر والكواكب معلومة لنا مُدرَكة دون أقطار الغيم، فإذا سار الغيم نرى[٢٠] القمر والكواكب كأنّها سائرة، لاتّصال الشعاع بالكل على وجه لا يتميّز. ولهذا، لو أمكن أن يحصل شعاع أعيننا ونجمعه نحو الكواكب أو القمر، لرأيناهما ثابتَين والسحاب سائراً[٢١].

وقد يتخيّل أحدنا أن القمر والكواكب يسيران إذا سار ناظراً إليهما، وذلك هو لاضطراب الشعاع وحركته. فلهذا، إذا وقف، زال ما يتخيّله.

فأما الكواكب، فلا نراها بالنهار ونراها بالليل لأن أحدنا إنما يرى عند قَدْر من الشعاع مخصوص، متى زاد لم تصح الرؤية. ومعلوم أن

[١٧] كذا.

[١٨] ص: نقطع واحد.

[١٩] كذا.

[٢٠] م: رُئِيَ.

[٢١] ص، م: سائر.

الشعاع الذي ينفصل من الشمس يقوى فيزيد على قَدْر الحاجة. ولهذا قد تبدو لنا الكواكب في بعض الحالات، وربّما نرى أكبر الكواكب عند انكساف الشمس. ومن كان يراها بأن ينزل بئراً عميقةً مُظلمةً، فلأن شعاع الشمس مفقود هناك، فصار هو[٢٢] المانع.

فإن قيل: «هلا جعلتم المانع شعاع الكواكب نفسه؟»، قيل له: لأنّا قد نرى الكواكب في بعض الحالات — وعلى هذا نرى المشتري لعظمه نهاراً — ولأن القمر يُرى وشعاعه أكثر من شعاع الكواكب. [م٢٢٩ أ]

فإن قيل: «فيجب، إذا حصل مثل شعاع الشمس ليلاً عند الشموع الكثيرة، أن تمتنع رؤية الكواكب»، قيل له: من المُحال أن يبلغ بذلك، وإن كثر، مبلغ شعاع الشمس. وعلى[٢٣] أنه لا فصل بين الشمعة الواحدة [ص١٥٧ أ] والشموع الكثيرة في رؤية ما نراه إذا قربنا منها. ومع ذلك فإنّا نفصل بين ما ندركه ليلاً وبين ما ندركه نهاراً. فصحت العلة التي قدّمناها.

فأما سقوط الظلّ عن الأشخاص، فهو لسترها المواضع التي قد وقع عليها الشعاع، ومتى صار الموضع مَحولاً بينه وبين الشعاع، فقد وُجد هناك ظلّ. وعند وجود مصباحَين، يسقط للشخص الواحد ظلاّن، لأنه يستر كل واحد من هذَين المصباحَين، فنرى كأن هناك ظلَّين.

وعلى هذه الطريقة، يتحرك أحدنا فيرى الظلّ كأنه يتحرك، لأنه يسير في كل حال ساتراً لغير ما كان ساتراً له من قبل. ويتخايل إليه، عند العدو، أن ظلّه يعدو[٢٤] معه.

فأما رؤية أحدنا ظلّ الشخص في حالتَي طلوع الشمس وغروبها أعظم مما يراه عند بلوغها كبد السماء، فلأن الشمس في هاتَين الحالتَين لا يخلص ضوؤها بل تُخالطها أجزاء من البخارات، فيزول ذلك عنها عند بلوغها وسط السماء، فيُرى[٢٥] أصغر.

[٢٢] م: هذا.
[٢٣] م: + هذا.
[٢٤] ص: يتحرك.
[٢٥] يعني الظلّ.

ولضُعف الشعاع وقوّته تأثير في هذا الباب. يُبيّن ذلك أن المصباح إذا قرب انطفاؤه، سقط عن الشخص ظلّ عظيم، وليس كذلك إذا كان قوي الشعاع. وهكذا فإذا قربنا من المصباح، سقط عن أشخاصنا ظلّ صغير، وإذا بعدنا عنه فضعُف شعاعه، سقط ظلّ عظيم.

والناظر في الماء يرى الأشخاص الواقفة والأشجار النابتة على ما حوله كأنها مُنكَّسة، لأن شعاع الماء يقع أوّلاً على أسفل الشجرة وعلى القَدَم من الشخص، ثم يتعدّى إلى الأعالي فيظنّ التنكيس. ولهذا يرى عند نظره في جانب من الفصّ كأن وجهه مُنكَّس، لأن شعاعه[٢٦] أوّلاً يقع على الذقن ثم على باقي الوجه، وفي شعاع هذا الفصّ انحراف فيرى الذقن ثم الجبهة.

وراكب السفينة، إذا نظر إلى شطّها وإلى الأشجار النابتة بقربها، يظنّ كأنها سائرة في خلاف جهة سيره، لأنه في كل ساعة يقع شعاعه على غير ما وقع عليه أوّلاً وينعرج إلى غيره، فيظنّها سائرةً في غير جهته. فأما الأشجار البعيدة عنه، فإنه يظنّها سائرةً بسير السفينة وفي الجهة التي يسير فيها، لأن شعاعه يقع على ما بَعُدَ بعد وقوعه على ما قرب، وقد ظنّ في القريب من الأشجار النابتة على الشطّ أنها سائرة في خلاف جهة سير السفينة. فإذا انفصل الشعاع إلى البعيد، ظنّه سائراً مع سير السفينة لأن شعاعه قد انعرج إليه.

فأما السراب، فيُخيَّل إليه أنه ماء لأن هناك أجزاءً من البخار قد ارتفعت، ولونها شبيه بلون الماء. فإذا وقع عليها شعاع الشمس، ظنّ ماءً.

فأما من بعينه يرقان، فإنه يظنّ فيما يراه أنه أصفر لأن الشعاع المنفصل من عينه تختلط به أجزاء صفر، فإذا وقع على ما يراه، تخايل إليه أنه أصفر. ولمثل هذا نرى الشمس إذا وقعت على الزجاج الذي في سقف الحمّام، فإن الشعاع الذي يسقط عنه في الحمّام يتلوّن بلون الزجاج.

وعلى مثل هذا، صح فيمن كانت به المِرّة الصفراء فتناول العسل، يجد[٢٧] هناك مرارةً لأن في مجاري الذوق [م٢٢٩ ب] أجزاءً مُرّةً، لا

[٢٦] أي شعاع الفصّ.

[٢٧] كذا، ولعل الصواب: أن يجد.

أنه يُدرِك العسل في الحقيقة مُرّاً. فيصير كمن يتناول اللوزة المُرّة ثم تناول بعدها سكّرةً، فإنه يجد مرارةً لبقاء[٢٨] أجزاء مُرّة من تلك اللوزة.

ويُرى المُرْدي، وقد اعتمد الملاّح عليه وهو في الماء، كأن فيه انكساراً. وإنما كان كذلك لأنه يضطرب الشعاع الواقع على الماء لاضطرابه، فيقع على بعضه بعد وقوعه على بعض، فظنّ فيه انكسارًا.

والنقطة الحمراء على قُطب الدوّامة أو الرحا، يظنّ عند إدارتها كأنها طوقٌ لما دار الشعاع المتّصل بها لدورانها، فيُخيَّل إلى الرائي أنها طوقٌ أحمر.

وفي النقوش الحاصلة على الجدران ما يحصل من خطوط مؤرَّبة، فيظنّ أنها ناتئة، وليس كذلك. والعلة اتّصال الشعاع بها على طريق التأريب، فيظنّ أنها ناتئة. ولهذا، إذا كانت خطوطاً مستقيمة، لم يظنّ نتوءها. وهي مع التأريب تختلف ألوانها، وفيها صقالة وبصبص يتردد فيها الشعاع.

ولا يُرى الهَباء إلا عند سقوط الشمس في كُوّة البيت ووقوع شعاعها عليه، لأنّا نحتاج في رؤيته إلى شعاع زائد للطافته، وإن كان حاصلاً في الجوّ على كل حال.

وأما في الظلمة، فإنما يرى[٢٩] مَن في الضوء وإن كان مَن في الضوء لا يراه، لأن شعاع أحدهما إذا انفصل وجد مادّةً فرأى معها، والآخر ينفصل شعاعه إلى[٣٠] الظلمة التي لا يُمَدّ[٣١] فيها فلا يرى مَن فيها. وهذا هو الوجه، دون ما تقوله الأشعرية إن ذلك هو لوجود الإدراك في أحدهما دون الآخر.

والعِرق، إذا رأيناه في وسط اللحم، فهو أكهب وإن كان أبيض، لأنه يجاور أجزاءً فيها ألوان مختلفة، فيُخيَّل إلينا أنه أكهب.

[٢٨] م: لبقايا.

[٢٩] أي من في الظلمة.

[٣٠] م: من.

[٣١] م: يمتدّ.

وزَبَد الماء نراه أبيض، وإذا[٣٢] سال لا نرى هذا البياض، لأنه لا يمتنع أن يكون في أجزاء الماء ما يتلوّن بلون البياض وإن كان الغالب خلافه، وعند السيلان تُغلَب هذه الأجزاء فلا نرى البياض.

وإذا جعلنا الخاتم في طست لا ماء فيه لم نره، وإذا[٣٣] جعلنا فيه ماءً رأيناه على بُعد، لما كان الماء [ص١٥٧ ب] يُمِدّ[٣٤] شعاع البصر، فإذا لم يكن فيه ماء لم تثبت هناك المادّة. ولهذا، لو كان بدل الماء حِبراً، لم نره في الطست لأنه لا حظّ له في إمداد[٣٥] شعاع العين.

ومن أدار نفسه مراراً كثيرةً، فإنه يرى الأرض عند ذلك كأنها تنخفض وترتفع. وليس هذا إلا لاضطراب شعاع عينه[٣٦] ودورانه بدوران الواحد منا، فيظنّ أن الأرض متحركة. وهذا أولى من أن يقال إنه تجتمع في رأسه أبخرة، لأنه قد يكون به دوران شديد ولا يظنّ ارتفاع الأرض وتطامُنها.

وقد بيّنّا في باب الأكوان أن أحدنا يفصل بين المتحرك والساكن وإن كانت الأكوان غير مُدرَكة، لأمر يرجع إلى أن الجسم متى تحرّك، استطال الشعاع بعد قصر أو انعرج بعد استقامة، ولولا ذلك لم يقع الفصل. ولهذا لم يقع الفصل بين المتحرك والساكن بأن لا تختلف حال الشعاع في الوجه الذي ذكرناه، كما يقال في السفينة السائرة إن راكبها يظنّها ساكنةً.

والعلة التي لأجلها لا يرى أحدنا، إذا غاص في الماء عند فتح عينَيه، أن العين فيها رقّة فتتألم بوصول الماء إليها، فلا يرى. وبهذا تُفارق عين السمكة، فإنها صلبة لا يؤثّر فيها الماء، فحالها فيما ترى في الماء كحالها خارج الماء.

[٣٢] م: وإن.

[٣٣] م: وإن.

[٣٤] م: يمتدّ.

[٣٥] م: امتداد.

[٣٦] ص: عينَيه.

ومتى خلط[٣٧] النِقس باللبن، رأى كأن هناك لوناً مُفَرداً[٣٨]، [م٢٣٠ أ] لما كان الشعاع كما يتّصل بالأسود يتّصل بما جاوره من الأبيض، فيصير كأنه راءٍ لبعض السواد وبعض البياض.

وإنما لا يرى أحدنا ما في الأواني الضيّقة الرأس إلا بعد التغميض لعينه، لأنه يحتاج في رؤيته لِما هذا سبيله إلى جمع الشعاع، فيجمعه بالتغميض.

وإذا غمسنا حلقة الخاتم في الماء، رأيناها أصغر مما هي لأن كل ما ينفصل من شعاع العين لا يتّصل بالخاتم عند الغمس، بل يُمنَع بعض الشعاع من الاتّصال، فيصير كالبُعد الذي يجعل الكبير صغيراً.

[٣٧] أي الواحد منا.

[٣٨] ص: منفرداً.

Christian Falsafa

YAḤYĀ B. ʿADĪ'S COLLOQUY *ON SEXUAL ABSTINENCE AND THE PHILOSOPHICAL LIFE*

SIDNEY H. GRIFFITH
The Catholic University of America

Like the philosophers of Late Antiquity from whom they borrowed so much, Yaḥyā b. ʿAdī and the Muslim and Christian members of his circle of mostly Aristotelian philosophers in Tenth Century Baghdad meant to live the philosophical life in the context of their religious commitments, and often in the service of their faith. Their concerns were not only with translating texts from Greek and Syriac into Arabic, and with the doctrines of their philosophical school. They also promoted the philosophical life through the cultivation of the virtues and the encouragement of appropriate spiritual exercises for maintaining the life of the mind. In Yaḥyā's case, his ideas about the appropriate dispositions for living the philosophical life come most to the fore in two of his works, the *Reformation of Morals*[1] and the composite text which, for reasons to be discussed below, the present writer calls *On Sexual Abstinence and the Philosophical Life*.[2] The specific purpose of the present study is to give an account of the latter work, which has hitherto not received much attention from scholars. In particular, the aim is to offer an outline of the text, to discuss its structure and contents in the context of the Muslim/Christian encounter of Tenth Century Baghdad, and to call attention to the work's unique character as a colloquy on how Yaḥyā b. ʿAdī thought it best to seek what in this work he called 'godly wisdom and true science'.

SEEKING GODLY WISDOM AND TRUE SCIENCE: YAḤYĀ B. ʿADĪ IN PURSUIT OF THE PHILOSOPHICAL LIFE

Yaḥyā b. ʿAdī was a logician (*manṭiqī*), a religious apologist/polemicist, and an Aristotelian philosopher. He was also a bookseller, a bibliophile,

[1] See YAḤYĀ B. ʿADĪ, *The Reformation of Morals* (*Eastern Christian Texts*, 1), ed. SAMIR KHALĪL KUSSAYM (SAMIR KHALĪL SAMIR), translated with an introduction by SIDNEY H. GRIFFITH, Provo: Brigham Young University Press, 2002.

[2] YAḤYĀ B. ʿADĪ, *Traité sur la continence* (*Studia Orientalia Christiana Collectanea*, 16), ed. and trans. VINCENT MISTRIH, Cairo: Éditions du Centre Franciscain d'Études Orientales Chrétiennes, 1981.

a copyist,[3] a translator[4] and a teacher. He was the master of a group of Muslim and Christian students of Aristotelian philosophy in Baghdad in the middle quarters of the Tenth Century who were simultaneously both practising Christians and Muslims, and passionate devotees of the philosophical life. In this context, in his *Reformation of Morals* Yaḥyā promoted as an ideal what he called 'humanity' (*al-insānīya*),[5] by which he meant not 'humanism' in the modern sense of the term, but, following his teacher al-Fārābī's understanding of the word, he meant,

> The quality that human beings have in common, or human nature; ... being truly human, in the sense of realizing the end or perfection of man qua man, often synonymous with the exercise of reason.[6]

Yaḥyā in fact viewed the cultivation of the life of reason as the very summit of human perfection. He speaks of mankind's distinguishing virtue and defining form as the rational power or soul[7] and for Yaḥyā its perfection consists in the acquisition of what he calls 'true science' (*al-ʿulūm al-ḥaqīqīya*) and 'godly wisdom' (*al-ḥikma al-ilāhīya*),[8] or as he sometimes also put it, 'the acquisition of science (*al-ʿulūm*) and

[3] See the entry on Yaḥyā in the bio-bibliography by his friend and contemporary Ibn al-Nadīm: *The Fihrist of al-Nadīm: A Tenth-Century Survey of Muslim Culture*, ed. and trans. BAYARD DODGE, II, New York - London: Columbia University Press, 1970, p. 631. According to Dimitri Gutas, it appears that Ibn al-Nadīm used Yaḥyā's notes for a good part of his bibliographical information on the Aristotelian corpus: see DIMITRI GUTAS, *Paul the Persian on the Classification of the Parts of Aristotle's Philosophy: A Milestone between Alexandria and Bagdad*, in: *Der Islam* 60 (1983), p. 253, n. 52, who in turn cites GERHARD ENDRESS, *The Works of Yaḥyā b. ʿAdī: An Analytical Inventory*, Wiesbaden: Dr. Ludwig Reichert Verlag, 1977, p. 6-7.

[4] In the Arabic sources there are varying estimations of Yaḥyā's prowess as a translator from the Syriac versions of originally Greek texts into Arabic. On the one hand, Ibn Abī Uṣaybiʿa said that Yaḥyā 'was outstanding (*jayyid*) in translation know-how (*jayyid al-maʿrifati bi-l-naql*)': IBN ABĪ UṢAYBIʿA, *Kitāb ʿUyūn al-Anbāʾ fī Ṭabaqāt al-Aṭibbāʾ*, ed. AUGUST MÜLLER, I, Cairo - Köningsberg: n.p., 1882-1884, p. 235. On the other hand, one of Yaḥyā's own students wrote that he produced ugly translations and bad interpretations: see ABŪ ḤAYYĀN AL-TAWḤĪDĪ, *Kitāb al-Imtāʿ wa-l-Muʾānasa*, ed. A. AMĪN and A. AL-ZAYN, I, Cairo: n.p., 1939-1944, p. 37.

[5] He uses the term in two places: *The Reformation of Morals*, p. 26, §15 and p. 106, §14.

[6] JOEL L. KRAEMER, *Humanism in the Renaissance of Islam: the Cultural Revival during the Buyid Age*, Leiden: Brill, 1986, p. 10, n. 14, defining al-Fārābī's understanding of the term.

[7] Yaḥyā b. ʿAdī, following the Neoplatonic tradition he inherited, distinguishes three faculties or powers (*quwā*) in the human soul, which powers he says 'are also named souls: the appetitive soul, the irascible soul, and the rational soul' (*The Reformation of Morals*, p. 14, §1).

[8] See *Traité sur la continence*, p. 14, §1.3-4, and p. 37, §65.4 (Arabic); p. 65 and 99 (French). In some passages Yaḥyā reverses the order and speaks of 'true wisdom and godly science': e.g., at p. 39, §74.2 (Arabic) and p. 101 (French).

knowledge (*al-maʿārif*) in act', this being the virtue, he says, that 'brings one closest to God'.[9]

As for how one should go about living the philosophical life of reason in pursuit of 'godly wisdom and true science', Yaḥyā b. ʿAdī had some very definite ideas. In the first place, seemingly following the teaching of his master al-Fārābī in his *Epistle on What Ought to Precede the Study of Philosophy*,[10] Yaḥyā proposes cultivating virtues and avoiding vices, following the programme he advocated in his treatise on *The Reformation of Morals*. There he describes the agenda of the 'complete man' who, according to Yaḥyā, has as his goal,

> To direct his attention to the study of 'true science' (*al-ʿulūm al-ḥaqīqīya*); to make it his aim to grasp the quiddities of existing things, to disclose their causes and occasions, and to search out their final ends and purposes. He shall not pause in his labour at any particular end without giving some consideration to what is beyond that end. He shall make it his badge of honor, night and day, to read books on morals, to scrutinize books of biographies and of conduct. He shall devote himself to implementing what virtuous people have bidden to be implemented and what the sages who have gone before have advised to be made habitual. He shall also acquire a modicum of the discipline of grammar and rhetoric and be endowed with a measure of eloquence and oratorical felicity. He shall always frequent the sessions (*majālis*) of scholars and sages and continually associate with modest and abstinent people.[11]

In addition to the obviously theoretical aspects of this program for 'one of reformed morals' (*al-muhadhdhab al-akhlāq*), who is Yaḥyā's 'perfect man' (*al-insān al-kāmil/al-tāmm*),[12] the reader cannot miss the equally obviously practical exercises that Yaḥyā recommends for such a man. Chief among them are frequenting the company of scholars and sages and reading books. The latter exercise in particular is not to be overlooked. After speaking of the importance of keeping good company, Yaḥyā says, 'One must also be continually studying books on morality and deportment as well as accounts of ascetics, monks, hermits and pious people'.[13] To do so is an indispensable part of advancing in the 'rational sciences' (*al-ʿulūm al-ʿaqlīya*), which Yaḥyā thinks are necessary for strengthening the rational soul. He says,

[9] See *Traité sur la continence*, p. 25, §33.2-3 and §34.5-7 (Arabic) and p. 81-82 (French).

[10] See THÉRÈSE-ANNE DRUART, *Al-Fārābī, Ethics, and First Intelligibles*, in: *Documenti e studi sulla tradizione filosofica medievale* 8 (1997), p. 403-423, esp. p. 410-411.

[11] *The Reformation of Morals*, p. 94, §4.

[12] *The Reformation of Morals*, p. xxxiv.

[13] *The Reformation of Morals*, p. 74, §11.

> When one studies the rational sciences, refines his study of them, examines the books on morality and deportment, and lingers over them, his soul will awaken, take cognizance of its appetites, recover from its indolence, perceive its virtues, and reject its vices.[14]

Finally in connection with reading books, Yaḥyā says, 'Anyone who has a love for his own morals must start with the study of the books on morals and deportment, then with schooling himself in true science'.[15] This program amounts to what he calls 'a tool for self-management' (*ālat al-siyāsa*), and a workable 'vehicle of practice' (*markab al-riyāḍa*).[16] Elsewhere he calls it 'a rule (*qānūn*) by means of which one might restrain oneself'.[17] The end result for such a man, says Yaḥyā, is that 'he will resemble the angels more than he resembles men', and he will be 'passionate for the image of perfection'.[18]

In *The Reformation of Morals* Yaḥyā b. ʿAdī's ideal men are not in fact the kings and leaders of whom he speaks so often in connection with the acquisition of virtues and the extirpation of vices. While he certainly meant to commend virtue to the members of the ruling classes of the pluralistic Islamic society in Baghdad in his day, it is clear that he considers 'scholars' (*ahl al-ʿilm*), 'monks' (*al-ruhbān*) and 'ascetics' (*al-zuhhād*) to be the truly estimable members of that society. He says that,

> What is to be considered good for them is clothing of hair and coarse material, travelling on foot, obscurity, attendance at churches and mosques and so forth, and abhorrence for luxurious living.[19]

Furthermore, their task is to 'give people an interest in eternal life'.[20] And Yaḥyā is insistent that the kings and leaders of whom he speaks so much in this treatise should give financial support to scholars and ascetics. Of kings he says that after consolidating their power,

> They should give to scholars according to their classes, they should assign them salaries from their own private monies, and they should reward anyone who perseveres in knowledge and refinement. They should deal kindly with the weak and the poor, and they should search out the strangers and the aliens. They should be solicitous for ascetics and devout people, and they should allot them proportionately a share of their goods and their flocks.[21]

[14] *The Reformation of Morals*, p. 82-84, §23.
[15] *The Reformation of Morals*, p. 84, §23.
[16] See *The Reformation of Morals*, p. 86, §25.
[17] *The Reformation of Morals*, p. 98, §7.
[18] *The Reformation of Morals*, p. 92-94, §2-3.
[19] *The Reformation of Morals*, p. 60, §43.
[20] *The Reformation of Morals*, p. 62, §45.
[21] *The Reformation of Morals*, p. 102, §5.11.

Yaḥyā's talk of scholars, monks and ascetics, churches and mosques in *The Reformation of Morals* evokes his view of the Islamochristian milieu in which he lived and worked. It invites the supposition that in his pursuit of philosophy in the interreligious company of Muslim, 'Jacobite', 'Nestorian', and 'Melkite' Christian teachers and students Yaḥyā hoped to cultivate among them all a sense of 'humanity'. That is what he called *al-insānīya*, the sense of which could foster the growth of a measure of mutual esteem between the upholders of religious convictions that are inherently critical of one another. He says,

> Men are a single tribe (*qabīl*), related to one another; humanity (*al-insānīya*) unites them. The adornment of the divine power is in all of them and in each one of them, and it is the rational soul. ... Since their souls are one, and love is only in the soul, all of them must then show affection for one another and love one another.[22]

Inevitably, in the social context in which Yaḥyā lived, even with the ideal of 'humanity' that he shared with his Muslim and Christian interlocutors, controversies arose over questions of values and moral practices involved in living the philosophical life. One constant point at issue between Muslims and Christians, and even between Christians of different denominations, was the issue of the practice of the virtue of 'continence' (*al-ʿiffa*), especially in the realm of sexuality and procreation. Already in the arguments about religion between Muslims and Christians in the first centuries of Islamic rule this issue of sexual morality and the differing norms regarding it in the two communities had become a focal point of interreligious polemics. Christian authors regularly charged Muslims with commending a lax sexual morality both in this world and in the hereafter. Muslims in turn, with an equally polemical intent regarding the Christian, monastic practice of total sexual abstinence, or celibacy, beginning already with the stricture registered in the Qur'ān against monasticism (Q. 57:27 [*al-Ḥadīd*]), resolutely gave currency to the alleged prophetic tradition according to which 'there is no "monasticism" (*rahbānīya*) in Islam'.[23] And among philosophers in Yaḥyā's day, both Christian and Muslim, there was an on-going debate about the degree of sexual renunciation that was appropriate for those seriously interested in pursuing the philosophical life.

[22] *The Reformation of Morals*, p. 106, §5.14-15.

[23] See the discussion of this tradition in LOUIS MASSIGNON, *Essay on the Origins of the Technical Language of Islamic Mysticism*, trans. BENJAMIN CLARK, Notre Dame, IN: University of Notre Dame Press, 1997, p. 98-104. See also the bibliography cited in n. 50 below.

Already among the Muslim scholars of the Ninth Century, the Muʿtazilite essayist Abū ʿUthmān ʿAmr b. Baḥr al-Jāḥiẓ (d. 255/868-9), in his famous work *Kitāb al-Ḥayawān*, in the context of a disquisition on castration and its effects, speaks at some length about the conscious 'desire for offspring' (*ṭalab al-walad*) that characterizes the sexual lives of human beings, by way of contrast with the simpler appetitive behavior of non-human animals. In the process he discusses the case of an aged eunuch who nevertheless still felt sexual desire for women. And in this connection al-Jāḥiẓ expressed it as his opinion that men do not have the ability 'to withhold themselves from wanting, needing and desiring women'. And as if he had in mind the controversy between Christians and Muslims on this very issue he goes on to say of male human beings that,

> God, who is most compassionate toward His creatures and most just toward His servants, is too exalted to encumber them with foregoing anything He had bestowed on their hearts and confirmed.[24]

Two centuries later the 'Nestorian' bishop of Nisibis, Elias bar Shīnāyā took this very passage as the point of departure for his *Risāla fī Faḍīlat al-ʿAfāf*, in which he defended the practicability of the virtue of continence precisely against al-Jāḥiẓ's contentions.[25]

In the meantime, there was controversy among philosophers about the requisite degree of the suppression of the natural desires that could be considered consistent with the determination to acquire knowledge and to practise virtue, which is to live the philosophical life. One finds this discussion most eloquently put in al-Rāzī's *Kitāb al-Sīra al-Falsafīya*.[26] Here al-Rāzī defends himself against a charge levelled against him by his adversaries to the effect that his lifestyle was not characterized by a sufficient degree of asceticism and the requisite suppression of the appetitive and irascible desires necessary to qualify him as a true philosopher. His response to his critics evokes the figure of Socrates, to whose example he appeals, making a distinction between two different phases of Socrates's life. In the first phase, according to al-Rāzī, Socrates practised an unreasonable degree of renunciation; foregoing

[24] AL-JĀḤIẒ, *Kitāb al-Ḥayawān*, I, Cairo: Maktabat Muṣṭafā l-Bābī al-Ḥalabī, 1938-1945, p. 128.

[25] See GEORGE RAḤMA AL-ANṬŪNĪ, Risāla fī Faḍīlat al-ʿAfāf *li-Īlīyā l-Niṣībīnī*, in: *Al-Machriq* 62 (1968), p. 5-74, esp. p. 14-15.

[26] See PAUL KRAUS, *Raziana I*, in: *Orientalia* 4 (1935), p. 300-334, including the Arabic text and a French translation. An English translation of the text is available in ABŪ BAKR MUḤAMMAD B. ZAKARĪYĀ AL-RĀZĪ, *The Book of the Philosophic Life*, trans. CHARLES E. BUTTERWORTH, in: *Interpretation* 20 (1992), p. 227-257.

gratifications which, according to al-Rāzī, when indulged in moderation would actually aid the acquisition of knowledge and the practice of justice. In the second phase of his life al-Rāzī says that Socrates in fact renounced the extremes to which he had earlier been prone in his spiritual exercises and lived more moderately. So al-Rāzī says that he emulates the Socrates of the second phase of his life, disagreeing not with the 'manner' (*kayfīya*) of Socrates' self-discipline, but with the 'degree' (*kammīya*) to which he practised it in the first phase of his life, going so far then as completely to renounce having any progeny (*nasl*), ever fighting enemies, and never attending entertainments.[27]

Al-Rāzī identifies Hindus and Manichaeans as groups who in his opinion regularly espouse unreasonable and reprehensible ascetical practices. And in this connection he goes on to say,

> What comes under this same heading, albeit far down the list, is what the Christians practise: living the monastic life and withdrawing into hermitages. Many Muslims too adopt the practice of staying in mosques, renouncing property, restricting themselves to a small amount of food, and then the most distasteful of it, to chafing clothing, and then the coarsest of it. All of this on their part is an outrage against themselves; it causes them pain, while weightier pain than it is not dispelled by means of it. Socrates pursued a way of life like this in the first phase of his lifetime, but he abandoned it in the second phase of his life, as we mentioned earlier.[28]

On the face of it, al-Rāzī's ideas about appropriate spiritual exercises for the philosopher, and for the Christian or Muslim ascetic, are somewhat out of sympathy with what Yaḥyā b. ʿAdī commends in *The Reformation of Morals*. And on one point in particular it is notably at variance with what Yaḥyā propounds in his composite treatise *On Sexual Abstinence and the Philosophical Life*, devoted to advocating the propriety and effectiveness of what he represents as the Christian practice of foregoing any desire for offspring or progeny on the part of anyone seriously interested in what he calls 'seeking godly wisdom and true science'.[29] A brief review of the arguments put forward in this treatise, and the manner in which Yaḥyā develops them, affords one an otherwise unavailable insight into both the ideals he entertained and the manner in which he discussed them in the course of his own pursuit of the philosophical life.

[27] See KRAUS, *Raziana I*, p. 310-311.
[28] KRAUS, *Raziana I*, p. 316.
[29] See notes 8 and 9 above.

SEXUAL ABSTINENCE AND PHILOSOPHY

Yaḥyā b. ʿAdī's work *On Sexual Abstinence and the Philosophical Life* is certainly not one his most important philosophical or theological texts. But it is somewhat unique among his works in that we find it in an unfinished state, incomplete both textually and intellectually, almost as if it were a work in progress, still in the process of circulating among his conversational partners, both Christian and Muslim, awaiting the resolution of significant criticisms of the thesis he seeks to defend. It is this very character of the work that affords the interested reader some insight not only into the ideas which Yaḥyā meant to commend but also some measure of understanding of the manner in which he pursued their clarification in colloquy with his colleagues, in his on-going effort to conceptualize the conditions for what he would consider a genuinely philosophical way of life. It will be best to examine the work first from the perspective of the text and its context and then to review the course of the arguments that Yaḥyā puts forth.

1. The Text, its Description and its Composite Format

As far as modern scholars have yet been able to discover, only one full copy of *On Sexual Abstinence and the Philosophical Life*, in the composite form in which Yaḥyā b. ʿAdī presumably left it, has survived. It is preserved in a manuscript compendium of a number of theological texts in Arabic by various authors that was copied in the year 1752 AD, and is now preserved in the library of the Coptic Orthodox Patriarchate in Cairo.[30] Two other, earlier manuscripts, now preserved in the Vatican Library, include much abbreviated epitomes of the text.[31] All three of

[30] See this manuscript described under no. 418 (578) in GEORG GRAF, *Catalogue de manuscripts arabes chrétiens conserves au Caire* (*Studi e Testi*, 63), Città del Vaticano: Biblioteca Apostolica Vaticana, 1934, p. 152-154; and under no. 370, Theol. 83, in MARCUS SIMAIKA PASHA, *Catalogue of the Coptic and Arabic Manuscripts in the Coptic Museum, the Patriarchate, the Principal Churches of Cairo and Alexandria and the Monasteries of Egypt*, II, Cairo: Government Press, Būlāq, 1939 and 1942, p. 161-162.

[31] They are Vatican Arabic MSS 115 and 134, described in ANGELUS MAI, *Scriptorum Veterum Nova Collectio e Vaticanis Codicibus Edita*, IV, Rome: Typis Vaticanis, 1831, p. 234-235, 259-260. Mai assigns MS 115 to 1200 AD (p. 235) and MS 134 to the fourteenth century (p. 260). Augustine Périer, on the basis of paleographical considerations, assigns MS 134 a date in the first half of the thirteenth century: See A. PÉRIER, *Yaḥyā ben ʿAdī, un philosophe arabe chrétien du Xe siècle*, Paris: Gabalda and Geuthner, 1920, p. 21.

them expressly attribute the work to Yaḥyā b. ʿAdī.[32] A brief introduction to the last section of the work itself mentions the date 10 Muḥarram 353 AH,[33] i.e., 28 January 964 AD, suggesting that the text was complete in the form in which we now have it ten years before Yaḥyā b. ʿAdī's death.

Over the years a considerable amount of confusion has attended the discussion of this work and in fact, until Vincent Mistrih's edition of the full text was published in 1981, previous scholars have scarcely recognized it as an integral work at all, nor have they had a very clear idea of its true character. No doubt the several names and descriptions of the work, and of portions of it, which have appeared in a number of places over the years, as well as the inclusion of the manuscript copies of the text in compendia of theological works, have all conspired to prevent the recognition of it as the record of a colloquy on sexual abstinence and the philosophical life.

As Augustin Périer suggested,[34] and Samir Khalil seconded,[35] the earliest reference to *On Sexual Abstinence and the Philosophical Life* may well be found in Ibn Abī Uṣaybiʿa's (d. 668/1270) bio-bibliography of famous physicians. At the very end of the entry on Yaḥyā b. ʿAdī, the text mentions, 'a book on the advantages and the disadvantages of sexual intercourse and the perspective from which to engage in it', and the text immediately adds the somewhat enigmatic concluding phrase, 'according to the conjecture[36] of the nobleman, Abū Ṭālib Nāṣir b. Ismaʿīl, the companion of the Sultan al-Qāʾim, in Constantinople'.[37] Presumably, Abū Ṭālib, whose mission to Byzantium in the eleventh century is in fact known to historians,[38] was the authority to whom Ibn Abī Uṣaybiʿa traced this bibliographical information, and not as Gerhard Endress has suggested, the one whom the bio-bibliographer claimed had commissioned the work in the first place, which, of course, is impossible given the eighty year span between Yaḥyā and the time of Abū Ṭālib, as Endress notes. In any event, from another perspective, Gerhard Endress, who in his own bibliography of Yaḥyā's works listed the work mentioned by Ibn ʿAbī Uṣaybiʿa under

[32] See Vincent Mistrih's introduction to the text in *Traité sur la continence*, p. 4-6.

[33] See *Traité sur la continence*, p. 40, §77 (Arabic) and p. 103 (French).

[34] See Périer, *Yaḥyā ben ʿAdī*, p. 71, n. 2.

[35] Samir Khalil, review of Endress, *The Works of Yaḥyā b. ʿAdī*, in: *Bulletin d'arabe chrétien* 3 (1979), p. 50.

[36] Endress, *The Works of Yaḥyā b. ʿAdī*, p. 124, interprets Ibn Abī Uṣaybiʿa's phrase, *bi-ḥasb iqtirāḥ al-sharīf*, to mean that Abū Ṭālib commissioned Yaḥyā to produce the work in question.

[37] Ibn Abī Uṣaybiʿa, *Ṭabaqat al-Aṭibbāʾ*, I, p. 235.

[38] See the reference to Ibn Khallikān in Endress, *The Works of Yaḥyā b. ʿAdī*, p. 124.

medical works, citing Yaḥyā's confessed incompetence in medicine, suggested that 'this treatise may have been ethical rather than strictly medical'.[39] But Vincent Mistrih, the editor of the complete, composite work, alluding to the title given by Ibn Abī Uṣaybiʿa, says:

> A juger de ce titre, il paraît qu'il s'agit d'un ouvrage tout à fait different. Car l'écrit sur la continence traite seulement indirectement des avantages et des inconvénients de la relation sexuelle.[40]

One can only say that in the judgement of the present reader, the text in fact has everything to do with the personal, social and philosophical advantages and disadvantages of sexual relations, on the part of someone who seeks 'true wisdom and godly science', albeit that it is not at all concerned with such physiological and pathological details of sexual engagement as the misleading listing of the text under medical works might at first suggest.

Much of the confusion surrounding the proper identification of this composite work by Yaḥyā b. ʿAdī seems in fact to spring from the several titles scholars have over the years assigned to the several parts of it, as well as to derive from their difficulties in recognizing its three parts as constituents of a single, composite work. Angelus Mai, not unreasonably, spoke of the text in its two abbreviated forms as being concerned with celibacy (*de caelibatu*).[41] Georg Graf, in his full description of the manuscript of the Coptic Patriarchate which contains the work, the parts of which he clearly recognizes, says somewhat inscrutably that it is a treatise by Yaḥyā b. ʿAdī 'sur la préférence des enfants et leur négligence', followed by 'trois questions qui lui furent posées par un ami, sur la procréation des enfants et leur predestination à aspirer à la science'.[42] Then in his monumental *Geschichte der christlichen arabischen Literatur*, when listing the works of Yaḥyā b. ʿAdī, Graf unaccountably mentions in one place only the two abbreviated recensions of the parts of the work in the two Vatican manuscripts, saying, after Mai, that they have to do with 'Rechtfertigung des Zölibates'. In another place in the *Geschichte*, citing the Cairo manuscript of the full text, he then supplies the misleading notice that the text is 'Über die Erziehung der Kinder'.[43]

[39] ENDRESS, *The Works of Yaḥyā b. ʿAdī*, p. 124.

[40] *Traité sur la continence*, p. 4.

[41] See MAI, *Scriptorum Veterum Nova Collectio*, IV, p. 234 and 260.

[42] GRAF, *Catalogue de manuscripts arabes chrétiens conservés au Caire*, p. 153.

[43] GEORG GRAF, *Geschichte der christlichen arabischen Literatur* (*Studi e Testi*, 118, 133, 146, 147 and 172), II, Città del Vaticano: Biblioteca Apostolica Vaticana, 1944-1953, p. 246 and 248.

Next, Samir Khalil, on the basis of a close analysis of the Vatican manuscript copies of the two abbreviations of Yaḥyā's work, identified what he called 'trois texts distincts: *maqāla fī ḥāl tark al-nasl*; *mukhāṭaba bayna ṣadīqayn fī maʿnā-hā*; et un *sans titre*'.[44] Finally, recognizing the integrity of the composite work, Vincent Mistrih speaks of it as Yaḥyā's *Traité sur la continence*. But this title, once again, by reason of its generality, obscures the full range of the text's actual subject matter. It is for this reason that the present writer assigns the work the descriptive title: *On Sexual Abstinence and the Philosophical Life*. This title, albeit that it includes none of Yaḥyā's own wording, at least has the virtue of suggesting the work's actual subject matter. It announces a discussion of the value of abstaining from seeking to procreate in the precise setting of the ongoing conversation among philosophers in Yaḥyā's milieu about how one who is determined to live the philosophical life should manage the human urge to procreate.

The three interrelated parts of the composite work are as follows:

1) An initial 'treatise' (*maqāla*) in which Yaḥyā b. ʿAdī sets out his line of reasoning in affirmation of the practice of abstaining from seeking to procreate on the part of those properly disposed to seek the happiness that is the attainment of 'true science and godly wisdom'.[45]
2) Quotations by Yaḥyā b. ʿAdī from a note or 'communication' (*mukhāṭaba*) from one of his friends to another one, followed by Yaḥyā's own comments on the issues raised in the correspondence. The anonymous writer of the communication had objected to the unknown addressee's understanding of arguments put forward by the writer in connection with the ideas advanced in Yaḥyā's treatise. At the end are three questions which Yaḥyā then posed for the correspondents on the subject in hand.[46]
3) A transcript or 'copy' (*nuskha*) of the interlocutor's reply to Yaḥyā's three questions, along with Yaḥyā's rebuttal of them and further clarifications of his main points.[47] It is at the beginning of this portion of the work that Yaḥyā mentions the date, 'the night of day two, the tenth night of *Muḥarram*, of the year 353',[48] i.e., Monday, 28 January

[44] SAMIR KHALIL, review of ENDRESS, *The Works of Yaḥyā b. ʿAdī*, p. 57.

[45] *Traité sur la continence*, p. 14-28, §§1-41 (Arabic) and p. 65-85 (French).

[46] *Traité sur la continence*, p. 28-40, §§42-77 (Arabic) and p. 86-103 (French).

[47] *Traité sur la continence*, p. 40-64, §§77-135 (Arabic) and p. 103-137 (French).

[48] *Traité sur la continence*, p. 40, §77 (Arabic) and p. 103 (French). Note that GRAF, *Catalogue de manuscripts arabes chrétiens*, p. 153, mistakenly identifies the day as Tuesday (*mardi*).

964 AD. At the end, Yaḥyā refers to 'the treatise (*maqāla*) I have produced on this subject',[49] presumably a reference to the initial portion of the composite work, which he now says he hopes his interlocutor will read with the conviction of its truthfulness, and with all his doubts dispelled.

This composite work in its several sections affords the modern reader a measure of historical insight into the process of interreligious, philosophical colloquy in Baghdad in the middle quarters of the Tenth Century, over an issue that was of concern to both Muslims and Christians, although each community had different points of view to commend in the matter. Religiously motivated celibacy, especially in the context of monasticism, had long been a highly esteemed value among Christians. Among the Muslims of Yaḥyā b. ʿAdī's day both Qur'ān and *Ḥadīth* were widely thought to reject monasticism and its privations, primarily celibacy, in the Qur'ān both nominally (e.g., in Q. 57:27 [*al-Ḥadīd*]) and in principle: 'Do not forbid the good things that Allah has made lawful to you' (Q. 5:87 [*al-Mā'ida*]); and in traditions variously stating the often quoted dictum, 'There is no monasticism in Islam'.[50] So it is not surprising that at the very beginning of his treatise Yaḥyā speaks of 'the Christian promoters' (*dāʿī l-naṣārā*)[51] of abstaining from seeking to propagate, the *daʿwa* of the Christians, as he then several times calls his position,[52] and of 'the opponents of the Christians' (*al-mukhālifū li-l-naṣārā*)[53] who are his presumably Muslim adversaries in this matter. But in spite of these kinds of religious allusions, mostly at the beginning of the treatise, the arguments on both sides are put forward along philosophical lines, as we shall see, including references to philosophical figures of the past such as the Arab philosopher Abū Yūsuf Yaʿqūb b. Isḥāq al-Kindī (d. ca 252/866),[54] and, of course, Socrates, Plato and Aristotle.[55] At one point Yaḥyā mentions a book that he presumes his interlocutors

[49] *Traité sur la continence*, p. 64, §135 (Arabic) and p. 136-137 (French).

[50] See in particular SARA SVIRI, Wa-rahbānīyatan ibtadaʿūhā: *an Analysis of Traditions Concerning the Origin and Evaluation of Christian Monasticism*, in: *Jerusalem Studies in Arabic and Islam* 13 (1990), p. 195-208. For further bibliography see n. 23 above and SIDNEY H. GRIFFITH, *Monasticism and Monks*, in: *Encyclopaedia of the Qur'ān*, ed. JANE D. MCAULIFFE, III, Leiden: E.J. Brill, 2003, p. 405-408.

[51] *Traité sur la continence*, p. 14, §1.8 (Arabic), p. 16, §9.8 (Arabic), p. 19, §15.1 (Arabic).

[52] *Traité sur la continence*, passim, p. 14-28 (Arabic).

[53] *Traité sur la continence*, p. 14, §2.1 (Arabic).

[54] See, e.g., *Traité sur la continence*, p. 43, §88.4 (Arabic) and p. 108 (French).

[55] See, e.g., *Traité sur la continence*, p. 46, §§95-96 (Arabic) and p. 112-113 (French).

know and respect, *The Book of the Syllogism* (*Kitāb al-Qiyās*), the Arabic title normally assigned at the time to Aristotle's *Prior Analytics*. Yaḥyā, his teacher Abū Bishr Mattā b. Yūnus, and presumably his students, were all involved in the effort to improve the Arabic version of this work and in commenting on the text.[56] At one point Yaḥyā, without mentioning Porphyry by name, refers to a passage in the *Eisagoge*, a work which he calls *al-Madkhal* ('the introduction') in Arabic,[57] rather than using the usual transliterated title, *Īsāghūjī*. Both Yaḥyā and one of his interlocutors mention the prophets and the Messiah;[58] there is an allusion to Muḥammad without naming him[59] and even a mention of Alexander the Great.[60] But the reasoning is neither religious nor theological; the persons mentioned are presented as models of the philosophical life.

A very interesting feature of the work is that Yaḥyā b. ʿAdī's treatise is textually presented together with the responses of his interlocutors, along with his replies back to them in turn, thereby allowing the modern reader a virtual glimpse into a living, inter-communal discourse from the past in progress, suggesting that for Yaḥyā and his friends the conversation was itself the philosophy, or perhaps that philosophy was the idiom of the conversation. One learns that notes were sent back and forth among conversation partners in reaction to a prepared text, and even that respondents were invited to write their responses on the backs of the pages that carried the thoughts to which they were reacting in the first place.[61] All the portions of the conversation are presented in their integrity in the ensemble, rather than just the gist of the several interventions being folded into the principal author's singular discourse. The composite format of the work preserves its character as a work rooted in the living, conversational give and take of a Tenth Century Baghdad philosophical circle in action. It is for

[56] See *Traité sur la continence*, p. 16, §9.3 (Arabic) and p. 69 (French). On Yaḥyā's role in the study and transmission of the Arabic version of the *Prior Analytics*, see RICHARD WALZER, *New Light on the Arabic Translations of Aristotle*, in: *Oriens* 6 (1953), p. 102-128, esp. p. 108-111. Vincent Mistrih, seemingly mistakenly, identifies the *Kitāb al-Qiyās* as a work of al-Fārābī: see *Traité sur la continence*, p. 69, n. 1.

[57] See *Traité sur la continence*, p. 52, §111.10 (Arabic) and p. 121 (French). Mistrih seems to have missed the reference. He simply translates *al-Madkhal* as 'prolegomènes', without comment.

[58] See, e.g., *Traité sur la continence*, p. 46, §95.6, p. 61, §129.3 and §130.6 (Arabic) and p. 112, 132, 133 (French).

[59] See *Traité sur la continence*, p. 46, §97.1 (Arabic) and p. 113 (French).

[60] See *Traité sur la continence*, p. 46, §95.8 (Arabic) and p. 112 (French).

[61] See *Traité sur la continence*, p. 40, §78.3 (Arabic) and p. 103 (French).

this reason that one may think of the finished, composite text not just as a transcript of an antecedent conversation, but as a discourse in its own right, a colloquy in writing on sexual abstinence and the philosophical life.

2. The Text and its Arguments

The Treatise

The treatise opens with a brief announcement of the *status quaestionis*. Yaḥyā says that philosophers (*ahl al-naẓar*) differ with one another in approving of what he calls 'being alone' (*tafarrud*) or 'staying single' (*tawaḥḥud*), which he then somewhat abstractly defines as 'avoiding involvement in seeking to procreate'.[62] He says that some people adopt this behaviour without any intention of cultivating a virtue that would lead them closer to God. Rather, he says, their purpose in remaining single is to acquire a virtue which is specific to man, i.e., 'to perfect his form, which is the rational power, and to bring it into practice by acquiring true science and godly wisdom'.[63] Other people, he says, make the generation of offspring an obligation and they claim that not to do so is contrary to what God intended when He equipped man with the generative power in the first place. And, according to Yaḥyā, these people take this fact to be proof that whoever abstains from procreation is thereby 'at variance with God, inimical to Him and loathsome to Him'.[64] As a matter of fact, Yaḥyā goes on to say, this is the very charge that is brought against the Christian promoters of abstinence. So, he states, 'it is our purpose in this treatise to clarify which of these two tenets is sound, and which of the two behaviours is virtuous'.[65] He unfolds his case in two parts in the main body of the treatise. In the first part he states the positions of his adversaries and offers refutations of them based on what he claims is their faulty logic;[66] in the second part he advances his own positive argument on behalf of what he represents as the Christian position.[67]

[62] *Traité sur la continence*, p. 14, §1.2 (Arabic) and p. 65 (French).
[63] *Traité sur la continence*, p. 14, §1.3-4 (Arabic) and p. 65 (French).
[64] *Traité sur la continence*, p. 14, §1.7 (Arabic) and p. 65 (French).
[65] *Traité sur la continence*, p. 14, §1.9 (Arabic) and p. 65-66 (French).
[66] See *Traité sur la continence*, p. 14-21, §§2-23 (Arabic) and p. 66-76 (French).
[67] See *Traité sur la continence*, p. 21-28, §§24-40 (Arabic) and p. 77-85 (French).

Part One

The first section of the first part of the treatise comprises Yaḥyā's rehearsal of the main lines of argument put forward by his adversaries. He summarizes them as consisting of four basic contentions. First the 'opponents of the Christians' are alleged to have argued that since both they and the Christians agree that God is 'wise' (*ḥakīm*), He could not therefore be thought to have done anything futile or profitless. The fact is, He created man with the power to generate offspring, the profitable benefit of which is the survival of progeny and the stability of the world. Whatever or whoever would prevent human reproduction is therefore opposed to God. So the 'Christian promoters' of abstinence may then be considered to be opposed to God and even 'detestable to Him' (*maqīt ʿinda-hu*).[68]

Next Yaḥyā says that the adversaries cite the truism that the existence of anything is better that its non-existence, entailing the consequence that whatever is not good for an existing thing is therefore detrimental to it. And from this premise they proceed to draw the conclusion that in regard to the existence of the human species, anything that would frustrate its continuance, such as the practice of abstaining from procreation, must therefore be considered to be detrimental to the human species.[69]

In this same connection, Yaḥyā goes on to say that the adversaries call upon the mutual affirmation of God's 'bountiful goodness' (*al-jūd*), which the divine attribute 'bountifully good' (*jawād*) bespeaks of Him, an affirmation which Yaḥyā says is explained in 'other places',[70] to argue that it is due to His bountiful goodness that God wills the existence of the human species. Therefore, anyone who would pose an obstacle to what God wills regarding the existence of the human species, such as proposing to abstain from procreation, would clearly be acting in opposition to God in His bountiful goodness and thereby such a person would become loathsome to God.[71]

[68] See *Traité sur la continence*, p. 14-15, §3.1-6, p. 14-15 (Arabic) and p. 66 (French).

[69] See *Traité sur la continence*, p. 15, §4.1-4 (Arabic) and p. 66-67 (French).

[70] This reference to 'other places' (*mawāḍiʿ ukhar*) seems to refer to other places in Yaḥyā b. ʿAdī's own works, in the context of his on-going discussions with Muslim intellectuals. The most likely place in this instance would be in his treatise on the unity of God, *al-tawḥīd*, where in fact he speaks at some length of God's 'bounteous goodness' precisely in the context of God's being the cause of bringing created beings into 'existence' from 'non-existence': See KHALIL SAMIR, *Le traité de l'unité de Yaḥyā b. ʿAdī (893-974)* (*Patrimoine Arabe Chrétien*, 2), Rome: Pontificio Istituto Orientale and Jounieh: Librairie Saint-Paul, 1980, p. 248-256 (Arabic). Vincent Mistrih also speaks of Yaḥyā's use of the concept of *jūd* in his apologetic treatises on the incarnation: see *Traité sur la continence*, p. 67, n. 1.

[71] *Traité sur la continence*, p. 15, §5.1-5 (Arabic) and p. 67 (French).

Finally, according to Yaḥyā, the adversaries contend that on the basis of the logical implications of the acceptance of the premise that existence is better than non-existence, in the matter of the existence of the human species, whoever contributes to its increase is good and whoever contributes to its decrease is bad. Therefore, those who will to engage in the propagation of the species are to be considered good, and pleasing to God, while those who espouse abstinence from procreation are to be considered bad, and inimical to God.[72]

Having thus given an account of 'the arguments of the opponents of the Christians', Yaḥyā says that he will proceed to expose 'the weakness of the fallacies of the opponents of the Christians', and to make clear 'the invalidity of their specious [arguments]', before 'affirming the true view, which will be a cure for their [sick] convictions'.[73] Then straightaway, Yaḥyā unveils the major argument he will deploy against the allegations of the adversaries, as he has presented them in the treatise. He says, 'all their syllogisms inevitably comprise false premisses'.[74] He then reminds the reader that it has already been made clear in *The Book of the Syllogism*[75] that syllogisms which are constructed in whole or in part of false premisses cannot yield true conclusions. And the principal false premise introduced by the adversaries in their first argument, Yaḥyā contends, is their allegation that the call of the Christians is absolutely and without qualification for abstinence from seeking to procreate. Rather, he says, the Christian appeal for this abstinence is made with the prior understanding that it calls people to practise it within the parameters of the need for everyone,

> To devote himself throughout his whole life to what is best for himself, which is to maximize the circumstances conducive to happiness (which is true science and godly wisdom) and not to be distracted from proceeding toward it unless by something inevitable, without which there would be no subsistence in his life. He should be eager to come to this point and to attain it.[76]

As the sequel will show the operative phrase here for Yaḥyā is: 'Not to be distracted ... unless by something inevitable (*illā bi-mā lā budd minhu*)'. For he goes on to argue that within the framework of the larger purpose, Christians promote abstinence from seeking to procreate as a

[72] *Traité sur la continence*, p. 15-16, §§6-7 (Arabic) and p. 67-68 (French).
[73] *Traité sur la continence*, p. 16, §8.1-7 (Arabic) and p. 68-69 (French).
[74] *Traité sur la continence*, p. 16, §9.2 (Arabic) and p. 69 (French).
[75] For the identity of this book see n. 56 above.
[76] *Traité sur la continence*, p. 16, §9.10-12 (Arabic) and p. 69-70 (French).

time and energy saving device in the pursuit of happiness. It is a practice 'to which necessity pushes whoever has the capacity for it and intends to do it'.[77] And it is a practice that one 'seeks and employs only for the sake of attaining something else by means of his employment of it'.[78] As a matter of fact, Yaḥyā says that not everyone has a capacity for sexual abstinence. He says that for some people abstention is easy and they avoid even thinking about sex, let alone being actually engaged in it. But other people are obsessed with sexual intercourse and 'if they curtail it, vehement maladies afflict them which encompass all their natural, animal and rational powers'.[79] So these people, Yaḥyā says, 'when they engage in it in proportion to their need for it, ... become more fit for achieving happiness than they would have been had they not made use of it'.[80] What is more, there are both categories of people in the world, according to Yaḥyā, so there is no danger that the propagation of the human species will in fact be neglected. Therefore, he argues, what the Christians promote in no way entails the extinction of the human species, and so they cannot on these grounds, rightly or logically be reckoned to be adversaries of God and consequently abominable in His sight.[81]

Likewise, Yaḥyā claims that the second argument put forward by his adversaries also rests on false or partially false premisses. To accept the truism absolutely that the existence of something is better than its non-existence, and to argue on this basis that whoever would impede the existence of what God prefers to exist, such as human progeny, is an adversary of God and hateful to Him, is logically false. For, Yaḥyā points out, one who does something God wants even more than He wants procreation, as is the case with one abstaining from the desire to procreate in the rational pursuit of happiness, is in no way to be at variance with God's will, nor to be abominable in His sight.[82]

According to Yaḥyā, his adversaries' third argument also rests on false premisses. It involves the allegation that since the non-existence of an entity can be considered an evil for it, those who renounce procreation are therefore engaged in bringing about the evil of the non-existence of

[77] *Traité sur la continence*, p. 17, §10.2 (Arabic) and p. 70 (French).
[78] *Traité sur la continence*, p. 17, §12.6 (Arabic) and p. 71 (French).
[79] *Traité sur la continence*, p. 18, §13.13 (Arabic) and p. 72 (French).
[80] *Traité sur la continence*, p. 18, §13.18 (Arabic) and p. 72 (French).
[81] See *Traité sur la continence*, p.18-19, §§14-15 (Arabic) and p. 72-73 (French).
[82] See *Traité sur la continence*, p. 19, §16 (Arabic) and p. 73 (French).

the human species. Yaḥyā says this is evidently not the case, because even if all those capable of foregoing involvement in the act of propagation were in fact to abstain from it, their action would not be sufficient to lead inevitably to the non-existence of human beings. He then offers a two-fold, corroborative line of reasoning for his rejection of this argument, on the one hand proceeding from the assumption that his adversary is a monotheist who rejects the philosophical doctrine of the eternity of the world, and on the other hand assuming that the adversary affirms that doctrine.

Yaḥyā points out that a monotheist, who to begin with espouses the doctrine of the divine creation of the world from non-being, could argue that even if *per impossible* everyone decided to devote his life to attaining happiness and therefore gave up procreation, if God nevertheless wanted the human race to continue, 'He could create individual human beings, just as He created the first father for humankind, Adam'.[83] Therefore, abstinence from procreation, even if everyone were to practise it, in no way necessarily entails the non-existence of the human species. Alternatively, a philosopher who accepts the doctrine that the world is 'eternal' or 'primordial' (*qadīm*), and wants to show that abstention from procreating does not inevitably require the non-existence of the human species, should know that the doctrine itself entails the corollary that all the natural species, mankind included, are likewise eternal/primordial and incorruptible (*ghayr fāsid*). For the doctrine of the eternity of the world, Yaḥyā argues, would make the agreement of every human person to abstain from procreating impossible. To abstain would be impossible for them, he says, 'due to the victory over them of the youthful drive (*ṣabwa*) [to procreate]'.[84] So, Yaḥyā reasons, the premise in his adversaries' argument claiming that personal abstention from propagation conduces to the non-existence of the human species is false.

Yaḥyā's evocation in this passage of both monotheists who acknowledge 'the coming-to-be of the world' (*ḥudūth al-ʿālam*), which he says is the case,[85] and of those for whom the world is eternal or primordial, is not just an anachronistic bid for logical completeness on his part. It reflects his awareness of the range of opinions current in his own philosophical milieu in tenth century Baghdad. Both al-Rāzī, and al-Fārābī, Yaḥyā's own teacher, espoused some form of the doctrine of the eternity

[83] *Traité sur la continence*, p. 20, §18.7 (Arabic) and p. 74 (French).
[84] *Traité sur la continence*, p. 20, §20.5 (Arabic) and p. 75 (French).
[85] See *Traité sur la continence*, p. 20, §18.4 (Arabic) and p. 74 (French).

of the world, and so presumably did some of their students who would have been Yaḥyā's contemporaries and dialogue partners.[86]

According to Yaḥyā b. ʿAdī, his adversaries' fourth argument includes premisses that he claims are false in part, and therefore he argues that they are incapable of yielding a true conclusion. The principal advanced by the adversaries alleges that 'to increase any good thing is good and to diminish it is bad'.[87] Yaḥyā then advances reasons why the premisses based on this principal are in his judgement partially false. In the first place, he points out that there are situations in which more is not better, nor is it less bad, but the contrary is in fact sometimes the case. He offers examples. Secondly, he argues that it would not be good for someone to engage in procreation if he were a person capable of foregoing it easily and without harm to himself, for the sake of the pursuit of happiness, for reasons already put forward. Thirdly, it is not true that everyone who abstains from procreating does something wrong, because, as was already shown, his action is predicated on the pursuit of a higher good, willed by God for everyone whom He has created capable of it.[88] Finally, Yaḥyā claims it is clear to anyone who understands the correct logic of the syllogism that a conclusion drawn from such flawed premisses as those he has exposed cannot necessarily be true. And he intends this judgement to apply to all four of the main arguments that he says his adversaries customarily mount against the Christian position. With this claim, the first part of the treatise comes to an end.

Part Two

Yaḥyā b. ʿAdī devotes the second part of the treatise to substantiating and commending what he says the Christians commend in the matter at hand:

> To be singly concerned to pursue happiness and to refrain from being distracted from it in pursuit of procreation.[89]

He begins with what he takes to be an unassailable truism, namely that 'the intellect is the most estimable [faculty] with which man is endowed'.[90] It is

[86] See JOEL L. KRAEMER, *Philosophy in the Renaissance of Islam: Abū Sulaymān al-Sijistānī and his Circle*, Leiden: E.J. Brill, 1986, p. 198-200; LENN EVAN GOODMAN, *Islamic Humanism*, Oxford: Oxford University Press, 2003, p. 130-132.

[87] *Traité sur la continence*, p. 21, §21.3 (Arabic) and p. 75 (French).

[88] See *Traité sur la continence*, p. 21, §§21-23 (Arabic) and p. 75-76 (French).

[89] See *Traité sur la continence*, p. 22, §24.2 (Arabic) and p. 77 (French).

[90] See *Traité sur la continence*, p. 22, §25 (Arabic) and p. 77 (French).

naturally fit for the reception of science and knowledge. And given the fact that a faculty is more estimable in act than in mere potency, it follows for Yaḥyā that the best human person would be the one actually most well equipped with science and knowledge. Now given the fact that God 'prefers, chooses and wills only that each human person attain what is best for him', it follows, according to Yaḥyā, that God does not will for anyone what would prevent him from attaining what is best for him. And at this point he raises the issue of how readily, in his judgement, a concern to procreate can present an obstacle to the pursuit of human happiness.

Yaḥyā goes into considerable detail in his description of the magnitude of the obstacle to the attainment of knowledge and science that child rearing and family life can pose for someone who in fact naturally has the capacity to abstain from it.[91] He makes the point that the impediments, some of which he goes on to mention, do not present just a small or moderate obstacle. 'Rather', he says, 'it is the highest degree of hindrance and the most extreme'.[92] So, given the premisses that, 'everything that helps the acquisition of a virtue is good, and everything which impedes the acquisition of the most virtuous virtue is bad',[93] and that whatever is bad is displeasing to God, Yaḥyā concludes that, 'everyone who brings children to birth in pursuit of progeny, when to do so is devoid of virtue, is detestable to God (*maqīt ʿinda Allāh*)'.[94] The reader immediately recognizes that with this conclusion Yaḥyā has reversed the charge that his philosophical adversaries, presumably Muslims, had initially leveled against the Christian position he supports, and in the very same words.[95] And so Yaḥyā comes to affirm what he says he wanted all along to make clear: 'Having children in pursuit of progeny, in the absence of any virtue that would bring one nearer to God, is not a virtue'.[96]

Finally, at the end of the treatise, Yaḥyā b. ʿAdī is concerned to show that the position defended by Christians in favor of the virtuous character of a lifelong abstention from procreation does not logically entail the acceptance of the theoretical possibility of the cessation of the human race, seemingly against God's apparent will to the contrary, as his adversaries had argued. He points out that God, in His infinite bounty (*jūd*),

[91] *Traité sur la continence*, p. 24, §§30-31 (Arabic) and p. 80-81 (French).

[92] *Traité sur la continence*, p. 24, §30.2 (Arabic) and p. 80 (French); p. 25, §32.3, (Arabic) and p. 81 (French).

[93] *Traité sur la continence*, p. 25, §34.2 (Arabic) and p. 82 (French).

[94] *Traité sur la continence*, p. 25, §34.9 (Arabic) and p. 82 (French).

[95] See the text cited at n. 63 above.

[96] *Traité sur la continence*, p. 26, §37.7 (Arabic) and p. 83 (French).

has created a world in which none of the species (*aṣnāf*) of His creatures has in fact ever been destroyed. That is because they are endowed with various temperaments (*amzija*), Yaḥyā says, according to which certain practices are easy for some of them to accomplish, while for others they are difficult. In the human instance, some people can easily practise sexual abstinence and others cannot, and this will always be the case. So Yaḥyā concludes, given the reality of this state of affairs, even if most people were to heed the call to choose what he thinks he has shown to be the better part and practise sexual abstention, there would remain the innate safeguard against the cessation of the human species and the decomposition of the world.[97] And therefore, he somewhat audaciously claims at the very end of the treatise, 'From what we have said, the invalidity of the opinion of the adversaries has become clear'.[98] And Yaḥyā gives praise to God.

3. The Communication of Objections

Once Yaḥyā b. ʿAdī's treatise was in circulation among his partners in philosophical conversation, one of them wrote to another about his thoughts on the subject. The communication came to Yaḥyā's attention and he wrote a report of the flow of the argumentation contained in it.

Yaḥyā's Report

The writer called attention to the role reproduction plays in safeguarding the species of living beings, but he protested that he did not in his own conversation mean that it is the noblest faculty. Rather, he agreed that one must perfect it and the other human faculties by means of the noblest enactment, 'that is the use of reason'.[99] And in connection with the God-given power of reproduction and child rearing, the writer reminded his addressee that 'human virtue is the mean between two extremes in every single human faculty'.[100] Consequently, he said that with the faculty of reproduction, 'continence (*al-ʿiffa*) ... is taking part in what one must take part in, in enacting this faculty, and not just abstention'.[101]

[97] See *Traité sur la continence*, p. 26-28, §§38-40 (Arabic) and p. 83-85 (French).
[98] *Traité sur la continence*, p. 28, §41.1 (Arabic) and p. 85 (French).
[99] *Traité sur la continence*, p. 29, §44.6 (Arabic) and p. 87 (French).
[100] *Traité sur la continence*, p. 29-30, §45.5 (Arabic) and p. 88 (French).
[101] *Traité sur la continence*, p. 30, §45.8 (Arabic) and p. 88 (French).

Finally, because of the nobility of the human species, the writer reasoned that it is better for there to be more rather than fewer human beings, because the well-being of the temporal order, he says, is proportional to the larger number of human beings. So an increase in the number of humans is an increase in good.[102] And he reasoned that it is a good that offsets whatever undesirable effects the vicissitudes of procreation and child rearing might generate. For, he wrote, he is not unmindful of the following doctrine:

> Of the works of philosophy, after the governance of the household there is then the governance of the city, then the governance of many cities, which is the apogee of the works of philosophy, in which the prophets specialize, peace be upon them, along with the just *imāms* and the righteous kings.[103]

The writer of the communication expressed his desire to discuss these matters in a face to face conversation, concluding in the light of the doctrine he had just enunciated that since procreation and child rearing are communal values and not just personal ones, it ought not be the case that 'we would abstain from enacting what is good for the majority, due to our fear of what is bad only rarely, I mean the minimal hindrance of child-bearing'.[104]

One notices in particular that the writer of the communication which Yāḥyā epitomizes brought the discussion of the moral value of abstention from procreation ultimately into the context of what he called 'the apogee of the works of philosophy'.[105] This frame of reference, that of the governance of cities, echoes one of the principal concerns of al-Fārābī,[106] the teacher *par excellence* of Yaḥyā's whole generation of philosophers. That the writer was a Muslim seems evident from the tenor of his remarks. Meanwhile, although Yaḥyā had the text of the writer's communication, he had no access to the text of the remarks of the writer's original addressee.[107]

[102] See *Traité sur la continence*, p. 30-31, §47.1-6 (Arabic) and p. 89 (French).

[103] *Traité sur la continence*, p. 31, §49.2-3 (Arabic) and p. 90 (French). MISTRIH translates this passage as follows: 'D'après (la classification) philosophique des activités, après le régime personnel vient celui de la maison, ensuite celui d'une ville et enfin celui de plusieurs villes, ce dernier étant le sommet de l'activité philosophique, reservée aux prophètes — à eux la paix! — aux imams justes et aux rois équitables'. I cannot find anything in the Arabic to correspond to the phrase: 'après le régime personnel'.

[104] *Traité sur la continence*, p. 31, §49.5 (Arabic) and p. 90 (French).

[105] *Traité sur la continence*, p. 31, §49.3 (Arabic) and p. 90 (French).

[106] See MUHSIN S. MAHDI, *Alfarabi and the Foundation of Islamic Political Philosophy*, Chicago: The University of Chicago Press, 2001, esp. p. 125-146.

[107] See Yaḥyā's complaint in this regard, registered in *Traité sur la continence*, p. 32, §52.5 (Arabic) and p. 91 (French).

Yaḥyā's Response

In his response to the text he has just summarized, Yaḥyā characterizes the contents of it as 'argumentation on behalf of the opinion of those who privilege the generation of children over abstention from it'.[108] And although he says he wishes he could win them over to his own point of view, he would yield to them, he says, if they could convince him otherwise. Then he proceeds to point out what he considers to be crucial logical fallacies in their arguments.

The first of the logical failures, Yaḥyā says, is that no proof is offered for the writer's allegation that 'the faculty of reproduction is [a feature of] genuine wisdom',[109] an assumption that grounds the opinion that privileges procreation over abstention as a work of philosophy. Even if it were true, he then argues, even along with an appeal to the assumption that God has not created any faculty for naught, it does not necessarily rule out the devotion of oneself to science, to the exclusion of procreation, as the better course of action.[110] Next Yaḥyā points out that the writer's appeal to the principle that 'virtue stands in the middle', cannot be used as a premise in a syllogism because it cannot be taken absolutely. Furthermore, he argues that given the fact that the pursuit of 'godly wisdom and true knowledge' is the highest human goal, and the fact that the vicissitudes of parenthood, when 'devoid of any virtue to bring one nearer to God',[111] constitute an obstacle to that pursuit, as shown in the *Treatise*, he concludes that one cannot then argue that moderation in procreation is preferable to abstention from it altogether.

It is only at this point in his remarks in response to his reader's reaction to his *Treatise* that Yaḥyā provides some insight into his own understanding of when the pursuit of procreation might be morally preferable to abstention. He says,

> [The pursuit of procreation] is devoid of any virtue to bring one closer to God when it is devoid of any intention to generate a prophet, a just king, a distinguished priest, or a skillful physician (*ḥakīm*), or any intention to eliminate an illness, or to take precautions against falling into a sickness, which would prevent anyone whom it would afflict from achieving the acquisition of the highest degree of true knowledge of which he is capable.[112]

[108] *Traité sur la continence*, p. 31, §50.1 (Arabic) and p. 90 (French).

[109] *Traité sur la continence*, p. 29 and 32, §44.1 and §52.2 (Arabic) and p. 87 and 91 (French): *quwwat al-ithmār hiya min maḥḍ al-ḥikma*.

[110] See *Traité sur la continence*, p. 32-33, §53.1-8 (Arabic) and p. 92-93 (French).

[111] *Traité sur la continence*, p. 35, §58.5 (Arabic) and p. 95 (French).

[112] *Traité sur la continence*, p. 35, §59.2-3 (Arabic) and p. 96 (French).

Put more positively, for Yaḥyā, procreation is only preferable to abstention from it when one intends to bring a prophet, priest or king to birth, or intends thereby to preserve his own health. The reader notes here in particular Yaḥyā's implicit reference to the concerns of his teacher, al-Fārābī for 'the virtuous city', noted above, and his introduction of a Christian motif, 'distinguished priest', alongside the Islamic provision for a prophet and a just king. In the sequel, Yaḥyā pursues a long digression in which he analyzes examples which the writer of the communication he is examining had used to clarify his meaning. Yaḥyā calls attention to what he argues are the shortcomings involved in the examples, and he reaffirms the positions he is confident of having established in his *Treatise*. He concludes that he has proven, at least to his own satisfaction, that

> A large number of human beings are not a good, if the large number conduces to the absence or weakening of wisdom, or lowering the number of those possessing it.[113]

He is speaking here, one supposes, about what, in his opinion, would be good or bad for the body politic at large.

Yaḥyā ends his response to the writer's communication by posing three questions to him. They may be paraphrased as follows: which of two men is the most virtuous, one who labours all his life for 'true wisdom and godly knowledge', abstaining from procreation so as to attain as much knowledge as possible, or one who is preoccupied with expending as much as is humanly possible on having children?[114] Which of two historical eras is the best, and which of two populations is happiest, those in which most people are concerned with the acquisition of knowledge, without giving much thought to procreation, or those in which people have as many children as possible, with no time left for the pursuit of knowledge?[115] Which is the best and happiest of human conditions (*aḥwāl*), that in which 'the number of wise men who do not procreate exceeds the number of unwise procreators' or the reverse?[116] Yaḥyā then closes this component of his composite work with an expression of confidence that his interlocutor will not think any differently in this matter than Yaḥyā himself thinks, once he has given it more careful consideration.

[113] *Traité sur la continence*, p. 39, §73.9-10 (Arabic) and p. 101 (French).
[114] See *Traité sur la continence*, p. 39, §74.1-4 (Arabic) and p. 101-102 (French).
[115] See *Traité sur la continence*, p. 39, §75.1-3 (Arabic) and p. 102 (French).
[116] See *Traité sur la continence*, p. 39, §76.1-4 (Arabic) and p. 102 (French).

The Interlocutor's Reply and Yaḥyā's Rebuttal

In due course, Yaḥyā b. ʿAdī's interlocutor replied to the three questions. Yaḥyā then followed his usual practice of first providing what he calls a 'copy' or 'transcript' (*nuskha*) of his friend's text, before offering his own rebuttal. In his prefatory remarks to this third, and longest component of the composite work, Yaḥyā recorded the date, 'Monday, the 10th night of Muḥarram, of the year 353',[117] i.e., 964 AD.

The Interlocutor's Reply

Yaḥyā's interlocutor asks for a private response from the master, preferably, he says, on the back of his own text.[118] He notes that the two of them are very close in their opinions, and he expresses his understanding that Yaḥyā does not promote abstention from procreation absolutely, but only according to the capacities of individual seekers after knowledge and wisdom. The writer makes a special plea for the case of a man of moderate constitution, whose bodily needs may be overly insistent. Surely, he reasons, such a person might responsibly devote a modicum of his time to procreation, thereby reserving the better part of his life-span for 'the works of the mind and of reflective discrimination'.[119]

The correspondent deals rather quickly with his reply to the three questions Yaḥyā had proposed. As for the first one, he says that it is impossible for anyone to devote himself fully to the pursuit of knowledge. The fact is, he insists, that everyone must spend some of his time meeting what he calls the 'animal' and 'vegetative' needs of his nature. Furthermore, and in this same connection, he offers the following definition of the virtue of 'continence' (*al-ʿiffa*). He says,

> Continence, which is the virtue proper to the 'vegetative' faculty in a human being, is keeping the mean in the exercise of the activity proper to this faculty. And the activity proper to this faculty is nourishment, growth and procreation.[120]

Following this definition, the writer reiterates the principle he had cited earlier, viz., 'virtue stands in the middle', and he offers the following application of it in the present instance. He says,

[117] *Traité sur la continence*, p. 40, §77.1 (Arabic) and p. 103 (French).
[118] See *Traité sur la continence*, p. 40, §78.3 (Arabic) and p. 103 (French).
[119] *Traité sur la continence*, p. 41, §80.3 (Arabic) and p. 104 (French).
[120] *Traité sur la continence*, p. 42, §82.7 (Arabic) and p. 106 (French).

> The continent man is neither the one who abstains completely from the activity proper to the vegetative faculty, nor is he the one who overstrains the impulse to it. Rather he is the one who is equable and who holds to the middle in regard to the impulse to these matters.[121]

The unnamed writer says that he considers the practice advocated by Yaḥyā possible only for superior, even celestial individuals.[122] For, he argues, the time available to human beings must be divided between both what is necessary and what is a matter of free choice, 'and it is not possible to devote all of it to matters of free choice (*al-umūr al-ikhtiyārīya*)'.[123]

The writer deals very summarily with his answer to the second question Yaḥyā had posed. He says simply that it is impossible and improbable that everyone would devote himself either to the pursuit of knowledge, or to the procreation of children.[124]

In answer to Yaḥyā's third question, the writer spends some time arguing on behalf of the thesis that the human condition is best served by the existence of as many human beings as possible in the world. Only in this case, he claims, with an increase in the population recognized as better than a decrease in their number, can one be sure of the greatest possible assembly of wise men in any given era, relative to the number of miscreants present. This situation, he alleges, best testifies to the 'goodness' (*jūd*), 'power' (*qudra*), and 'wisdom' (*ḥikma*) of God, who of course is the one who has equipped human beings with the ability to bring about the increase through the faculty to procreate, which He created in mankind.[125]

In support of this line of reasoning, Yaḥyā's correspondent refers to one of the treatises of the philosopher al-Kindī (d. 252/866), which, he says, 'may be interpreted to be about the farthest celestial sphere's (*al-falak al-aqṣā*) worship of God'.[126] This work is no doubt al-Kindī's, *Risāla fī l-Ibāna ʿan Sujūd al-Jirm al-Aqṣā wa-Ṭāʿati-hi li-Allāh*,[127] in

[121] *Traité sur la continence*, p. 42, §84.7 (Arabic) and p. 107 (French).

[122] See *Traité sur la continence*, p. 42, §85.2 (Arabic) and p. 107 (French): *al-ashkhāṣ al-ʿāliya al-falakīya*.

[123] *Traité sur la continence*, p. 42, §85.4 (Arabic) and p. 107 (French).

[124] *Traité sur la continence*, p. 43, §86.1-2 (Arabic) and p. 107 (French).

[125] See *Traité sur la continence*, p. 43-44, §§87-89 (Arabic) and p. 107-109 (French).

[126] *Traité sur la continence*, p. 43, §88.4 (Arabic) and p. 108 (French): *bi-sujūd al-falak al-aqṣā li-Allāh*.

[127] See the edition and French translation in: *Œuvres philosophiques et scientifiques d'al-Kindī: II, Métaphysique et cosmologie*, ed. Roshdi Rashed and Jean Jolivet, Leiden: Brill, 1998, p. 173-199.

which the philosopher makes it clear that the 'body' (*al-jirm*) of which he speaks is in fact a 'celestial sphere' (*al-falak*), endowed, as he supposes, with a rational nature.[128] In the context, al-Kindī offers an explanation of the rational qualities and capabilities of human and celestial individuals (*ashkhāṣ*), in terms of their suitability for obediently paying worship to God.[129] Yaḥyā's correspondent cites this passage, even echoing its wording, in confirmation of his own evocation of God's generosity, power and wisdom in creating celestial and human individuals, 'who, by means of their godly intellectual powers acquire a knowledge of the sciences and of the skills of craftsmanship and industry'.[130]

Having answered Yaḥyā's three questions, the correspondent concludes his reply with a comparison of the careers of two hypothetical individuals, both of whom, he says, are endowed with the highest human potential. He describes the first one of them in language which clearly envisions the vocation of a Christian monk or ascetic, whose life is characterized by a lonely, celibate search for wisdom in solitude in the wilderness, amidst hardship and deprivation. The correspondent says that in his opinion this man's career is 'a life that hampers and holds its protagonist back from every virtue'.[131] He mentions that in his destitute situation such a person misses the opportunity for access to what the correspondent calls 'philosophical knowledge and its utilization'.[132] The second, highly favoured individual, by way of contrast, lives his life in community with others. He seeks knowledge wherever he can find it, especially 'from reading established books which, over the courses of the ages, the most virtuous men have spent their lifetimes writing, augmenting and enhancing'.[133] Such a man has 'wealth, offspring, slaves and a wife'.[134] The correspondent says that in his opinion this man's career is 'a humane, rich life, the best of lives, the basis of which is the right ordering of the mind'.[135]

[128] See *Œuvres philosophiques*, II, p. 181. Al-Kindī wrote the *risāla* in response to a query about a passage in Q. 55.6 (*al-Raḥmān*), where the Qur'ān says, *wa-l-najmu wa-l-shajaru yasjudāni*. Clearly he interprets the term *al-najmu* in its astronomical meaning and not in the sense of 'shrubs' or 'herbs', as the context implies and as many interpreters over the centuries have in fact understood the term.

[129] See *Œuvres philosophiques*, II, esp. p. 181.

[130] YAḤYĀ B. ʿADĪ, *Traité sur la continence*, p. 43, §88.6 (Arabic) and p. 108 (French).

[131] *Traité sur la continence*, p. 45, §92.1 (Arabic) and p. 110 (French).

[132] *Traité sur la continence*, p. 45, §93.3 (Arabic) and p. 111 (French).

[133] *Traité sur la continence*, p. 44, §91.6-7 (Arabic) and p. 110 (French).

[134] *Traité sur la continence*, p. 45, §91.9 (Arabic) and p. 110 (French).

[135] *Traité sur la continence*, p. 45, §93.1 (Arabic) and p. 111 (French); p. 45, §92.2 (Arabic) and p. 110 (French).

As exemplary individuals, the correspondent mentions first the names of Socrates, Plato and Aristotle. He points out that they 'lived their whole lives as citizens and humanists, abundantly supplied with associates and disciples; they were authors of books and of all kinds of philosophy, its sciences and its exercises'.[136] Of course, they were married, with households, children, slaves and goods. He says that Aristotle was the most illustrious of them all, living virtually a royal life. But there is also the example of the prophets and law-givers, among whom only the Messiah was not married, but even he did not require that his apostles and disciples be celibate, according to Yaḥyā's correspondent. Among the many other philosophers, prophets, lawgivers and just kings whom one might recall, he names only Alexander (the Great). Then finally, in a kind of thought-experiment, he mentions two groups of three men each, the first of them being those he calls the best of Christ's apostles, whom he names as Simon, John and Luke. The second group he mentions is made up, he says, of the choice practitioners of philosophy, by which he means the three ancient philosophers he named above. The correspondent then says that faced with the question of which of these two groups is the most virtuous, whose lives are the worthiest, 'I think that Aristotle, Plato and Socrates, more than all the other practitioners of philosophy and devotees of religion, are the most virtuous in moral choice, and the most perfect in conduct and gentility'.[137] Almost as an afterthought he then quickly says that what his own thinking in these matters, his own creed (*madhhab*), requires of him is that he also say 'our prophet, may God's prayer be with him, is the most virtuous of prophets and his companions are the most virtuous of companions'.[138] The correspondent then boasts that not a single one of them ever,

> Commanded something that would conduce to the reduction of the number of individuals, the destruction of cities, or the invalidation of the better part of the exercises of philosophy and their sublime purposes.[139]

Yaḥyā's correspondent brings his reply to a close with the observation that he agrees with Yaḥyā's contention that any exercise of the faculty of procreation which is 'devoid of virtue' is an evil.[140] However, he claims that its exercise within the parameters of continence and the

[136] *Traité sur la continence*, p. 46, §95.3 (Arabic) and p. 112 (French).
[137] *Traité sur la continence*, p. 46, §96.3 (Arabic) and p. 112-113 (French).
[138] *Traité sur la continence*, p. 46, §97.1 (Arabic) and p. 113 (French).
[139] *Traité sur la continence*, p. 47, §97.3 (Arabic) and p. 113 (French).
[140] See Yaḥyā's earlier espousal of this principle in *Traité sur la continence*, p. 25, §34.7 (Arabic) and p. 82 (French).

need to preserve the human species do not discount virtue. Rather, he reminds Yaḥyā that virtue is a matter of moderation and that both absolute renunciation and excessive indulgence are vices. So, in the correspondent's view, Yaḥyā's position requires further clarification. For, he maintains, the pleasures of procreation and the pains and disabilities of its neglect, are designed by God to prompt men to moderation. And he reminds Yaḥyā that 'most individuals do not actually exercise the faculty of reason in the matter of the wisdom and the discernment of the mean specific to it, in what pertains to the vegetative faculty and the animal faculty'.[141]

The correspondent's line of reasoning, with its high appreciation of the theory and practice of philosophy, along with his merely perfunctory nod to the authority of Muḥammad and the Islamic prophetic tradition, fairly accurately reflects the views expressed by Muḥammad b. Zakarīyā' al-Rāzī in his *Kitāb al-Sīra al-Falsafīya*, which was briefly discussed above.[142] Yaḥyā's engagement with these views, his careful report of their expression, and his concern seriously to discuss them testifies to the importance he assigns not just to the defence of the traditional Christian ascetical practice of celibacy, but to his concern for the appropriate spiritual exercises of philosophy in his own day, in the inter-religious milieu of Baghdad in the Tenth Century.

Yaḥyā's Rebuttal

Yaḥyā begins his rebuttal with a reaffirmation of the position he had put forward earlier about the conditions which in his view would legitimate a philosopher's engagement in the act of procreation. He had originally specified these conditions in the context of his comments on the note from one of his friends on the occasion of his reading of Yaḥyā's initial treatise 'on clarifying the state of abstaining from seeking to procreate', which is the first component of the composite work, *On Sexual Abstinence and the Philosophical Life*. Yaḥyā's report of the note's contents and his critique of the arguments advanced in it, one will recall, make up the second component of Yaḥyā's composite work. Now in the third component, at the beginning of his rebuttal against the interlocutor's reply to the three questions Yaḥyā had posed at the end of the second component, he rephrases the position he had articulated in the earlier place. He now says,

[141] *Traité sur la continence*, p. 47-48, §100.2 (Arabic) and p. 114 (French).
[142] See the texts cited in n. 26 above.

> Any act of procreation which fails to move toward giving birth to a prophet, or to a purely honest man, or to an eminent physician, or a just king, or which would free one from distress or save one from falling into an illness is a vice.[143]

In this short paragraph, Yaḥyā b. ʿAdī provides a succinct re-statement of what he will hereinafter consistently invoke as the 'six values' (*al-maʿānī al-sitta*)[144] which alone, he contends, can legitimate a philosopher's engagement in the physical processes of procreation. He first articulates his principle in what he calls a 'universal judgement' (*ḥukm kullī*), which, in response to his interlocutor's evocation of the principle of moderation in continence, Yaḥyā says applies whether a man is of an 'equable temperament' (*muʿtadil al-mizāj*) or not. 'It is necessarily the case', Yaḥyā goes on to say,

> That if one's act of procreation moves toward one of these [aforementioned] six values, it is permissible and to be considered morally good. If it is devoid of all of them, it is morally wrong and to be considered a vice.[145]

Throughout his rebuttal, Yaḥyā b. ʿAdī follows the method of quoting passages verbatim from his interlocutor's replies to the three questions Yaḥyā had himself previously proposed.[146] He deals first with the interlocutor's contention that by reason of the principle of moderation, 'the virtue of continence (*al-ʿiffa*) is in no way attributable to someone who by his own free choice utterly abandons procreation'.[147] In reply, Yaḥyā contends that the interlocutor has misconstrued what the philosophers have had to say about keeping to the mean in the management of one's concupiscent and irascible faculties. The requisite 'moderation' (*iʿtidāl*), Yaḥyā points out, is not to be predicated of the exercise of the two faculties themselves, but rather it is to be predicated of the human being who controls the action of the faculties. The two faculties 'are only two tools', he says,

143 *Traité sur la continence*, p. 48, §102.4 (Arabic) and p. 115 (French). See the earlier phrasing at p. 35, §59.2-3 (Arabic) and p. 96 (French). Yaḥyā repeats the first four conditions of his second list at p. 62, §132.9 (Arabic) and p. 135 (French).

144 *Traité sur la continence*, p. 48-49, §103.4 (Arabic) and p. 116 (French). Eight times in all in the course of his rebuttal Yaḥyā b. ʿAdī refers to these six, philosophically acceptable purposes for procreation. Only here does he call them 'values' (*al-maʿānī*). In two places he calls them 'reasons' or 'motives' (*al-asbāb*), at p. 51, §108.2 and p. 60, §128.1 (Arabic) and p. 118-119 and p. 132 (French). In five places he calls them 'aims' or 'purposes' (*al-wujūh*), at p. 56, §118.6, p. 57, §120.5 and 7, p. 58, §121.3 and §123.2 (Arabic) and p.127, 128, 129 (French).

145 *Traité sur la continence*, p. 48-49, §103.4 (Arabic) and p. 116 (French).

146 See the three questions as reported above, at notes 113, 114 and 115, and the interlocutor's answers summarized in the text annotated in notes 119-129 above.

147 *Traité sur la continence*, p. 49, §105.3 (Arabic) and p. 117 (French).

> Which one's soul, which is the rational soul, puts to use in connection with anything one needs, whenever one needs it, according to the measure of the need, and it abandons its deployment of them when it is free of the need.[148]

So moderation is a function of the rational soul, according to Yaḥyā, and not a function of the activities of the concupiscent and irascible faculties themselves. As such, it is nothing more than the virtue by means of which the faculties are moved to comply with the direction of the rational soul.[149] And so, on this basis Yaḥyā can claim that permanently abstaining from enacting the faculty of procreation does not necessarily deprive one of moderation.[150] He says he cannot understand why his interlocutor ignores the philosophers' definition of the appropriate moderation of the three human faculties. Yaḥyā then quotes the definition as, 'movement toward what one must acquire, and abstention from movement toward what is not necessary to acquire'.[151] As for what one must or must not acquire, Yaḥyā says,

> We know that in the human being these two faculties [i.e., the appetitive and the irascible] are the ones which a man controls by his reason, which is his very soul. It is by means of his reason that he abstains from whatever of theirs he determines he must abstain from.[152]

It is just this point that Yaḥyā says his interlocutor forgets. Yaḥyā complains that the interlocutor avoids answering his questions directly because he does not want to own up to the fact that he really does wrongly put procreation ahead of knowledge.[153] He esteems having children better than acquiring knowledge. And this is the reason why he

[148] *Traité sur la continence*, p. 50, §106.2-3 (Arabic) and p. 118 (French).

[149] See *Traité sur la continence*, p. 51, §108.4 (Arabic) and p. 119 (French).

[150] See *Traité sur la continence*, p. 51, §109.5 (Arabic) and p. 119 (French).

[151] *Traité sur la continence*, p. 51, §110.2 (Arabic) and p. 119 (French). Yaḥyā does not cite a source for this definition.

[152] *Traité sur la continence*, p. 51, §110.3 (Arabic) and p. 119-120 (French).

[153] It is in this context of his complaint about the interlocutor's failure to give a direct answer to the three questions because he thought their scenarios impossible that Yahyā refers to a passage in Porphyry's *Eisagoge*. He asks his interlocutor, 'How have you failed to heed, God help you, what use was made in *The Introduction* (*al-Madkhal*) of imagining a crow whose blackness had disappeared from it? This is something whose existence is impossible, but to imagine (*tawahhum*) it is not absurd': *Traité sur la continence*, p. 52, §111.10 (Arabic) and p. 121 (French); see n. 57 above. The reference is to a line in the *Eisagoge* which says, 'black is an accident, inseparably belonging to the crow and the negro (*al-zanjī*), although it is perhaps possible to imagine (*yatawahhamu*) a white crow and a Negro whose colour has left him'. See the Arabic version of the text, which Yaḥyā b. ʿAdī may have used, in Abū ʿUthmān ad-Dimashqī's (d. after 914) version of PORPHYRY, *Īsāghūjī*, ed. AḤMAD QAWWĀR AL-AHWĀNĪ, Cairo: Dār Iḥyā' al-Kutub al-ʿArabīya, 1952, p. 82.

mistakenly thinks that a greater number of people in the world is better than a smaller number. Whereas, according to Yaḥyā, the opposite is in fact the truth. He says that in spite of the world's large population over the course of time only a few outstanding philosophers, such as 'Plato, Aristotle, and those who follow their example',[154] have in fact appeared, and bad people have far outnumbered the virtuous. Accordingly, a sound mind can only determine, Yaḥyā says, that,

> The healthiest thing, and the most virtuous, both for the human race and for its individual members, is that their number should be reduced.[155]

As for which of two men is the most virtuous, he who, abstaining from procreation, labours all his life for 'true wisdom and godly knowledge', or he who is preoccupied with having and bringing up children, Yaḥyā gives his considered judgement as follows:

> The most virtuous way of life is to spend one's time gaining knowledge, to devote oneself to it according to one's ability, and not to be concerned with consorting with a wife, nor with having children, unless it would be to achieve one of the six purposes we have already prescribed. It is to spend what goods one has by the labour of others for one's own well-being and nourishment, without which one could not maintain one's life in a manner which would suffice for devoting one's time to gaining knowledge. It is to spend the remainder on whatever would help one to achieve the maximum of knowledge, such as books and teachers and whatever else follows the same course, without being concerned to seek offspring, save for the six purposes.[156]

Against what he considers to be the prejudices of his interlocutor, who had mentioned the behavior of the ancient philosophers and prophets in support of his views, Yaḥyā argues that in fact their lives and works uphold his own position. He cites Plato's allegory of the cave in the *Republic*, to show that the majority of people are unwilling to turn toward the light.[157] He evokes the life of Socrates, who said he married only to give himself the opportunity to practise the virtue of patience and thereby to help in the acquisition of wisdom.[158] He mentions Plato and Aristotle as exemplars of virtue. He says that if, as they say, Aristotle had a daughter, it may well have been the case that he undertook that course of action 'either in search of deliverance from a disease or as a

[154] *Traité sur la continence*, p. 54, §114.3 (Arabic) and p. 123 (French).
[155] *Traité sur la continence*, p. 54, §115.6 (Arabic) and p. 124 (French).
[156] *Traité sur la continence*, p. 57, §120.4-7 (Arabic) and p. 127-128 (French).
[157] *Traité sur la continence*, p. 59, §124.7-10 (Arabic) and p. 130 (French).
[158] *Traité sur la continence*, p. 59-60, §§125-126 (Arabic) and p. 130-131 (French).

precaution against falling into one'.[159] As for the prophets and the just men of old, who were married and had children, Yaḥyā says that,

> The intelligent man would approve the opinion that they did that only intending thereby one of the six reasons which bring one closer to God, exalted and mighty be He.[160]

Finally, for Yaḥyā b. ʿAdī, the life and practice of Christ are of special significance for his argument against the position of his interlocutor, who contended that lifelong celibacy is inconsistent with the practice of the virtue of continence (*al-ʿiffa*). Yaḥyā points out that Christ was a lifelong celibate and he commended the practice to his 'associates' (*aṣḥāb*) and 'apostles' (*ḥawārīyūn*), along with other renunciations. What is more, Yaḥyā says,

> You too have no doubt about his virtue of continence and the continence of his associates, and that he perfectly fulfilled to the utmost the four virtues which are continence, courage (*shajāʿa*), wisdom (*ḥikma*), and justice (*ʿadl*).[161]

Yaḥyā proceeds to use this agreement as the basis for his argument that since Christ and his companions possessed the virtue of continence to perfection, one cannot then logically argue that lifelong celibacy and abstention from procreation are incompatible with this virtue. Therefore, it is necessarily true, Yaḥyā argues,

> That not everyone who by his own choice abstains from what is lawful (*mashrūʿ*) in the matter of generating children is without continence. This is what we wanted to make clear.[162]

Yaḥyā brings his rebuttal to a conclusion by reaffirming his fundamental conviction. He says,

> The truth is, may God grant you strength and perseverance, that the virtue of man by means of which he is a man, is but wisdom (*al-ḥikma*) alone. That is because it is the virtue after which all the other virtues in him follow. When he has it to perfection, the perfection of right self-management redounds to him. And the health of the soul consists solely in his mind's and his soul's mastery, which is its perfection, over the remaining two faculties. I mean the concupiscent faculty and the irascible faculty, and the mind's guidance of the two of them, with the result that they are motivated only toward what it motivates the two of them, so they do only what it prompts them to do.[163]

[159] *Traité sur la continence*, p. 60, §127.4 (Arabic) and p. 131-132 (French).
[160] *Traité sur la continence*, p. 60, §128.1 (Arabic) and p. 132 (French).
[161] *Traité sur la continence*, p. 61, §129.4 (Arabic) and p. 132-133 (French).
[162] *Traité sur la continence*, p. 62, §130.10 (Arabic) and p. 133-134 (French).
[163] *Traité sur la continence*, p. 62, §132.4-7 (Arabic) and p. 134-135 (French).

Needless to say, Yaḥyā b. ʿAdī goes on to conclude that having and raising children uses up the time that could otherwise be better spent in the acquisition of 'godly wisdom and true science', unless one would engage in procreation for one of the six valid reasons for it he proposed earlier. In that case, he says, God's attachment of pleasure to the sexual act as an inducement to engage in it for the sake of producing offspring, as the interlocutor had claimed, is no argument against the practice of abstaining from it altogether for higher purposes, nor does it mean that complete abstention from it compromises the virtue of continence. At the end Yaḥyā expresses his conviction that with these thoughts in mind his interlocutor will now, with God's help, find the treatise which Yaḥyā had originally composed on this subject completely convincing.

THE PHILOSOPHICAL LIFE IN TENTH CENTURY BAGHDAD

Yaḥyā b. ʿAdī's colloquy with his Muslim interlocutors on the role of sexual abstinence in pursuit of the philosophical life has much to teach the modern reader about the cultivation of philosophy in Baghdad in the Tenth Century, especially on the part of a Christian philosopher in an Islamic society. While it is true that in the initial treatise Yaḥyā represents the position he espouses regarding the legitimacy of lifelong celibacy as something his presumably Muslim adversaries regard as a distinctively 'Christian claim' (*daʿwat al-naṣārā*),[164] it is immediately clear that he means to justify it not as a religious observance, but as a legitimate philosophical exercise. And in this context it appears that for his Christian apologetic purposes, he means to argue on behalf of a traditionally monastic, ascetical practice in the context of a debate already current among Muslim philosophers and religious thinkers in his milieu about the role of sexual abstinence and continence in the philosophical life. One recalls in this connection the earlier Christian usage of presenting monasticism as 'Christian Philosophy' or the 'Philosophy of Christ',[165] an idea which resonates well with Yaḥyā's thinking, especially in the final rebuttal of his interlocutor's position. It seems that Yaḥyā advocated living the philosophical life, in the Late Antique sense

[164] See, e.g., *Traité sur la continence*, p. 15, §3.4-6 (Arabic) and p. 66 (French).

[165] See ANNE-MARIE MALINGREY, Philosophia*: étude d'un groupe de mots dans la littérature grecque, des Présocratiques au IVe siècle après J.-C.*, Paris: Librairie C. Klincksieck, 1961, esp. p. 289-301.

of the expression,[166] as a personal vocation in Tenth Century Baghdad and that in the context of his other Christian apologetic works he also meant to claim that the profession of his own 'Jacobite' Christology provided the best available religious option to foster anyone's ambition to live the philosophical life.

It seems that Yaḥyā b. ʿAdī regarded philosophy as a realm of discourse in which both Christians and Muslims could participate, in the conviction that in the end reason would serve the interests of revelation, and in the meantime devotion to philosophy would preserve the decencies of life in common. When one reads the colloquy on sexual abstinence and the philosophical life from this point of view, and not just as if it were merely a Christian tract on celibacy, one catches a glimpse of what the philosophical life meant to at least one Christian philosopher in Baghdad in the Tenth Century. After all, his argument is that sexual abstinence best suits the interests of the cultivation of reason, and as Yaḥyā once wrote,

> Men are a single tribe (*qabīl*), related to one another; humanity unites them. The adornment of the divine power is in all of them and in each one of them, and it is the rational soul.[167]

[166] In this connection, see the studies of PIERRE HADOT, *Philosophy as a Way of Life*, trans. MICHAEL CHASE, Oxford: Blackwell, 1995; *What is Ancient Philosophy?*, trans. MICHAEL CHASE, Cambridge, MA: Harvard University Press, 2002.

[167] YAḤYĀ B. ʿADĪ, *The Reformation of Morals*, p. 106 and 107, §5.14.

Avicenna and Beyond

IMAGINATION AND TRANSCENDENTAL KNOWLEDGE IN AVICENNA*

DIMITRI GUTAS
Yale University

The role of the internal sense of imagination (*al-takhayyul*, *al-mutakhayyila*) in the acquisition and processing of knowledge that humans receive from and about the supernal world[1] is crucial and ubiquitous in Avicenna's epistemology. This role clearly derives ultimately from Aristotle's fateful statements about thinking and imagination in *De Anima* 403a8-9 and elsewhere,[2] but my concern here is not with its history and pedigree but with the precise epistemological function and modalities of human imagination in Avicenna's thought.[3] Avicenna never wrote an independent treatise on the subject, so his theory has to be pieced together from the many (and sometimes, though perhaps only seemingly, inconsistent)

* It is a distinct pleasure to dedicate this article on Avicenna's thought to Richard M. Frank, a subject for the significance of which he showed rare appreciation and about which we enjoyed many a spirited talk. I would also like to thank here Alexander Treiger for a number of very incisive comments and helpful suggestions, and James Montgomery for his masterful blend of impeccable but self-effacing scholarship and uncommon editorial skill.

[1] I will be using this term to refer to the realm of the transcendental, i.e., to what is called the supralunar world in Aristotelian and the realm of the divine in religious terms.

[2] See the statement in that passage that thinking 'too is a form of imagination or does not exist apart from imagination', καὶ τοῦτο [i.e. τὸ νοεῖν] φαντασία τις ἢ μὴ ἄνευ φαντασίας. The extant early Arabic translation renders this passage as *ʿaraḍa [i.e., al-idrāk bi-l-ʿaql] bi-ḍarb min ḍurūb al-tawahhum am lam yakun bi-ghayri tawahhum* (in: ARISṬŪṬĀLĪS, *Fī l-Nafs*, ed. ʿA. BADAWĪ, Cairo, 1954 [reprint: Kuwayt - Beirut, 1980], p. 5), while the Latin version of Isḥāq's lost translation, which Avicenna used, reads *hoc [i.e., intelligere] etiam est ymaginatio, aut non potest esse sine ymaginatione* (in: *Averrois Cordubensis Commentarium Magnum in Aristotelis* De Anima *Libros*, ed. F.S. CRAWFORD, Cambridge, Mass., 1953, p. 16), where *ymaginatio* is almost certainly rendering *takhayyul* rather than *tawahhum* as in the old translation. The medieval Hebrew translation of Isḥāq's Arabic by Zĕraḥyāh ben Yiṣḥāq Ḥēn uses the term *dimyān*, which also seems to translate *takhayyul* rather than *tawahhum*: see G. BOS, *Aristotle's* De Anima *Translated into Hebrew*, Leiden, 1994, p. 47.

[3] This paper is a companion piece to my *Intellect without Limits: The Absence of Mysticism in Avicenna*, in: *Intellect and Imagination in Medieval Philosophy*, ed. M.C. PACHECO and J.F. MEIRINHOS, I, Turnhout: Brepols, 2006. In that paper I discuss the objects of the transcendental knowledge gained with the help of the intellect and imagination, none of which turns out to be mystical. This paper focuses on the mechanics of the process whereby the imagination acquires such objects of knowledge.

accounts in his various works composed at different stages in his career. This task was largely accomplished by Y. Michot in his monograph on the afterlife in Avicenna, but because his focus in that work was primarily eschatological and not epistemological, the subject bears a more sharply delineated presentation along the lines I suggest here.[4]

It is important to note at the outset that for Avicenna imagination is one of the five internal senses that belong to the animal soul, the other four being the common sense (*al-ḥiss al-mushtarak*), the form-bearing faculty (*al-muṣawwira*) or imagery (*al-khayāl*), the estimation (*al-wahm*), and memory (*al-ḥāfiẓa*) or recollection (*al-mutadhakkira*). They are all material faculties and located in the brain, front to back, in the order listed, with imagination placed in the centre, between imagery and estimation. As such the animal soul is mortal and dies with the death of the body, just like the vegetative soul. Humans have this latter soul in common with animals and plants, and the animal soul only in common with animals. It is only the rational soul, an immaterial substance which characterizes humans exclusively, that is immortal.[5]

Avicenna differentiated between two major aspects of the role of imagination in the acquisition of knowledge of and from the supernal world already in his works composed during what I have called his transition period (ca. 1013-1014).[6] This differentiation is based on the nature and source of the supernal knowledge: it consists either of intelligible universal concepts which are thought eternally by the active intellect (the tenth intellect — that of the earthly realm — in Avicenna's emanative cosmology), or of forms of particulars (referring to past, present, and especially future events and things on earth) which are generated, and hence also thought, by the souls of the celestial spheres. These latter objects of knowledge Avicenna consistently refers to as 'unseen things' (*al-mughayyabāt*) or things of the 'unseen' (*al-ghayb*).[7] An early formulation of Avicenna's position is found in his work from that period, *Provenance and Destination* (*al-Mabdaʾ wa-l-Maʿād*), which brings out

[4] J.R. MICHOT, *La destinée de l'homme selon Avicenne*, Louvain, 1986, p. 118-133. Furthermore, the section in which Michot discusses the subject is entitled *La faculté prophétique*, which may mislead the casual reader into thinking that the presentation of the epistemological functions of imagination applies to prophets only and is not valid for human knowledge in general.

[5] See the more extensive discussion of the internal senses, with references to pertinent literature, in GUTAS, *Intellect without Limits*, Part II.

[6] D. GUTAS, *Avicenna and the Aristotelian Tradition*, Leiden, 1988, p. 99 and 145.

[7] See the detailed discussion of this subject, in connection with Avicenna's alleged 'mystical' knowledge in GUTAS, *Intellect without Limits*, Part III.

both this differentiation and some basic problems related to it. The acquisition of knowledge from the souls of the celestial spheres is described as follows:[8]

> As for the reason for the knowledge of [future] events (*al-kā'ināt*), it is the contact of the human soul with the souls of the celestial bodies which... know what happens in the world of the elements.... For the most part, these [human] souls come into contact with them [the souls of the celestial spheres] by virtue precisely of a congeneric similarity (*mujānasa*) between them. The congeneric similarity is that thing (*al-ma'nā*) which, there [in the heavens], is close to the concerns of these [human souls]. So most of what is seen [by the human souls] of what is to be found there [in the heavens] is congeneric to the states of the bodies of these [human] souls or to the states of one who is close to these bodies. And although the contact [of the human souls with the celestial souls] is total, the majority of the influence they receive from them is for the most part close to just their [own] concerns. This contact comes about on the part (*min jiha*) of the estimation and imagination (*al-khayāl*)[9] and through their use, and concerns particular things, whereas contact by means of the intellect is something else, which is not our subject here.[10]

Avicenna broaches the subject of contact by means of the intellect a couple of pages later in the same treatise:

> He who has a very powerful imagination and a very powerful [rational] soul [i.e., here, the prophet] is not completely distracted or engrossed by the sensibles. That part of him [i.e., his intellect] which misses no opportunity to come into contact with that [supernal] realm is abundant — it being possible for it [to effect this contact] also in the waking state — and it pulls the imagination along with it and sees the truth and retains it, while the imagination does its work: it represents what [the intellect] sees in images, in the form of a visible and audible object of the senses.... The imagination of the prophet does not do this when [it is] in contact with the principles of future things [i.e., the souls of the celestial spheres], but rather when the active intellect radiates upon its [rational] soul and illuminates it with the intelligibles. The imagination then begins to represent these intelligibles and depict them in the common sense at which time the senses perceive an indescribable grandeur and power that belongs to God. Such a person then possesses both perfect rational soul and perfect imagination.[11]

[8] In this and all translations given below, the words in square brackets were added by me to help intelligibility.

[9] Avicenna uses the term *khayāl* in this passage for imagination and not *al-mutakhayyila*, as he was to do later, but it is clear that his mature and precise terminology had not yet developed at this stage; at the end of this passage (p. 118.4) he refers to the same faculty as *al-takhayyul*. See further GUTAS, *Intellect without Limits*, note 19.

[10] IBN SĪNĀ, *al-Mabda' wa-l-Ma'ād*, ed. 'A. NŪRĀNĪ, Tehran, 1363/1984, p. 117. Cf. the French translation of this passage in MICHOT, *La destinée de l'homme*, p. 121, note 70.

[11] IBN SĪNĀ, *al-Mabda' wa-l-Ma'ād*, p. 119.

These two passages make statements about a number of things in varying degrees of explicitness. First of all, what is made absolutely clear is the different natures and sources of the two kinds of knowledge: as mentioned above, one consists of the intelligibles, which come with the active intellect, and the other, knowledge about particular events on earth, comes from the souls of the celestial spheres. What is not as clear, and this is the main problem that is the focus of this investigation, is the human faculty which receives these two kinds of knowledge.

To begin with the faculty that receives the intelligibles from the active intellect, Avicenna says in the second passage above that it is the man's (or, in this particular case, the prophet's) 'soul', without further specification; only at the end of the passage does he indicate that this is the 'rational soul'. But he does not mention the intellect explicitly, and in the first part of the passage he chooses to refer to it by one of its characteristics: that part of man, he says, which 'misses no opportunity to come into contact with' the supernal realm, i.e., the active intellect. Thus there is no doubt that Avicenna is actually referring here to the human intellect, and the purpose behind this circumlocution must be Avicenna's desire to point thereby to the underlying basis for the possibility of this contact: the human intellect, an immaterial and immortal substance, is identical with the equally immaterial and immortal intellects of the celestial spheres, and hence has a natural proclivity for contact with the last of them, the active intellect.

Less clear is the way in which Avicenna expresses himself with regard to the faculty which receives the second kind of knowledge, the faculty that comes into contact with the souls of the celestial bodies. Although at the beginning of the first paragraph above he starts by saying that it is the human, i.e., rational, souls that come into contact with the souls of the celestial bodies, toward the end he says specifically that 'this contact comes about on the part of the estimation and imagination and through their use'. But the internal senses of imagination and estimation are part of the animal, not human soul, and, as already mentioned, they are located in the brain and hence material and mortal. There is thus a number of problems with this formulation. First, there is the obvious contradiction in the two statements: is it the human or animal soul that receives knowledge from the souls of the celestial spheres? Second, and most importantly, if indeed it is the animal soul that receives this knowledge, how is it possible for a material and mortal substance to be in contact with the divine and immortal supernal world? And third, if it is the rational soul that receives this knowledge, how then can the intellect, which can only know universals, receive this knowledge about particulars from the souls of the spheres? These problems, though not actually as severe as formulated here, were nevertheless to remain with Avicenna, particularly on account of imprecise formulations in his various works, and we will meet them again later.

Most unfortunately, these problems contributed to a false understanding of Avicenna's basic position and led to the belief in modern scholarship that

> Imagination... may enter conjunction with the active intellect and receive the emanation of the active intellect directly.[12]

But this cannot be correct, as Dag Hasse pointedly remarks: the animal soul cannot receive knowledge from the supernal realm and it cannot have this prophetic property because, 'if this were correct... animals could become prophets as well'.[13] In other words, if the imagination, which is part of the mortal and material animal soul, could come into direct contact with the souls of the celestial spheres (let alone with the active intellect — as Davidson would have it — which is an immaterial and immortal substance), then the role and nature of the intellect are severely compromised, as is the entire metaphysical and irreducible distinction between material and immaterial substance and the divine and the mundane, and there ensue such absurd consequences as the possibility for dumb animals to have knowledge of the future and

[12] H. DAVIDSON, *Alfarabi, Avicenna, and Averroes on Intellect*, New York - Oxford, 1992, p. 123; similarly, p. 119: 'the compositive imaginative faculty enters "conjunction" with the "supernal region"'; and p. 121: it is possible for imagination to have 'reception of intelligible thoughts from a supernal source, without the participation of the human intellect'. See also IBN SĪNĀ, *Fī Ithbāt al-Nubuwwāt*, ed. M. MARMURA, Beirut, 1968, p. xiii: 'The first type [of prophetic knowledge] involves the reception by a prophet's imaginative faculty of particular imaged knowledge from the celestial souls'; and p. xiv: 'Prophets of the first type receive the particular knowledge possessed by the celestial souls as impressions on their imaginative faculty'. The position described in these statements is not that of Avicenna but of al-Fārābī: 'When a man's faculty of imagination (*al-mutakhayyila*) reaches its utmost perfection he will receive in his waking life from the active intellect present and future particulars... and the imitations of the separate intelligibles.... This man will obtain, through the particulars which he receives and sees, prophecy with respect to present and future events, and through the intelligibles which he receives, prophecy with respect to things divine. This is the highest rank of perfection which the faculty of imagination can reach' (R. WALZER, *Al-Farabi on the Perfect State*, Oxford, 1985, pp. 224-225, translation adopted with slight modifications). Avicenna clearly borrowed the concept from al-Fārābī, but it appears that he eventually modified it precisely in order to avoid the problems in this position I just mentioned.

[13] D. HASSE, *Avicenna's* De Anima *in the Latin West*, London - Turin, 2000, p. 159. See the related questions also raised by MICHOT, *La destinée de l'homme*, p. 122-123.

become themselves prophets, since animals have all the internal senses, with estimation being their highest faculty.[14] If, then, Avicenna could not have meant to maintain such a philosophically untenable position, how are we to understand his statement that the contact between human and celestial souls 'comes about on the part of the estimation and imagination'?

The answer is provided, as Michot pointed out, by Avicenna himself in a work that is roughly contemporary with *The Provenance and Destination*, i.e., also dating from his 'transition period', *The State of the Human Soul* (*Ḥāl al-Nafs al-Insānīya*).[15] In this work Avicenna has a lengthy chapter on prophecy (*fī ithbāt al-nubuwwa*) in which he gives an explicit account of all aspects of the issue.[16] Here too he distinguishes between the two kinds of supernal knowledge — one consisting of the forms of particular events that are caused by the various motions of the heavenly spheres, and the other of intellective forms, of intelligibles — and he says the following about the human faculty that receives them:

> As for the intellective forms, contact with them comes about by means of the theoretical intellect, but as for these forms which are the subject of our discussion [i.e., the forms of particular events], the soul conceives them by means of just another faculty, the practical intellect, which is served in this respect by the imagination. Thus the soul, by means of its faculty which is called practical intellect, acquires particular things from the substances of the supernal souls, while by means of its faculty which is called theoretical intellect it acquires universal things from the substances of the supernal intellects for which it is impossible that they should ever contain anything of the particular forms.[17]

[14] See *Avicenna's* De Anima, *Being the Psychological Part of* Kitāb al-Shifā', ed. F. RAHMAN, London, 1959, p. 167.1: estimation 'is the principal faculty for judgment in animals'.

[15] MICHOT, *La destinée de l'homme*, p. 123. For bibliographical references to this work of Avicenna see MICHOT, *La destinée de l'homme*, p. xvii-xviii. In an earlier article, *Prophétie et divination selon Avicenne. Présentation, essai de traduction critique et index de l'*«Epître de l'âme de la sphère», in: *Revue Philosophique de Louvain* 83 (1985), p. 507-535, Y. MICHOT advanced the view that this work, being a 'patchwork philosophique' drawn from the *Shifā'* and the *Najāh*, is posterior to them in age, i.e. written toward the end of his life (i.e., between 1030-1037: see p. 507, note 3). In my own work, *Avicenna and the Aristotelian Tradition*, which was essentially completed before I could benefit from these publications by Michot, I proposed (p. 99-100) an earlier date for this work, as above, a view to which I continue to subscribe: given the patchwork nature of the *Shifā'* and the *Najāh* themselves, it is rather they that are posterior, as I maintain on my chronological chart, p. 145.

[16] There is an annotated French translation of this chapter in MICHOT, *Prophétie et divination*, p. 512-522.

[17] IBN SĪNĀ, *Aḥwāl al-Nafs*, ed. A.F. AL-AHWĀNĪ, Cairo, 1371/1952, p. 117. Cf. the French translation in MICHOT, *Prophétie et divination*, p. 517.

The distinction between the theoretical and practical intellect is primary in Avicenna and helps him regulate and define the human rational soul's relationship to what lies above and below it, i.e., to the supernal world and the intelligibles on the one hand and to its own body and the animal and vegetative souls on the other.[18] It is this distinction which he brings to bear in this context also, in establishing the precise manner by which humans receive knowledge from the supernal world. The two sources of this knowledge, the active intellect and the souls of the heavenly spheres, are in contact each with an aspect of the human rational soul, the former with the theoretical intellect and the latter with the practical intellect. Now the practical intellect, Avicenna says at the beginning of this same treatise, has three functions: one with respect to the impelling faculty of the animal soul (*nuzūʿīya*), another with respect to the imaginative and estimative faculties of the animal soul, and a third with respect to itself.[19] The function which is directed toward the souls of the heavenly spheres and which consists in receiving from them knowledge of particular things on earth is clearly then that which it has with respect to the imaginative and estimative faculties of the animal soul, for, as he says in the passage cited above, the imagination 'serves' the practical intellect in accomplishing this function. Accordingly, the passage in Avicenna's *The Provenance and Destination*, the very first one that was cited above, in which he says that the contact with the souls of the spheres 'comes about on the part of the estimation and imagination' is to be understood as meaning that the contact comes about on the part of the practical intellect as it is assisted by the imagination and estimation. Thus understood, the inconsistencies in Avicenna's account and theory I referred to above are removed: it is the intellect which is, ultimately, in contact with the eternal supernal world and not the animal soul and its faculties.

We can also be sure that this is what Avicenna really meant in *The Provenance and Destination* and that he simply expressed himself elliptically in the sentence in question when we consider carefully his words, because in the first passage from that work cited above he says that the contact between the souls of the celestial spheres and the human soul

[18] This distinction also is ultimately derived from Aristotle, *De Anima*, 433a14-15, πρακτικός and θεωρητικὸς νοῦς. Avicenna first set forth his description of the nature and functions of the theoretical and practical intellect in *The State of the Human Soul* (AL-AHWĀNĪ, p. 63-65), a passage which he later repeated in both the *Shifā'* (RAHMAN, p. 45-49) and the *Najāh*, Cairo, 1331, p. 267-270.

[19] *Aḥwāl al-Nafs*, p. 63, repeated in *Najāh*, p. 267 and *Shifā'*, p. 46.

comes about on account of a congeneric similarity (*mujānasa*) between them. If the contact were established *directly* between the imagination and the celestial souls, this would mean that the animal soul in humans and the celestial souls would share the same genus of substance, which is absurd; the animal soul is material (in the sense that it is based on the four sublunar elements) and mortal, while the celestial souls, though corporeal, are so through the celestial supralunar substance and are immortal. The inference is thus that the celestial souls are congeneric with the practical intellect. And this is precisely what Avicenna maintains in the *Metaphysics* of the *Shifā'* where he says that the souls which move the celestial spheres are 'like our practical intellect' (*ka-l-ʿaql al-ʿamalī fī-nā*).[20] Thus the congeneric similarity between the practical intellect and the souls of the celestial spheres at once explains the basis for the possibility of contact between the two and ensures that it is indeed the practical intellect (and not the imagination) that effects the contact.[21]

The imagination aids the practical intellect during its contact with the celestial souls by 'serving' it, or, as Avicenna says in the *Dāneshnāmah*, by acting as its instrument (*āla*).[22] In fact, the imagination may also help the theoretical intellect during its contact with the active intellect. In both cases the imagination converts this knowledge into audible and visible images, but when the contents of the knowledge are the divine message of revelation, this is conveyed to people as a recited holy text, while the knowledge about particular events manifests itself in dreams or, in the case of people with strong imagination, even during their waking moments, as intimations and such.

[20] IBN SĪNĀ, *al-Ilāhīyāt*, ed. M.Y. MOUSSA et al., Cairo, 1960, p. 387.7. Further on Avicenna calls the souls of the celestial spheres 'the practical/efficacious angels' (*al-malā'ika al-ʿamala*): p. 435.8.

[21] It is to be noted, though, that in the case of the souls of the celestial spheres whose bodies are eternal, their practical intellect, which is responsible for the particularization of the universal knowledge they receive from the intellects of the spheres, is tantamount to their imagination: in the *Aḥwāl al-Nafs*, p. 114-115, Avicenna says that the celestial souls 'perceive the particulars either through imagination or through a practical intellection which is higher than the imagination' (*tudrik umūran juz'īyatan idrākan immā an yakūn takhayyulan aw-taʿaqqulan ʿamalīyan huwa arfaʿu min al-takhayyul*: see the correct text as given by Michot, *Prophétie et divination*, p. 513). In a passage from the late work *Glosses*, Avicenna (if it is indeed Avicenna) equates practical intellect and imagination in the celestial spheres: *al-taʿaqqul ay al-takhayyul* (*al-Taʿlīqāt*, ed. ʿA. BADAWĪ, Cairo, 1973, p. 129.3). For a discussion of the knowledge of particulars by the celestial spheres, with further references to Avicenna's texts, see MICHOT, *La destinée de l'homme*, p. 110-118.

[22] *Al-Ṭabīʿīyāt*, ed. M. MESHKĀT, Tehran 1331SH/1371AH, p. 135.8; cf. AVICENNE, *Le livre de science*, transl. H. MASSÉ and M. ACHENA, Paris, 1986, II, p. 84.

The two passages from the *Provenance and Destination* cited at the beginning have their counterparts in the *Shifā'* in the appropriate sections of the book on the soul. The second passage, on the reception of intellective knowledge from the active intellect, corresponds to the following description of the process in the *Shifā'* in the chapter on the intellect, Book V, Chapter 6:

> [The material intellect of some people is so strong] that they do not need great effort, or training and instruction, in order to make contact with the active intellect;... indeed it seems as if they know everything of themselves.... In this state the material intellect ought to be called 'sacred intellect', since it partakes of the genus of dispositional intellect (*bi-l-malaka*), except that it is so lofty that it is not something shared by all people. It is not unlikely that some of these acts pertaining to the sacred spirit because of their powerful and overwhelming nature deluge the imagination which then reproduces them in terms of perceptible and audible linguistic images.[23]

The first passage on the knowledge of particulars received by the practical intellect has its counterpart in the *Shifā'* in the chapter on the internal senses, Book IV, Chapter 2:

> In some people, the faculty of imagination may happen to have been created so very strong and dominant that the senses cannot overpower it and the form-bearing [faculty] cannot disobey it. The[ir rational] soul also is strong, so that its attending to the intellect and what is with[24] the intellect does not paralyse its application to the senses.[25] Such people experience in their wake what others experience in their sleep, namely, the state we will talk about later [in this section] — this is the state of the sleeper who perceives the unseen things (*al-mughayyabāt*) by ascertaining[26] them either as they are in themselves or through any images for them — for the same thing may happen to those people in their wake.... Many times they see a thing as it is, and many times there appears to them its image for the same reason that an image of what someone has seen appears to him in sleep.... Frequently [also] a figure of a person presents itself to them and they imagine that what they perceive is an address from that figure by means of audible utterances that can be memorized and recited; this is the prophethood

[23] RAHMAN, *Avicenna's* De Anima, p. 248-249.

[24] *Qibala*, i.e., 'in the presence of the intellect', referring to the intelligibles.

[25] Reading, along with the Latin translator and against Rahman, *iltifātu... inṣibāba*. The rational soul, which is the subject here, naturally turns towards, or attends to, the intellect. If it is strong, then its proper activity, attending to the intellect, does not preoccupy it completely so that it is able at the same time to do something in addition, pay attention to the senses. See the translation by HASSE, *Avicenna's* De Anima, p. 159.

[26] See the significance of the wording with *taḥaqquq* here in GUTAS, Avicenna, p. 183-184, 188.

that is the property specifically of the imagination.[27] There are also other prophecies, whose nature will become clear later.[28]

These passages in the *Shifā'* elaborate upon and amplify the two passages from the *Provenance and Destination* cited at the beginning. And yet, when it comes to the question of identifying the specific faculty that makes contact with the celestial souls to receive the supernal knowledge — whether it is the faculty of the imagination or the rational soul (the practical intellect) — an issue that was formulated in a problematic way by Avicenna in the the *Provenance and Destination* but stated explicitly in *The State of the Human Soul*, Avicenna still uses in the *Shifā'* an occasional turn of phrase that is ambiguous. One passage which is very explicit about both this question and the next one, about the nature and modalities of the connection between the rational soul and the supernal world, deserves quoting in full:

> In order to receive the effluence of the unseen (*fayḍ al-ghayb*), the [rational] soul needs the internal faculties for two reasons. The first is in order to form in them concepts of particulars that will be stored in memory, and the second is so that these faculties will help the [rational] soul and work with it in the direction of its will, and not distract it or pull it in their own direction.[29] There is need [a] for a connection between the unseen on the one hand and the [rational] soul and the internal faculty of imagination on the other, and [b] for a connection between the [rational] soul and the internal faculty of imagination. If the senses use it [imagination] or the intellect uses it in the intellective way we mentioned, then it will not be free for other things; like a mirror [which,] when it is distracted from one direction and is moved toward another, many things whose nature it is to be impressed unexpectedly and suddenly on that mirror on account of a certain connection between them [those things and the mirror], they will not be impressed. No matter whether this distraction comes from the senses or the control of the intellect, when one of them is removed, then the necessary connection between the unseen on the one hand and the [rational] soul and the faculty of the imagination on the other is ready to occur, as is also [the connection] between the [rational] soul and the faculty of the imagination, and something appears in it [the imagination] in the way in which it appears.[30]

[27] *Wa-hādhihi huwa l-nubuwwa al-khāṣṣa bi-l-quwwa al-mutakhayyila*. Cf. the translation of this sentence in RAHMAN, *Prophecy*, p. 72, note 30.

[28] Discussed in RAHMAN, *Avicenna's* De Anima, p. 201.6 (prophecy related to the motive faculties of the soul producing telekinesis), 250.2 (prophecy related to the intellect).

[29] For the will, see IBN SĪNĀ, *al-Ishārāt wa-l-Tanbīhāt*, ed. S. DUNYĀ, Cairo, 1968, Part IV, *Namaṭ* IX,7, p. 76: i.e., the rational soul desires to have this connection with the unseen, and the internal faculties should work with it toward that goal, not distract it toward other concerns.

[30] *Avicenna's* De Anima, p. 177.20-178.10.

Several things need to be emphasized about this passage. First, it unequivocally says that it is the *rational* soul that receives the 'effluence of the unseen', and not the faculty of the imagination in the animal soul. It is true that the text says just 'the soul', but it is clear that here, as in all these passages in the *Shifā'*, Avicenna means the rational soul. In any case, there could be no doubt in the present passage:

> In order to receive the effluence of the unseen, the soul needs the internal faculties (*fa-inna l-nafs muḥtāja fī talaqqī fayḍ al-ghayb ilā l-quwā l-bāṭina*) (p. 177.20-21).

If the word 'soul' in this sentence meant the animal soul, then the sentence would be tautological: the animal soul *is* the internal senses, so there would be no meaning in stating that it needs itself in order to receive the unseen. This position is consistent with the nature of the rational soul overall: since it needs the internal faculties even in intellection and in order to perfect itself, it follows that it should also need them in this different sort of cognition, i.e., contact with the supernal intelligences.

Avicenna uses expressions that indicate that it is the rational soul that comes into contact with the supernal world elsewhere in this chapter,[31] and most tellingly also in the following passage:

> Not all imitation (*muḥākāt*) of the faculty of imagination is strictly of that which emanates upon the [rational] soul from the Realm of [Divine] Sovereignty (*malakūt*).[32]

For if it were the imagination that received the emanated forms, the text should have said 'emanates upon itself' and not 'emanates upon the soul'.[33] It thus seems clear that Avicenna in the *Shifā'* is acknowledging more explicitly that it is the rational soul that comes into contact with the supernal world, despite at least one formulation, as I mentioned, where the wording implies that it is the imagination that effects the contact:

[31] See, e.g., the following: 'When it happens that in a waking state the soul perceives (*adraka*) something [of the unseen things], or that in a state of sleep it comes into contact with the Realm of [Divine] Sovereignty (*ittaṣalat bi-l-malakūt*), if this faculty [the imagination], either because it is quiescent or subdued, enables [the soul] to record well whatever imaginings appear in it and does not overpower the soul in a crippling way (*muqaṣṣiratan ʿalay-hā*) at the time of recording, that form [that is so recorded] is in the best position to be remembered well as such ...' (*Avicenna's* De Anima, p. 175.14-176.1).

[32] *Avicenna's* De Anima, p. 179.6.

[33] See further *Avicenna's* De Anima, p. 177.2-3: *min ghayr an takūna l-nafs ittaṣalat bi-l-malakūt*.

> The celestial bodies may drop forms into the imagination in accordance with [its] predisposition' (*fa-inna-hā qad tūqiʿu … ṣuwaran fī l-takhayyul bi-ḥasab al-istiʿdād*) (p. 180.5-6),

though it could also be claimed that what is intended here is that the celestial bodies cause these forms to fall into the imagination through the mediation of the practical intellect aspect of the rational soul — the practical intellect, that is, which, as discussed above, is aided and 'served' by the imagination.[34] We can thus understand Avicenna in the passage just quoted that it is the rational soul which receives the knowledge of the unseen.

The second thing that this passage does is that it answers the question about the modalities of this particular kind of knowledge: it establishes [a] a rationale for its transmission, [b] a hierarchy for it, and [c] the conditions for it.

[a] The rationale is that for this knowledge to be transmitted, there must come about a necessary relation or connection (*nisba*) between the source of this knowledge, the supernal world, and its recipient, the rational soul and the imagination as a unit, and also, since this knowledge manifests itself through the imagination, between the rational soul and the imagination. In other words, what in the *Provenance and Destination* had been a congeneric similarity between the upper world and the human soul here is expressed as a connection or relation between the two. And this connection is effected, as Avicenna says throughout the chapter, through contacts between them: *ittiṣālāt* (p. 174.3, 175.15, 177.2-3).

[b] The hierarchy of transmission is clear: from the supernal world to the rational soul, and from the rational soul to the imagination.

[34] In any case, it is clear that for Avicenna practical intellect and imagination are closely related in humans, and in the case of the souls of the celestial spheres they are practically identical (see above, note 21). This is why Avicenna can say that the perception of particulars by the celestial souls is 'a perception that is not purely intellectual' (*idrāk ghayr ʿaqlī maḥḍ*: *al-Ilāhīyāt*, p. 436.15); that is, it depends on the practical intellect of the celestial souls and is thus quasi-imaginative. Furthermore, while the intellects of the celestial spheres, as pure intellects, know particulars in a universal manner, the souls of the spheres 'know them in a particular manner as if they were being directly perceived or in a manner that is conducive to direct perception and observation': *ʿalā naḥw juzʾī ka-l-mubāshar aw al-mutaʾaddī ilā l-mubāshar aw al-mushāhad* (*al-Ilāhīyāt*, p. 437.10, and see RAHMAN, *Prophecy*, p. 75, note 33). This would appear to mean that the practical intellects or imaginations of the celestial spheres create representations of the particulars and thus one could say that they know them 'as if they were being directly perceived'. This knowledge is transmitted to the practical intellect of humans which perceives apparently the same representations through the help of imagination.

[c] In order for this transmission to occur, though, the major condition to be fulfilled is that the imagination must be free from distractions, regardless whether these distractions come from the senses or the intellect. Once this is done, the necessary connection between the souls of the spheres and the rational soul, and between the rational soul and the imagination, is just ready to come about (*awshaka an tattafiq*, p. 178.8) and the knowledge that was transmitted appears in some form in the imagination. The specific form in which this knowledge appears is left vague in Avicenna's formulation at the end of this passage: 'something appears in it [the imagination] in the way in which it appears', but he provides the answer earlier in this chapter: 'Those [perceptions, i.e. of the unseen] may be of any kind — they may be intelligibles, or warnings,[35] or poetry, or anything else, in accordance with [the individual's] predisposition, habits, or character'.[36]

Finally, another distinguishing characteristic of this kind of knowledge is explicitly stated in this chapter of the *Shifā'*: most important for understanding the nature of this cognitive process is that this kind of knowledge received from the supernal world comes to one unsolicited; it comes, once the conditions just mentioned are fulfilled, 'unexpectedly and suddenly' (*mughāfaṣatan wa-mubāghatatan*, p. 178.6). Avicenna takes this to be an observed fact, and his efforts in this chapter of the *Shifā'* are directed precisely at trying to elucidate it. He says:

> There is not a single person who has not had his share of [veridical] dreams [while asleep] and perceptions [of unknown and future events] while awake, for the cause of the discrete ideas (*khawāṭir*) that occur all at once to the [rational] soul is nothing else but certain contacts, and one is conscious neither of these contacts [themselves] nor of that with which contacts have been made, either before or after them.[37]

And this is the major difference, it seems, between this form of knowledge and intellectual knowledge. Thinking, and the wish to discover the middle terms of syllogisms, i.e., establish contact with the active intellect, are voluntary acts of cognition; the contacts with the supernal world, by contrast, are involuntary, because they happen at any time: during sleep, when one's intellect is dormant, or during waking hours, when one is engaged in other activities, and also in states of sickness or

[35] The word used here is *indhārāt*, the same word used repeatedly by Avicenna to describe part of the contents of the knowledge received from the celestial souls; see Gutas, *Intellect without Limits*, *passim*.

[36] *Avicenna's* De Anima, p. 174.5-7.

[37] *Avicenna's* De Anima, p. 174.1-4.

fear, when the intellect again is in abeyance, or in fools, simpletons, and madmen.[38] Avicenna continues:

> These notions [i.e., these perceptions of the supernal world] come about for reasons which arise in the [rational] soul for the most part furtively; they are like stolen intimations which do not stay long enough to be remembered unless the [rational] soul acts quickly with the intent to retain them, and what it does most is to preoccupy the imagination with the sort [of activity] that is unrelated to what it [the imagination] had been doing.[39]

That is, the imagination normally combines and separates images and concepts which it finds in the imagery and in memory. What the rational soul in this instance, i.e., when it receives the knowledge of the unseen, is asking the imagination to do is to convert or 'imitate' the new data from the supernal world to some form or image that can be stored in the memory or the imagery. This is vital for the retention of the received form because, as mentioned earlier, the intellect, that is the rational soul when it thinks, cannot store concepts: it has no retentive powers. This illustrates the major role that imagination plays in this process, and it is this aspect of the process that led Avicenna to call this kind of prophecy — when it is prophecy — or this kind of knowledge, knowledge that is proper to the faculty of the imagination.[40]

What is essential to comprehend here is the extreme variability of the manifestations of this knowledge of past, present, and future events. It can come to prophets, of course, but also to every man, even simpletons and fools — and this fact alone is enough to guarantee that this is not any kind of knowledge of divine or mystical secrets; it can come while one is asleep or awake, or in a state of semi-consciousness; and it can manifest itself in all forms: as dreams that need interpretation and dreams that do not, as visions of individuals talking to one, as simple warnings about events, as poetry, and even as intelligible concepts. This bewildering variety of manifestations is due both to the great complexity of the apparatus of the internal senses that Avicenna describes — the imagination, the estimation, and the imagery and the common sense

[38] See *Avicenna's* De Anima, p. 171.12-16: 'That which happens to the [rational] soul, namely, not to be preoccupied with the function of any one faculty or faculties, may come about on account of some damage or infirmity distracting from full performance — as it happens in the case of sickness and in the case of fear — and it comes about either on account of some relaxation — as in the case of sleep — or on account of excessive zeal to employ that faculty exclusively'.

[39] *Avicenna's* De Anima, p. 174.7-10.

[40] *Avicenna's* De Anima, p. 173.20-21.

must all have certain relations to each other and all of them collectively to the rational soul, relations which sometime inhibit and sometime support the process — and to the multiformity of combinations of individual constitutions, strengths of the soul, state of preparedness, and so on. Avicenna, keenly aware as a scientist of the multiformity of psychic and mental experience, tries to account for all these states within a comprehensive theory in a truly scientific spirit. It may not be an exaggeration to suggest that the entire Book IV (of the *Kitāb al-Nafs* of the *Shifāʾ*) on the internal senses deserves to be considered as the first modern treatise of psychology.

Avicenna revisits these themes in his final philosophical summa, *Pointers and Reminders*, but this time in a more allusive manner, as is to be expected of this highly suggestive work. The modalities of transmision of the knowledge from the supernal world are not discussed at all but simply depicted through the metaphor of 'engraving' — *intiqāsh*, *naqsh*, something which in his other works Avicenna refers to as impression, *inṭibāʿ*, *irtisām* — which leaves its 'trace', *athar*, on the soul, i.e., the knowledge from the unseen is 'engraved' upon the soul of the person. Avicenna says:

> It is in the nature of your soul to be engraved with the engravings of that [supernal] realm in accordance with [its] predisposition and the withdrawal of obstacles. You know this, so do not deny that some of the unseen (*al-ghayb*) from its realm will be engraved on [your soul].[41]

When received, this knowledge is again manifested in a variety of ways, as before. Avicenna says:

> The 'trace' [from the unseen] becomes observable and visible, or a cry that calls out, or other things; and sometimes it becomes an image with a perfectly developed form, or speech with a definite metrical structure, and sometimes it is in a state of the greatest beauty.[42]

Further on, Avicenna elaborates even more about the manifestations of the unseen. When the contact between the human soul and the supernal world takes place, it may take the following forms:

> [a] Sometimes, the fleeting glance of the unseen is a sort of strong opinion; [b] sometimes, it resembles the address of a genie or a call from someone absent; [c] and sometimes it takes place with something coming to view face to face, with the result that we actually observe the form of the unseen.[43]

[41] *Ishārāt*, X.10, p. 124-125.
[42] *Ishārāt*, IX.19, p. 139.
[43] *Ishārāt*, X.23, p. 148.

All these manifestations Avicenna finally categorizes into three categories. They are, he says, either (a) inspiration (*ilhām*), (b) pure revelation (*waḥy*), or (c) dreams (*ḥulm*).[44]

The ambiguity with regard to which faculty receives this knowledge, this 'trace' of the unseen, remains somewhat. In the majority of passages it is quite clear that the recipient is the rational soul, as distinct from the imagination. Avicenna says, 'When an engraving descends upon the soul unexpectedly, the imagination is roused to go to it and it receives it as well'.[45] This is self-explanatory. But on one occasion Avicenna also expresses himself as follows:

> When the substance of the soul is powerful ... it is not unlikely that seizing such an opportunity [of coming into contact with the supernal world] may befall it in the waking state. Sometimes the 'trace' [of the unseen] alights upon the memory and then stops there; but sometimes the impression becomes overpowering and then shines very clearly on the [faculty of] imagery.

This would indicate that not only the imagination, but even the other internal senses, memory and imagery — the storing places of sensible forms — may receive directly this celestial influence, if the term used, *nazala* (to alight, to descend upon, used of someone getting off a horse), implies a direct descending without the intermediacy of the rational soul. But given the allusive nature of this work, it may not be necessary to give too much literal significance to Avicenna's formulation in this passage.

Avicenna concludes his discussion of knowledge with a statement that summarizes his scientific approach and philosophical method in this regard. He says:

> Know that the way to profess and attest to these things is not [to say], 'they are merely plausible conjectures at which one arrives from intelligible matters only', even though this would have been something to rely upon, had it been [the case]; rather they are experiences of which, once confirmed, one seeks the causes.[46] One of the instances of happiness that is vouchsafed to

[44] *Ishārāt*, X.22, p. 144.

[45] *Ishārāt*, X.18, p. 138.

[46] The structure of this rather difficult sentence is not immediately apparent due to the syntactic peculiarity that the whole sentence *innamā ... faqaṭ* functions as a noun that serves as a predicate of *laysa*. Otherwise the basic structure has the form of a 'not ... but' sentence (*laysa ... wa-lākin*), studied and inventoried by M. Ullmann, *Nicht nur ... sondern auch ...*, in: *Der Islam* 60 (1983), p. 3-36, paradigm XXXIII, p. 27. The words *innamā* and *faqaṭ* occur within the embedded sentence that functions as predicate of *laysa* and are thus unrelated to the *laysa ... wa-lākin* structure of the main sentence. The structure of the sentence has been misunderstood by all translators (A.F. Mehren, A.-M. Goichon, S.

lovers of [philosophical] reflection is both that these states should occur to them personally and that they should observe them several times successively in others, to the point that all this becomes an experience, of relevance to the establishment of something marvellous that has sound existence, and an incentive to seek its cause. When it [this marvellous something] is elucidated, the [rational] soul finds reassurance in the existence of these causes, while the estimation yields and does not oppose the intellect in its vanguard function relating to the [investigation of] these [causes].[47]

This is Avicenna in his least dogmatic moment — it is the most explicit acknowledgement of empiricism that one finds in his works. The whole subject of knowledge (including prophetic knowledge) through the intermediacy of the imagination, centered as it is on the issue of knowledge of future events, presents formidable problems, some of which were mentioned in the preceding analysis of Avicenna's positions, notably the matter of the faculty that receives the particulars from on high (intellect or imagination), and the precise modes of the transmission of this knowledge. None of the three ways that Avicenna proposes is fully analytical or really explanatory: (a) congeneric similarity or (b) a certain connection between the souls of the spheres and the human soul are merely statements without analysis, let alone proof, while (c) the metaphor of 'engraving', for all its allusiveness, is hardly a philosophical concept — to say nothing of the problem of knowledge of particulars by the celestial souls. Avicenna must have been painfully aware of these problems and the shortcomings of his analyses,[48] and here he explicitly

Inati), perhaps understandably; what is inexcusable is the failure to render properly the expression *qāla bi-* (in *al-qawl bi-hā*): A.-M. GOICHON translated the first line as, 'il n'y a pas moyen de parler de ces choses': *Livre des directives et remarques*, Beirut - Paris, 1951, p. 519; and S . INATI as, 'are in no way the subject of speech': *Ibn Sīnā and Mysticism*, New York - London, 1996, p. 103. They both disregarded the fact that *qāla bi-* means to profess a doctrine and not 'to speak about' something, a mistranslation upon which was based the mistaken notion that Avicenna is talking about 'ineffable' things here. MEHREN did not make this particular mistake (and thus Goichon and Inati should have consulted his version), but his misunderstanding of the structure of the sentence as a whole again led to a misleading paraphrase: 'Tout ce que nous venons d'exposer ici ne peut être envisagé comme doctrine prouvée': *Traités mystiques ... d'Avicenne*, Leiden, 1891, Fasc. II, p. 19. Interestingly enough, the medieval commentators refrained from commenting on the passage. Quṭb al-Dīn al-Rāzī did not comment at all on the last two *namaṭ*s of the *Ishārāt*, while Fakhr al-Dīn al-Rāzī said that 'these sections are in no need of exegesis'! (*hādhihi l-fuṣūl ghanīya ʿan al-tafsīr*): *Sharḥay al-Ishārāt li- … al-Ṭūsī wa- … Fakhr al-Dīn al-Rāzī*, II, Cairo, 1325, p. 139.4). Al-Ṭūsī did make a few lexical remarks on some of the words in this section, but for the rest he, too, said that the meaning was obvious (*wa-bāqī l-faṣl ẓāhir*): *Ishārāt*, X.24, p. 149. I am indebted to Alexander Treiger for a fruitful discussion of this passage that led to the resolution of its ambiguities.

47 *Ishārāt*, X.24, p. 149.

48 Cf. MICHOT, *La destinée de l'homme*, p. 115 and note 45.

states why this is so. These things, he says, do not have their starting points in 'intelligible matters', i.e., in intelligible premisses, which could give rise to 'plausible conjectures' that could be proven or disproven syllogistically. Rather, he says, these things are empirical facts, based on indisputable human experience, both our own and that of others. People have experiences (dreams, visions, premonitions — and of course, prophecy) which in fact do inform them of the past, present, and future events. These are empirical truths which one then has to try and explain, using one's intellect and letting it take the lead, be the vanguard. This search for causes through the use of rational investigation in Avicenna, what we might otherwise call his scientific attitude, is what makes his philosophy so penetrating. It is also very interesting to see, at the end of his last major work (and one indeed that is considered to be mystical) that Avicenna is rejecting the dogmatic and otherworldly approach of Plotinus for the scientific and logical one of Aristotle.

AVICENNA'S CRITIQUE OF PLATONISTS IN BOOK VII, CHAPTER 2 OF THE *METAPHYSICS* OF HIS *HEALING*

MICHAEL E. MARMURA
University of Toronto

I

Notwithstanding the Neoplatonic setting of Avicenna's theory of universals, it remains at core Aristotelian. It negates any doctrine affirming the existence of the Platonic forms or related entities in an autonomous realm of their own, separate from the particulars of sense. This negation is for the most part implicit in Avicenna's detailed exposition of his theory of universals in Book V of the *Metaphysics* of his *Healing*, surfacing there briefly, though not insignificantly.[1] The detailed rebuttal of Platonist doctrines is postponed to the second and third chapters of Book VII.[2] The third chapter, dependent on the second, is a comprehensive critique of Platonist and Pythagorean philosophies of mathematics, already touched on in the second chapter.

Our main concern will be with the second chapter, particularly with the five arguments with which Avicenna concludes it. These are aimed not only at Plato's theory of forms as we know it from the *Phaedo* and *The Republic*, for example. They are also directed against various theories of unnamed Platonists according to which, in one way or another, mathematical objects and their logically prior principles, their *mabādi'*, become the separate entities. The mathematical entities themselves are also referred to as *mabādi'*, this time as the principles that help engender the natural forms of the particulars of sense. What these theories, including Plato's theory of forms, have in common is their affirmation that there are related entities that are separate from the particulars of sense. The five arguments, as Avicenna explicitly states, are intended to refute all such theories.

While the main line of reasoning of these arguments is not difficult to grasp, it is not entirely devoid of the problematic. We will indicate this

[1] IBN SĪNĀ (AVICENNA), *al-Shifā'* (*Healing*): *al-Ilāhīyāt* (*Metaphysics*), ed. G.C. ANAWATI, S. DUNYA and S. ZAYID, Cairo, 1960, p. 202-204 — see Section IV below. Hereafter this text will be cited as *Ilāhīyāt* in the notes and *Metaphysics* in the text.

[2] *Ilāhīyāt*, p. 310-324.

in Section III, below, where we will offer a translation of the arguments with commentary. We will then conclude (Section IV) with a critical discussion of the pivotal concept, namely the concept of a quiddity considered strictly in itself, that underlies Avicenna's theory of universals and hence his five arguments. But first, something must be said about the theories Avicenna's five arguments purport to refute.

II

The theories Avicenna discusses are varied, some touched on only briefly. We will confine ourselves to those that seem most pertinent to his critique. The tone of his descriptions and criticisms of the Platonist theories is set early in the chapter where he writes:

> When [Greek philosophers] first made the transition from what is apprehended by the senses to what is apprehended by the intellect they became confused. A group[3] thought that the division necessitates the existence of two things in each thing, as for example, two humans in the idea of humanity — a corruptible, sensible human, and an intellectually apprehended, separate, eternal and changeless human … It was known that Plato and his teacher Socrates went to excess in upholding this view, saying that there belongs to humanity one existing idea in which individuals participate and which continues to exist with their ceasing to exist. This, [they held], is not the sensible, multiple and corruptible meaning and is therefore the intelligible, separable meaning.[4]

As already indicated, apart from mentioning Socrates and Plato in connection with the theory of separate forms, Avicenna does not name the authors of the other theories.[5] After this brief mention of Plato and Socrates, and before resuming discussion of the theory of forms, Avicenna writes:

> Another group (*qawm*) did not perceive a separable existence for this [Platonic] form, but only for its principles. They rendered the mathematical entities that are separable in definition deserving to be separable in existence. They made those forms that are not separable in definition not separable in

[3] *Qawm*, more literally, 'people', 'folk', referred to by Avicenna in the plural. Henceforth *qawm* will be translated as 'group'.

[4] *Ilāhīyāt*, p. 310.13 - p. 311.8.

[5] Avicenna's accounts, which must derive from the body of Aristotelian commentary available to him in translation, reflect Aristotle's discussions in his *Metaphyiscs*, particularly Book I (Chapters 6 and 9), Books II, XIII and XIV. For a translation of the last two books (with a substantial introduction and detailed notes), see JULIA ANNAS, *Aristotle's Metaphysics, Books M and N*, Oxford, 1976.

> essence. They [further] made the natural forms to be generated only through the connection of these mathematical forms with matter, as for example, concavity. For it is a mathematical idea: once it connects with matter, it becomes 'snub-noseness' (*fuṭūsa*) and becomes a natural idea. It is then for concavity inasmuch as it is mathematical to separate [in existence], even though inasmuch as it is natural it is not for it to separate.[6]

When Avicenna states that this group 'did not perceive a separable existence for this [Platonic] form, but only for its principles', these presumably include the principle of the One and the indefinite Dyad — the Dyad consisting of the great and the small.[7] But then he immediately speaks of the separate mathematical entities as 'the principles' that help generate the natural forms — a shift in what the term 'principles' refers to. This shift in meaning becomes explicit when, after interrupting discussion of the above theory by turning to Plato's theory of forms, he resumes discussion of the former. 'As for the others (*wa-amma l-ākharūn*)', a reference to 'the group' he had been discussing earlier, he writes, 'they rendered the principles of natural things mathematical objects, rendered them the things that are in truth the intelligibles, rendered them in truth the separable entities [in existence]'. He continues:

> They stated that if they strip the corporeal states from matter, then only magnitudes,[8] shapes and numbers remain. This is because the passive qualities that [fall] under affections derive from the nine [*sic*] categories, positive dispositions (*al-malakāt*), power and absence of power being matters that belong to things possessing affections, positive dispositions and powers. As for relation, the things [in this category] that are connected with the likes of [the above] are also material. Hence there remains 'place', which is quantitative, 'time', which is quantitative and 'situation', which is quantitative. As for action and affection, it is material. The result of [all] this is that everything that is not quantitative is attached to matter. [But] the principle of what is attached to matter is [itself] not attached to matter. Hence, mathematical things become the principles and the things that are in truth the intelligibles, everything else being not an intelligible. For this reason no one gives a definition of colour, taste and the like that is worthy of attention. For [such a thing] is related to a [sensible] apprehending faculty; as such, the mind (according to them) does not apprehend it intellectually — it is only imagined by the imaginative faculty following sensation.[9]

[6] *Ilāhīyāt*, p. 311.7-13.

[7] For Aristotle's reference to the great and the small, see *Metaphysics*, I, 6, 987b22-23.

[8] Reading *aʿẓām* (as in one manuscript reading) instead of *aqṭār*, which in the context can be translated as '[spatial] areas'.

[9] *Ilāhīyāt*, p. 312.6-15.

We have quoted this particular theory that Avicenna reports in full for a number of reasons. One reason is that, as we shall see, this is a specific theory Avicenna targets in the last of the five arguments against the theories of separate entities. A second, because it raises the question of identifying 'the group' upholding this theory. (It seems to consist of the followers of Speusippus, noted for abandoning the Platonic forms for numbers.) A third reason is that it reveals Aristotelian elements in this theory, indicating that its advocates utilize Aristotelian concepts for their own non-Aristotelian ends. This is seen, for example, in the discussion of definition and the example of concavity as a separate mathematical entity which has a background in Aristotle's discussions of definition in his *Metaphysics* (Book VI, 1, 1025b, 26-1026a, 5). A further reason is the elaboration of the theory in terms of the Aristotelian categories.[10]

Closer to the principle of the great and the small is suggested when Avicenna speaks of another group as making 'the principles [consisting of] the excessive, the deficient and the equal'. Some, he goes on to say, 'made the equal take the place of *hyle*'. Another group, he then states, 'made [the equal] take the place of form because [form] is restricted and limited, whereas there is no limit to the excessive and the deficient'.[11] Avicenna also refers to another group, stating that 'some make for every numerical mathematical rank a form corresponding to an existing form',[12] so that 'when abstraction takes place and when mixture with matter takes place there will be the form of man or horse ... [another] group hold that there is a difference between these numerical forms and the exemplars'. This is suggestive of views in the traditions of Xenocrates (who identified the forms with numbers) and Speusippus who, as stated earlier, forsook the Platonic forms for numbers.

In the discussion of all these theories of unnamed authorship, the interest is with the mathematical nature of the separable entities. The Pythagorean influence on these is evident, but Avicenna makes it clear that the theories of the latter do not assign a separate existence for the

[10] All this suggests that members of 'the group' belong to a post-Aristotelian period, though perhaps not exclusively — Aristotle was for a long time a member of the Academy and it seems most unlikely that ideas associated with him were not discussed in the Academy. Modern scholars have also often spoken of 'Aristotle's Platonism'. For a discussion of the ambiguity of this appellation, see G.E.L. OWEN, *The Platonism of Aristotle*, in: *Studies in the Philosophy of Thought and Action*, ed. P.F. STRAWSON, London, 1968, p. 147-174.

[11] *Ilāhīyāt*, p. 313.1-3.

[12] *Ilāhīyāt*, p. 313.17-314.3.

mathematical entities.[13] Avicenna's discussions evoke the question of where Plato stands in all these. Is there any suggestion in these discussions that Plato himself was moving in the direction of rendering the separate entities exclusively mathematical, the issue intensely debated in modern scholarship?

When discussing Plato, Avicenna tells us that 'most of his inclination (*akthar mayli-hi*) was [towards the view] that it is the forms that are separate'. The phrase, 'most of his inclination', suggests that Avicenna was aware that Plato may have had an inclination towards other views.[14] Still, his exposition of Plato is very much in tune with what he holds in *The Republic*, particularly about the place of mathematics in an intermediary position between the forms and the world of the senses: 'regarding mathematical [entities]', Avicenna writes, 'these for [Plato] were [intermediary] ideas between forms and natural things'.[15] His account of Plato's theory of ideas accords with Aristotle's exposition in *Metaphysics* I, 6, on which it seems to be based, though perhaps not exclusively.

III

Turning to the five arguments, these presuppose Avicenna's theory of universals. The aspect of this theory immediately relevant to understanding these arguments is the ontological (discussed in the first two of the nine chapters of Book V of his *Metaphysics*).[16] The key idea underlying this ontology is that of a quiddity or nature considered strictly in itself. A consideration of the quiddity, the *māhīya*, 'the what it is', of a thing does not yield the knowledge that the thing defined or described exists. The quiddity pure and simple excludes the idea of existence. To use Avicenna's well known example with reference to the quiddity, 'horseness (*al-farasīya*)', he declares, 'is simply horseness' — 'in itself it is neither one nor many and exists neither in concrete things nor in the soul, existing in none of such things either potentially or actually'.[17]

[13] *Ilāhīyāt*, p. 312.14-15.

[14] He could have gathered this not only from reading (between the lines) parts of Aristotle's *Metaphysics*, but from other works — for example from the *De Anima*, I, 2, 404b24-25, where it is stated that Plato maintained the identity of forms and numbers, or from Aristotle's one allusion (*Physics*, IV, 2, 209b15) to Plato's 'unwritten doctrine'.

[15] *Ilāhīyāt*, p. 311.14-15.

[16] *Ilāhīyāt*, p. 195-212.

[17] *Ilāhīyāt*, p. 196.10-12.

The mention of the one and the many is of particular relevance to understanding the five arguments. The one and the many, together with universality and particularity, are the necessary concomitants of existence. But as concomitants of existence they are not included in the quiddity considered as such. He thus uses this idea — that is, that the one and the many, as concomitants of existence, are not included in the quiddity as such — to resolve a major problem facing his theory of universals. How can a quiddity such as humanity be common to many humans without itself becoming many? Avicenna's answer is that inasmuch as humanity is simply humanity it is neither one nor many. Hence the problem does not arise. His resolution of this problem is not without its ingenuity, though — as we shall try to show — not without its ambiguity.

*

* *

The first of the five arguments is the longest and begins as follows:

> [1] One of [the causes of their error] is the belief that if a thing is abstracted such that a consideration of another thing is not connected with it, then it is separate from it in existence. It is as though if attention is paid to the thing alone, [a thing] that has an associate, in a manner that gives no attention to the associate, [this] would render it not adjoining its associate. In short, if it is considered without the condition of [its] conjunction with another, it is believed that it is considered with the condition that there is no conjunction [with another], so that [according to this view], it was only suitable to be examined because it was not conjoined, but separate. For this reason, it was believed that since the mind attains the intelligibles existing without attending to what is conjoined to them, the mind attains nothing but [what is] separate among them. This, however, is not the case. Rather, for each thing with respect to itself there is one consideration and with respect to its relatedness to something conjoining it there is another consideration.[18]

The argument thus far is quite clear: the error lies in concluding that when something is abstracted from its necessary concomitants it therefore has an existence separate from them. That the concomitants Avicenna is referring to are the objects of sense is implicit in what he says. It is stated more explicitly in his expression of this idea at the beginning of the chapter where, as we have indicated earlier, he stated that when people 'first made the transition from what is apprehended by the senses to what is apprehended by the mind they became confused', thinking that 'the division necessitates the existence of two things in each thing,

[18] *Ilāhīyāt*, p. 314.9-15.

for example, two humans in the idea of humanity — a corruptible, sensible human, and an intellectually apprehended, separate, eternal and changeless human'.[19]

Avicenna's stance in all this is Aristotelian and continues to be so as he expands on what he had said:

> If we apprehend intellectually the form of the human, for example, inasmuch as it is the form of the human alone, we would have apprehended intellectually an existent alone with respect to its self.[20] But inasmuch as we have [so] apprehended it, it does not necessarily follow that it alone is separate [in existence]. For that which is mixed with another, inasmuch as it is itself, is inseparable from [the other][21] by way of negation, not by way of equipolence (*al-ʿudūl*), in terms of which separation in subsistence is understood.[22]

The Arabic of this last sentence is problematic[23] and, at first sight, it is not immediately clear how the concept of equipolence fits in. Basically, this concept means the denial, not of a statement as a whole, but only of either its subject or (usually) its predicate. To take as an example the case of a predicate consisting of one term, its denial can acquire a positive meaning for which a verbal equivalence can be found. Thus,

[19] *Ilāhīyāt*, p. 310.13 - p. 311.2.

[20] *Bi-dhāti-hi*, alternatively, 'to its essence'.

[21] That is, the other component of the mixture.

[22] *Ilāhīyāt*, p. 314.16 - p. 325.2.

[23] The passage in the Arabic reads *fa-inna l-mukhāliṭ min ḥaythu huwa huwa 'ghayr mufāriq' ʿalā jihat al-salb lā ʿalā jihat al-ʿudūl alladhī yufhamu min-hu l-mufāriq bi-l-qiwām*. The key expression here is *ghayr mufāriq*. One naturally tends to read it vowelled as *ghayru mufāriqin*. This, though not the only vowelling possible, seems to be the one that is intended. It could be vowelled as *ghayrun mufāriqun*, which would form the predicate of *huwa huwa* in the compound nominal sentence. The sentence would then translate something as follows:

> 'For that which is mixed with another, inasmuch as it is itself, is "an other", separable from [the other component] by way of negation, not by way of equipolence, in terms of which separation in subsistence is understood'.

In this translation, the shift is towards identity. Thus if we have two distinct but inseparable things, A and B, the denial in the statement 'Not (A is B)' is a denial only of identity, not of separability. Denial by equipolence would take the form '(A is not-B)', which would mean for Avicenna the separation of A and B 'in subsistence', a denial he is rejecting. The British Museum manuscript cited in the *apparatus criticus* gives the alternative reading *al-muqārin*, 'the connected [with]', instead of *al-mufāriq*, 'the separable', which does not seem to make good sense. It is followed by the statement: 'some of them have understood it thus'. For 'it is inseparable (*ghayr mufāriq*) [?]' not in that it is said that it is separable [in existence] because equipolence is an expression of the privation of an existing attribute; its privation is part of its existence. Privation hence necessarily requires existence, unlike absolute negation'. This interpolation, itself not entirely clear, hints at the difficulty encountered in following the wording and the thought of this passage.

for Avicenna, the statement, 'Zayd is not-seeing', translates into 'Zayd is blind'.[24]

Turning to the problematic sentence above, Avicenna is concerned with the inseparability of the two components of a mixture 'in subsistence', allowing, however, their separability in abstraction. In the case of the mixture of two things, A and B, the denial of their separability 'by way of negation', can be expressed by the statement, 'A is not separable from B'. The predicate here would be 'not separable from B'. Negation by way of equipolence would mean the negation of the predicate, thus we would have the statement: 'A is not (not separable from B)', thereby affirming its separability. And this is what Avicenna is rejecting. He continues:

> It is not difficult for us to direct attention through perception or some other state to one or two things whose role is not to separate from its companion in subsistence, even though it separates from it in definition, meaning and reality, since its reality is not entered in the reality of the other. For conjunction necessitates connectedness, not permeation in meaning.[25]

The thought here is quite clear: the separateness, or otherness, of two things in terms of their definition, does not mean that they are separate in existence. In other words, if these two are necessary concomitants, they cannot separate in existence, only in abstraction. This indicates that Avicenna is not speaking of the necessary components of one and the same definition, where 'the reality' of one enters 'in the reality of the other'. For example, when we define man as a rational animal, we cannot in this definition separate by abstraction his rationality from his animality, which in turn, cannot be separated from the corporeality of being an animal.[26] In this instance, we are speaking about matter in a generic sense.

[24] IBN SĪNĀ, *Kitāb al-Ishārāt wa-l-Tanbīhāt*, ed. G. FORGET, Leiden, 1892, p. 239-240; in S.C. INATI'S translation, IBN SĪNĀ, *Remarks and Admonitions Part I: Logic*, Toronto, 1984, p. 83 ff.; IBN SĪNĀ, *al- Najāh*, ed. M. FAKHRY, Beirut, 1985, p. 54-55. The example appears in passing in Avicenna's lengthy discussion of statements relating to equipolence in his *Kitāb al-ʿIbāra* (*De Interpretatione*) of the *Shifāʾ*, ed. M. KHUDAYRI, Cairo, 1970, Book II, Chapter 1, p. 76-87 (p. 81, lines 10-11). For discussions of composite expressions, see S.C. INATI, *Ibn Sīnā on Single Expressions*, in: *Islamic Theology and Philosophy*, ed. M.E. MARMURA, Albany, 1984, p. 148-159. For a discussion of *ʿudūl* and its antecedents in Greek thought, particularly in Theophrastus, see F.W. ZIMMERMANN, *Al-Farābi's Commentary and Short Treatise on Aristotle's* De Interpretatione, Oxford, 1981, p. lxxxi, and note i, where *ʿudūl* is translated as 'metathetic', and p. 98, note l.

[25] *Ilāhīyāt*, p. 315, lines 2-5.

[26] As Avicenna puts it elsewhere, we cannot understand 'man' without understanding that man is composed of flesh and bones: *Fī Aqsām al-ʿUlūm* (*On The Division of the Sciences*) in: *Tisʿ Rasāʾil*, Cairo, 1908, p. 106.

The abstraction that Avicenna talks about in this entire argument seems to be the act of 'extracting' the form from a particular existent, where, after receiving the image of the particular through the external sense of sight, the mind denudes it from its material attachments. Avicenna's concern remains with the particular, the Aristotelian substance, the composite of form and matter.

*

* *

> [2] The second cause is their error concerning the one. For when we say that humanity is one meaning, we do not intend by this that it is one meaning which is the very one found in many and thus becomes many through relation, as in the case of one father that happens to be [a father] of many; rather, it is akin to [many] fathers in [relation] to diverse sons. We have discussed this fully in other places.
>
> These people did not know that we say of many things that their meaning is one, meaning by this that if we suppose any one of them to occur first to matter which is of the same state as it is for the other, there would ensue from it this one individual. Similarly, if any one of them comes first to the intellect, becoming imprinted in it, then that one meaning would result from it. If, [on the other hand], one comes first [to the mind], the other becomes inoperative: it would not enact anything. [This would be] like warmth. If it occurs to matter that has moisture in it, it would cause another meaning, or if it occurs to a mind in which the idea [of] moisture and its intelligible has first come to it, it would enact a different meaning.
>
> Had they understood the meaning of 'one' in this, this would have sufficed them. This [misunderstanding of what 'one' means] is what led them astray.[27]

Underlying this argument is Avicenna's concept of the quiddity considered in itself. Considered in itself, the quiddity does not include existence and its concomitants, the one and the many. This helps us understand his example of fatherhood as a relation. If fatherhood refers to one father in relation to many sons, there is a sense in which his being the father of this son, of that son, and so on, can be taken as entailing multiplicity in the relation, fatherhood. In the example of the many fathers to various sons, fatherhood, now considered as a quiddity in itself, is neither one nor many. When it is referred to as 'one', this is not in any numerical sense, but in the sense of being one and the same, that is the identical nature common to all fathers in relation to all sons.

[27] *Ilāhīyāt*, p. 315.6-14.

Avicenna in the above indicates the epistemological side of this, which he discusses more fully in the *Psychology* of the *Healing*.[28] When from seeing any member of a species, for example, an individual human, the image resides in the soul, the mind abstracts the form humanity. When it perceives another particular human, the mind does not 'take from it some other form of the species', since this had already been abstracted. As Avicenna puts it, 'if the sense presents to the imagination and the imagination to the intellect some form, the intellect takes from it a meaning'. If, then, the imagination presents to the intellect 'another form of that species, it being another only in number, the intellect will not take from it at all some other form of that species other than the one it had already taken'.[29]

*

* *

> [3] The third [error] consists in their ignorance that our statement 'that such and such inasmuch as it is such and such is some other thing differing from it in definition' is a contradictory statement. This is similar to the statement of an erring person who if asked, 'is the human inasmuch as he is the human, one or many?', answers, 'he is either one or many'. For the human inasmuch as he is the human is only the human. Inasmuch as he is the human he is nothing other than the human. Oneness and multiplicity are other than the human. We have finished with explaining this.[30]

The Arabic of the first sentence, reproduced almost literally in the translation, is cryptic. Its sense is explained in the example that follows. What is intended is that whatever is considered strictly in itself does not include anything else which would differ from it in definition. Again, at the base of this argument is Avicenna's concept of the quiddity considered in itself. It does not include existence, nor any of its concomitants such as unity and multiplicity. Thus in the example, humanity inasmuch as it is humanity is neither one nor many.

*

* *

> [4] Their fourth [error] is their supposition that if we say that humanity exists always, permanently, this is the same as our saying [that] humanity is either one or many. This would only be the case if our saying, 'humanity',

[28] Ibn Sīnā, *al-Shifā'*: *al-Ṭabī'īyāt* (*Physics*); *al-Nafs* (*De Anima*), ed. G.C. Anawati and S. Zayed, Cairo, 1975, V, 5, p. 209-210.

[29] Ibn Sīnā, *al-Nafs*, p. 209, lines 17-21.

[30] *Ilāhīyāt*, p. 315.15 - p. 316.4.

> and [our saying] 'humanity is either one or many', are one and the same meaning. Similarly, they must not suppose that if they admit to themselves that humanity is permanent, then they are necessarily [committed to the view] that the one specific humanity is permanent so as to posit an eternal humanity.[31]

Once again the underlying premise of this argument is the quiddity considered strictly in itself. The first part of the above denies that by maintaining the humanity, permanent in existence, is either one or many. It is neither. The second part, beginning with 'similarly' above, is less clear. But Avicenna's intention here is that if one erroneously thinks of humanity as being numerically one, then one is committed to the view that there is a numerically one humanity which is permanent. This relates to Avicenna's statement (which we referred to earlier) about the confusion of those who posit the existence of separate forms, where, taking the example, 'humanity', he maintains that they in effect, uphold the existence of 'two humans in the idea of humanity — a corruptible, sensible human, and an intellectually apprehended, separate, eternal and changeless human'.[32]

*

* *

> [5] The fifth [error] is their belief that if material things are caused, then their causes are necessarily any of the things that separate. For it is not the case that if material things are caused and mathematical things are separate then it follows necessarily that the mathematical things are their causes. Rather, [their causes] may be other substances that are not among the nine categories.
>
> Nor have they arrived at the heart of the ascertaining of the truth that the definitions of the geometrical [figures] among mathematical [objects] cannot dispense with matter, even though they can do without some kind of matter. It seems that these are things for whose ascertainment [certain] principles we have already discussed suffice.[33]

This passage is directed specifically at theories that maintain that the separate mathematical entities cause the natural forms without which material things cannot exist. Avicenna's point is that if material things have non-material causes, these need not be the separate mathematical entities (supposing, for the sake of argument, that there are such separate

[31] *Ilāhīyāt*, p. 316.5-8.

[32] *Ilāhīyāt*, p. 311.2-3; already quoted in discussing the 'first error' above.

[33] *Ilāhīyāt*, p. 311.9-14.

mathematical entities). They may have as causes substances 'that are not among the nine categories'. What then are these substances? As we see it, these must be the immaterial celestial intelligences of Avicenna's cosmology, particularly the active intellect, 'the bestower of forms' (*wāhib al-ṣuwar*), from which the forms in the sublunar sphere emanate. This, then would be the one place in this chapter where Avicenna's Neoplatonism seems to emerge.

In the second paragraph of the passage above Avicenna alludes to his having discussed the ontological status of geometrical figures. He had discussed this in several places, particularly in the *Isagoge* of the *Logic* of the *Healing*.[34] Like the objects of knowledge of physics, the objects of mathematical knowledge cannot be dissociated from matter. Mathematics, however, differs from physics in that its object of knowledge is not confined to one specific kind of matter. To take such a geometrical figure as a triangle, it has to exist in some kind of matter. (A triangle can be wooden, made of iron, or of some other substance). The mind, however, can abstract it and view it in its own right, so to speak, probing its mathematical properties without reference to the matter in which it happens to be.

Put in another way, there are no perfect triangles or circles that have an autonomous existence, dissociated from matter. These can have an existence dissociated from matter only as abstractions in a mind.

IV

As already indicated, Avicenna's arguments rest on his own theory of universals. The key operative idea in this theory is the concept of a quiddity considered strictly in itself, which Avicenna uses to resolve certain problems, particularly that of the one and the many. His discussions of this concept, however, do not seem to be free from ambiguities[35] which,

[34] IBN SĪNĀ, *al-Shifā'*: *al-Manṭiq* (*Logic*) I: *al-Madkhal* (*Isagoge*), ed. M. KHUDAYRI, G.C. ANAWATI and A.F. AHWANI, Cairo, 1953, I, p. 12.14 - p. 13.4; *Fī Aqsām al-'Ulūm*, p. 105-107; *Ilāhīyāt*, p. 3; *al-Shifā'*: *al-Manṭiq*, V: *al-Burhān* (*Demonstration*), ed. A.E. AFFIFI, Cairo, 1956, p. 187-188. For a translation of the *Isagoge* chapter with a commentary, see my article, *Avicenna on the Divisions of the Sciences in the* Isagoge *of his* Shifā', in: *Journal of the History of Arabic Science* 4 (1980), p. 241-251.

[35] For a discussion of some of these ambiguities, see my articles, *Avicenna's Chapter on Universals in the* Isagoge *of his* Shifā', in: *Islam: Past Influences and Present Challenge*, ed. A.T. WELCH and P. CACHIA, Edinburgh, 1979, p. 34-56; and *Quiddity and Universality in Avicenna*, in: *Studies in Neoplatonism*, ed. P. MOREWEDGE, Albany, 1992, p. 77-78.

left unresolved, weaken his arguments against the Platonists: they also tend to blur the basic insight Avicenna offers in his doctrine of essence. As we see it, the main ambiguity in this theory pertains to the relation of the quiddity considered in itself to existence. Existence is not included in the quiddity as such. Yet quiddities have to exist, either in a mind or extramentally. This existence, according to Avicenna, is a necessary concomitant of the quiddity.

There are two key passages in Book V of the *Metaphysics* of the *Healing* that sum up Avicenna's view of how quiddities (considered in themselves, as such) exist in individual things. Their existence 'with another', he argues in both passages, does not deprive them of their identity, of what they are in themselves. He begins one of the passages as follows:

> [The fact] that the animal existing in the individual is a certain animal (*ḥayawān mā*) does not prevent animal inasmuch as it is animal — [that is], not through its being an animal in some state (*bi-ḥāl mā*)[36] — from existing in it. [This is] because, if this individual is a certain animal, then a certain animal exists. Hence, animal [inasmuch as it is animal] which is part of a certain animal exists.

Avicenna thus asserts that a quiddity in itself exists in an individual as 'part' of it. This is a point he elaborates in the second passage which we will be quoting and commenting on shortly. In the second part of the passage above he gives an example to show how this existence does not deprive the quiddity of its being what it is. He writes:

> This is like whiteness. For, even though not separable from matter, it exists in its whiteness in matter as something else, considered in itself, having its own reality, even though it so happens that this reality is conjoined in existence with something else.[37]

Now this example of whiteness in a material object (which Avicenna has used elsewhere)[38] is simply an analogy. Taken literally, it can be misleading. The whiteness he is speaking about in the example is a particular quality of a particular material object. The real question here would be the relation of the quiddity, whiteness, to the particular white quality of a particular material object. In what sense can the quiddity considered in itself be said to exist in this particular quality?

[36] That is, in some state other than its being a quiddity considered strictly in itself.

[37] *Ilāhīyāt*, p. 202.3-8.

[38] This an example which Avicenna had also used in *Isagoge*, Book I, Chapter 12, p. 66.8-10.

This brings us to the second passage where Avicenna gives a fuller discussion of the view that the quiddity considered in itself exists in an individual, without losing its identity, so to speak. In this discussion, he brings in another element, namely the priority 'in existence' of such a quiddity to the individual it associates with:

> Considering animal in itself would be permissible even though it exists with another because [it] itself with another is [still] itself. Its essence belongs to it itself and its being with another is either an accidental matter that occurs to it or some necessary concomitant to its nature. Considered in this way it is prior in existence (*mutaqaddim fī l-wujūd*) to the animal which is either particular by [reason of] its accidents or universal, existing [as a particular extramentally] or [as a universal in the mind], in the way the simple is prior to the complex and the part to the whole. In this [mode of existence] it is neither genus nor species, neither individual, one nor many. But in this [mode] of existence it is only animal and only human.[39]

In what sense, then, is one to understand this priority 'in existence to the animal which is either particular by [reason of] its accidents or universal, existing ... extramentally' on in the mind? To say that this priority is similar to the priority of the simple to the complex and the part to the whole, is suggestive that we are speaking here of an amalgam of individual entities, a composite of individual existents. But, perhaps more to the point, is a dilemma we seem to be facing: to be considered simply in itself, a quiddity must first exist either in a mind, in things, or in both. Its existence is then prior to its being considered strictly in itself. How, then, is its being considered in itself prior in existence to its existence in things? The sense in which the expression 'prior in existence' is used is not clarified.[40]

[39] *Ilāhīyāt*, p. 201.8-13.

[40] In seeking a clarification here, one may turn to two aspects of Avicennan thought. The first is his emanative system. A quiddity like humanity, for example, exists in the active intellect, 'the bestower of forms', and then emanates on the terrestrial world where it becomes 'dispersed' (*muntashira*), particularised in individuals. In this sense its existence in the active intellect is prior to its dispersed existence terrestrially. But this is not the question here. The concern is with the quiddity, not as an existent, but as something considered in itself where it does not include the idea of existence. The question, then, can take the form: how can that which excludes existence from being what it is, be prior 'in existence' to an existing individual with which it associates? The second is to invoke Avicenna's distinction between 'affirmative existence' (*al-wujūd al-ithbātī*) and 'special existence' (*al-wujūd al-khāṣṣ*). In *Ilāhīyāt*, I, 5, p. 31.5-8, he states: 'to everything there is a reality by virtue of which it is what it is. The triangle thus has a reality in that it is a triangle, and whiteness a reality in being whiteness. We should perhaps call this "special existence", not intending by this the meaning given to "affirmative existence"'. But once

Moreover, when Avicenna speaks of a quiddity or a nature considered in itself as 'existing' 'in', 'with', or as 'part of', an individual, one has also to ask how does this accord with his statement about a quiddity like 'horseness' — which, in itself 'neither one nor many, exists neither externally nor in the soul'? Taken at face value, there seems to be inconsistency here. What Avicenna, however, intends by his statement about 'horseness' is that such a quiddity, considered as such, does not include the notion of existence. Existence is hence not predicated of the quiddity 'horseness'. For those who maintain that existence is not a predicate this would be a significant insight. And, as we see it, contrary to criticisms that Avicenna regards existence as an accident, this represents Avicenna's position.

But then, we do have the statement in the paragraph quoted above that the quiddity like animality in itself exists 'with another' as 'either an accidental matter that occurs to it or some necessary concomitant of its nature'. This is not fully explained. The statement, as it stands, raises all sorts of questions. It raises, for example, the question (which caused controversy in post-Avicennan Islamic philosophy) of whether or not existence is prior to essence. Its language also suggests what could be interpreted as a move in the direction of regarding existence as a predicate, and would thus blur the Avicennan insight, indicated above, that it is not.

In brief, Avicenna's theory of universals, ingenious and historically significant as it is, leaves many a point not clarified. If, as with Santayana, one in an imaginary trip were to visit limbo and have a chat with Avicenna, there would be a number of questions about his theory that one would want to ask.

we consider what this 'special existence' stands for, we find that it is really identical with the quiddity considered in itself. The sense of the expression 'prior in existence' remains not clarified. Put in another way, in what sense is a thing's 'special existence' prior to its 'affirmative existence'? Would it not be prior to it in the affirmative sense?

READING AVICENNA IN THE MADRASA: INTELLECTUAL GENEALOGIES AND CHAINS OF TRANSMISSION OF PHILOSOPHY AND THE SCIENCES IN THE ISLAMIC EAST

GERHARD ENDRESS
Ruhr-Universität Bochum

> The reasons for the 'hellenization' of the Aš'arite and Maturidite *kalâm* in the late period and for the ultimate demise of the Mu'tazilite school in Sunnî Islam are extremely complex and involve the whole web of Islam's religious and intellectual development in that and in the preceding period. The assumption — to put it in its most extreme form — that the 'Aristotelianized' *kalâm* of al-Ghazzâlî, aš-Šahrastânî, Fakhr ad-Dîn ar-Râzî, and al-Ğurğânî followed through a kind of mutation of the natural intellectual maturity and perfection of that of the earlier period, while the *kalâm* of al-Aš'arî and al-Bâqillânî, abû Hâšim, and 'Abd al-Ğabbâr formed an intermediate stage of the process — a sort of holding operation — between the intellectual ferment of the early period and the introduction of the Aristotelian and Neoplatonic elements into the *kalâm* at the beginning of the twelfth century, must give rise to a number of serious questions'.[1]

The continuity of philosophical teaching, and the persistence of discourse on God and the World, on matter and form, on body and soul, are constituted by authors, by the works taught by authors and their schools, and through the transmission of their teaching in institutions of learning. Richard M. Frank has shown us the driving forces behind this in the commerce and struggle of ideas. I would like to offer a much more pedestrian approach in looking at the transmission and reading of texts. The close connection between textual transmission and teaching tradition, between personal authority and the written document, the spreading of global networks under the impact of authorities, schools of learning, and hence, the integration of teaching traditions through common canons of knowledge, discourse and method, is the very essence of Islamic civilization from the early Middle Ages until today.

The chains and networks of learning can be followed up through the evidence of extant manuscripts, the indications of the biographical litera-

[1] RICHARD M. FRANK, *Beings and their Attributes: the Teaching of the Basrian School of the Mu'tazila in the Classical Period*, Albany: SUNY, 1978, p. 2.

ture, and through the succession of commentaries and glosses on the basic manuals evolving in the later period. I propose to consider how, on the basis of examples taken from mathematics, medicine, and philosophy, these traditions first evolved independently within each of the disciplines and within separate institutions, and then converged into an epistemic community of *ʿulūm ʿaqlīya*, practical and theoretical, until finally the teaching of *ḥikma* and *riyāḍīyāt* joined the teaching of the law, *Uṣūl al-Fiqh* and *Kalām* (*ʿulūm al-dīn*) in the canon and cursus of the *madrasa*.

In the early period, from the Eighth to the Tenth Century, traditions of learning concur and compete: on the one side, the epistemic community of Islamic tradition, on the way towards defining and delimiting the sources of valid decisions in law and the faith — and on the other side, scientists, translators and administrators collecting and elaborating canons of readings in the service of individual disciplines of mathematics, astronomy, natural science and medicine, and of the philosophical paradigms accompanying these traditions. Choosing, adding and eliminating elements of the Iranian and Greek traditions of learning, merging and harmonizing these elements in the first works of synthesis, Arabic authors — mathematicians, astronomers, physicians — each defined a cursus of studies, adopted to individual methodologies and philosophical models, and taught on the basis of a canon of authoritative texts. An integration and consolidation of such canons was first brought about within individual scientific communities. Simultaneously, and in successive approaches, Muslim intellectuals trained in the rational sciences, close to the administration of the central and provincial courts, and to the authorities of the religious community, defended and integrated the rational sciences in systematic expositions. By infringing upon the domains of religious hermeneutics and legal reasoning, these provoked the first exchanges across borders, and challenged grammarians and jurists to redefine their principles (*uṣūl*) of reasoning.

But the way to the study of rationalist methodology, epistemology and theology in the schools of law was paved when philosophy was emancipated from the applied arts, and philosophers set out to interpret religious knowledge rationally, and to answer the aporias of theology autonomously and universally. After the early approaches of al-Kindī and his school, elaborated by Abū Zayd al-Balkhī and established in the social framework of the *kuttāb* by the *udabāʾ al-falāsifa* of the Tenth Century — approaches aiming at cautious delimitation rather than bold integration — a more comprehensive, and in its subordination of religion and law under the theoretical sciences, more radical outline of the

'Principles of the Views of the Inhabitants of the Virtuous City' was drafted by al-Fārābī (with his theory of religious language and political discourse, and his construction of a new canon involving the subsumption of the particular religious disciplines under the universals of rational knowledge); while the Christian translators and commentators of Aristotle, the *ruʾasāʾ al-manṭiq* from Abū Bishr Mattā to Yahyā b. ʿAdī and ʿĪsā b. Zurʿa still kept within the confines of their own cognitive system. In the long run, it was al-Fārābī's model which carried the day, and led on to an Islamic philosophy in its own right. Al-Fārābī's goal was fully achieved, and a new *summa philosophiae* worked out, by Ibn Sīnā. It was the work of Avicenna, the doctor and philosopher from Bukhara, the most critical, and the most creative reader of his predecessors — the Christian translators of Aristotle, the schools of al-Kindī, al-Balkhī, al-Fārābī, among scientists, courtiers and *kuttāb* — who first, not only conceived, but wrote out a comprehensive canon of the rational sciences. Through a two-century succession of critics and defenders, this was received and transformed into great *summae* of knowledge in the schools of Fakhr al-Dīn al-Rāzī, of Naṣīr al-Dīn al-Ṭūsī, and of the Sunnī and Shiʿite scholasticism of the Ottoman, Safavid and Mughal empires.

1. Early contacts across borders: Scribes, books and readers

The themes, paradigms and canons of rational science and demonstrative philosophy, even after an increasing interchange and interaction had started to take place between the first recipients of Hellenistic concepts and the direct readers of Greek texts in translation, remained apart from those of the religious disciplines in the first period, up to the crisis of the caliphate and the dissolution of the empire during the Tenth Century. The teachers of the Sharīʿa, Islamic tradition and Islamic law, first started to develop institutions of learning, as taught in the *ḥalaqāt* of the *jāmiʿ* mosques and (once these started to develop in the East) the colleges of law (*madāris*); the first were, in terms of institutions, restricted to professional spheres of activity — some of them close to the courts and the centres of administration, such as observatories, hospitals, and libraries.

In distinction to the conditions prevailing in the *ʿulūm sharʿīya*, the path from author to reader in the Hellenistic sciences was not controlled beyond the immediate circle of students. In the transmission of *Ḥadīth* and of legal materials — the standards of which were transferred to philology, grammar, and the syllabus of literary education current in the higher échelons of administration called *adab* — books passed to the open market only via the outermost circle of users. The books of scientists, doctors and philosophers were made available, evaluated and distributed by the book market. Important holdings were kept and made accessible by private libraries, beginning with the most famous *Bayt al-Ḥikma* of the ʿAbbasid court. But even the *Bayt al-Ḥikma* was just a library, not an 'academy', as it has been occasionally called; neither here nor elsewhere, did the transmitters of the Hellenistic heritage have institutions of learning to call their own, let alone exercising strictures of authority. It is significant that their means of expression were as uncontrolled by the standards of philology (grammar being the primary *ancilla* of the religious sciences) as the dissemination of their teaching was uncontrolled by the standards of *taḥammul al-ʿilm*: it is here, apart from the documents of Christian Arabic and Judæo-Arabic, that we find the earliest examples of what is called Middle Arabic by historians of the Arabic language.

But the osmosis between fields of learning took place through the practical interests of the scholars and their patrons. While we are lucky enough, in many cases, to find direct witnesses of the reception and proliferation of texts in extant manuscripts, it is not easy to assess, except in individual cases, the availability of books and the stocks of libraries. We have to rely on biographers and bibliographers to round out our picture, and to derive additional evidence from the authors' statements and from source analysis, in order to form a reliable picture of the dissemination of texts in a given field.

Al-Jāḥiẓ, the early master of Arabic erudition (*adab*), heaped scorn and disdain upon the translators from Greek and Syriac because their Arabic was bad[2] — but he continued to use their work. On the other side, Ḥunayn b. Isḥāq, the famous translator of medical and other scientific and philosophical Greek works, engaged a scribe (at a meagre pay in relation to the princely salary he received himself) who was an expert in Arabic grammar: al-Aḥwal, a grammarian of the generation of Thaʿlab (fl. ca. 250 AH), considered one of the *imām*s of the *ʿarabīya*. He became interested in what he copied, and himself wrote a *Kitāb ʿUlūm al-Awāʾil* on the 'sciences of the Ancients'.[3]

[2] AL-JĀḤIẒ, *Kitāb al-Ḥayawān*, ed. ʿABD AL-SALĀM MUḤAMMAD HĀRŪN, I, Cairo: Maktabat Muṣṭafā al-Bābī al-Ḥalabī, 1938-45, p. 75-78; VI, p. 19; VI, p. 280.3-11.

[3] The Banū Mūsā, mathematicians in the service of the ʿAbbasid court, payed to the likes of Ḥunayn b. Isḥāq, Ḥubaysh b. al-Ḥasan, and Thābit b. Qurra, the best translators of Greek medical and mathematical works in their day, five hundred *dīnār*s per month 'for translation and assiduity'; see IBN AL-NADĪM, *al-Fihrist*, ed. G. FLÜGEL, Leipzig: Vogel, 1871, p. 250. On Ḥunayn's *warrāq*, Muḥammad b. al-Ḥasan al-Aḥwal, who was

We are told by the biographers of Abū Saʿīd al-Sīrāfī, the advocate of grammar in the well-known encounter with the Christian translator and logician Mattā b. Yūnus,[4] that he studied with some success 'the science of the *Almagest*, Euclid, and logic'.[5] But the categories, definitions and divisions of logic which some of his colleagues were tempted to adopt for grammar (as is evident in the *Uṣūl al-Naḥw* of Ibn al-Sarrāj (d. 316/928) and *al-Īḍāḥ fī ʿIlal al-Naḥw* of al-Zajjājī (d. ca. 337-40/948-951) were unacceptable to him, because they were incompatible with the concepts of the tradition on which his authority rested. The readers of *Falsafa* had been infected by their reading matter. The multicultural and polyethnic diversity of early ʿAbbasid urbanism was divided into schools, orthodoxy lined up against heresy — in the sciences as well as in the issues of theology which since the death of the Prophet had shaped the fate of the empire.

But the study of arithmetic, algebra and astronomy was considered a duty, if not a work of love, by many of the professionals of court and chancery, even though they were primarily trained in the *ʿUlūm al-Sharīʿa*. Even Ibn Qutayba (213-276/828-889) who in the programmatic introduction to his *Adab al-Kātib*, denounced those of the *kuttāb* who indulged in the study of *Kalām* and natural philosophy, logic and gnomic sayings, while neglecting the Qurʾān, *Ḥadīth*, and the grammar and lexicography of pure Arabic, and in the same vein, attacked the fake authority of the founder of logic as opposed to the true authority of the Prophet — in the same text, recommends a thorough knowledge of the applied sciences.

paid twenty dirhams for copying out a hundred leaves, see AL-ṢAFADĪ, *al-Wāfī bi-l-Wafayāt*, II, ed. H. RITTER, Istanbul: Milli Eğitim Basımevi, 1949, p. 345.3; on his teachers and his own works, see p. 344 f., and AL-QIFṬĪ, *Inbāh al-Ruwāh fī Anbāʾ al-Nuḥāh*, ed. MUḤAMMAD ABŪ L-FAḌL IBRĀHĪM, III, Cairo: Dār al-Kutub al-Miṣrīya, 1950-1973, p. 91 f.: *kāna nāsikhan yuwāriqu li-Ḥunayn bn Isḥāq fī manqūlāti-hi.*

[4] See G. ENDRESS, *Grammatik und Logik: arabische Philologie und griechische Philosophie im Widerstreit*, in: *Sprachphilosophie in Antike und Mittelalter*, ed. B. MOJSISCH, Amsterdam: Grüner, 1986, p. 163-299.

[5] AL-ZUBAYDĪ (d. 397/989), *Ṭabaqāt al-Naḥwīyīn wa-l-Lughawīyīn*, ed. MUḤAMMAD ABŪ L-FAḌL IBRĀHĪM, Cairo: Dār al-Maʿārif, 1973, p. 119.12: *wa-huwa lladhī fassara kitāb Sībawayh, wa-yantaḥilu l-ʿilm bi-l-Majisṭī wa-Uqlīdis wa-l-manṭiq*; AL-QIFṬĪ, *Inbāh al-Ruwāh*, I, p. 323.5-6: *kāna yadrus al-Qurʾān wa-l-qirāʾāt wa-ʿulūm al-Qurʾān wa-l-naḥw wa-l-lugha wa-l-fiqh wa-l-farāʾiḍ wa-l-kalām wa-l-shiʿr wa-l-ʿarūḍ wa-l-qawāfī wa-l-ḥisāb*; 323.9-10: *wa-qaraʾa ʿalā Abī Bakr Ibn al-Sarrāj wa-ʿalā Abī Bakr al-Mabramān al-naḥw, wa-qaraʾa ʿalay-hi aḥadu-humā l-qirāʾāt, wa-darasa l-ākhar ʿalay-hi l-ḥisāb*; AL-SUYŪṬĪ, *Bughyat al-Wuʿāh fī Ṭabaqāt al-Lughawīyīn wa-l-Nuḥāh*, ed. MUḤAMMAD ABŪ L-FAḌL IBRĀHĪM, I, Cairo: al-Ḥalabī, 1964, p. 507.14-16 (quoting from Abū Ḥayyān al-Tawḥīdī, *Taqrīẓ al-Jāḥiẓ*): *Abū Saʿīd al-Sīrāfī ... imām al-aʾimma maʿrifatan bi-l-naḥw ... wa-l-ḥisāb wa-l-handasa.*

Many a jurist studied algebra for solutions of the more intricate problems of *farā'iḍ*, many a *kātib* of the *dīwān al-kharāj* was an expert on applied mathematics, arithmetic, geometry, and practical astronomy to be applied in accounting, surveying and geodesy.[6] An *ignoramus* like Ibn Thawāba, who — according to a satire in the shape of a (fictitious) correspondence, presented by Abū Ḥayyān al-Tawḥīdī in his own style — held geometrical constructions to be illicit sorcery,[7] was never taken seriously.

Even after the rise of the traditionist movement, a Ḥanbalite student of law would take classes 'in the distribution of shares (*farā'iḍ*), arithmetic, algebra, geometry' as a matter of course — a single example must suffice: Abū Bakr Qāḍī al-Māristān (d. 535/1140-41, a pupil of the famous *qāḍī* Abū Yaʿlā al-Farrā' (d. 458/1065), who 'excelled in all of these'.[8]

2. Philosophers and scientists on their own

During the first two centuries of reception of the Greek intellectual heritage into the Arabic culture of the Near East, the Christian translators remained outside the emerging Islamic institutions, and among themselves. But inside these circles, the Arabic manuscript tradition of some of the most important works of Aristotle provides impressive documentary evidence of philosophy reading in a coherent teaching tradition. The Paris manuscript of Aristotle's *Organon*[9] is an authentic testimony of the

[6] Ulrich Rebstock, *Rechnen im islamischen Orient: die literarischen Spuren der praktischen Rechnenkunst*, Darmstadt: Wissenschaftliche Buchgesellschaft, 1992, p. 59-80 ('Rechnen als berufliche Qualifikation').

[7] Abū l-ʿAbbās Aḥmad b. Yaḥyā Ibn Thawāba (died in 273/886-7 or 277/890-1). The text is reproduced by Abū Ḥayyān al-Tawḥīdī on the authority of al-Kindī's disciple al-Sarakhsī, in his satire on al-Ṣāḥib Ibn ʿAbbād, whom he accused of similar ignorance, in: *Akhlāq al-Wazīrayn*, ed. Muḥammad b. Tāwīt al-Ṭanjī; quoted by Yāqūt in the entry on Ibn Thawāba in his *Irshād al-Arīb*, ed. D.S. Margoliouth, II, London: Luzac, 1923-31, p. 36-51; = ed. Aḥmad Farīd Rifāʿī, IV, Cairo: ʿĪsā l-Bābī al-Ḥalabī, 1936-1938, p. 160-74), who discusses the authenticity of this report, and suspects a forgery on the part of al-Tawḥīdī (p. 50 f./174). See Franz Rosenthal, *Aḥmad b. aṭ-Ṭayyib as-Saraḫsî* (*American Oriental Series*, 26), New Haven, Conn.: American Oriental Society, 1954, p. 86-94; Everett K. Rowson, *A Muslim Philosopher on the Soul and its Fate: al-ʿĀmirī's* Kitāb al-Amad ʿalā l-Abad (*American Oriental Series*, 70), New Haven, Conn.: American Oriental Society, 1988, p. 289-293.

[8] Ibn Rajab al-Baghdādī (d. 795/1393), *Kitāb al-Dhayl ʿalā Ṭabaqāt al-Ḥanābila* (*Histoire des Ḥanbalites*): *I: 460-540/1067-1145*, ed. Henri Laoust and Sami Dahan, Damascus: Institut Français de Damas, 1951, no. 91, p. 231.16-18.

[9] Paris, Bibliothèque nationale, fonds arabe 2346; *Manṭiq Arisṭū*, ed. ʿAbd al-Raḥmān Badawī, Cairo: Dār al-Kutub al-Miṣrīya, 1950-1952; see also *Manṭiq Arisṭū*, ed. Farīd Jabr, Beirut: Dār al-Fikr al-Lubnānī, 1999. The texts in question include the *Cat-*

Aristotle reading of the Tenth-Century Christian Arab theologian and philosopher Yaḥyā b. ʿAdī (d. 363/974) and his (mainly Christian) pupils, going back to the holograph exemplars of Ibn ʿAdī, of his immediate follower ʿĪsā b. Isḥāq b. Zurʿa (d. 398/1008), and of Ibn Zurʿa's pupil al-Ḥasan b. Suwār (Ibn al-Khammār, d. p.p. 407/1017). The latter's autograph provided the direct source of our manuscript, and was annotated with lecture notes taken down from Ibn Suwār's teachers.[10]

The next generation of the same school is represented by the Leiden manuscript[11] of Aristotle's *Physics*, and provides an instructive glimpse of the gradual shift in make-up of the reading public concerned with such studies. The manuscript goes back to a copy taken in 395/1004 by the *mutakallim* Abū l-Ḥusayn al-Baṣrī, who again had recourse to the exemplar of Yaḥyā b. ʿAdī; and the text of the *Physics* is accompanied with a chain of school commentaries by the Christian Alexandrian John Philoponus and the school of Yaḥyā b. ʿAdī. The tradition of Aristotle reading is still that of the Christian transmitters of the Alexandrian school, the type of commentary being perhaps modelled on the *hypomnēmata* of the lecture course[12] and the *catenæ patrum* of the Christian biblical literature. But the student-copyist of the ancestor of our manuscript was a Muʿtazilite theologian who followed the lecture-course of

egoriæ, De Interpretatione, Analytica priora et posteriora, Topica, and *Sophistici Elenchi*, while the *Poetica* and *Rhetorica*, also bound into the volume, are of a different provenance and later date; on the Rhetoric — copied from the copy of Ibn al-Samḥ (see below) and thereby belonging to the same tradition of Baghdadi Christian teachers of logic, see S. M. STERN, *Ibn al-Samḥ*, in: *Journal of the Royal Asiatic Society* (1956), p. 314.

[10] The teaching tradition of the Arabic *Organon* was first analyzed on the basis of the Paris manuscript by RICHARD WALZER, *New Light on the Arabic Translations of Aristotle*, in: *Oriens* 5 (1954), p. 91-142. A new analysis has been put forward by HENRI HUGONNARD-ROCHE, *Une ancienne 'édition' arabe de l'Organon d'Aristote: problèmes de traduction et de transmission*, in: *Les problèmes posés par l'édition critique des textes anciens et médiévaux*, ed. J. HAMESSE, Louvain-la-Neuve: Université Catholique de Louvain, 1992, p. 139-157; see p. 156: 'À juger d'après les colophons du Parisinus, les traités de l'*Organon* ont été édités avec le souci de puiser les textes aux meilleures sources, et une attention particulière a été portée à la généalogie des copies qui ont servi à ces 'éditions'. Pourtant l'étude des notes marginales ou interlinéaires a montré que ces textes ont subi des corrections ou des remaniements, qui paraissent aller, aux yeux d'un éditeur moderne, à l'encontre du désir d'assurer l'exactitude des textes transmis par le soin mis à contrôler la chaîne de leur transmission'.

[11] MS. Leiden, Univ. or. 583 Warner; see J.J. WITKAM, *Seven Specimins of Arabic Manuscripts Preserved in the Library of the University of Leiden*, Leiden: Brill, 1978, p. 15.

[12] See ODILE GOULET-CASÉ, *Plotin, professeur de philosopie*, in: *Porpyhre, La vie de Plotin*, ed. LUC BRISSON et al., Paris: Vrin, 1982-1992, I, p. 257-276, and p. 272 f.; II, p. 283.

Abū ʿAlī al-Ḥasan b. al-Samḥ (d. 418/1027):[13] Abū l-Ḥusayn (or Abū l-Ḥasan) al-Baṣrī (d. 436/1044), a black sheep in the fold of Muʿtazilite theology and disliked for his interest in the sciences of the Ancients (*ʿulūm al-awāʾil*), but an unflinching follower of the methods of the *falāsifa*.[14]

A copy of al-Baṣrī's apographon was made in the Karkh quarter of Baghdad in 470/1077; but for the second half of Book VII to the end of Book VIII, this is based on an exemplar containing commentaries by the Tenth/Eleventh century physician, and *kātib* of the Katholikos of the Iraqi Nestorians, Abū l-Faraj b. al-Ṭayyib (d. 434/1043)[15] — a faithful continuator of the Alexandrian lecture course, with its divison into *praxeis* (Arabic, *taʿālīm*). The Karkh copy, finally, served the scribe of the Leiden manuscript: Abū l-Ḥakam al-Maghribī (d. 549/1155), a physician and man of letters who also fulfilled public functions in Baghdad under Saljuqid rule, and who copied for himself the *Physica* in the course of the year 524/1129-30 in Baghdad and during his journeys in Khuzistan.[16]

Continuing interest in Aristotle's *Physics* is attested by the 13th century bibliographer al-Qifṭī, *qāḍī al-akram* of Aleppo, who acquired a copy of the full commentary on the *Physics* by the Christian Alexandrian John Philoponus, a copy which ʿĪsā b. ʿAlī (d. 391/1001), son of the famous vizier ʿAlī b. ʿĪsā,[17] had studied with Yaḥyā b. ʿAdī, and which was annotated by a student of Ibn al-Ṭayyib using excerpts from the commentary of Themistius.

The above examples serve to demonstrate two concurrent phenomena: the nature of a teaching tradition based on the book, and the implications of an open market — a market of books as well as a market of ideas. Teaching and study in philosophy and the sciences was not connected with specific institutions of learning, but with technical and sci-

[13] See Stern, *Ibn al-Samḥ*, p. 314; Al-Qifṭī, *Taʾrīkh al-Ḥukamāʾ*, ed. A. Müller and J. Lippert, Leipzig: Dieterich, 1903, p. 411 f.; he is mentioned among the *shuyūkh al-Naṣārā* by Abū Ḥayyān al-Tawḥīdī, *al-Muqābasāt*, ed. Muḥammad Tawfīq Ḥusayn, Baghdad: Maṭbaʿat al-Irshād, 1970, p. 85), and like Ibn ʿAdī, seems to have been a bookseller in the Bāb al-Ṭāq quarter of Baghdad (*Muqābasāt*, p. 109.2, see Stern, *Ibn al-Samḥ*, p. 31 f.).

[14] See Stern, *Ibn al-Samḥ*, p. 36-38, referring to Ibn al-Murtaḍā (after al-Bayhaqī, *Sharḥ ʿUyūn al-Masāʾil*), and other sources.

[15] See below, p. 382-383.

[16] Stern, *Ibn al-Samḥ*, 34-36.

[17] He died in 334/946: 'He had two sons, probably by different wives: Ibrāhīm, who became secretary to the caliph al-Muṭīʿ in 347/958-9 and died in 350/961; and ʿĪsā (b. 302/914-5), who likewise became secretary to al-Ṭāʾiʿ, earned some repute as a traditionist and student of the "Greek" sciences, and died in 391/1001' (H. Bowen, *ʿAlī b. ʿĪsā*, *EI2*, I, p. 387).

entific praxis and the application of learning in hospitals, observatories, and the adminstrative tasks of the *dīwān al-kharāj* and other offices of the central and provincial administrations. Before returning to the changing readership of the philosophers, widening from scientists and physicians to include administrators and literary figures, and finally, to the teachers of the *Sharīʿa*, we shall dwell on the circles of philosophers: even here, we have to do, not with a single chain of reception and development of the sources, but with multiple and concurrent traditions and innovations of *Falsafa*.

3. The new canon and its readers in the scientific community

Al-Fārābī drafted a new canon of the rational sciences, not unprecedented as a genre, but in scope and systematic coherence. Ibn Sīnā continued, but also refounded the transmission of the *ʿulūm al-awāʾil* under the premisses of a new metaphysics, and exposed them in a full *summa* of the philosophical arts and sciences. Departing from al-Fārābī's paradigm of demonstrative science, he renewed the philosophical basis of rational scientific theory and practice, and set out to develop philosophy — *ḥikma* — as a metaphor of religious knowledge. Departing from the encyclopedic and courteous/administrative/*adab* tradition of al-Kindī/al-Balkhī, he reviewed the old canon of the theoretical sciences, he created a new encyclopedia of the method and matter of philosophy — of the classical *curriculum studiorum* of ethical propaedeutics, logical hermeneutics, demonstrative logic, physics and metaphysics, including the elementary matter of mathematics and astronomy, and adding — outside the philosophical canon proper — a manual of theoretical and practical medicine. It was through him that the *Falsafa* came to be and to stay an integral and living part of Arabic Islamic thought — in the scientific community, both Muslim and non-Muslim, as a universal religion for intellectuals, and then also in the religious community, where grammarians, jurists and theologians adopted from demonstrative science the guidelines of their *uṣūl*.

In the first instance, readers of al-Fārābī and Ibn Sīnā are explicitly attested, or found as transmitters of extant manuscripts, among physicians, Muslims as well as Christians. This brings to the mind Ibn Sīnā's owner's note on the title page of his copy of Galen's *De Sectis* (ms. Paris, *Bibliothèque nationale*, fonds arabe 2859), where he calls himself a doctor (*mutaṭabbib*).

The earliest manuscript extant of al-Fārābī's *Mabādi' Arā' Ahl al-Madīna al-Fāḍila*, one of the deeds of foundation of Islamic philosophy in its own right, was copied in 463/1071 by a young Christian doctor from Mayyāfāriqīn, Yaḥyā b. ʿAbd al-Masīḥ, whose philosophical learning we can trace back to the Christian school of logic led in Tenth Century Baghdad by Yaḥyā b. ʿAdī and ʿĪsā b. Zurʿa (mentioned before in connexion with the reading of Aristotle's *Organon*).[18]

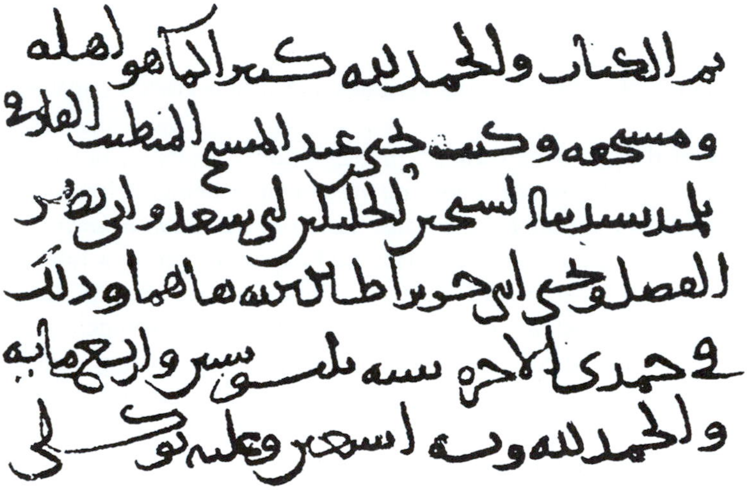

Expl. of Ms. Tehran, Kitābkhāna-ī Millī-i Malik 149, dated 463 AH., containing al-Fārābī, Mabādi' Ārā' Ahl al-Madīna al-Fāḍila

[18] See R. Walzer, *Al-Farabi on the Perfect State: Abū Naṣr al-Fārābī's* Mabādi' Ārā' Ahl al-Madīna al-Fāḍila, Oxford: Clarendon Press, 1985, p. 22 f., but correct Walzer's information on the copyist; the colophon (see our illustration) says: 'written by Yaḥyā b. ʿAbd al-Masīḥ, physician of Mayyāfāriqīn, the disciple of our illustrious masters Abū Saʿīd and Abū Naṣr, al-Faḍl and Yaḥyā the sons of Jarīr, may God grant them life ...'. On the Christian Arab theologian Abū Naṣr Yaḥyā b. Jarīr (d. after 472/1079-80), see Ibn Abī Uṣaybiʿa, Muwaffaq al-Dīn Aḥmad b. al-Qāsim (d. 668/1270), *ʿUyūn al-Anbā' fī Ṭabaqāt al-Aṭibbā'*, ed. Imra' al-Qays b. al-Ṭaḥḥān (i.e., August Müller), I, Cairo: Maṭbaʿat al-Wahbī, 1299/1882, p. 243.25-28 (with Vorwort, Lesarten, Indices [under the title], *Ibn Abi Useibia*, Königsberg, 1884); Georg Graf, *Geschichte der christlichen arabischen Literatur*, II, Città del Vaticano: Pontificio Istituto Orientale, 1944-1953, p. 259. On his brother, Abū Saʿīd al-Faḍl, see Ibn Abī Uṣaybiʿa, *ʿUyūn*, I, p. 243.29-32; he was court physician to Naṣīr al-Dawla, the last Marwanid emir of Mayyāfāriqīn and Āmid (r. 472-478/1079-1085), while his brother Yaḥyā served the vizier Kāfī al-Kufāh b. Jahīr who from 478/1083 brought the emirate under Seljuqid control (see C. Hillenbrand, *Marwānids*, in: *EI2*, VI, p. 626 ff.). Also contained in this manuscript is the Arabic version of Theophrastus's *Metaphysics*.

Incidentally, a brother of Yaḥyā b. ʿAdī, Ibrāhīm, seems to have been active in spreading al-Fārābī's writings in Iran.[19] — One branch of the manuscript tradition of the Arabic version of Aristotle's *De Caelo* goes back to a revised text made by on the basis of the Syriac version by the Christian physician Mihrān b. Manṣūr, working in the service of the Artuqid Najm al-Dīn Alpï (547-572/1152-1176) of Diyārbakr.[20]

Ms. Mashhad, Āstān-i Quds-i Raḍawī, 149

[19] Abū l-Ḥasan al-Bayhaqī, *Tatimmat Ṣiwān al-Ḥikma*, ed. Muḥammad Shafīʿ, Lahore: Panjab University, 1935, p. 102; see G. Endress, *The Works of Yaḥyā b. ʿAdī*, Wiesbaden: Reichert, 1977, p. 50.

[20] See G. Endress, *Die arabischen Übersetzungen von Aristoteles' Schrift* De caelo, Frankfurt am Main: J.W. Goethe-Universität, 1966, p. 27 f.

We must wait for the Iranian *madāris* of the Seljuqid period in order to encounter witnesses of mathematical and philosophical studies under the roof of the law college. The mere existence of a book in the holdings of a *madrasa* library does not justify conclusions as to its use and study. Even though banned from institutionalized religious learning in *waqf* institutions, books of the 'foreign' sciences, *Falsafa* and rationalistic theology (*Kalām*), could be donated to libraries and given the sanction of *waqf* for the benefit of the institutions' students.[21]

It is interesting to note mention of the works of Ibn Sīnā's school in the Niẓāmīya of Nishapur by Ẓahīr al-Dīn al-Bayhaqī (488-565/1095-1169): a 'Book on Animals' (in Persian) by Ibn Sīnā's disciple and biographer Abū ʿUbayd al-Jūzjānī, and a treatise (or treatises) by Ibn Sīnā's favourite pupil, Abū ʿAbd Allāh al-Maʿṣūmī, 'On the separata, and the number of the intelligences and the spheres, and the order of created beings'.[22]

But we do have manuscripts of the rational sciences, and especially of mathematics, which were not only preserved, but copied in one of the *madāris*, and we may safely assume that the contents were studied by one of the professors of law (or whatever his discipline among the *ʿulūm sharʿīya* may have been). Indeed, it is in the lifetime of Fakhr al-Dīn al-Rāzī that we encounter the first examples of scientific works copied in the Niẓāmīya college of Baghdad. We have a *majmūʿa* of mathematical treatises, bearing the following subscription:

> The treatise is completed, with the praise of God, and by his help and gracious support, in Baghdad the City of Peace. I added it to my course of studies (*ʿallaqtu-hu*) in the Niẓāmīya within the first ten days of the year 556 of the Hijra [December 30, 1160-January 8, 1161].[23]

[21] See George Makdisi, *The Rise of Humanism in Islam and the Christian West*, Edinburgh: Edinburgh University Press, 1990, p. 67 ff. (Chapter Three, 'Books and the Law of *Waqf*').

[22] Ẓahīr al-Dīn ʿAlī b. Zayd al-Bayhaqī, *Tatimmat Ṣiwān al-Ḥikma*, ed. Muḥammad Shafīʿ, Lahore: Panjab University, 1351/1932 [1935], no. 51 (=*Taʾrīkh Ḥukamāʾ al-Islām*, ed. Muḥammad Kurd ʿAlī, Damascus: al-Majmaʿ al-ʿIlmī al-ʿArabī, 1976 [1946], p. 101.1; no. 52 = p. 102.11-14; see Max Meyerhof, *ʿAlī al-Bayhaqī's* Tatimmat Ṣiwān al-Ḥikma*: a Biographical Work on the Learned Men of Islam*, in: *Osiris* 8 (1948), p. 122–217 (p. 162, 163).

[23] Anton M. Heinen, *An Unknown Treatise by Sanad b. ʿAlī on the Relative Magnitudes of the Sun, Earth and Moon*, in: *From Deferent to Equant: a Volume of Studies in the History of Science in the Ancient and Medieval Near East in Honor of E. S. Kennedy* (*Annals of the New York Academy of Sciences*, 500), ed. David A. King and George Saliba, New York: New York Academy of Sciences, 1987, p. 167, 171/173. The manuscript used by the editor, now in private possession at Lahore (Pakistan), contains several treatises ending with the statement that they were copied at the Niẓāmīya colleges of Mosul and of Baghdad.

The use of the term *ʿallaqtu-hu* is significant, pointing out that the readings contained in the manuscript were part of a *taʿlīqa*, a course of set papers which the anonymous student had copied for his own use.[24]

From the next generation, we have a 'splendid and unique' copy of geometrical tracts by the Tenth Century mathematician Abū Saʿīd al-Sijzī, dated 612/1215 in the Niẓāmīya *madrasa* of Baghdad — the very place where al-Ghazālī had been teaching Shafiʿite law, and transformed Ashʿarite theology to become the mainstay of Sunnī dogmatics. The compiler of the manuscript was al-Ḥasan b. al-Ḥasan b. Muḥammad b. ʿAlī b. Aḥmad, a direct descendant of he illustrious vizier and founder of the *madrasa*, Niẓām al-Mulk (d. 485/1092).[25]

Such testimonies are but the sparse external evidence of a process which began when the secretaries, as well as the grammarians and jurists aspired after competence in the sciences. In the early period, the 'rise of colleges' — depicted in copious detail by George Makdisi[26] — began but slowly to admit study of the *humaniora* beyond the language, exegesis and application of the Scripture.

4. Doctors reading Avicenna: The physicians' philosophy and the philosophers' physick

Avicenna's immediate public, his readers and interpreters, were members of the scientific professions: physicians — who for their intellectual instruction and enlightenment adopted his *Shifāʾ* and his *al-Ishārāt wa-l-Tanbīhāt* as eagerly as they read his medical *Qānūn* — and astronomers, Muslims and non-Muslims who found the principles of their science explained in the frame of his philosophic encyclopedia.

While the physicians took to reading Ibn Sīnā's *Qānūn*, the philosophers, and the philosopher-theologians starting with Fakhr al-Dīn al-Rāzī, in their turn started reading theoretical medicine in the *kullīyāt* of Avicenna's ever more popular handbook. We are specially well-informed about these exchanges between medicine and the rational

[24] See George Makdisi, *The Rise of Colleges: Institutions of Learning in Islam and the West*, Edinburgh: Edinburgh University Press, 1981, p. 111-128, and index *s.v.*, on the *taʿlīqa*, 'reportatio' of the law school.

[25] MS Dublin, Chester Beatty Library, no. 3652; see A.J. Arberry, *The Chester Beatty Library: a Handlist of the Arabic Manuscripts*, III, Dublin: Chester Beatty Library, 1955-1964, p. 58-60 and description of plate 85. On al-Sijzī, see F. Sezgin, *Geschichte des arabischen Schrifttums*, V, Leiden: Brill, 1974, p. 329-334.

[26] Makdisi, *The Rise of Colleges*; Makdisi, *The Rise of Humanism*.

sciences, and the growing interest taken by teachers of the religious disciplines, by a Damascene oculist who in his life, formation and activity was a living example of this outlook: Muwaffaq al-Dīn b. Abī Uṣaybiʿa (d. 668/1270), author of the invaluable biographical lexicon of the 'Generations of Physicians' (see also below, p. 389).[27]

Before the advent of the *Qānūn*, the authoritative handbooks of medicine had been the *Kitāb al-Malakī*, dedicated by ʿAlī b. al-ʿAbbās al-Majūsī (d. between 372/982 and 384/995) to the Buyid *malik* ʿAḍud al-Dawla, founder of the Bīmāristān al-ʿAḍudī of Baghdad in 372/982, and the *Kitāb al-Mi'a* of Abū Sahl ʿĪsā b. Yaḥyā al-Masīḥī (d. 401/1010).[28] A Jacobite Christian, Abū Sahl had come to Baghdad for study, and afterwards was active in Khorasan and with the Ma'munids of Gurgānj;[29] there he met al-Bīrūnī and above all, his greatest pupil, Ibn Sīnā.[30] Soon, the *Qānūn fī l-Ṭibb* of Ibn Sīnā surpassed the fame of his teacher's *Kitāb al-Mi'a*, and eventually replaced it even while preserving through its influence the heritage of that tradition.

From the East, but also from Damascus and from farther afar, people went to Baghdad for the study of medicine. Among the teachers of the Bīmāristān were influential philosopher-physicians: the Nestorian Abū l-Faraj b. al-Ṭayyib (d. 435/1043)[31] — much abused by Ibn Sīnā for his slavish aderence to the Alexandrian tradition of Aristotelian commentaries — and his pupils throughout two generations, such as al-Mukhtār b. al-Ḥasan b. Buṭlān,[32] best known through the encounters with his Egyptian competitor Ibn Riḍwān. In its turn, the Galenic tradition of the Baghdad school returned to Damascus through the physicians who had studied with the last eminent teacher of the ʿAḍudī hospital: with Amīn al-Dawla Hibat Allāh b. al-Tilmīdh (who died, nearly

[27] IBN ABĪ UṢAYBIʿA, *ʿUyūn*; see also M. ULLMANN, *Die Medizin im Islam*, Leiden: Brill, 1970, p. 231 f.

[28] IBN ABĪ UṢAYBIʿA, *ʿUyūn*, I, p. 327 f.; F. SEZGIN, *Geschichte des arabischen Schrifttums*, III, Leiden: Brill, 1970, p. 326; ULLMANN, *Medizin*, p. 151 f.

[29] IBN ABĪ UṢAYBIʿA, *ʿUyūn*, I, p. 327 f. (mentions the accusation of plagiarism raised against Ibn Sīnā: p. 328.16); Sezgin, *GAS*, III, p. 326; ULLMANN, *Medizin*, p. 151.

[30] YAḤYĀ MAHDAWĪ, *Fihrist-i nuskhahā-i muṣannafāt-i Ibn-i Sīnā*, Teheran: Dānishgāh-i Tihrān, 1333 HSh/1954, p. 187, no. 98.

[31] IBN ABĪ UṢAYBIʿA, *ʿUyūn*, I, p. 239.20-21, records his teaching activity: *yuqri' ṣināʿat al-ṭibb fī l-Bīmāristān al-ʿAḍudī*, and mentions a manuscript of Galen's *Ad Glauconem* read under Ibn al-Ṭayyib in the Bīmāristān on 11 Ramaḍān, 406 AH; ULLMANN, *Medizin*, p. 156-158.

[32] ULLMANN, *Medizin*, p. 157.

a hundred years old, in 560/1165).[33] The Nestorian Ibn at-Tilmīdh had completed his studies in Iran before coming to Baghdad, where he became chief physician (with the old Syriac title of *sāʿūr*), as well as personal physician to the caliphs — and for this matter, a notorious rival of the Jewish doctor Abū l-Barakāt Hibat Allāh b. Malkā (d. between 550/1155 and 560/1165), a doctor with strong philosophical leanings, and a highly original mind.[34] Ibn al-Tilmīdh, while keeping offices as a dignitary of his church, was well-versed in the Arabic Islamic tradition, a true *adīb*, and on excellent terms with the *fuqahāʾ* of the Madrasa Niẓāmīya situated behind his own house.[35]

Ibn al-Tilmīdh's dispensatory (*Aqrābādhīn*) replaced the old Ninth Century manual of Sābūr b. Sahl, and it was he who introduced Ibn Sīnā's *Qānūn* into the study of medicine. Hibat Allāh b. Jumayʿ (d. 594/1198, see below p. 384), a commentator of the *Qānūn* in his tradition, praised his painstaking study of the text:

> Someone mentioned that Abū l-Ḥasan Hibat Allāh Ṣāʿid [sic] al-Baghdādī, the physician known by the name Ibn al-Tilmīdh, owned a copy [of the *Qānūn*] which, he says, he corrected on the basis of [a collation against] the author's original copy (*dastūr al-muṣannif*), and appended his own notes to it. This copy (so the report said) was renowned for its correctness, was sold in Baghdad after his death, and later was transferred to Syria.[36]

[33] AL-QIFṬĪ, *Taʾrīkh al-Ḥukamāʾ*, p. 340-342; IBN ABĪ UṢAYBIʿA, *ʿUyūn*, I, p. 259-276; MAX MEYERHOF, *Ibn al-Tilmīdh*, in *EI*2, III, p. 956 ff. He was court physician under the caliphs al-Muktafī (r. 1136-60) and al-Mustanjid (r. 1160-70). On his rivalry with Abū l-Barakāt at the court of al-Mustaḍīʾ (before the latter's coming to office, r. 1170-80), see IBN ABĪ UṢAYBIʿA, *ʿUyūn*, I, p. 259.30 f. (according to AL-QIFṬĪ, *Tārīkh al-Ḥukamāʾ*, p. 341.14, while he was personal physician to al-Muktafī). See also ULLMANN, *Medizin*, p. 163, and ALBERT Z. ISKANDAR, *An Autograph of Ibn al-Tilmīdh's Marginal Commentary of Ibn Sīnā's Canon of Medicine*, in: *Le Museón* 90 (1977), p. 177-236, with copious references.

[34] IBN ABĪ UṢAYBIʿA, *ʿUyūn*, I, p. 278-280; p. 255.3-4; AL-QIFṬĪ, *Taʾrīkh al-Ḥukamāʾ*, p. 343-346; see SH. PINES, *Abū ʾl-Barakāt al-Baghdādī*, *EI*2, I, p. 111-113.

[35] IBN ABĪ UṢAYBIʿA, *ʿUyūn*, I, p. 260.25-26, on the authority of Muwaffaq al-Dīn ʿAbd al-Laṭīf al-Baghdādī (d. 629/1231), the eminent scholar in both the religious and the philosophical studies, whose father had been a professor at the Niẓāmīya: *wa-min murūwati-hi anna ẓahra dāri-hi kāna yalī l-Niẓāmīya, fa-idhā mariḍa faqīh naqala-hu ilay-hi wa-qāma fī maraḍi-hi ʿalay-hi fa-idhā aballa wahaba la-hu dīnārayni wa-ṣarafa-hū*. See ISKANDAR, p. 178.

[36] From the introduction of IBN JUMAYʿ, *al-Taṣrīḥ bi-l-Maknūn fī Tanqīḥ al-Qānūn*; see ALBERT Z. ISKANDAR, *A Catalogue of Arabic Manuscripts on Medicine and Science in the Wellcome Historical Medical Library*, London: Wellcome Library, 1967, p. 51-53; passage quoted by Iskandar from ms. Oxford, Bodl., Marsh 390, f. 3b16-4a1, in ISKANDAR, *Autograph*, p. 180.

His glosses on the *Qānūn*, discusssing the terminology, especially of the *materia medica*, of the text, have survived in an autograph manuscript, or one based on the autograph.[37]

But then, some of the best minds of the next generation went to Damascus. There, Nūr al-Dīn b. Zangī (r. 1146-1175) had founded a new center of medical practice and science — according to the historians, the initiator of the *Jihād* against the Franks had endowed the ransom money of one of the Crusader knights as a *waqf* towards its foundation — al-Bīmāristān al-Nūrī, equipped with a library, and ever since its inauguration in 551/1156, also a school of medicine.[38] The Kurdish general of Nūr al-Dīn, later on the powerful opponent of the Zangids, the great Ayyubid Ṣalāḥ al-Dīn, put an end to the Fatimid dynasty of Cairo in 567/1171, and soon afterwards (577/1181) founded there another *bīmāristān*, called al-Nāṣirī after his regnal title; the first hospital had been founded by Aḥmad b. Ṭūlūn in Fusṭāṭ.[39]

Among the physicians — Christians, Jews, and Muslims — who brought the medical teaching of Baghdad to Damascus, and then, through their disciples, further to Cairo, were:

(a) Raḍī al-Dīn al-Raḥbī (d. 631/1233),[40] from 555/1160 director of the polyclinic of the Nūrī hospital, later one of the physicians of Saladin and of his brother and successor al-Malik al-ʿĀdil;

(b) the Jew Hibat Allāh Ibn Jumayʿ (d. 594/1198),[41] like al-Raḥbī — who associated with him during a stay in Egypt[42] — personal physician to Salāḥ al-Dīn;

[37] Ibn Abī Uṣaybiʿa, *ʿUyūn*, I, p. 276.26, mentions *ḥawāshī* on the *Qānūn*, next to *ḥawāshī* on al-Masʿūdī's *Kitāb al-Miʾa*. Those on the *Qānūn* are extant in manuscript, see Iskandar, *An Autograph.*

[38] Sibṭ Ibn al-Jawzī, *Mirʾāt al-Zamān*, I, Hyderabad: Dāʾirat al-Maʿārif al-ʿUthmānīya, 1951, p. 248; al-Maqrīzī, *al-Khiṭaṭ*, II, Būlāq: al-Maṭbaʿa al-Amīrīya, 1270/1853, p. 408.5-7; see O. Spies and H. Müller-Bütow, *Anatomie und Chirurgie des Schädels ... nach Ibn al-Quff*, Berlin: De Gruyter, 1971, p. 11-18, 22 ff., texts on the physicians of the Bīmāristān from Ibn Abī Uṣaybiʿa.

[39] On the physicians in Saladin's entourage, see Samira Jadon, *The Physicians of Syria during the Reign of Ṣalāḥ al-Dīn, 570-589 AH/1174-1193 AD*, in: *Journal of the History of Medicine and Allied Sciences* 25 (1970), p. 323-340; Samira Jadon, *A Comparison of the Wealth, Prestige, and Medical Works of the Physicians of Ṣalāḥ al-Dīn in Egypt and Syria*, in: *Bulletin of the History of Medicine* 44 (1970), p. 64-75.

[40] Ibn Abī Uṣaybiʿa, *ʿUyūn*, II, p. 192-194; p. 243.9-16.

[41] Ibn Abī Uṣaybiʿa, *ʿUyūn*, II, p. 112-115.

[42] Ibn Abī Uṣaybiʿa, *ʿUyūn*, II, p. 193.8.

Amīn al-Dawla Ibn al-Tilmīdh
and the Teaching of Ibn Sīnā's Qānūn *in Baghdad and Damascus*

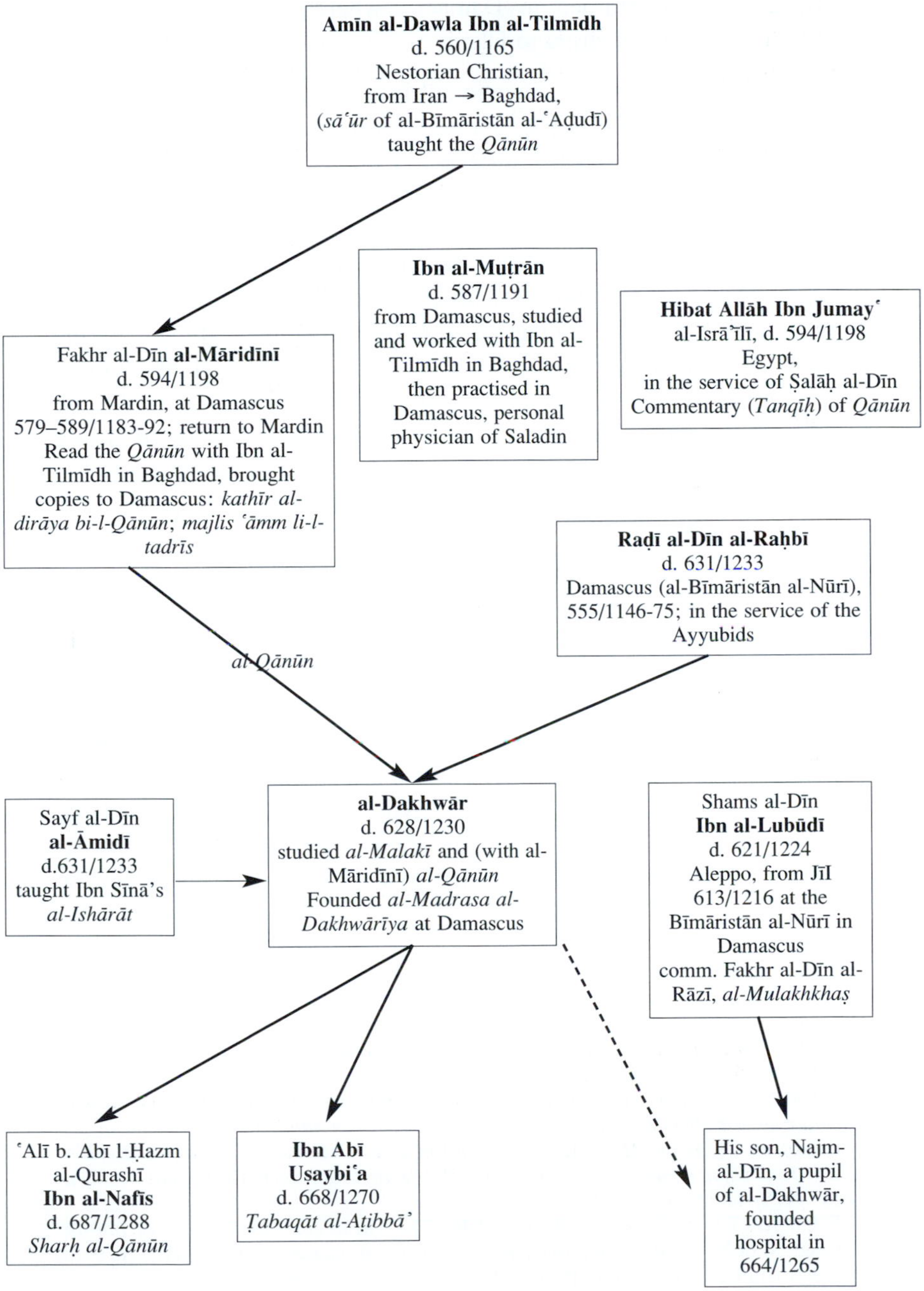

(c) Muwaffaq al-Dīn b. al-Muṭrān (d. 587/1191),[43] a native of Damascus who studied in Byzantium, then worked with Ibn al-Tilmīdh in Baghdad, and returned to Damacus where he became Saladin's physician, and converted to Islam.

Their teaching activities are mentioned by Ibn Abī Uṣaybiʿa at several instances: Raḍī al-Dīn al-Raḥbī rarely ever taught for non-Muslims (*dhimma*);[44] a pupil of Ibn al-Muṭrān held a *majlis ʿāmm li-l-mushtaghilīn ʿalay-hi bi-l-ṭibb*.[45] As a basic manual, Avicenna's *Qānūn* still competed with al-Majūsī's *Malakī* — the latter exists in a copy with al-Raḥbī's own *qirāʾa* notice of 577/1181[46] — but soon gained general dominance. Ibn Jumayʿ was quoted above for his praise of Ibn al-Tilmīdh's revised copy in his 'Refinement' (*Tanqīḥ al-Qānūn*). Another student of the medical school of Baghdad was Fakhr al-Dīn al-Māridīnī (d. 594/1198); after years of service with the Artuqid court in his native Mardin, he came to Damascus for a decade (579-589/1183-1193), where he gave a public lecture (*majlis ʿāmm li-l-tadrīs*) and read with his students Ibn Sīnā's *Qānūn*, which he had studied in his own time at Baghdad with Ibn al-Tilmīdh [47] — and at the same time, Ibn al-Tilmīdh studied Avicenna's logic with al-Māridīnī![48] He was competent in all of the *ʿulūm ḥikmīya*, in philosophy and mathematics a student of Abū l-Futūḥ Aḥmad b. al-Sarī (Ibn al-Salāḥ, d. 548/1153, who had come to the Artuqid court from Hamadhān, and later also went to Damascus).[49]

His most devoted disciple was Muhadhdhib al-Dīn al-Dakhwār (d. 628/1230),[50] who became personal physician to al-Malik al-ʿĀdil and (in Damascus) of al-Ashraf, holder of a chair of medicine and chief physician (*raʾīs al-aṭibbāʾ*) of Syria and Egypt. Al-Dakhwār had read the *Malakī* of al-Majūsī with al-Raḥbī, and the *Qānūn* with Fakhr al-Dīn al-Māridīnī.[51] When al-Māridīnī decided to return to his home town, he

[43] IBN ABĪ UṢAYBIʿA, *ʿUyūn*, II, p. 175-81.
[44] IBN ABĪ UṢAYBIʿA, *ʿUyūn*, II, p. 193.28.
[45] Muwaffq al-Dīn b. ʿAbd al-ʿAzīz, see IBN ABĪ UṢAYBIʿA, *ʿUyūn*, II, p. 192.3.
[46] Ms. Paris, Bibliothèque nationale, fonds arabe 2874, dated 545 AH.
[47] IBN ABĪ UṢAYBIʿA, *ʿUyūn*, II, p. 299-301.
[48] IBN ABĪ UṢAYBIʿA, *ʿUyūn*, I, p. 300.5-6 (not quite clear: *wa-mimmā qaraʾa ʿalay-hi fī dhālika kitāb al-Mukhtaṣar al-awsaṭ li-l-Jurjānī [!] li-bn Sīnā*).
[49] IBN ABĪ UṢAYBIʿA, *ʿUyūn*, II, p. 164; on Ibn al-Sarī, see PAUL KUNITZSCH, *Zur Kritik der Koordinatenüberlieferung im Sternkatalog des Almagest*, Göttingen: Vandenhoeck, 1975), and SEZGIN, *GAS*, VI, p. 92 f.
[50] IBN ABĪ UṢAYBIʿA, *ʿUyūn*, II, p. 239-46; *The Theologus Autodidactus of Ibn an-Nafīs*, ed. MAX MAYERHOF and JOSEPH SCHACHT, Oxford: Clarendon Press, 1968, p. 9-10.
[51] IBN ABĪ UṢAYBIʿA, *ʿUyūn*, II, p. 239.7, 239.19-21; I, p. 300.12.

pressed him to stay and to finish his reading of the *Qānūn*, offering him a generous salary, but could not be persuaded: *al-ʿilm lā yubāʿ aṣlan*.[52] He was a devoted teacher, but here as elsewhere in his time, this seems to have been a private initiative, not a professional obligation. When he finished his daily work at the Bīmāristān, and had taken care of his patients among the princes of the dynasty and other notables, he would go to his home: *yaʾtī ilā dāri-hi thumma yashraʿu fī l-qirāʾā wa-l-dars wa-l-muṭālaʿa*, copied the manuscripts he needed to study, and then opened his *majlis* for physicians and other students interested in his teaching, reading the texts and explaining difficult passages.[53] Only shortly before his death, the Malik al-Ashraf appointed him *raʾīs al-aṭibbāʾ* and created for him a chair of medicine (*majlis li-tadrīs ṣināʿat al-ṭibb*).[54] In his old age, he endowed his estate and his library for the foundation of a school of medicine, the renowned Madrasa al-Dakhwārīya (opened in 628/1231).[55] Two other doctors of the Nūrī hospital followed this praiseworthy example in the next decades: Najm al-Dīn al-Lubūdī (al-Madrasa al-Lubūdīya, founded in 664/1265)[56] and ʿImād al-Din al-Dunayṣirī (al-Madrasa al-Dunayṣirīya or al-Rabaʿīya, in 686/1287).[57] The ingenious physician, philosopher and natural scientist, ʿAbd al-Laṭīf b. Yūsuf al-Baghdādī (557-629/1162-1231) — in medicine an admirer, while in philosophy a critic of Avicenna — taught in Damascus during his several sojourns there,[58] as did the famous pharmacologist Ibn al-Bayṭār from Malaga (d. 646/1248), who was chief botanist under al-Malik al-Kāmil, and went to Cairo after his death.[59]

From the same generation, we have a manuscript of the *Qānūn*, copied in 593-597/1196-1201 and collated with the exemplar of a certain Abū ʿImrān Mūsā — none other than Maimonides, the great Jewish philosopher, theologian and jurist who by that time practised and taught medicine in Cairo.[60]

52 Ibn Abī Uṣaybiʿa, *ʿUyūn*, I, p. 300.14-17.

53 Ibn Abī Uṣaybiʿa, *ʿUyūn*, II, p. 243.19-25.

54 Ibn Abī Uṣaybiʿa, *ʿUyūn*, II, p. 244.12.

55 Ibn Abī Uṣaybiʿa, *ʿUyūn*, II, p. 244.20-245.2; al-Nuʿaymī, *Al-Dāris fī Taʾrīkh al-Madāris*, ed. Jaʿfar al-Ḥasanī, II, Damascus: al-Majmaʿ al-ʿIlmī al-ʿArabī, 1367-1370/1948-1951, p. 127-133.

56 Ibn Abī Uṣaybiʿa, *ʿUyūn*, II, p. 185-159; al-Nuʿaymī, *Al-Dāris*, II, p. 135.5-138.7.

57 Ibn Abī Uṣaybiʿa, *ʿUyūn*, II, p. 367-372; al-Nuʿaymī, *Al-Dāris*, II, p. 133-135.

58 Ibn Abī Uṣaybiʿa, *ʿUyūn*, II, p. 201-213, including ʿAbd al-Laṭīf's autobiography.

59 Ibn Abī Uṣaybiʿa, *ʿUyūn*, II, p. 133.23-24.

60 Abū ʿImrān Mūsā b. ʿUbayd Allāh Ibn Maymūn, born 534/1139 in Cordoba, died 601/1204 in Cairo; see Ullmann, *Medizin*, p. 167-169. The manuscript is Paris, Bibliothèque nationale, fonds arabe 2885-2891, containing *al-Qānūn*, parts I.1–VI.5.

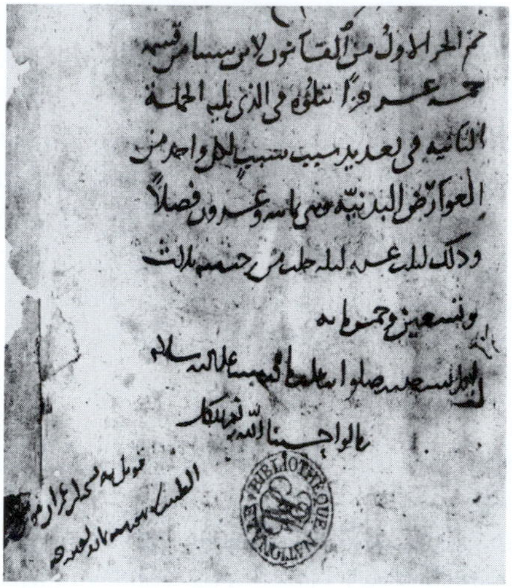

Ibn Sīnā, al-Qānūn fī l-Ṭibb, MS *Paris, Bibl. nat. ar. 2885*

Among the students of al-Dakhwār who worked in Damascus and Cairo, we find Ibn al-Nafīs (d. 687/1288), a commentator of Hippocrates, and a critic of Galen, in philosophy as in medicine a follower of Ibn Sīnā.[61] After concluding his study and training, he went to Cairo and was appointed *raʾīs al-aṭibbāʾ* of Egypt under the first Mamluks. Through his compendium (*Mūjiz*) and his great commentary on Ibn Sīnā's *Qānūn,* he succeeded in establishing this work firmly in the medical schools of the East. In a separate commentary devoted to the anatomical part of the work (*Sharḥ Tashrīḥ al-Qānūn*), he made his famous observations on the blood circulation, refuting the Galenic model (while maintaining his general physiology), and based on sober empirical observations, for the first time postulated the existence of the pulmonary circulation.

While Ibn Sīnā's medical work was esteemed by doctors and — for its theoretical *kullīyāt* — by philosophers alike as a systematical foundation and a complete *summa* of natural science and the medical applications, learned physicians looked for an exposition of the principles of being, and the method of deduction, in his manuals of natural philosophy and of logic — and for a legitimation of rational science in the

[61] Ullmann, *Medizin*, p. 280-283; Meyerhof and Schacht, *Ibn al-Nafīs*, p. 10-22; Albert Z. Iskandar, *Nafīs, Ibn al-*, in: *Dictionary of Scientific Biography*, IX, New York: Scribner, 1970-1980, p. 602-606.

epistemic community of Islam, in his works of philosophical theology: above all, in his *Ishārāt wa-l-Tanbīhāt*, and in his earlier work on the 'Beginning and the Return' of intellect and the rational soul, *al-Mabda' wa-l-Maʿād*. The earliest manuscript of the latter work was copied by a medical student, who 'attached it' (*ʿallaqa-hu*) to his course of studies.[62]

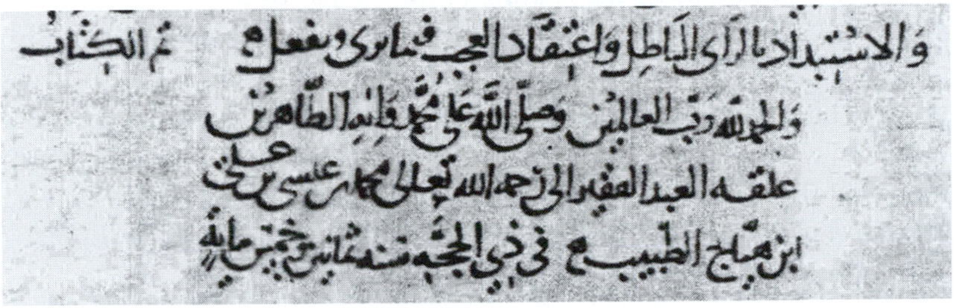
والحمد لله رب العالمين وصلى الله على محمد وآله الطاهرين
في ذي الحجة سنة ثمانين وخمسمائة

Ibn Sīnā, al-Mabda' wa-l-Maʿād
expl. of ms. Istanbul, Tokapı Saray, Ahmet III, 3268, f. 110, dat. 580/1185

The principal teacher of logic, of natural philosophy, and philosophical theology (*ḥikma*) in Damascus under the Ayyubids, Sayf al-Dīn al-Āmidī (d. 631/1233, see below, p. 405, 406-408) read his interpretation of Avicennian philosophy with the learned doctors of his time: with al-Dakhwār, including his defence of Ibn Sīnā's *Ishārāt* against Fakhr al-Dīn al-Rāzī's critical *Sharḥ*; [63] with the author of the *Ṭabaqāt al-Aṭibbā'* himself, Ibn Abī Uṣaybiʿa (d. 668/1270), al-Āmidī read his own shorter manual of philosophy, the *Kitāb Rumūz al-Kunūz*, 'and this was due to the deep friendship between him and my father'.[64]

Turning to the philosophers, and philosopher-theologians, we find them reading and commenting upon Ibn Sīnā's *al-Qānūn fī l-Ṭibb*, mostly, it is true confining themselves to the part on theoretical medicine, *al-Kullīyāt*. The jurists and theologians who were fascinated by his writings of philosophical theology, criticising while commenting, and struggling with the obstacles it presented for the faith, found in the *Qānūn* a welcome exposition of natural and medical sciences. A long sequence of 'philosophers', philosopher-scientists and philosopher-jurists, starting from Ibn Sīnā's own pupils, wrote commentaries, epitomes and *quaestiones* on his

[62] See MAKDISI, *The Rise of Colleges* and footnote 24, p. 381 above.
[63] IBN ABĪ UṢAYBIʿA, *ʿUyūn*, II, p. 243.pu.-244.2.
[64] IBN ABĪ UṢAYBIʿA, *ʿUyūn*, II, p. 174.19.

physiological and medical theory.[65] Ibn Sīnā's disciple Muḥammad b. Yūsuf al-Īlāqī wrote *Fuṣūl* on certain passages of the *Qānūn*.[66] Close-linked chains of commentators started from the work of Fakhr al-Dīn al-Rāzī, and are found among the following of Naṣīr al-Dīn al-Ṭūsī. We shall meet their authors in the following sections of our survey: Fakhr al-Dīn al-Rāzī himself,[67] Nāmwar al-Khūnajī,[68] Quṭb al-Dīn al-Miṣrī.[69] A remarkable testimony of the reading of the *Qānūn* in these schools is the *Sharḥ Kullīyāt al-Qānūn* of al-Ṭūsī's polymath pupil Quṭb al-Dīn al-Shīrāzī (d. 710/1310), not for its originality, but for the survey of sources given in his preface, where he lists all previous commentaries of the work which he could lay his hands on during his travels in the East, or which were sent on his demand by the Mamluk Sultan Qalāwūn (such as, e.g., the *Sharḥ* of Ibn al-Nafīs, though not the latter's *Sharḥ al-Tashrīḥ*).[70]

5. Mathematics and the law

With the learned physicians of Baghdad and Damascus who took to reading Ibn Sīnā's works both in medicine and in philosophy, we have reached the generation of the key figures of this develoment, teachers of Shafiʿite law who brought the rational sciences to the class-rooms of the *madrasa*: Fakhr al-Dīn al-Rāzī (543-606/1149-1209) and Kamāl al-Dīn b. Yūnus (551-639/1156-1242).

Through their example, and the activity of their contemporaries and disciples, philosopher-physicians, philosopher-scientists and philosopher-jurists, the discussion about philosophical issues, the defense of philosophy and the further expansion of philosophical concepts and methods became, not so much an issue between separate circles of the Arabo-Islamic and the Hellenistic traditions, but a matter of debate inside the religious community. After the integration of the diverse traditions of philosophical and scientific thought, achieved by Ibn Sīnā, the final integration in what we might call an Islamic scholasticism was achieved by scientists who by training and partly also by

65 See the survey given in the introduction of Iskandar, *Catalogue*, p. 33 ff.

66 Iskandar, *Catalogue*, p. 37; on his biographical data see Rudolf Sellheim, *Materialien zur arabischen Literaturgeschichte* (*Verzeichnis der orientalischen Handschriften in Deutschland*, 17, Reihe A), I, Wiesbaden: Steiner, 1976-1987, p. 147.

67 Iskandar, *Catalogue*, p. 33; see below p. 401.

68 Iskandar, *Catalogue*, p. 34; see below p. 404.

69 Iskandar, *Catalogue*, p. 33; see below p. 403-404.

70 Iskandar, *Catalogue*, p. 49; an autograph copy is MS. Oxford, Bodl. Hunt. 263.

their professional activity belonged to the milieu of the *ʿulūm sharʿīya*, and taught in the *madrasa*, the college of law.

The social background of this development was the rise of a rank of scholars assuming universal competence: the philosopher-scientist, and at the same time philosopher-theologian, at home in the courts as well as in the *madrasa*. Until the first half of the twelfth century, teaching of the *ʿaqlīyāt* was kept out of the *madrasa*, and restricted to the libraries, observatories, hospitals and private circles of professional scholars where physicians, and astronomers, Christians, Jews and Muslims used to cooperate. While such learning began to spread more widely among Muslim scholars who as a matter of course had graduated from one of the schools of law, more and more eminent representatives of logic, of medicine, of mathematics and of spherical astronomy are found among the professors of the law college. Still, it took a long time before the teaching of these subjects was admitted into the traditional institutions of learning of the *ʿulūm sharʿīya*. The basic cursus, *taʿlīqa*, of jurisprudence, after the isagogic elements of grammar, *Qirāʾa*, and *Tafsīr*, was confined to the set books of the *uṣūl* and *furūʿ* of law, and the *majālis al-baḥth*: disputation of the *ikhtilāf al-fuqahāʾ*, i.e. questions disputed among the *madhāhib* of legal authority. The *ʿulūm al-awāʾil*, the Sciences of the Ancients, could only be taught outside the *madrasa*, in hospitals, observatories, and through the private instruction of scholars.

In pursuing the line of *fuqahāʾ* who took pains to keep rational demonstration and legal reasoning in different compartments, and who taught inside the *madrasa* on the one hand, and outside on the other, we will start with the mathematician. Kamāl al-Dīn b. Yūnus[71] went from Mosul to Baghdad for the study of Shafiʿite law at the Niẓāmīya *madrasa*, and on returning to his home town, spent his life teaching law at a succession of Mawṣilī colleges, whither he attracted students from all regions of the Dār al-Islām.

Ibn Khallikān (608-681/1211-1282), who was his personal student from 626 AH, is full of praise for his rank and authority both as *faqīh* and as mathematical genius:

[71] Mūsā b. Abī l-Faḍl Yūnus b. Muḥammad b. Manaʿa b. Mālik b. Muḥammad b. Saʿd b. Saʿīd b. ʿĀṣim: see IBN ABĪ UṢAYBIʿA, *ʿUyūn*, I, p. 306; ṬĀSHKUBRĀZĀDE, *Miftāḥ al-Saʿāda*, ed. KĀMIL KĀMIL BAKRĪ and ʿABD AL-WAHHĀB ABŪ L-NŪR, II, Cairo, 1968, p. 356, 358; IBN KHALLIKĀN, *Wafayāt al-Aʿyān*, ed. IḤSĀN ʿABBĀS, V, Beirut: Dār al-Thaqāfa, 1968-1972, p. 311-318; AL-SUBKĪ, *Ṭabaqāt al-Shāfiʿīya al-Kubrā*, ed. ʿABD AL-FATTĀḤ MUḤAMMAD AL-ḤULW and MAḤMŪD MUḤAMMAD AL-ṬANĀḤĪ, VIII, Cairo: ʿĪsā l-Bābī al-Ḥalabī, 1974-1976, p. 378-386 (mainly based on Ibn Khallikān).

> When his excellence became known, the students of jurisprudence crowded around him because of his profound learning in all the disciplines of knowledge; indeed, he united a knowledge of the sciences as nobody before him had, and stood out in the science of mathematics.[72]

Even Ḥanafites came to work with him on their *madhhab*, where he offered his own solutions of some difficult *quaestiones* in al-Shaybānī's *al-Jāmiʿ al-Kabīr*. What is more remarkable, and a testimony to his reputation as an open mind, is that 'the *ahl al-dhimma* used to study the Torah and the Gospel under him, and he explained these two scriptures to them, and they would admit that they could find nobody to expound them as he did'.[73] The physician and polymath ʿAbd al-Laṭīf al-Baghdādī gave a detailed account in his autobiography of a year of studies (585/1189) he spent at Mosul; even while taken aback by some of Kamāl al-Dīn's leanings, somewhat eccentric in his eyes, towards alchemy, magic, and the mystical 'illumination' of the *Shaykh al-Ishrāq* al-Suhrawardī, he could not but admire him for his brilliant scholarship.[74] When Fakhr al-Dīn al-Rāzī's works became available in Mosul, no one among the learned community understood his terminology except Kamāl al-Dīn.[75]

But his fame, spreading through the East of the Muslim world, was based on his supreme competence in the rational sciences (*ḥikma*): logic, natural philosophy, metaphysics, medicine, and especially mathematics. He taught Euclid's *Elements* on geometry, the 'Middle Books',[76] the *Conica* (according to Apollonius), theoretical astronomy (*al-hay'a*) and mathematical astronomy, simply called *al-Majisṭī* after Ptolemy's basic manual. The list of his readings given by his younger contemporary Ibn Khallikān reads like a full catalogue of the sciences;[77] in mathematics, this covered basic arithmetic (*al-ḥisāb al-maftūḥ*),[78] algebra, arithmology (*arithmāṭīqī*, probably number theory on the lines of Nicomachus's *Introductio* as opposed to simple *ʿilm al-ḥisāb*), the 'method of the two errors' (*ṭarīq al-khaṭa'ayn*), the theory of musical harmonies (*al-mūsīqī*), and geodesy (*al-misāḥa*). In the

[72] IBN KHALLIKĀN, *Wafayāt*, V, p. 311.

[73] IBN KHALLIKĀN, *Wafayāt*, V, p. 312.19-313.1.

[74] IBN ABĪ UṢAYBIʿA, *ʿUyūn*, II, p. 204.

[75] IBN KHALLIKĀN, *Wafayāt*, V, p. 312.4 f.

[76] *Al-Mutawassiṭāt*, sc. the 'Middle Books' of the mathematical sciences, optics and mechanics.

[77] IBN KHALLIKĀN, *Wafayāt*, V, p.312 f.

[78] I. e. the calculus of rational numbers (*al-ʿadad al-maftūḥ*), versus irrational numbers (*al-aṣamm*), like certain roots and proportions.

science of *awfāq*, the calculus of 'magical squares',[79] he found methods nobody had detected before him.

His teacher in mathematics had been Sharaf al-Dīn al-Ṭūsī (d. 582/1186), who had taught in Damascus and Aleppo and also for some time in Mosul. His biographer, al-Subkī, found a copy of the first book of Euclid's *Elements*, in the Arabic translation revised by Thābit b. Qurra, with a reading notice in the hand of Kamāl al-Dīn, referring to his teacher in the traditional form of *qirā'a ʿalā l-shaykh*:

> I have read this volume before the *shaykh*, the learned, chaste and pious Imām, Sharaf al-Dīn ... Abū l-Muẓaffar — may God prolong his days — after his return from Ṭūs, and I analyzed its problems (*ḥallaltu-hu*) with him, as also — by myself — those of the *Almagest*, and part of the *Conica*.[80] And I asked him to fulfil his promise to present to us the book of *Aporias*,[81] so he brought it, and I made a copy of it. Written by Mūsā b. Yūnus b. Muḥammad b. Manaʿa, at the given date, viz. the 19th Rabīʿ I, 576.[82]

His written work on subjects of mathematics, however, is small; even less has come down to us. Best known (through indirect tradition) are his answers to the questions on mathematics and optics which the emperor Frederick II Hohenstaufen submitted to the Muslim Arab scientists.[83]

His own teaching of such matters, it seems, did not take place inside the *madrasa*. Indeed,

> his orthodoxy was suspected (*kāna yuttahamu fī dīni-hi*), because the rational sciences were foremost in his mind, and at times, he committed mistakes, his thoughts being occupied because of these sciences.[84]

[79] See MOHAMED SOUISSI, *La langue des mathématiques en arabe*, Tunis: Université de Tunis, 1968, p. 353, no. 1898.

[80] *Kitāb al-Makhrūṭāt*, i.e. the *Conica* of Apollonius.

[81] *Kitāb al-Shukūk*, probably the *Shukūk ʿalā Baṭlamyūs* by Ibn al-Haytham.

[82] AL-SUBKĪ, *Ṭabaqāt*, V, p. 386.9-15.

[83] On his *Risāla fī l-Burhān ʿalā ['ttikhādh] al-Muqaddima allatī Ahmalahā Arshimīdis fī Kitābi-hī fī Tasbīʿ al-Dā'ira wa-Kayfīyat Ittikhādh dhālika* (Epistle on the proof of the assumption of the lemma, which [proof] Archimedes left out in his book on the division of the circle into seven equal parts, and how that can be achieved), and further works of geometrical analysis, see JAN P. HOGENDIJK, *Greek and Arabic Constructions of the Regular Heptagon*, in: *Archive for History of Exact Sciences* 30 (1984), p. 197-330. On the contacts between Frederick and al-Abharī in the context of the eastern Islamic tradition of the rational sciences, see also D.N. HASSE, *Mosul and Frederick II Hohenstaufen: notes on Aṯīraddīn al-Abharī and Sirāǧaddīn al-Urmawī*, in: *Occident et Proche-Orient: contacts scientifiques au temps des Croisades. Actes du colloque de Louvain-la-Neuve, 1997*, ed. I. DRAELANTS, A. TIHON and B. VAN ABEELE, Turnhout: Brepols, 2000, p. 145-63.

[84] IBN KHALLIKĀN, *Wafayāt*, V, p. 316.ult.-317.2.

The well-known traditionist, Taqī al-Dīn Ibn al-Ṣalāḥ (d. 643/1245), asked him to give lessons in logic (*sa'ala-hu an yaqra'a ʿalay-hi shay'an min al-manṭiq*) — *sirran,* in secret (or just 'in private'?) — but after repeated entreaties, the master talked him out of it: 'Look,' he told him, 'people think well of you, but they will connect everybody who engages in this discipline with unbelief, so it will end up ruining your reputation, and no profit will come to you from this art'.[85]

Notwithstanding such reservations, students from afar travelled to Mosul to study under his guidance.

(a) The Shafiʿite Athīr al-Dīn al-Mufaḍḍal b. ʿUmar al-Abharī (d. 663/1265?), already a distinguished teacher of law as well as of astronomy (*ṣāḥib al-taʿlīqa fī l-khilāf wa-l-zīj wa-l-taṣānīf al-mashhūra*),[86] despite his eminence, went to study with Kamāl al-Dīn b. Yūnus around 625-626/1227-1228, took his copy of the *Almagest* and went to sit in his class and worked as his famulus (*muʿīd*) like any student. Kamāl al-Dīn did not think all too highly of him, missing the challenge of critical brilliance.[87] This did not lessen al-Abharī's respect; his biographer, Ibn Khallikān, has transmitted his eulogy upon Ibn Yūnus. It is true that al-Abharī's own fame rests on rather pedestrian manuals of the philosophical encyclopedia of *ḥikma*, of logic, and of astronomy — manuals which, however, maintained a place in the syllabus of the *madrasa* until the Twentieth Century.

(b) His most eminent student, however, was the Shiʿite Naṣīr al-Dīn al-Ṭūsī (597-672/1201-1274), who came to Mosul as a young man about the same time,[88] after preliminary studies in law and theology in Egypt, to study the mathematical sciences with Ibn Yūnus. But we will come back to his own tradition of learning and teaching in science, philosophy and theology (see below, section 8, p. 414 ff.

85 Ibn Khallikān, *Wafayāt*, V, 314.

86 Ibn Khallikān, *Wafayāt*, IV, 396-501.

87 Ibn Khallikān, *Wafayāt*, V, p. 313, a report based on personal encounters with al-Abharī and other contemporaries.

88 Al-Ṣafadī, *al-Wāfī*, I, p. 181.21-22, on the authority of Shams al-Dīn b. al-Muʿayyad al-ʿUrḍī, one of the astronomers who worked with al-Ṭūsī in the observatory of Marāgha (the son of Mu'ayyad al-Dīn al-ʿUrḍī); see Muḥammad b. Shākir al-Kutubī, *Fawāt al-Wafayāt*, ed. Muḥyī al-Dīn ʿAbd al-Ḥamīd, II, Cairo: Maktabat al-Nahḍa al-Miṣrīya, 1951, p. 141; Al-Ṣafadī, *al-Wāfī*, I, p. 182.12-13 (from a report of Shams al-Dīn al-Jazarī on the activity in Marāgha around al-Ṭūsī).

(c) Among his students in the rational sciences was the Jacobite Christian physician Theodore of Antioch (Thadhārā al-Anṭākī) who wrote on the ancient sciences in both Syriac and 'Latin' (*al-lāṭinīya*, Byzantine Greek, or the Latin he may have practiced at the court of Sicily?). From Antioch, he came to Mosul, and read with Kamāl al-Dīn b. Yūnus 'the writings of al-Fārābī and Ibn Sīnā and the analysis (*ḥall*) of Euclid and the Almagest'. Returning to Antioch, he deemed his competence still insufficient, and went to Mosul a second time in order to continue reading with Ibn Yūnus. After serving as a physician at various courts in Baghdad and Armenia, he went to the King of the Franks, Frederick II Hohenstaufen, who held him in high esteem and provided him with a profitable living.[89]

6. Philosophy for Theologians: The School of Fakhr al-Dīn al-Rāzī and its Competitors

It is Fakhr al-Dīn al-Rāzī who is held mainly responsible for making jurists and theologians read, comment, refute and defend the works of Ibn Sīnā. Among the things deemed worthy of remark about the jurist-scientist Kamāl al-Dīn b. Yūsuf by one of his contemporaries, was his ability to understand the writings of Fakhr al-Dīn al-Rāzī when these first came to be known in Mosul.[90]

It is true that in this respect, the way had been prepared by al-Ghazālī, and even before the *Ḥujjat al-Islām*, by his teachers — as we begin to see more clearly now:

> Al-Ghazālī's role in the 'philosophizing' of Sunnī theology was not a lonely struggle by a single genius, but part of a broader trend that seems to have begun during Avicenna's lifetime and that picked up speed in the first and second generations after Avicenna's death in 1037, with the work of al-Ghazālī's teacher, the Ashʿarite al-Juwaynī (d. 1085), as well as of the Maturidite al-Bazdawī.[91]

'It is clear', as Richard Frank had already written in 1992,

> that in some of the elements of al-Ghazâlî's theology that we shall discuss he follows and elaborates material that was found already in al-Juwaynî's

[89] Ibn al-ʿIbrī, *Ta'rīkh Mukhtaṣar al-Duwal*, ed. Anṭūn Ṣāliḥānī, Beirut: al-Maktaba al-Kāthūlīkīya, 1958, p. 273.4-17.

[90] See above p. 392.

[91] Robert Wisnovsky, *One Aspect of the Avicennian Turn in Sunnī Theology*, in: *Arabic Sciences and Philosophy* 14 (2004), p. 65-100 (p. 65).

> *R. al-Niẓâmiyya* and, consequently, that he was not necessarily dependent upon Avicenna (certaily not directly) for the theses and concepts. There remains however, as we shall see, rather conspicuous evidence, that al-Ghazâlî was deeply and constantly preoccupied with the challenge which Avicenna and his writings posed for him.[92]

Al-Ghazālī took the decisive steps:

> While rejecting significant elements of Avicenna's cosmology, al-Ghazâlî adopted several basic principles and theses that set his theology in fundamental opposition to that of the classical Ashʿarite tradition.[93]

Indeed, it was he who gave to Muslim theologians a philosophy answering questions of *Kalām*: *fides quaerens intellectum*. It was the philosophy of Ibn Sīnā, epitomized,[94] assimilated and refuted by al-Ghazālī, expurgated in an extensive critical exposition by al-Rāzī, and instrumentalized, in several approaches and interpretations, by the schools of Sunnī and Shīʿī scholasticism. But it was through al-Rāzī, the 'Son of the Preacher of Rayy', *ibn khaṭīb al-Rayy*, as he would be called by his contemporaries, that Ibn Sīnā entered the *madrasa*.

Through Avicenna's new metaphysics and epistemology, exposed as a demonstrative science, the influence of philosophy and the Greek encyclopedia of rational sciences spread (a) beyond the closed circles of experts trained in the disciplines of the Greek tradition, and (b) beyond the higher echelons of the central and provincial administrations where the school of al-Kindī and later proponents of Islamic Platonism — Abū Zayd al-Balkhī, Abū l-Ḥasan al-ʿĀmirī, Miskawayh — had become established. With the rise of philosophy, *ḥikma*, and its *Organon* of logic as an instrument of scriptural hermeneutics, in the religious community, the clear-cut division between non-Arab and non-Muslim transmitters of the sciences on the one hand and the representatives of the Islamic schools had already been blurred, and soon ceased to exist (albeit the presence and prestige of Jews and Christians in the medical professions continued to be acknowledged, and also to be resented). The scientists themselves had put their knowledge at the service of religion, such as the astronomers working as time-keepers of the *jāmiʿ* mosques. A growing

[92] RICHARD M. FRANK, *Creation and the Cosmic System: al-Ghazâlî and Avicenna* (*Abhandlungen der Heidelberger Akademie der Wissenschaften, Phil.-hist. Kl.*, 1992, 1), Heidelberg: Carl Winter, 1992, p. 10 n. 1.

[93] FRANK, *Creation and the Cosmic System*, p. 11.

[94] Al-Ghazālī's *Maqāṣid al-Falāsifa* is primarily based on Ibn Sīnā's shorter *summa* of the philosophical cursus, written in Persian, the *Dānishnāma-i ʿAlāʾī*: see JULES JANSSENS, *Le* Dānesh-nāmeh *d'Ibn Sīnā: un texte à revoir?*, in: *Bulletin de philosophie médiévale* 28 (1986), p. 163-177.

number of educated Muslims, not a few of them judges and professors of law already in the generation of Avicenna's immediate pupils, felt attracted by his work which promised a comprehensive explanation of the world, a view of demonstrable truth in the dilemma between the odium of schism and traditionist reaction, and a view of cosmic order in the face of chaos. They made his philosophy their *credo*, and they read the Koran in the light of his philosophical exegesis.

The consequence of this tremendous success was that from the Seljuqid period, most discussion about philosophy was

(a) either a polemic against philosophy *qua* Avicennian philosophy as used — or rather, according to some, abused — by al-Ghazālī, al-Rāzī and his school, and his competitors, such as Sayf al-Dīn al-Āmidī;

(b) or a polemic against Avicenna's wrong understanding of true philosophy which made philosophy susceptible to such criticism (uttered most vehemently by Ibn Rushd);

(c) or a renewed attempt to eliminate from the Avicennian paradigm of philosophy the crucial offences it presented to religious belief (the paradigm of later *Kalām*) while adopting the conceptual framework of his metaphysics (essence and existence).

On the other hand, the very refutation of *Falsafa* hellenized the language of *Kalām*: making philosophical concepts and arguments available to theological discourse, raising *Kalām* to equal rank in the esteem of the *mutafalsifūn*. Following his example, the theologians grasped for the instruments of logical argument commended by al-Ghazālī the philosopher, in matters of physics and metaphysics, and refuted the *falāsifa* in their own language: the language of demonstration.

While Ibn Sīnā treated the symbols of the revealed Scripture as an allegory of the intelligible universals, his later critics — Fakhr al-Dīn al-Rāzī, and the critics and metacritics in his wake — treated the concepts of *Falsafa* as hermeneutical contrivances appropriate for conciliating the universal claim of rationalism with scriptural exegesis. At the same time, the Ṣūfīya, following the *Shaykh al-Ishrāq*, Shihāb al-Dīn al-Suhrawardī, re-interpreted the concepts of *Falsafa* as a metalanguage of mystical illumination.

From the philosophical theology of Avicenna grew a religious philosophy which canonized the discourse of Avicennian *Falsafa* in the very process of eliminating the old stumbling-blocks of Aristotelian physics.[95] This philosophy provided answers to the aporias of *Kalām* theology for the benefit of the religious community. Members of the same community began to regard rational demonstration as an indispensable, firm basis of sound argument in the service of Islam, and prepared the way for an Islamic scholasticism, adopted as propædeutics and methodology by the teachers of theology and law. At first outside rather than inside the religious community, but increasingly within the colleges of law — in Mongol and post-Mongol Iran, and then in late empires of the Ottomans and of Mughal India — the rational sciences joined the Islamic disciplines of the Sharīʿa, and in building a theology made scientific, paved the way to a philosophy made religious. This was accepted but slowly and grudgingly by the *ahl al-sunna wa-l-jamāʿa*, and never fully integrated but on a heavy ground of dissonant voices — produced, it is true, not (or not only) by narrow-minded traditionists, but by experts in both fields (Ibn Taymīya, for example, is both the most radical and the most proficient among the critics of logic). Acceptance for these tendencies was better prepared in the milieu of Shafiʿite jurists and Ashʿarite theologians of the Muslim East, and was renewed and systematized by the ideologues of the Imamite Shīʿa as a philosophical paradigm of their spiritual cosmology, and instrumentalized to establish the religious-political claims in their communities — a claim consummated in the religious institutions of the Safavid state of Iran.[96]

a) Fakhr al-Din al-Rāzī[97]

Born in Rayy in 543 or 544, son of the *khaṭīb* Ḍiyā' al-Dīn ʿUmar b. al-Ḥusayn b. al-Ḥasan (hence his *shuhra* Ibn al-Khaṭīb) he began initial studies of the *sharʿīyāt* with his father, who had studied with Abū l-Qāsim

[95] See FRANK, *Creation and the Cosmic System*.

[96] See now AYMAN SHIHADEH, *From al-Ghazālī to al-Rāzī: 6th/12th Century Developments in Muslim Philosophical Theology*, in: *Arabic Sciences and Philosophy* 15 (2005), p. 141-179, which contains additional material with regard to this and the following section, but which appeared after submission of the present article.

[97] AL-QIFṬĪ, *Ta'rīkh al-Ḥukamā'*, p. 291–293; ABŪ SHĀMA, *Dhayl al-Rawḍatayn*, ed. MUḤAMMAD ZĀHID B. AL-ḤASAN AL-KAWTHARĪ, Beirut: Dār al-Jīl, 1974 [1947], p. 68; KHWĀNSĀRĪ, *Rawḍat al-Jannāt*, p. 190-192; AL-SUBKĪ, *Ṭabaqāt*, VIII, p. 81-96 (and further sources from listed p. 81, note); IBN ABĪ UṢAYBIʿA, *ʿUyūn*, II, p. 23-30; ṬĀSHKUBRĀZĀDE, *Miftāḥ al-Saʿāda*, p. 445-451; IBN KHALLIKĀN, *Wafayāt al-Aʿyān*, III, p. 381-385; AL-ṢAFADĪ, *al-Wāfī*, V, p. 248-59. G.C. ANAWATI, *Fakhr al-Dīn al-Rāzī: Tamhīd li-Dirāsat Ḥayāti-hi wa-Muʾallafāti-hi*, in: *Ilā Ṭāhā Ḥusain*, ed. ʿABD AL-RAḤMĀN AL-BADAWĪ, Cairo: Dār al-Maʿārif, 1962, p. 193-234; G.C. ANAWATI, *Fakhr al-Dīn al-Rāzī*, in: *EI2*, III, p. 751-755; TONY STREET, *Concerning the Life and Works of Fakhr al-Din al-Razi*, in: *Islam: Essays on Scripture, Thought and Society. A Festschrift in Honour of Anthony H. Johns*, ed. P.G. RIDDELL and TONY STREET, Leiden: Brill, 1997, p. 135-146.

al-Anṣārī, a personal disciple of the Imām al-Ḥaramayn, al-Juwaynī. Through this tradition, Fakhr al-Dīn embraced Ashʿarite theology at an early age, and learnt al-Juwaynī's *Shāmil* by heart. In Marāgha, Fakhr al-Dīn al-Rāzī received his instruction in the rational sciences from Majd al-Dīn al-Jabalī (al-Jīlī?).

The teaching of mathematics and astronomy at Marāgha, long before the foundation of the observatory by Naṣīr al-Dīn al-Ṭūsī in 1259, is also attested by notes of transmission in manuscripts, such as the ms. Oxford, Hunt. 677 of Apollonius's *Conica* (*Kitāb al-Makhrūṭāt*), copied at Marāgha in 462/1070.[98] It is a remarkable manuscript in that it contains a testimony of al-Ṭūsī's own teaching: from a marginal note, we learn that a certain Aḥmad b. ʿAlī, known as Ibn al-Bawwāb, from Baghdad copied into this manuscript, in 662/1263-4, the comments and corrections which al-Ṭūsī himself had noted in his own copy of the *Conica* in 645/1247-8.[99]

Henceforth, al-Rāzī included the whole range of the philosophical-scientific encylopedia into his teaching. Incidentally, it is in his lifetime that we encounter the first examples of scientific works copied in the Niẓāmīya *madrasa* of Baghdad (see above, p. 380-381).

All his life, Fakhr al-Dīn moved among the power centers of eastern Iran: from Khwārazm to Transoxania, engaging in relentless controversies wherever he went, and staying nowhere for long — first going back to Rayy, then seeking the favours of the Ghurid Shihāb al-Dīn (569-599/1173-1203) of Ghazna, who heaped honours and fortunes upon him. He then served the Khwārazm-Shāh ʿAlāʾ al-Dīn Muḥammad b. Tekish, and after another interlude in Transoxania (Bukhara, in 580/1184) finally settled in Herat under the Ghurid Ghiyāth al-Dīn. There he died on Monday, 1st Shawwāl 606/29 March 1210. Through his authority as a *faqīh*, he served the powers of his age (who served him in turn by giving him chairs and institutions for his teaching) in supporting the mainstream of orthodoxy, tipping the balance in favour of Shafiʿite law and Ashʿarite theology where the Muʿtazila upheld its influence, fighting the anti-intellectual 'fundamentalism' of the Karrāmīya (the *Ḥashwīya*, or anthropomorphists),[100] fighting with sharp reasoning as well as with

[98] Described by G. Toomer in APOLLONIUS, *Conics, Books V to VII: the Arabic Translation of the Lost Greek Original in the Version of the Banū Mūsā*, ed. GERALD J. TOOMER, I, New York: PUBLISHER, 1990, p. lxxxv-lxxxvii.

[99] See TOOMER, *Conics*, p. lxxxvi, n. 1; A.F.L. BEESTON, *The Marsh Manuscript of Apollonius's* Conica, in: *The Bodleian Library Record* 4 (1952-1953), p. 76-77.

[100] When passing Fērūzkūh on his way to Bukhara in 580, a riot was organized against him by the Karrāmīya who attacked him for corrupting Islam with the doctrines of Aristotle, al-Fārābī and Ibn Sīnā; see G.C. ANAWATI, *Fakhr al-Dīn al-Rāzī*, in: *EI*2, III, p. 752.

inspiring preaching,[101] and — what is important for our present inquiry — made *ḥikma*, the demonstrative reasoning and the scientific concepts of the *falāsifa*, an instrument of converting courtiers, men of science, physicians and astrologers, to his cause. His vast learning and numerous writings in the fields of law and its ancillaries on the one hand, his enormous oeuvre on the encyclopedia of philosophy and the rational sciences on the other, served this encompassing ambition.

What in al-Ghazālī's thought had been successive phases of a thinker's convictions, albeit not uninfluenced by the vicissitudes of time and the virulence of heterodoxy, were coinciding methods and paradigms in al-Rāzī's: a conscious, simultaneous use of a variegated arsenal of intellectual and spiritual weaponry. The fusion between the two traditions of rational exegesis, philosophical and theological, was in the eyes of many contemporaries of al-Rāzī and of the following generations of scholastics in Sunnī Islam, a confusion, and was a matter of controversy in his own time, and not undisputed even among his school. He provided systematic treatments of the whole range of the *cursus studiorum*, in separate manuals, including a theology which in using logical method and the Peripatetic concept of demonstrative science, defined and defended the stance of orthodoxy as he saw it. For the philosophical encyclopedia of al-Rāzī and his successors as well as for the polymath scientists of Iran from al-Ṭūsī to the Ṣafavid schools, both of Avicenna's divisions of philosophy serve as alternative models: the tripartite division of the classical canon beside the four-part division presented in the introduction of the *Kitāb al-Mashriqīyīn*; logic in many cases is separately mentioned in the titles of such handbooks, or treated in separate manuals. Al-Rāzī gives both the *ḥikma* part of his *Mulakhkhaṣ fī l-Ḥikma wa-l-Manṭiq*[102] (written in 579/1184) and his *Mabāḥith al-Mashriqīya*[103] the same division (i.e. tripartite, without the logic): he relegates the First Philosophy, the ontology and doctrine of principles of the old metaphysics to the beginning: the doctrine of the universals (*al-umūr al-ʿāmmīya*); he goes on with the doctrine of substances and of natural processes of physics — categories (*aʿrāḍ*), and substances (*jawāhir:* body, soul, intellect) — a physical theory which in

[101] On Fakhr al-Dīn al-Rāzī as a preacher in both Arabic and Persian, see AL-ṢAFADĪ, *al-Wāfī*, IV, p. 249.7.

[102] See SELLHEIM, *Materialien zur arabischen Literaturgeschichte,* I, p. 141 f.

[103] Detailed table of contents in WILHELM AHLWARDT, *Verzeichniss der arabischen Handschriften* (*Die Handschriften-Verzeichnisse der Königlichen Bibliothek zu Berlin,* 17), IV, Berlin: Asher, 1887-1899, p. 403-415, no. 5064.

its principles of movement and causality eliminates the old stumbling-blocks of the philosophers' doctrine of the eternity of the world. In the final part, he crowns the *cursus studiorum* with the theology of the *Kalām* ('the pure divinalia', *al-ilāhīyāt al-maḥḍa*).

In the wake of al-Rāzī's achievement, on the one hand, the treatment of theology in the terms and through the concepts of philosophy opened the whole field of the sciences to Islamic scholasticism; on the other hand, the reduction of the rational sciences to theology, and the elimination of the outrage of Aristotelian physics, prevented Muslim scientists, despite enormous progress in observation and calculus, to transcend the paradigms of ancient science.

His basis in philosophy were those works of Ibn Sīnā which were conceived as, or could be read as, a hermeneutic of the Qur'anic message, and as an answer to the aporias of Ashʿarite *Kalām*. His pioneering achievement in this repect is the *Sharḥ al-Ishārāt*, a commentary on the physics and metaphysics in the *Kitāb al-Ishārāt wa-l-Tanbīhāt* of Ibn Sīnā; in addition he wrote a summary, *Lubāb al-Ishārāt*. Following Ibn Sīnā as a guide, he also studied those of the natural sciences which had been given a theoretical framework and a systematic position among the rational sciences by the *Shaykh al-Raʾīs*. In this way, he commented upon the general part of Ibn Sīnā's handbook of medicine in his *Sharḥ Kullīyāt al-Qānūn*.[104]

He took a special interest in the popular natural sciences (but, unlike many later protagonists of the *ʿaqlīyāt* in the Shafiʿite and Shiʿite schools of the era dawning in the next generation, not in mathematics). Even though some of the works ascribed to him on astrology, oneiromancy, and other topics neighbouring on the occult may be spurious, there is no reason to doubt the authenticity of others such as his Physiognomy, *Kitāb al-Firāsa*.

b) Disciples and Competitors of Fakhr al-Dīn al-Rāzī

Abū l-Faraj Ibn al-ʿIbrī (the Jacobite Christian Gregorius Barhebraeus, d. 685/1286) — the Christian theologian, historian, and astronomer, who worked with Naṣīr al-Dīn al-Ṭūsī in Marāgha[105] for some time — wrote a survey of scholarly life under the caliphate of al-Mustanṣir (d.

[104] Written in 580/1280 during a stay in Sarakhs, in the house of the physician Thiqat al-Dīn ʿAbd al-Raḥmān al-Sarakhsī, in the course of a journey to Bukhārā; see SELLHEIM, *Materialien zur arabischen Literaturgeschichte,* I, p. 201, no. 55 (Ms. Berlin, or.8° 1466, dated 627/1230).

[105] On his life and his works in Syriac, see ANTON BAUMSTARK, *Geschichte der syrischen Literatur*, Bonn, 1922, p. 312-320.

The School of Fakhr al-Dīn al-Rāzī
fī l-manṭiq wa-l-ḥikma
Ibn al-ʿIbrī, *Ta'rīkh Mukhtaṣar al-Duwal*, p. 254

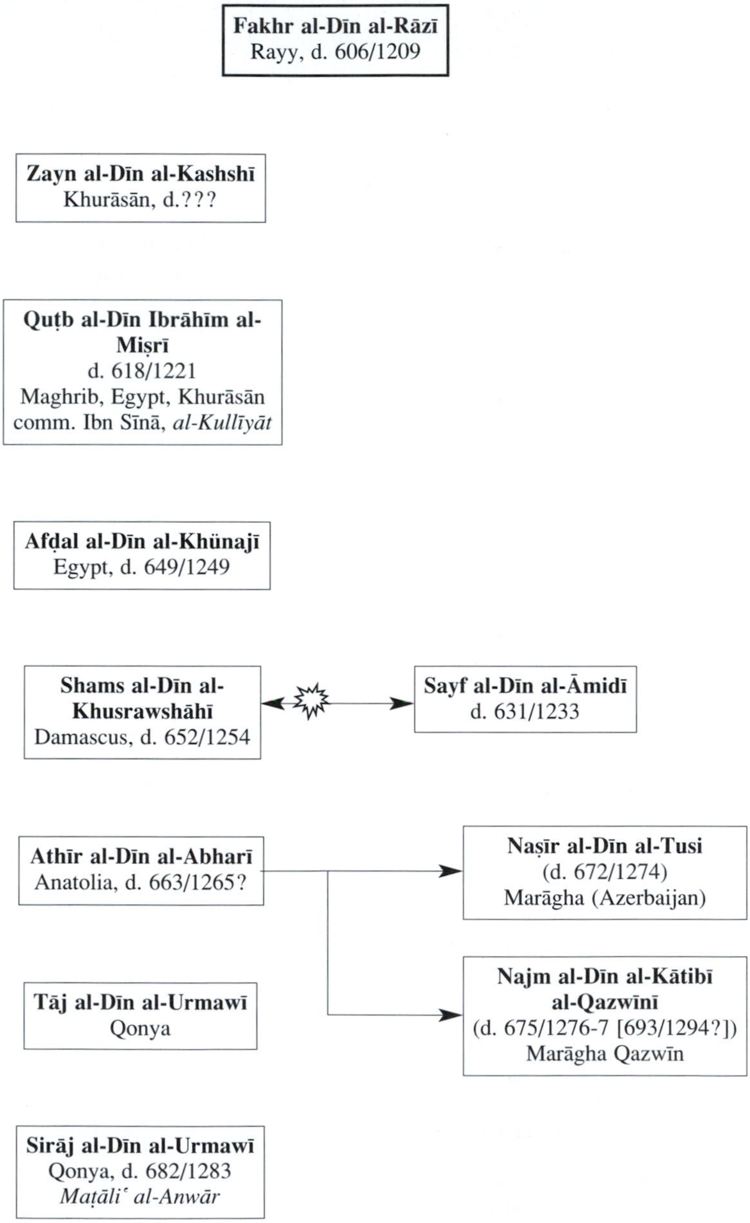

623/1226) in his *Ta'rīkh Mukhtaṣar al-Duwal.*[106] He portrays the school of Fakhr al-Dīn al-Rāzī, *sādāt fuḍalā' aṣḥāb taṣānīf jalīla fī l-manṭiq wa-l-ḥikma*, as represented by scholars in all of the Orient, from eastern Iran to Egypt, Syria and Anatolia:

- in Khurāsān, Quṭb al-Dīn al-Miṣrī (d. 618/1221);
- in Egypt, Afḍal al-Dīn al-Khūnajī (d. 649/1249);
- in Damascus, Shams al-Dīn al-Khusrawshāhī (d. 652/1254) and Athīr al-Dīn al-Abharī (d. 663/1265?);
- in Anatolia (Rūm), Tāj al-Dīn al-Urmawī and (in Qonya) Sirāj al-Dīn al-Urmawī (d. 682/1283).

i) Quṭb al-Dīn Abū l-Ḥārith Ibrāhīm b. ʿAlī b. Muḥammad al-Sulamī al-Miṣrī al-Maghribī, is referred to as *al-ḥakīm,* and *al-imām fī l-ʿaqlīyāt.* After travels in Egypt, he went to Khurāsān to study with Fakhr al-Dīn al-Rāzī and was respected, and praised by the master himself, as one of his eminent disciples (*ṣāra min kibār talāmidhati-hi*). Together with Ibn al-ʿIbrī, in his *Ta'rīkh Mukhtaṣar al-Duwal,* Ibn Abī Uṣaybiʿa mentions him as one of the eminent disciples of al-Rāzī. His reputation rested on his competence in the *ʿaqlīyāt*, Avicennian philosophy and theoretical science. He was killed in 618/1221, a victim of the Mongol invasion of Khurāsān, during the sack of Nishapur.[107] 'He wrote many books', his biographers say, but the only title named is his commentary on the *Kullīyāt* of Ibn Sīnā's *Qānūn fī l-Ṭibb.*[108] The relation of his commentary to al-Rāzī's is detailed by Ibn Abī Uṣaybiʿa in his notice:

> In the *Sharḥ al-Kullīyāt*, I found him to give precedence to al-Masīḥī [i.e. Abū Sahl ʿĪsā b. Yaḥyā al-Masīḥī al-Jurjānī, forerunner and teacher of Ibn Sīnā, and author of the famous *Kitāb al-Mi'a* [mentioned above, p. 382], while Ibn al-Khaṭīb [Ibn Khaṭīb al-Rayy, i.e. Fakhr al-Dīn al-Rāzī] favours the *Shaykh* Abū ʿAlī b. Sīnā. These are his own words: The Masīḥī is more knowledgeable about the art of medicine, and our teachers used to give him

[106] Ed. ANṬŪN ṢĀLIḤĀNĪ, Beirut: al-Maṭbaʿa al-Kāthūlīkīya, 1958, p. 254.14-17.

[107] See IBN ABĪ UṢAYBIʿA, *ʿUyūn*, II, p. 30.18-30; IBN AL-ʿIBRĪ, *Ta'rīkh Mukhtaṣar al-Duwal,* p. 445; AL-SUBKI, *Ṭabaqāt al-Shāfiʿīya*, VIII, p. 121, no. 1109; IBN AL-FUWAṬĪ, *Majmaʿ al-Ādāb fī Muʿjam al-Alqāb*, ed. MUṢṬAFĀ JAWĀD, IV, Baghdād: Wizārat al-Thaqāfa, 1967, p. 611 f. (quoting a couplet of poetry by Quṭb al-Dīn on the authority of 'our *mawlā*, Naṣīr al-Dīn Abū Jaʿfar M. b. M. b. al-Ḥ. al-Ṭūsī'); AL-ṢAFADĪ, *al-Wāfī*, VI, p. 69-70 (based mainly on Ibn Abī Uṣaybiʿa); AL-DHAHABĪ, *Ta'rīkh,* sub anno 618. The *Ta'rīkh Maqābir Shīrāz*, p. 354 (quoted by the editor in IBN AL-FUWAṬĪ, *Majmaʿ al-Ādāb*, p. 611, n. 1), mentions him as a teacher of the *qāḍī* Jamāl al-Dīn Abū Bakr b. Yūsuf al-Miṣrī in the latter's biography. See also ʿUMAR RIḌĀ KAḤḤĀLA, *al-Aʿlām,* III, Damascus: Maṭbaʿat al-Taraqqī, p. 260.

[108] Mss. of his commentary on the *Qānūn* see BROCKELMANN, *GALS*, I, p. 824, no. 82 (f).

> precedence over many others, whom they deemed more competent than Abū ʿAlī in this art. He also said: The expression of al-Masīḥī is clearer and more lucid than the discourse of the Shaykh.[109]

As a student of Ibn Sīnā's philosophy in the tradition of al-Rāzī, he also shows up in an *isnād* of readers of Ibn Sīnā's *al-Ishārāt wa-l-Tanbīhāt*, reported by al-Ṣafadī[110] on the authority of Ibn al-Akfānī (to be discussed in detail in Section 7 below, p. 409-414). Here he appears here as a direct student of Fakhr al-Dīn al-Rāzī, and Athīr al-Dīn al-Abharī, in his turn, refers to him as his *shaykh* for the reading of the *Ishārāt*.

ii) Afḍal al-Dīn Abū ʿAbd Allāh Muḥammad b. Nāmawār (Nāmwar) al-Khūnajī (d. 646/1248) was respected as a philosopher and a physician.[111] He wrote a compendium of logic and a commentary on the *Kullīyāt* of Ibn Sīnā's *Qānūn fī l-Ṭibb*. Ibn Abī Uṣaybiʿa read the latter text with him during his studies in Cairo in 632.[112]

iii) Shams al-Dīn ʿAbd al-Ḥamīd b. ʿĪsā al-Khusrawshāhī (from Khusrawshāh, a *ḍayʿa* near Tabrīz, d. 652/1254), excelled in the rational sciences, but was an authority in Shafiʿite law as well. He was acknowledged as one of the most brilliant personal disciples of Fakhr al-Dīn al-Rāzī. In Syria, he entered the service of the Ayyubid Sultan al-Malik al-Nāṣir Ṣalāḥ al-Dīn Dāwūd,[113] staying with him in al-Karak, and held in great esteem by this prince. Afterwards, he went to Damascus, where he stayed until his death in Shawwāl 652, and was buried on the Jabal Qāsiyūn.[114]

Ibn Abī Uṣaybiʿa met with him personally when he moved to Damascus, and found him to be *shaykh ḥasan al-samt malīḥ al-kalām*, a sound scholar and an accomplished expert in the sciences: 'One day, I saw him when a Persian scholar brought him a book written in a subtle hand, in Baghdādī size and Muʿtazilī cut.[115] When he opened it, he proceeded to kiss it and put it upon his head. I asked him about this, and he said: This

[109] IBN ABĪ UṢAYBIʿA, *ʿUyūn*, II, p. 30.22-26.

[110] AL-ṢAFADĪ, *al-Wāfī*, II, p. 142.15-143.2.

[111] IBN ABĪ UṢAYBIʿA, *ʿUyūn*, II, p. 120; BROCKELMANN, *GAL*(2), I, p. 607; *GALS*, I, p. 838.

[112] IBN ABĪ UṢAYBIʿA, *ʿUyūn*, II, p. 120.22-23.

[113] Ayyubid ruler of Damascus 615-624/1218-1227 (as governor 597-615/1201-1218).

[114] IBN ABĪ UṢAYBIʿA, *ʿUyūn*, II, p. 173.1-12; AL-SUBKĪ, *Ṭabaqāt al-Shāfiʿīya*, VIII, p. 161.

[115] *Thumn baghdādī, taqṭīʿ muʿtazilī*: see ADAM GACEK, *The Arabic Manuscript Tradition: A Glossary of Technical Terms and Bibliography* (*Handbook of Oriental Studies*, 58), Leiden: Brill, 2001, under *th-m-n*, *q-ṭ-ʿ*. Abū Ḥanīfa recommended a square shape for textbooks: see p. 117, reference to BURHĀN AL-DĪN AL-ZARNŪJĪ, *Taʿlīm al-Mutaʿallim*, Beirut: al-Maktab al-Islāmī, 1981, p. 85.

is the handwriting of our *shaykh*, the Imām Fakhr al-Dīn, son of the *khaṭīb*, may God have mercy on him. My esteem for him grew because of his reverence for his *shaykh*.

Khusrawshāhī was a prominent figure in the entourage of the Ayyubid Sultan of Damascus, al-Malik al-Nāṣir (son of al-Malik al-Muʿaẓẓam, r. 624-626/1227-1229), being named as his *shaykh* by the historian Ibn Wāṣil.[116] Against his fiercest competitor, Sayf al-Dīn al-Āmidī (see below, p. 406-408) — who was a favourite of al-Malik al-Muʿaẓẓam — he sought to spread al-Rāzī's teaching.

Ibn al-ʿIbrī has an anecdote illustrating his prestige with the Ayyubid prince, a patron of philosophical learning in his time:

> al-Najīb al-Rāhib al-Miṣrī al-Ḥāsib reported in Damascus that al-Malik al-Nāṣir Dāwūd b. al-Malik al-Muʿaẓẓam b. al-Malik al-ʿĀdil b. Ayyūb, the lord of Karak, told him that he used to frequent Shams al-Dīn al-Khusrawshāhī in order to read with him the book *ʿUyun al-Ḥikma* of the *shaykh* Abū ʿAlī b. Sīnā.When he arrived in front of the quarter where Shams al-Dīn al-Khusrawshāhī lived, he beckoned to those of his following and of the Mamluks who were with him to remain standing in their place, while he got down on his feet, took his book wrapped in a cloth (*mindīl*) under his armpit, and went to the house of the *ḥakīm*, and when the door was opened to him, entered, went through his readings, asked about what came to his mind, and then stood up to go, and never permitted the *shaykh* to stand up before him.[117]

In the opinion of his contemporaries, he was equally competent in the rational sciences (*al-ʿulūm al-ḥikmīya*), in theoretical medicine (*al-uṣūl al-ṭibbīya*) and the Islamic disciplines (*al-ʿulūm al-sharʿīya*), and indeed, was one of the most eminent disciples of Fakhr al-Dīn al-Rāzī.[118] He also wrote a compendium (*mukhtaṣar*) of several treatises of Ibn Sīnā, commented upon al-Rāzī's *al-Āyāt al-Bayyināt* as well as on Avicenna's *Shifāʾ* and *ʿUyūn al-Ḥikma*.

iv) Athīr al-Dīn al-Abharī (d. 663/1265?), the renowned teacher of logic, *ḥikma,* and *uṣūl al-dīn* — we have met him among the students of Kamāl al-Dīn b. Yūnus (above, p. 394) —, worked with Naṣīr al-Dīn al-Ṭūsī as an astronomer in Marāgha; more will be said about him in connection with the Rāzī-Ṭūsī Tradition (p. 410, 414-416).

[116] Jamāl al-Dīn Muḥammad b. Sālim b. Wāṣil, *Mufarrij al-Kurūb fī Akhbār Banī Ayyūb*, ed. Ḥasanayn M. Rabīʿ and Jamāl al-Dīn al-Shayyal, V, Cairo: Dār al-Kutub, 1973, p. 15.

[117] Ibn al-ʿIbrī, *Taʾrīkh*, p. 254.17-23.

[118] Ibn Abī Uṣaybiʿa, *ʿUyūn*, II, p. 173.1-4;7.

v) The Anatolian (Rūmī) scholars, Tāj al-Dīn al-Urmawī and (in Qonya) Sirāj al-Dīn al-Urmawī (d. 682/1283), wrote manuals and commentaries of logic and theology in the tradition of al-Rāzī. Sirāj al-Dīn al-Urmawī[119] is best known for his manual of logic, *Maṭāliʿ al-Anwār fī l-Manṭiq*, and he wrote a compendium of al-Rāzī's *al-Maḥṣūl fī Uṣūl al-Fiqh* under the title *al-Taḥṣīl*. As a commentator of Ibn Sīnā's *Kitāb al-Ishārāt wa-l-Tanbīhāt*, he enters the lineage of readers and critics of this all-important work in al-Rāzī's tradition, of which more will be said in connection with the Abharī-Ṭūsī line of philosophical teaching (Sections 7–8, below).

Tāj al-Dīn al-Urmawī is mentioned by Ibn Abī Uṣaybiʿa as one of his teachers; in the bibliography of Fakhr-al-Dīn al-Rāzī, he lists the *Risāla al-Kamālīya fī l-Ḥaqāʾiq al-Ilāhīya*, written in Persian for Kamāl al-Dīn Muḥammad b. Mīkāʾīl, 'and I found that our *shaykh*, the learned *imām*, Tāj al-Dīn Muḥammad al-Urmawī had translated it into Arabic in the year 625 [1228], in Damascus'.

vi) The Competitor: al-Āmidī

Through his work, Fakhr al-Dīn al-Rāzī had endowed a tradition of both exposing and criticizing philosophy in a commentary upon Avicenna's seminal text, the *Kitāb al-Ishārāt wa-l-Tanbīhāt*. But, as al-Ṭūsī said in the introduction to his commentary, al-Rāzī's *sharḥ* was rather a *jarḥ*, an attack rather than a fair exposition. The first to reply to such 'misrepresentations in the form of commentary', *al-Tamwīhāt fī Sharḥ al-Tanbīhāt*, was a jurist, theologian and philosopher who did not hail from al-Rāzī's line of tradition, but who emerged as a competitor against the growing influence of his school: Sayf al-Dīn al-Āmidī, from Āmid in upper Mesopotamia (551-631/1156-1233).[120] He was a Ḥanbalite who converted in Baghdad to Shafiʿite *fiqh* and Ashʿarite theology, who privately learned philosophy from Jewish and Christian teachers in the Karkh quarter of Baghdad, who taught in Egypt until he had to flee from accusations against his infecting religion with his philosophical tenets,

[119] Abū l-Thanāʾ Maḥmūd b. Abī Bakr: see AL-SUBKĪ, *Ṭabaqāt al-Shāfiʿīya*, VIII, p. 371; BROCKELMANN, *GAL*(2), I, p. 614 f., 667, no. II (b); *GALS*, I, p. 817, 848, 921, no. 3 (b); SELLHEIM, *Materialien zur arabischen Literaturgeschichte*, I, p. 154 f.

[120] Biographical sources: IBN KHALLIKĀN, *al-Wāfī*, III, p. 293-294; AL-QIFṬĪ, *Taʾrīkh al-Ḥukamāʾ*, p. 240-241; IBN ABĪ UṢAYBIʿA, *ʿUyūn*, II, p. 174-175; AL-SUBKĪ, *Ṭabaqāt al-Shāfiʿīya*, VIII, p. 306-308; IBN AL-ʿIMĀD, *Shadharāt al-Dhahab*, V, Cairo: Maktabat al-Qudsī, p. 144; AL-YĀFIʿĪ, *Mirʾāt al-Janān*, IV, Beirut: Muʾassasat al-Risāla, 1970 [1919-1921], p. 73; IBN WĀṢIL, *Mufarrij al-Kurūb*, V, p. 35-41; *GAL*, I, p. 393 ([2] p. 494); *GALS*, I, p. 678.

and then went to Syria for the rest of his life. Among his considerable œuvre are three full treatments of *Uṣūl al-Fiqh* (the *Iḥkām al-Ḥukkām fī Uṣūl al-Aḥkām*), of *Uṣūl al-Dīn* (under the title of *Abkār al-Afkār fī Uṣūl al-Dīn*), and a treatment of *ḥikma*, philosophy, on the lines of Avicenna's paradigm and system, *al-Nūr al-Bāhir fī l-Ḥikam al-Zawāhir*, divided into logic, physics, and metaphysics.[121] Each of the three manuals, we should add, has its own treatment of logic: the legal reasoning of *qiyās*, the methodology of theological *naẓar*, and the syllogistic logic of the Aristotelian *Analytics*.[122] But like Fakhr al-Dīn al-Rāzī, al-Āmidī did not integrate all of the hermeneutical, and rational disciplines into one comprehensive and systematic 'enyclopedia'; he had to face public persecution, and fled Egypt, because of his propagating philosophy in his teaching of the *uṣūlān*.

After returning from Egypt, he settled in Ḥamāh, where in 615/1218-19, he placed himself at the service of the Ayyubid sovereign al-Malik al-Manṣūr Muḥammad (regn. 587-617/1191-1221)[123] — to whom he had dedicated already in 605/1208 his commentary on the *Ishārāt* —, and received a comfortable salary. On the death of al-Manṣūr in 617/1221, he went to Damascus, where the Ayyubid ruler, al-Malik al-Muʿaẓẓam (the son of al-Malik al-ʿĀdil, r. 615-624/1218-1227) conferred his favours upon him, and appointed him to the chair of the Madrasa al-ʿAzīzīya. Here he became a celebrated teacher of law, famous for his versatility in learned discussion on the disputed questions of the law schools, and also of the rational sciences — 'and it was uncommon that someone should teach anything of the philosophical sciences'.[124] Among his students at Damascus, we have already met the physicians Ibn Abī Uṣaybiʿa and al-Dakhwār (d. 628/1230).[125]

'He railed against Fakhr al-Dīn, the son of the Khaṭīb of Rayy, and when he mentions him in his writings, then [anonymously] with the words "one of the recent authors said", and reviles and attacks him excessively — doing this, it seems to me, out of jealousy for Fakhr al-Dīn'.[126]

[121] Facsimile ed. of MS Ankara, Ismail Saib 4830 (of the original five volumes, only four are extant) by F. Sezgin, *Splendid Light on Bright Wisdom: al-Nūr al-Bāhir fī l-Ḥikam al-Zawāhir* (*Publications of the Institute for the History of Arabic Islamic Science*, Series C, 67), Frankfurt am Main, 2001. His shorter manual of *ḥikma*, *Rumūz al-Kunūz*, still unpublished, closely corresponds to the layout and sequence of topics of the larger work.

[122] See G. Endress, *Die dreifache Ancilla: Hermeneutik und Logik im Werk des Sayf-al-Dīn al-Āmidī*, in: *Logik und Theologie: das* Organon *im arabischen und im lateinischen Mittelalter*, ed. D. Perler and U. Rudolph, Leiden: Brill, 2005, p. 117-145.

[123] Ibn Abī Uṣaybiʿa, *ʿUyūn*, II, p. 174.

[124] Ibn Abī Uṣaybiʿa, *ʿUyūn*, II, p. 174.18.

[125] See above p. 389.

[126] Ibn Wāṣil, *Mufarrij al-Kurūb*, V, p. 36.

This judgement of the contemporary historian Ibn Wāṣil, in its turn, is marked by the struggle for influence at the Ayyubid courts of Syria, where al-Āmidī encountered Shams al-Dīn al-Khusrawshāhī — al-Rāzī's disciple who managed to win over the Ayyubid prince for al-Rāzī's philosophy (see above, p. 404-405). To increase his jealousy, al-Āmidī had heard — as Ibn Wāṣil adds maliciously — that the Khwārazmshāh ʿAlāʾ al-Dīn Muḥammad b. Tekish (r. 596-617/1200-1220) had delegated somebody to the service of Fakhr al-Dīn al-Rāzī, took his instruction, and heaped him with favours.

On the accession of al-Malik al-Ashraf Mūsā (626/1229), he first kept his chair, but was dismissed shortly before his death (631/1231) — according to some,[127] denounced because of his philosophical leanings: when the Sultan acceeded to the throne in Damascus, he decreed that no *faqīh* was to devote himself to anything else but *Ḥadīth, Tafsīr,* and *Fiqh*, and whoever would meddle with logic and the sciences of the ancients, was to be exiled.[128]

7. THE READING OF AVICENNA'S *KITĀB AL-ISHĀRĀT WA-L-TANBĪHĀT* IN COMMENTARY, REFUTATION, AND ARBITRATION

One of the main vehicles of discussion, approach and delimitation between philosophers and theologians is the commentary on Ibn Sīnā's *al-Ishārāt wa-l-Tanbīhāt*, expositions, attacks, apologies, and 'arbitrations' between Avicenna and his opponents. It it this work in which the *Shaykh al-Raʾīs* pursued his programme of interpreting religious language as a metaphor of universal apodeixis, and in which — as also in many others of his *summae* and treatises — he replied to question of *Kalām* in a philosophical discourse on being, essence, categories, attributes, and the all-important concept of the divine First Cause as first Necessary Being (*wājib al-wujūd*). Against the criticism in the *Sharḥ al-Ishārāt wa-l-Tanbīhāt* of Fakhr al-Dīn al-Rāzī, we find, in the generation of his disciples, the metacriticism of Sayf al-Dīn al-Āmidī in his *Kashf al-Tamwīhāt fī Sharḥ al-Tanbīhāt* (above, p. 406) and — again in the

[127] But according to his younger contemporary, al-Qifṭī (*qāḍī akram* of Aleppo, d. 646/1248), and Ibn Wāṣil, because of a political intrigue: he led clandestine negotiations behind the back of the Ayyubid princes with the lord of Āmid, his home town, for the position of judge, after Āmid had been conquered by al-Malik al-Kāmil, together with al-Ashraf, in 630/1232, and its Artuqid sovereign deposed.

[128] HENRI SAUVAIRE, *Description de Damas* (according to ʿAbd al-Basīṭ al-Dimashqī al-ʿAlmāwī, *Mukhtaṣar*), in: *Journal Asiatique*, s.9, 6 (1895), p. 263.

next generation — the *Sharḥ* of Naṣīr al-Dīn al-Ṭūsī, who from the same school had received his philosophical and theological learning: called the *Ḥall Mushkilāt al-Ishārāt*. This text, in its turn, was the point of departure of a school tradition.[129]

The study of Ibn Sīnā's philosophy, on the basis of his *Kitāb al-Ishārāt wa-l-Tanbīhāt*, in the tradition of Fakhr al-Dīn al-Rāzī and his school, is illustrated by a chain of transmission — an *isnād* in the style of traditionist *qirā'a* notices — reported by al-Ṣafadī on the authority of his own teacher in the rational sciences, the Egyptian physician and polymath, Shams al-Dīn Ibn al-Akfānī (d. 749/1348). With Ibn al-Akfānī, al-Ṣafadī himself had read the first part of the *Ishārāt*.[130] It is reported in his notice of the astronomer and *ṣūfī*, Shams al-Dīn al-Shurwānī (d. 699/1299-1300):

> The *shaykh* and *imām* Shams al-Dīn Muḥammad b. Ibrāhīm known as Ibn al-Akfānī, mentioned before, told me:
>
> I have read the *Ishārāt* of Abū ʿAlī b. Sīnā under the *shaykh*, the *imām* Shams al-Dīn Muḥammad b. Aḥmad al-Shurwānī, the *ṣūfī*, at the Khānqāh of Saʿīd al-Suʿadāʾ inside Cairo, by the end of the year 698 and in early 699 [1298], and he reported:
>
> I have read the work and its commentary with the commentator, the Khwāja Naṣīr al-Dīn Muḥammad al-Ṭūsī; and the latter said:
>
> I have read it with the *imām* Athīr al-Dīn al-Mufaḍḍal al-Abharī, who said:
>
> I read it with the *shaykh* Quṭb al-Dīn Ibrāhīm al-Miṣrī, and he said:
>
> I have read it with the *imām* Fakhr al-Dīn Muḥammad al-Rāzī, who said:
>
> I have read it with Sharaf al-Dīn Muḥammad al-Masʿūdī, and he said:
>
> I have read it with the *shaykh* Abū l-Fatḥ Muḥammad known as Ibn al-Khayyāmī, who said:
>
> I have read it with Bahmanyār, the disciple of the *Shaykh al-Raʾīs*, and he said:
>
> I have read it under the author, the *raʾīs* Abū ʿAlī b. Sīnā.

We shall pursue this lineage from Ibn Sīnā and his school — a virtual *isnād* of his philosophical tradition, its is true, rather than based on actual *qirā'a* notices —, dealing but briefly with the first generations, and then taking up the thread among the contemporaries of Fakhr al-Dīn al-Rāzī.

a) Bahmanyār b. al-Marzubān, 'the disciple of the *Shaykh al-Raʾīs*', was a secretary in the Buyid bureaucracy whom Ibn Sīnā may have

[129] See below, p. 413.

[130] *Al-Wāfī*, II, p. 25.13-14. On Ibn al-Akfānī, see further below, p. 411.

first met when coming to Rayy in 404-405/1014-1015, and his immediate continuator through philosophical works of some repute.[131]

b) Abū l-Fatḥ Muḥammad 'known as Ibn al-Khayyāmī' is not otherwise known. Roshdi Rashed seems to identify this scholar with the mathematician and philosopher ʿUmar al-Khayyām[ī] (d. 517/1123-4).[132]

c) Sharaf al-Dīn Muḥammad al-Masʿūdī (d. shortly after 582/1186), was a mathematician, contemporary of Fakhr al-Dīn al-Rāzī.[133]

d) Sharaf al-Dīn in his turn had studied the work with al-Rāzī.

e) We have already met Quṭb al-Dīn Ibrāhīm al-Miṣrī (d. 618/1221) among the students of al-Rāzī, mentioned by Barhebraeus.

f) Athīr al-Dīn al-Mufaḍḍal al-Abharī (d. 663/1265?, see above, p. 394, 405), a slightly older contemporary of al-Ṭūsī, is named here as his teacher in *Falsafa*. Al-Abharī's introduction to logic, *al-Īsāghūjī fī l-Manṭiq*, and his manual of philosophy, *Kitāb Hidāyat al-Ḥikma*, along with many commentaries and glosses remained popular textbooks of the *madrasa* for several centuries.[134]

g) The Khwāja Naṣīr al-Dīn Muḥammad al-Ṭūsī (d. 672/1274), finally, is the source of Avicenna reading for many subsequent generations, not only in the Shiʿite schools of the East, but also in the Sunnī *madrasa*.

h) Shams al-Dīn Muḥammad b. Aḥmad al-Shurwānī, Ibn al-Akfānī's teacher in philosophy with whom he read the *Kitāb al-Ishārāt wa-l-Tanbīhāt*, was also an astronomer with general interests in the rational sciences.[135] He is mentioned among the group of astronomers

[131] David C. Reisman, *The Making of the Avicennan Tradition: the Transmission, Contents, and Structure of Ibn Sīnā's* al-Mubāḥaṯāt *(The Discussions)* (*Islamic Philosophy, Theology and Science*, 49), Leiden: Brill, 2002, p. 185-196, esp. p. 192.

[132] Roshdi Rashed, *Sharaf al-Dīn al-Ṭūsī: œuvres mathématiques: algèbre et géometrie au XIIe siècle*, Paris: Les Belles Lettres, 1986, p. xxxii, n.17.

[133] On the biographical data of Sharaf al-Dīn Muḥammad al-Masʿūdī, see Roshdi Rashed, *Sharaf al-Dīn al-Ṭūsī*, p. xxxii-xxxiii, n. 17: According to Fakhr al-Dīn al-Rāzī, he was alive in 582/1186, when he met him personally: 'Je suis entré là où était Sharaf al-Dīn al-Masʿūdī, et cela était l'année 582' (quoting al-Rāzī, *Les dialogues du savant al-Rāzī*, MSS A & K 136, Salar Jung, Hyderabad, f.12v).

[134] G. Endress, *Die wissenschaftliche Literatur*, in: *Grundriss der arabischen Philologie*, ed. W. Fischer and H. Gätje, III, Wiesbaden: Reichert, 1992, p. 56, 60 f.

[135] Al-Ṣafadī, *al-Wāfī*, II, p. 142.11-143.3. The vocalisation al-Shurwānī is confirmed by Al-Ṣafadī, *al-Wāfī*, II, p. 143.2.

working with Naṣīr al-Dīn al-Ṭūsī's son, Ṣadr al-Dīn, in the observatory at Marāgha in a contemporary report, quoted by al-Ṣafadī, of Ḥasan b. Aḥmad,[136] who gives a lively picture of the activities and the instruments used by the astronomers.[137]

i) Shams al-Dīn Muḥammad b. Ibrāhīm Ibn al-Akfānī (d. 749/1348), the source of our *isnād*, was an Egyptian physician, and a polymath well-versed in the mathematical and natural sciences and the disciplines of philosophical rationalism, apart from traditional Islamic learning.[138] He is best known for his survey and classification of the sciences, *Irshād al-Qāṣid ilā Asnā l-Maqāṣid,* which bears ample testimony to his catholic learning in all of the religious and rational sciences, and through his listing of the basic textbooks for each discipline provides a valuable testimony of the authorities and the actual teaching tradition in the various disciplines.[139] For logic, physical philosophy and metaphysics (*kutub al-manṭiq majmūʿa maʿa kutub* [*al-ʿilm*] *al-ṭabīʿī wa-l-ilāhī*), these are the works of Fakhr al-Dīn al-Rāzī, Naṣīr al-Dīn al-Ṭūsī and the latter's contemporaries — Athīr al-Din al-Abharī, Sirāj al-Dīn al-Urmawī (see above, p. 406), Ibn Kammūna, Najm al-Dīn al-Kātibī al-Qazwīnī (see further below, Section 8). The 'full expositions' (*al-mabsūṭāt*) of philosophy, among which is Ibn Sīnā's *Shifā'*, close with al-Ṭūsī's *Sharḥ al-Ishārāt wa-l-Tanbīhāt*, taking the place of Avicenna's basic work, and serving as a textbook for the accomplished student of philosophy — as our source, al-Ṣafadī, reports in his biographies of the *shaykh*.[140]

[136] Possibly ʿIzz al-Dīn al-Irbilī, a physician with philosophical leanings (d. 726 AH): AL-ṢAFADĪ, *al-Wāfī*, XI, 1981, p. 399, no. 574, on the authority of Shams al-Dīn al-Jazarī who calls him *ṣāḥibu-nā*.

[137] AL-ṢAFADĪ, *al-Wāfī*, I, p. 182.13; see AYDIN SAYILI, *The Observatory in Islam*, Ankara: Türk Tarih Kurumu, 1960, p. 216.

[138] IBN AL-AKFANI, *De egyptische arts Ibn al-Akfānī (gest. 749/1348) en zijn indeling van de wetenschapen: editie van het* Kitāb Irshād al-Qāṣid ilā Asnā al-Maqāṣid *met en inleiding over het leven en werk van de auteur,* proefschrift, Rijksuniversiteit te Leiden, ed. JANUARIUS JUSTUS WITKAM, Leiden: Ter Lugt Pers, 1989, p. 23 ff., esp. p. 28-44 on the biographical material from al-Ṣafadī whose biographical works are our main source on his contemporary teacher and friend: *al-Wāfī*, II, p. 25-27; and the *Aʿyān al-ʿAṣr*, quoted from the MS and translated by Witkam.

[139] The *Irshād* is the main source of the Ottoman encyclopaedist Aḥmad b. Muṣṭafā Tāshköprüzāda (901-968/1495-1561) for the systematic layout of his *Miftāḥ al-Saʿāda fī Mawḍūʿāt al-ʿUlūm*, though this work is many times the size of its predecessor; see WITKAM, *De egyptische arts*, p. 269-276.

[140] AL-ṢAFADĪ, *al-Wāfī*, II, p. 25.14.

Ibn al-Akfānī's isnād *of Ibn Sīnā's* Ishārāt

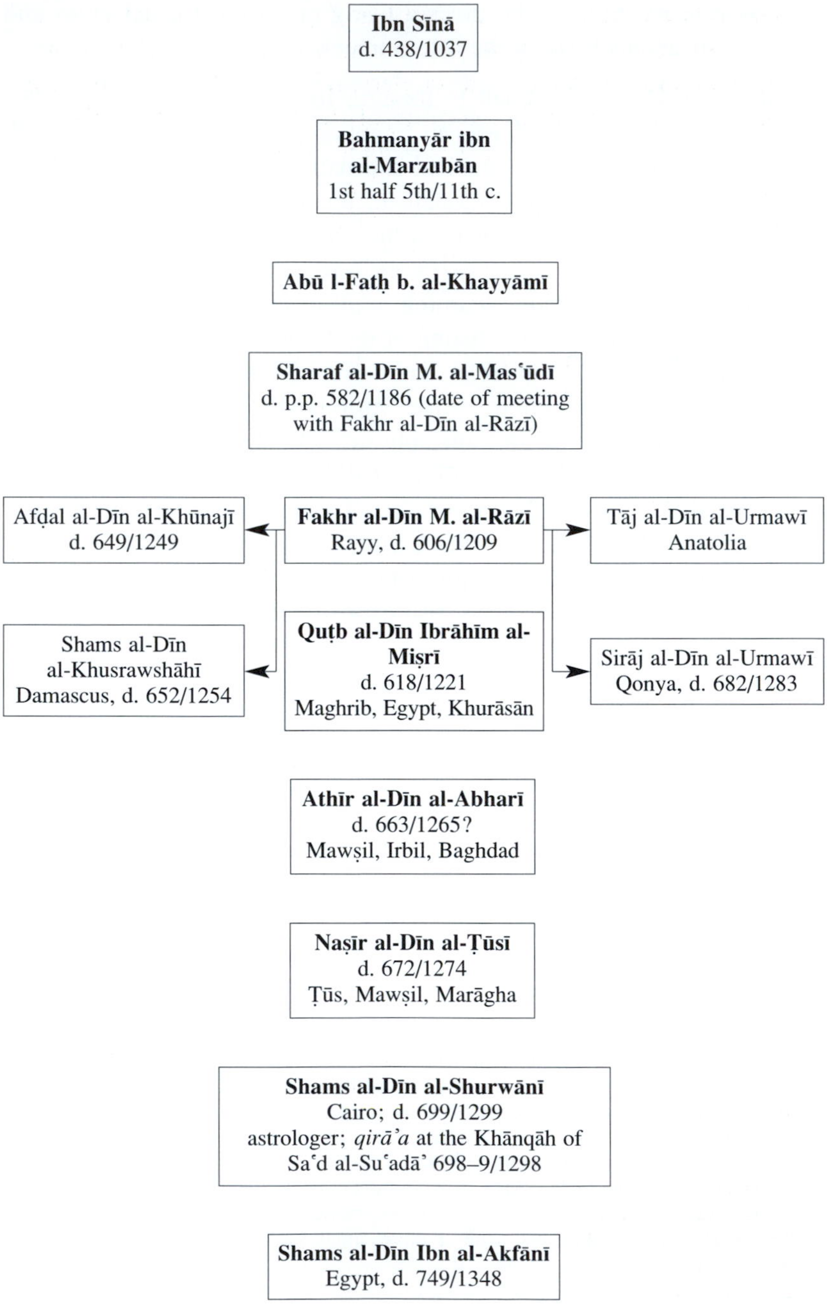

j) Ṣalāḥ al-Dīn Khalīl b. Aybak al-Ṣafadī (d. 764/1363), the historian and biographer, studied philosophy with Ibn al-Akfānī. His eulogies on the broad and deep learning of his teacher are found both in *al-Wāfī bi-l-Wafayāt* and in his biographical lexicon of contemporary notables and scholars, *Aʿyān al-ʿAṣr*[141] — in the latter text, playing on the wording of the titles of Ibn Sīnā's main works: *law ra'ā-hu l-Ra'īs, la-kānat ilayhi Ishāratu-hu wa-bi-hi ṣaḥḥa Shifā'u-hu wa-tammat Najātu-hu*, and continuing in the same vein in a comparison of his mathematical learning with the authority of the great philosopher-scientist, Naṣīr al-Dīn al-Ṭūsī.[142]

In the Islamic East, the tradition proceeding from Naṣīr al-Dīn al-Ṭūsī (d. 672/1274) can be followed up in a series of texts proceeding from Ibn Sīnā's *Ishārāt* and al-Ṭūsī's *Ḥall Mushkilāt al-Ishārāt*, mostly written by the same authors who, on the other hand, continued al-Ṭūsī's teaching in commenting, glossing and elaborating on his own writings on *ḥikma* as well as *Kalām* (to be covered briefly in our concluding section). From al-Ṭūsī's own generation is the physician Aḥmad b. Abī Bakr al-Nakhjuwānī (fl. ca. 651/1253,[143] the date of his *Ḥall Shukūk al-Qānūn*). Quṭb al-Dīn al-Rāzī al-Buwayhī (d. 766/1365), Shiʿite philosopher and theologian, is only one of several authors to write a *muḥākama*, an 'arbitration', between Ibn Sīnā, his critics like Fakhr al-Dīn al-Rāzī and his defenders following al-Ṭūsī. The principal continuator of al-Ṭūsī's dogmatic theology and one of the main authorities in later Shiʿite *Kalām*, Ḥasan b. Yūsuf b. al-Muṭahhar al-ʿAllāma al-Ḥillī (d. 726/1325) alone wrote three expositions of the *Ishārāt* and its difficulties.[144]

141 AL-ṢAFADĪ, *Aʿyān al-ʿAṣr*, in the facsimile edition of MS Atif 1809: FUAT SEZGIN (ed.), *The Important Persons of the Age: Aʿyān al-ʿAṣr wa-Aʿwān al-Naṣr*, Frankfurt am Main: Institute for the History of Arabic-Islamic Science, 1990, Part 2, p. 406-410.

142 See the text, with Dutch translation, of al-Ṣafadī's notice from the *Aʿyān al-ʿAṣr*: WITKAM, *De egyptische arts*, p. 31.

143 KAḤḤĀLA, *al-Aʿlām*, I, p. 178b.

144 Commentaries and refutations on Ibn Sīnās *al-Ishārāt wa-l-Tanbīhāt* are listed by YAḤYĀ MAHDAWĪ, *Fihrist-i nuskhahā-i muṣannafāt-i Ibn-i Sīnā*, Teheran: Dānishgāh-i Tihrān, 1333 HSh/1954), p. 35 f.

8. Philosophy, theology and science in the tradition of Naṣīr al-Dīn al-Ṭūsī and the schools of post-Mongol Iran

Also in the Ashʿarite-Shafiʿite schools of the East, the tradition of Fakhr al-Dīn al-Rāzī had a wide following, and was developed and presented in great *summae* of encylopedic dimensions — in constant interchange and discussion with the Shiʿite *Kalām* of al-Ṭūsī and his following, and at the same time, penetrated by the mystical philosophy of the *Shaykh al-Ishrāq* Shihāb al-Dīn al-Suhrawardī (d. 587/1191) — in a sense, a gnostical allegory of the Avicennian paradigm. We can only mention by name some of the protagonists, all of them known through their 'encyclopedic' handbooks of logic, scholastic theology and philosophy: after al-Abharī, whom we have already met in al-Ṭūsī's circle, we find his pupil Najm al-Dīn al-Kātibī al-Qazwīnī (d. 675/1276-7), with al-Ṭūsī in Marāgha — see further below); in the following century, ʿAḍud al-Dīn al-Ījī (d. 746/1345), the latter's disciple Saʿd al-Dīn al-Taftazānī (d. 792/1390), and al-Taftazānī's jealous competitor at the court of Timur, the Sayyid al-Sharīf al-Jurjānī (d. 816/1413). Best known among al-Jurjānī's pupils is Jalāl al-Dīn al-Dawānī (d. 908/1502-3, see below, p. 416-417). The chains of commentaries and compendia spreading out from al-Abharī, al-Kātibī and their disciples constitute the school-traditions in philosophy of several centuries.[145]

The tradition of mystical philosophy ties in with the basic works of *Ishrāq* by Shihāb al-Dīn al-Suhrawardī and his following; and then also, of Muḥyī al-Dīn Ibn al-ʿArabī (d. 645/1240) and his Anatolian spokesmen. Here as in *Falsafa* and *Kalām*, we encounter the genre of commentary as evidence of a school tradition. On al-Suhrawardī's *Talwīḥāt*, e.g., we find the commentaries of Shams al-Dīn al-Shahrazūrī (d. p.p. 687/1288)[146] and of his Jewish contemporary, Saʿd b. Manṣūr Ibn Kammūna (d. 683/1284).[147] It does not come as a surprise that the latter also wrote a commentary on Ibn Sīnā's *al-Ishārāt wa-l-Tanbīhāt*.[148] Another

145 Endress, *Die wissenschaftliche Literatur*, p. 56, 60 f. On al-Abharī and al-Kātibī, see also Hasse, *Mosul and Frederick II Hohenstaufen*.

146 P. Lory, *Al-Shahrazūrī, Shams al-Dīn Muḥammad b. Maḥmūd*, in: *EI*2, IX, p. 219-220.

147 Sabine Schmidtke, *Ibn Abī Ǧumhūr, Theologie, Philosophie und Mystik im zwölferschiitischen Islam des 9./15. Jahrhunderts: die Gedankenwelten des Ibn Abī Ǧumhūr al-Aḥsāʾī (um 838/1434-35 — nach 906/1501)* (*Islamic Philosophy, Theology and Science*, 39), Leiden: Brill: 2000, 7, n. 34; Sabine Schmidtke, *Studies on Saʿd b. Manṣūr Ibn Kammūna (d. 683/1284): Beginnings, Achievements, and Perspectives*, in: *Persica* 29 (2003), p. 107-123; and Y. Tzvi Langermann, *Ibn Kammūna and the 'New Wisdom' of the Thirteenth Century*, in: *Arabic Sciences and Philosophy* 15 (2005), p. 277-327.

148 See the inventory of his known œuvre compiled by Schmidtke, *Studies*, as quoted in the previous note.

medium of intellectual encounter in this field is the *murāsala*, a disputation in the form of an exchange of epistles, such as the one between al-Ṭūsī and the archdisciple, and stepson, of Ibn al-ʿArabī, Ṣadr al-Dīn al-Qōnawī (d. 673/1274), the eminent transmitter of the mystic of Murcia to the later schools of mystical philosophy.[149]

In his turn, Naṣīr al-Dīn al-Ṭūsī[150] took up the traditions of both Sunnī and Shiʿite *Kalām* (including the latter's Muʿtazilite heritage), the philosophy of Ibn Sīnā, and of a mathematical science put into the service of Islam. Among his closest companions were philosophers like Afḍal al-Dīn (Bābā Afḍal) al-Kāshānī (first half of the Seventh/Thirteenth Century),[151] Athīr al-Dīn al-Abharī (mentioned on several occasions previously), and Najm al-Dīn ʿAlī al-Kātibī al-Qazwīnī, called *dabīrān*, 'the secretary', (d. 675/1277?), author of the much-read manual of philosophical-mystical theology, *Ḥikmat al-ʿAyn*.[152] Al-Ṭūsī's and al-Kātibī's most eminent disciple was Quṭb al-Dīn Maḥmūd b. Masʿūd al-Shīrāzī (630-710/1232-1311)[153] — both a philosopher and a mathematician of genius. After working with al-Ṭūsī and al-Kātibī in Marāgha, he went to Anatolia, where he studied with Ibn al-ʿArabī's follower, Ṣadr al-Dīn al-Qōnawī, in 673/1274,[154] and became *qāḍī* of Sīwās, and finally retired to Tabrīz. As a philosopher, he merged Ibn Sīnā's systematic approach

[149] Ed. of the Persian text and annotated summary by GUDRUN SCHUBERT, *Annäherungen: der mystisch-philosophische Briefwechsel zwischen Ṣadr ud-Dīn-i Qônawī und Naṣīr ud-Dīn-i Ṭūsī* (*Bibliotheca Islamica*, 43), Beirut — Stuttgart: Steiner, 1995.

[150] On his biography and bibliography, see the detailed work of MUḤAMMAD TAQĪ MUDARRIS RAŻAWĪ, *Aḥwāl wa-Āthār-i Khwāja Naṣīr al-Dīn al-Ṭūsī*, Tehran: Asāṭīr, 1370 HSh/19922.

[151] MUDARRIS RAŻAWĪ, *Aḥwāl wa-Āthār*, p. 205-210; MUḤAMMAD TAQĪ DĀNĪSHPĀZHUH, *Niwishtahā-i Bābā Afḍal*, in: *Mihr* 8 (1953), p. 433-461, 499-502.

[152] Najm al-Dīn ʿAlī b. ʿUmar al-Kātibī al-Qazwīnī; see MAHDI MOHAGHEGH, *Al-Kātibī*, in: *EI2*, p. 762; MUDARRIS RAŻAWĪ, *Aḥwāl wa-Āthār*, p. 226-228; on a philosophical correspondence with al-Ṭūsī *fī ithbāt al-wājib*: MUDARRIS RAŻAWĪ, *Aḥwāl wa-Āthār*, p. 468-475, no. 59; *Muṭāraḥāt Falsafīya bayna Naṣīr al-Dīn al-Ṭūsī wa-Najm al-Dīn al-Kātibī* (*Nafāʾis al-Makhṭūṭāt*, 7), ed. MUḤAMMAD ḤASAN ĀL YĀSĪN, Baghdad: Maktabat al-Nahḍa, 1956; *Muṭāraḥāt Manṭiqīya bayna Najm al-Dīn al-Kātibī al-Qazwīnī wa-Naṣīr al-Dīn al-Ṭūsī*, ed. ʿABD ALLĀH NŪRĀNĪ, in: *Manṭiq wa-Mabāḥith-i Alfāẓ: Majmūʿa-i Mutūn-i Maqālāt-i Taḥqīqī* (*Collected Texts and Papers on Logic and Language*) (*Silsila-i Dānish-i Īrānī*, 8), ed. MAHDĪ MUḤAQQIQ, Tehran: Dānishgāh-i Tihrān, 1353 HSh/1974, p. 277-286. For a later dating of his death (693/1294), see SELLHEIM, *Materialen*, II, p. 119.

[153] IBN AL-FUWAṬĪ, *Majmaʿ al-Ādāb fī Muʿjam al-Alqāb*, ed. MUṢṬAFĀ JAWĀD, Baghdad, 1967, IV.4, p. 616 f. no. 2927; see the article *Quṭb al-Dīn al-Shīrāzī*, in *Dictionary of Scientific Biography*, II, p. 247-253. —We have mentioned his commentary on the *Kullīyāt* of Ibn Sīnā's *Qānūn fī l-Ṭibb*, extant in his autograph copy (see above, p. 390).

[154] See HELLMUT RITTER, *Autographs in Turkish Libraries*, in: *Oriens* 6 (1953), p. 63-90 (p. 71, 77 f.).

with the philosophical theology of *Ishrāq*,[155] and gave a *summa* of the rational sciences, modelled on Avicenna's *Shifā'* but written in Persian, in his monumental *Durrat al-Tāj li-Ghurrat al-Dubāj*.[156] In Shiʿite theology, al-Ṭūsī's most respected follower was al-ʿAllāma (Ḥasan b. Yūsuf b. al-Muṭahhar) al-Ḥillī (d. 726/1325),[157] while in the philosophy of Imamite-Shiʿite orientation it was Quṭb al-Dīn al-Rāzī al-Buwayhī (d. 766/1365).[158]

From al-Ṭūsī's companions at Marāgha to the last offsprings of his school and Timurid and Ṣafavid Iran, many of these scholars combine the threefold proficiency of the Khwāja: mathematical science, demonstrative philosophy, and dogmatic theology. Such universal competence in all of the disciplines of the intellectual and the religious learning pervades the development of Islamic schools of Iran in Mongol and post-Mongol periods. This tradition is leading us to the theologian-scientists working at the observatory of the Timurid Ulugh-Bek in Fifteenth Century Samarqand, and, by the end of that century, to Jalāl al-Dīn al-Dawānī, who from al-Abharī, al-Shahrazūrī and Quṭb al-Dīn al-Shīrāzī took the fusion of Ibn Sīnā's rational and al-Suhrawardī's mystical philosophy into the Sunnī *madrasa*.[159]

Chains of commentaries and reworkings of al-Ṭūsī's seminal works permit us to pursue the genealogy of this teaching tradition. As in philosophy his elaboration of the Avicennian proof of the First Cause *qua* first necessary being, *ithbāt wājib al-wujūd*, al-Ṭūsī's dogmatic work, *Tajrīd al-Kalām fī Taḥrīr ʿAqā'id al-Islām* (in short *Tajrīd al-ʿAqā'id*) is at the beginning of a long sequence of commentaries and glosses (*ḥawāshī*). The first among these were canonized as well as the basic text: the *Kashf al-Murād* of al-ʿAllāma al-Ḥillī, the *Taʿrīḍ* of Shams al-Dīn al-Isfarāʾīnī al-Bayhaqī, the *Tasdīd* of Shams al-Dīn Maḥmūd b. ʿAbd al-Raḥmān al-Iṣfahānī (d. 749/1348), called *al-sharḥ al-qadīm*, the 'old' preceding the 'new' one: *al-*

155 JOHN T. WALBRIDGE, *The Science of Mystic Lights: Quṭb al-Dīn Shīrāzī and the Illuminationist Tradition in Islamic Philosophy* (*Harvard Middle Eastern Monographs*, 26), Cambridge, Mass.: Harvard University Press, 1992; HENRY CORBIN, *Le livre de la sagesse orientale* (Ḥikmat al-Ishrāq) *de Sohrawardi: commentaires de Qoṭboddin Shīrāzī et Mollā Ṣadrā Shīrāzī*, Lagrasse: Verdier, 1986.

156 Ed. MUḤAMMAD MISHKĀT, Tehran: Majlis-i Shūrā-i Millī, 1939-1945.

157 See SABINE SCHMIDTKE, *The Theology of al-ʿAllāma al-Ḥillī* (*Islamkundliche Untersuchungen*, 152), Berlin: Schwarz, 1991.

158 A survey of these traditions in Shiʿite theology and its philosophical and mystical components is given by SCHMIDTKE, *Ibn Abī Ǧumhūr*, 1-13.

159 For an inventory on his works on *Kalām*, philosophy, and *ishraqī* mysticism, see RIḌĀ PŪRJAWĀDĪ, *Kitābshināsī-i āthār-i Jalāl al-Dīn-i Dawānī*, in: *Maʿārif* 43-44 = 15/1-2 (1377 HSh/1998), p. 81-138.

sharḥ al-jadīd of ʿAlāʾ al-Dīn al-Qūshjī (d. 879/1474), and on the latter there are three *ḥawāshī* alone by Jalāl al-Dīn al-Dawānī (d. 908/1502-3).[160]

Among the commentators of al-Ṭūsī's dogmatic *Tajrīd al-ʿAqāʾid* we find, at the same time, his disciples and followers in philosophy and the mathematical sciences; but then, instead of treating the *ʿaqīda*, the *ithbāt al-wāʾib* and the philosophical theology of *al-Ishārāt wa-l-Tanbīhāt* in different compartments, not only theology is clad in the language of philosophy, but all of the rational sciences are put under the ægis of *ḥikma*. Indeed, the merging of the paradigms of rational knowledge left permanent traces in the final integration of the Greek traditions of rational science with the Islamic view of the First Cause, origin and order of the world, and the conditions and limits of rational knowledge. Ridding astronomy of the strictures of Aristotelian cosmology— as in the theory of planetary motions put forward by one of the scientist-theologians of Samarqand ʿAlī b. Muḥammad al-Qūshjī (d. 879/1474) in his Glosses on al-Ṭūsī's *Tajrīd al-ʿAqāʾid*[161] —, and ridding theology of the strictures of a philosophy regarding the essence, but disregarding the will of God —, the philosopher-scientists of the Eastern schools let us perceive the dawning of a new picture of the world. But on this final glimpse of new departures, we are leaving the confines of an intellectual identity embracing the whole of Muslim civilization.

ʿAlī b. Muḥammad al-Qūshjī was a scholar close to the Timurid court at Samarqand, and worked at the famous observatory which Ulugh-Beg had built as a successor to al-Ṭūsī's observatory of Marāgha. His commentary on al-Ṭūsī's dogmatic *Tajrīd al-Kalām fī Taḥrīr ʿAqāʾid al-Islām* remained influential until the Ṣafavid schools of Shīrāz and Iṣfahān, quoted by Mullā Ṣadrā (Ṣadr al-Dīn al-Shīrāzī). — In the next generation, Shams al-Dīn al-Khafrī (d. 935/1528-9, or 957/1550?), another Shiʿite theologian and astronomer in the tradition of the Marāgha scholars, and a disciple of Sayyid Ṣadr al-Dīn Dashtakī Shīrāzī (d. 903/1497), who lived under the Ṣafavid Shāh Ismāʿīl, wrote at Shīrāz one of the most respected glosses — after that of Dashtakī, his teacher — on al-Ṭūsī's *Tajrīd al-ʿAqāʾid*; he also commented on the scholastic theology *Ḥikmat al-ʿAyn* of

160 PŪRJAWĀDĪ, *Kitābshināsī*, p. 113 f., a survey of thirteen *shurūḥ*, regarded as authoritative in the school, and numerous supercommentaries and glosses (*ḥawāshī*) is given in ĀGHĀ BUZURG, *al-Dharīʿa fī Taṣānīf al-Shīʿa*, III, Najaf: Teheran, 1936-1978, p. 352 ff., no. 1278.

161 F. JAMIL RAGEP, *Freeing Astronomy from Philosophy: an Aspect of Islamic Influence on Science*, in: *Osiris* 16 (2001), p. 49-71. In general, see also A.I. SABRA, *Science, Philosophy and Theology in Islam: the Evidence of the Fourteenth Century*, in: *Zeitschrift für Geschichte der Islamisch-Arabischen Wissenschaften* 9 (1994), p. 1-42.

Philosophy, Theology and Science in the Tradition of Naṣīr al-Dīn al-Ṭūsī

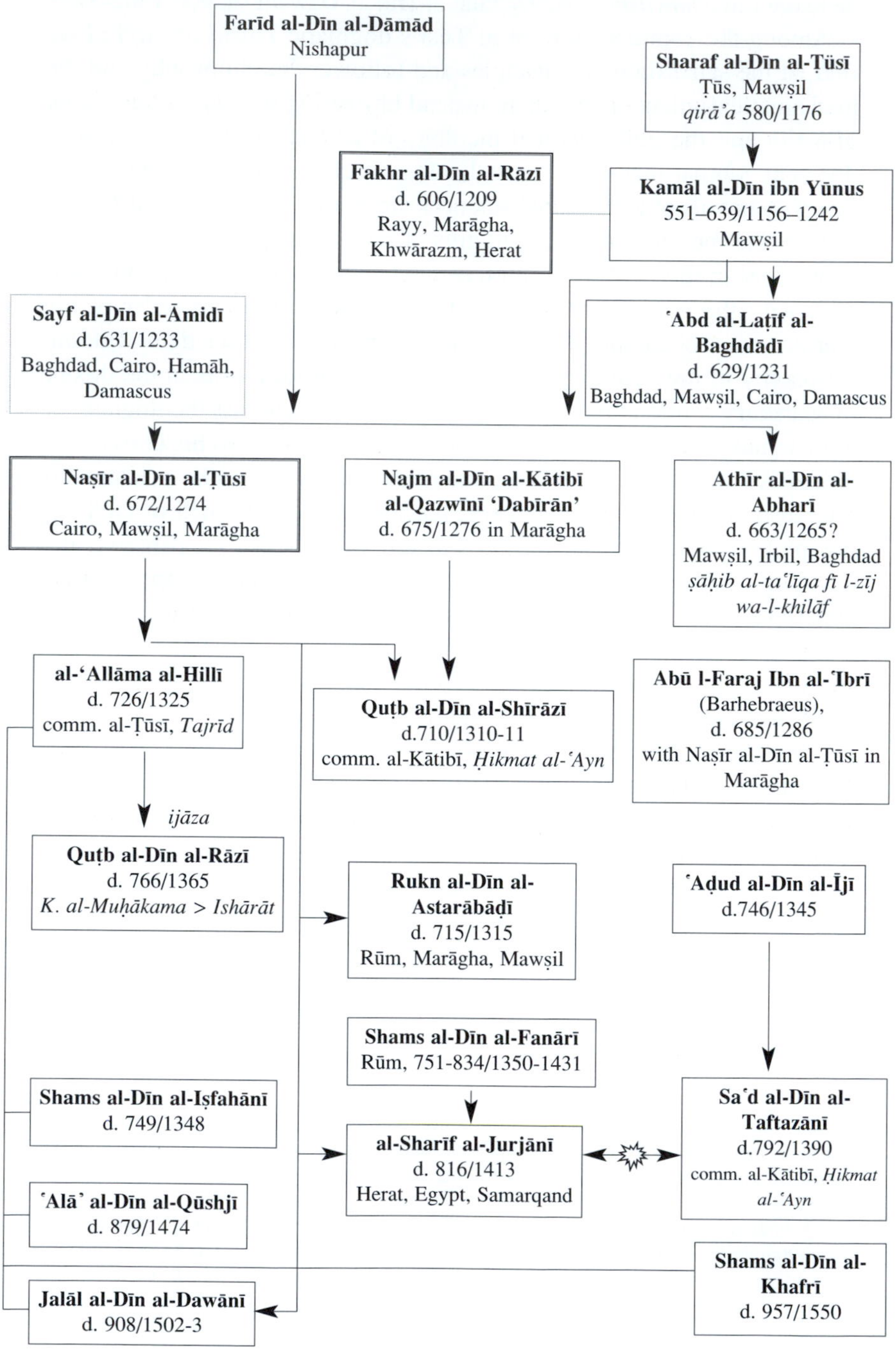
Farīd al-Dīn al-Dāmād
Nishapur
Sharaf al-Dīn al-Ṭūsī
Ṭūs, Mawṣil
qirā'a 580/1176
Fakhr al-Dīn al-Rāzī
d. 606/1209
Rayy, Marāgha, Khwārazm, Herat
Kamāl al-Dīn ibn Yūnus
551–639/1156–1242
Mawṣil
Sayf al-Dīn al-Āmidī
d. 631/1233
Baghdad, Cairo, Ḥamāh, Damascus
ʿAbd al-Laṭīf al-Baghdādī
d. 629/1231
Baghdad, Mawṣil, Cairo, Damascus
Naṣīr al-Dīn al-Ṭūsī
d. 672/1274
Cairo, Mawṣil, Marāgha
Najm al-Dīn al-Kātibī al-Qazwīnī 'Dabīrān'
d. 675/1276 in Marāgha
Athīr al-Dīn al-Abharī
d. 663/1265?
Mawṣil, Irbil, Baghdad
ṣāḥib al-taʿlīqa fī l-zīj wa-l-khilāf
al-'Allāma al-Ḥillī
d. 726/1325
comm. al-Ṭūsī, *Tajrīd*
Quṭb al-Dīn al-Shīrāzī
d.710/1310-11
comm. al-Kātibī, *Ḥikmat al-ʿAyn*
Abū l-Faraj Ibn al-ʿIbrī
(Barhebraeus),
d. 685/1286
with Naṣīr al-Dīn al-Ṭūsī in Marāgha
ijāza
Quṭb al-Dīn al-Rāzī
d. 766/1365
K. al-Muḥākama > Ishārāt
Rukn al-Dīn al-Astarābāḍī
d. 715/1315
Rūm, Marāgha, Mawṣil
ʿAḍud al-Dīn al-Ījī
d.746/1345
Shams al-Dīn al-Fanārī
Rūm, 751-834/1350-1431
Shams al-Dīn al-Iṣfahānī
d. 749/1348
al-Sharīf al-Jurjānī
d. 816/1413
Herat, Egypt, Samarqand
Saʿd al-Dīn al-Taftazānī
d.792/1390
comm. al-Kātibī, *Ḥikmat al-ʿAyn*
ʿAlāʾ al-Dīn al-Qūshjī
d. 879/1474
Shams al-Dīn al-Khafrī
d. 957/1550
Jalāl al-Dīn al-Dawānī
d. 908/1502-3

Najm al-Dīn al-Kātibī al-Qazwīnī, and in philosophy, treated the topic of *ithbāt al-wājib* at least four times. Among his works of mathematical astronomy, he produced a *Takmila* on al-Ṭūsī's *Tadhkira fī ʿIlm al-Hayʾa*, laid out as a supercommentary on the basis of the commentary of al-Sharīf al-Jurjānī, and a commentary on Quṭb al-Dīn al-Shīrāzī's *al-Tuḥfa al-Shāhīya*, called *Muntahā l-Idrāk fī Madrak al-Aflāk.*[162]

The Ṣafavid philosopher-theologians of the school of the Mīr-i Dāmād and Ṣadr al-Dīn al-Shīrāzī (Mullā Sadrā) from the Fifteenth to the Seventeenth Century not only read Avicenna and his commentators, but retraced the chain of transmitters and commentators of their spriritual and intellectual traditions, to its origins in the various fields of theology, philosophy, mysticism, and — depending on their professional competence — of mathematics and astronomy. Beyond their immediate curricular traditions, however, they fell back on the texts of gnostical and Neoplatonic *ḥikma* from the first period of reception and translation of the original Greek sources, and on the founders of *Falsafa* in the Arabic Islamic milieu: on al-Kindī, on the Baghdadi commentators of the Peripatetic tradition — Yaḥyā b. ʿAdī, ʿĪsā b. Zurʿa, among them Ibn Sīnā's most important forerunner al-Fārābī —, and indeed, on Ibn Rushd's compendia of Aristotle's logical and physical works. Here, the tradition recorded in our manuscripts and in a library of biographical testimonies of a living and variegated practice, can be traced as a continuous, coherent and widely disseminated teaching tradition form the generation of Ibn Sīnā's disciples until the Eighteenth Century. Notwithstanding the differences of persuasion between *ahl al-sunna, ithnā ʿasharī* and *sabʿī* Shiʿism, between the *madhāhib* of law and the schools of *Kalām* — Ashʿarīya, Muʿtazila and the latter's continuation in the Imāmīya, and between the basic attitudes towards philosophy, ranging from Ibn Sīnā's school of *Falsafa* to its Ashʿarite critics, and from the Ashʿarite sympathizers with philosophy to its

162 On this work, see GEORGE SALIBA, *A Sixteenth-Century Critique of Ptolemaic Astronomy: the Work of Shams al-Dīn al-Khafrī*, in: *Journal for the History of Astronomy* 25 (1994), p. 15-38; *A Redeployment of Mathematics in a Sixteenth-Century Arabic Critique of Ptolemaic Astronomy*, in: *Perpectives arabes et médiévales sur la tradition scientifique grecque: Actes du colloque de la SIHSPAI, 1993*, Leuven and Paris: Peeters and Institut du Monde Arabe, 1997, p. 105-122; on another discussion of planetary theories: *The Ultimate Challenge to Greek Astronomy:* Ḥall mā lā yanḥall *of Shams al-Dīn al-Khafrī (d. 1550)*, in: *Sic itur ad astra — Studien zur Geschichte der Mathematik und Naturwissenschaften: Festschrift für den Arabisten Paul Kunitzsch zum 70. Geburtstag*, ed. MENSO FOLKERTS and RICHARD LORCH, Wiesbaden: Harrassowitz, 2000, p. 490-505.

Ḥanbalite opponents: for all of them, the language of philosophy — the language of demonstration — is familiar ground. In this way, the reading of Avicenna, his commentators, epitomators, and theological critics became an integral part of Muslim thought.

Al-Ghazālī on Causality

AL-GHAZĀLĪ'S CONCEPTION OF THE AGENT IN THE *TAHĀFUT* AND THE *IQTIṢĀD*: ARE PEOPLE REALLY AGENTS?

THÉRÈSE-ANNE DRUART
The Catholic University of America

Al-Ghazālī claims that his opposition to some 'Aristotelian' tenets stems from a different conception of causation. Various scholars, for instance L.E. Goodman, I. Alon, R. Bahlul, and G. Giacaman, have discussed whether al-Ghazālī denies causation to any being other than God in the Seventeenth Discussion of the *Tahāfut*. As this passage presents two distinct theories in opposition to that of the philosophers,[1] these scholars tried to determine which of these theories, if any, al-Ghazālī endorses. Such determination is a rather risky venture since al-Ghazālī repeatedly warns us that the positions he uses in the *Tahāfut* in order to combat the *falāsifa* are not necessarily his own.

More recently, scholars such as B. Abrahamov, R.M. Frank, and M.E. Marmura have examined various works of al-Ghazālī in order to discover his own views on causation and to determine whether or not he defends a strict occasionalism and, therefore, is a strict Ashʿarite.[2] Consensus is elusive on this point and the complexity of al-Ghazālī's position gives rise to interpretations that sharply diverge. Frank contends, for example, that al-Ghazālī views the world as a deterministic system, in

[1] L.E. GOODMAN, *Did al-Ghazâlî Deny Causality*, in: *Studia Islamica* 47 (1978), p. 83-120; I. ALON, *Al-Ghazālī on Causality*, in: *Journal of the American Oriental Society* 100 (1980), p. 397-405; R. BAHLUL, *Miracles and Ghazali's First Theory of Causation*, in: *Philosophy and Theology* 5 (1990-91), p. 137-150; G. GIACAMAN and R. BAHLUL, *Ghazali on Miracles and Necessary Connection*, in: *Medieval Philosophy and Theology* 9 (2000), p. 39-50.

[2] B. ABRAHAMOV, *Al-Ghazālī's Theory of Causality*, in: *Studia Islamica* 67 (1988), p. 75-98; R.M. FRANK, *Creation and the Cosmic System: Al-Ghazâlî & Avicenna* (*Abhandlungen der Heidelberger Akademie der Wissenschaften, Philosophisch-historische Klasse, Jahrgang 1992,* 1. Abhandlung), Heidelberg, 1992, and *Al-Ghazālī and the Ashʿarite School* (*Duke Monographs in Medieval and Renaissance Studies*, 15), Durham — London, 1994; M.E. MARMURA, *Al-Ghazālī on Bodily Resurrection and Causality in* Tahāfut *and the* Iqtiṣād, in: *Aligarh Journal of Islamic Thought* 2 (1989), p. 46-75, reprinted in his *Probing in Islamic Philosophy: Studies in the Philosophies of Ibn Sīnā, al-Ghazālī and other Major Muslim Thinkers*, Binghampton, NY, 2005, p. 273-299. *Ghazali's Chapter on Divine Power in the* Iqtiṣād, in: *Arabic Sciences and Philosophy* 4 (1994), p. 279-315; *Ghazālian Causes and Intermediaries*, in: *Journal of the American Oriental Society* 115 (1995), p. 89-100 (a review article of FRANK's *Creation and the Cosmic System*) and *Ghazali and Ashʿarism Revisited*, in: *Arabic Sciences and Philosophy* 12 (2002), p. 91-110.

which secondary causes have their place, while Marmura denies any causation to secondary causes.

These discussions led to two new detailed interpretations of the famous Seventeenth Discussion: one by U. Rudolph and the other by O. Lizzini. Both scholars focus on physical causation, taking up the famous example of fire burning a piece of cotton and al-Ghazālī's denial of agency to the inanimate.[3]

In this paper, I would like to return to al-Ghazālī's claim that the whole dispute with the *falāsifa* turns on a different conception of causation in order to examine whether his views on voluntary causation in the *Tahāfut* and the *Iqtiṣād* argue for the same position since the former is a work of refutation that may not represent his own conceptions, while the latter is a work of *Kalām*. Since most scholars have focused on physical causation, such as the burning of a piece of cotton, our attention to voluntary action hopes to shed new light on the question. Already in the 1980s Frank had attracted the attention of scholars to human agency in *Kalām* texts, but few followed in his footsteps.[4]

Al-Ghazālī reproaches philosophers for not providing a good account of voluntary action and, in particular, God's action. For him the philosophers present a God who does not act voluntarily, but rather by a natural necessity; not knowingly and by choice, but in keeping with the Neoplatonic view of necessary emanationism. This view depicts a God who does not really act, for a true agent must be endowed with knowledge of the object of his action and with will. These two requirements of knowledge and will explain why al-Ghazālī insists that the inanimate is inert and does not act. As the philosophers deny proper cognition and will to God, they reduce His causation to that of the inanimate and they do not acknowledge Him as a living being, who is, therefore, a true agent, but rather liken Him to something inert or dead. Aristotle's prime mover as final cause neither really acts nor really moves the heavens; the heavenly bodies move on their own, since, being alive and endowed with knowledge and will, they act in moving through their desire to imitate the unmoved mover. Therefore, Aristotle and his followers have ensouled the

[3] ULRICH RUDOLPH in: D. PERL and U. RUDOLPH, *Occasionalismus. Theorien der Kausalität im arabisch-islamischen und im europäischen Denken*, Göttingen, 2000, p. 63-73; O. LIZZINI, *Occasionalismo e causalità filosofica: la discussione della causalità in al-Gazâlî*, in: *Quaestio* 2 (2002), p. 155-183.

[4] *The Autonomy of the Human Agent in the Teaching of ʿAbd al-Ǧabbâr*, in: *Le Muséon* 95 (1982), p. 323-355; *Two Islamic Views of Human Agency*, in: *La notion de liberté au Moyen Age: Islam, Byzance, Occident* (*Penn-Paris-Dumbarton Oaks Colloquia*, 4: Session des 12-15 octobre 1982), Paris, 1985, p. 37-49.

celestial bodies, making them alive and animals, whereas for al-Ghazālī they are inanimate. As al-Ghazālī's contentions rest on a contrast between God, the agent *par excellence*, and inanimate things, one needs to determine more precisely whether he grants some kind of agency to animate beings, such as animals and human beings. This latter question calls to mind the theological debate between the 'determinist' and the Muʿtazilite schools of thought, as well as al-Ashʿarī's doctrine of acquisition, often presented, even by al-Ghazālī, as a mid position between these two extremes. Our choice for a *Kalām* text of the chapter on 'power' of the *Iqtiṣād* stems from R. Frank's description of it as perhaps 'the most tortuous and difficult section of *Iqtiṣād*', a section 'in which he talks about (and round about) the question of the human power of action'.[5]

The problem

In a work posterior to the *Tahāfut*, *al-Munqidh*, al-Ghazālī reviews the various philosophical disciplines. While praising the natural sciences, particularly those linked to medicine and anatomy, he indicates that his main concern is the philosophers' view that nature has an inner principle of motion and rest. For him nature is inert and the Creator simply uses it as a tool. To illustrate his point, al-Ghazālī refers to the celestial bodies: 'the sun, moon, stars and the elements are subject to God's command: none of them does any act (*fiʿl*) by itself or from itself'.[6] Notice that al-Ghazālī puts the celestial bodies on the same level as the elements, which he sees both as inanimate and completely inert.

Al-Ghazālī thinks that, had the philosophers realised that nature is purely inert and that God is the agent, they would have avoided the three metaphysical positions that make them unbelievers. He discusses these positions in some detail in the section on metaphysics following that on physics; briefly stated, they are: 1) the denial of bodily resurrection and, therefore, physical rewards and punishments in the afterlife; 2) the eternity of the world; and 3) the denial of God's knowledge of particulars.

[5] *Al-Ghazālī and the Ashʿarite School*, p. 42.

[6] AL-GHAZĀLĪ, *al-Munqidh min al-Ḍalāl (Erreur et Délivrance)*, ed. F. JABRE, Beirut, 1969, p. 23 of the Arabic. Recently STEPHEN MENN has argued that the *Munqidh* belongs to a Galenic tradition of autobiography (*The* Discourse on the Method *and the Tradition of Intellectual Autobiography*, in: *Hellenistic and Early Modern Philosophy*, ed. by J. MILLER and B. INWOOD, Cambridge, 2003, p. 141-91) and the passage on natural sciences recalls Galen's texts as well as al-Rāzī's own intellectual autobiography.

Agency in the *Tahāfut*

In the *Tahāfut* metaphysical considerations precede those of natural sciences and, therefore, the famous Seventeenth Discussion and its analysis of the burning of a piece of cotton.[7] Yet, interestingly, most of the examples in this discussion involve some deliberate action on the part of animate beings, such as the quenching of thirst by drinking, and of satiety by eating. There is also discussion of deliberate human actions, such as healing by drinking some medicine and other actions in medicine, arts, and crafts, but this voluntary aspect is left aside.[8] The question whether God's agency excludes any human agency is raised at the end, when al-Ghazālī's adversaries comment about God moving the hand of a dead man so that he writes something intelligible. If God can do so, then, how can we distinguish a tremor from a voluntary movement of the hand? Al-Ghazālī simply indicates that tremor happens without the human being having power over it, whereas voluntary action requires it, though God creates this human power too.[9] Al-Ghazālī assumes that the linguistic distinction between 'tremor' and 'voluntary movement' reflects an ontological difference: the tremor is directly produced by God, but the voluntary movement requires an intermediary, a human 'power', though what difference this 'power' makes remains unexplained. The *Iqtiṣād*, too, also assumes this view that somehow our way of speaking reflects reality.

The *Tahāfut*[10] begins with a discussion of the eternity of the world, the first consideration of which rests on an analysis of the will. The philosophers do not pay enough attention to the will and so do not properly distinguish action, which requires both knowledge and will, from 'mechanical' or natural causation in which knowledge and will have no role. Nature 'does' nothing.

The first discussion gives us a definition of the will: 'the will [is] an attribute whose function is to differentiate a thing from its similar',[11] i.e.,

[7] All references to the *Tahāfut* will be to Al-Ghazālī, *The Incoherence of the Philosophers*, translated, introduced, and annotated by M.E. Marmura, Provo, Utah, 1997. The text is subdivided in numbered sections in both the Arabic and the English. We will refer to this numbering.

[8] *Tahāfut*, p. 170, §1.

[9] *Tahāfut*, p. 180-181, §§ 38-39.

[10] For a more detailed analysis of agency in the *Tahāfut*, see my article, *Algazali*, in: *A Companion to Philosophy in the Middle Ages* (*Blackwell Companions to Philosophy*), ed. J.J. E. Gracía and T.B. Noone, London: Blackwell, 2003, p. 120-125.

[11] *Tahāfut*, p. 22.1-2, §41 (Marmura's translation).

the ability to differentiate between indiscernibles. Just as someone hungry selects one of two identical dates to begin eating, God selects one among the infinity of indiscernible possible instants 'to begin' to create. The will is self-determining and does not depend on the intellect's inability to distinguish between indiscernibles. The philosophers' objection that what allows someone thirsty to select one of two identical glasses of water is a difference in weight simply reveals their inability to conceive of true indiscernibles or to accept that the will is self-determining.

The third discussion argues that the philosophers fail to show that God is the agent and maker of the world. As K. Gyekye showed in his analysis of this section, a true action must include will and knowledge.[12] As the philosophers deprive God of will or even knowledge of particulars, they fail to show that He is agent and maker on three counts: 1) the agent's will; 2) the act's temporal origination; and 3) through their acceptance of a relationship common to act and agent, i.e., that as the agent is one, so should the act be.

Addressing the first point, i.e., the agent's will, al-Ghazālī begins with defining agent (*fā'il*). An agent is a person (*man*) 'from whom the act proceeds, together with the will to act by way of choice and the knowledge of what is willed'.[13] This definition implies that inanimate beings, since they are deprived of both knowledge and will, cannot really act, except in a metaphorical way. It thus allows us to distinguish between an agent and a natural cause or instrument. Al-Ghazālī justifies his claim that only people — and eventually animals — can truly act in analysing the way we speak of an event that combines voluntary and natural causation:

> … if we suppose that a temporal event depends for its occurrence on two things, one voluntary and the other not, the intellect relates the act to the voluntary. The same goes for the way we speak. For if someone throws another into the fire and [the latter] dies, one says that the [former], not the fire is the killer.[14]

One attributes the killing to the person, who knowingly and, therefore, voluntarily threw another into the fire, but not to the fire the efficacy (*ta'thīr* rather than *fi'l*) of which does not involve the will. Al-Ghazālī counts among the well-known and true universal principles the affirmation that 'act does not belong to what is inanimate', but rather to what is

[12] K. GYEKYE, *Al-Ghazâlî on Action*, in: *Ghazâlî, la raison et le miracle* (Paris, 1987), p. 83-91.

[13] *Tahāfut*, p. 57, §4 (Marmura's translation).

[14] *Tahāfut*, p. 59, §13 (Marmura's translation with some modifications).

animate.[15] This analysis of the way we speak reminds us of al-Ghazālī's remarks in the Seventeenth Discussion about the difference between tremor and a voluntary movement of the hand.

Moving to the second point, the act's temporal origination, al-Ghazālī then gives a definition of 'act'. An act is 'the bringing forth of something from non-being to being by means of its temporal origination'.[16] Therefore, an act — or more exactly its effect — cannot be eternal. The condition of temporal origination certainly holds in the case of human makers, such as the tailor, weaver, and builder to whom al-Ghazālī refers in the next discussion about the *falāsifa*'s inability to show that God is the maker of the world.[17] Observation shows that a maker or craftsman is an agent who chooses between alternative courses of action and then acts after not having acted. How this requirement would fit with God's immutability remains unexplained. Though the philosophers call God a maker, they do so only by sheer metaphor. Al-Ghazālī hints here that, on the contrary, God is the 'maker' and 'agent' *par excellence*, because of his knowledge, will, and power, whereas the philosophers have voided such terms of any meaning when applying them to God.

The third point deals with the philosophers' uncritical acceptance of a common relation between the agent and act, i.e., that both the agent and its effect must be one. This stems from a Neoplatonic dictum that from the one only the one proceeds. The philosophers deem God to be one in every respect and the Neoplatonic dictum does not allow them to explain multiplicity of effects. Having shown that application of this dictum leads to endless inconsistencies, al-Ghazālī concludes that the philosophers' attempt to magnify God's greatness in removing Him from knowledge of particulars in all their pettiness paradoxically undermines God's status, depriving Him of what everyone understands by greatness, i.e., knowledge of all beings:

> They have rendered His state approximating that of the dead person who has no information about what takes place in the world, differing from the dead, however, only in His self-awareness.[18]

The God of the philosophers is 'half-dead', so to speak, not really alive, and, therefore, no true agent. This goes counter to God's beautiful name

[15] *Tahāfut*, p. 58, §8.
[16] *Tahāfut*, p. 61, §18.
[17] *Tahāfut*, p. 79, §4.
[18] *Tahāfut*, p. 71-72, §58 (Marmura's translation).

of the Living, as an examination of *al-Maqṣad al-Asnā* will confirm. Al-Ghazālī, then, wonders:

> What is there to prevent one from saying that the First Principle is knowing, powerful, willing; that He does [or acts] as He wishes, governs what He wills, creates things that are varied as well as things that are homogeneous as He wills and in the way He wills?[19]

In the Fourth Discussion al-Ghazālī simply shows that claiming that all bodies are temporally originated because they are never devoid of temporal events is a coherent and intelligible view requiring that such bodies have a maker and a cause. On the other hand, the eternity of the world becomes intelligible only if one assumes that the world does not depend at all on a cause or maker, instead of arguing for its eternal dependence on a 'necessary being', a notion dear to Avicenna that al-Ghazālī deems unintelligible.

Finally, the Fourteenth Discussion attacks the philosophers' claim that the heaven is an animal that obeys God through circular motion. As our will moves our bodies to its goals by means of motion of the soul, so, say the philosophers, does the heavenly animal whose essential motion is to worship the Lord of the world. Having denied purposive, voluntary agency to God, the philosophers to al-Ghazālī's disgust now grant it to the heavens, making of it an animal, which wills and knows. They eliminate the alternative that such motion is caused by God and compulsory by arguing that such compulsory motion would entail God treating that body differently from the way He treats all the other bodies and, therefore, an ability to differentiate between indiscernibles, though for al-Ghazālī, as we have seen, the ability to differentiate between indiscernibles is just what will is and does.

In conclusion, al-Ghazālī criticizes the philosophers for blurring the distinction between natural and voluntary causes and for depriving God of agency or voluntary causation and, therefore, demoting him to a level close to inanimate things, which cannot act, whereas God surely does. In the *Tahāfut* the way we speak of human beings acting reveals how we should speak of God. The whole contrast is between animate and inanimate and does not in any way exclude that living beings, be they animal or human, are agents at least in some way. We need, therefore, to examine al-Ghazālī's view on God's beautiful name of the Living in order to determine whether in this religious view the contrast between 'alive' and 'inanimate' or 'dead' that we have highlighted in the *Tahāfut* is purely

[19] *Tahāfut*, p. 77, §79 (Marmura's translation with slight modifications).

for rhetorical and eristic purposes or whether it reflects al-Ghazālī's own views. We should also examine the way in which all living beings are said to be alive.

AL-MAQṢAD AL-ASNĀ ON THE 'LIVING' AND THE 'POWERFUL'

Al-Maqṣad is posterior to both the *Tahāfut* and the *Iqtiṣād*, but probably anterior to the *Munqidh*.[20] *Al-Maqṣad* is an important text since, according to what al-Ghazālī says in *al-Arbaʿīn fī Uṣūl al-Dīn,* in it he knocks at the door of gnosis.[21] The section on *al-Ḥayy*, the Living, is brief but enlightening; right from the very beginning al-Ghazālī emphasizes the contrast between alive and dead or inanimate:[22]

> The living is the acting (*al-faʿʿāl*) and the perceiving (*al-darrāk*) since the one who does not act at all and does not perceive is dead.[23]

Interestingly, the form of *faʿala* used to speak of the acting or the agent is no longer the present participle ordinarily used to refer to the agent in the *Tahāfut*, but the intensive adjectival form, used by the philosophers for the Agent Intellect. Al-Ghazālī may hint that what the philosophers denied to God they have granted to the Agent Intellect, though in their emanationist system it is only the tenth Intelligence.

Once the basic contrast has been set, al-Ghazālī begins to establish a hierarchy among the living beings in contrasting the lowest and highest levels of perception and, therefore, of life:

> The lowest level of perception is awareness of itself, for what is not aware of itself is inanimate and dead. The perfect and absolute living is the one who encompasses all that is perceptible under his perception as well as all beings under his action so that nothing perceptible escapes his knowledge and no effect his action and this is God.[24]

Recall that in the *Tahāfut* al-Ghazālī had complained that philosophers had only granted self-awareness to God and, therefore, could only attribute agency to him in a metaphorical sense. Pursuing his hierarchy

[20] See G.F. HOURANI, *A Revised Chronology of Ghazālī's Writings*, in: *Journal of the American Oriental Society* 104 (1984), p. 298.

[21] See MARMURA, *Ghazali and Ashʿarism Revisited*, p. 100.

[22] AL-GHAZĀLĪ, *al-Maqṣad al-Asnā fī Sharḥ Maʿānī Asmāʾ Allāh al-Ḥusnā*, ed. F.A. SHEHADI, Beirut: Dar el-Machreq, 1982, p. 142.

[23] AL-GHAZĀLĪ, *Maqṣad*, p. 142.12-13.

[24] AL-GHAZĀLĪ, *Maqṣad*, p. 142.13-16.

of the living beings, al-Ghazālī now gives us more details in order to establish intermediaries between the two extremes:

> [God] is the Living in the absolute sense. As for any other living being, its life is in proportion to its perception and action. All this is narrowed down to its deficiency [in perception and action]. Living beings differ in deficiency and these differences determine their ranks.[25]

Al-Ghazālī concludes by presenting the hierarchy in descending order: angels, human beings, and beasts.

As in the *Iqtiṣād* the important section for our purpose is that on power, one may have expected that such would also be the case in *al-Maqṣad al-Asnā*. In fact the section on the 'Powerful' is not much longer than that on the 'Living' and al-Ghazālī ends by disclaiming he should reveal much of this issue in this book. For the emphasis on perception it substitutes an emphasis on will and knowledge. The powerful is defined as 'the one who, when he wills, does, and, when he wills, does not'.[26] It insists on the all encompassing power of God who is powerful in the absolute sense, since he can 'invent' every being by an invention of which He alone is endowed and for which He does not need any help. On the other hand, human beings have only a deficient power that encompasses only some possibles and does not include 'invention'. Whatever human beings do requires the intervention of God's power. Al-Ghazālī does not seem here to deny that human beings are endowed with some power and can, therefore, be considered agents in some sense. But obviously he does not want to discuss a complex issue in a more popular treatise. The *Maqṣad* does not indicate where the issue is discussed, but we can find such a discussion in the *Iqtiṣād*, a *Kalām* treatise posterior to the *Tahāfut* but anterior to the *Maqṣad*.[27]

THE *IQTIṢĀD*: AL-GHAZĀLĪ ON THE 'AGENCY' OF SPIDERS, BEES AND HUMAN BEINGS

In the *Tahāfut* al-Ghazālī argues that by denying knowledge of particulars and will to God the philosophers are unable to show that God is a true agent or maker. Since nature as such is inert, only animate or living beings are agents and the text emphasizes similarities between human

[25] AL-GHAZĀLĪ, *Maqṣad*, p. 142.16-18.
[26] AL-GHAZĀLĪ, *Maqṣad*, p. 145.3.
[27] See HOURANI, *Chronology*, p. 289-302.

beings and God. On the other hand, the *Iqtiṣād* grants real causative power to God but only 'acquisitive' power to human beings. This raises the question whether for al-Ghazālī human beings are really agents and if not, why they are not. I shall argue that in the *Iqtiṣād* not only does al-Ghazālī refuse to consider human beings as agents in the strict sense, he does not even strongly distinguish between animals and human beings, despite, as we saw, arguing for a hierarchy between living beings in the *Maqṣad*.[28]

For al-Ghazālī the philosophers have reduced God to a nearly inanimate being, a nearly 'dead person who has no information of what takes place in the world, differing from the dead, however, only in his self-awareness' (*Tahāfut*, p. 71-72, §58). Yet, one of the main Islamic names for God is the 'Living'. The *Iqtiṣād*, like the *Maqṣad*, provides a definition of this attribute: 'living' means 'being self-aware, knowing oneself and others, knowing all beings'.[29] In depriving God of knowledge of particulars, the philosophers also deprive Him of will, since knowledge, though not the cause of the will, is its necessary condition. This new definition seems to require not only some degree of knowledge, as did that in the *Maqṣad*, but rather knowledge of all beings, a condition inaccessible to human beings, if this means exhaustive knowledge of all the particulars, and not simply 'universal' knowledge. The *Iqtiṣād* takes the fact that God is the all-knowing and all-powerful Living Being as so obvious that this attribute is dealt with in five lines and says nothing of the word applying to any other being.

In the *Tahāfut* in order to distinguish voluntary from natural causation, al-Ghazālī had considered the way we speak, noting that if a person throws another in the fire, we call that person a killer, not the fire. He also argued that we perceive the difference between a tremor and a voluntary motion of the hand. In the section of *Iqtiṣād* dealing with power, al-Ghazālī often calls on the way Arabic speakers use words to build his argument, emphasizing the similarities between God and human beings and, more generally, all animate beings, including animals. In the *Tahāfut* the only difference al-Ghazālī had mentioned is that human beings act for an end, whereas God does not, since He cannot depend on an end external to Him. Besides, the definition of the agent given in the *Tahāfut* (p. 57, §4), at first view applies to both God and human beings: an

[28] For the *Iqtiṣād* see AL-GHAZĀLĪ, *al-Iqtiṣād fī l-I'tiqād*, ed. I.A. ÇUBUÇKÜ and H. ATAY, Ankara: Nur Matbaasi, 1962. The chapter on divine power has been translated by M.E. MARMURA in his article, *Ghazali's Chapter on Divine Power* (see note 2 above).

[29] AL-GHAZĀLĪ, *Iqtiṣād*, p. 100-101.

agent is 'one from whom the act proceeds together with the will to act by way of choice and the knowledge of what is willed'. Such a definition states nothing about whether an agent acts or does not act for an end and, therefore, seems to fit both God and human beings. Yet, the definition seems to exclude animals as agents since it states that the act proceeds with the will to act by way of choice and generally animals are not considered to have choice, even if one grants them a certain level of cognition.

In the chapter on power of the *Iqtiṣād*, al-Ghazālī examines the views of the determinists and the Muʿtazilites and tries to find a midway position thanks to the Ashʿarite theory of acquisition (*kasb*). Marmura comments on this section but does not directly address the question whether animate beings other than God can be called agents in any way. Al-Ghazālī begins his examination of divine power by claiming that the originator of the world is powerful

> Because the world is an act that is well designed, organized, perfected, ordered, comprising [different kinds] of *wonders* and *signs*.[30]

He then clarifies what he means by the world being well-designed, i.e.,

> Its organization, its orderliness, and its symmetry. Whoever looks into his organs, external and internal, there will become manifest for him of the *wonders* of perfection that whose enumeration would be lengthy. This, then, is a premise, which is apprehended, known through the senses and observation. It is hence impossible to deny.[31]

Power is a divine attribute additional to God's essence in order to ensure creation in time since '"power", according to the convention of language is an expression of the attribute by which the act is rendered ready for the agent and through which the act comes about'.[32] For al-Ghazālī, if God were to create by His essence, the world would be eternal.

Al-Ghazālī then asks whether 'the contrary of what is known [will happen] is [enactable] by [divine] power?'[33] If God has foreknowledge that Zayd will die on Saturday morning, is it in God's power to create life for Zayd on this same Saturday morning? In itself Zayd's life is

[30] Marmura's translation: *Ghazali's Chapter on Divine Power*, p. 296; AL-GHAZĀLĪ, *Iqtiṣād*, p. 80.

[31] Italics added for emphasis. Marmura's translation: *Ghazali's Chapter on Divine Power*, p. 296; AL-GHAZĀLĪ, *Iqtiṣād*, p. 80.

[32] Marmura's translation: *Ghazali's Chapter on Divine Power*, p. 297; AL-GHAZĀLĪ, *Iqtiṣād*, p. 81.

[33] Marmura's translation: *Ghazali's Chapter on Divine Power*, p. 299; AL-GHAZĀLĪ, *Iqtiṣād*, p. 83.

possible, but is now made impossible in terms of its connection with God's knowledge. Then, God's inability to create life in Zayd does not stem from slackness or weakness in His power, but from a connection to His own will that has made it impossible. This section ends with al-Ghazālī once again going back to the correct linguistic use of the word for power:

> It is clear that the correct thing is to use this term ['power']. For people say that so and so has the power to move or to remain still — if he wishes he moves and if he wishes he stays still.[34]

Once again, divine and human powers seem very similar and the term appears to be used univocally.

The second issue al-Ghazālī raises in connection with the pervasiveness of divine power in its connection to all possibles is that of the power of animals and of the rest of the living creatures. If what these beings enact is not enactable by divine power, then, divine power is not all pervasive. On the other hand, if what these beings enact is also enactable by God, then, one will need:

> To affirm an object of power, [enacted by] two possessors of power, which is impossible, or else to deny that man and the rest of the animals have power, which is a denial of necessary [knowledge] and a denial of the demands of the religious law, since demanding that which is not within one's power is impossible.[35]

Notice that human beings and animals are put on the same level, despite a reference to religious law.

In order to differentiate a spasmodic movement, say a tremor, from a voluntary movement, al-Ghazālī claims that one and the same object of power may be enacted by two possessors of power, on the condition that such powers be connected differently to that single object. This prevents a violation of the principle of non contradiction. Divine power is causally connected to the object, whereas human power is not. 'Power', therefore, is not used univocally of both God and created beings, such as human beings, animals, angels, jinn, and devils. From created power no true creation or 'invention' (*ikhtirāʿ*) can arise. Why are invention and creation denied to animate creatures, such as human beings and animals? Recall that here human beings and animals are grouped together.

[34] Marmura's translation: *Ghazali's Chapter on Divine Power*, p. 302; AL-GHAZĀLĪ, *Iqtiṣād*, p. 86.

[35] Marmura's translation: *Ghazali's Chapter on Divine Power*, p. 303; AL-GHAZĀLĪ, *Iqtiṣād*, p. 86-87.

Al-Ghazālī claims that creation or invention belongs only to agents who know what they create:

> For, [in the case of] motions that proceed from the human being and the rest of animals, if asked about their number, details and amount, [the individual] would have no information about them.[36]

As an example of this absence of information, he describes an infant boy who crawls *by choice* to his mother's breast and sucks, just as the new born kitten crawls to its mother's teat, though its eyes have not yet opened. Notice that the infant boy, though deprived of knowledge, is said to crawl *by choice*.

Leaving aside infants, al-Ghazālī moves to reflections on the building activities of spiders and bees, which defy the knowledge of most people and even at times geometricians.

First, the spiders. They weave

> By way of webs wondrous shapes that astound the geometricians by their circularity, the parallelism of the sides of [their concentric shapes] and the symmetry of their organization.[37]

Though they do not 'know' what they are doing, spiders manage to act 'as if they knew' what geometricians themselves *are unable to know*. It is not that spiders 'know' better than specialists in geometry; rather it is God's power enacting such 'knowledge' in them. The knowledge displayed thus belongs to God; He alone may be said to be acting.

Second, the bees, on which al-Ghazālī spends much time. The bees build hexagonal cells as the most efficient way to deal with limited space. As they are nearly circular, the bees require cells of a shape close to that of circle, but if they were building circular cells, much empty space would be lost between these cells. Besides, if hexagonal cells are stacked properly, there is no empty space left, while this would not be the case, if they were octagons or pentagons. Of course, building square cells would also prevent empty space, but squares encompass much less of the area of the corresponding circle, than hexagons do. Bees maximize the use of space. This time al-Ghazālī acknowledges that geometricians proved that bees make the most efficient use of space, but contends that most rational beings fall short of apprehending such complexities.

[36] Marmura's translation: *Ghazali's Chapter on Divine Power*, p. 304: AL-GHAZĀLĪ, *Iqtiṣād*, p. 87-88.

[37] Marmura's translation: *Ghazali's Chapter on Divine Power*, p. 304: AL-GHAZĀLĪ, *Iqtiṣād*, p. 88.

Therefore, if most people do not apprehend the bees' geometric efficiency, the bees must not grasp it either and the knowledge guiding their action is in fact that of God, who, therefore, is the true agent. Al-Ghazālī does not hesitate to assert that 'God ... has forced [the bees] *to choose* the hexagonal shape in crafting their cells'.[38] The bees do not apprehend the reasons for their building hexagonal cells and, hence, have no power for resisting what God enacts in them. Suddenly lyrical, al-Ghazālī proclaims:

> Indeed, there are in the crafts of animals wonders which if I were to relate a portion thereof, the breasts would be filled with the greatness of God ... Woe then to those who stray from the path of God, who are conceitedly deceived by their inadequate power and weak ability, who think they participate with God in creation, invention, and the innovating of such *wonders and signs*.[39]

Al-Ghazālī must have more admiration for spiders and bees than for human beings, because he never tackles directly an example of the agency of an adult human being. Notice too that he attributes 'choice' to both the infant boy and the bees, which are forced to choose. Is al-Ghazālī hinting that since bees act for an end, proper knowledge of the best means to the end determines the action? His understanding of choice is certainly not the Aristotelian one. God does not act for an end and, therefore, His knowledge, though a necessary condition for His will, does not determine it and allows Him to specify one among several indiscernibles.

Human and divine powers differ and both God and human beings can be said to be agents, but what makes the act of the human being possible is that it is created. Examining the difference between tremor and voluntary motion, al-Ghazālī denies that the difference between divine and human powers is one of degree. Rather, God 'invents' the human power and its object. The object of power is not 'through' the power of the 'servant', even though it exists 'with' it. The connection between the human being and the object of power is not causal, just as the connection between knowledge and will is not causal, though the former is a necessary condition for the latter. God's knowledge does not determine His will, as His ability to specify one among many indiscernibles shows. There are, therefore, different types of connection between a power and

[38] Marmura's translation: *Ghazali's Chapter on Divine Power*, p. 305: AL-GHAZĀLĪ, *Iqtiṣād*, p. 89.

[39] Marmura's translation: *Ghazali's Chapter on Divine Power*, p. 305; AL-GHAZĀLĪ, *Iqtiṣād*, p. 89-90.

its object. In the case of God it is causal, but not in the case of human beings or animals, regardless of their level of knowledge. Whether the connection between a created power and its object is a necessary condition for God's habitual exercise of power is not really stated, but is assumed.

In the *Iqtiṣād* al-Ghazālī grants little knowledge to human beings and still less to bees and even spiders. God creates knowledge in human beings and, therefore, we are not agents in exactly the same way as God is. We seem to be agents simply in a metaphorical way, whatever he says about normal linguistic usage. Animate beings, be they animal or human, are alive and in some way aware of themselves and have some self-knowledge as well as knowledge of something other than themselves, but only God 'knows *all* the beings and has power over *all* objects of power' (the emphasis is mine). The kind of power one has seems determined by one's cognitive level, even if al-Ghazālī does not want to grant differences of degrees.

In the *Arbaʿīn* al-Ghazālī describes the *Iqtiṣād* as going 'deeper in ascertaining [the truth] and ... closer to knocking at the doors of gnosis', than the usual *Kalām* books.[40] Something very similar had been said of the *Maqṣad*; yet, the former seems to deny any sort of hierarchy between living beings, while the latter does.

BEYOND PHILOSOPHY AND *KALĀM*

Marmura's recent study of 'choice' in the *Iḥyāʾ ʿUlūm al-Dīn* shows that there too al-Ghazālī presents himself as trying to find a midway position between the determinists and the Muʿtazilites, thanks to the theory of acquisition. But this theory does not seem to leave space for any true human agency, for in the *Iḥyāʾ* al-Ghazālī claims, 'choice is also God's creation and the servant is compelled in the choice he has'.[41]

For al-Ghazālī philosophers may present a God who is barely alive, whereas he alone presents God as fully alive because He knows all that can be objects of power. As both human beings and animals have low cognitional levels, the geometric skills of bees and spiders show that in

[40] Marmura's translation in: *Ghazali and Ashʿarism*, p. 100.

[41] Marmura's translation in: *Ghazali and Ashʿarism*, p. 106. Timothy J. Gianotti in a paper delivered in Seattle on April 3, 2004 at the annual meeting of the Medieval Academy argued that in the *Iḥyāʾ* al-Ghazālī seems to deny any agency to any being other than God.

fact the one who knows such properties is God; and it is He alone who acts. Whether there is much difference between human beings and geometrically minded animals remains unclear. Geometricians may have a better grasp but even this grasp is directly created by God. Spiders and bees exhibit more clearly the 'wonders and signs' God can accomplish through human beings and animals who both turn out to be barely alive.

OCCASIONALISM, NATURAL CAUSATION AND SCIENCE IN AL-GHAZĀLĪ*

JON MCGINNIS
University of Missouri, St. Louis

The present study suggests a metaphysical model for understanding al-Ghazālī's account of causal powers. The model explains al-Ghazālī's position on natural, efficient causation as found in his *Tahāfut al-Falāsifa* and certain theological works, as well as grounds his belief that one can have scientific knowledge of the world in the rich sense described by Aristotle and the Arabic *falāsifa*. Concerning these points, the works of Richard Frank and Michael Marmura have greatly enhanced our understanding of al-Ghazālī, and yet their interpretations of al-Ghazālī on efficient causation are diametrically opposed. Frank in two monographs, *Creation and the Cosmic System: Al-Ghazâlî & Avicenna* and *Al-Ghazālī and the Ashʿarite School*, has forcefully, and I believe convincingly, argued that al-Ghazālī posited efficacious, causal powers in created things in opposition to traditional Ashʿarite occasionalism.[1] In contrast, Marmura in several articles as well as the notes to his translation of al-Ghazālī's *Tahāfut* has argued that al-Ghazālī maintained the traditional occasionalism of Ashʿarite *Kalām*, and suggested how al-Ghazālī modified his philosophical understanding of science to accommodate this occasionalism.[2] The

* I am thankful to Tony Street and Shane Duarte for their willingness to discuss various technical points that arose during my research of this study. I would like also to acknowledge the University of Missouri Research Board, who provided research funds for this project, as well as the Center for International Study at the University of Missouri, St. Louis, who made possible a trip to the 38th International Congress on Medieval Studies at Kalamazoo, where a portion of this paper was presented. As always, any errors are solely my own.

[1] *Creation and the Cosmic System: Al-Ghazâlî & Avicenna* (*Abhandlungen der Heidelberger Akademie der Wissenschaften, Philosophisch-historische Klasse*, 1. Abhandlung), Heidelberg, 1992; *Al-Ghazālī and the Ashʿarite School* (*Duke Monographs in Medieval and Renaissance Studies*, 15), Durham — London, 1994. A similar thesis has been argued in less detail by B. ABRAHAMOV, *Al-Ghazālī's Theory of Causality*, in: *Studia Islamica* 67 (1988), p. 75-98.

[2] *Ghazali and Demonstrative Science*, in: *Journal of the History of Philosophy* 3 (1965), p. 183-204; *Ghazali's Chapter on Divine Power in the* Iqtiṣād, in: *Arabic Science and Philosophy* 4 (1994), p. 279-315; *Ghazālian Causes and Intermediaries*, in: *Journal of the American Oriental Society* 115 (1995), p. 89-100 (a review article of FRANK's *Creation and the Cosmic System*); and AL-GHAZĀLĪ, *The Incoherence of the Philosophers*, translated, introduced, and annotated by M.E. MARMURA, Provo, 1997.

model of causal powers, which I suggest, reconciles the textual evidence put forth on both sides by Frank and Marmura as well as grounds al-Ghazālī's belief that true science is possible.

Al-Ghazālī, I submit, holds an intermediate position between traditional Ashʿarite occasionalism and the *falāsifa*'s theory of efficient causation. The suggested interpretation makes all causal processes immediately dependent upon a divine, or at least angelic, volitional act, as al-Ghazālī's fellow *mutakallimūn* held, and yet leaves room for natural, efficient causation through secondary causes, akin to the position of the *falāsifa*. To anticipate my arguments, I suggest that for al-Ghazālī created things have causal natures, but understood as the passive powers to act or to be acted upon. Thus God, or some volitional agent, is required at every moment to actualize the passive power to act in a created thing such that the thing itself in turn acts as an efficient cause on something possessing a properly disposed passive power to be acted upon. Thus, while I agree with Frank, and others, that al-Ghazālī allows for natural, secondary causation, I disagree that his break with traditional Ashʿarite occasionalism is as sharp as some believe.

To this end, I begin with the historical and philosophical background to al-Ghazālī's account of efficient causation: first, Avicenna's arguments for necessary causal relations among natural things, and second, a traditional Ashʿarite *Kalām* argument for occasionalism. In the first section I also consider an Ashʿarite critique of Avicenna's arguments, which purports to show that there are no epistemological grounds for accepting a premise that Avicenna's arguments require, which I follow with a possible Avicennan response. In the second section I consider al-Ghazālī's account of natural, efficient causation in the Seventeenth Discussion of his *Tahāfut*, where I suggest that al-Ghazālī's main concern is to provide a basis for scientific knowledge in light of the philosophers' critique of occasionalism. In the third, and final, section I again consider al-Ghazālī's view of natural, efficient causation in certain theological works. Although the evidence produced in these last two sections for my thesis is circumstantial, it nonetheless is suggestive in that it offers a reconciliation of various apparently contradictory claims in al-Ghazālī.

Historical background

One of the most significant sources of al-Ghazālī's own position concerning efficient causation, both as a source of inspiration and an ostensive object of criticism,[3] was Avicenna. For Avicenna effects followed as necessary consequences of their causes; thus Avicenna's cosmic system was an overall closed and deterministic one. His arguments for necessary, causal relations are found in his metaphysical writings discussing the necessary in itself, the possible in itself and a hybrid of these two, the possible in itself, but necessary through another.[4]

This last classification, i.e., the possible in itself, but necessary through another, is our primary concern. The argument Avicenna most frequently invokes for necessary causal relations, and the one regularly referred to in the secondary literature,[5] observes that the possible considered in itself is indeterminate with respect to being.[6] In other words, merely considered in itself there is nothing that requires that what is possible in itself should either exist or not exist. Consequently, if something merely possible in itself actually exists, then there must be something that gives to the possible in itself a preponderance of or determinately selects (*murajjiḥ*) its existence. In other words, if something merely possible in itself, and so of itself indeterminate with respect to existence, actually exists, then there must be something that causes it to exist determinately, when it actually exists. Now if in the presence of this cause the possible in itself were still to remain possible in itself, then it would still be indeterminate with respect to existence or non-existence, and one would have to posit yet another cause that determinately selects or gives preponderance to existence over non existence, and the same holds true as long as the possible in itself remains merely possible in itself. Avicenna blocks the regress by asserting that when the possible in itself

[3] Jules Janssens has argued that al-Ghazālī's *Tahāfut* is not in fact, as is often believed, an outright refutation of Avicenna's philosophy, but instead is directed at a slavish conformity to the ancients. This thesis is partially borne out in the Seventeenth Discussion of the *Tahāfut*, but it would also seem that al-Ghazālī has in mind some variant of Avicenna's account of necessary, causal relations as well. See J. JANSSENS, *Al-Ghazālī's* Tahāfut: *Is It Really a Rejection of Ibn Sīnā's Philosophy?*, in: *Journal of Islamic Studies* 12 (2001), p. 1-17.

[4] The pertinent Avicennan texts associated with this topic have been collected and translated by George F. Hourani; see G.F. HOURANI, *Ibn Sīnā on Necessary and Possible Existence*, in: *The Philosophical Forum* 4 (1972), p. 74-86.

[5] See G. SMITH, *Avicenna and the Possibles,* in: *The New Scholasticism* 17 (1943), p. 340-357; B.H. ZEDLER, *Another Look at Avicenna*, in: *The New Scholasticism* 50 (1976), p. 504-521; B.H. ZEDLER, *Why are the Possibles Possible?*, in: *The New Scholasticism* 55 (1981), p. 113-130; and M.E. MARMURA, *The Metaphysics of Efficient Causality in Avicenna (Ibn Sina)*, in: *Islamic Theology and Philosophy: Studies in Honor of George F. Hourani*, ed. M.E. MARMURA, Albany, 1984, p. 172-187, and p. 304-305 (notes).

[6] The argument can be found in AVICENNA, *Shifā': al-Ilāhīyāt*, ed. G.C. ANAWATI and S. ZAYED, I, Cairo, 1960, I, 6, p. 38-39; and *Najāh*, ed. M.T. DANISHPAZHUH, Tehran, 1985, XI.2.ii, p. 547-548.

actually exists, then its existence is necessary through another, namely, its cause. In short, in the presence of the requisite causes, effects issue forth necessarily.

This is the standard Avicennan argument for necessary causal relations, but Avicenna also suggests a second, and I believe more 'elegant', argument.[7] In fact, it is this second, less appreciated, argument that appears to be the object of al-Ghazālī's critique in the Seventeenth Discussion of the *Tahāfut* rather than the one just mentioned, despite the former's greater popularity. Avicenna's second argument for the necessity of causal relations is again in his discussion of the necessary and the possible in itself, albeit only implicitly. Unlike the first argument, which began with an analysis of the possible in itself, the second argument begins with an analysis of necessity. At least one criterion for being necessary, according to Avicenna, is that its opposite implies a contradiction. Thus, assume a certain proposition. If that assumed proposition entails a contradiction, then that proposition's opposite must be necessary.

For Avicenna, to assume that certain causes do *not* necessitate their effects leads to an explicit contradiction. Avicenna gives the following example. From repeated observations we know that fire has the active causal power to burn, whereas cotton has the passive power to be burned. Now let fire, with its active causal power to burn, be put in contact with cotton, with its passive causal power to be burned, and assume that the expected effect, the burning of the cotton, does not occur. In this case either one of two things would explain the non occurrence of burning. Either that which in fact has the active causal power to burn, namely, the fire, does not in fact have the active causal power to burn, which is clearly a contradiction — for the fire cannot simultaneously have and not have the active power to burn. Or, similarly, that which in fact has the passive causal power to be burned, namely, the cotton, does not in fact have the passive causal power to be burned, and there again is a contradiction. Thus, the assumption that the effect is not necessitated by its causes leads to an explicit contradiction; however, in that case, its opposite must be necessary, and so causes must necessitate their effects. The argument's contentious premise is that there are active and passive causal powers, which will be the very point that the *mutakallimūn* find objectionable.

Before considering the *mutakallimūn*'s objection, we should consider their diametrically opposed theory of causation, namely, occasionalism.

[7] See AVICENNA, *Najāh*, XI.2.i, p. 546-547.

Islamic occasionalism, briefly, is the view that at every moment God re-creates the world *in toto*, both the atoms that make up the world as well as the accidents that determine the attributes that atoms have.[8] Medieval Islamic speculative theologians had various arguments for their theory of occasionalism, of which I offer one.[9] The basis of the argument is the Ashʿarite claim that the very capacity (*istiṭāʿa*) to act must come to be simultaneously with its correlative action and cannot pre-exist that action. The standard argument for this thesis, found in al-Ashʿarī, as well as others, is that a non-active or non-acting capacity to act entails a contradiction.[10] We can philosophically flesh this argument out as follows. A non-active capacity to act would be a mere possibility to act; however, insofar as something is merely a possibility it presently is not existing, even if purportedly it will be something existing at some later point. Thus, to claim that there presently exists a non-active capacity, i.e., a mere possibility to act, is just to say there presently exists something that presently is not existing, a patent contradiction. Consequently, at every moment a thing acts the thing must have both its capacity to act and its action created for it by God. In short, the successive occurrence of events we experience is in fact just God's continuous re-creation of the world and events at every moment.

Two corollaries follow from Islamic occasionalism. The first is that the apparent orderly sequence of events is not due to changes of states in an enduring substance causally being acted upon by another substance, but due solely to God's habit (*ʿāda*) or custom (*sunna*) of regularly conjoining certain essentially unrelated events with others. The second is that natures, as understood by Aristotle and the Arabic *falāsifa* who followed him, could not be real. Aristotelian natures, understood as an internal principle of change and being at rest belonging to a thing essentially and not accidentally, were intended as causal powers within a thing.[11] A thing's nature indicates either its formal or material cause,

[8] Concerning *Kalām* proofs for the existence of atoms and accidents, see AL-BĀQILLĀNĪ, *Kitāb al-Tamhīd*, ed. R.J. MCCARTHY, Beirut, 1957, p. 17-21, paragraphs 27-36; and AL-JUWAYNĪ, *Kitāb al-Irshād ilā Qawāṭiʿ al-Adilla fī Uṣūl al-Iʿtiqād*, Cairo, 1950, p. 17-27.

[9] R. J. McCarthy refers to AL-BĀQILLĀNĪ, *Inṣāf*, ed. M. AL-KAWTHARĪ, Cairo, 1950, p. 127-139, as providing a specific argument for occasionalism in his *The Theology of al-Ashʿarī*, ed. R.J. MCCARTHY, Beirut, 1953, p. 35, fn. 5. Unfortunately, I was unable to consult the *Inṣāf*.

[10] See AL-ASHʿARĪ, *al-Lumaʿ*, in: *The Theology of al-Ashʿarī*, Chapter 3, p. 33-44; AL-BĀQILLĀNĪ, *Tamhīd*, p. 286-287, paragraphs 487-489; and AL-JUWAYNĪ, *Irshād*, p. 215-225.

[11] See ARISTOTLE, *Physics* II, 1, 192b21-23.

where the formal cause explains a natural thing's being or acting in a specific way. For example, the reason that fire burns is that it belongs to the nature of fire, *qua* the form of fire, to burn. Indeed, Avicenna's second argument for necessary, causal relations, which we saw above, is founded on the claim that things have natures with accompanying causal powers.

Thus, not surprisingly, the *mutakallimūn* adamantly rejected the natures of the philosophers with their purported inherent causal powers. For instance, in al-Bāqillānī's *Kitāb al-Tamhīd* one sees an argument apparently directed specifically at Avicenna's claim that one can know that things like fire and cotton have the causal powers to burn and to be burned respectively:

> Concerning what [the philosophers] are in such a stir about, namely that they know by sense perception and necessarily that the burning … occurs from the fire, it is tremendous ignorance. That is because that which we observe and perceive sensibly is only a change of state of the body with … the fire's contacting … and [the contacted thing's] being burned and changed from what it was, no more. As for the knowledge that this newly occurring state is from the action of whatever, [this agency] is not observed; rather it is something grasped through rigorous inquiry and examination.[12]

When one observes fire's contacting cotton and the cotton's burning one neither experiences the internal mechanism by which the fire purportedly causes the burning, nor does it seem that a mere conceptual analysis of fire would logically require that it burns cotton. Thus, one has no reason, whether *a posteriori* or *a priori*, for thinking that the cotton's burning is due to the fire. On the other hand, since the Ashʿarites believe that there is a scriptural basis for reserving all agency to God alone, they subsequently claim to know with certainty that it is God who regularly produces fire in cotton on the occasion of fire's being in contact with cotton.

Avicenna seems to have been aware of, or at the very least anticipated, this critique and its challenge to his overall theory of causal necessity. For Avicenna, following Aristotle, one has science or knowledge in the truest sense (Greek *epistēmē*, Arabic *ʿilm*) if and only if one recognizes with certainty and necessity that a given predicate belongs to its subject; however, a given predicate will belong to its subject necessarily and certainly if and only if there is a causal relation linking the predicate to the subject, where this causal relation between subject and

[12] AL-BĀQILLĀNĪ, *Tamhīd*, p. 43, paragraph 77.

predicate is in turn explained by the thing's nature.[13] Thus, to deny natures and their accompanying necessary, causal relations is to undermine the very possibility of science. Hence to the extent that one believes that we do have science or knowledge, one must be committed to the reality of causal relations and natures. For Avicenna these causal relations and natures are known either directly through intellectual insight (*ḥads*)[14] or a process of experimental testing (*tajriba*),[15] and indeed are known with necessity and certainty. Consequently, for Avicenna we do have science and knowledge in the truest sense, whereas for the Ashʿarites, according to Avicenna's argument, there cannot be knowledge and science. This argument, as we shall see, exercised al-Ghazālī and, I believe, played an important role in al-Ghazālī's own formulation of causation.

Avicenna's necessitarianism and Islamic occasionalism represent the major competing theories of causation that provide the context of al-Ghazālī's own theory. The latter reserves all causal efficacy for God alone, whereas the former gives the natures of created things causal powers. In the remaining two sections I want to suggest that al-Ghazālī's account of causation is a compromise between these two, ensuring God's or some angelic intermediary's on-going, even immediate, role in causal relations, but likewise making natures, with their accompanying causal powers, necessary causes of events.

AL-GHAZĀLĪ ON NATURAL EFFICIENT CAUSATION IN THE *TAHĀFUT*

Before turning to the details of al-Ghazālī's arguments concerning efficient causation, I shall make one global observation about the Seventeenth Discussion. Nowhere in this discussion, as far as I can discern, does al-Ghazālī take up Avicenna's first and better known argument for causes' necessitating their effects. The argument again in brief was that

[13] See AVICENNA, *Shifā'*: *Kitāb al-Burhān*, ed. A.E. AFIFI, Cairo, 1956, I, 8, p. 85-92.

[14] I prefer 'intellectual insight' as a translation for *ḥads* over the more standard translation 'intuition'. 'Intuition' can connote the idea of 'guessing', even if accurately, at the way things might be; however *ḥads* should not be confused with guessing, even if accurately. In contrast, 'insight' suggests an assessment of the true and real nature of a situation, which, I believe, more closely approximates Avicenna's intended meaning of *ḥads*. See D. GUTAS, *Avicenna and the Aristotelian Tradition. Introduction to Reading Avicenna's Philosophical Works,* Leiden, 1988, p. 159-176 for a discussion of *ḥads*.

[15] For a discussion of Avicenna's notion of *tajriba* see my *Scientific Methodologies in Medieval Islam*, in: *Journal of the History of Philosophy* 41 (2003), p. 307-327; JULES J. JANSSENS, *Experience* (Tajriba) *in Classical Arabic Philosophy (al-Fārābī-Avicenna)*, in: *Quaestio* 4 (2004), p. 45-62.

if causes were not to necessitate their effects, there would be an infinite regress of causes. If the intent of the Seventeenth Discussion were to undermine the philosophers', and particularly Avicenna's, position on natural, necessary causation, then one should expect some specific statement and critique of this argument, and again such is not the case. The reason for this omission is that the argument is innocuous for al-Ghazālī's own theory of efficient causation, as I understand it. There is nothing in the argument that precludes either multiple causes jointly necessitating an effect or one of those causes acting through volition.

In contrast, Avicenna's second argument, to which al-Ghazālī does respond, concluded that if the active and passive powers *alone* did not necessitate their effect, then an explicit contradiction would follow. Thus, Avicenna concludes that active and passive powers necessarily produce their effect. This argument presents a threat to al-Ghazālī, since it undermines the need for a volitional agent in a given causal relation, and the absolute exclusion of a volitional agent in a causal process is what al-Ghazālī truly wants to deny. In short, the overall intent of al-Ghazālī's critique of efficient causation, I contend, is not to deny either that there are natures or that natures have causal powers, as traditional Ashʿarite *mutakallimūn* would have it, but to deny that these causes *alone*, independent of any volitional agent, can necessitate their causes. To this end I now turn to al-Ghazālī's arguments.

Al-Ghazālī explicitly addresses two positions concerning efficient causation: 1) that the cause of the effect is a single cause and that that cause alone brings about its effect, giving the example 'the agent of the burning is only (*faqaṭ*) the fire' (*Tahāfut*, p. 171, §4); and 2) the effect requires the matter's being properly prepared to receive the forms, where this preparation is brought about by the normally observed causes, but in addition it also requires 'principles of temporal events' (*mabādi' al-ḥawādith*), one of which is identified with Avicenna's giver of forms (*wāhib al-ṣuwar*). Furthermore, the second position maintains that 'from these principles things proceed by necessity and naturally (*bi-l-luzūm wa-l-ṭabʿ*), *not by way of deliberation and choice*' (*Tahāfut*, p. 172, §9).

The first position al-Ghazālī considers, which is closely akin to the Muʿtazilites' doctrine of *tawlīd*, maintains that a created thing can alone be a cause without reference to any additional causal principle. Al-Ghazālī proceeds by considering the example of fire's causing the cotton to burn and that the fire is the *only* cause. His criticism of this position uses what initially appears to be al-Bāqillānī's argument, namely that the only proof one has that fire is the cause of the burning is observations, and yet observations cannot guarantee causal connections, but only constant conjunctions. In fact, though, there is a subtle, but important, difference between al-Bāqillānī's version of the argument and al-Ghazālī's. Al-Ghazālī's argument runs:

> As for fire, which is inanimate, it has no action; for what indication is there that it is an agent? There is no indication except the observation of the occurrence of the burning with the contact of the fire. The observation indicates the occurrence with it, but not the occurrence by it *and that there is no cause except it* (*Tahāfut*, p. 171, §5).

Whereas al-Bāqillānī concluded that one simply could not know that the fire is the cause of the burning, al-Ghazālī's conclusion is that one cannot know that the burning is by the fire *and only by the fire*. The reason for this 'weaker' conclusion, I believe, is that he thinks that one can know that the fire is *a* cause of the burning; however, observation cannot prove that the fire is the sole cause. He concludes his discussion of the first position by observing that the more exacting philosophers did think that there is an additional causal factor other than just the fire, namely, the giver of forms, which leads to his critique of the second position.

The second position, again, is that things in the sublunar realm do act as causes inasmuch as they prepare the matter to receive form, with the form's being in turn emanated from some additional principle or principles, for instance, Avicenna's 'giver of forms,' i.e., the intellect associated with the moon. To this extent, I think that al-Ghazālī would agree with the philosophers — where he takes umbrage is their further claim that this principle or principles emanates a form through its nature (*bi-l-ṭabʿ*) and so the form issues forth 'mechanically' or of necessity and essentially, without their being any volitional element.

In presenting the philosophers' argument for this position al-Ghazālī provides a variant of Avicenna's second argument mentioned above, namely, when there is no will involved, as in the case of fire's burning cotton, then it is inconceivable, i.e., it involves a contradiction, that fire be brought into contact with two identical pieces of cotton and that one would burn and the other not (*Tahāfut*, p. 173, §9). Here, al-Ghazālī's additional rider that 'no will is involved' is telling; for this is what he truly finds objectionable about Avicenna's argument, not, I hazard, its claim to show that natures are causes or that they are necessary for their effects.

Al-Ghazālī considers two approaches to respond to this argument. In laying out the first approach (*Tahāfut*, p. 173-175, §§11-17) al-Ghazālī asserts two theses: one, that there can be a volitional element in natural, causal processes, and, two, that the introduction of volition into natural, causal processes does not entail certain purported absurdities that would undermine the possibility of science. He defends the first thesis by referring the reader to Discussion One of the *Tahāfut*, where he argued that God and the principles, or angels, do act by choice and voluntarily, and I shall not rehearse those arguments here.

Al-Ghazālī takes up the second thesis in response to a potential objection to the first thesis. The objection, which is a variation of the Avicennan response to al-Bāqillānī's critique, claims that 'when one denies the necessity of the effects from their causes and [the effects] are related to the volition of their creator (*mukhtari'*), and moreover the volition has no specifically imposed course, but [the course] can be diverse and of various kinds', then every conceivable possibility would be realised; for example a boy's becoming a dog, or ashes musk or common stones gold or a piece of fruit a human (*Tahāfut*, p. 173-174, §13). In short, there would be no necessary and certain causal relations between things, and so one could never have scientific knowledge.

Al-Ghazālī's response is in fact a philosophical 'bait and switch'. The underlying philosophical issue concerns the very possibility of having scientific knowledge, whereas al-Ghazālī shifts the focus to an analysis of possibility. Al-Ghazālī's variation of the objection assumed a temporal frequency model of modalities. For our purposes this would involve the repressed premise that whatever is possible will at some time be realised. Al-Ghazālī is somewhat justified in introducing this premise, even if contentiously; for in his logical works Avicenna maintains that modalities and temporalities are isomorphic, that is to say modal propositions can be mapped on to temporal propositions exactly, and vise versa. Thus within the context of Avicenna's syllogistic one can say that *x* is possible, in at least one sense, if and only if it exists at some future time.[16] Al-Ghazālī

[16] To be more exact, the square of opposition formed by temporal propositions in Avicenna's syllogistic have exactly the same form as the square formed by their modal analogues. Thus, for Avicenna a general possible (*mumkina 'āmma*) has the form '*x* is possible, iff *x* exists at some future time', and a special possible (*mumkina khāṣṣa*) has the form '*x* is possible, iff *x* exists at some future time and does not exist at another future time'. Also, one should note that Avicenna is fairly careful to keep modalities as analysed in his metaphysical treatises separate from syllogistic modalities as found in his logical treatises, and does not really see his modal logic as having much direct bearing on his metaphysics; rather, his aim in the logical works is to provide an interpretation of modalities for Aristotle's system in the *Prior Analytics*. See T. STREET, *Fakhraddīn ar-Rāzī's Critique of Avicennan Logic*, in: U. RUDOLPH and D. PERLER, *Logik und Theologie. Das* Organon *im arabischen und im lateinischen Mittelalter*, Leiden, forthcoming. I am grateful to Dr. Street for providing me with an advanced copy of this article, as well as his willingness to discuss this point with me.

considers this notion of possibility, and not the more pressing issue of the possibility of scientific knowledge, in his response, and thus he subtly shifts the focus of the objection.

Al-Ghazālī's response observes that the philosophers have not established that the possible as such may or may not occur, and thus the absurd possibilities mentioned in the objection need never be realised. Moreover, in contrast to the objection's claim to the contrary, al-Ghazālī maintains that on the basis of having observed time after time that natural events follow a set course, we can have unshakable knowledge that they will continue to do so:

> By means of continuous custom (*ʿāda*),[17] [observing certain events' occurring] time after time, there is firmly fixed in our minds their course according to past custom, being firmly fixed in such a way that they do not depart from it (*Tahāfut*, p. 174, §15).[18]

Al-Ghazālī's response is tailored in such a way as to allow both that natural processes can have an element of choice and yet that one can have scientific, i.e., necessary and causal, knowledge of these processes. Indeed, in summing up these sections, al-Ghazālī virtually suggests as much:

> Therefore, nothing precludes that something, within the scope of God's powers, is possible, and [that] His former knowledge has come to pass that He will not actualize it despite its being possible at certain given moments, and [that] He determines for us the knowledge that he will not actualize it at that moment (*Tahāfut*, p. 175, §17).

Admittedly, the over-all impression one gets from al-Ghazālī's 'first approach' is that he subscribes to traditional Ashʿarite occasionalism, but this is certainly a red herring. His comments about what falls within the scope of the divine power must be supplemented by later comments

[17] See FRANK, *Creation and the Cosmic System*, p. 59 for a discussion of al-Ghazālī's non-traditional use of this term.

[18] Despite certain similarities with al-Bāqillānī, this passage also has certain affinities with Avicenna's account of *tajriba*, i.e., experimentation or empirical testing, especially in its claim that repeated observations can fix something firmly in our minds: 'Experimentation is like our judging that the scammony plant is a purgative of bile; for since this [phenomenon] is repeated many times, one abandons that it is among the things that occur by chance, so the mind judges and concedes that it belongs to the character of scammony to purge bile, that is, purging bile is an intrinsic characteristic belonging to scammony' (*Kitāb al-Burhān*, I, 9, p. 95). Given that, in the immediate context of al-Ghazālī's discussion, his intention is to show that one can know that the purported absurdities will not follow, and that al-Bāqillānī's claim is not strong enough to give one this conclusion, there is a strong temptation to see al-Ghazālī referring back to Avicenna's account of *tajriba* and not to his Ashʿarite predecessor, although I shall not insist upon this point.

he makes in his second approach, where he again takes up a variant of the same Avicennan objection, namely that occasionalism undermines the very possibility of science (*Tahāfut*, p. 178-179, §27). Again al-Ghazālī does not take the objection head on, but instead fleshes out the notion of impossibility (*muḥāl*), and thus by extension how one should understand possibility.[19]

The impossible, we are told, is

> the affirmation of something simultaneous with its denial, or the affirmation of the more specific simultaneous with the denial of the more general, or the affirmation of two things simultaneous with the denial of one, whereas whatever does not reduce to this, then is not impossible, and what is not impossible is [within God's] power (*Tahāfut*, p. 179, §29).

Despite the appearance of a standard Ashʿarite account of impossibility, when al-Ghazālī gives examples to clarify his meaning he goes further. For instance, he indicates that when a thing changes, there must be a common substrate, which he identifies with matter, and where there is no common matter, then a change from one thing to another is also impossible (*Tahāfut*, p. 180, §§35-36). Not only does this addition go beyond his initial account of impossibility, but also, as al-Ghazālī himself acknowledges, is at odds with the position of some of his fellow *mutakallimūn*. Thus, al-Ghazālī, in contrast to certain *mutakallimūn*, denies that it is possible for God to change something from one categorical genus to a different categorical genus (*Tahāfut*, p. 179-180, §§34-35). He gives as an example that not even God can turn blackness into a cooking pot; for there is no common matter to underlie the transition from one genus to the other.

The role matter plays in al-Ghazālī's notions of possibility and impossibility has far-reaching implications concerning his attitude towards occasionalism and account of miracles. For if traditional Islamic occasionalism is correct, then anything short of an impossibility, understood as concept incompatibility, falls within the scope of divine power; for instance, according to traditional Ashʿarite occasionalism it is possible that what at one moment was a piece of fruit God could in the next moment make to be a boy. Such a view is certainly what a traditional

[19] For a further elaboration of al-Ghazālī's view of modalities in the *Tahāfut* see T. KUKKONEN, *Possible Worlds in the* Tahāfut al-Falāsifa*: Al-Ghazālī on Creation and Contingency*, in: *Journal of the History of Philosophy* 38 (2000), p. 479-502; and B. DUTTON, *Al-Ghazālī on Possibility and the Critique of Causality*, in: *Medieval Philosophy and Theology* 10 (2001), p. 23-46. Both articles should be supplemented with Frank's comments in *Creation and the Cosmic System*, §4.

Ashʿarite *mutakallim* would want and expect from a fellow Ashʿarite; for it makes sensible the number of miracles described in the Koran, such as Moses' staff's being transformed into a serpent.

In contrast to the traditional Ashʿarite account of miracles, al-Ghazālī appeals to matter's receptivity to different forms, arguing that God can make the matter go through the discrete stages of a natural process in an imperceptible period of time:

> Likewise … the transformation of the staff into a serpent is possible in this way, namely that the matter is receptive of everything. Thus, earth and the rest of the elements undergo alteration into a plant, and the plant undergoes alteration, when animals eat [it], into blood, and then blood undergoes alteration into semen, and then the semen is made ready in the womb and so is changed into an animal, where this, in the judgment of custom, occurs over a long time. So why do the opponents make it impossible that within God's power the matter rotates through these stages in a time shorter than one is aware, and when it is possible in a shorter time, then nothing restrains it from being the shortest. Thus, these powers are accelerated in their action, and through [this process] the prophet's miracle happens (*Tahāfut*, p. 176, §19).

The view of substantial change al-Ghazālī presents here is essentially the view that Avicenna articulates in both his *Physics* and biological work, *The Book of Animals*.[20] Avicenna's view is that through a gradual process of alteration the material of a given substance is suitably prepared to receive a new substantial form, which emerges all at once. Thus, for example, when semen becomes a human, there are a number of discrete stages in the process, but during each stage the matter is gradually prepared such that it can take on another substantial form, which occurs in a punctuated leap (*ikhtilāja*). This position is just the one al-Ghazālī is putting forward, with the exception that al-Ghazālī makes it explicit that there is nothing that precludes this natural process, with its various discrete stages, from occurring at such an accelerated rate that the process is not observed. What is particularly noteworthy here is that nothing in al-Ghazālī's account of miracles requires a violation of the regular natural processes; they merely occur in a period of time that is so short that they go unnoticed. Indeed, al-Ghazālī goes as far as to say that miracles are consistent with science and the scientific method of induction:

[20] See AVICENNA, *Shifāʾ*: *Kitāb as-Samʿ al-Ṭabīʿī*, ed. S. ZAYED, Cairo, 1983, II, 3, p. 101.2-7; and *Shifāʾ*: *Kitāb al-Ḥayawān*, ed. A. MONTASIR, S. ZAYED and A. ISMĀʿĪL, Cairo, 1970, IX, 5, especially, p. 172.3-8 and p. 176.17-19.

> Who ever investigates the wonders of the sciences through induction, will not deem what is related of the prophets' miracles remote from the power of God in any way whatsoever (*Tahāfut*, p. 178, §25).

To summarize al-Ghazālī's first approach, it is primarily negative in that it shows that the philosophers have not demonstrated that there cannot be a volitional element in natural, causal processes nor that by introducing such a volitional element science needs be undermined. We have fleshed out these negative conclusions with some of al-Ghazālī's positive comments from his second approach, namely, the place of matter in assessing impossibility and possibility, as well as how miracles need not transgress the bounds of natural processes and yet still be miraculous. Two further points should be noted. First, nowhere has al-Ghazālī personally endorsed traditional Islamic occasionalism; the introduction of occasionalism only came in with the philosophers' objection that if volition is allowed a role in natural, causal processes, then any sort of random, arbitrary and disjointed conjunctions would occur, and so science would be impossible. Second, al-Ghazālī's response to this objection is not the traditional Ashʿarite response one might expect; rather, his response involves modifying both the notion of possibility and impossibility, and consequently how to understand the scope of divine power, as well as what constitutes a miracle. Without these very non-traditional modifications, the initial objection that traditional occasionalism makes science impossible still stands.

Having presented his first approach, he now considers a second, positive approach to responding to the philosophers' position. The philosophers' position again is that natural, sublunary causes prepare the matter such that it is receptive to a form emanated from a separate principle, which emanates the form necessarily and essentially without any volitional element. In response, al-Ghazālī writes:

> The second approach … is that we grant that the fire is created such that when two similar pieces of cotton come into contact with it, it ignites them and makes no distinction between them when they are similar in every respect; however, despite this, we allow a prophet's being flung into a fire and not being burned, either through a change of an attribute of the fire or a change of an attribute of the prophet. Thus, from either God or an angel there comes to be an attribute in the fire which restricts its heat to its body inasmuch as it does not go beyond it, and so its heat remains together with it, but is [still] according to the form (*ṣūra*) and true nature (*ḥaqīqa*) of fire; or there comes to be in the body of the prophet an attribute that does not exclude his being flesh and bone, but repels the influence of the fire (*Tahāfut*, p. 175, §18).

The demonstration that underwrites the philosophers' claim to causal necessity is again Avicenna's second proof presented in the first section. The argument in a nutshell was that if one assumes the absence of burning under the conditions that something with the actual power to burn is in contact with something with the actual power to be burned, then a contradiction follows. As a direct response to Avicenna's argument, al-Ghazālī's position, if taken at face value, is a non starter. It assumes, in the case of fire, that there can be the form and true nature of fire and yet the fire not burn; however, on the common philosophical analysis of natures to burn just is the specific activity of the form of fire. To be fire is to have the specific activity of burning under the proper conditions. In other words, if an instance of the substance fire is stripped of its power to burn, then it is only homonymously fire, but in fact is no longer the substance fire, just as a corpse is not in fact a human, but only homonymously a human. In effect, al-Ghazālī's argument has only claimed that what is no longer essentially fire need not burn, and this claim of course the philosophers would accept. What they will not take as proven is that in the actual presence of fire and a properly disposed material, the effect will not necessarily follow.

I think that there is a way to reconstruct al-Ghazālī's position that in fact gives it more bite. There are two advantages to the interpretation I shall offer. First, it provides al-Ghazālī with a stronger argument in the present context than is immediately apparent. Second, it gives a principled means of explaining al-Ghazālī's frequent shifts between occasionalistic and natural, causal language both within the *Tahāfut* and other works rather than having to treat each instance on an *ad hoc* basis so as to harmonize it with either a purely occasionalistic or natural, causal interpretation.

I submit that al-Ghazālī has a new interpretation of natures at play. On the standard reading of natures as found in Aristotle's *Physics* II, natural things have both an active nature, which is identified with the thing's form, and a passive nature, which is identified with the thing's material. Thus, if we consider, for example, a piece of cotton's burning, the cotton, *qua* the material nature, has the passive power to be burned, whereas, fire, *qua* the formal nature, has the *active* power to burn. In contrast, I suggest that al-Ghazālī construes both formal and material natures as passive, i.e., the cotton has the passive power to be burned and the fire has the *passive power* to burn: in other words, the fire only burns once another cause actualizes the fire's passive power to burn, such that it then has the active power to burn. Once the fire's passive power to burn is actualized, the fire of itself actualizes the cotton's passive power to be burned, such that there is burning; however, there still must be an additional cause other than either the fire or cotton that actualizes the fire's passive power to burn. This additional cause on the present interpretation cannot act on account of a nature; for since all natures are passive on this interpretation, there would need to be yet another cause, and so on *ad infinitum*, should one only appeal to things acting through their natures. The way to avoid the regress is to appeal to a cause that does not act by nature, but acts by volition or will, which is exactly what al-Ghazālī wants to show.

The argument that I am suggesting al-Ghazālī adopts is analogous to Avicenna's first proof for necessary, causal relations. Al-Ghazālī needs just to replace Avicenna's 'possible in itself' with 'passive natures' and Avicenna's 'necessary' with 'voluntary'. All natural processes, then, must terminate in a cause that does not itself act through a nature, but acts through volition, otherwise, just as in Avicenna's argument, an infinite regress of causes, now acting only through their natures, would result. Indeed, part of the process of converting Avicenna's first argument to one in terms of willful agents was already undertaken by al-Ghazālī's teacher, al-Juwaynī, in his *Kitāb al-Irshād*, albeit in a different context:

> When something required in addition to the atom (*jawhar*) is affirmed and it is determined that it is different from the [atom], then either it is a choosing agent (*fāʿil mukhtār*) or it is a necessitating account (*maʿnā mūjib*). If it is a necessitating account, then its bringing about the subsistence of the atom specific in its respect is particular [to it alone], since if the specificity it has were not through it, then the status it has through its necessitating would be no more fitting than its necessitating any other.[21]

Whereas al-Juwaynī took this argument to show that for any given effect the cause can only be a willful agent, namely, God, al-Ghazālī sees the argument's conclusion as more modest, namely, a willful agent must always be present in any causal nexus. Such a conclusion does not preclude other non-willing causes as being part of the nexus, merely that no natural causal process will be totally devoid of some cause acting through volition. Indeed, al-Ghazālī suggest as much in his *Iḥyāʾ ʿUlūm al-Dīn*, *Kitāb al-Tawḥīd wa-l-Tawakkul*:

> Whenever the will (*al-mashīʾa*), which turns (*taṣrifu*) the power to [the power's] potential object (*maqdūri-hā*), exists, then the power is inevitably

[21] AL-JUWAYNĪ, *Irshād*, p. 19.

> turned (*inṣarafat*), having no means to do differently. Thus, through the power the motion necessarily follows, and the power is necessarily moved together with the determination of the will.[22]

Here the verb *ṣarafa, yaṣrifu*, and the seventh form *inṣarafa, yanṣarifu*, have the sense of 'to turn something from one state to another', where I suggest that the power is turned from a passive state to an active state through the actualisation of the willful agent.[23]

The present model of al-Ghazālī's account of causal powers has the advantage of explaining his frequent occasionalistic language; for all events do require an act of volition, whether on the part of God or an angelic intermediary. Moreover, this interpretation likewise explains al-Ghazālī's natural, causal language; for it is the causal natures within things that act and bring about their effects, albeit only together with an act of divine or angelic volition. More immediately, the suggested interpretation makes sense of al-Ghazālī's second approach in light of the objection presented above. Again the objection was that on the standard understanding of natures it is inconsistent for al-Ghazālī to claim that fire can retain its form and true nature and yet have its heat restricted such that it does not burn; for to burn, on the traditional reading of natures, just is the specific, defining act of fire. If, as the present interpretation suggests, the form and true nature of fire is not to have the *active* power to burn, but to have the *passive* power to burn, then even in the case where fire's heat is restricted it is still fire; for it still possesses the form of fire *qua* passive power to burn.

Again, al-Ghazālī's overall concern in the Seventeenth Discussion, I contend, is to harmonize natural, causal processes' having an element of volition with the possibility of science, understood as knowing that certain causal relations obtain and that those relations are necessary. I have suggested in what sense al-Ghazālī might believe these causal relations obtain. What is left is to explain in what sense one can know that these relations are necessary. Clearly, the relation cannot be necessary by nature or essentially; for the inclusion of volition precludes just this type of necessity. Still, there is another sense of necessity that al-Ghazālī can appeal to and which yet does not undermine the role of volition in natural, causal processes.[24]

[22] AL-GHAZĀLĪ, *Iḥyā'*: *Kitāb al-Tawḥīd wa-l-Tawakkul*, ed. A. KHĀLIDĪ, IV, Beirut, 1998, p. 331.

[23] See Lane, *Lexicon*, s.v.

[24] The notion of necessity I am ascribing to al-Ghazālī relies heavily upon Frank's careful analysis in *Creation and the Cosmic System*, §§4.2-4.3, p. 52-77.

To make clear the type of necessity that I believe that al-Ghazālī has in mind, let us consider an example taken from human actions. I have a certain end I want to accomplish, for instance, to be a good husband. In order to achieve this end, there are a number of things I must either do or not do, such as be faithful, spend time with my wife and the like. Clearly, it is within the scope of my power to choose to be unfaithful or spend all my time at the office and never at home with my wife; however, I cannot choose both to be a good husband and to do these latter actions. There are certain things that I must do of necessity, if I am to be a good husband, but such necessity does not violate my power to choose, i.e., my having other possibilities open to me that I choose not to realise. Indeed, in a sense the very fact that I have other possibilities open to me that I do not chose, is part of my being a good husband.

The case is similar for God, whose design as a measure of His liberality and justice is that His creation be good (perhaps even the best). In order to ensure this order of the good, God must of necessity make actual certain possibilities, where the possibilities that he actualizes just are the natural, causal processes one constantly experiences. Such a necessity, one must note, in no way puts God under compulsion, even if God acts in a given way necessarily. Frank finds this notion of necessity in later theological writings by al-Ghazālī;[25] however, it is already implicit in the *Tahāfut*, where al-Ghazālī states with respect to miracles that in addition to the matter's being properly prepared, the miracle must also further the order of the good (*niẓām al-khayr*):

> The moment demanding (*istiḥqāq*) the occurrence of [miraculous events] is [when] the prophet's attention is devoted to them and the order of the good is obvious in their appearance in order for the divine law to continue. Hence, that [i.e., the order of the good] is something selectively determining (*murajjiḥ*) on the side of existence, where the event (*shay'*) in itself is possible and the principle is munificent and generous through [the event]. The event does not emanate from it, however, except when the need selectively determines its existence and the good becomes obvious in it. The good, though, does not become obvious in it, except when a prophet, in establishing his prophethood, needs it in order to emanate the good (*Tahāfut*, p. 176, §21).

The most relevant point for our purposes is that even miracles are the result of a certain necessity, namely, what is necessary for the order of the good, and so *a fortiori* mundane, natural processes will be neces-

[25] Among Frank's many reference two are indicative of the general trend: AL-GHAZĀLĪ, *Iḥyā'*, I, Cairo, 1957, p. 90, and IV, p. 249 f.

sary for this order as well. One further note, although this passage, taken in isolation, suggests that God might bring about a certain event in a manner outside the natural order of causal processes, the immediately preceding context indicates otherwise. For al-Ghazālī observes that even the philosophers allow that prophets might bring about certain unexpected meteorological events, albeit in a way that is consistent with the orderly procession of natural, causal processes. In short, all natural, causal processes are necessary, namely, necessary for the order of the good established by God, and such a necessity in no way undermines a place for volition in the causal nexus. Consequently, for al-Ghazālī one can know that certain natural, causal relations obtain and that these relations are necessary. Thus one can have scientific knowledge despite the inclusion of volition in the causal nexus, the proof of which was al-Ghazālī's primary intention in the Seventeenth Discussion.[26]

AL-GHAZĀLĪ ON NATURAL EFFICIENT CAUSATION IN CERTAIN THEOLOGICAL WORKS

The teleological necessity discussed above has been well documented by Frank, and I let his comments suffice. In contrast, the modified occasionalism that I have suggested above has not been documented, and so I want to consider further implicit expressions of it in some of al-Ghazālī's theological manuals, of which I merely mention certain passages from *al-Maqṣad al-Asnā*[27] and *al-Iqtiṣād fī l-Iʿtiqād*.[28]

[26] Although this teleological account of necessity can ground the necessity of causal processes in the cosmos, it is not immediately clear how it can underwrite the necessity of scientific demonstrations. For no term can appear in the conclusion of a demonstrative syllogism that is not contained in its premises, and yet in most cases of scientific demonstrations neither God nor the order of the good appear as terms in the initial premises. Al-Ghazālī seems to be aware of this difficulty and so in *Miyʿār al-ʿIlm* he grounds the necessity of scientific demonstrations on logical necessity in a way very much like the hypothetical-deductive model of scientific explanation put forth by Twentieth Century philosophers of science. Briefly, the idea is that the major premise will state a causal law that is a generalization of the form 'all M are P', the minor premise will be some empirical observation of the form 'S is M' from which it follows of *logical necessity* that 'S is P'. See MARMURA, *Ghazali and Demonstrative Science*, for further details. One should note, though, that what ultimately grounds the major premise's generalisation, and so gives the demonstration its ontological import, is teleological necessity.

[27] AL-GHAZĀLĪ, *Al-Maqṣad al-Asnā fī Sharḥ Maʿānī Asmāʾ Allāh al-Ḥusnā*, ed. F.A. SHEHADI, Beirut, 1986.

[28] AL-GHAZĀLĪ, *Al-Iqtiṣād fī l-Iʿtiqād*, Cairo, 1966.

The first instance I shall consider is a frequent analogy Ghazālī gives between God and light. The analogy, I contend, must be placed within its proper historical and scientific context in order to be appreciated fully. Al-Ghazālī provides a detailed description of the analogy in the *Maqṣad* during his discussion of the name *al-ẓāhir*, the Manifest.[29] God is likened to light not only in that light is the most manifest, but also that through light everything else becomes manifest. Here a fuller understanding of ancient and medieval theory of sight gives us a better purchase on understanding the analogy. According to these theories, sight required more than simply having a properly functioning organ of sight, i.e., something with the power to see, and an object of sight, i.e., something with the power to be seen. In addition, there had to be light that acts in such a way as to make the medium transparent, and thus make what was only potentially visible actually visible and what was only potentially seeing actually seeing. Moreover, light is necessary at every moment there is sight, that is, as long as there is the actualization of both the power to see and the power to be seen, then light is present. Although I shall not push this analogy too far, it is noteworthy that al-Ghazālī would not have been ignorant of this scientific point concerning light and sight, and it exactly maps onto the account of efficient causation I have suggested.

Two further pieces of evidence can be found in the *Maqṣad* in al-Ghazālī's discussion of the name *al-ḥāfiẓ*, the Mindful or the Preserver.[30] Here al-Ghazālī talks directly about God's relation to the inanimate elements — earth, air, fire and water — that make up composites in the sublunar realm. Again, using ancient and medieval scientific theories to flesh out al-Ghazālī's claims, associated with each element are two powers, one active and one passive, which are themselves taken from two sets of basic contraries: hot/cold (active powers) and wet/dry (passive powers). Thus, earth has the powers cold/dry, water cold/wet, air hot/wet and fire hot/dry. Now, observes al-Ghazālī, these powers are mutually destructive — for heat destroys cold and wet destroys dry and *vice versa*; however, since composite bodies are a properly proportioned mixture of all these elements with their mutually destructive powers, if these powers considered in themselves were fully actualised, then bodies should not be able to cohere, but be rent asunder by the mutually destructive powers. The reason that bodies do cohere, according to al-

[29] AL-GHAZĀLĪ, *Maqṣad*, p. 147-149.
[30] AL-GHAZĀLĪ, *Maqṣad*, p. 119-122.

Ghazālī, is that God moderates the various powers respectively. To put it in terms of my thesis, God only actualizes the inherent passive powers of the elements of composite things to the extent that is needed for there to be a balance such that the composite is well constituted.

Moreover, in this same section, al-Ghazālī also considers a water drop's hanging from a finger tip. The nature of the water is such that it should fall, and yet if it falls while still very small, the ambient air would destroy it and change it into air. What one experiences, though, is that the drop of water remains on the finger tip until it is large enough to drop through the air without being destroyed and transformed into air:

> Concerning [the drop of water], that is not a preservation belonging to it of itself from knowing its weakness and its contrary's power and [knowing] its need to draw upon the remaining moisture; that is only a preservation from an angel put in charge over it through the intermediacy of an account that is a capacity of the being of [the drop of water] itself (*yatamakkanu min dhāti-hā*).[31]

Once more, I shall not make too much of this example, but it is suggestive. Here al-Ghazālī claims that it belongs to the very nature of the water to fall and yet that power is only actualised through the operation of a willful agent in conjunction with an account (*maʿnā*) that belongs to the water itself. Again, the example perfectly maps onto the suggested model of efficient causation.

I take the final piece of evidence from al-Ghazālī's *Iqtiṣād*, which is paralleled in less detail in the *Kitāb Qawāʿid al-ʿAqāʾid* of the *Iḥyāʾ*, and its discussion of divine power and the power of creatures with its accompanying discussion of *kasb*, acquisition or performance.[32] In this discussion al-Ghazālī adjudicates between two competing theories concerning the power of creatures, namely, the determinists (*mujbira*), who deny creatures have any power, and the Muʿtazilites, who assert that certain creatures have active causal powers, which act without the direct influence of God. Al-Ghazālī sees himself holding a middle position between these two extremes:

> The truth is only to assert two powers over a single act and to defend a potential (*maqdūr*) related to two powers. So nothing remains but the apparent improbability of two powers coinciding over a single act, which is improbable only when the connection of the two powers is according to

[31] AL-GHAZĀLĪ, *Maqṣad*, p. 122.

[32] AL-GHAZĀLĪ, *Iqtiṣād*, p. 45-49; *Iḥyāʾ*: *Kitāb Qawāʿid al-ʿAqāʾid*, ed. A. KHĀLIDĪ, I, Beirut, 1998, p. 166-167.

> one [and the same] mode. Thus, if the two powers differ and the mode of their connection is different, then the coinciding of two powers over a single thing is not impossible, as we shall make clear.[33]

I simply note that for al-Ghazālī a certain potential (*maqdūr*), i.e. the object of power (*qudra*), is the object of two powers, one belonging to God and the other to creatures, where the two powers are related to the action according to two distinct modes. I submit that the different modes are just power considered as actualized by God, and power considered as passive, belonging to the creatures themselves. Unfortunately, al-Ghazālī does not provide a positive account of what the different modes exactly are, but only a negative account denying certain possible connections proposed by the Muʿtazilites. Still, even his negative comments are telling.

According to the Muʿtazilites as presented by al-Ghazālī

> the relation of the power and the potential are only intelligible inasmuch as there is the production of an effect (*al-ta'thīr*), and the bringing into existence and the determinate occurrence of the potential through [the power] (*ījād wa-ḥuṣūl al-maqdūr bi-hi*) (*Iʿtiqād*, p. 48).

Al-Ghazālī adds that for the Muʿtazilites this relation can only be that of an (actual) causal power to its effect. Al-Ghazālī responds in a way analogous to the traditional Ashʿarite argument against created things' having a capacity (*istiṭāʿa*); however, I suggest that in al-Ghazālī's hands the argument is no longer directed at powers or capacities absolutely understood, but only at active causal powers, not passive powers. Thus, the argument runs: if created things had active causal powers, then they would always be necessitating their effects and one could not explain how they sometimes act, while at other times do not act. In contrast, we should note, if created things only had passive powers, then they would only necessitate their effects when God, or some angelic intermediary, actualized that power, and otherwise not.[34]

[33] AL-GHAZĀLĪ, *Iqtiṣād*, p. 46-47. For an alternative interpretation of the arguments to be considered here see MARMURA, *Ghazali's Chapter on Divine Power in the* Iqtiṣād, which provides a detailed analysis and translation of this chapter.

[34] The Ashʿarites' initial concern that non-acting capacities or powers would imply the contradiction that something presently exists that does not presently exist was addressed by the philosophers' gloss on the notion of potentiality. Potentiality for philosophers such as Avicenna was not viewed as simply a possibility, but was explained in terms of matter's preparedness. Thus a potentiality refers not to a presently non-existing possibility, but to the actually present structure of a thing, where that structure is predisposed to being acted upon by an actually existing cause.

This interpretation has the added benefit of also explaining the traditional doctrine of *kasb*, or how it is that created things can be said to acquire or perform their respective actions without appealing to the *ad hoc bi-lā kayf* of al-Ashʿarī. When a created thing's passive power to act has been actualised, then the action follows of necessity from the actualised power. Thus in a real sense the created thing acquires or performs its actions, since it is the immediate source of the action. The action belongs to the created thing as the created thing's own effect, not simply *bi-lā kayf*.

A detailed account of this chapter is beyond the purview of the present study, but I do hope to have sketched out a way of reading al-Ghazālī's account of power and potency in the *Iqtiṣād* that is consistent as well as consonant with his other claims concerning causal efficacy. Likewise I hope that this sampling of passages from some of al-Ghazālī's theological works provides some evidence that al-Ghazālī was not a traditional Islamic occasionalist, but a modified occasionalist, allowing to a certain degree natural, secondary causation similar to the medieval Arabic philosophers' view.

In conclusion, the modified occasionalism which I have ascribed to al-Ghazālī, on the one hand, gives voice to the Ashʿarite belief that all processes result from an act of divine (or perhaps angelic) volition, and so (contrary to the philosophers) the world is not a closed, deterministic system, where events issue forth necessarily and essentially from the natures of created things and their principles. All natures for al-Ghazālī, I suggest, are passive powers, whether as a passive power to act or to be acted on, and insofar as they are passive they require something that actualizes them as a matter of volition. On the other hand, al-Ghazālī's modified occasionalism upholds the belief that one can and does have knowledge of necessary, causal relations, and thus fulfills the requirements of the philosophical definition of science. The necessity in question, however, is not a necessity that flows mechanically from causal natures, but one that makes room for volition, and yet this volitional element in no way undermines the causal efficacy of natural things. The fire's power to burn is in fact the cause of the cotton's burning, once the fire's passive power to burn has been actualized by a willful agent, either directly on the part of God or through some angelic intermediary.

ORIENTALIA LOVANIENSIA ANALECTA

1. E. LIPIŃSKI, Studies in Aramaic Inscriptions and Onomastics I.
2. J. QUAEGEBEUR, Le dieu égyptien Shaï dans la religion et l'onomastique.
3. P.H.L. EGGERMONT, Alexander's Campaigns in Sind and Baluchistan and the Siege of the Brahmin Town of Harmatelia.
4. W.M. CALLEWAERT, The Sarvāṅgī of the Dādūpanthī Rajab.
5. E. LIPIŃSKI (ed.), State and Temple Economy in the Ancient Near East I.
6. E. LIPIŃSKI (ed.), State and Temple Economy in the Ancient Near East II.
7. M.-C. DE GRAEVE, The Ships of the Ancient Near East (c. 2000-500 B.C.).
8. W.M. CALLEWAERT (ed.), Early Hindī Devotional Literature in Current Research.
9. F.L. DAMEN, Crisis and Religious Renewal in the Brahmo Samaj Movement (1860-1884).
10. R.Y. EBIED - A. VAN ROEY - L.R. WICKHAM, Peter of Callinicum, Anti-Tritheist Dossier.
11. A. RAMMANT-PEETERS, Les pyramidions égyptiens du Nouvel Empire.
12. S. SCHEERS (ed.), Studia Paulo Naster Oblata I. Numismatica Antiqua.
13. J. QUAEGEBEUR (ed.), Studia Paulo Naster Oblata II. Orientalia Antiqua.
14. E. PLATTI, Yaḥyā ibn ʿAdī, théologien chrétien et philosophe arabe.
15. E. GUBEL - E. LIPIŃSKI - B. SERVAIS-SOYEZ (eds.), Studia Phoenicia I-II.
16. W. SKALMOWSKI - A. VAN TONGERLOO (ed.), Middle Iranian Studies.
17. M. VAN MOL, Handboek Modern Arabisch.
18. C. LAGA - J.A. MUNITIZ - L. VAN ROMPAY (eds.), After Chalcedon. Studies in Theology and Church History.
19. E. LIPIŃSKI (ed.), The Land of Israel: Cross-Roads of Civilizations.
20. S. WACHSMANN, Aegeans in the Theban Tombs.
21. K. VAN LERBERGHE, Old Babylonian Legal and Administrative Texts from Philadelphia.
22. E. LIPIŃSKI (ed.), Phoenicia and the East Mediterranean in the First Millennium B.C.
23. M. HELTZER - E. LIPIŃSKI (eds.), Society and Economy in the Eastern Mediterranean (1500-1000 B.C.).
24. M. VAN DE MIEROOP, Crafts in the Early Isin Period.
25. G. POLLET (ed.), India and the Ancient World.
26. E. LIPIŃSKI (ed.), Carthago.
27. E. VERREET, Modi Ugaritici.
28. R. ZADOK, The Pre-Hellenistic Israelite Anthroponomy and Prosopography.
29. W. CALLEWAERT - M. LATH, The Hindī Songs of Nāmdev.
30. A. SHISHA-HALEVY, Coptic Grammatical Chrestomathy.
31. N. BAUM, Arbres et arbustes de l'Égypte ancienne.
32. J.-M. KRUCHTEN, Les Annales des prêtres de Karnak.
33. H. DEVIJVER - E. LIPIŃSKI (eds.), Punic Wars.
34. E. VASSILIKA, Ptolemaic Philae.
35. A. GHAITH, La Pensée Religieuse chez Ǧubrân Ḫalil Ǧubrân et Miḫâʾîl Nuʿayma.
36. N. BEAUX, Le Cabinet de curiosités de Thoutmosis III.
37. G. POLLET - P. EGGERMONT - G. VAN DAMME, Archaeological Sites of Ancient India.
38. S.-A. NAGUIB, Le Clergé féminin d'Amon thébain à la 21e dynastie.
39. U. VERHOEVEN - E. GRAEFE (eds.), Religion und Philosophie im Alten Ägypten.
40. A.R. GEORGE, Babylonian Topographical Texts.
41. A. SCHOORS, The Preacher Sought to Find Pleasing Words. Part I.
42. G. REININK - H.E.J. VAN STIPHOUT (eds.), Dispute Poems and Dialogues in the Ancient and Mediaeval Near East.

43. C. TRAUNECKER, Coptos. Hommes et dieux sur le parvis de Geb.
44. E. LIPIŃSKI (ed.), Phoenicia and the Bible.
45. L. ISEBAERT (ed.), Studia Etymologica Indoeuropaea Memoriae A.J. Van Windekens dicata.
46. F. BRIQUEL-CHATONNET, Les relations entre les cités de la côte phénicienne et les royaumes d'Israël et de Juda.
47. W.J. VAN BEKKUM, A Hebrew Alexander Romance according to MS London, Jews' College no. 145.
48. W. SKALMOWSKI - A. VAN TONGERLOO (eds.), Medioiranica.
49. L. LAUWERS, Igor'-Severjanin, His Life and Work — The Formal Aspects of His Poetry.
50. R.L. VOS, The Apis Embalming Ritual. P. Vindob. 3873.
51. Fr. LABRIQUE, Stylistique et Théologie à Edfou. Le rituel de l'offrande de la campagne: étude de la composition.
52. F. DE JONG (ed.), Miscellanea Arabica et Islamica.
53. G. BREYER, Etruskisches Sprachgut im Lateinischen unter Ausschluß des spezifisch onomastischen Bereiches.
54. P.H.L. EGGERMONT, Alexander's Campaign in Southern Punjab.
55. J. QUAEGEBEUR (ed.), Ritual and Sacrifice in the Ancient Near East.
56. A. VAN ROEY - P. ALLEN, Monophysite Texts of the Sixth Century.
57. E. LIPIŃSKI, Studies in Aramaic Inscriptions and Onomastics II.
58. F.R. HERBIN, Le livre de parcourir l'éternité.
59. K. GEUS, Prosopographie der literarisch bezeugten Karthager.
60. A. SCHOORS - P. VAN DEUN (eds.), Philohistor. Miscellanea in honorem Caroli Laga septuagenarii.
61. M. KRAUSE - S. GIVERSEN - P. NAGEL (eds.), Coptology. Past, Present and Future. Studies in Honour of R. Kasser.
62. C. LEITZ, Altägyptische Sternuhren.
63. J.J. CLÈRE, Les Chauves d'Hathor.
64. E. LIPIŃSKI, Dieux et déesses de l'univers phénicien et punique.
65. K. VAN LERBERGHE - A. SCHOORS (eds.), Immigration and Emigration within the Ancient Near East. Festschrift E. Lipiński.
66. G. POLLET (ed.), Indian Epic Values. *Rāmāyaṇa* and its impact.
67. D. DE SMET, La quiétude de l'Intellect. Néoplatonisme et gnose ismaélienne dans l'œuvre de Ḥamîd ad-Dîn al-Kirmânî (Xe-XIe s.).
68. M.L. FOLMER, The Aramaic Language in the Achaemenid Period. A Study in Linguistic Variation.
69. S. IKRAM, Choice Cuts: Meat Production in Ancient Egypt.
70. H. WILLEMS, The Coffin of Heqata (Cairo JdE 36418). A Case Study of Egyptian Funerary Culture of the Early Middle Kingdom.
71. C. EDER, Die Ägyptischen Motive in der Glyptik des Östlichen Mittelmeerraumes zu Anfang des 2. Jts. v. Chr.
72. J. THIRY, Le Sahara libyen dans l'Afrique du Nord médiévale.
73. U. VERMEULEN - D. DE SMET (eds.), Egypt and Syria in the Fatimid, Ayyubid and Mamluk Eras. Proceedings of the 1st, 2nd and 3rd International Colloquium organized at the Katholieke Universiteit Leuven in May 1992, 1993 and 1994.
74. P. ARÈNES, La déesse Sgrol-Ma (Tara). Recherches sur la nature et le statut d'une divinité du bouddhisme tibétain.
75. K. CIGGAAR - A. DAVIDS - H. TEULE (eds.), East and West in the Crusader States. Context - Contacts - Confrontations. Acta of the Congress Held at Hernen Castle in May 1993.
76. M. BROZE, Mythe et Roman en Egypte ancienne. Les Aventures d'Horus et Seth dans le papyrus Chester Beatty I.
77. L. DEPUYDT, Civil Calendar and Lunar Calendar in Ancient Egypt.
78. P. WILSON, A Ptolemaic Lexikon. A Lexicographical Study of the Texts in the Temple of Edfu.
79. A. HASNAWI - A. ELAMRANI - M. JAMAL - M. AOUAD (eds.), Perspectives arabes et médiévales sur le tradition scientifique et philosophique grecque.

80. E. LIPIŃSKI, Semitic Languages: Outline of a Comparative Grammar.
81. S. CAUVILLE, Dendara I. Traduction.
82. C. EYRE (ed.), Proceedings of the Seventh International Congress of Egyptologists.
83. U. VERMEULEN - D. DE SMET (eds.), Egypt and Syria in the Fatimid, Ayyubid and Mamluk Eras II.
84-85. W. CLARYSSE - A. SCHOORS - H. WILLEMS (eds.), Egyptian Religion. The Last Thousand Years.
86. U. VERMEULEN - J.M. VAN REETH (eds.), Law, Christianity and Modernism in Islamic Society.
87. D. DE SMET - U. VERMEULEN (eds.), Philosophy and Acts in the Islamic World Proceedings of the Eighteenth Congress of the Union européenne des Arabisants et Islamisants held at the Katholieke Universiteit Leuven.
88. S. CAUVILLE, Dendara II. Traduction.
89. G.J. REININK - A.C. KLUGKIST (eds.), After Bardaisan. Studies on Continuity and Change in Syriac Christianity in Honour of Professor Han J.W. Drijvers.
90. C.R. KRAHMALKOV, Phoenician-Punic Dictionary.
91. M. TAHTAH, Entre pragmatisme, réformisme et modernisme. Le rôle politico-religieux des Khattabi dans le Rif (Maroc) jusqu'à 1926.
92. K. CIGGAAR - H. TEULE (eds.), East and West in the Crusader States. Context — Contact — Confrontations II. Acta of the Congress held at Hernen Castle, the Netherlands, in May 1997.
93. A.C.J. VERHEIJ, Bits, Bytes, and Binyanim. A Quantitative Study of Verbal Lexeme Formations in the Hebrew Bible.
94. W.M. CALLEWAERT - D. TAILLIEU - F. LALEMAN, A Descriptive Bibliography of Allama Muhammad Iqbal (1877-1938).
95. S. CAUVILLE, Dendara III. Traduction.
96. K. VAN LERBERGHE - G. VOET (eds.), Languages and Cultures in Contact: At the Crossroads of Civilizations in the Syro-Mesopotamian Realm.
97. A. CABROL, Les voies processionnelles de Thèbes.
98. J. PATRICH, The Sabaite Heritage in the Orthodox Church from the Fifth Century to the Present. Monastic Life, Liturgy, Theology, Literature, Art, Archaeology.
99. U. VERHOEVEN, Untersuchungen zur Späthieratischen Buchschrift.
100. E. LIPIŃSKI, The Aramaeans: Their Ancient History, Culture, Religion.
101. S. CAUVILLE, Dendara IV. Traduction.
102. U. VERMEULEN - J. VAN STEENBERGEN (eds.), Egypt and Syria in the Fatimid, Ayyubid and Mamluk Eras.
103. H. WILLEMS (ed.), Social Aspects of Funerary Culture in the Egyptian Old and Middle Kingdoms.
104. K. GEUS - K. ZIMMERMANN (eds.), Punica — Libyca — Ptolemaica. Festschrift für Werner Huß, zum 65. Geburtstag dargebracht von Schülern, Freunden und Kollegen.
105. S. CAUVILLE, Dendara. Les fêtes d'Hathor.
106. R. PREYS, Les complexes de la demeure du sistre et du trône de Rê. Théologie et décoration dans le temple d'Hathor à Dendera.
107. A. BLASIUS - B.U. SCHIPPER (eds.), Apokalyptik und Ägypten. Eine kritische Analyse der relevanten Texte aus dem griechisch-römischen Ägypten.
108. S. LEDER (ed.), Studies in Arabic and Islam.
109. A. GODDEERIS, Economy and Society in Northern Babylonia in the Early Old Babylonian Period (ca. 2000-1800 BC).
110. C. LEITZ (ed.), Lexikon der ägyptischen Götter und Götterbezeichnungen, Band I.
111. C. LEITZ (ed.), Lexikon der ägyptischen Götter und Götterbezeichnungen, Band II.
112. C. LEITZ (ed.), Lexikon der ägyptischen Götter und Götterbezeichnungen, Band III.

113. C. LEITZ (ed.), Lexikon der ägyptischen Götter und Götterbezeichnungen, Band IV.
114. C. LEITZ (ed.), Lexikon der ägyptischen Götter und Götterbezeichnungen, Band V.
115. C. LEITZ (ed.), Lexikon der ägyptischen Götter und Götterbezeichnungen, Band VI.
116. C. LEITZ (ed.), Lexikon der ägyptischen Götter und Götterbezeichnungen, Band VII.
117. M. VAN MOL, Variation in Modern Standard Arabic in Radio News Broadcasts.
118. M.F.J. BAASTEN - W.Th VAN PEURSEN (eds.), Hamlet on a Hill. Semitic and Greek Studies Presented to Professor T. Muraoka on the Occasion of his Sixty-Fifth Birthday.
119. O.E. KAPER, The Egyptian God Tutu. A Study of the Sphinx-God and Master of Demons with a Corpus of Monuments.
120. E. WARDINI, Lebanese Place-Names (Mount Lebanon and North Lebanon).
121. J. VAN DER VLIET, Catalogue of the Coptic Inscriptions in the Sudan National Museum at Khartoum (I. Khartoum Copt).
122. A. ŁAJTAR, Catalogue of the Greek Inscriptions in the Sudan National Museum at Khartoum (I. Khartoum Greek).
123. H. NIEHR, Ba'alšamem. Studien zu Herkunft, Geschichte und Rezeptionsgeschichte eines phönizischen Gottes.
124. H. WILLEMS - F. COPPENS - M. DE MEYER - P. DILS, The Temple of Shanhûr. Volume I : The Sanctuary, The *Wabet*, and the Gates of the Central Hall and the Great Vestibule (1-98).
125. K. CIGGAAR - H.G.B. TEULE (eds.), East and West in the Crusader States. Context – Contacts – Confrontations III.
126. T. SOLDATJENKOVA - E. WAEGEMANS (eds.), For East is East. Liber Amicorum Wojciech Skalmowski.
127. E. LIPIŃSKI, Itineraria Phoenicia.
128. D. BUDDE, S. SANDRI, U. VERHOEVEN (eds.), Kindgötter im Ägypten der griechisch-römischen Zeit. Zeugnisse aus Stadt und Tempel als Spiegel des Interkulturellen Kontakts.
129. C. LEITZ (ed.), Lexikon der ägyptischen Götter und Götterbezeichnungen, Band VIII.
130. E.J. VAN DER STEEN, Tribes and Territories in Transition.
131. S. CAUVILLE, Dendara V-VI. Traduction. Les cryptes du temple d'Hathor.
132. S. CAUVILLE, Dendara V-VI. Index phraséologique. Les cryptes du temple d'Hathor.
133. M. IMMERZEEL, J. VAN DER VLIET, M. KERSTEN, C. VAN ZOEST (eds.), Coptic Studies on the Threshold of a New Millennium. Proceedings of the Seventh International Congress of Coptic Studies. Leiden, August 27 - September 2, 2000.
134. J.J. VAN GINKEL, H.L. MURRE-VAN DEN BERG, T.M. VAN LINT (eds.), Redefining Christian Identity. Cultural Interaction in the Middle East since the Rise of Islam.
135. J. MONTGOMERY (ed.), 'Abbasid Studies. Occasional Papers of the School of 'Abbasid Studies, Cambridge, 6-10 July 2002.
136. T. BOIY, Late Achaemenid and Hellenistic Babylon.
137. B. JANSSENS, B. ROOSEN, P. VAN DEUN (eds.), Philomathestatos. Studies in Greek Patristic and Byzantine Texts Presented to Jacques Noret for his Sixty-Fifth Birthday.
138. S. HENDRICKX, R.F. FRIEDMAN, K.M. CIAŁOWICZ, M. CHŁODNICKI (eds.), Egypt at its Origins. Studies in Memory of Barbara Adams.
139. R. ARNZEN, J. THIELMANN (eds.), Words, Texts and Concepts Cruising the Mediterranean Sea. Studies on the Sources, Contents and Influences of Islamic Civilization and Arabic Philosophy and Science.

140. U. VERMEULEN, J. VAN STEENBERGEN (eds.), Egypt and Syria in the Fatimid, Ayyubid and Mamluk Eras IV.
141. H.T. DAVIES, Yūsuf al-Shirbīnī's Kitāb Hazz al-Qūḥuf bi-Sharḥ Qaṣīd Abī Shādūf.
142. P. VAN NUFFELEN, Un héritage de paix et de piété. Étude sur les histoires ecclésiastiques de Socrate et de Sozomène.
143. A. SCHOORS, The Preacher Sought to Find Pleasing Words II. A Study of the Language of Qoheleth. Part II: Vocabulary.
144. M.E. STONE, Apocrypha, Pseudepigrapha and Armenian Studies. Collected Papers: Volume 1.
145. M.E. STONE, Apocrypha, Pseudepigrapha and Armenian Studies. Collected Papers: Volume 2.
146. M. CACOUROS, M.-H. CONGOURDEAU (eds.), Philosophie et sciences à Byzance de 1204 à 1453. Les textes, les doctrines et leur transmission.
147. K. CIGGAAR, M. METCALF (eds.), East and West in the Medieval Eastern Mediterranean I.
148. B. MICHALAK-PIKULSKA, A. PIKULSKI (eds.), Authority, Privacy and Public Order in Islam.
149. E. CZERNY, I. HEIN, H. HUNGER, D. MELMAN, A. SCHWAB (eds.), Timelines. Studies in Honour of Manfred Bietak.
150. J.Cl. GOYON et C. CARDIN (eds.), Proceedings of the ninth international congress of Egyptologists. Actes du neuvième congrès international des Égyptologues. Grenoble, 6-12 septembre 2004.
151. S. SANDRI, Har-pa-chered (Harpokrates). Die Genese eines ägyptischen Götterkindes.
152. J.E. MONTGOMERY (ed.), Arabic Theology, Arabic Philosophy. From the Many to the One: Essays in Celebration of Richard M. Frank.
153. E. LIPIŃSKI, On the Skirts of Canaan in the Iron Age. Historical and Topographical Researches.
154. M. MINAS-NERPEL, Der Gott Chepri. Untersuchungen zu Schriftzeugnissen und ikonographischen Quellen vom Alten Reich bis in griechisch-römische Zeit.

PRINTED ON PERMANENT PAPER • IMPRIME SUR PAPIER PERMANENT • GEDRUKT OP DUURZAAM PAPIER - ISO 9706
N.V. PEETERS S.A., WAROTSTRAAT 50, B-3020 HERENT